9th International Operational Modal Analysis Conference (IOMAC 2022)

Vancouver, Canada
3 - 6 July 2022

Editors:

Carlos E. Ventura
Mehrtash Motamedi
Alexander Mendler
Manuel Aenlle-Lopez

ISBN: 978-1-7138-7348-8

Printed from e-media with permission by:

Curran Associates, Inc.
57 Morehouse Lane
Red Hook, NY 12571

CURRAN ASSOCIATES INC. proceedings.com

Some format issues inherent in the e-media version may also appear in this print version.

Printed by Curran Associates, Inc. (2024)

International Operational Modal Analysis Conference (IOMAC)
University of Oviedo
Department of Construction and Manufacturing Engineering
C/ Pedro Puig Adam
Edificio Oeste. Módulo 7
Campus de Gijón
33204, Gijón
Spain

Phone: +34 985 182057
Fax: +34 985 182033

iomac@uniovi.es

Additional copies of this publication are available from:

Curran Associates, Inc.
57 Morehouse Lane
Red Hook, NY 12571 USA
Phone: 845-758-0400
Fax: 845-758-2633
Email: curran@proceedings.com
Web: www.proceedings.com

9th IOMAC INTERNATIONAL **OPERATIONAL MODAL ANALYSIS** CONFERENCE

Proceedings

Vancouver – Canada
3-6 July 2022

Editors:

Carlos E. Ventura, Mehrtash Motamedi, Alexander Mendler and Manuel Aenlle-López

SPONSORS IOMAC 2022

HBK

OMMATIDIA
A NEW LOOK AT LIDAR

STRUCTURAL ENGINEERS ASSOCIATION
SEA
BRITISH COLUMBIA

Structural Vibration Solutions

PUBLISHING INFORMATION

Editors:

Carlos E. Ventura
Mehrtash Motamedi
Alexander Mendler
Manuel Aenlle-López

Title: Proceedings of the 9th International Operational Modal Analysis Conference (IOMAC)

INTERNATIONAL GROUP OF OPERATIONAL MODAL ANALYSIS
Campus de Gijón
C/ Pedro Puig Adam s/n, Edificio 7
32204, Gijón, Spain
Email: iomac@uniovi.es
www.iomac.eu

ACKNOWLEDGEMENTS:

The Steering Committee would like to acknowledge support provided by:

Mona Amer, Felix Yao, Leila Katebi, Ashritha Kedarisetti, Terry Moser, Tomás Núñez, Yuxin Pan, Indira Pandey and Alireza Taale

A message from your Conference Chair

The first ever International Operational Modal Analysis Conference, IOMAC, was held in the beautiful city of Copenhagen in Denmark in 2005. Since then, every two years, IOMAC has been held in other beautiful and exciting cities in like Portonovo, Italy, Istanbul, Turkey, Guimaraes, Portugal, Gijón, Spain, and Ingolstadt, Germany. All these European cities have hosted IOMAC and have seen how this conference has matured over the years, and has been the catalyst to make Operational Modal Analysis, OMA, a practical and useful tool for evaluating the dynamic behaviour of all kinds of structures. When IOMAC started in 2005, the main purpose of the conference was to provide a venue for people interested in OMA to exchange experiences and research results in this field. At that time OMA was still considered a new field and there was a clear need to better understand what OMA was about and its potential to be useful in many areas of structural vibrations. Over the ensuing years, the IOMAC conferences have continued to be an excellent venue to exchange experiences on how to use OMA for a variety of applications, to report and discuss findings about the advantages and challenges of the technology and to share new research and advances on the applicability of OMA to many fields where vibrations are an issue.

As a departure from the traditional way of having IOMAC in the "Old Continent," this time the 9th IOMAC will be held in Vancouver, one of the most beautiful and vibrant cities of the "New Continent." The conference will be held from the 3rd to the 6th of July 2022. In, addition to the conference, several pre-conference courses will be offered to people interested in gaining a deeper understanding of various aspects of OMA. As it has been a tradition with past conferences, the conference will include the "Lecture of Honor" and the Keynote Lecture. The sessions during the conference will cover all major aspects of OMA, with focus on the following topics: Identification Techniques, Measurement Techniques, Applications in Civil Structures, Applications in Mechanical Structures, Comparison with Traditional Modal Analysis, Model Validation and Model Updating, Structural Modification, Structural Health Monitoring and Wind Turbines.

The theme of the conference is "***Reaching Beyond Borders***" and reflects the fact that OMA is not limited by any type of borders, physical or intellectual, and that there is a tremendous opportunity to explore new applications of the technology, so it is natural to join together to explore these new challenges. This includes researchers, practicing engineers and technicians, students, equipment vendors, and software developers. All will have the opportunity to share their knowledge in this rather fascinating field and to improve their specific skills.

We expect that the 9th IOMAC will be a source of both professional fruits and lasting friendships for all participants. We also expect that it will serve to identify topics of cooperation that will help the IOMAC Organization to fulfill its mission of promoting the interchange of information and technical cooperation. Above all, I hope it will contribute to create and strengthen our human and professional ties in goal to make OMA a useful and practical tool.

Dr. Carlos E. Ventura
Professor of Civil Engineering and Director of EERF
The University of British Columbia, Vancouver, BC, Canada

STEERING COMMITTEE

Dr. Carlos E. Ventura, Chair
University of British Columbia
Dr. Manuel Aenlle-López
University of Oviedo
Dr. Palle Andersen
Structural Vibration Solutions A/S (SVS)
Dr. Niels-Jørgen Jacobsen
Hottinger Brüel & Kjær (HBK)

Dr. Alexander Mendler
Technical University of Munich
Dr. Mehrtash Motamedi
University of British Columbia
Dr. Salman Soleimani-Dashtaki
University of British Columbia

PERMANENT IOMAC COMMITTEE

Manuel Aenlle-Lópezc (Chair)
University of Oviedo
Carlos E. Ventura
University of British Columbia
Palle Andersen
Structural Vibration Solutions

Pelayo Fernández Fernández (Vice-Chair)
University of Oviedo
Niels-Jørgen Jacobsen
Brüel & Kjær
Carmelo Gentile
Politecnico de Torino

INTERNATIONAL SCIENTIFIC COMMITTEE

Manuel Aenlle-López, Spain
Palle Andersen, Denmark
Joerg Bienert, Germany
Ruben Boroscheck, Chile
Anders Brandt, Denmark
Rune Brincker, Denmark
Reto Cantieni, Switzerland
Javier Cara Cañas, Spain
Giuliano Coppotelli, Italy
Álvaro Cunha, Spain
Eddy Dascotte, Belgium
Guido De Roeck, Belgium
Michael Döhler, France
Pelayo Fernández Fernández, Spain

Dora Foti, Italy
Carmelo Gentile, Italy
Jacek Grosel, Poland
Niels-Jørgen Jacobsen, Denmark
Jyrki Kullaa, Helsinki
Thomas Lagö, USA
Filipe Magalhães, Portugal
Bart Peeters, Belgium
Carlo Rainieri, Italy
Julie Regnier, France
Thomas Schmidt, Germany
Dmitri Tcherniak, Denmark
Carlos E. Ventura, Canada

CONFERENCE SECRETARIAT

c/o Venue West Conference Services Ltd.
PO Box 98144, Yaletown RPO
Vancouver, BC, V6Z 2Z7, Canada

Dr. Carlos Ventura

Conference Chair

Dr. Carlos Ventura is currently the Director of the Earthquake Engineering Research Facility (EERF) at UBC and has more than 30 years of experience as a structural engineer. Dr. Ventura's areas of research are in Structural Dynamics and Earthquake Engineering. He has been conducting research on the dynamic behavior and analysis of structural systems subjected to extreme dynamic loads, including severe ground shaking for more than twenty years. His research work includes experimental studies in the field and in the laboratory of structural systems and components. Research developments have included development and implementation of performance-based design methods for seismic retrofit of low rise school buildings, novel techniques for regional estimation of damage to structures during earthquakes, detailed studies on nonlinear dynamic analysis of structures and methods to evaluate the dynamic characteristics of large Civil Engineering structures. His current research is focused on the development of performance-based guidelines for seismic retrofit of schools, on methods to evaluate the interaction between critical infrastructure vulnerable to natural and man-made hazards, and on structural health monitoring of building, bridges and dams. Dr. Ventura has written over 400 technical papers and reports related to the seismic behavior of structures, and has received numerous awards for his research accomplishments, including the Lieutenant Governor's Award of Excellence (2013), the Innovation Award of the Canadian Society of Civil Engineering (2010) and the APEGBC Meritorious Achievement Award (2006). He is a member of several national and international professional societies and advisory committees. He is a member of the Canadian Academy of Engineering and Fellow of Engineers Canada. He is also a member of several building and bridge code committees. In addition to his academic activities, Dr. Ventura is a recognized international consultant on structural vibrations and safety of large Civil Engineering structures.

Dr. Manuel Aenlle López

Dr. Manuel Aenlle-López is a mechanical engineer and received his M.Sc and Ph.D. from the University of Oviedo in 1994 and 2001, respectively. He is employed as full professor at the University of Oviedo (Spain). In 1995 he was a pre-doctoral fellow at the structural dynamics department of the research institute ISMES.sPa (Bergamo-Italy) and a post-doctoral fellow at the Aalborg University (2004), Aarhus University (2013) and Technical University of Denmark (2017). He has been the chair of the permanent committee of the International Operational Modal Analysis Conference (IOMAC) since 2015. His research has been focused on operational modal analysis (OMA), dynamic behavior of laminated glass elements, and fatigue of structures. Manuel Aenlle López has published 38 journal papers, more than 90 papers in national and international conferences, and he has been the principal investigator of 5 research projects funded by the Spanish Ministers of Research.

Niels-Jorgen Jacobsen

Mr. Jacobsen joined Brüel & Kjær (now Hottinger Brüel & Kjær (HBK) in 1986 as a Digital Signal Processing software developer on analyzer systems. Later job positions include project manager, application specialist, vibration group manager and product manager as which he is currently working with responsibility for HBK's structural dynamics solutions. Mr. Jacobsen has worked intensively with both theoretical and practical aspects in the fields of structural dynamics, machine diagnostics and industrial acoustics. He has been the author of several technical papers and articles and is frequently lecturing worldwide. Mr. Jacobsen holds a B.Sc. in Electronic Engineering from the Technical University of Denmark and a B.Sc. in International Business from Copenhagen Business School.

Dr. Palle Andersen

Dr. Palle Andersen is a Civil Engineer with specializations in computational methods for structural dynamics. He got his M.Sc. in 1993 from Department of Civil Engineering at Aalborg University, and his Ph.D. in 1997. Since 1999 he has been the managing director and co-founder of Structural Vibration Solutions A/S. He is the senior developer of the ARTeMIS software for Operational Modal Analysis. For more than 20 years, he has been giving lectures and courses on Operational Modal Analysis and the use of ARTeMIS software worldwide. He is the author and co-author of more than 100 papers and articles on Operational Modal Analysis and Damage Detection, and the co-inventor of the Frequency Domain Decomposition patent. Today one of the most used techniques for Operational Modal Analysis.

Alexander Mendler

Dr. Alexander Mendler is a Postdoctoral Fellow and Habilitation Candidate at the Technical University of Munich (TUM), Germany. He graduated from TUM with a B.Sc. in civil engineering (2013) and a M.Sc. in structural engineering (2016). In 2020, he received his Ph.D. from the University of British Columbia in structural and earthquake engineering. Alexander's area of research is in structural dynamics and vibration analysis of structures. He specialized on the analysis of ambient vibrations, operational modal analysis, non-destructive testing, and structural health monitoring. The goal of his research is to develop new methods for the performance assessment, sensor placement optimization, and quality control of monitoring systems

Mehrtash Motamedi

Dr. Mehrtash Motamedi, P.Eng. is Research Associate at the Department of Civil Engineering and EERF Engineering Manager at the University of British Columbia, Vancouver, Canada. He is an expert in seismic design and retrofitting of structures and nonstructural components, and has 20 years of experience in experimental research projects in Earthquake and Structural Engineering area. Dr. Motamedi closely collaborates with professionals from the Association of Professional Engineers and Geoscientists of British Columbia to provide the supportive testing materials for the innovative retrofit guidelines for school buildings titled, "Seismic Retrofit Guidelines." As part of these guidelines, Dr. Motamedi has coordinated several testing programs to generate the unique test data and verification for analytical models used for the performance-based seismic assessment and retrofit of school building in BC.

Dr. Salman Soleimani-Dashtaki

Dr. Salman Soleimani-Dashtaki obtained his PhD in civil engineering from the University of British Columbia in 2018, working on Seismic Strengthening of Unreinforced Masonry Walls Using Sprayable Ecofriendly Ductile Cementitious Composite (EDCC). He received his BASc with a minor in commerce from the Sauder School of Business at UBC. Dr. Soleimani has been an active member of the both UBC and BC chapters of the Earthquake Engineering Research Institute (EERI), and he now serves on the Board of Directors of the BC EERI Chapter. He is currently working as a postdoctoral fellow and a sessional lecturer at the Civil Engineering Department of the University of British Columbia, in Vancouver.

INVITED SPEAKERS

OPENING KEYNOTE: Dr. Erdal Şafak_New Approaches to Analyze Vibration Records from Buildings

Dr. Erdal Şafak is a retired Professor at the Earthquake Engineering Department of Kandilli Observatory and Earthquake Research Institute of Bogazici University in Istanbul, Turkey. He received his Ph.D. in Structural Engineering in 1980 from the University of Illinois at Urbana-Champaign in the U.S., and was a researcher with the U.S. Geological Survey for 22 years, specializing on structural response to earthquakes, ground motion modeling, structural monitoring, and data analysis. He taught part-time classes at Stanford University in Palo Alto, Colorado School of Mines in Golden, Colorado and The George Washington University in Washington, DC. In August 2006, he joined to Boğaziçi University, and was the Head of the Earthquake Engineering Department at Kandilli Observatory and Earthquake Research Institute until July 2018, retiring in February of 2020. His scientific work includes over 60 papers on referred journals, more than one hundred conference papers, and over 2,800 citations to his publications.

LECTURE OF HONOUR: Dr. Ruben Boroschek_SHM in a Seismic Environment

Dr. Ruben Boroschek obtained his engineering degree from the University of Costa Rica and his PhD degree at the University of California Berkeley. He has been a Professor at the University of Chile since 1992. His areas of research are seismic hazard, experimental dynamic and structural health monitoring, vulnerability assessment of critical facilities, base isolation and passive energy dissipation. Also, he has developed a carrier in the industry in areas of structural health monitoring and structural review of industrial facilities. In 2017 he was designated Engineer of The Year by the Chilean Structural Engineers Association and the Best Industrial project of the year 2019 by the same association. He is an honorary professor at National University of San Antonio Abad of Cusco Peru, Corresponding Member of the Mexican Academy of Engineering, and representative of the Anti-Seismic System International Society for central and south America. He is the ex-President of the Consortium of Organization for Strong Motion Observation Systems (COSMOS).

TABLE OF CONTENTS

APPLICATIONS IN CIVIL ENGINEERING

9th International Operational Modal Analysis Conference
iomac
July 3 - 6, 2022
Vancouver, Canada

DEMONSTRATION OF TUNED MASS DAMPER EFFECTIVENESS VIA LONG-TERM STRUCTURAL MONITORING

Ronwaldo Aquino[1], J. Shayne Love[2], Trevor Haskett[3], Gary Clarke[4], and Derek Kelly[5]

[1] Senior Engineer, Motioneering Inc., ron.aquino@motioneering.ca
[2] Technical Director, Motioneering Inc., shayne.love@motioneering.ca
[3] Senior Technical Director, Motioneering Inc., trevor.haskett@motioneering.ca
[4] Senior Project Manager, Motioneering Inc., gary.clarke@motioneering.ca
[5] Principal, RWDI, derek.kelly@rwdi.com

ABSTRACT

The wind tunnel study of a super tall and slender skyscraper predicted that occupants may experience motion comfort issues during common wind events. As such, a tuned mass damper (TMD) was designed and installed inside the skyscraper. A structural monitoring system was subsequently installed to continually record bi-axial responses of both the building and the TMD. The monitoring recorded building and TMD accelerations during both ambient (calm) and significant wind conditions, with maximum gust speeds reaching 77 km/hr at the nearby airport. Using the ambient data, the natural frequencies and, to some extent, the inherent damping of the building were identified even with a TMD installed. Under high wind conditions, the approximated total effective damping and the spectral shape of the responses visibly change from the ambient results, indicating that the TMD is functioning as designed. The continuous data recording also captured comparative responses during a series of consecutive events wherein the TMD was briefly locked out one morning while gust speeds reached 56 km/hr. When the TMD was later released on the same morning, the gust speeds reached a comparable 57 km/hr from approximately the same direction. The responses captured were compared with those from when the TMD was locked out, indicating the total effective damping introduced by the TMD, thus demonstrating its effectiveness.

Keywords: Super tall building, tuned mass damper (TMD), long-term structural monitoring, performance verification, total effective damping

1. INTRODUCTION

1.1. The Study Building

The Council on Tall Buildings and Urban Habitat (CTBUH) defines a super tall building as one that is more than 300 m in height [1]. The construction of one such super tall skyscraper has recently been completed. The building is a very slender tower, as well, with a slenderness (height-to-minimum-width) ratio of 16. A building may be considered slender if the slenderness ratio is higher than 6, which various international wind loading codes would treat as very dynamically wind sensitive (e.g. [2]).

During the design stage, a wind tunnel study was carried out for the building and predicted that occupants may experience motion comfort issues during common wind events, and that a supplemental damping system (SDS) was needed to increase the total effective damping and meet occupant comfort criteria. Numerous iterations in architectural and structural design followed suit to reduce the wind-induced responses, and a final design was arrived at and analysed together with the latest wind tunnel test data. Figure 1 shows the results of the latest wind tunnel study without and with proposed SDS, wherein a tuned mass damper (TMD) system was selected because it required the least amount of space within the building. Note that while the TMD would provide damping sufficient to bring down the predicted peak total accelerations to well below criteria under annual and 10-year return period events, an additional criterion to reduce monthly accelerations to below 7 milli-g was also included and governed the TMD design. Note that the accelerations shown in Figure 1 are peak total accelerations, which were governed by the more dominant North-South tower motion.

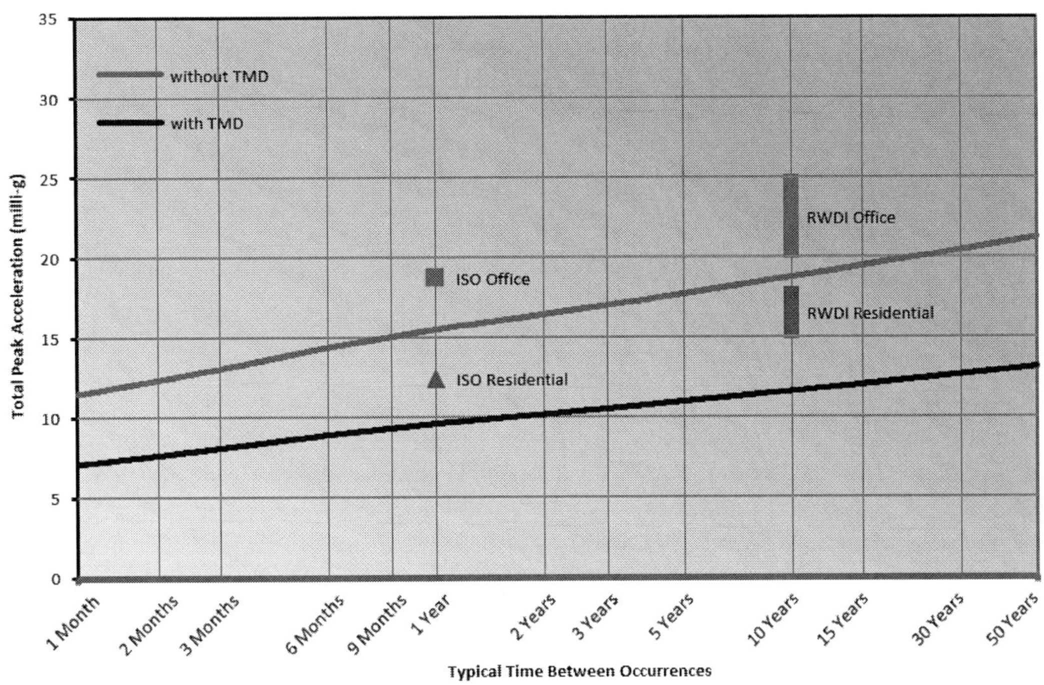

Figure 1. Predicted peak total accelerations from wind tunnel study and initial TMD concept design

1.2. Tuned Mass Dampers

A TMD is a mechanical device that absorbs the vibration energy of the building or structure wherein it is installed. Physically, it consists primarily of a large, suspended mass that is tuned to swing at a period close to the targeted building period. It also includes viscous damping devices which convert the vibration energy from the building into heat. Without the TMD, the building would vibrate at higher amplitudes than if the properly designed TMD was installed and enabled. If the building motions were higher than standard limits for occupant comfort, building residents might sense these motions and potentially file complaints. The TMD reduces these motions and the frequency of such complaints.

Theoretically, TMDs are tuned to an individual vibrational mode of the building. If a mode of the building is represented by a 1DOF (one-degree-of-freedom) system modelled using the target mode's generalized mass, stiffness, and damping coefficient (Figure 2a), then a building with a TMD would be equivalent to a 2DOF system with a 2nd DOF representing the TMD's mass, stiffness, and damping coefficient (Figure 2b). Therefore, under random excitation such as wind loading, the expected frequency responses would look similar to Figure 3 for the without TMD (1 peak) and with TMD (2 peaks) cases. Figure 3 also illustrates a building with a slightly mistuned TMD with one peak dominating over the other.

In some buildings, the TMD may be bi-tuned or tuned to two orthogonal modes. For the current study building, the first two fundamental sway natural frequencies of the building are closely spaced, and thus one TMD natural frequency can control both fundamental sway modes (i.e. building X and Y axes). As expected, the TMD frequency is slightly mistuned against one building mode but better tuned against the other. Figure 4 shows the predicted spectral shapes for the modal responses

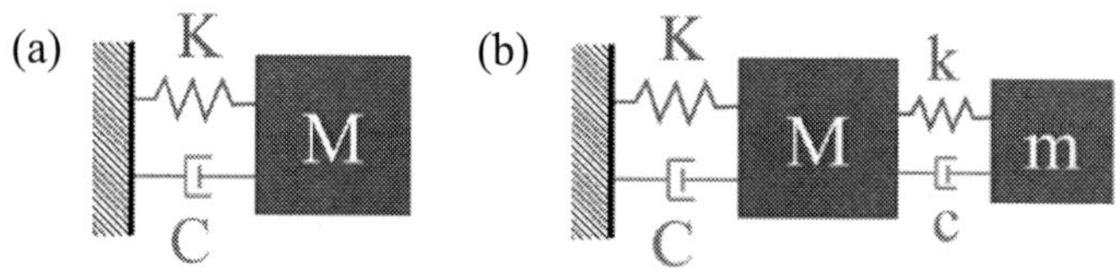

Figure 2. (a) 1-degree-of-freedom representation of a building vibration mode, and (b) 2-degree-of-freedom representation of building mode and TMD system.

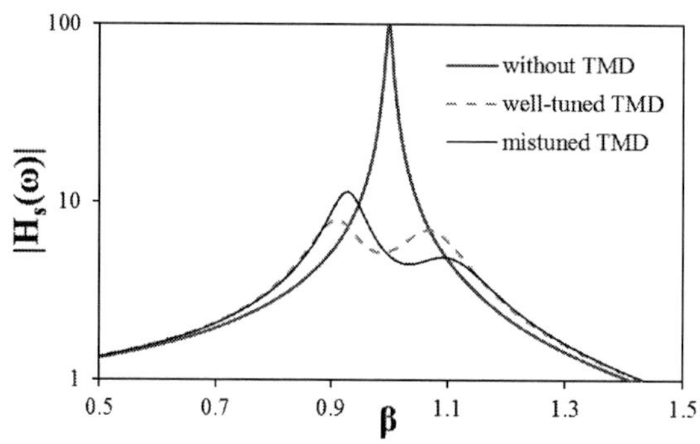

Figure 3. Theoretical spectral shape of building modal response without TMD, with well-tuned TMD, and with slightly mistuned TMD. β indicates ratio of excitation frequency

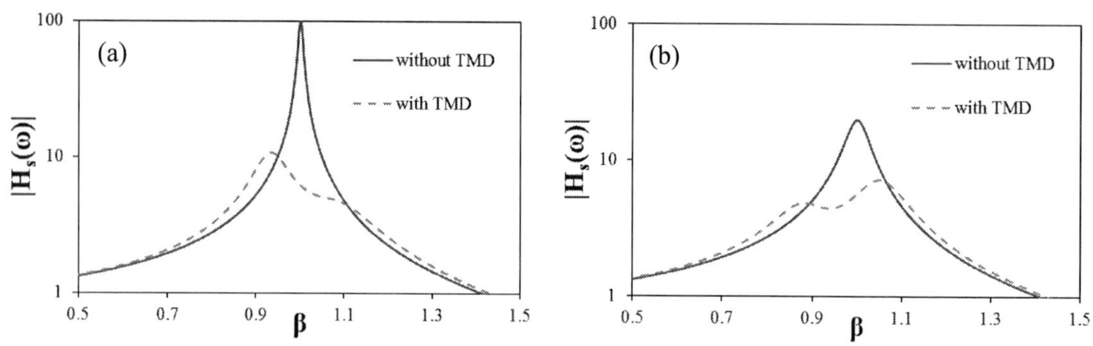

Figure 4. Predicted spectral shapes of study building's responses without and with TMD for (a) Mode 1 (Y-direction / North-South), and (b) Mode 2 (X-direction / East-West).

2. STRUCTURAL MONITORING

2.1. Set-Up

A structural monitoring system was installed at the building after the TMD had been installed to continually capture responses of both the building and the TMD. The monitoring recorded bi-axial building and TMD acceleration data under ambient (calm) wind conditions. It also recorded responses during significant wind events corresponding to gust speeds up to 77 km/hr recorded at the nearby airport. The monitoring set-up consisted of two tri-axial MEMS accelerometers (Make: SENSR, Model: CX1) connected to a network-enabled data acquisition system that can be accessed remotely for data transfer over the Internet. One accelerometer was mounted on the building's top mechanical floor (above the TMD room floor) and the second was mounted on the underside of the TMD itself. The building sensor was aligned such that its +Y axis points toward Project North, consistent with the structural axis convention. Figure 5 shows photos of the monitoring system components.

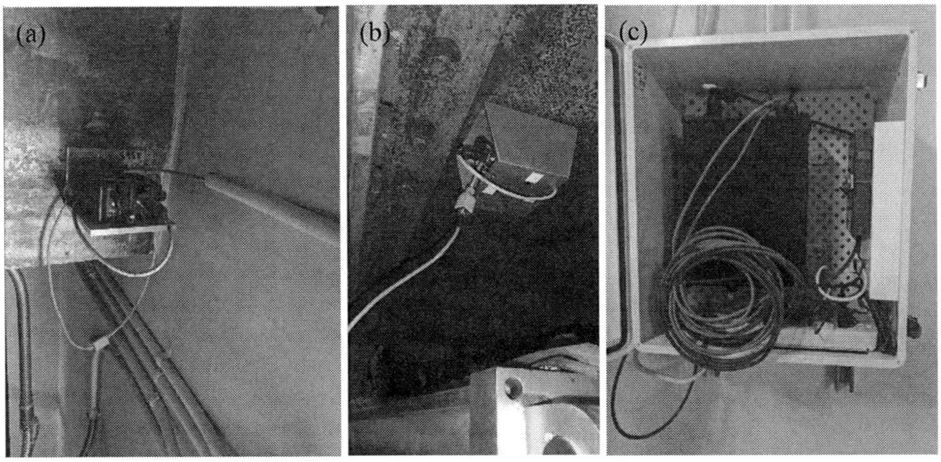

Figure 5. Photos of (a) SENSR CX1 accelerometer mounted on bracket attached to structural wall, (b) underside of mounting bracket with accelerometer attached to the TMD, and (c) data acquisition unit.

2.2. Limitations

With the available measurements, data processing can generate spectral responses comparable to the plots in Figure 3, and therefore indicate dominant response frequencies. Data filtering can isolate the first two fundamental sway modes (frequencies and response amplitudes) from higher order mode contribution. Further processing may also allow to estimate the inherent damping in the tower, as well as total effective damping that accounts for the supplemental damping provided by the TMD system.

Having only one sensor on one floor of the building, any system identification or modal analysis carried out will not be able to approximate building mode shapes. Likewise, the torsional modes may not be adequately identifiable from the current setup, but are known to exist at frequencies above this range of interest from earlier work while commissioning the TMD. However, mode shapes and torsional response are irrelevant for the purposes of this study. The TMD was designed to address only the sway modes. Additionally, the current study effectively assumes that the structural engineer's finite element model of the tower correctly predicts the fundamental mode shapes of the building. The general modal directions can be identified (e.g. Mode 1 is approximately 20° clockwise from the +Y axis), but for the purposes of this paper, the 1st mode is treated as being primarily Y-direction or North-South motion, and the 2nd mode as being primarily X-direction or East-West motion.

3. DATA PROCESSING

3.1. Preliminary Processing

As mentioned above, the data was first adjusted so that Y accelerations were aligned North-South and X accelerations aligned East-West. The data was then subjected to a Butterworth bandpass filter from 0.3 to 0.9 rad/s, effectively removing any low frequency components associated with signal "drift". The time domain data was transformed into the frequency domain using Welch's method [3], generating power spectral density plots corresponding to each data set. Peak responses were selected from the time domain data, while peak frequencies were picked from the spectral density plots. For the discussion in this paper, data from the dates listed in Table 1 were extracted, corresponding to the hours with largest wind speeds (except for record #1, which is for calm weather).

Table 1. Date and time of analyzed data with corresponding wind speed data courtesy of Weather Underground

Record #	Local Date	Local Time	Peak gust speed (km/hr)	Wind direction	Notes
1	2021/04/27	00:00-23:59	N/A	NW	No gustiness reported
2	2021/04/30	00:00-23:59	74	NW	
3	2021/07/06	16:00-19:00	93	NW	Thunderstorm
4	2021/11/12	07:00-09:00	56	SSE	TMD disabled
5	2021/11/12	09:00-11:00	57	S	

3.2. Results and Discussion

Table 2 summarizes the peak recorded accelerations from the full filtered time series data for Records #1 to #5. Figure 6 to Figure 10 show the corresponding spectral density plots for Records #1 to #5.

Table 2. Peak recorded accelerations from filtered time series data

Record #	Tower Peak Accelerations (milli-g)		TMD Peak Accelerations (milli-g)	
	E-W	N-S	E-W	N-S
1	0.4	0.8	0.5	0.8
2	4.1	7.8	13	20
3	3.0	7.9	8.8	18
4	7.6	13	9.7	13
5	5.0	4.1	14	11

A few expected observations can be drawn from Table 2. First, that building response and an enabled TMD's response both increase with wind speed – except perhaps when the type of wind storm is a thunderstorm, which acts differently on structures than "normal" synoptic winds. Second, wind direction has some impact as well on building responses. Third, that TMD absolute acceleration is generally much higher than tower response – except when the TMD is not working, such as under "ambient" or very low conditions (Record #1, when TMD internal friction has not yet been overcome) or when the TMD is intentionally, temporarily disabled (Record #4). Record #3 illustrates that the TMD is also working somewhat during a thunderstorm. Lastly but most importantly, the building response increases when the TMD is disabled versus when the TMD is enabled, for a given very similar wind speed and direction. This last point suggests that the TMD is functioning as intended.

Similar observations can be made from Figure 6 to Figure 10. A correlation can be seen between the peak spectral accelerations from these plots and the peak accelerations in Table 2. Most importantly, it can be observed that, for Records #1 (Figure 6) and #4 (Figure 9), the spectral shapes are more similar to the "without TMD" spectral shape shown in Figure 4. Meanwhile, the spectral shapes for Records #2, #3, and #5 (**Figure** 7, 8, and 10, respectively) are very different and better resemble the wider-band response for the "with TMD" cases in Figure 4. Note that Records #1 and #4 show a secondary component in the other direction (e.g. there is an E-W component for the N-S-dominant frequency).

This is due to the actual building modes not exactly aligned with the building and the accelerometers' X and Y axes.

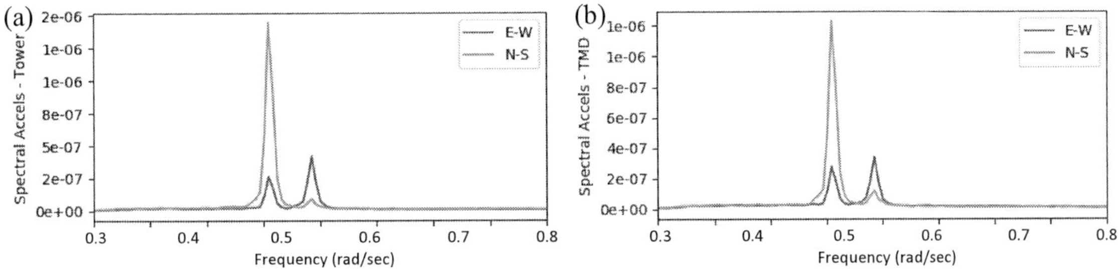

Figure 6. Power spectral density plots for (a) tower and (b) TMD for Record #1 (full day).

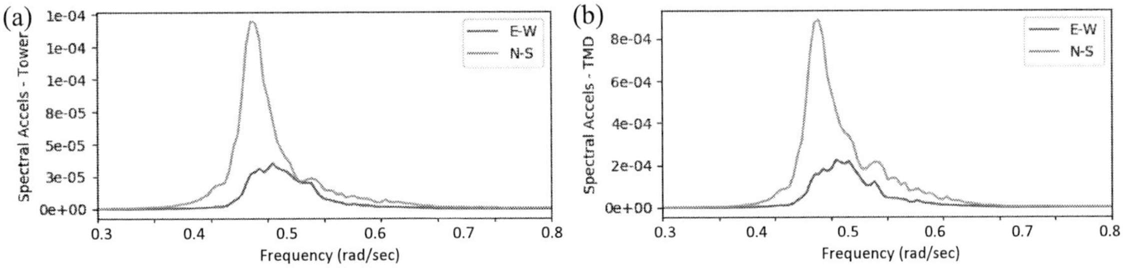

Figure 7. Power spectral density plots for (a) tower and (b) TMD for Record #2 (full day).

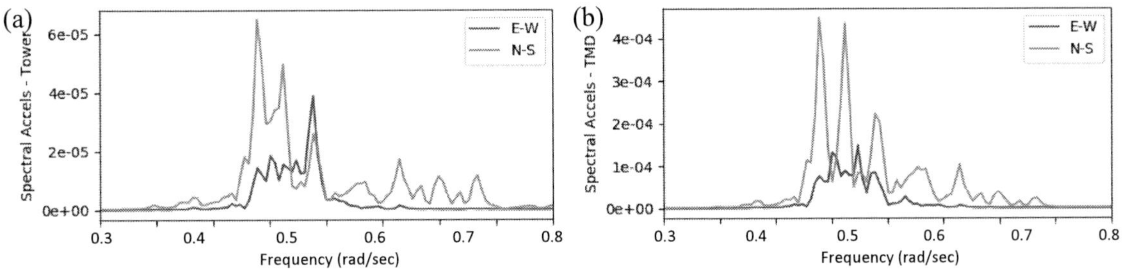

Figure 8. Power spectral density plots for (a) tower and (b) TMD for Record #3 (3 hours).

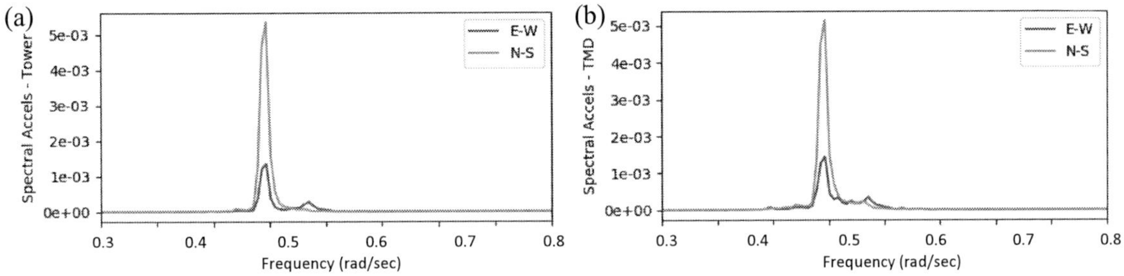

Figure 9. Power spectral density plots for (a) tower and (b) TMD for Record #4 (2 hours).

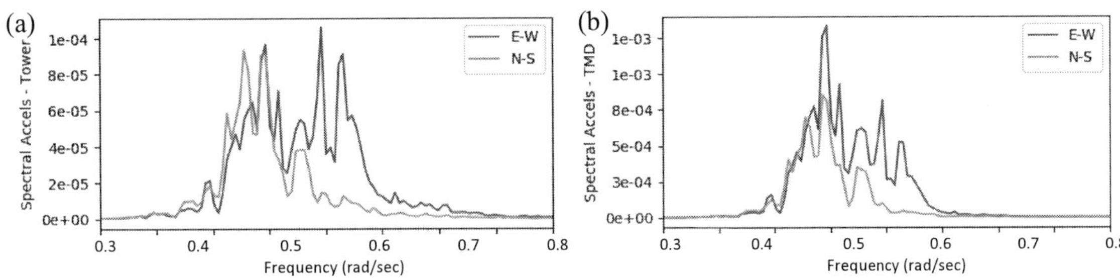

Figure 10. Power spectral density plots for (a) tower and (b) TMD for Record #5 (2 hours).

Short segments of the time series data are shown in Figure 11 for the recorded Y-direction (N-S) component motions of tower and TMD for the 5 records, as an example to illustrate how the tower and TMD motions are tracking each other. Again, similar conclusions can be made as from Table 2 and Figure 6 thru Figure 10. When the TMD is not working during very low wind conditions (Record #1) or when the TMD was disabled (Record #4), the tower and TMD motion track each other very closely with practically zero phase lag. Meanwhile, for Records #2, #3, and #5, a visible approximate 90 degree phase lag can be observed, which is expected of TMD behaviour within a structure.

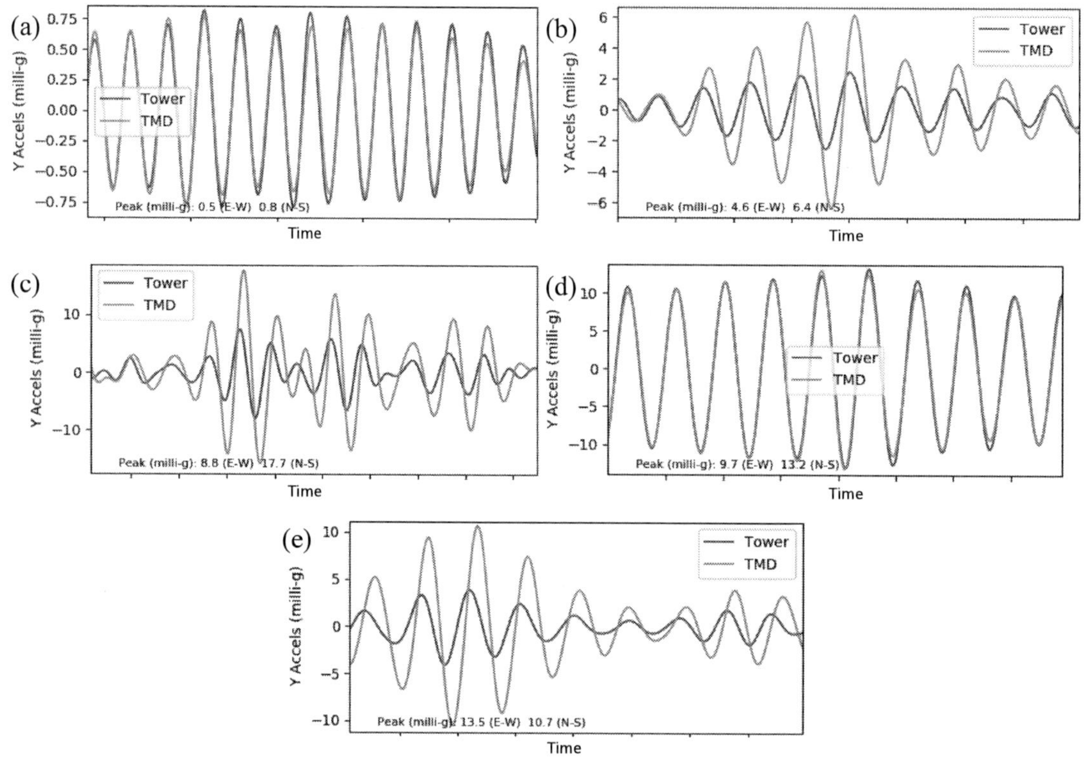

Figure 11. Short segments of Y-direction (N-S) accelerations of tower and TMD for (a) Record #1, (b) Record #2, (c) Record #3, (d) Record #4, and (e) Record #5.

4. TUNED MASS DAMPER EFFECTIVENESS

4.1. Estimate of inherent and total effective damping via autocorrelation

For a structure without a TMD (or with a TMD that is immobile due to friction or lock-out), the autocorrelation function of a time series data will yield what is very similar to a free decay response, from which the inherent structural damping can be calculated. However, this is not an acceptable approach for a structure equipped with an operable TMD [4]. Instead, the added effective damping that the TMD provides to the structure may be computed as [5]:

$$\zeta_{add} = \pi f_s \mu E[\ddot{X}\dot{x}_r]/E[\ddot{X}^2] \tag{1}$$

where f_s is the modal structural frequency, μ is the TMD-structure mass ratio, $\ddot{X}$ is the tower acceleration, $\dot{x}_r$ is the TMD relative velocity, and $E[\ ]$ denotes the expected value operation. The total effective damping may then be computed as the summation of the inherent structural damping and the added effective damping provided by the TMD: $\zeta_{eff} = \zeta_s + \zeta_{add}$.

Figure 12 shows the generated autocorrelation functions for the two records (#1 and #4) in which the TMD was immobile, as well as the free decay envelope associated with the predicted damping ratio, which is given by:

$$FDE = \pm e^{-2\pi f_s \zeta_s t} \tag{2}$$

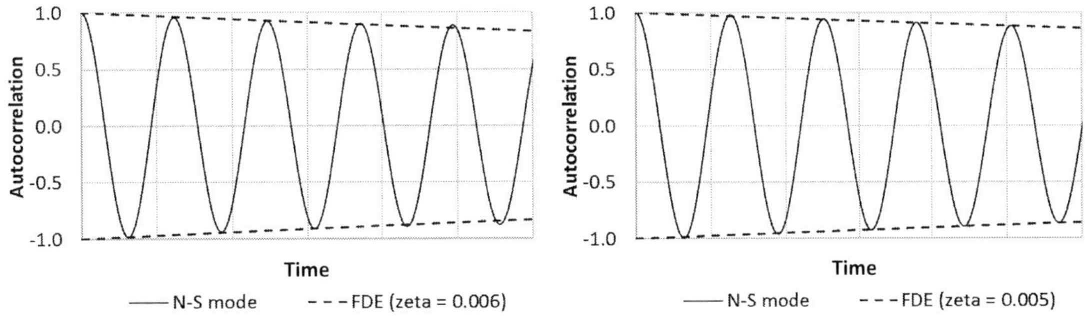

Figure 12. Autocorrelation functions of (N-S) accelerations of tower for (a) Record #1, (b) Record #4.

Table 3. Estimated N-S modal damping ratios

Record #	Peak Accel. (milli-g)	Estimated Damping Ratio	Peak gust speed (km/hr)	Wind direction	Notes
1	0.8	0.6%	N/A	NW	No gustiness
2	7.8	2.9%	74	NW	
3	7.9	3.0%	93	NW	Thunderstorm
4	13	0.5%	56	SSE	TMD disabled
5	4.1	4.9%	57	S	

Table 3 summarizes the estimated damping ratios based on the best-fit *FDE* curves applied to the autocorrelation functions shown in Figure 12, as well as the application of Eq. (1) when the TMD is operational. The inherent structural damping ratio is low (0.5%). When the TMD is operational, the damping ratios are considerably higher (2.9%-4.9%).

4.2. Estimate of total effective damping via response reduction

Records #4 and #5 have very similar wind conditions, therefore the total effective damping may also be estimated by comparing the building response amplitude when the TMD is operational vs. when the TMD is immobile according to the relationship:

$$\zeta_{eff} = \zeta_s \left(\frac{D_{withoutTMD}}{D_{withTMD}} \right)^2 \tag{3}$$

Based on the data for Records #4 and #5 in Table 3, and using an assumed inherent structural damping ratio of 0.5%, the total effective damping ratio can be calculated as 5.0%. The independently calculated total effective damping ratios are both in agreement with expectations for this TMD design, and confirm the TMD will reduce accelerations to acceptable levels for occupant comfort.

5. SUMMARY

The wind tunnel study of a super tall and slender skyscraper predicted that occupants may experience motion comfort issues under common wind events. A tuned mass damper (TMD) was then designed and installed in the building. Subsequently, a long-term structural monitoring system was installed that captured building and TMD responses under various wind conditions. Processing of the monitoring data from five example events has revealed that the inherent damping ratio is 0.5%~0.6%. The analysis results also revealed that southerly winds with up to 57 km/hr gusts can allow the TMD to provide a total effective damping ratio of approximately 5%, indicating that the TMD is performing as designed. The TMD therefore enables the super tall building to achieve occupant motion comfort criteria during common wind events.

REFERENCES

[1] Council on Tall Buildings and Urban Habitat. CTBUH Height Criteria for Measuring & Defining Tall Buildings. *https://cloud.ctbuh.org/CTBUH_HeightCriteria.pdf*, retrieved: 8 April 2022.

[2] Canadian Commission on Building and Fire Codes (2015). *National Building Code of Canada 2015*. Ottawa, National Research Council of Canada.

[3] Welch, P. (1967) The use of the fast Fourier transform for the estimation of power spectra: A method based on time averaging over short, modified periodograms. *IEEE Trans. Audio Electroacoust*, 15, 70-73.

[4] Love, J.S., and Morava, B. (2021) Practical experience with full-scale performance verification of dynamic vibration absorbers installed in tall buildings. *International Journal of High-Rise Buildings*, 10(2), 85-92.

[5] Love, J.S., and Tait, M.J. (2017) Estimating the added effective damping of SDOF systems incorporating multiple dynamic vibration absorbers with nonlinear damping. *Engineering Structures*, 130, 154-161.

9th International Operational Modal Analysis Conference
iomac
July 3 - 6, 2022
Vancouver, Canada

DYNAMIC RESPONSE OF LAMINATED GLASS ELEMENTS IN TIME DOMAIN

Manuel Aenlle-López[1], F. Pelayo[2], Natalia García-Fernández[3], Miguel. Muniz-Calvente[4], M.J. Lamela-Rey[5].

[1] *Professor, University of Oviedo, aenlle@uniovi.es*
[2] Associate Professor, University of Oviedo, fernandezpelayo@uniovi.es
[3] PhD Student, University of Oviedo, garciafnatalia@uniovi.es
[4] Associate Professor, University of Oviedo, munizcmiguel@uniovi.es
[5] Associate Professor, University of Oviedo, mjesuslr@uniovi.es

ABSTRACT

Laminated glass consists of two or more layers of monolithic glass and one or more interlayers of a polymeric material, the polyvinyl butyral (PVB) being the most used interlayer material. In the last years, the concept of effective thickness was proposed to simplify the calculation of these elements subject to static loadings, which consists of using a monolithic model with mechanical properties equal to those of the laminated element. However, when laminated glass is subject to dynamic loadings, the mechanical properties of the monolithic model have to be defined time and temperature dependent, which complicates the use of this technique in numerical models.

In this paper, expressions for obtaining the modal parameters of a laminated glass beam using a monolithic model are presented. On the other hand, a time domain effective stress thickness is defined and used to predict the dynamic response of laminated glass beams The proposed techniques are, firstly, validated comparing the analytical response of a laminated glass beam with the numerical results obtained with numerical model assembled in ABAQUS. Secondly, the dynamic responses are estimated and compared with experimental tests carried out on a laminated glass beam, where the modal parameters were estimated with operational modal analysis.

Keywords: Viscoelasticity, Dynamic Behaviour, Laminated Glass Elements.

1. INTRODUCTION

Laminated glass is a layered material that consists of two or more plies of monolithic glass and one or more polymeric interlayer material subject to high pressure and temperature in autoclave. All polymeric interlayers present a viscoelastic behavior, i.e. their mechanical properties are time and temperature dependent [1, 2]. In analytical and numerical models, glass mechanical behavior is usually modelled as linear-elastic whereas the PVB is commonly considered as linear-viscoelastic [3, 4, 5].

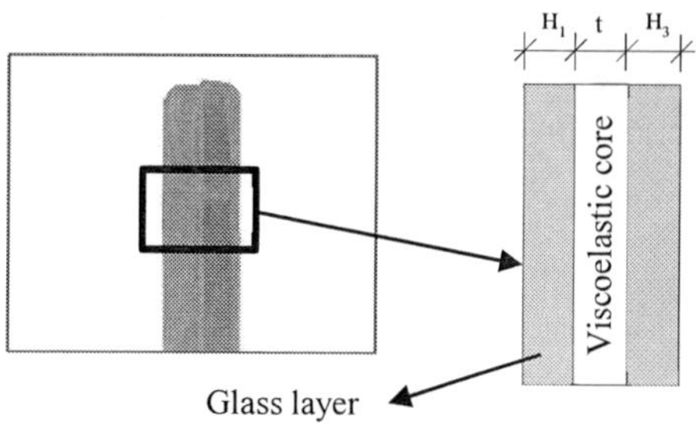

Figure 1: Example of laminated glass in sandwich configuration.

In order to obtain the dynamic behaviour of laminated glass element, a finite element analysis can be assembled. However, these methods are high time consuming because the viscoelasticity (time and temperature dependence) of the interlayers cannot be considered with modal superposition techniques.

In the last years, the concept of effective thickness has been proposed to estimate deflections and stresses in laminated glass beams using simplified monolithic models which thickness is time and temperature dependent [3, 4, 5]

In this work, expressions and techniques to predict the dynamic response of laminated glass beams are presented. The technique combines the modal parameters and a linear elastic monolithic model. The method is validated by analytical and numerical simulation as well as experimentally.

2. BASIC THEORY

2.1. Modal Parameters of laminated glass beams

The natural frequencies ω_{mon} of a monolithic beam with stiffness EI_{mon} and constant mass per unit length are given by:

$$\omega_{mon}^2 = k_I^4 \frac{EI_{mon}}{m_{mon}} \tag{1}$$

where the wavenumber k_I is constant for each mode. The stiffness EI_{mon} is expressed as:

$$EI_{mon} = (EbH_{TOT}^3)/12 \tag{2}$$

with b being the width of the beam, H_{TOT} the total thickness and E the Young's modulus.

The mass per unit length can be calculated with:

$$m_{mon} = \rho_{mon} H_{TOT} \tag{3}$$

where ρ_{mon} is the mass-density

The natural frequencies and loss factors of a laminated glass beam can be obtained from the expression [6-9]:

$$\omega^2(1 + j\eta) = \omega_{mon} \frac{\rho_{mon}}{\rho} \frac{E_{eff}^*(\omega, T)}{E} \tag{4}$$

Where the term $E^*_{eff}(\omega, T)$is an effective frequency domain stiffness [10]:

$$E^*_{eff}(\omega, T) = \frac{E}{1+Y}\left(1 + \frac{Y}{1 + \frac{E H_1 t H_2 k_I^2(\omega, T)}{G_t^*(\omega, T)(H_1 + H_2)}}\right) \tag{5}$$

A description of the parameters in Eq. (5) are presented in Appendix.

With respect de mode shapes, it has been experimentally demonstrated [11] that there are not discrepancies between the mode shapes of monolithic beam and a laminated glass beam with same geometry and boundary conditions, i.e:

$$\psi \cong \psi_{mon} \tag{6}$$

where ψ and ψ_{mon} are mode shapes normalized to the largest component equal to unity.

2.2. Dynamic response in Time Domain

In structural dynamics, the responses of the system can be decomposed in terms of modal coordinates using the mode superposition method, i.e. [12]:

$$w(x, t) = \sum_{i=1}^{Nmodes} \phi_i(x) q_i(t) \tag{7}$$

Where $\phi_i(x)$ and $q_i(t, T)$ are the i-th mode shape and the i-th modal coordinate, respectively. For a laminated glass beam, the maximun stresses in the glass layers can be obtained with the following expressions [7, 13]:

$$\sigma_1(x, t, T) \cong \frac{H_1}{2} \cdot \sum_{i=1}^{Nmodes} E_{1\sigma i}(T) \cdot \phi_i''(x) \cdot q_i(t, T) \tag{8}$$

Whereas the stresses at the bottom of layer 3 are obtained from:

$$\sigma_2(x, t, T) \cong \frac{H_2}{2} \cdot \sum_{i=1}^{Nmodes} E_{1\sigma i}(T) \cdot \phi_i''(x) \cdot q_i(t, T) \tag{9}$$

Where $E_{1\sigma i}(T)$ and $E_{2\sigma i}(T)$ are constant time domain stress effective Young modulus [7], which are dependent on the geometry and the mechanical properties of the glass and the interlayer [14]. These time domain stress effective Young modulus can be obtained with the equations:

$$E_{1\sigma i}(T) = E_{1\sigma eff}(\omega_i, T) \tag{10}$$

$$E_{2\sigma i}(T) = E_{2\sigma eff}(\omega_i, T) \tag{11}$$

where ω_i is the natural frequency of the i-th mode, and $E_{1\sigma eff}(\omega_i, T)$ and $E_{2\sigma eff}(\omega_i, T)$ are frequency domain effective Young modulus whose expressions can be retreived from literature [9].

If the experimental modal parameters of the beam (natural frequencies, mode shapes and damping ratios) are known, i.e. by modal analysis, and the experimental response time histories $w(x,t)$ are measured at several points of the structure, the vector of experimental modal coordinates $\{q_x(t,T)\}$ can be estimated by:

$$\{q_x(t,T)\} = [\phi_x]^{-1}\{w_x(t,T)\} \tag{12}$$

Where subscript 'x' indicates experimental data, $[\phi_x(x)]^{-1}$represents the inverse matrix of the experimental mode shapes and $\{w_x(t,T)\}$ the vector of experimental responses. If Eq. (12) is substituted in Eqs. (8) and (9), the stresses at any point of the layer 1 can be obtained with the expression [13]:

$$\sigma_1(x,t,T) \cong \frac{H_1}{2} \cdot \sum_{i=1}^{Nmodes} E_{1\sigma i}(T) \cdot \phi''_{xpi} \cdot q_{xi}(t,T) \tag{13}$$

and at the bottom of layer 3 with:

$$\sigma_2(x,t,T) = \frac{H_2}{2} \cdot \sum_{i=1}^{Nmodes} E_{2\sigma i}(T) \cdot \phi''_{xpi} \cdot q_{xi}(t,T) \tag{14}$$

Where ϕ''_{xpi} are the experimental mode shapes expanded to the unmeasured DOF's using one of the techniques proposed in the literature [15].

3. EXAMPLES OF APPLICATION IN A LAMINATED GLASS BEAM

3.1. Modal parameter of a laminated glass beam

In order to validate the technique proposed in this paper, the modal parameters of a simply supported laminated glass beam, made of annealed glass layers, PVB core and with the following geometrical data: $L = 1$ m, $H_1 = 4$ mm, $t = 0.76$ mm, $H_2 = 4$ mm, $b = 0.1$ m, were predicted at 25^oC using Eq. (4) and validated with a numerical model assembled in ABAQUS.

As a first step, two numerical models were assembled using available mechanical properties for glass and PVB [14]. The details of the models used are:

- A simply supported monolithic glass model with thickness $H_{TOT} = H_1 + t + H_2 = 8.76\ mm$.. The beam was meshed using quadratic hexahedral elements (20 nodes per element) with an approximate size of 4 mm.

- A layered model with glass layers modelled as linear elastic and the PVB interlayer model as linear viscoelastic, was also meshed using 3 quadratic hexahedral elements through the beam thickness (one element for each material layer).

The natural frequencies ω_{mon}, corresponding to the first four bending modes of the monolithic model, were obtained solving the eigenvalue problem, and the results are presented in Table 1 for a temperature of 25°C. The wavenumbers k_I were estimated from the monolithic model using Eq. (1).

The natural frequencies and the corresponding loss factors were estimated from the frequency response function (FRF), which was isolated around the peaks of resonance and taken to the time domain using the Inverse Discrete Fourier Transform (IDFT). The resonance frequency is obtained by determining the zero crossing times, and the damping by the logarithmic decrement of the corresponding free decay. The predicted natural frequencies and loss factors at 25ºC are shown in Tables 1, respectively.

Table 1. Modal parameters at 25º C.

Mode	Monolithic glass beam	Laminated glass beam			
	Nat. freq	Nat. freq		Loss factor	
	[Hz]	Eq. (4)	FEM Visco	Eq. (4)	FEM Visco
1	21.31	21.60	21.62	0.0154	0.0157
2	85.24	85.86	84.95	0.0305	0.0306
3	191.72	186.49	186.81	0.0497	0.0488
4	340.48	323.81	324.50	0.0683	0.0715

From Table 1, it is concluded that the modal parameters have been predicted with a good accuracy. Although damping estimation in laminated glass panels using Eq. (13) are not accurate, in this particular case (simply supported beam) $k_R = 0$ for all the modes (which is the assumption considered for deriving Eq. (4)), which explains the large precision of the predictions.

3.2. Stresses estimation in a laminated glass beam under impact loading

3.2.1 Modal Analysis

A laminated glass beam was used in the experiments. The dimensions of the beam were 1000 mm x 100 x 6.38 mm, being the thicknesses of glass H_1 and H_2 three milimeters and the thickness of PVB interlayer t=0.38 mm. The total mass of the beam was 1.544 kg. The beam was clamped at both ends between rubbery bands in a glass standard impact frame [16] (see Figure 2).

The modal parameters of the beam were experimentally determined by operational modal analysis at 22 ºC. The responses of the beam were measured with 7 accelerometers with a sensitivity of 10 mV/g which were uniformly distributed along the beam and seven strain gages using a sampling frequency of 2132 Hz (see Figure 2), the test duration being approximately 2 minutes. The modal parameters were estimated in the frequency domain using the ARTEMIS Modal Pro software. The singular value decomposition of the experimental responses is presented in Figure 3. The first five experimental natural frequencies and the corresponding damping ratios are presented in Table 2. The mode shapes for the beam are those presented in Table 2.

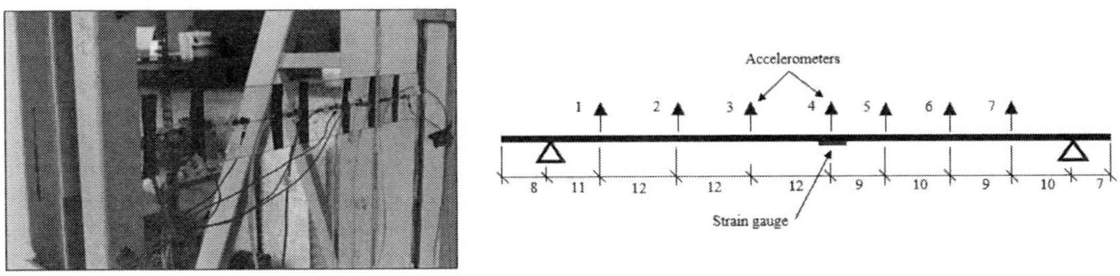

Figure 2. Experimental set-up for the laminated glass beam (distances in cm).

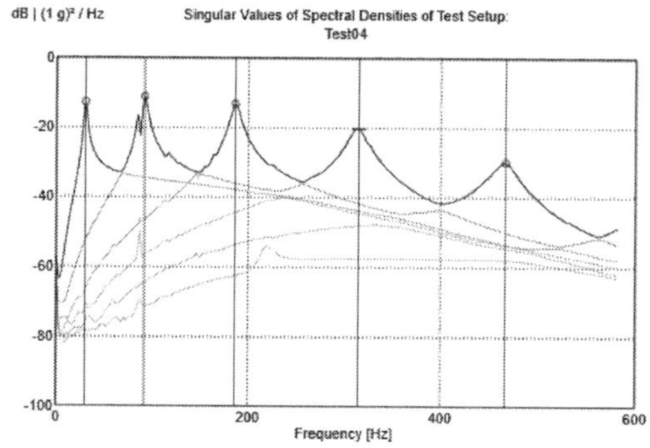

Figure 3. Singular value decomposition of the spectral densities for the OMA in the beam.

3.2.2 Impact tests

The beam was also subjected to an impact test using an impact hammer with a medium stiffness head and the additional mass of 75 grams. The response of the beam was measured with the same configuration used in modal analysis tests (Fig. 2).

Table 2. Modal parameters of the laminated glass beam.

Mode	Natural frequencies [Hz]	Exp. Damp. [%]	Experimental mode Shape
1	30.16	4.28	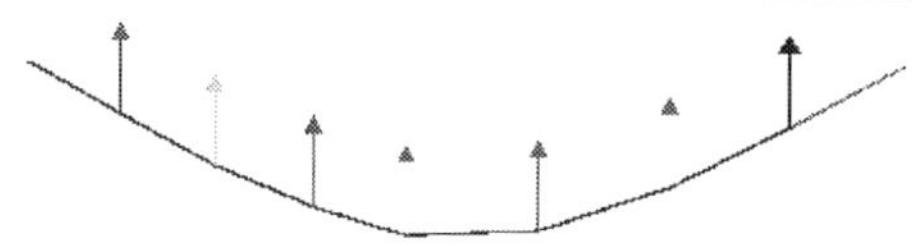
2	92.70	3.23	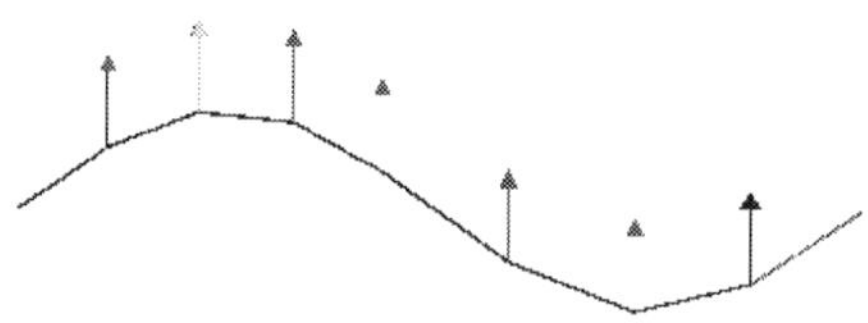
3	186.49	2.92	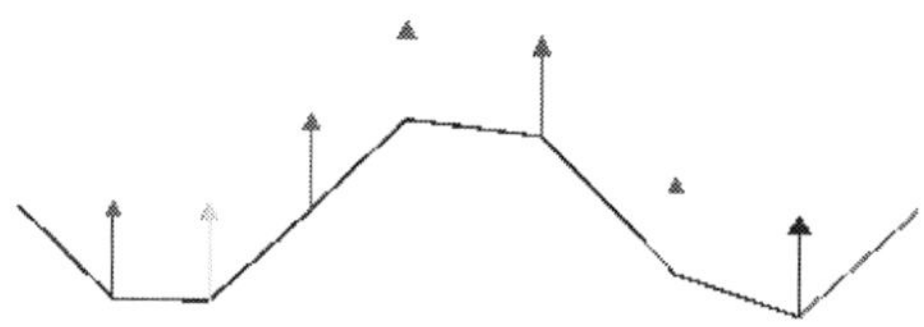
4	313.41	2.89	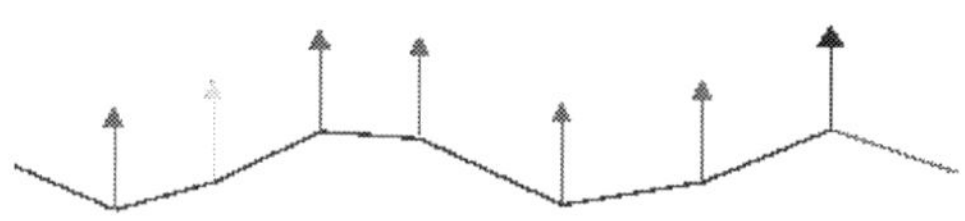
5	465.53	2.82	

3.2.3 Analytical Predictions

From the experimental responses and the experimental mode shapes, the modal coordinates were estimated using Eq. (12). Then, the experimental mode shapes were expanded using a monolithic 1D finite element model of the beam assembled in ABAQUS. In order to take into account the effect the rubbery at the supports, the finite element model was updated with elastic fixed supports.

The stresses at the midpoint of the bottom of layer H_2 , predicted with Eq. (14) is presented in Fig (4) together with those obtained with the strain gage at the same point. The effective Young modulus $E_{2\sigma i}(T)$ at temperature $T = 22^oC$ was calculated with Eq. (11) [7].
It can be observed that the calculated stresses are predicted with an error less than 6 % demonstrating that a reasonable good accuracy can be obtained with this technique.

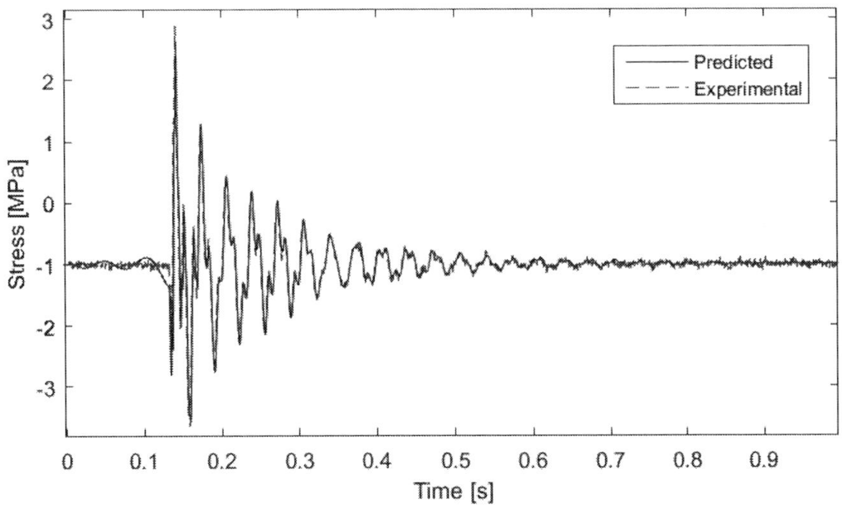

Figure 4. Predicted and experimental stresses for a laminated glass beam under soft impact loading (mid-point).

4. CONCLUSIONS

- In this paper, a methodology to predict the dynamic response of laminated glass elements using a linear-elastic monolithic model, has been proposed and validated.
- The method for obtaining the dynamic responses was also validated comparing the stresses estimated on a laminated glass subjected to an impact loading. The errors between the two models are less than 6%, which demonstrates that the technique can be used to predict with a good accuracy the dynamic response of laminated glass elements.

ACKNOWLEDGEMENTS

The financial support given by the Spanish Ministry of Education through the projects BIA201453774-R and MCI-20-PID2019-105593GB-I00/AEI/10.13039/501100011033 are gratefully appreciated.

REFERENCES

[1] Ferry, J.D., (1980) *Viscoelastic Properties of Polymers*, Third ed., John Wiley & Sons, Ltd., New York.

[2] Benninson, S., M.HX, Q. and Davies, P., (2008) High-performance laminated glass for structurally efficient glazing. *Innovative Light-weight Structures and Sustainable Facades*, Hong Kong, May.

[3] Ross, D., Ungar, E.E., and Kerwin, E.M., (1959) Damping of Plate Flexural Vibrations by Means of Viscoelastic Laminate, *Structural Damping*, ASME, p. 49-88.

[4] DiTaranto, R.A., and McGraw, Jr, J.R., (1969) Vibratory Bending of Damped Laminated Plates, *J Eng Ind*, 91(4):1081-1090.

[5] López-Aenlle, M., Pelayo, F., 2013) Frequency Response of Laminated Glass Elements: Analytical Modelling and Effective Thickness, *Appl Mech Rev*, 65(2), 020802 (13 pages).

[6] Mead, D. J.; Markus, S. The forced vibration of a three-layer, damped sandwich beam with arbitrary boundary conditions. J Sound Vib, 10(2):163–175, 1969.

[7] Aenlle López M, Fernández P, Álvarez-Vázquez A, García-Fernández N, Muñiz-Calvente M. Response of laminated glass elements subject to dynamic loadings using a monolithic model and a stress effective Young's modulus. Journal of Sandwich Structures & Materials. 2022;24(4):1771-1789. doi:10.1177/10996362221084636

[8] Lopez-Aenlle, M., Pelayo, F., Frequency Response of Laminated Glass Elements: Analytical′ Modelling and Effective Thickness. Appl Mech Rev, 65(2):020802, 2013.

[9] Lopez-Aenlle, M.; Pelayo, F. Dynamic effective thickness in laminated-glass beams and′ plates. Compos Part B-Eng, 67:332–347, 2014.

[10] Aenlle, M. L.; Pelayo, F.; Ismael, G. An effective thickness to estimate stresses in laminated glass beams under dynamic loadings. Compos Part B-Eng 82:1–12, 2015.

[11] Blasón, S.; López-Aenlle, M.; Pelayo, F. Influence of temperature on the modal parameters of′ laminated glass beams. In Proc. of the 11th International Conference on Vibration Problems (ICOVP), Lisbon, Portugal, 2013.

[12] Clough Ray W, Penzien J. Dynamics of structures, 2nd edition, McGraw-Hill, New York. 1993.

[13] Ismael, G., Manuel L. Aenlle and Pelayo, F. A Time Domain Effective Young's Modulus to Estimate Stresses in Laminated Glass Beams under Dynamic Loadings. 4th International Conference on Mechanics of Composites, Madrid, 9 - 12 July 2018.

[14] Pelayo, F., M.J. Lamela-Rey, M. Muniz-Calvente, M. López-Aenlle, A. Álvarez-Vázquez, A. Fernández-Canteli. Study of the time-temperature-dependent behaviour of the PVT: Application to laminated glass elements. Thin-Walled Structures. 119:324-331, 2017

[15] Friswell, M.I., Mottershead, J.E. Finite element model updating in structural dynamics. Kluwer Academic Publishers. 1995.

[16] UNE-EN 12600-2003. Glass in Building. Pendulum test. Impact test method and classification for flat glass.

Appendix

List of Parameters and Symbols

$$H_0 = t + \left(\frac{H_1 + H_2}{2}\right)$$

$$Y = \frac{H_0^2 E_1 H_1 E_2 H_2}{EI_T(E_1 H_1 + E_2 H_2)}$$

$$I_T = I_1 + I_2 = \frac{H_1^3 + H_2^3}{12}$$

$$I_1 = \frac{H_1^3}{12}$$

$$I_2 = \frac{H_2^3}{12}$$

E	Young's modulus of glass layers
ρ	Mass-density of the glass layers.
$G_t^*(\omega)$	Complex shear modulus for the polymeric interlayer
$k_I^2(\omega, T)$	Wavenumber of the beam

9th International Operational Modal Analysis Conference
iomac
July 3 - 6, 2022
Vancouver, Canada

MODAL IDENTIFICATION OF DAMS USING AMBIENT VIBRATION TESTS AND MODAL RESPONSE ANALYSIS

Mehrtash Motamedi[1], and Carlos E. Ventura[2]

[1] Research Associate, University of British Columbia, mmotamedi@civil.ubc.ca.
[2] Professor, University of British Columbia, ventura@civil.ubc.ca.

ABSTRACT

This paper describes how the modal properties of dams can be identified by ambient vibration tests and modal analysis. For this purpose, a typical concrete dam in the Province of British Columbia, Canada was selected and subjected to a series of ambient vibration measurements. Modal response analysis was then performed to identify the dynamic properties of the structure, including predominant natural frequencies and the corresponding mode shapes to support seismic assessment and upgrading of the dam. The testing program consisted of several setups on multiple locations of the structure including crest, piers, spillway ogee, hoist structure and abutments. Tromino® velocity/acceleration wireless sensors were used for the measurements which were placed on predetermined locations as planned. The computer program ARTeMIS was used to perform the system identification of the structure. The software allows to develop a 3D model of the structure and test points; the resulting mode shapes are displayed using this geometry. Two different techniques were used for modal identification: the Enhanced Frequency Domain Decomposition (EFDD) and the Stochastic Subspace Identification (SSI). These two modal identification techniques were used to cross-validate the results. The joint analysis of the signals measured in various strategic points of the structure made it possible to identify the modal configurations and the corresponding natural frequencies. As the results of this study, the vibration modes of the dam in upstream-downstream and cross-canyon directions, as well as the motions of the hoist structure were discussed. Also, the natural frequencies and corresponding dynamic mode shapes were presented.

Keywords: Ambient vibration tests, Modal analysis, Dams, Modal frequencies, Mode shapes.

1. INTRODUCTION

Ambient Vibration Test (AVT) technique has been employed for structural system identification during past decades and is growing very fast recently [1 and 2]. This paper also describes a series of AVTs conducted at a selected concrete dam in the province of British Columbia, Canada in order to determine the modal frequencies and the mode shapes of the dam. Prior to the AVTs, a site visit to the dam was conducted to determine the location of the measurements and develop a test plan. The test plan included measurements at the crest of the dam, at the galleries inside the dam, and on top of the concrete piers.

The selected dam is located on a river, and holds back the dam lake, also known as a reservoir, for storing a portion of the drinking water. The selected dam is a concrete structure consisting of a reinforced concrete wall and a spillway concrete bridge at the crest supported by a buttress concrete section. The concrete dam is about 189 m wide in the cross-canyon direction. The height varies from 92.1 m at the river valley location to 21 m at the east side and west side abutments. The roadway crown is located at elevation of 148.93 m.

The central section of the dam comprises a concrete deck and buttress structure. It contains a 24.4 m wide overflow spillway bay. The crest of the dam (top of parapet walls) is located at elevation of 150.38 m. At the west and east ends, the concrete structure is connected to the bedrock at the sides of the valley by two core walls. The transition blocks transfer the lateral load from the water reservoir and any lateral seismic loads from the concrete structure to the bedrock foundation.

Figure 1 shows a satellite view of the selected dam and Figure 2 illustrates the plan view of the dam.

Figure 1. Satellite view of the dam (Source: Google Map).

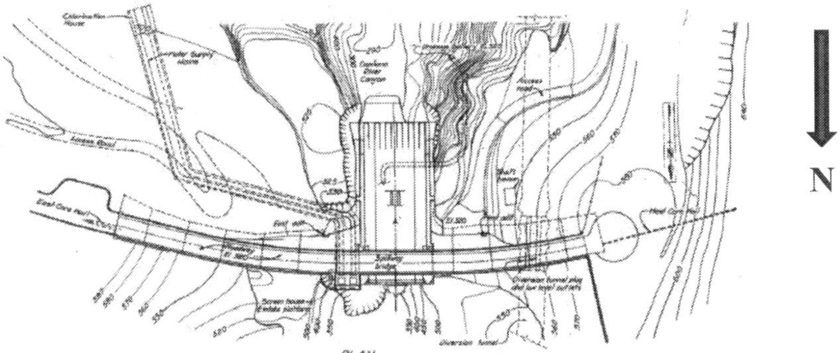

Figure 2. Drawings of the selected dam: Plan view (Source Metro Vancouver).

2. AMBIENT VIBRATION TESTS

The Ambient Vibration Tests (AVT) were conducted at a selected dam in order to determine the dynamic modal properties (modal frequencies and mode shapes) of the dam. The starting and ending time of the test setups, number of the sensors in each setup, recording time for each setup, and the reservoir level at the time of the ambient vibration tests and also the average temperature at the time of the tests are presented in Table 1.

Table 1: Test information for each setup.

	Setup 1	Setup 2	Setup 3	Setup 4	Setup 5	Setup 6	Setup7
Date of the Test		17 April 2018			11 May 2018		
Time of the Test	11:06:32	12:11:31	12:53:13	8:26:17	9:31:56	10:38:50	12:36:36
No. of the Sensors	8	8	8	7	7	4	4
Recording Duration (min.)	40	32	32	40	40	40	30
Temperature (C)	9	11	13	12	13	14	17
Reservoir Level (m)		144.91				144.90	

Tromino® velocity/acceleration sensors were used to carry out these AVTs [3]. The collected records were time synchronized with a radio antenna and amplifier in each sensor. This allowed the synchronization of the recordings both within each measurement setup and between setups. The Tromino sensors are suitable for high-resolution ambient vibration tests as they are fully portable, wireless, compact, and light instruments. Each sensor is equipped with two sets of three orthogonal high-resolution electrodynamics sensors (high gain and low gain velocity meter) and one set of three orthogonal digital accelerometers with a frequency range of 0.1 to 300 Hz. For these tests the high-gain velocity data was used for the modal identification process.

The testing program consisted of seven measurement setups: three linear arrays (at about 10 m spacing) of eight sensors on the top of the crest of the dam (setups 1, 2, and 3); an array of seven sensors inside the upper gallery at west side (Setup 4); an array of seven sensors inside the east side of upper gallery and the intermediate gallery (Setup 5); one set of four sensors inside the lower gallery (Setup 6); and one setup of four sensors at top of the piers (Setup 7). Figures 3 and 4 show the schematic upstream and downstream elevation of the dam and the location of the measurement setups at the crest and inside the galleries. One stationary reference sensor was used for all setups (Shown in Figures 3 and 4).

The first three setups are shown in Figure 5-a and provided data to determine the global dynamic response of the dam at the crest level. Sensors S5, S6, and S7 of setup 2 were located on top of the bridge and were not used for modal analysis of the dam. Instead, the readings from setup 7 were used to verify the predominant frequency of the dam. In this setup, Sensor S3 was placed on top of the bridge and was used only for radio communication between sensors and the data extracted from this sensor was not used for modal identification of the dam. Figure 5-b and 5-c show the setups 6 and 7 inside the lower gallery and on top of the piers, respectively.

The sampling frequency of the recordings at each setup was 512 samples per second (sps), and the total recording duration for each setup was about 30 to 40 minutes. This testing approach allows to capture the most important vibration modes up to a frequency of about 256Hz. The north component of each sensor has been oriented perpendicular to crest canyon direction of the dam for all of the measurement setups (Figure 5).

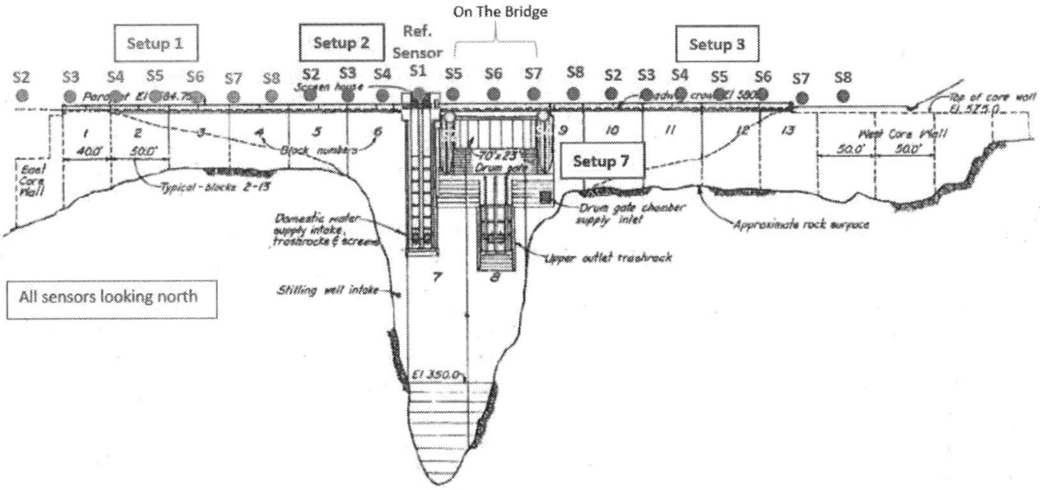

Figure 3: Upstream elevation of the dam and location of measurement setups on the crest (Setup 1, 2, and 3), and location of sensors on the concrete piers (Setup 7).

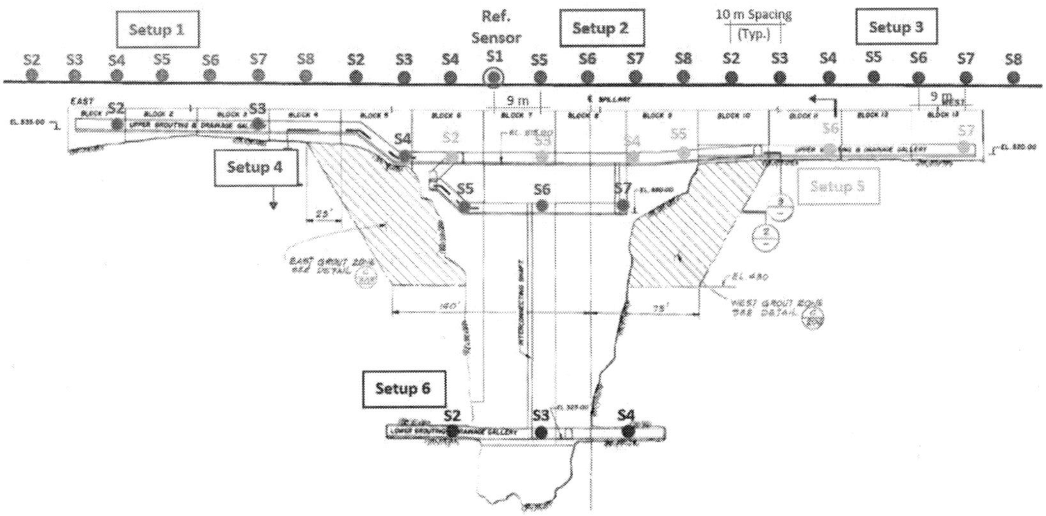

Figure 4: Downstream elevation of the dam and location of sensors on the crest, and location of measurements setup inside the galleries (Setup 4, 5 and 6).

(a) (b) (c)

Figure 5: Location of sensors: a) at the crest (setup 3); b) Lower gallery (Setup 6); c) Top of the piers (Setup 7).

3. METHODOLOGY AND DATA PROCESSING

The computer program ARTeMIS version 4 [4], was used to perform the modal identification of the dam. The software allows the user to develop a 3D model of the structure and test points; the resulting mode shapes are displayed using this geometry. Two different, complementary techniques are usually used for modal identification [5]: the Enhanced Frequency Domain Decomposition (EFDD) and the Stochastic Subspace Identification (SSI). These two modal identification techniques are used to cross-validate the results. The joint analysis of the signals measured in various strategic points of the structure makes it possible to identify the modal configurations and the corresponding natural frequencies.

The EFDD technique is an enhanced frequency domain method and the procedure consists of decomposing the system output into a set of systems of a specific degree of freedom, which are independent for each mode. The singular values are estimated from the spectral density of the specific degree of freedom system and the configuration of the modes is estimated from the singular vectors by selecting the highest peaks of the responses.

The SSI technique is a time domain method which consists of adjusting a parametric model to the time series recorded by the sensors. SSI method takes a matrix of the time history data, and performs a series of geometric manipulations which results in a set of mathematical models that represent the system that produces the data; the analysis provides modes based on those models. The advantage of the SSI is more accurate modal estimations, especially in the lower frequencies when the data is properly decimated. The disadvantage is that the SSI method takes a considerable amount of time for analysis, and is not easily applied to broadband data. In contrast, the FDD method is very quick and allows for the user to picks modes anywhere in the frequency range of interest.

Ambient vibration data recorded on and off the dam contains both noise and the response of the dam under ambient vibrations. The noise component of the recorded data is mainly due to mechanical imperfections in the sensors, instrument noise, installation, and other aspects in the sensor such as digitalization. The noise components of the vibration data, by its nature, usually appear as a random phenomenon in the data; however, the response of the dam is not random, but consistent at certain frequencies due to resonance effects of the dam to environmental excitations. Removing the noise components from the data is generally achieved by using signal processing tools such as decimation, filtering, and data averaging.

The data collected at all measurement locations on the crest, inside the galleries, and top of the piers was processed and analysed with ARTeMIS Modal. A 3D model (for animation purposes only) of the dam was created using the structural geometry. The model includes the discretized locations of 37 measurement points on the crest of the dam and inside the galleries including the reference and roving sensors as seen in Figure 6. The blue arrows represent the location and orientation the of reference sensor for setups 1 to 7, while the green and pink arrows represent the location and orientation of the roving sensors. This estimation would be correct since the readings from all of the sensors had been fully synchronized. Therefore, this method would provide a reliable estimation of a mode shape.

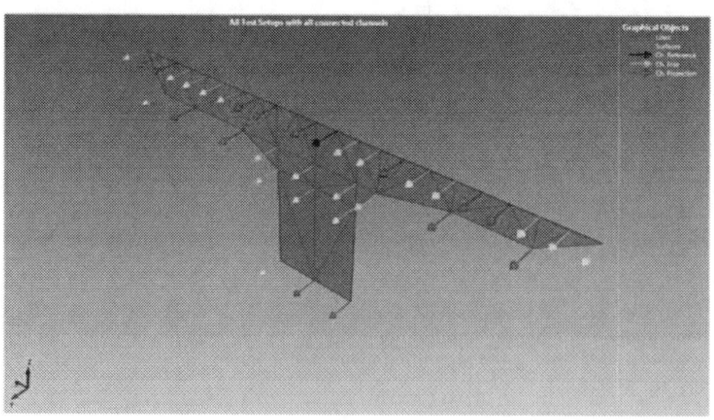

Figure 6: 3D ARTeMIS model showing the locations of the measurement points at the crest and the galleries of the dam (Only measurements conducted in the North-South direction are shown for simplicity).

4. TEST RESULTS

The results of the analysis using the Enhanced Frequency Domain Decomposition method (EFDD) are shown in Figure 7. This figure shows a plot of the spectral density of the peak singular values of all the data from setups 1 to 7 as a function of frequency. The peak values in this plot can be associated to dominant frequencies in the datasets, and some of these correspond to modal frequencies. Since the data is only from the crest of the dam and the galleries in limited locations, some of the peaks may be associated to local or higher order modes. However, the results of the analysis of the data using the SSI method can be used to determine with greater certainty the most dominant frequencies in the dataset. Figure 8 shows the Stabilization Diagram of all the data from setup 1. The vertical red dotted lines indicate the frequencies at which the modal frequencies are stable and can be associated to natural modes of the structure. By combining the results from both methods, it is possible to determine what of the peaks in Figure 7 are associated to modal frequencies of the dam [5].

Based on this analysis, the predominant frequency (the first natural frequency) of the structure is estimated to be 9.29 Hz, and it corresponds to the fundamental mode of the dam in the upstream-downstream direction. The corresponding mode-shape is shown in Figure 9. The second modal frequency is at 13.09 Hz, and it corresponds to a mode of the dam in the upstream-downstream direction, as shown in Figure 10. Frequencies of some of the higher order modes (third and fourth modes) of the dam were also identified as 19.71 and 21.30 Hz.

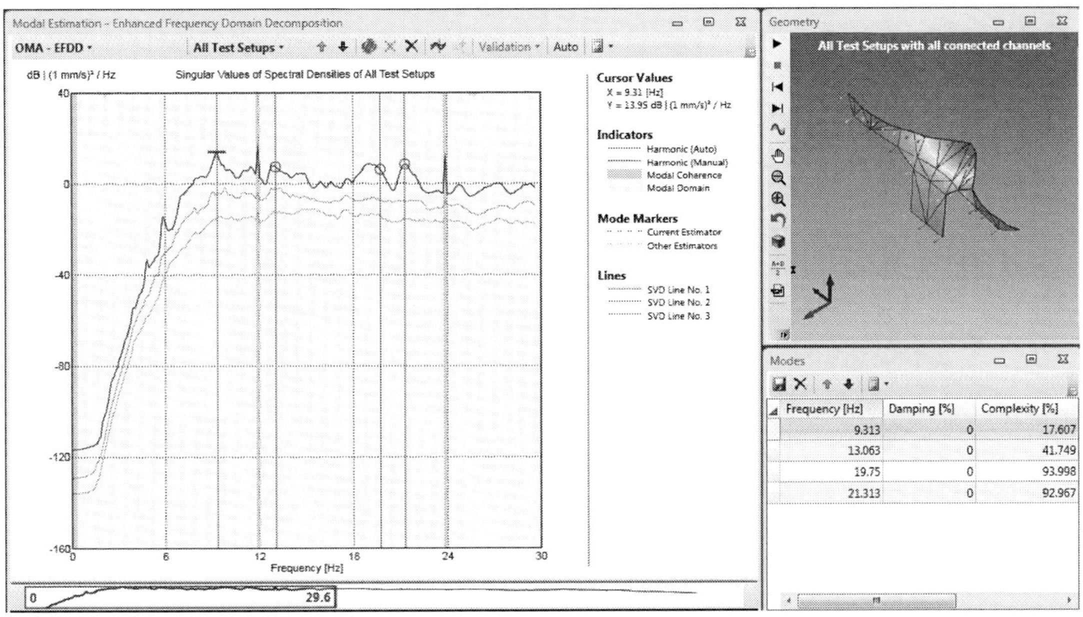

Figure 7: Singular Values of Spectral Densities of all test setups in the frequency range of 0 to 30 Hz using EFDD.

Table 2 summarizes the modal frequencies extracted from the vibration data for which the confidence on the results is high from both the EFDD and SSI-UPC methods. Figures 11 and 12 show the third and fourth mode of the dam corresponding to 19.71 Hz and 21.30 Hz, respectively.

Table 2: Modal frequencies obtained from modal analysis estimated by EFDD and SSI methods (Hz).

	EFDD Method	SSI – UPC Merged Method
1st Mode	9.31	9.26
2nd Mode	13.06	13.11
3rd Mode	19.75	19.67
4th Mode	21.31	21.29

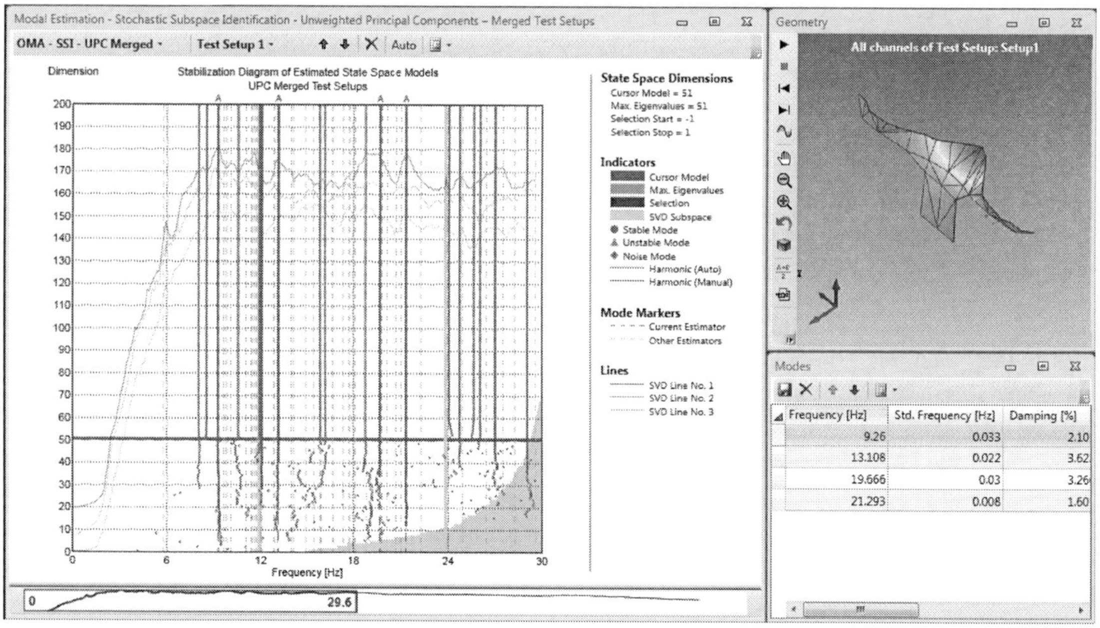

Figure 8: Stabilization Diagram of Estimated State Space Models from all the data in setup 1. This plot is for the Unweighted Principal Components (UPC)-Merged Test Setups in the frequency range of 0 to 30 Hz.

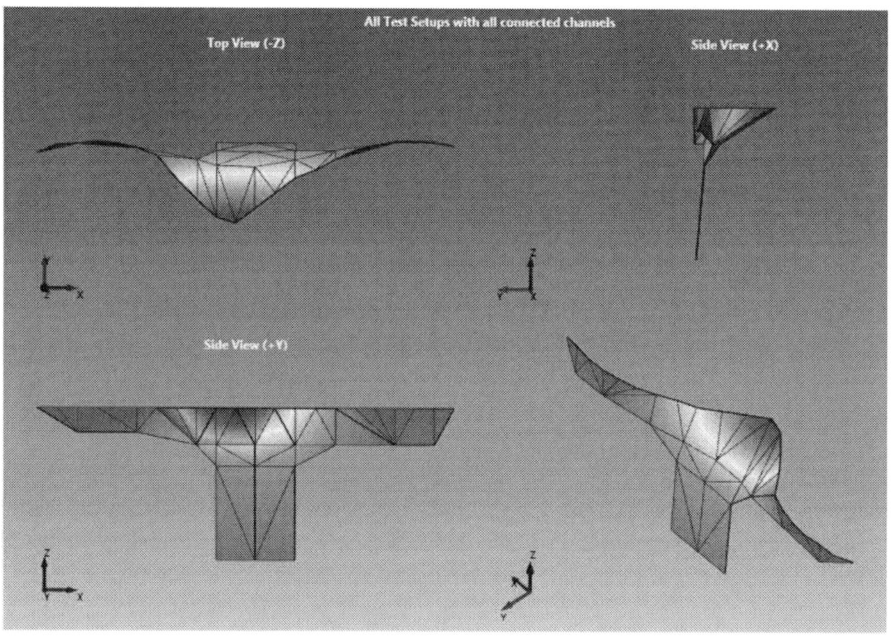

Figure 9: First mode shape of the dam in upstream-downstream direction (f=9.31 Hz) – Quad view.

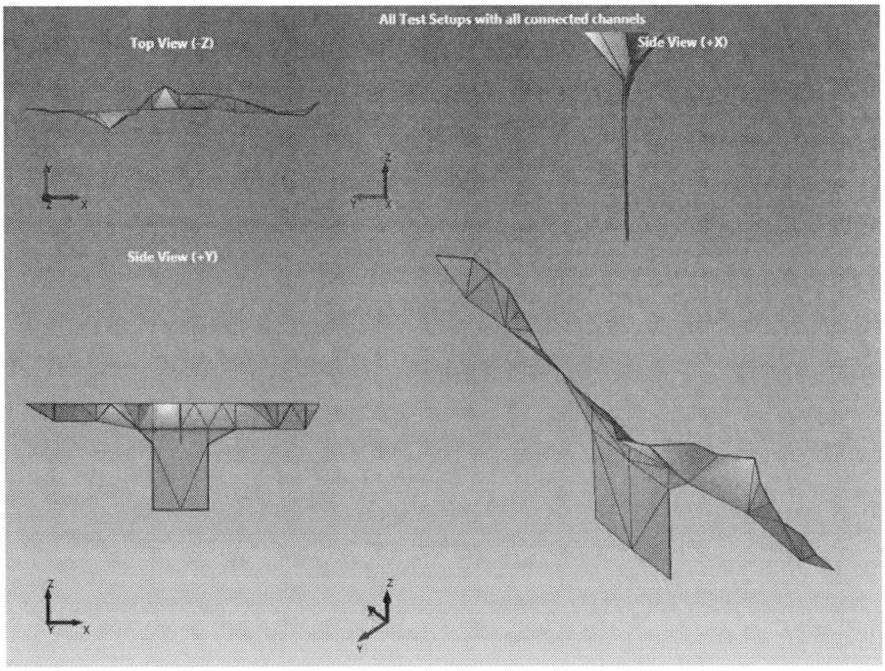

Figure 10: Second mode shape of the dam in upstream-downstream direction (f=13.06 Hz) - Quad view.

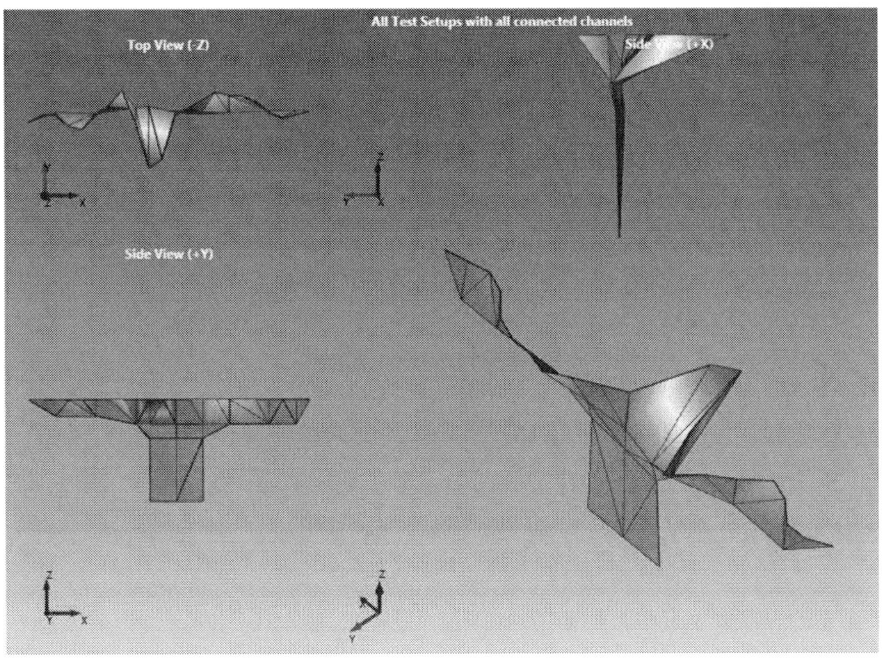

Figure 11: Third mode shape of the dam in upstream-downstream direction (f=19.75 Hz) - Quad view.

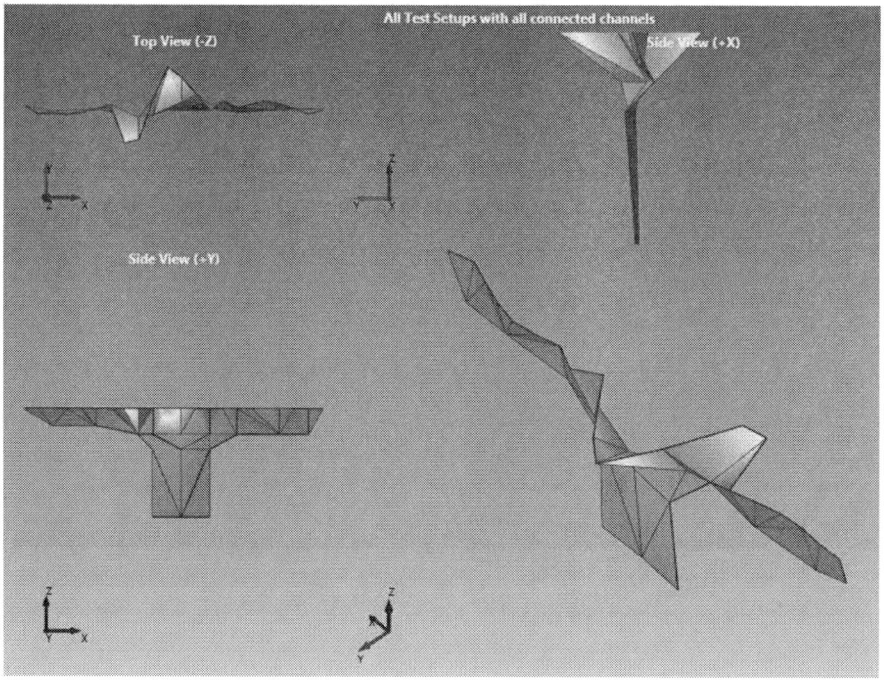

Figure 12: Forth mode shape of the Dam in upstream-downstream direction (f=21.31 Hz) - Quad view.

Different modal identification techniques were used to identify the modes of the dam. The results were cross-validated in terms of frequencies and mode shapes [5]. Figure 13 presents a validation diagram of the results. This diagram shows the Modal Assurance Criterion values of the estimated frequencies by EFDD and SSI-UPC Merged methods. This comparison validates the existence of the predominant frequency at 9.29 Hz, which was obtained from all setups (Table 3).

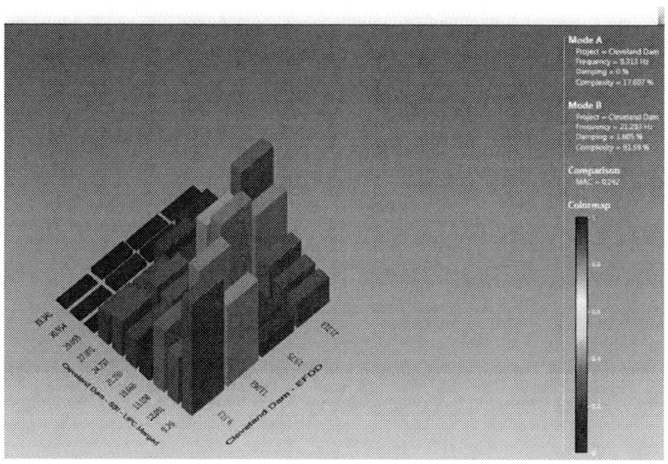

Figure 13: Validation diagram of the results; Modal Assurance Criterion Values for EFDD and SSI-UPC Merged methods.

5. CONCLUSIONS

A series of ambient vibration tests was conducted on a selected dam in April 2018. The testing program consisted of seven measurement setups using wireless digital seismometers: three of these were linear arrays on top of the crest of the concrete dam; another setup was an array inside the upper gallery; another setup was an array inside the intermediate gallery; and eight single-sensor measurement located inside the galleries of the concrete dam. Vibration of the dam was recorded for approximately 30-40 minutes for each setup.

The results from the modal analyses indicated that the fundamental frequency of the dam in the upstream-downstream direction is 9.29 Hz. The frequencies corresponding to second, third and fourth modes of vibration of the dam are 13.09 Hz, 19.71 Hz and 21.30 Hz, respectively. The identified frequencies and periods of the dam are also summarized in the Table 3. The main direction of the associated mode shapes is included in the table.

Table 3: Summary of modal periods obtained from the ambient vibration tests.

Mode #	Frequency (Hz)	Period (Sec.)	Mode & Direction
1	9.29	0.108	1st Upstream – Downstream
2	13.09	0.076	2nd Upstream – Downstream
3	19.71	0.051	3rd Upstream – Downstream
4	21.30	0.047	4th Upstream – Downstream

ACKNOWLEDGEMENTS

The ambient vibration tests and modal response analysis described in this paper have been performed with collaboration of Dr. Alexander Mendler and Mr. Felix Yao from the University of British Columbia. Their contribution and technical support are gratefully acknowledged.

REFERENCES

[1] Miquel, B. & Verret, D. (2019) The use of ambient vibration instrumentation for dams at Hydro-Québec. In: *Proc. 12th Canadian Conf. on Earthquake Engineering,* Quebec, Canada.

[2] Peeters, B. (2000) *System identification and damage detection in civil engineering*. Ph.D. Thesis, Katholieke University of Leuven, Belgium.

[3] Micromed (2012) *Tromino: Portable ultra-light acquisition system for seismic noise and vibration- User's manual*, Macromed, Italy.

[4] Structural Vibration Solutions (2014) *ARTeMIS Modal Software*, Version 4.

[5] Brincker, R., and Ventura, C.E. (2015) *Introduction to operational modal analysis.* John Wiley & Sons, Ltd, United Kingdom.

APPLICATIONS IN CIVIL ENGINEERING/MODAL UPDATING

9th International Operational Modal Analysis Conference
iomac
July 3 - 6, 2022
Vancouver, Canada

ON THE INITIAL PERFORMANCE ASSESSMENT OF A FREQUENCY-DOMAIN MAXIMUM LIKELIHOOD FORMULATED IN Z-DOMAIN

Sandro D. R. Amador[1], *Simona Miraglia*[2], *Umberto Alibrandi*[3] *and Rune Brincker*[4]

[1] Assistant Professor, Technical University of Denmark (DTU), Denmark, sdio@byg.dtu.dk.

[2] Dr. Simona Miraglia, Bane Denmark, Denmark, smrl@bane.dk.

[3] Associate Professor, Aarhus University, Denmark, ua@cae.au.dk.

[4] Professor Rune Brincker, Brincker Monitoring ApS, rune@brincker-monitoring.com.

ABSTRACT

In frequency domain experimental modal identification, the main goal is to extract the modal properties from the measured transfer function or power spectral densities. The modal parameter estimation can be carried out in a Linear Least Squares (LLS) sense by means of parametric identification methods. When the accuracy of such estimates is not accurate enough, non-linear identification methods based on Maximum Likelihood (ML) can by employed to improve precision of the LLS estimates in an iterative manner. One the main advantages of the ML-based optimization techniques is that, apart from providing more accurate estimates, they are also capable of estimating the uncertainties on the optimized estimates if the noise information is also taken in account in the optimization process. In this paper, the performance of a new frequency-domain ML-based technique formulated in Z-domain modal is investigated by means of a simulated example.

Keywords: Maximum Likelihood, Non-Linear Least Squares, Modal Identification, Modal Parameter Estimation, Frequency Domain, Modal Analysis, Identification Technique

1. INTRODUCTION

When it comes to **E**xperimental and **O**perational **M**odal **A**nalysis (**EMA** and **OMA**) the main challenge is the extract the physical properties of the dynamic system being tested from the measured vibration data. The vibration properties' estimation can be carried either in time or in frequency domain using the so-called parametric identification based on **L**inear **L**east **S**quares model (**LLS**) fitting. Several identification methods exist for this purpose as, for instance, the **p**oly-reference **L**east **S**quares **C**omplex **F**requency

Domain (**pLSCF**) [1] formulated in frequency domain and the **S**tochastic **S**ystem **I**dentification (**SSI**) algorithms developed to estimate the modal parameters from the measured responses [2], the **I**brahim **T**ime **D**omain (**ITD**) [3, 4] and the **p**oly-reference **L**east **S**quares **C**omplex **E**xponential (**pLSCE**) (also known as **LSCE**-Prony) [5, 6].

It turns out that, in some circumstances, the accuracy of the **LLS** methods is not good enough due several sources of errors such as noise and estimation errors. In these circumstances, the **N**on-**L**inear **L**east **S**quares (**NLLS**) techniques such as those based in **M**aximum **L**ikelihood (**ML**) can be employed to iteratively improve the accuracy of **LLS** estimates for the modal properties. The underlying idea of the **NLLS** identification with the **ML**-based approaches is to use the estimates from a **LLS** technique as a starting guess to iteratively improve their accuracy by minimizing the cost function computed from the difference between the measure data and model synthesized from the estimates obtained in each iteration. In the case of **ML**-based methods, this is achieved by making use of the so-called Gaussian-Newton algorithm in combination with the Levenberg–Marquardt [7] approach to prevent the cost function to converge to local minima.

In [9–11] a frequency domain **ML** estimator is introduced to iteratively optimize the invariants of the Frequency Response Function (**FRF**) in Laplace-domain, i.e., the mode shape vectors, continuous time poles, modal participation factor vector and out-of-band residuals. The idea behind this approach is to use the estimates from a previous **LLS** Modal Parameter Estimation (**MPE**) as starting guess. Then, after performing some Gauss-Newton iterations, the **ML**-based approach yields the optimized estimates. Afterwards, the authors formulated another **ML**-based technique in Laplace-domain to optimize the **LLS** modal properties in the cases where reciprocity in considered [12]. One of the main advantages of the **ML**-based **MPE** algorithms is that it considers both the measured vibration data and the noise information in the optimization process. Therefore, apart from providing optimized estimates for the modal properties, they also compute the confidence bounds for these estimates.

In this paper, an initial performance assessment of a new **ML**-based estimator is presented. The **ML** estimator herein introduced is formulated in z-domain Modal Model, hence the acronym **ML-ZMM**. Differently from the **ML-MM** described in [9, 10], the **ML-ZMM** aims at improving the estimates for the discrete-time poles after some Gauss-Newton iterations, rather than the continuous-time poles. Apart from assessing the ability of providing optimized estimates for the natural frequencies and damping coefficients, the robustness in predicting confidence bounds for this properties is also evaluated in this paper.

2. DERIVATION OF THE ML-ZMM

Once the modal parameters are estimated with a **LLS** algorithm, they can be optimized by means of the Maximum Likelihood algorithm formulated using the modal model in z-domain. If displacement responses are measured during the vibration test, the **FRF** matrix $H(z) \in \mathbb{C}^{N_o \times N_i}$ with N_i inputs and N_o outputs is modeled in z-domain by

$$H(z) = \sum_{m=1}^{N_m} \frac{\phi_m l_m^T}{z - \mu_m} + \frac{\phi_m^* l_i^H}{z - \mu_m^*} \tag{1}$$

with N_m denoting the number of vibration modes, $\mu_m \in \mathbb{C}$, $\phi_m \in \mathbb{C}^{N_o \times 1}$, $l_m \in \mathbb{C}^{N_i \times 1}$ stand for the discrete-time poles, mode shape and the operational factor vectors corresponding to the mth vibration mode; $z = e^{j\omega \Delta t}$ is the z-domain variable, with $j = \sqrt{-1}$ denoting the imaginary unit and $\omega = 2\pi f$ is the angular frequency, where f designates the frequency in cycles per second (Hertz); and the operators $(\bullet)^*$ and $(\bullet)^H$ denote the conjugate and Hermitian of a complex matrix, respectively. The continuous-time poles, $\lambda_m \in \mathbb{C}$, are related to their discrete-time counterparts as $\mu_m = e^{\lambda_m \Delta t}$, with $\Delta t \in \mathbb{R}$ standing for the sampling interval. The poles λ_m occur in complex-conjugated pairs and are related to the eigenfrequencies ω_{n_m} and damping ratios ξ_{n_m} as:

$$\lambda_m, \lambda_m^* = -\omega_{nm}\xi_{nm} \pm j\sqrt{1-\xi_{nm}^2}\omega_{nm} \tag{2}$$

Compared to conventional **LLS**-based approaches, **ML**-based algorithms have the advantage of taking into account not only the measured **FRFs**, but also the noise information during the parametric identification process, and thus, apart from providing the optimized estimates of modal parameters, they also yield the confidence intervals of these estimates. The optimization of the starting parameters with the **ML-ZMM** is accomplished by minimizing the following (negative) log-like cost function

$$\sum_{o=1}^{N_o}\sum_{f=1}^{N_f} l(\Theta)_{ML-ZMM} = E_o(\Theta, z_f)E_o^H(\Theta, z_f) \tag{3}$$

with N_f the number of frequency lines, $z_f = e^{j\omega_f \Delta t}$ the z-domain variable evaluated at frequency line f and $E_o(\Theta, z_f)$ the row vector error between the measured and the estimated **FRF** for the oth measured output, which is calculated as:

$$E_o(\Theta, z_f) = \left(\frac{\hat{H}_{o1}(\Theta, z_f) - H_{o1}(z_f)}{\sigma_{H_{o1}(z_f)}} \cdots \frac{\hat{H}_{oN_i}(\Theta, z_f) - H_{oN_i}(z_f)}{\sigma_{H_{oN_i}(z_f)}}\right) \tag{4}$$

where $\hat{H}_o(\Theta, z_f) \in \mathbb{C}^{1\times N_i}$, $H_o(z_f) \in \mathbb{C}^{1\times N_i}$ and $\sigma_{H_o(z_f)} \in \mathbb{R}^{1\times N_i}$ are the oth row of the **FRF** in modal model formulation (1), and of the measured **FRF** and its corresponding standard deviation, respectively. The parameter Θ is a column vector with all the parameters to be optimized by means of the Gauss-Newton Newton algorithm and is given by:

$$\Theta = \begin{bmatrix}\theta_1 & \theta_2 & \cdots & \theta_{N_o} & \theta_{L\mu}\end{bmatrix}^T \in \mathbb{R}^{2N_m(N_i+N_o)} \tag{5}$$

with

$$\theta_{L\mu} = \begin{bmatrix}\theta_L & \theta_\mu\end{bmatrix} \in \mathbb{C}^{2N_mN_i} \tag{6}$$

The parameter $\theta_o \in \mathbb{C}^{2N_m}$ is a vector with the real and imaginary parts of the mode shape ordinates corresponding to the oth output, given by

$$\theta_o = \begin{bmatrix}\mathfrak{Re}(\phi_{o1}) & \mathfrak{Re}(\phi_{o2}) & \cdots & \mathfrak{Re}(\phi_{oN_m}) & \mathfrak{Im}(\phi_{o1}) & \mathfrak{Im}(\phi_{o2}) & \cdots & \mathfrak{Im}(\phi_{oN_m})\end{bmatrix} \in \mathbb{R}^{2N_m} \tag{7}$$

where $\mathfrak{Re}(\bullet)$ and $\mathfrak{Im}(\bullet)$ stand for the real and imaginary parts of a complex number. The parameters $\theta_L \in \mathbb{R}^{2N_m(N_i-1)}$ and $\theta_\mu \in \mathbb{C}^{2N_m}$ in eq. (6) are columns vectors containing, respectively, the real and imaginary parts of all the operational factors elements, and the real and imaginary parts of the discrete-time poles. These parameters are defined, respectively, as:

$$\theta_L = \begin{bmatrix}\mathfrak{Re}(L_{11}) & \cdots & \mathfrak{Re}(L_{N_k1}) & \mathfrak{Re}(L_{11}) & \cdots & \mathfrak{Im}(L_{N_k1}) & \cdots \\ \cdots & \mathfrak{Re}(L_{1N_m}) & \cdots & \mathfrak{Re}(L_{N_kN_m}) & \mathfrak{Re}(L_{1N_m}) & \cdots & \mathfrak{Im}(L_{N_kN_m})\end{bmatrix} \tag{8}$$

and

$$\theta_\mu = \left[\Re e\left(\mu_1\right) \;\; \Re e\left(\mu_2\right) \;\; \cdots \;\; \Re e\left(\mu_{N_m}\right) \;\; \Im m\left(\mu_1\right) \;\; \Im m\left(\mu_2\right) \;\; \cdots \;\; \Im m\left(\mu_{N_m}\right)\right] \in \mathbb{R}^{2N_m} \tag{9}$$

where $L_{km} \in \mathbb{C}$ is the kth element of the operational factor vector of the mth vibration mode $l_m \in \mathbb{C}^{N_i \times 1}$, with $k = 1, 2, \cdots, N_k$, and $N_k = N_i - 1$, which means that only the operational factors that differ from 1 are optimized by the algorithm during the performed iterations. As the identified operational factors are normalized with regard to the maximum element of each mode in the identification with the **pLSCF**, the derivatives of the elements that equals 1 are not evaluated and, therefore, are not included in the vector defined by eq. (8). In fact, this works like a constraint, since the operational factors elements that equal 1 are not updated during the minimization of the cost function (3). The maximum likelihood optimization of the parameters Θ is accomplished by minimizing the cost function (3) in a non-linear least squares sense. This is performed by means of the Gauss-Newton optimization algorithm combined with Levenberg–Marquardt approach [7], which forces the cost function to decrease with the performed iterations. The Gauss-Newton iteration is basically divided in two steps:

1. Solve the normal equations

$$J_i^H J_i \text{vec}(\Delta\Theta_i) = -J_i^H E_i \quad for \quad \text{vec}(\Delta\Theta_i). \tag{10}$$

2. Compute an update of the previous solution

$$\Theta_{i+1} = \Theta_i + \Delta\Theta_i \tag{11}$$

where $\text{vec}(\Delta\Theta_i) \in \mathbb{R}^{2N_m(N_o+N_i)}$ is the perturbation on the modal parameters, E_i is the error between the measured quantity and the parametric model (i.e. **FRF** equation in z-domain modal model formulation (1)), J_i is the Jacobian matrix evaluated at the ith iteration, and the vec($\bullet$) stands for the column stacking operator. The equation error calculated at the ith iteration $E_i = E(\Theta_i)$ is given by

$$E_i = \begin{Bmatrix} \text{vec}(E_1(\Theta_i)) \\ \text{vec}(E_2(\Theta_i)) \\ \vdots \\ \text{vec}(E_{N_o}(\Theta_i)) \end{Bmatrix} \in \mathbb{R}^{N_f N_o N_i \times 1}, \quad E_o(\Theta_i) = \begin{bmatrix} E_o(\omega_1, \Theta_i) \\ E_o(\omega_2, \Theta_i) \\ \vdots \\ E_o(\omega_{N_f}, \Theta_i) \end{bmatrix} \in \mathbb{R}^{N_f \times N_i} \tag{12}$$

and the corresponding Jacobian matrix by

$$J_i = \left[\frac{\partial E(\Theta_i)}{\partial \Theta_i}\right] \in \mathbb{R}^{N_f N_o N_i \times 2N_m(N_o+N_i)} \tag{13}$$

with Θ_i representing the parameters given by eq. (5) at the ith iteration. This matrix has the following structure:

$$J = \begin{bmatrix} Y_1 & 0 & \cdots & 0 & X_1 \\ 0 & Y_2 & \cdots & 0 & X_2 \\ \vdots & \vdots & \ddots & \vdots & \vdots \\ 0 & 0 & \cdots & Y_{N_o} & X_{N_o} \end{bmatrix} \tag{14}$$

where X_o is a matrix with the derivatives of the equation error (4) with regard to the discreet-time poles and operational factors, and Y_o is a matrix with the derivatives with respect to the mode shapes. The matrix X_o is computed as:

$$X_o = \begin{bmatrix} X_L & X_\mu \end{bmatrix} \tag{15}$$

where the entries X_L and X_μ are sub-matrices containing the derivatives of the equation error (4) with respect to the real and imaginary of the operational factors, real and imaginary parts of the discreet-time poles, respectively. The sub-matrix X_L is computed as:

$$X_L = \begin{bmatrix} X_{L_1} & X_{L_2} & \cdots & X_{L_{Nm}} \end{bmatrix} \tag{16}$$

with X_{L_m} containing the derivatives of the equation error with respect to the real and imaginary parts of the elements of the operational factor of the mth mode. The sub-matrix X_μ is calculated as:

$$X_\mu = \left[\text{vec}\left\{ \frac{\partial E_o(\Theta)}{\partial \mathfrak{Re}(\mu_1)} \right\} \quad \cdots \quad \text{vec}\left\{ \frac{\partial E_o(\Theta)}{\partial \mathfrak{Re}(\mu_{Nm})} \right\} \quad \text{vec}\left\{ \frac{\partial E_o(\Theta)}{\partial \mathfrak{Im}(\mu_1)} \right\} \quad \cdots \quad \text{vec}\left\{ \frac{\partial E_o(\Theta)}{\partial \mathfrak{Im}(\mu_{Nm})} \right\} \right] \tag{17}$$

The sub-matrices X_{L_m} in eq. (16) are defined by

$$X_{L_m} = \left[\text{vec}\left\{ \frac{\partial E_o(\Theta)}{\partial \mathfrak{Re}(L_{1m})} \right\} \quad \cdots \quad \text{vec}\left\{ \frac{\partial E_o(\Theta)}{\partial \mathfrak{Re}(L_{N_k m})} \right\} \quad \text{vec}\left\{ \frac{\partial E_o(\Theta)}{\partial \mathfrak{Im}(L_{1m})} \right\} \quad \cdots \quad \text{vec}\left\{ \frac{\partial E_o(\Theta)}{\partial \mathfrak{Im}(L_{N_k m})} \right\} \right] \tag{18}$$

with $N_k = N_i - 1$. It is worth noting that the same constraint strategy used in the definition of eq. (8) must be used to calculate the derivatives in eq. (18). Therefore, only the derivatives with respect to the operational factors elements which are different from 1 are included in this equation. In eq. (14), Y_o is a sub-matrix with the derivatives of the equation error with respect to the real and imaginary parts of the oth mode shape vector

$$Y_o = \left[\text{vec}\left\{ \frac{\partial E_o(\Theta)}{\partial \mathfrak{Re}(\phi_{o1})} \right\} \quad \cdots \quad \text{vec}\left\{ \frac{\partial E_o(\Theta)}{\partial \mathfrak{Re}(\phi_{oNm})} \right\} \quad \text{vec}\left\{ \frac{\partial E_o(\Theta)}{\partial \mathfrak{Im}(\phi_{o1})} \right\} \quad \cdots \quad \text{vec}\left\{ \frac{\partial E_o(\Theta)}{\partial \mathfrak{Im}(\phi_{oNm})} \right\} \right] \tag{19}$$

It is worth noting that, apart from the measured **FRF**s, the variance of the noise is also taken into account during the parametric identification with **ML**-based algorithms. In the context of **EMA**, the variance is estimated by means of the so-called $H1$ **FRF** estimator [7]. In case of single-input measurements (i.e **SISO** and **SIMO** systems), the variance can be calculated as:

$$\sigma^2_{H_{oi}} = \frac{1}{N_b} \left(\frac{1 - \gamma^2_{oi}}{\gamma^2_{oi}} \right) |H_{oi}|^2 \tag{20}$$

where N_b and γ^2_{oi} stand for the number of averaged data blocks used to estimate the **FRF** and the coherence function, respectively. Given the block structure of the Jacobian matrix, the normal equations (10) are rewritten as follows

$$\begin{bmatrix} R_1 & 0 & \cdots & 0 & S_1 \\ 0 & R_2 & \cdots & 0 & S_2 \\ \vdots & \vdots & \ddots & \vdots & \vdots \\ 0 & 0 & \cdots & R_{N_o} & S_{N_o} \\ S_1^T & S_1^T & \cdots & S_{N_o}^T & \sum_{o=1}^{N_o} T_o \end{bmatrix} \begin{Bmatrix} \text{vec}(\Delta\theta_1) \\ \text{vec}(\Delta\theta_2) \\ \vdots \\ \text{vec}(\Delta\theta_{N_o}) \\ \text{vec}(\Delta\theta_{L\mu}) \end{Bmatrix} = - \begin{Bmatrix} \mathfrak{Re}\left(Y_1^H E_1\right) \\ \mathfrak{Re}\left(Y_2^H E_2\right) \\ \vdots \\ \mathfrak{Re}\left(Y_{N_o}^H E_{N_o}\right) \\ \sum_{o=1}^{N_o} \mathfrak{Re}\left(X_o^H E_o\right) \end{Bmatrix} \tag{21}$$

with

$$R_o = \mathfrak{Re}\left(Y_o^H Y_o\right) \in \mathbb{R}^{(2N_m N_i)\times(2N_m N_i)}$$
$$S_o = \mathfrak{Re}\left(Y_o^H X_o\right) \in \mathbb{R}^{(2N_m N_i)\times(2N_m N_i)}$$
$$T_o = \mathfrak{Re}\left(X_o^H X_o\right) \in \mathbb{R}^{(2N_m N_i)\times(2N_m N_i)}$$

From eqs. (21), the perturbation on the coefficients $\text{vec}(\Delta\theta_o)$ (i.e., the perturbations on the real and imaginary parts of the mode shape vectors) can be written as a function of the perturbation on the natural frequencies, damping ratios, operational factors, $\text{vec}(\Delta\theta_{L\mu})$, as:

$$\text{vec}(\Delta\theta_o) = -R_o^{-1}(\mathfrak{Re}\left(Y_o^H E_o\right) + S_o\text{vec}(\Delta\theta_{L\mu})) \tag{22}$$

and the perturbations $\text{vec}(\Delta\theta_o)$ can be eliminated from the last set of equations in (21) by means of eq. (22), yielding

$$\sum_{o=1}^{N_o}(T_o - S_o^T R_o^{-1} S_o)\text{vec}(\Delta\theta_{L\mu}) = -\sum_{o=1}^{N_o}(\mathfrak{Re}\left(X_o^H E_o\right) - S_o^T R_o^{-1}\mathfrak{Re}\left(Y_o^H E_o\right)) \tag{23}$$

or in a more compact form

$$M_1\text{vec}(\Delta\theta_{L\mu}) = M_2 \tag{24}$$

with

$$M_1 = \left(T_o - S_o^T R_o^{-1} S_o\right), \quad M_2 = \sum_{o=1}^{N_o}\left(S_o^T R_o^{-1}\mathfrak{Re}\left(Y_o^H E_o\right) - \mathfrak{Re}\left(X_o^H E_o\right)\right) \tag{25}$$

This elimination reduces the memory required to run the algorithm. An efficient implementation of the **ML-ZMM** is only possible if the variances are taken into account in the cost function (3). Once the perturbations on the discrete-time poles and operational factors are calculated in the last iteration by means of eq. (23), then perturbations on the mode shape vectors are computed using eq. (22).

2.1. Estimation of the uncertainty bounds

One of the main advantages of the **ML**-based algorithms is the possibility to estimate the confidence intervals for the identified modal parameters using the noise information measured together with the **FRF**s during the vibration tests. As shown in [7], a good approximation of the covariance of the **ML** parameters Θ_{ML-MM} is obtained by

$$\text{Cov}(\phi, L, \mu) \simeq \frac{1}{2}\mathfrak{Re}\left(\left[J_l^H J_l\right]\right)^{-1} \tag{26}$$

with J_l the Jacobian matrix evaluated in the last iteration of the Gaussian-Newton algorithm. Taking advantage of the structure of the Jacobian matrix and using the matrix inversion lemma [8], the covariance of the natural frequencies, damping ratios and the operational factors can be estimated independently as follows

$$\text{Cov}(L, \mu) \simeq \frac{1}{2} M_1^{-1} \tag{27}$$

Therefore, it is not necessary to invert the full matrix in eq. (21). Once the uncertainties on the discrete-time poles are found from (27), they can be propagated to the natural frequencies and damping ratios by means of the following linearization formulas [13]:

$$\begin{aligned} \text{Var}(F_{n_m}) &\simeq \left[\frac{\partial f_{nm}\left(\theta_{\mu m}\right)}{\partial \hat{\theta}_{\mu m}}\right] \text{Cov}(\hat{\theta}_{\mu_m}) \left[\frac{\partial f_{nm}\left(\theta_{\mu m}\right)}{\partial \hat{\theta}_{\mu m}}\right]^T \\ \text{Var}(\xi_{n_m}) &\simeq \left[\frac{\partial \xi_{nm}\left(\theta_{\mu m}\right)}{\partial \hat{\theta}_{\mu m}}\right] \text{Cov}(\hat{\theta}_{\mu_m}) \left[\frac{\partial \xi_{nm}\left(\theta_{\mu m}\right)}{\partial \hat{\theta}_{\mu m}}\right]^T \end{aligned} \tag{28}$$

Given the structure of the Jacobian matrix, it is straightforward to apply matrix inversion lemma [8] and derive the covariance of the mode shapes, yielding

$$\text{Cov}(\phi_o) \simeq R_o^{-1} + R_o^{-1} S_o M_1^{-1} S_o^T R_o^{-1} \tag{29}$$

3. VALIDATION OF THE ML-ZMM IMPLEMENTATION

The example used to validate the **ML**-based approach discussed in Section 2. is illustrated in Fig. 1. This system was used by [14] to compare different modal parameter estimation techniques in terms of their sensitivity to statistical errors. It comprises five masses supported by cantilever beams which are connected among themselves by arch springs. The exact natural frequencies, damping ratios and modal masses of the system are given in Tab. 1, whereas the real modes are shown in Tab. 2. These properties were used to generate the **FRF**s used in simulated **EMA**.

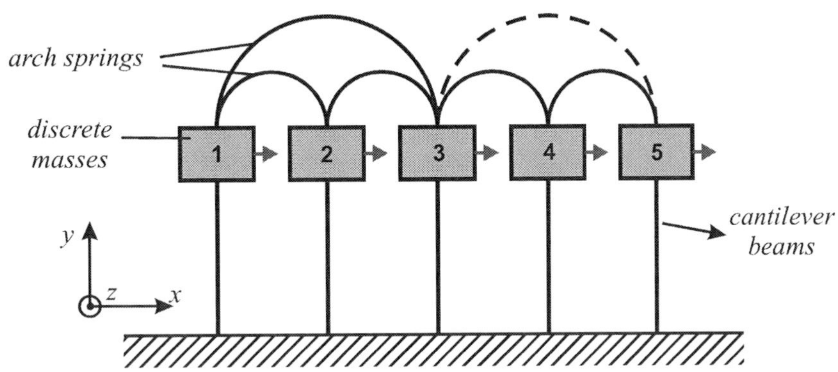

Figure 1: Five-**DOF** system connected with arch springs [14]

The system was excited by a white Gaussian noise at masses 1 and 2, and the responses were measured at all **DOF**s, resulting in **FRF** matrix with two columns and five rows. The **FRF** was calculated in the frequency range of 0-80 Hz with a resolution of 0.1 Hz. Afterwards, a colored noise was added to the **FRF** matrix with a standard deviation of 10%. The noise was added to the real and imaginary parts independently, and was calculated as a percentage of the absolute value of the **FRF** at each frequency line. This was achieved by adding a complex random number to the **FRF** at each frequency line. This number was computed so that its amplitude is a random number of a normal distribution and its phase is an uniform random number between 0 and 2π.

Table 1: Eigenfrequencies, damping ratios and modal masses of the five-**DOF** system

Mode	f_n [Hz]	ξ_n [%]	m_i [Kg]
1	26.06	2	2.52
2	36.84	2	2.97
3	51.47	2	0.90
4	56.21	2	1.09
5	62.60	2	1.05

Table 2: Real modes of the five-**DOF** system

DOF/Mode	1	2	3	4	5
1	0.7147	1.0000	-0.0911	-0.9230	-0.6083
2	0.7166	0.9999	-0.1493	1.0000	-0.1937
3	0.7981	0.2257	0.1554	-0.1518	1.0000
4	0.8518	-0.5166	1.0000	0.1231	-0.3936
5	1.0000	-0.8590	-0.5860	0.0196	-0.2041

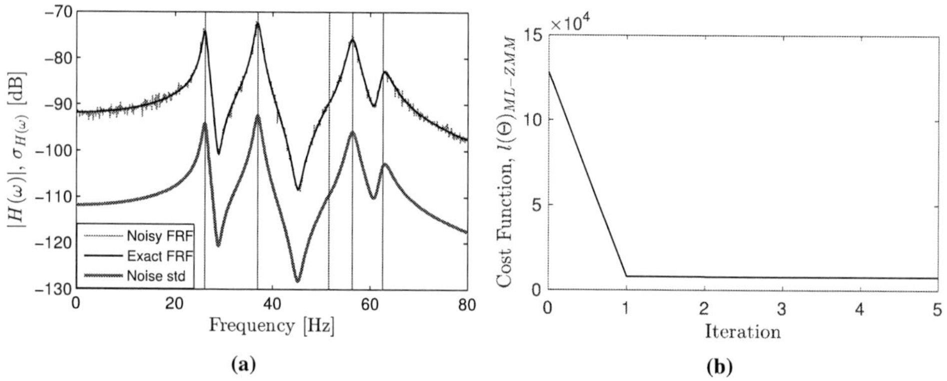

Figure 2: Element(1,1) of the **FRF** matrix contaminated with 10% noise: exact (black line) and noisy (red line) **FRF**, noise standard deviation (green line) and exact natural frequencies (vertical lines) (a); and cost function variation over the performed **ML-ZMM** iterations

The exact and noisy element(1,1) of the **FRF** matrix, and the corresponding "exact" standard deviation of the noise are shown in Fig. 2a. A set of 500 **FRF**s with 800 frequency lines contaminated with noise was generated to perform Monte Carlo simulations in order to assess the efficiency of the proposed **ML-ZMM**. The modal parameters of each dataset were identified with the **pLSCF** and **LSFD** estimators and then used as starting values to be optimized by the **ML-ZMM** algorithm. The identification of each dataset was performed using the full frequency band, i.e., with no upper and lower residual terms. In Fig. 2b, it is shown that variation of the cost function, $l(\Theta)_{ML-ZMM}$, over the five performed iterations in a typical Monte Carlo realization.

The variations of the **pLSCF** and **ML-ZMM** estimates for the 3rd natural frequency and damping ratio over the Monte Carlo simulations are shown in Figs. 3. These results show that the bias on the **pLSCF** estimates is removed after only 5 Gauss-Newton iterations of **ML-ZMM**. Apart from its optimization capabilities, the **ML**-based techniques have also the advantage of predicting the confidence bounds for the optimized estimates if the noise information is taken into account in the optimization process. In Figs. 4, the standard deviations of the 3rd natural frequency and damping ratio (estimated after 5 iterations of the **ML-ZMM** in each Monte Carlo realization) are compared to the respective sample standard deviation. It is clear from these figures that the **ML-ZMM** provides accurate estimates for the sample standard deviations of such modal properties.

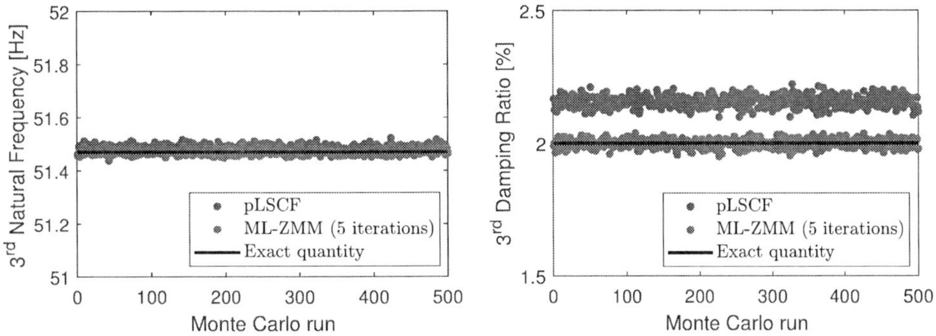

(a) (b)

Figure 3: Estimates for natural frequency (a) and damping ratio (b) of the 3rd vibration mode obtained with the **pLSCF** (blue dots) and **ML-ZMM** after 5 iterations (red dots)

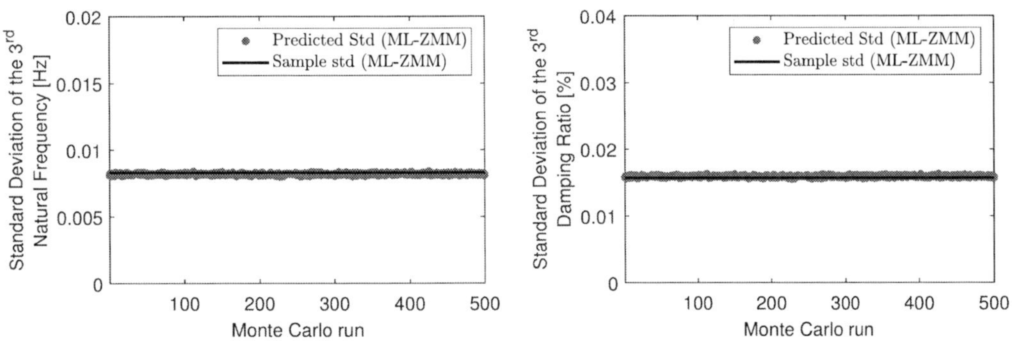

(a) (b)

Figure 4: Estimates for the standard deviation of the natural frequency (a) and damping ratio (b) of the 3rd vibration mode obtained after 5 **ML-ZMM** iterations (red dots) and sample standard deviation (solid black line)

4. CONCLUSIONS

In this paper, an initial performance assessment of a **ML**-based estimator formulated in z-domain modal model is presented. Just like any other **ML**-based approach, the **ML-ZMM** requires a good starting guess to assure convergence over the performed Gauss-Newton iterations. Despite the fact that any **LLS**-based identification technique can be used to provide the starting guess, the proposed **ML** approach is combined with the **pLSCF** estimator to retain the multi-reference information and improve the accuracy of the **LLS** estimates. The main difference of the **ML-ZMM** herein introduced with regards to the **ML-MM** described in [10] is that the former optimizes the discrete-time rather than the continuous-time poles. The efficiency of the **ML-ZMM** was assessed by means a simulated application example with no upper and lower residuals. The results obtained from such simulations show that not only did the **ML-ZMM** reduce the bias on the estimates for the natural frequencies and damping ratios, but it also provided accurate estimates for the confidence intervals of those estimates.

5. ACKNOWLEDGEMENTS

The authors acknowledge all the support received from Danish Offishore Center (**DOC**) at the **T**echnical **U**niversity of Denmark (**DTU**).

REFERENCES

[1] P. Guillaume, P. Verboven, S. Vanlanduit, H. Van-der-Auweraer and B. Peeters, "A Poly–reference Implementation of the Least-squares Complex Frequency–domain Estimator", *In Proceedings of the International Conference on Noise and Vibration Engineering*, Leuven, Belgium, 2003.

[2] B. Peeters, "System Identification and Damage Detection in Civil Engineering. Katholieke Universiteit Leuven, Belgium", *PhD thesis*, Katholieke Universiteit Leuven, Leuven, Belgium, 2000.

[3] Ibrahim, S. R., Milkulcik, E. C., A Method for Direct Identification of Vibration Parameters from Free Response. *Shock and Vibration Bulletin*, 47, (pp. 183–196) 1977.

[4] Brincker R, Olsen P, Amador S, Juul M, Malekjafarian A, Ashory M., Modal participation in multiple input Ibrahim time domain identification. *Mathematics and Mechanics of Solids, vol. 24, issue 1, (pp. 168–180)* 2019.

[5] Vold, H., Kundrat, J., Rocklin, G. T., Russel, R., A Multi-input Modal Estimation Algorithm for Mini-computers. *In SAE Technical Paper Number 820194.* 1982.

[6] Vold, H., Rocklin, G. T., The Numerical Implementation of a Multi-input Modal Estimation Algorithm for Mini-computers. *In proceedings of the 1st International Modal Analysis Conference*, Orlando, FL., USA, 1982.

[7] R. Pintelon and J. Schoukens, "System Identification: A Frequency Domain Approach". *IEEE Press*, vol. 1, ed. 1, Piscataway, 2001.

[8] T. Kailath, "Linear Systems". *Prentice–Hall*, vol. 1, ed. 1, 1998.

[9] M. El–Kafafy, T. De–Troyer, B. Peeters, and P. Guillaume, "Fast maximum-likelihood identification of modal parameters with uncertainty intervals: A modal model–based formulation". *Mechanical Systems and Signal Processing*, vol. 37, pp. 422–439, 2013.

[10] M. El–Kafafy, T. De–Troyer and P. Guillaume, "Fast maximum-likelihood identification of modal parameters with uncertainty intervals: A modal model formulation with enhanced residual term". *Mechanical Systems and Signal Processing*, vol. 48, pp. 49–66, 2014.

[11] Amador, S., El-Kafafy, M., Cunha, Á. and Brincker, R., "A New Maximum Likelihood Estimator Formulated in Pole-Residue Modal Model" *Applied Sciencies*, 9, 3120, 2019.

[12] M. El–Kafafy, B. Peeters, P. Guillaume and T. De–Troyer, "Constrained maximum likelihood modal parameter identification applied to structural dynamics". *Mechanical Systems and Signal Processing*, vol. 72–73, pp. 567–589, 2016.

[13] R. Pintelon, P. Guillaume and J. Schoukens, "Uncertainty calculation in (operational) modal analysis". *Mechanical Systems and Signal Processing*, vol. 21, pp. 2359–2373, 2007.

[14] M. Böswald, D. Göge, U. Füllekrug and Y. Govers, "A review of experimental modal analysis methods with respect to their applicability to test data of large aircraft", *In Proceedings of the International Conference on Noise and Vibration Engineering* Leuven, Belgium, 2006.

9th International Operational Modal Analysis Conference
iomac
July 3 - 6, 2022
Vancouver, Canada

OPERATIONAL MODAL ANALYSIS AND NUMERICAL MODELLING OF A FOOTBRIDGE GALLERY LINKING TWO BUILDINGS

N. García-Fernández[1], F. Pelayo[2] and M. Aenlle[3]

[1] PhD student, University of Oviedo, garciafnatalia@uniovi.es
[2] Professor, University of Oviedo, fernandezpelayo@uniovi.es
[3] Professor, University of Oviedo, aenlle@uniovi.es

ABSTRACT

The dynamic behavior of structures can be studied using numerical models, from which the numerical modal parameters can be extracted, or through the experimental modal parameters estimated with classical or operational modal analysis (OMA). On the one side, several identification methods proposed for operational modal analysis are easy to automate, which makes OMA an effective method for structural health monitoring and vibration serviceability. On the other side, numerical models can be used to predict the response of structures in operation. In this paper, the dynamic behavior of the footbridge located at the Milan's campus (Oviedo, Spain) is studied. This lattice structure links two buildings at a height of 12 meters, and it has a complete glass enclosure, which favors the influence of the wind, and may therefore be subjected to greater dynamic loads than those predicted in the design of the structure. The experimental modal parameters of this structure were estimated with operational modal analysis and used to update a numerical model assembled in ABAQUS.

Keywords: Footbridge, Modal Analysis, OMA, Numerical Analysis, Model Updating.

1. INTRODUCTION

It is well known that Operational modal analysis (OMA) is an useful technique for estimating the modal parameters (natural frequencies, mode shapes and damping ratios) of medium/large structures [1-4] using natural and operational loads.

This paper reports the operational modal tests and anlayis applied to a footbride gallery (see Fig. 1). This footbridge structure was constructed between the late 80s and early 90s, with the objective of linking the two main buildings of the "Campus of Milán" at the University of Oviedo (Spain). The pedestrian footbridge was assembled in factory and then placed on the buildings with a crane. The structure is located at approximately 12 metres from the base of the building. The footbridge is a steel structure composed of two lateral Pratt trusses, which are connected through the top part by a gable roof.

The pedestrian bridge also has a glass cover on the top and in both lateral sides, which was not considered during the structural design. No information about the time when this enclosure was placed is available. This area of the city is subjected to moderate winds, and the glass cover can influence the dynamic behavior predicted for the structure. An updated finite element model could be useful to study the influence of the enclosure in the dynamic behavior of this structure.

Figure 1. Pedestrian Footbridge at the Milan's campus.

The trusses are made of steel S275. UNP280 profiles, in a box-welded configuration, were used in the top and bottom chords, whereas the diagonals and the vertical posts were constructed with UNP140 profiles, also in a box-welded configuration. The total length of the structure is 34 meters, and it is supported in both buildings for a length of 5 meters. The width of the footbridge is 4.35 metres and the height 3.4 metres. These dimensions were measured in situ, and they are not consistent with the information provided by the original project of the structure (Fig. 2). Information about how the structure is supported in the buildings is not available either. The deck of the footbridge is made of concrete and supported by concrete T beams.

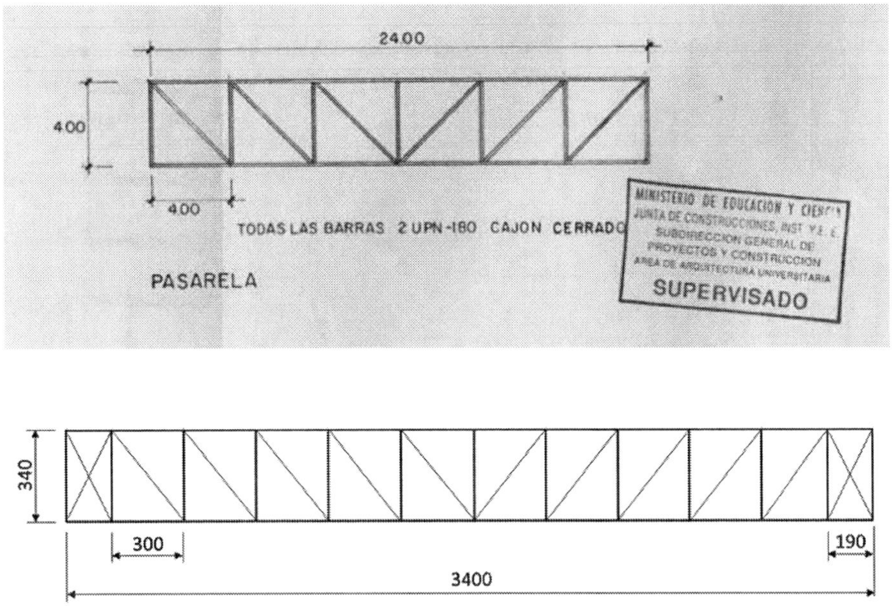

Figure 2. Real dimensions of the built (bottom image) structure and original drawings (top image).

In this work, a finite element model of the structure was assembled and updated with the experimental modal parameters estimated with operational modal analysis. The experimental modal parameters will be used for a future periodic structural health monitoring (SHM) of the footbridge, and the structural behavior with and without glass cover will be investigated with the updated finite element model.

2. OPERATIONAL MODAL ANALYIS

The experimental odal parameters (natural frequencies, mode shapes and damping ratios) of the structure, in the range 0-50Hz, were estimated with Operational Modal Analysis (OMA).

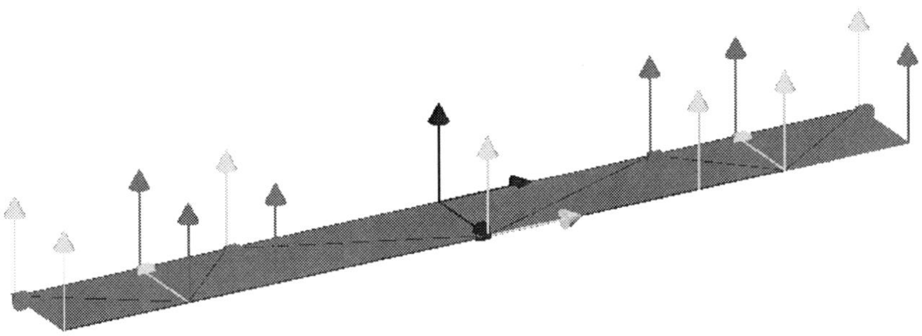

Figure 3. Experimental DataSet

The experimental responses were measured in 14 nodes and 23 DOF's (Fig. 3) using 6 accelerometers (PCB 393B31) with a sensitivity of 10 V/g (Fig .4) using 3 data sets. The responses were measured with a TEAC-LX 120 acquisition system using a sampling frequency of 100 Hz. The responses were measured for approximately 20 minutes in each data set Apart from the natural excitation, the structure was also excited by 3 people walking and jumping randomly over the structure.

Figure 4. PCB 393B31 accelerometers

The modal identification was performed using the Artemis Modal software and the modal parameters were estimated with the CFDD (Curve-fit frequency domain decomposition) and SSI (subspace stochastic identification) techniques [5]. The singular value decomposition of the SSI stabilization diagram is presented in Figure 5 for the vertical DOF's.

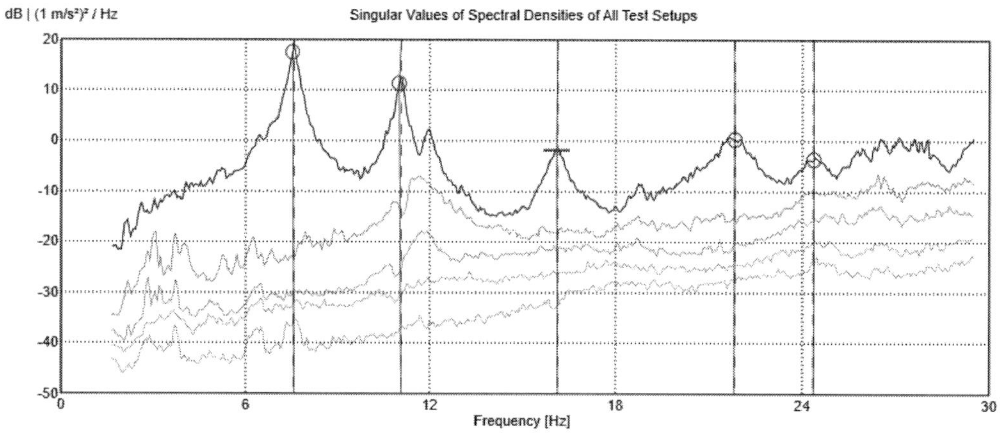

Figure 5.SVD of the acceleration vertical responses.

2.1. Experimental results in vertical direction

The experimental mode shapes in the vertical direction, obtained with the CFDD technique, are presented in Figure 6, whereas the natural frequencies are presented in Table 1.

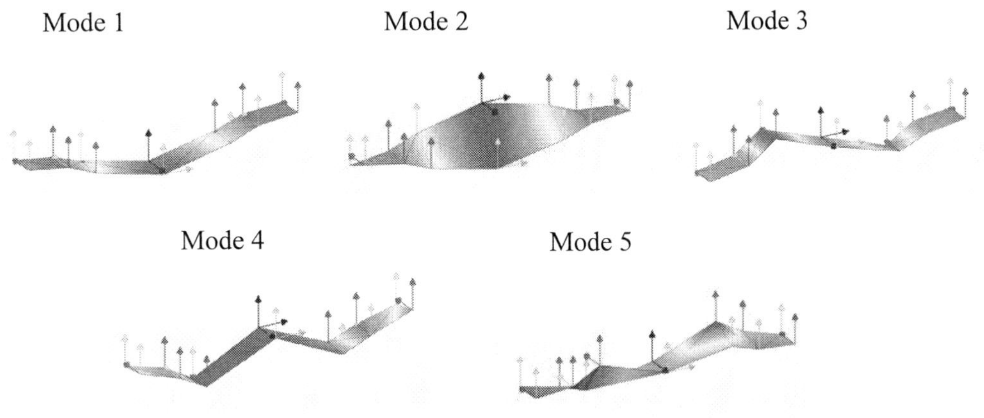

Figure 6. Experimental mode shapes

As it can be observed, the DOF's located in the supporting area are moving in the vertical direction, which means that the footbridge is not completely fixed to the buildings, i.e. there is a non-linear relative motion of the footbridge with respect to the buildings.

2.2. Experimental results in lateral direction

With respect to the lateral modes, the analysis is more complex, because no sensors were attached to the buildings. Moreover, the gable roof introduces additional local lateral modes which are dificult to identify considering only the sensors located at the deck. Only three lateral modes were identified with a reasonable reliability. The natural frequencies correspoding to these modes are presented in Table 2 and the mode shapes in Figure 8.

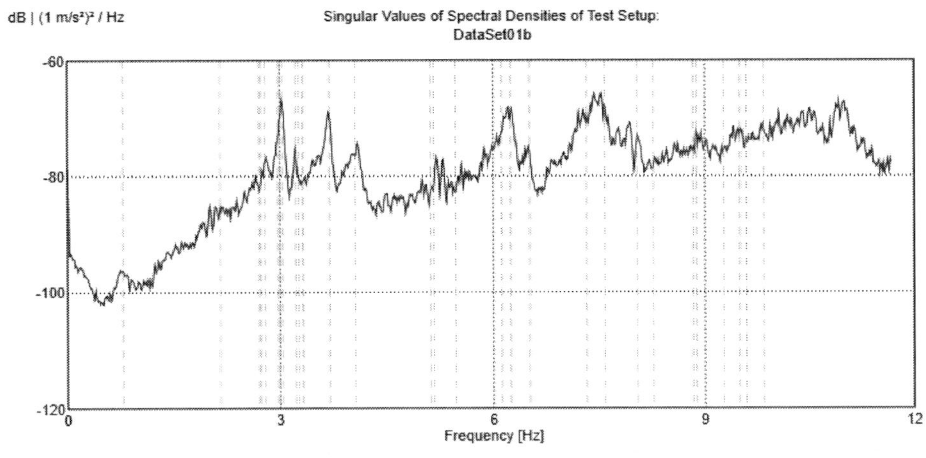

Figure 7. First singular value of the acceleration lateral responses.

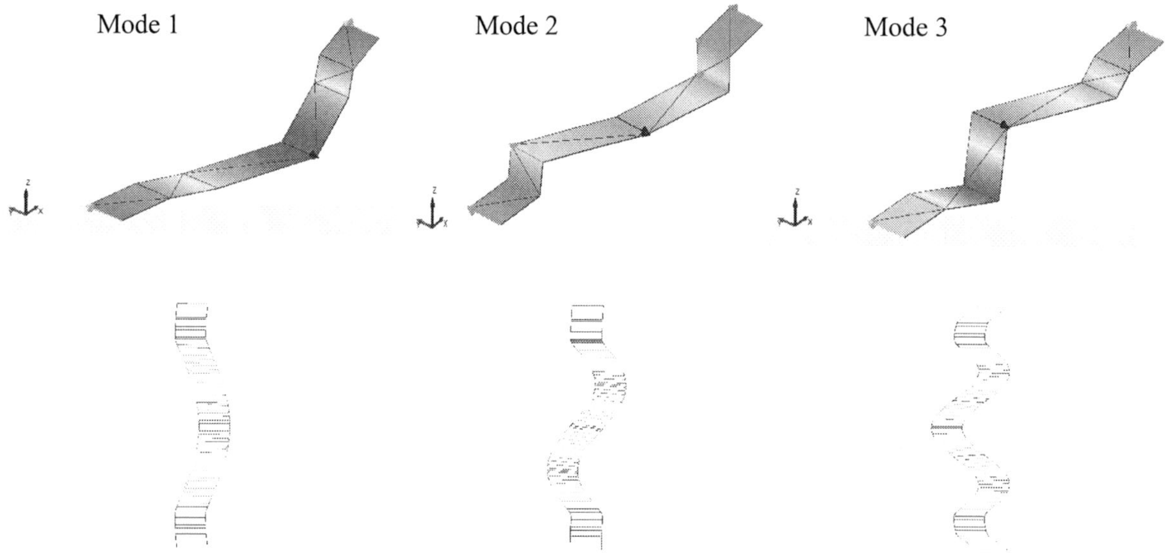

Figure 8. Experimental and numerical lateral modes

3. FINITE ELEMENT MODEL

3.1. First finite element model

The finite element model of the pedestrian footbridge was modeled in ABAQUS CAE. The model was meshed using 1-D beams elements (B3D3) for all the structural elements (see Fig. 9). The mass of the footbridge enclosure (glass + aluminum frames) were modeled as point-masses, whereas its effect on the stiffness of the structure was not considered.

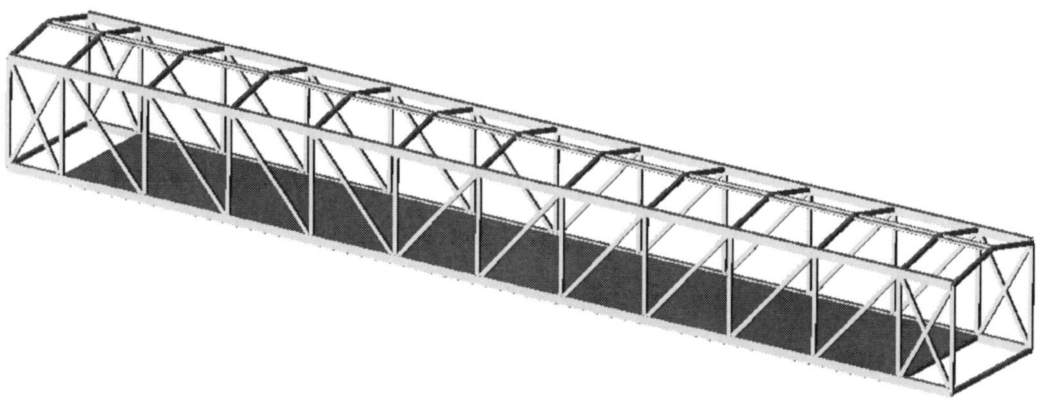

Figure 9. Finite element model of the structure

As it was previously mentioned, the boundary conditions are not known in detail. Pin supports were considered along the 4,9 meters of the bottom chords resting on the buildings (see Figure 10) The numerical natural frequencies corresponding to the vertical modes are presented in Table 1, whereas the those corresponding to the lateral modes are shown in Table 2.

Table 1. Experimental and numerical natural frequencies for the vertical modes.

Mode	Frequency		
	Experimental [Hz]	Numerical [Hz]	Error [%]
1 (bending)	7.56	7.43	1.67
2 (torsion)	11.05	11.11	0.52
3 (bending)	15.87	14.67	9.19
4 (bending)	21.79	19.17	12.02
5 (bending)	24.32	23.46	3.52

It can be observed in Table 1 that a good correlation exists for the modes 1,2 and 5, the errors being less than 3.5%, whereas a larger error has been obtained for modes 3 and 4. With respect to the lateral modes (see Table 2) the discrepancies are significantly large, which can attribuited to the boundary conditions assumed in the numerical model.

Table 2. Experimental and numerical natural frequencies for the lateral modes.

Mode	Frequency		
	Experimental [Hz]	Numerical [Hz]	Error [%]
1	4.06	4.35	7.14
2	8.09	13.68	69.08
3	15.14	20.64	36.32

3.2. Model updating

In order to get a better numerical-experimental correlation, the numerical model was manually updated [6] using the modal parameters estimated with OMA. Only the boundary conditions were modified in the updating process (see Fig. 10), diminishing the length and the number of the pin supports. This changes mainly affect the lateral modes decreasing the stiffness in this direction.

After the updating process, a good correlation was obtained for the vertical modes, the errors being less than 5.1% (see Table 3). With respect to the lateral modes (See Table 4), the numerical-experimental discrepancies also decrease significantly, confirming the fact that the structure is not firmly or fully attached to the buildings. However, although the errors were reduced for the identified lateral modes, the second bending mode (see Figure 8) still presents a large error (33 %).

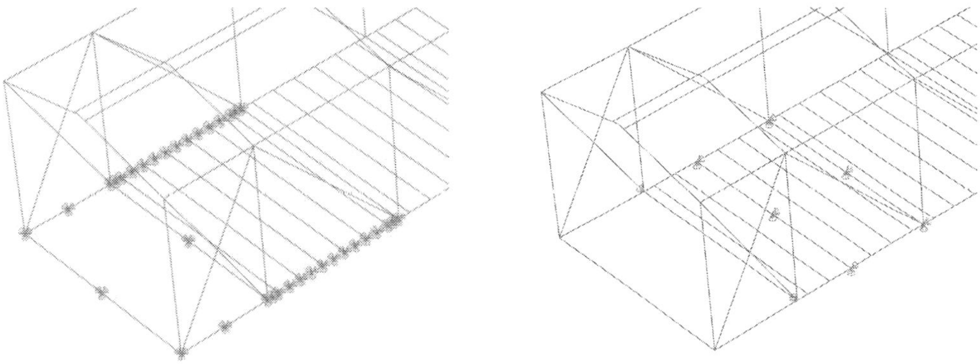

Figure 10. Original (left) and updated (right) boundary conditions used in the FEM model.

Table 3. Experimental and updated numerical natural frequencies for the vertical modes.

Mode	Frequency		
	Experimental [Hz]	Numerical [Hz]	Error [%]
1 (bending)	7.56	7.50	0.81
2 (torsion)	11.05	11.21	1.46
3 (bending)	15.87	15.06	5.10
4 (bending)	21.79	21.50	1.32
5 (bending)	24.32	24.11	0.86

Table 4. Experimental and updated numerical natural frequencies for the lateral modes.

Mode	Frequency		
	Experimental [Hz]	Numerical [Hz]	Error [%]
1	4.06	4.02	0.98
2	8.09	10,76	33.01
3	15.14	16.28	7.52

4. CONCLUSIONS

- A footbridge connecting two builinding in the Campus of Milan (University of Oviedo) was modelled in ABAQUS and the numerical modal parameters were correlated with the experimental modal parameters estimated with operational modal analysis (OMA).
- The boundary conditions were not known in detail and the numerical model was manually updated using the experimental modal parameters in both lateral and vertical directors, in order to get a better correlation.
- From the updated numerical model, it is concluded that the structure is not fully fixed to the buildings.
- Further studies, numerical and experimental, will be carried out in order to model this structure more accurately.
- A fatigue analysis should be carried out in order to identify damage and to stablish an initial state for the future structural health monitoring of the footbridge.

ACKNOWLEDGEMENTS

The economic support given by the Spanish Ministry of Education through the project MCI-20-PID2019-105593GB-I00/AEI/10.13039/501100011033 is gratefully appreciated.

REFERENCES

[1] Gentile, C., & Gallino, N. (2008). Ambient vibration testing and structural evaluation of an historic suspension footbridge. *Advances in Engineering Software, 39*(4), 356–366. https://doi.org/10.1016/j.advengsoft.2007.01.001

[2] Hu, W.-H., Caetano, E., & Cunha, Á. (2013). Structural health monitoring of a stress-ribbon footbridge. *Engineering Structures, 57*, 578–593. https://doi.org/10.1016/j.engstruct.2012.06.051

[3] Reynders, E., Degrauwe, D., De Roeck, G., Magalhães, F., & Caetano, E. (2010). Combined Experimental-Operational Modal Testing of Footbridges. *Journal of Engineering Mechanics, 136*(6), 687–696. https://doi.org/10.1061/(ASCE)EM.1943-7889.0000119

[4] Brincker, R., & Ventura, C. (2015). Introduction to Operational Modal Analysis (Wiley).

[5] Chen, H.-P., & Ni, Y.-Q. (2018). Structural Health Monitoring of Large Civil Engineering Structures (Wiley-Blac). John Wiley & Sons, Ltd. https://doi.org/10.1002/9781119166641

[6] Friswell, M. I., & Mottershead, J. E. (1995). Finite Element Model Updating in Structural Dynamics (Vol. 38). Springer Netherlands. https://doi.org/10.1007/978-94-015-8508-8

AMBIENT VIBRATION TEST AND MODAL RESPONSE ANALYSIS OF A UNIVERSITY BUILDING IN A SEISMIC REGION

Víctor Carol Hernández Monzón [1], Carlos E. Ventura[2]

Summary

This article emphasizes the analysis of environmental vibration and its response of an educational building that has been developed by the University of San Carlos de Guatemala – USAC – [1], since 1970. This structural model has been used as a parameter for most of their constructions in many buildings nationwide. For this project one of the main approaches is to be able to carry out a modal response analysis of this type of building. Considering that the study carried out is located in a seismic zone with a very high frequency of seismic events, such as the expulsion of degassing from the Santiaguito volcano which is located in the south of Quetzaltenango city. And also the movement of tectonic plates, in this particular case The Cocos subduction plate, which is a young oceanic tectonic plate beneath the Pacific Ocean off the west coast of Central America where there is a frecuent sismic activity.

The building taken as a sample is a 3-level reinforced concrete building consisting of moment-resistant frames, with a flat slab, which is symmetrical in its structural footprint as well as vertically in its main elements, and also has an opening of 18 x 36 m., to separate the rooms (classrooms and laboratories) of the building. Masonry walls were done in its construction, which were decoupled from the main elements such as beams and columns.

For this, environmental vibration tests were carried out to obtain natural frequencies, mode shapes and damping ratios. These parameters have been obtained using the Artemis software version 7.2.0.0 Likewise, an FEM model of the structure is established for which the ETABS – CSI- [2] software was used in order to compare the results obtained from the environmental vibrations, for this several hypotheses and comparisons of the analytical and experimental results are presented.

This work has been developed with professors of the Civil Engineering department who have helped to take the corresponding captures. As well the Consejo Superior Universitario Centroamericano -CSUCA- [3] Dr. Carlos Alvarado Cerezo and Centro de Coordinación para la Prevención de los Desastres en América Central y República Dominicana [4] and its Executive Secretary Licda. Claudia Herrera, as well as the Swiss Cooperation- COSUDE- [5] for the equipment and software donated to the Civil Engineering course at the Centro Universitario De Occidente, within the framework of the Effect 3 Project "Project to strengthen the governance of Disaster Risk Management in Central America" as part of the Insertion of Gestión Integral de Riesgo (GIRD) and resilient adaptation to climate change (ACC) as a transversal axis of the Civil Engineering career".

1 - Professor, Civil Engineering Department, USAC CUNOC Guatemala – hernandez.victor@usac.edu.gt
2 - Professor, Civil Engineering Department, UBC, ventura@ubc.ca

Introduction

During the last years, this type of studies has been carried out worldwide in a very efficient way, both to be able to establish the monitoring of the structural health of structures as well as to be able to calibrate the analytical and experimental models, which is the development of this work, the desire to establish and to define the differences between the natural period of vibration (analytical) and experimentally, this type of study has not been carried out so far in Guatemala, being one of the first where the Modal Operational Analysis is applied. Ventura [6],

The structural typology is disclosed, the type of building used by the Centro Universitario de Occidente -.CUNOC- [7], as well as the definition of the loads that are currently defined in the NSE regulations -Structural Safety Standards- established by the Coordinadora Nacional de Desastres -Conred- [8], through the Association of Structural and Seismic Engineering -AGIES v.2018 [9]-

The methodology used displays the steps taken into account for the development of this work, showing in a very simplified way the development of the data sampled in the experimental part, especially to establish the context of the dynamic analysis.

To develop the sampling of this type of structural footprint, it was established on how the sampling would be done so as not to use equations or extrapolation in the model -ARTeMIS- to simplify the configuration of the dynamic model in txt format.

Until now, this type of study has not been carried out in Guatemala since there was no equipment or knowledge to make this type of analysis, therefore this is a pioneer in research that will have a lot of outcomes on teaching-learning, both at the level of undergraduate and graduate of the University Center of the University of San Carlos de Guatemala. These environmental vibration tests are easy to carry out, taking into consideration some important things such as the placement of devices, connection with the program that the devices bring by default, as well as the transfer of data in programs such as Viewwave [10], Seismosignal [11], this last one for the baseline correction and define the Setup of each sampling point taken into account.

These environmental tests have several advantages: They are simple to carry out, the external excitation is due to the environmental noise. As a result of the pandemic the building at the time of sampling was completely empty with no humans beings inside. (01.31.2022), so only the vibrations found are due to the traffic, which comes from the north of the building, the west side and as well as the wind.

Modal identification is the determination of modal parameters of structures constructed from experimental data. Modal identification of output-only structures is typically used to identify modal parameters from the natural responses of many structures (civil, spatial, and mechanical). In these cases, the loads are unknown, and the identification process is carried out based only on the responses. Typically, the identification process is based on ambient vibration testing, and assumes that a structure can be adequately excited by natural forms such as wind, human activities, and the result of motions that can be easily measured with highly sensitive instruments. Applications in civil engineering structures can be found in Ventura, Brincker, Cunha [12].

The Finite Element Model (FEM) of the building is explained as they were analyzed to obtain approximate results in relation of the models. The results of the dynamic analysis are compared with experimental data such as fundamental frequencies and mode shapes, they are tabulated and discussed.

Building Description

The building consists of three levels with a height of 10.65 m, each level with a height of 3.55 m, the slab used is ribbed with reinforced ribs 0.27 m thick and filled with a block specially manufactured for this purpose, the construction took place in 2005 with the standards and norms of that time. Located in the west of Guatemala, Occupation of the educational type building, Seismicity Index of the place 4.1, Spectral ordinate for short period Scr. 1.5g, Spectral ordinate period of 1 second 0.55 s. AGIES [13] Structural system defined by reinforced concrete frames E-1, the components of the structural system as special frames columns-beams.slabs.

A very special characteristic of this type of structure is that it is used in the vast majority of donut-type University buildings, that is; with a hole in the central part of 18 x 27 m, the dimensions of the building are 45 m long and 36 meters short length, the structural system is considered in the AGIES regulations as Important Works within category III, distance between columns of 9.0 m to axes, columns of 0.70 x 0.70, beams of 0.60 x 0.40 m. To establish the divisions between the classrooms were built with masonry walls of 0.15 for the first level of brick with pines and walls on the second and third levels of pine block, separated from the structural frames of one inch of separation. Borders were used for the perimeter enclosure with shotcrete and pinned, likewise in the overhangs in the internal part, borders are used in the same way as the perimeter enclosure.

Moreover, in order to control what is stipulated in the plans is actually built, complementary studies were carried out, such as:

- Standard penetration test (SPT), to verify the speed of short waves at different stratigraphic levels.
- Vertical electrical survey, to be able to establish the resistivity of the soil,
- Radiography of beams, columns and slab to establish the steel used.

The main façade/front, the floor plan and seismic hazard characterization Fig. 2 are presented due to its location in the city, likewise there is a study that places the city in two scenarios for seismic risk, establishing a 7.6 earthquake for a Chixoy fault -Polochic located to the north of the department, and a 7.7 scenario for a subduction earthquake Fig. 3.

Fig.1 : Buildings view

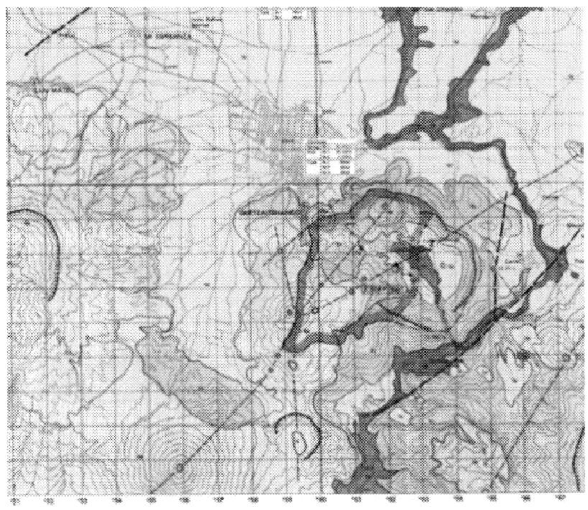

Fig. 2: The study on groundwater development in the central plateau in Guatemala 1,995 Kokusai Kogyio Co., Ltd, Japan International Cooperation Agency (Cooperation, 2022)

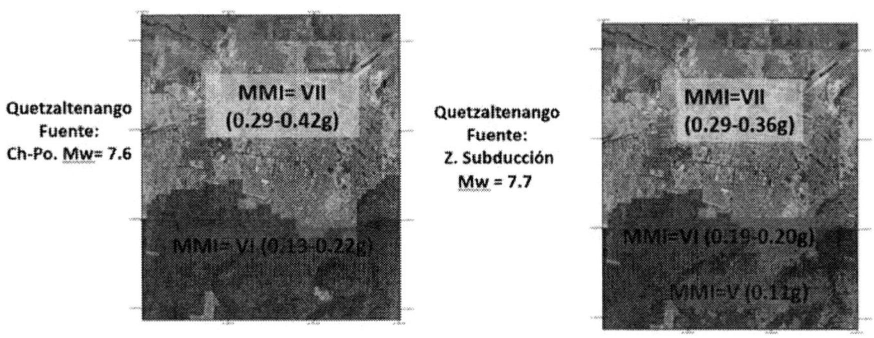

Fig. 3: Seismic Prediction in Quetzaltenango, according to Japan International Cooperation Agency study

The understanding of the dynamics of structures was the main object of this study through the instrumentation program for the understanding and behavior of structural damage to earthquake loads. In the elastic range of structures with environmental noise, in order to establish a better understanding of the finite element programs that were used at the time and that today both the sensors and the software have advanced enormously for a better understanding of what the user projects in the analytical models and compare them with the vibration of environmental noise of the structural, is the most important for a better understanding of structures.

Finite Model Element

To enter information into the analytical model, all available information was sought, as well as complementary studies in order to have an approximation from the structure as equal as possible, which was entered directly into the finite element model (FEM), using ETABS. Previously to obtain results of the different modes of vibration of the structure. Several models were made to improve the corresponding analysis. Different types of structural systems were analyzed, in each of them the fundamental period of said analysis is defined, being the following:

1. Structural frames fig. 4
2. Structural frames including articulated walls and stands module fig. 5
3. Structural frames including articulated walls and stands module fig. 6

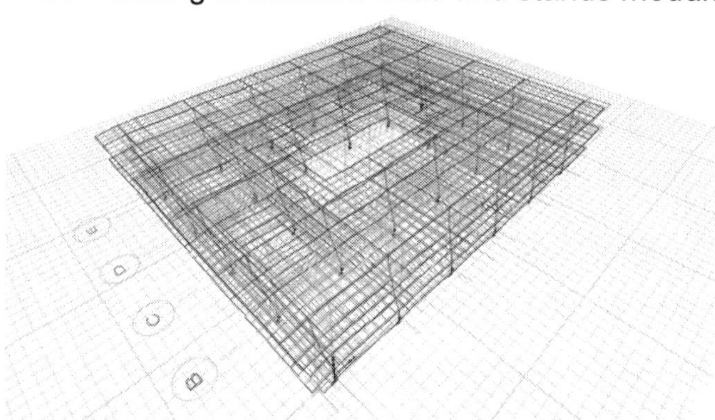

Fig. 4: 3D elevation view of the finite element model. Structural frames only Fundamental mode 0.48 sec.

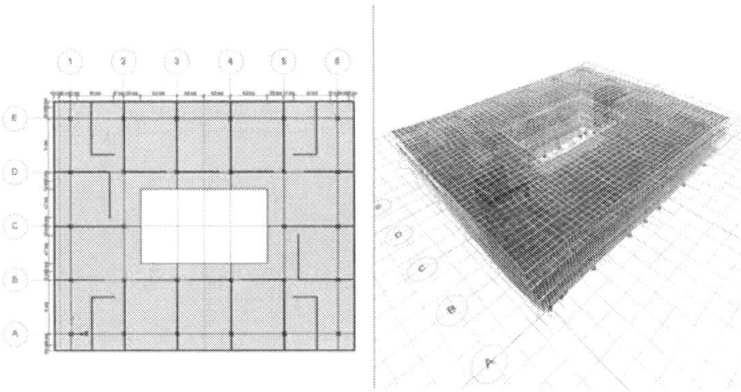

Fig. 5: 3D elevation view of the finite element model. Including stands and walls without connecting them to the frame system. Fundamental mode 0.20 sec.

The results obtained with FEM were used to choose the appropriate sensor location for environmental vibration tests. The experimental results were used to update the FEM, introducing a slight variation of the modulus of elasticity, in order to coincide with the analytical and experimental results (see Table 1).

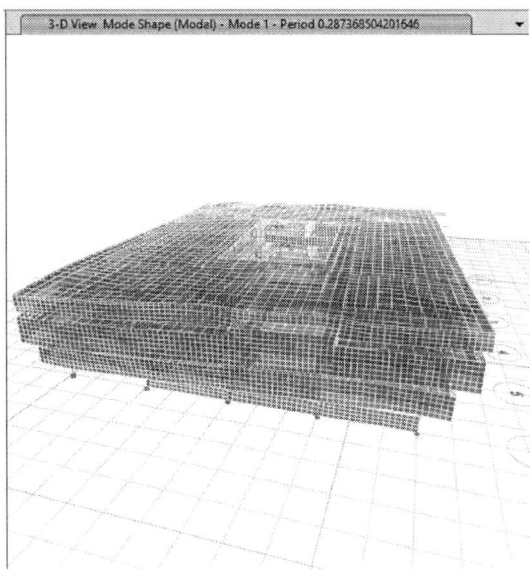

Fig. 6: Building modeled with articulated walls fundamental mode (without connection and without module of stairs)

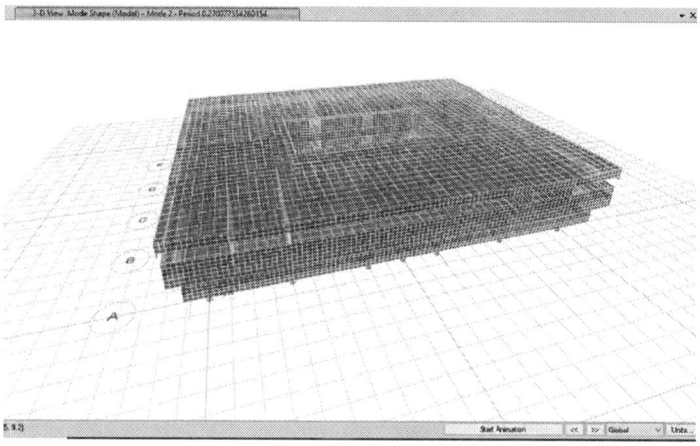

Fig. 7: Modeled building with hinged walls 2nd mode (without connection and without stairs)

N.º	Mode shape	Updated Model
1	1st torsion	3.479 Hz
2	2nd NS	3.70 Hz
3	3nd WE	4.44 Hz

Table 1: Main modes of the structure

Environmental Vibration Tests

Environmental vibration test-based analysis is a methodology used to characterize the dynamic behavior of a structure excited by low-amplitude vibrations. The information obtained can be useful for calibrating and updating finite element models of the building, or can be also used for monitoring the health of the building. The importance of the environmental analysis Celebi [14] is given by the elastic properties of the structure and the behavior before a severe seismic event to the structure can pass to the non-linear range and it is much easier to predict it. The procedures and the main results obtained for the environmental vibration tests are described below.

Instrumentation

For the present work, three Etna2 [15] figure 8 accelerographs were used, calibrated for + 1g, with 200 sps, having as reference, type: triaxial episensor forced balance accelerometers, digitizer: 3 to 24 bit sensor channel for internal sensor band-optimized 32- bit data path, Dynamic range: -130 db at 100 sps, earthquake early warning low latency 0.1 s packets reade.

Fig. 8 Etna2 de Kinemetrics

The response of the structure was recorded at various places in the building; the location of the sensors Fig. 9., three 3-component accelerometers (triaxial) were used, one was used as a reference sensor and the other two were located in different positions in such a way that they moved parallel both on the roof, 3rd level, and 2nd level , considering a rigid base at floor level, according to the SPT study and the AGIES standard classification, It has to be facing N in order to obtain the NS, EW and Z (vertical) components, in this case they are obtained for each setup 09 components out of a total of 12 setup that are entered in the ARTeMIS configuration, since it is much easier to enter the information through the config. extension of the software.

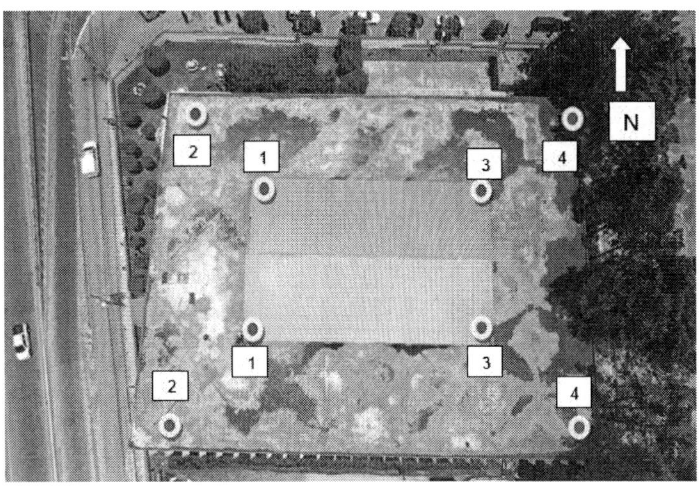

Fig. 9: Positioning of sensors on the roof

Experimental Settings

The acceleration data was recorded 07 minutes, to guarantee that all the modes of interest are excited, taking as reference the values of $1000 < T < 2000$, where T is the time to define the sampling time according to the main parameter of the Fundamental Period of the building approaching 0.30 second taken from rule of thumb N/10 which is equal to 0.30 sec. The sample rate is 200 Hz. The results presented here were obtained using a decimation factor of 10 for the 200 Hz sample rate and averaged over 1024 sample points. This value corresponds to eliminating all frequencies above 10 Hz in the spectra. These frequencies are eliminated since they are not considered to be outside the study range.

Spectral Analysis

Modal identification is used to identify the modal parameters of a structure using measurements of experimental data. The building is subjected to environmental vibrations generated by "unknown" loads, such as wind, human activity, traffic parallel to the North and West building, etc. The whole system is assumed to be driven by Cunha white noise . In these cases, the structural modes are identified, as well as what are called operational modes. The main focus of output-only analysis is to be able to distinguish structural modes from operational modes, in the process of modal identification.

The ARTeMIS version 7.2.0.0 [16] software was used to perform the modal identification of the structure. Two different techniques were used for modal identification: the Frequency Domain Decomposition (FDD) and the Stochastic Subspace Identification (SSI) technique given by Van Overschee and Me Moor. These two modal identification techniques are used to validate the results.

Point selection

The sensors that have been moved from position on each floor carrying a sequence on the three levels in such a way that their position with the roof was maintained (see fig. 10). To simulate the modal configurations, the rigid movement of the body of the floor slabs is assumed and the registered movements are translated into the equivalent movement of the three points used to simulate the rectangular shape of the structure, in ARTeMIS, trying to define a geometric figure that more similar to the analytical model to resemble its shape.

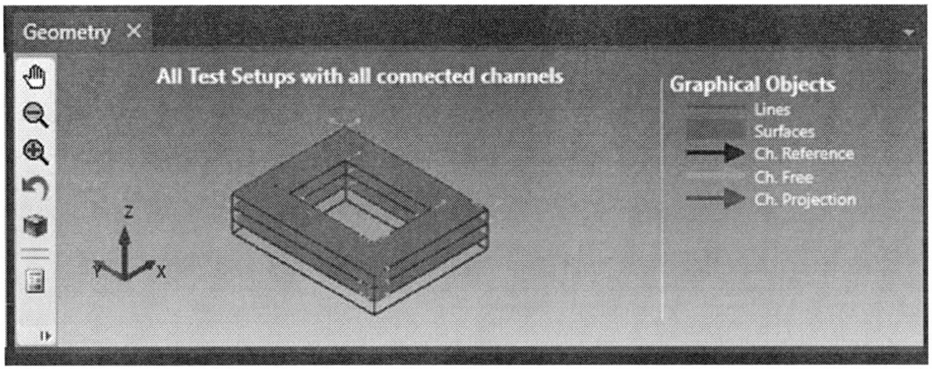

Fig. 10. Model in ARTeMIS with view of the sensors

Data processing consists of the following steps in a summarized way:

- Examine the accelerograms of the same recording to evaluate their quality and to synchronize them based on the common time signal.
- It is necessary to define that for each Setup in the configuration program nine registers are defined in each of the NS, EO, Vertical directions.
- Baseline correction is performed to determine the zero acceleration axis, and thus eliminate the frequency components that are not of interest when applying a filter between 2 and 10 Hz.
- Integration of the corrected accelerograms to obtain the histories in time, speeds and displacements. (Viewwave, Seismosignal)

For the study of the behavior of the instrumented building, data must be analyzed in the time and frequency domain, to establish the structural characteristics, such as frequencies and natural modes of vibration; comparing them with various models that were developed. Throughout this work, given the uncertainty of taking these variables into consideration or not, such as the perimeter borders, cantilevered borders, connection of the walls, and the placement of the stands in the analytical model.
On the other hand, it is important to highlight that the sections considered were taken as gross sections without cracking since the building has not suffered damage over time, only in the walls, but this is due to the fact that in some places the expansion joint is not the best so that in the face of severe seismic events that they have had; If they have shown cracking, as a result of the differences in stiffness between the walls and the structural system used, considering that the masonry walls are not totally disconnected mainly in the 3rd . Level.

The FDD technique roughly decomposes the density spectral matrix of the system response in an ensemble of SDOF systems using singular value decomposition (SVD) within a frequency range to discard values that do not have a very specific relationship. The singular values are estimations of the spectral density of the systems see fig. 11., SDOF, and the singular vectors are estimates of the mode shapes.

The SSI technique consists of fitting a parametric model to the raw temporal data series collected by the sensors. Using a specific representation of the transfer function, all modal parameters are exposed. Therefore, the natural frequency damping ratios and mode shapes can be extracted.

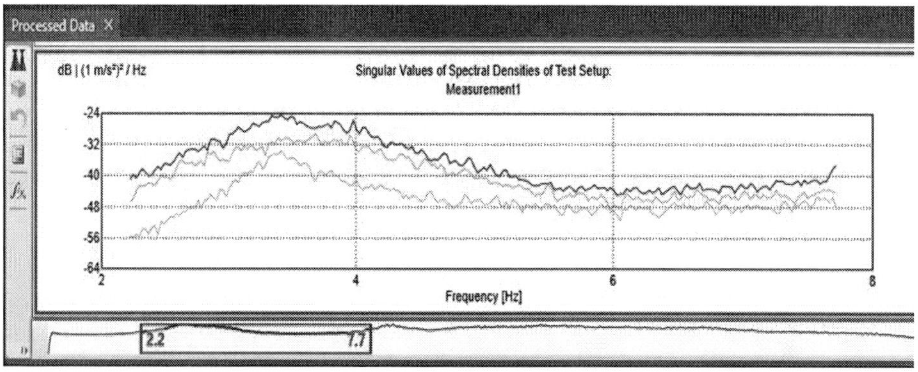

Fig: 11, Singular values of the spectral density sampling.

Experimental Results

The results of the FDD peak collection method are presented in Fig. 12. The identification of three peaks is clear: they are structural modes and represent natural frequencies of the building, and they are compared with the values obtained in the analytical model.

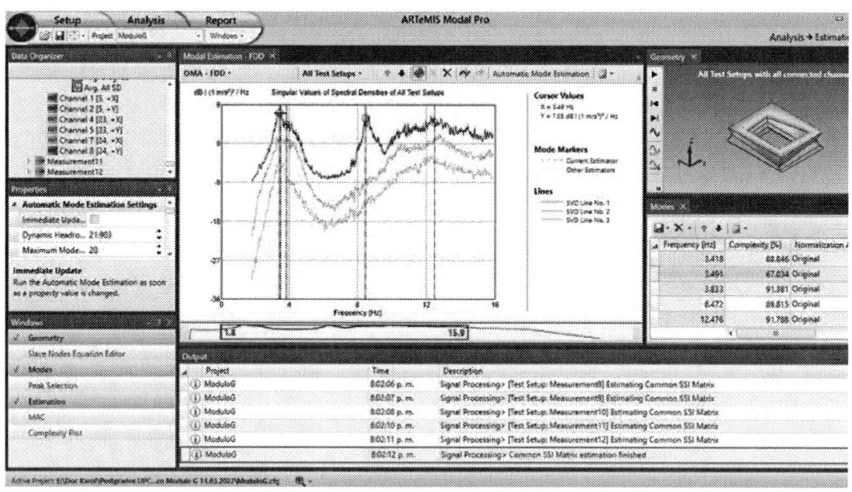

Fig. 12, Frequency analysis to identify vibration modes

Nº	Mode shape	Numerical results	EFDD
1	1st Torsion	3.418 Hz	3.48 Hz
2	1st NS	3.491 Hz	3.70 Hz
3	1st NS	3.833 Hz	4.44 Hz

Table 2: Comparison of fundamental frequencies

CONCLUSIONS

The environmental vibration tests provide a very proximate estimate of the values of the analytical model. due to the information processed, other important parameters must continue to be established in order to have closer approximations in the experimental and analytical frequencies. As well as referencing the sampling points so that in the future the post-earthquake conditions of the studied structure can be evaluated and see how it can be degraded, although it can be seen that in the University Center there are other modules very similar to the structural system of the building under observation and it can be seen that after 40 or 50 years they have only had problems of differential and non-structural settlements (2nd Order), for which the information must be safeguarded to see possible changes in stiffness in the elements when is subjected to seismic excitations, this contributes to the teaching - learning that must be made known in undergraduate and postgraduate students so that they can take as a reference and that they can learn from this type of building that fundamentally in its first mode is rotation due to the large opening in the center.

It should be noted that when considering the non-structural elements in the building, the correlations and the approximation to the fundamental mode in the elastic mathematical model and experimental values are consistent, taking into consideration all the structural elements and the so-called non-structural elements that in a certain way They contribute significantly to the stiffness and mass of the structure and this is demonstrated by the closeness of the values of the ambient vibration modes and those in the analytical model.

It is important to point out that a soil-structure interaction study must be carried out in order to better determine if there are changes in the fundamental frequency of the building, and to determine transfer and coherence functions that allow a better approximation of the values calculated in this work.

Acknowledgement

The authors would like to thank the following people who have contributed by making the appropriate sample recollection: Ing. Daniel Quintana, Ing. Luis Hernández, Ing. Carlos Julián Hernández, Ing. Pavel Cifuentes, Ing. Erick Calderón and Mr. David López, for their logistical support during field operations in the building and head of maintenance of the Centro Universitario de Occidente Ing. Jorge Mario González for the support provided in access to the building, as well as the Coordinator of the Civil Engineering Career, Ing. Nery Pérez. , to Prof. Frances López Almansa for his scientific collaboration and comments on the results, in the course of Earthquake Resistant Design and Rehabilitation of Buildings and Bridges of the Polytechnic University of Catalonia, and Dr. Mario Rodríguez of Seminar I of the Doctorate of Research in Education .

REFERENCES

1. Universidad de San Carlos de Guatemala -USAC- www.usac.edu.gt
2. Computers Structures Inc., "*ETABS Integrated Finite Element Analysis and Design of Structures*", Berkeley, California, USA, (2001).
3. Consejo Superior Universitario Centroamericano -CSUCA- https://csuca.org/es/
4. Centro de coordinación para la Prevención de los Desastres en América Central y República Dominicana -CEPREDENAC- https://cepredenac.org/
5. Cooperación Suiza para America Central -COSUDE- https://www.eda.admin.ch/deza/es/home/paises/america-central.html
6. Centro Universitario de Occidente – CUNOC- www.ingenieria.cunoc.usac.edu.gt
7. Ventura. C.E., Brincker R., "*Introduction to Operational Modal Analysis*" Wiley 2015
8. Coordinadora para la Reducción de Desastres -CONRED- https://conred.gob.gt/
9. Asociación Guatemalteca de Ingeniería Estructural y Sismica -AGIES https://www.agies.org
10. ViewWave https://iisee.kenken.go.jp/staff/kashima/viewwave.html
11. SeismoSignal License Educational https://seismosoft.com

12. Ventura C. E., Brincker R., Dascotte E., Andersen P., 2001. "*FEM Updating of the Heritage Court Building Structure*", Proceedings of the 19th International Modal Analysis Conference (IMAC), Kissimmee, Florida, pp.324-330, 2001

13. "Asociación Guatemalteca de Ingeniería Estructural y Sismica" NSE 2- Edición 2018 Actualización 15.07.2020

14. Celebi Mehmet, Safak Erdal, Brady Gerald A, Maley Richard, and Sotoudeth Vahid, "*Integrated Instrumentation Plan for Assesing the Seismic Response of Structure A Review of the Current USGS Program*", U.S. Geological Survey Circular 1,987

15. Kinemetrics Inc. Rock + series. Etna2 "*Accelerograph User Manual*" pp 33, 2017

16. SVBs, Structural Vibration Solutions "ARTeMIS Extractor, Release 7.1.1 User's Manual", Denmark, 2022.

APPLICATIONS IN MECHANICAL ENGINEERING

9th International Operational Modal Analysis Conference
iomac
July 3 - 6, 2022
Vancouver, Canada

BAYESIAN UPDATING FOR DISCRETE-TIME DOMAIN MODEL OF CHATTER IN TURNING

Keivan Ahmadi[1]

[1] *Department of Mechanical Engineering, University of Victoria, Victoria, British Columbia, Canada V8W 2Y2*

ABSTRACT

Dynamics of the turning process include a natural delayed feedback loop which may destabilize the process vibrations and cause chatter. Identification of the machine tool's modal parameters is essential for model-based optimization of the machining parameters to prevent chatter. Operational Modal Analysis (OMA) can effectively be used to identify the modal parameters from the vibration signals measured under machining conditions, however, the identified parameters are strongly affected by the feedback loop in the process dynamics. In this work, we use Bayesian inference to extract the machine tool's modal parameters from the (closed-loop) system poles estimated by OMA. A discrete-time domain model of turning dynamics is used to relate the machine tool's modal parameters to the system poles estimated by OMA. Bayesian inference is then used to determine the posterior probability distribution of the modal parameters. The resulting probability distribution functions are also used in the chatter model to establish probabilistic chatter limits for the machining parameters. An experimental example is presented to show that the predicted chatter limits are more accurate than those obtained by traditional methods based on modal testing under non-operational conditions.

Keywords: *Operational Modal Analysis, Bayesian Model Updating, Chatter*

1. INTRODUCTION

Machining forces are proportional to the thickness of the removed chip, which is in turn modulated by the tool or workpiece vibrations that are caused by those forces. This feedback from vibrations into the forces that cause them creates a natural delayed feedback loop in the machining dynamics. If machining parameters such as spindle speed and cutting width (or depth) are not selected properly, the process vibrations become unstable and cause chatter, damaging the tool or the machined surface[1]. Stable machining conditions can be identified by the bifurcation analysis of chatter models that describe the system dynamics with delay differential equations [2]. Existing chatter models require accurate knowledge of the machine tool's Frequency Response Function (FRF) at the tool's tip or the modal parameters extracted from the FRF. The machine tool's FRF or its modal parameters are usually obtained by traditional modal testing (e.g. impulse hammer) when the machine tool is in idle condition.

However, the machine tool's dynamics change considerably under operational machining conditions—for example, due to spindle rotation, bearing preload, or process damping. Operational Modal Analysis (OMA) is a more suitable method for identifying the machine tool's dynamics, but important challenges such as strong harmonics in the response (due to spindle rotation), mode-shape scaling, and the natural feedback in the process dynamics limit the application of OMA in machining.

Instead of common excitation methods (e.g. hammer or shaker) in modal testing, Minis et al. [3] used the machining forces as the excitation source in the identification of the dynamics of a turning machine. Because the input machining forces were measured by a dynamometer and used to identify the system dynamics, this method can be classified as a hybrid experimental-operational modal testing. To expand the bandwidth of the excitation forces, a pseudo-random binary pattern was created on the workpiece surface to add a strong random component to the harmonic forces generated at the spindle revolution frequency. A similar approach was later adopted by Ozsahin et al. [4] for milling operations. Inverse stability analysis in the works of Ozsahin et al. [5], Grossi et al. [6], Eynian [7], and Liu and Altintas [8] also provide an operational method for identifying the dynamics of the machine tool. This method uses the experimentally identified chatter limits of the machine tool in the corresponding chatter model to identify the machine tool's dynamics inversely. Following a similar concept, Postel et al. [9] use the experimentally identified chatter limits in machine learning methods to identify the machine tool's modal parameters. The accuracy of these methods strongly depends on the ability to detect vibration instability in the experiments, which is difficult, especially when the system is close to the border of stability and is affected by several random and nonlinear phenomena.

Operational modal analysis in its traditional sense (i.e. output only—without measuring the input machining forces) was also studied by Zaghbani and Songmene for milling operations [10]. Modal frequency and damping values were shown to vary considerably by spindle speed, but mode shape scaling and removing the effect of the feedback loop from the identified modal parameters were not discussed. Kim and Ahmadi used an OMA method to identify the dynamics of the machining system from the acceleration signals measured under turning force [11]. They showed that the modal frequency and damping values identified under stable machining conditions represent the dominant poles of the closed-loop system. Similarly, Kiss et al. [12], [13] identified the closed-loop dynamics of the machining system by perturbing its stable orbits during the process (using impact test). Because the stability of the closed-loop system depends on the modal damping corresponding to its dominant pole, the identified modal damping ratios can be used to accurately quantify the level of stability under the tested condition. However, improving the accuracy of chatter models requires the identification of the open-loop modal parameters of the machine tool (or workpiece) under operational conditions. Ahmadi [14] used Bayesian inference to update the machine tool's modal parameters in a frequency domain chatter model. The experimental data needed for Bayesian updating were obtained by the OMA of the closed-loop system, as presented in [11]. The updated probability distributions of the modal parameters were then used in a discrete-time domain model of chatter to determine the probability of chatter occurrence under given machining conditions. The resulting stability predictions were shown to be more accurate after model updating.

This paper improves the method in [14] by using the discrete-time domain model in both of the updating and stability prediction stages. Because updating the discrete-time domain requires computing the eigenvalues of its transition matrix at each likelihood function evaluation, which can be computationally intractable, the method presented in [14] uses a frequency domain model in parameter updating; but then a discrete-time domain model must be used for predicting the system stability using the updated parameter distributions. As a result, the predicted system stability is still affected by the discretization error of the discrete-time domain model. To circumvent this problem, in this work, we use a surrogate of the discrete-time domain model to evaluate the likelihood function and use the discrete-time domain method in both of the model updating and stability prediction stages. Therefore, the updated parameters also compensate for the discretization error and result in more accurate stability predictions.

The discrete-time domain model of machining chatter in turning is described in the next section, followed by a brief description of the Bayesian model updating method in Section 3. Formulating the likelihood function based on the surrogate of the discrete-time domain model is also discussed in

Section 3, and an experimental case study is presented in Section 4 to demonstrate the implementation of the presented model updating approach.

2. CHATTER MODEL

Consider the turning setup shown in Figure 1. The tool is fixed to the table of a Computer Numerical Control (CNC) machine tool and a cylindrical workpiece is mounted in the spindle that rotates at the fixed speed of $60/\tau$ revolutions per minute. The general equation of elastic vibrations of the tool in this setup is as follows:

$$\ddot{\boldsymbol{q}}(t) + 2\boldsymbol{\Omega}\boldsymbol{Z}\dot{\boldsymbol{q}}(t) + \boldsymbol{\Omega}^2\boldsymbol{q}(t) = a\boldsymbol{\Phi}^T\boldsymbol{K}_c\boldsymbol{\Phi}\big(\boldsymbol{q}(t-\tau) - \boldsymbol{q}(t)\big) \quad (1)$$

where $\boldsymbol{q}(t)$ is the vector of modal coordinates, $\boldsymbol{K}_c = [k_{fc}, \quad k_{tc}]^T[1, \quad 0]$ is the matrix of cutting force constants, and a is cutting width. The delay term on the right-hand side of the equation represents chip thickness modulation due to the surface waves generated by vibrations in the preceding pass, as illustrated schematically in Figure 1(a). The block diagram of the closed-loop system dynamics is shown in Figure 1(c). In the example used in this work, the tool is axially rigid and its lateral vibrations are measured by accelerometers mounted at M points in Z-direction and N points in Y-direction, as shown in Figure 1(a). The workpiece is also flexible in Y-direction, but its deflections in that direction do not affect chip modulation and can be omitted from the equation of motion.

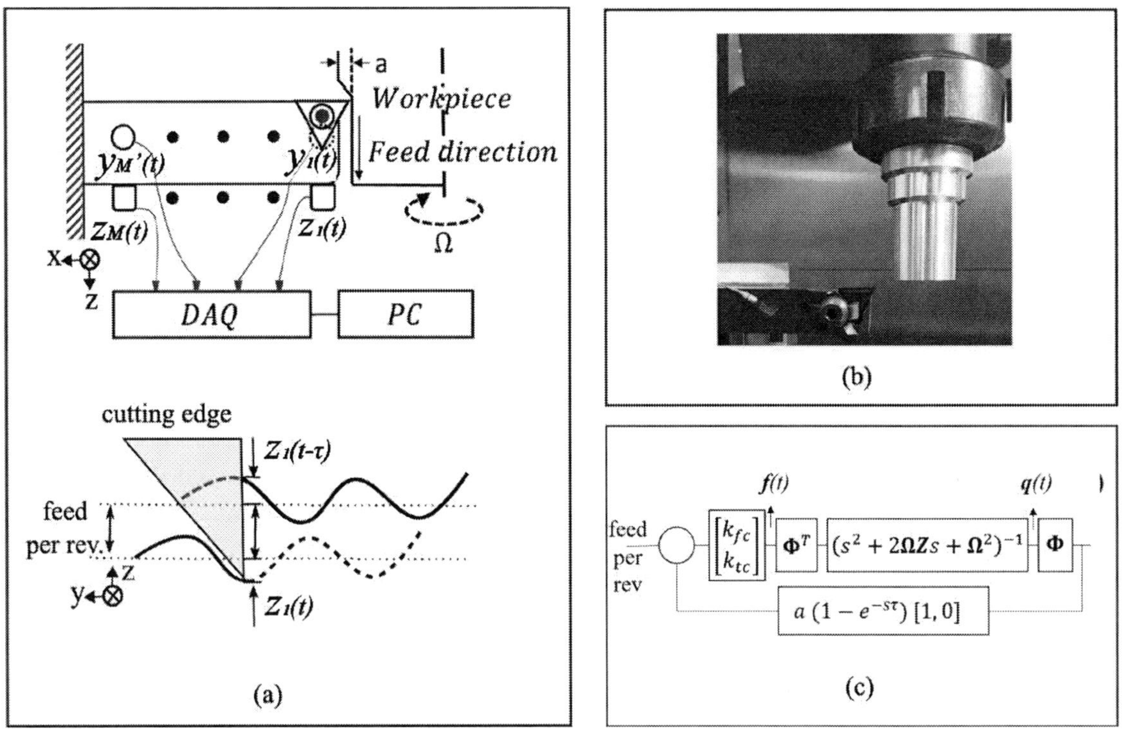

Figure 1: a) schematic of the test setup and chip regeneration in turning, b) picture of the test setup, and c) block diagram of closed-loop dynamics in turning [14]

In Eq.(1), $\boldsymbol{\Omega}$ is the diagonal matrix of modal frequencies, ω_n, $\boldsymbol{Z}$ is the diagonal matrix of modal damping ratios, ζ_n, and $\boldsymbol{\Phi}$ is the matrix of mass-normalized mode shapes, ϕ_n. Traditionally, these parameters are measured by modal testing such as impulse hammer tests when the machine is in idle condition. However, these parameters strongly depend on the operational conditions (e.g. due to process damping) and therefore are better described by the following random variables:

$$\omega_n = \bar{\omega}_n(1+\theta_{\omega n}),\quad \zeta_n = \bar{\zeta}_n(1+\theta_{\zeta n}),\quad \boldsymbol{\phi}_n = \bar{\boldsymbol{\phi}}_n(1+\theta_{\phi n}),\ n=1..N \tag{2}$$

where overbar designates the nominal values and $\theta_{\omega n}$, $\theta_{\zeta n}$, and $\theta_{\phi n}$ are random variables representing the variations of the nominal modal parameters. Notice that the mode shapes are assumed to remain constant but their mass-normalization factor are variable. The goal of this work is to determine the joint probability distribution of $\boldsymbol{\theta}_m=[\theta_{\omega n}, \theta_{\zeta n}, \theta_{\phi n}]^T$ based on the OMA of the closed-loop machining system.

The continuous-time distributed-parameter system in Eq.(1) can be approximated by a lumped-parameter system in the discrete-time domain, where the delay term τ is divided into m time-intervals of Δt seconds ($\tau=m\Delta t$) and the system is assumed to be subjected to constant forces within each interval [15]. As a result of discretization, the dynamics of the approximated lumped-parameter system is expressed by the following equation:

$$\boldsymbol{u}_{i+1} = \boldsymbol{G}(a,\tau,\boldsymbol{\theta}_m)\boldsymbol{u}_i \tag{3}$$

where $\boldsymbol{u}_i = \boldsymbol{u}(i\Delta t)$ is the state vector for the approximate lumped system, and $\boldsymbol{G}(a,\tau,\boldsymbol{\theta}_m)$ is the corresponding state transition matrix. The compositions of the state vector and transition matrix depend on the applied discretization method. With the full-discretization method used in this work [16], the transition matrix is expressed as follows:

$$\boldsymbol{G}(a,\tau,\boldsymbol{\theta}_m) = \begin{bmatrix} \Phi_0 & \mathbf{0} & \mathbf{0} & \cdots & \mathbf{0} & \left(\boldsymbol{\Phi}_1 - \frac{1}{\Delta t}\boldsymbol{\Phi}_2\right)\boldsymbol{B} & \frac{1}{\Delta t}\boldsymbol{\Phi}_2\boldsymbol{B} \\ \mathbf{I} & \mathbf{0} & \mathbf{0} & \cdots & \mathbf{0} & \mathbf{0} & \mathbf{0} \\ \mathbf{0} & \mathbf{I} & \mathbf{0} & \cdots & \mathbf{0} & \mathbf{0} & \mathbf{0} \\ \vdots & \vdots & \vdots & \ddots & \vdots & \vdots & \vdots \\ \mathbf{0} & \mathbf{0} & \mathbf{0} & \cdots & \mathbf{0} & \mathbf{0} & \mathbf{0} \\ \mathbf{0} & \mathbf{0} & \mathbf{0} & \cdots & \mathbf{I} & \mathbf{0} & \mathbf{0} \\ \mathbf{0} & \mathbf{0} & \mathbf{0} & \cdots & \mathbf{0} & \mathbf{I} & \mathbf{0} \end{bmatrix} \tag{4}$$

where

$$\boldsymbol{\Phi}_0 = e^{\boldsymbol{A}\Delta t};\ \boldsymbol{\Phi}_1 = \boldsymbol{A}^{-1}(\boldsymbol{\Phi}_0 - \boldsymbol{I});\ \boldsymbol{\Phi}_2 = \boldsymbol{A}^{-1}(\Delta t\boldsymbol{\Phi}_0 - \boldsymbol{\Phi}_1) \tag{5}$$

and

$$\boldsymbol{A} = \begin{bmatrix} \mathbf{0} & \boldsymbol{I} \\ -\boldsymbol{\Omega}^2 - \boldsymbol{\Phi}^T a\boldsymbol{K}_c\boldsymbol{\Phi} & -2\boldsymbol{\Omega} \end{bmatrix};\ \boldsymbol{B} = \begin{bmatrix} \mathbf{0} & \mathbf{0} \\ \boldsymbol{\Phi}^T a\boldsymbol{K}_c\boldsymbol{\Phi} & \mathbf{0} \end{bmatrix} \tag{6}$$

At each combination of spindle rotation period and cutting width, τ and a, stability of the linear system in Eq.(3) is determined by the eigenvalues of the transition matrix, $\boldsymbol{G}(a,\tau,\boldsymbol{\theta}_m)$. If all of the eigenvalues are inside the unit circle on the complex plane, the system is stable, otherwise, it is unstable (i.e. chatter occurs). Since modal parameters ($\boldsymbol{\theta}_m$) are random, according to Eq.(2), eigenvalues of the transition matrix are also random. Assuming that the modal parameters are normally distributed around their nominal values, second-order perturbation method can be used to determine the mean and variance of the eigenvalues of the associated transition matrix. Because the system stability is determined by the eigenvalue that has the greatest moduli, we will only consider that eigenvalue hereafter. Let $\mu_r(\boldsymbol{\theta}_m)$ be the largest eigenvalue of the transition matrix for spindle rotation period τ_r and cutting width a_r, i.e. $\boldsymbol{G}(a_r,\tau_r,\boldsymbol{\theta}_m)$. The probability distribution of this eigenvalue is then normal with the following mean and variance [17]:

$$\begin{gathered} \bar{\mu}_m = \mathbb{E}[\mu_m(\boldsymbol{\theta}_m)] = \mu_m(0) + \frac{1}{2}\mathrm{Trace}(\boldsymbol{\Sigma}_\theta\mathbf{D}_\mu) \\ \mathbb{E}[(\mu_m(\boldsymbol{\theta}_m) - \bar{\mu}_m)(\mu_m(\boldsymbol{\theta}_m) - \bar{\mu}_m)^*] = \boldsymbol{d}_\mu^T\boldsymbol{\Sigma}_\theta\boldsymbol{d}_{\mu^*} + \frac{1}{2}\mathrm{Trace}(\boldsymbol{\Sigma}_\theta\mathbf{D}_\mu\Sigma_\theta\mathbf{D}_{\mu^*}) \end{gathered} \tag{7}$$

where $\mathbf{\Sigma}_\theta$ is the covariance matrix for the joint normal distribution of $\boldsymbol{\theta}_m$, and $\boldsymbol{d}_\mu$ and $\mathbf{D}_\mu$ are the gradient vector and Hessian matrix of eigenvalue derivatives with respect to $\boldsymbol{\theta}_m$, respectively. Note that, the eigenvalues of the real-valued transition matrix consist of complex conjugate pairs that are designated μ_r and μ_r^*. The equivalent continuous-time frequency (ω_r) and damping ratio (ζ_r) of each eigenvalue (discrete-time pole) are

$$\omega_r(\boldsymbol{\theta}_m) = \sqrt{\lambda_r(\boldsymbol{\theta}_m)\lambda_r^*(\boldsymbol{\theta}_m)}, \quad \zeta_r(\boldsymbol{\theta}_m) = \frac{-\Re(\lambda_r(\boldsymbol{\theta}_m))}{\omega_r(\boldsymbol{\theta}_m)} \tag{8}$$

where $\lambda_r(\boldsymbol{\theta}_m) = \ln \mu_r(\boldsymbol{\theta}_m)/\Delta t$ is the equivalent continuous-time pole and $\Re$ stands for the real part of a complex number. Note that, ω and ζ denote both the parameters of the closed-loop pole and modal parameters of the open-loop system in Eq.2; indices r and n are used to distinguish between the open and close loop parameters. In the next section, the closed-loop pole will be identified for a set of $r=1..N_r$ combinations of spindle rotation period and width of cut (τ_r, a_r).

3. BAYESIAN MODEL UPDATING

Let $\widehat{\omega}_{rs}$ and $\hat{\zeta}_{rs}$ be the frequency and damping ratio values of the dominant closed-loop pole identified by OMA of acceleration signals measured at $r=1..N_r$ combinations of spindle rotation period and width of cut (τ_r, a_r). At each combination, OMA is repeated $s=1..N_s$ times. Each of the identified closed-loop poles can be predicted by substituting a given set of $\boldsymbol{\theta}_m$ in the discrete-time domain model of Section 2:

$$\frac{\widehat{\omega}_{rs}}{\omega_r(\boldsymbol{\theta}_m)} = 1 + \varepsilon_{rs}; \quad \frac{\hat{\zeta}_{rs}}{\zeta_r(\boldsymbol{\theta}_m)} = 1 + e_{rs} \tag{9}$$

where ε_{rs} and e_{rs} are frequency and damping prediction errors. Following the Maximum Entropy theorem, we assume both ε_{rs} and e_{rs} are independently zero-mean Gaussian processes with known covariance values, σ_ω^2 and σ_ζ^2,:

$$p(\varepsilon_{rs}, e_{rs}) = \mathcal{N}\left(\begin{bmatrix}0\\0\end{bmatrix}, \begin{bmatrix}\sigma_\omega^2 & 0\\ 0 & \sigma_\zeta^2\end{bmatrix}\right) \tag{10}$$

Consequently, the measured closed-loop poles can also be assumed normally distributed (and left-truncated at zero):

$$\begin{aligned} p(\widehat{\omega}_{rs} \mid \boldsymbol{\theta}_m, \boldsymbol{M}) &= c_\omega \exp\left[-\frac{1}{2}\left(\frac{1-\widehat{\omega}_{rs}/\omega_r(\boldsymbol{\theta}_m)}{\sigma_\omega}\right)^2\right] \\ p(\hat{\zeta}_{rs} \mid \boldsymbol{\theta}_m, \boldsymbol{M}) &= c_\zeta \exp\left[-\frac{1}{2}\left(\frac{1-\hat{\zeta}_{rs}/\zeta_r(\boldsymbol{\theta}_m)}{\sigma_\zeta}\right)^2\right] \end{aligned} \tag{11}$$

Since the identified damping and frequencies are assumed statically independent, the joint conditional probability distribution of the observed experimental data $\boldsymbol{D} = [\omega_{rs}, \zeta_{rs}]^T, r = 1..N_r$ and $s = 1..N_s$, is expressed as follows:

$$p(\boldsymbol{D} \mid \boldsymbol{\theta}_m, \sigma_\omega, \sigma_\zeta) = \text{c} \exp\left(-\frac{1}{2}\sum_{j=1}^{N_s}\sum_{r=1}^{N_r}\left(\frac{\left(1-\frac{\widehat{\omega}_{rs}}{\omega_r(\boldsymbol{\theta}_m)}\right)^2}{\sigma_\omega^2} + \frac{\left(1-\frac{\hat{\zeta}_{rs}}{\zeta_r(\boldsymbol{\theta}_m)}\right)^2}{\sigma_\zeta^2}\right)\right) \tag{12}$$

with the constant c normalizing the integration of the probability distribution function to unity. Equation (12) represents the likelihood of the identified poles given the model parameters $\boldsymbol{\theta}_m$. Prediction error covariances, σ_ω^2 and σ_ζ^2, determine the weights of contributions from frequency and damping prediction errors to the likelihood function. If the contribution weight from either of those two sources dominates the likelihood function, the information gained from the other source might be unused in the parameter updating process. To avoid this, following the approach presented by Goller et al. in [18], we introduce a new parameter $\alpha = \sigma_\zeta / \sigma_\omega$ and use that to generate various model classes such that:

$$p(\boldsymbol{D} \mid \boldsymbol{\theta}, \mathrm{M_k}) = \mathrm{c} \exp\left(-\frac{1}{2} \sum_{j=1}^{N_s} \sum_{r=1}^{N_r} \left(\frac{\left(1 - \frac{\widehat{\omega}_{rs}}{\omega_r(\boldsymbol{\theta}_m)}\right)^2}{\sigma_\omega^2} + \frac{\left(1 - \frac{\hat{\zeta}_{rs}}{\zeta_r(\boldsymbol{\theta}_m)}\right)^2}{\alpha^2 \sigma_\omega^2} \right) \right) \tag{13}$$

where $\boldsymbol{\theta} = [\boldsymbol{\theta}_m, \sigma_\omega]^T$ is the vector of model parameters to be updated, and M_k shows the class of models with α_k^2 ratio between covariance of frequency and damping prediction errors. A set of model classes with $\alpha_1, .., \alpha_K$ are considered and the most plausible class (according to the observed data) is chosen for updating. Therefore, the overall model updating process consists of two steps. The first step updates the model parameters $\boldsymbol{\theta}$ within each model class M_k, and the second step determines the model class that better describes the observed data. Both of these two steps apply Bayes' rule, as explained in the following sections.

3.1. Updating of model parameters

Starting with a prior probability distribution for the model parameters, $p(\boldsymbol{\theta} \mid M_k)$, we use the general Bayes' rule to determine their posterior probability distribution based on the information gained from experimental (OMA) observations, as follows:

$$p(\boldsymbol{\theta} \mid \boldsymbol{D}, M_k) = \frac{p(\boldsymbol{D} \mid \boldsymbol{\theta}, M_k) p(\boldsymbol{\theta} \mid M_k)}{p(\boldsymbol{D} \mid M_k)} \tag{14}$$

where $p(\boldsymbol{D} \mid M_k) = \int p(\boldsymbol{D} \mid \boldsymbol{\theta}, M_k) p(\boldsymbol{\theta} \mid M_k) d\boldsymbol{\theta}$ is marginal likelihood or model evidence. Marginal likelihood is a normalizing constant that forces the integral of $p(\boldsymbol{\theta} \mid \boldsymbol{D}, M_k)$ to be equal to unity, but it also has great importance in selecting the most plausible model class among the considered classes (i.e. model selection). Numerical or analytical computation of model evidence becomes intractable when the likelihood function includes multiple model parameters and is highly peaked. Instead, Transitional Markov Chain Monte Carlo algorithm is used to estimate the model evidence while also generating samples from the posterior distribution $p(\boldsymbol{\theta} \mid \boldsymbol{D}, M_k)$ as demonstrated in the examples presented in Section 4 [19].

3.2. Model class selection

Bayes' rule can also be applied to determine the probability (plausibility) of a certain model class describing the observed data. Consider the set of *K* model classes $\boldsymbol{M} = \{M_1, \dots, M_K\}$ with a uniform prior probability for each model class. Similar to Eq. (14), the posterior probability of each model class is obtained by applying the general Bayes' rule:

$$p(M_k \mid \boldsymbol{D}) = \frac{p(\boldsymbol{D}|M_k)}{p(\boldsymbol{D})} \tag{15}$$

Because the denominator of Eq.(15) is a normalizing constant, the model class with the greatest evidence (marginal likelihood), $p(\boldsymbol{D}|M_k)$, has the highest posterior probability conditioned on the observed experimental data.

4. EXPERIMENTAL RESULTS

The turning setup shown in Figure 1 was used in [11] to identify the dominant closed-loop poles of the system dynamics by OMA. In this work, we use the same identified poles for updating the modal parameters of the tool, which were initially measured by impulse hammer tests and are shown in Table 1. The workpiece material was Aluminium 6061 with cutting force coefficients $k_{tc} = 635$ and $k_{fc} = 159$ MPa. Acceleration response to the machining forces was measured using *M*=2 accelerometers mounted in Z-direction and *M'*=2 accelerometers in Z-direction. Modified Least Squares Complex Exponential (LSCE) method was used to identify the frequency and damping of the dominant closed-loop pole under a set of operational conditions [11], [20]. Because the rotational speed of the spindle is precisely regulated at the commanded value, the modified LSCE method can effectively remove the un-damped harmonics from the system response and identify its damped poles. The dominant pole was identified at N_r=5 combinations of spindle speed and width of cut, and identification was repeated N_s=10 times at each combination by using randomly selected segments of the measured response. The mean value and standard deviation of the identified poles are shown in

Table 2. Sensitivity analysis in [14] showed that the closed-loop poles in

Table 2 are mainly affected by variations in the parameters of the second mode shown in Table 1; therefore, only $\theta_{\omega 2}, \theta_{\zeta 2}$, and $\theta_{\phi 2}$ will be updated based on the identified poles.

Table 1. Modal parameters of the tool obtained by impulse hammer test under non-operational conditions.

Mode	Frequency		
n	$\omega_n/2\pi$ [Hz]	ζ_n [-]	$\boldsymbol{\phi}_n^T = [Z_1, Y_1]$ [$\sqrt{Kg^{-1}}$]
1	1842	0.021	[2.8,-0.9]
2	2445	0.009	[0.9,2.6]

Table 2: Dominant closed-loop poles identified by modified LSCE at $\boldsymbol{r} = \mathbf{1..5}$ spindle speed and cutting width combinations. Mean values and standard deviations are computed based on $\boldsymbol{N_s} = \mathbf{10}$ repetitions of the identification using randomly selected segments of the recorded acceleration signals

r	$\frac{60}{\tau_r}$ [rev/min]	a_r[mm]	$\hat{\omega}_{rs}/2\pi$ [Hz]	$\hat{\zeta}_{rs}$
1	7150	2.286	2473±0.56	0.12±0.014
2	7150	2.54	2477±0.28	0.06±0.005
3	6950	2.54	2508±0.30	0.19±0.007
4	7500	2.032	2476±0.33	0.09±0.005
5	7500	2.54	2476±0.39	0.02±0.004

Similar to [14], the prior distribution of $\theta_{\omega 2}$ is assumed to be zero-mean normal with 0.001 variances and truncated at ± 0.03. The prior distributions of $\theta_{\zeta 2}$ and $\theta_{\phi 2}$ are also assumed to be zero-mean normal with 0.05 variance and truncated at ± 0.8. The prior distribution of prediction error variance, σ_ω, is assumed to be uniform across 1×10^{-10} and 5×10^{-6}.

The improved Transitional Markov Chain Monte Carlo (iTMCMC) algorithm presented in [19] was used to generate samples from the posterior distribution of the model parameters according to the assumed priors and the likelihood function defined in Eq.(13). To generate one sample by iTMCMC, the likelihood function and thereby the eigenvalues of the corresponding transition matrix ($\boldsymbol{G}$) must be computed several times for different model parameters ($\boldsymbol{\theta}$). The transition matrix usually has large dimensions depending on the resolution of time discretization. In this example, the system poles converge with acceptable accuracy when the delay period is divided into *m=200* time intervals, which would lead to an 804×804 transition matrix. Considering the large dimension of the transition matrix and the fact that generating thousands of samples by iTMCMC requires several thousands of times evaluating the eigenvalues of the transition matrix at various values of $\boldsymbol{\theta}$, the direct computation of the eigenvalues is computationally inhibiting and surrogate models of $\omega_r(\boldsymbol{\theta}_m)$ and $\zeta_r(\boldsymbol{\theta}_m)$ must replace direct computation. In this work, we use Gaussian Process Regression (GPR) with a squared exponential kernel to build surrogate models based on the eigenvalues computed for a uniform grid of model parameters within the truncation limits of their prior distribution [21]. The GPR model is then used to predict the closed-loop frequency and damping at any arbitrary combination of model parameters. Note that generating the training data in this approach still requires eigenvalue computation at many combinations of modal parameters (4096 eigenvalue computations in this work), which is very time-consuming (about two hours using a consumer-grade computer). However, this computation is performed only once and the trained GPR model can be used any time the closed-loop poles at an arbitrary combination of modal parameters are needed in the iTMCMC algorithm.

The iTMCMC algorithm was used to generate 5000 samples from the posterior distribution of the model parameters for 12 model classes with $\alpha_i = 2^{i+2}, i = 1..12$. Model evidence (log marginal likelihood) for each model class was also computed by iTMCMC and is shown in Figure 2. Model evidence becomes maximum at $\alpha = 512$, indicating the highest plausibility of this model compared to the other 11 model classes. Therefore, this model class is selected for parameter updating.

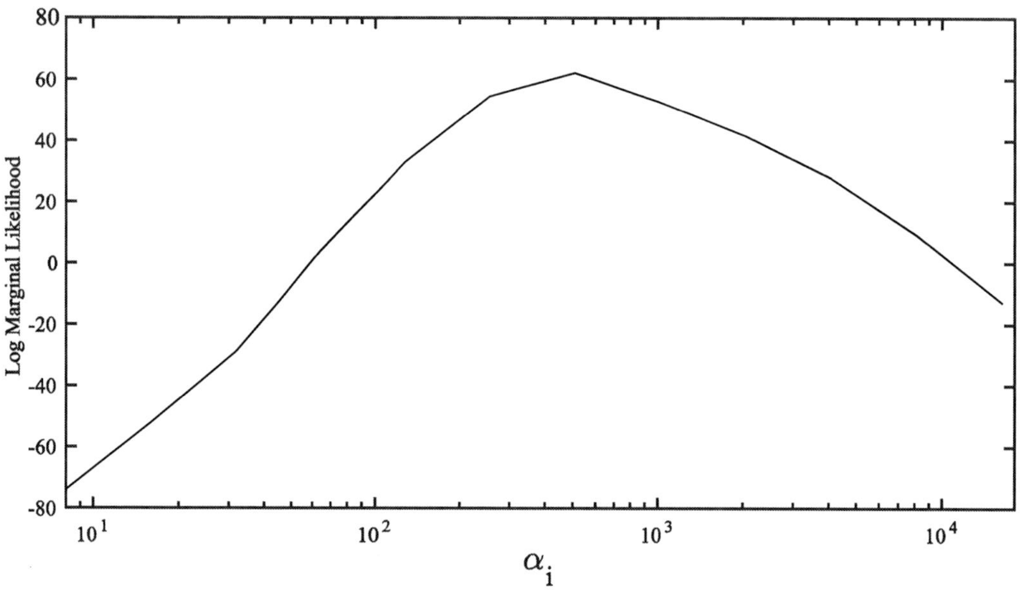

Figure 2: Model evidence (Log marginal likelihood) for model classes with $\boldsymbol{\alpha_i = 2^{i+2}, i = 1..12}$

For the selected model class, 25000 samples were generated from the posterior distribution of the four model parameters. Parts (a-d) of Figure 3 show the histograms of each model parameter and the other parts show 2-D views of the joint distribution. Samples generated from prior distributions are also shown with light grey points in the same figure. The posterior distribution is densely concentrated around the updated model parameter values. Although there are two distinct peaks in the distribution, one of the peaks is significantly larger than the other, indicating the higher probability of the corresponding model parameters describing the identified poles.

Figure 4 shows samples of the posterior distributions for the same example, except that the prior for all of the four model parameters are assumed to be uniform across their truncation ranges. This figure also shows that the updating process considerably reduces the parameter uncertainty in the prior distribution, however, the probability of the parameters at the two peaks are now similar to one another and more data is needed to further reduce parameter uncertainty. This additional data was provided by the normal prior defined based on impulse hammer test results in Figure 3; when hammer test results are not available, additional information can be obtained by OMA under additional cutting width and spindle speed combinations.

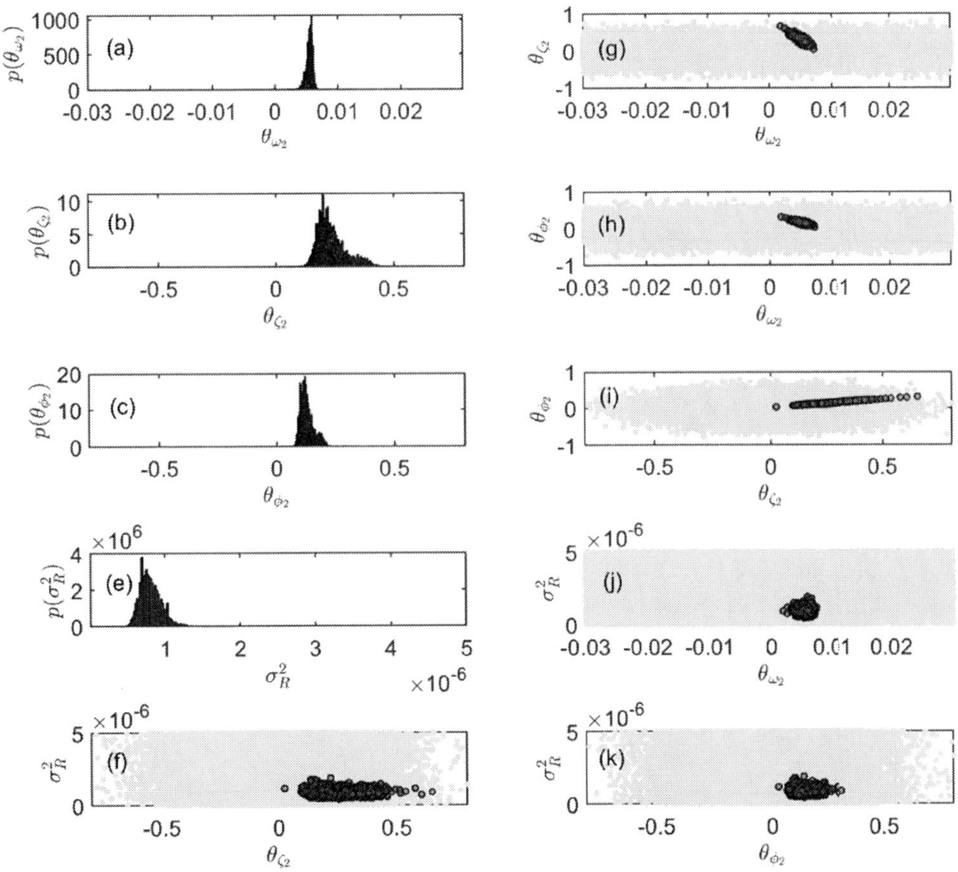

Figure 3: Samples from *normal* prior and updated posterior distributions of model parameters for model class with $\boldsymbol{\alpha} = \mathbf{512}$

The posterior distribution of model parameters shown in Figure 3 resembles multi-modal Gaussian. A two-mode Gaussian mixture model was fitted to the samples in that figure and the parameters of the first peak (with higher probability) were used to represent the probability distribution of the model parameters after updating:

$$\begin{bmatrix}\theta_{\omega 2}\\ \theta_{\zeta 2}\\ \theta_{\phi 2}\end{bmatrix} = N\left(\begin{bmatrix}0.0057\\ 0.2112\\ 0.1158\end{bmatrix}, \begin{bmatrix}0.00012 & -0.00638 & -0.00260\\ -0.00638 & 1.1710 & 0.52401\\ -0.00260 & 0.52401 & 0.26105\end{bmatrix} \times 10^{-3}\right) \quad (16)$$

A grid of points was considered on the spindle speed and cutting width plane and the mean and variance of the largest eigenvalue of the transition matrix at each point were obtained by substituting the mean and variances from Eq.(16) in Eq.(7). Figure 5 shows the border between the points with unstable eigenvalues and those with entirely stable eigenvalues. The curve of the mean values is the contour plot of the eigenvalues with unit modulus. The upper/lower credibility bounds are determined by the contour plot of the eigenvalues plus/minus one standard deviation equal to unity. Also shown in this figure are experimentally determined stable (circles) and unstable (crosses) combinations of speed and width, all of which agree with the stability borders established by the updated model parameters. For comparison, the mean curve of the stability diagrams obtained by the prior estimate of modal parameters (Table 1) is also shown in this figure, which over-estimates the stability limit at 7300 rev/min spindle speed. Notice that only five of the stable points (P1-P5) were used in updating and the points at 7300 rev/min were used only for validation.

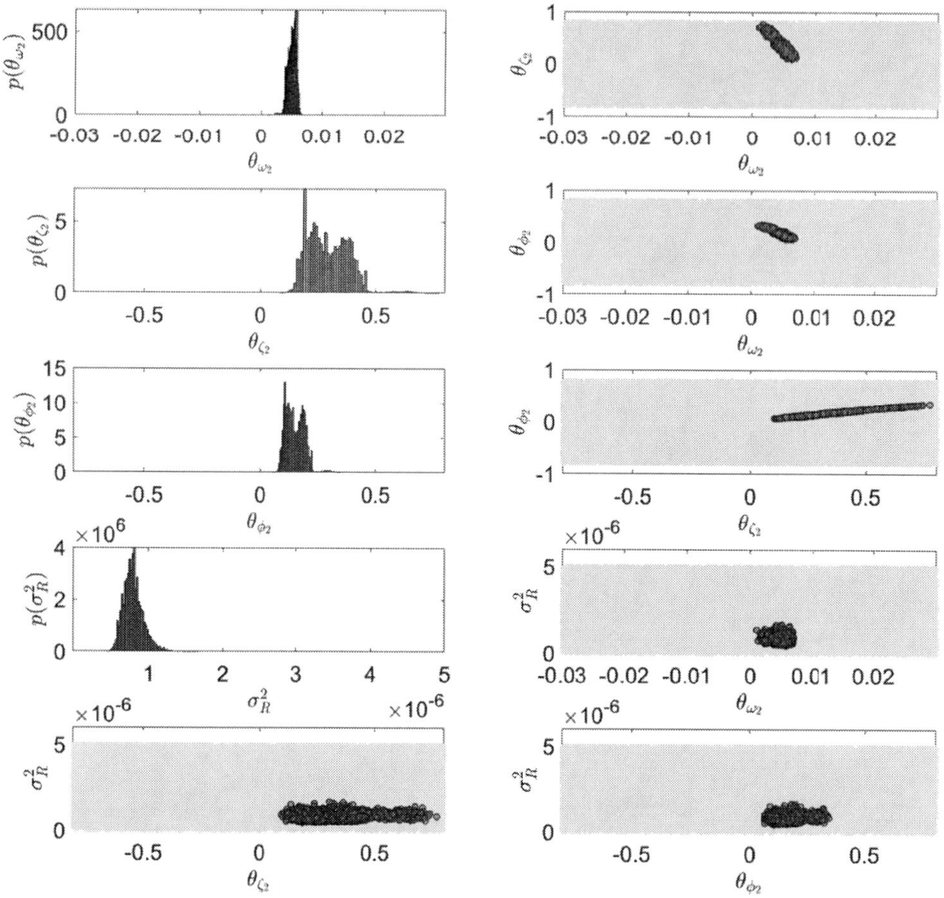

Figure 4: Samples from a *uniform* prior and updated posterior distributions of model parameters for model class with $\boldsymbol{\alpha} = \mathbf{512}$

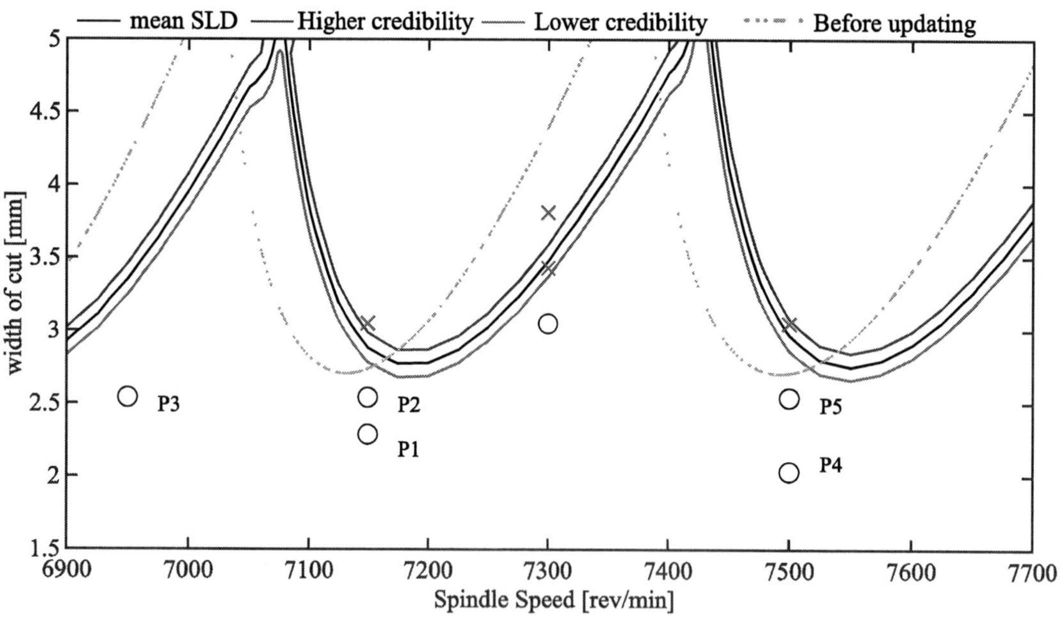

Figure 5: Stability Lobe Diagrams (SLD) with credibility bounds. Circles and crosses are experimentally determined stable and unstable points, respectively. P1-P5 are the stable points used in model updating

5. CONCLUSIONS

Bayesian model updating was used to determine the probability distributions of the tool modal parameters in a discrete-time domain model of chatter in turning. The likelihood function in Bayesian updating was defined based on the surrogate of the discrete-time domain model to circumvent computationally expensive eigenvalue computations. The updated chatter model was used to determine the probabilistic limits of chatter on the plane of spindle speed and cutting width.

The presented model was shown to considerably improve the accuracy of the chatter model. However, the updated parameters depend on their assumed prior distribution when sufficient experimental data is not available (from OMA). The tool modal parameters obtained from impulse hammer tests can provide a reasonable assumption for the prior distribution. Alternatively, the automated OMA of the vibration signals during the process can inject new information into the updating process to progressively reduce uncertainty in the distributions of the modal parameters. Automated OMA in machining is difficult because of the dominance of undammed harmonics generated by the spindle rotation, and this remains a key challenge to be addressed in future.

ACKNOWLEDGEMENTS

This work was completed during the author's study leave at the Institute for Machine Tools and Industrial Management (iwb) at the Technical University of Munich (TUM). I thank Prof. Michael Zaeh and the *iwb* colleagues for their support.

REFERENCES

[1] Y. Altintas and M. Weck, "Chatter Stability of Metal Cutting and Grinding," *CIRP Ann.*, vol. 53, no. 2, pp. 619–642, Jan. 2004, doi: 10.1016/S0007-8506(07)60032-8.

[2] Y. Altintas, G. Stepan, E. Budak, T. Schmitz, and Z. M. Kilic, "Chatter Stability of Machining Operations," *J. Manuf. Sci. Eng. Trans. ASME*, vol. 142, no. 11, Nov. 2020, doi: 10.1115/1.4047391/1084163.

[3] I. E. Minis, E. B. Magrab, and I. O. Pandelidis, "Improved methods for the prediction of chatter in turning, Part 2: Determination of cutting process parameters," *J. Manuf. Sci. Eng. Trans. ASME*, vol. 112, no. 1, pp. 21–27, 1990, doi: 10.1115/1.2899291.

[4] O. Özşahin, E. Budak, and H. N. Özgüven, "Investigating dynamics of machine tool spindles under operational conditions," *Adv. Mater. Res.*, vol. 223, pp. 610–621, 2011, doi: 10.4028/www.scientific.net/AMR.223.610.

[5] L. Ljung, "System identification-theory for the user 2nd edition ptr prentice-hall," *Up. Saddle River, NJ*, 1999.

[6] N. Grossi, L. Sallese, A. Scippa, and G. Campatelli, "Improved experimental-analytical approach to compute speed-varying tool-tip FRF," *Precis. Eng.*, vol. 48, pp. 114–122, 2017, doi: 10.1016/j.precisioneng.2016.11.011.

[7] M. Eynian, "In-process identification of modal parameters using dimensionless relationships in milling chatter," *Int. J. Mach. Tools Manuf.*, vol. 143, no. December 2018, pp. 49–62, 2019, doi: 10.1016/j.ijmachtools.2019.04.003.

[8] Y. P. Liu and Y. Altintas, "In-process identification of machine tool dynamics," *CIRP J. Manuf. Sci. Technol.*, vol. 32, pp. 322–337, 2021, doi: 10.1016/j.cirpj.2021.01.007.

[9] M. Postel, B. Bugdayci, F. Kuster, and K. Wegener, "Neural network supported inverse parameter identification for stability predictions in milling," *CIRP J. Manuf. Sci. Technol.*, vol. 29, pp. 71–87, 2020, doi: 10.1016/j.cirpj.2020.02.004.

[10] I. Zaghbani and V. Songmene, "Estimation of machine-tool dynamic parameters during machining operation through operational modal analysis," *Int. J. Mach. Tools Manuf.*, vol. 49, no. 12–13, pp. 947–957, 2009, doi: 10.1016/j.ijmachtools.2009.06.010.

[11] S. Kim and K. Ahmadi, "Estimation of vibration stability in turning using operational modal analysis," *Mech. Syst. Signal Process.*, vol. 130, 2019, doi: 10.1016/j.ymssp.2019.04.057.

[12] A. K. Kiss, D. Hajdu, D. Bachrathy, G. Stepan, and Z. Dombovari, "In-process impulse response of milling to identify stability properties by signal processing," *J. Sound Vib.*, vol. 527, p. 116849, Jun. 2022, doi: 10.1016/J.JSV.2022.116849.

[13] A. K. Kiss, D. Hajdu, D. Bachrathy, and G. Stepan, "Operational stability prediction in milling based on impact tests," *Mech. Syst. Signal Process.*, vol. 103, pp. 327–339, Mar. 2018, doi: 10.1016/J.YMSSP.2017.10.019.

[14] K. Ahmadi, "Bayesian Interference for Updating Chatter Model Parameters in Turning," 2022. https://dspace.library.uvic.ca/handle/1828/13904 (accessed Apr. 29, 2022).

[15] T. Insperger and G. Stépán, "Semi-discretization method for delayed systems," *Int. J. Numer. Methods Eng.*, vol. 55, no. 5, pp. 503–518, Oct. 2002, doi: 10.1002/NME.505.

[16] Y. Ding, L. M. Zhu, X. J. Zhang, and H. Ding, "A full-discretization method for prediction of milling stability," *Int. J. Mach. Tools Manuf.*, vol. 50, no. 5, pp. 502–509, May 2010, doi: 10.1016/J.IJMACHTOOLS.2010.01.003.

[17] A. Nobari, H. Ouyang, and P. Bannister, "Statistics of complex eigenvalues in friction-induced vibration," *J. Sound Vib.*, vol. 338, pp. 169–183, 2015, doi: 10.1016/j.jsv.2014.10.017.

[18] B. Goller, J. L. Beck, and G. I. Schuëller, "Evidence-Based Identification of Weighting Factors in Bayesian Model Updating Using Modal Data," *J. Eng. Mech.*, vol. 138, no. 5, pp. 430–440, 2012, doi: 10.1061/(asce)em.1943-7889.0000351.

[19] W. Betz, I. Papaioannou, and D. Straub, "Transitional Markov Chain Monte Carlo: Observations and Improvements," *J. Eng. Mech.*, vol. 142, no. 5, p. 04016016, 2016, doi: 10.1061/(asce)em.1943-7889.0001066.

[20] P. Mohanty and D. J. Rixen, "Operational modal analysis in the presence of harmonic excitation," *J. Sound Vib.*, vol. 270, no. 1–2, pp. 93–109, Feb. 2004, doi: 10.1016/S0022-460X(03)00485-1.

[21] C. E. Rasmussen, "Gaussian processes in machine learning," in *Summer school on machine learning*, 2003, pp. 63–71.

9th International Operational Modal Analysis Conference
iomac
July 3 - 6, 2022
Vancouver, Canada

COMPARISON OF DIFFERENT OMA TECHNIQUES AND THEIR APPLICATION TO AN AXIAL COMPRESSOR TEST RIG

Mona Amer[1], *Joerg Wallaschek*[2], *Joerg R. Seume*[3], *Carlos E. Ventura*[4]

[1] Institute of Turbomachinery and Fluid Dynamics, Leibniz University Hannover, amer@tfd.uni-hannover.de
[2] Institute of Dynamics and Vibration Research, Leibniz University Hannover, joerg.wallaschek@ids.uni-hannover.de
[3] Institute of Turbomachinery and Fluid Dynamics, Leibniz University Hannover, seume@tfd.uni-hannover.de
[4] Civil Engineering Department, University of British Columbia, ventura@civil.ubc.ca

ABSTRACT

Identifying the modal properties of mechanical engineering systems while these are under operating conditions is still associated with major challenges, especially when said operation is induced by rotation of components. In this case, ambient vibration excitation, which is typically assumed for the application of output only techniques, is superposed by a deterministic periodic excitation component. This paper studies different techniques to perform an operational modal analysis in this particular situation. The methods are applied to an axial compressor test rig at the Institute of Turbomachinery and Fluid-Dynamics. Among them, three approaches, the Hilbert-Huang transform, the Bayesian OMA, and the stochastic subspace identification, are investigated. For the stochastic subspace identification, two different pole picking techniques to automatize the selection of stable poles from the stability diagram are studied. Furthermore, various approaches to deal with the harmonic excitation, which can lead to falsely identified modal parameters in the analysis process, are presented and applied to the data sets. Measurements at different rotational speeds of the rotor were collected and are used for the analysis. The results are summarized and the relative strengths and weaknesses of the different methods are discussed. The results obtained in this study are a first step towards a digital model to monitor the vibration behavior of rotating machinery using OMA techniques.

Keywords: axial compressor, Hilbert-Huang transform, stochastic subspace identification, pole picking, harmonic detection

1. INTRODUCTION

Operational modal analysis (OMA) has been broadly used in the civil engineering domain throughout the last decades to determine the modal parameters of structures, such as high rise buildings, towers, bridges, dams, and wind turbines. OMA is gaining more and more attention in the mechanical engineering domain, where it is for example used for the identification of light weight structures such as in the aerospace industry [1, 2]. Especially, the development of the stochastic subspace identification (SSI) [3], considered a robust technique to perform the analysis on in-operation data, encouraged the spread of OMA in different sectors. A challenge is caused by the existence of periodic excitation that occurs for rotating machinery. In particular, closely spaced frequencies – eigenfrequencies and periodic excitation frequencies – can lead to an erroneous evaluation [4]. For this reason, there are various methods dealing with the elimination of the disruptive effect or the identification of harmonic modes, which are categorized by Motte et al. [5]. Some of these procedures will be presented and discussed in more detail in the following section.

Some examples for the application of OMA to mechanical engineering structures also in the presence of rotation are given in the literature. Wilkes et al. studied the application and adaptation of OMA to a centrifugal compressor [6]. The focus was on flow-induced excitation and the effects and structural behavior of the five-stage rotor using proximity probes, examining different operating conditions, e.g. different pressure fields. Arjmand and Bratek performed an OMA on different case studies such as a reciprocating compressor and a steel pile foundation [7]. The relevant rotational speed was at a low range between 270-330 rpm. Clarke et al. studied diesel engines of ship structures and discussed the problems related to modal identification in the presence of harmonic excitation [8]. Carden and Lindblad showed that even torsional modes of a reciprocating compressor, which are usually not speed dependent, have different characteristics in standstill conditions than in operation. Their contribution proposes OMA as a valuable method because other numeric tools such as finite element analyses partly fail to predict the real operational behavior.

While the application of OMA has been studied on a number of real applications, in most cases only a comparison between OMA (in general) and classical experimental modal analysis (EMA) has been performed. The literature is lacking a comparison of different OMA techniques which can incorporate the mentioned challenges. This should support finding a suitable method in order to treat data from a high speed rotating application as accurately as possible. In addition, most research focuses on isolated components, whereas a holistic approach taking into account the casing and foundation is often missing. For this reason, different techniques from the literature were implemented and applied to a high speed axial compressor test rig at the Institute of Turbomachinery and Fluid-Dynamics (TFD), Leibniz University Hannover. This test rig consists of a rotor, assembled casing components, and a concrete and steel foundation. The results gained from the different methods are discussed and compared amongst each other. The ultimate purpose of this research and the modal identification in operation, is to contribute to structural health monitoring (SHM). This contribution, brings the long term objective of a digital twin, which is increasingly demanded by the industry for the reliable operation of complex capital goods, a step closer.

2. METHODOLOGY

As explained in the introduction, different techniques have been implemented in a toolbox in order to analyze the axial compressor data from the test rig at TFD. The studied configuration consists of a single stage rotor with a nominal speed of 17100 rpm. Previous results, as well as the setup of the test rig can be found in [9, 10]. For the analysis, data from different rotational speeds were measured at stationary operating conditions with a sampling rate of 25.6 kHz. In the following, three OMA techniques are implemented; afterwards, two applied clustering techniques are described, and finally, several methods for the harmonic detection are presented.

Hilbert-Huang Transform

The Hilbert-Huang transform (HHT) is based on the empirical mode decomposition, which decomposes the time signal into intrinsic mode functions (IMF) [11]. In a consecutive step, an estimate of the free vibration response is extracted from the IMF using the random decrement technique (RDT) [12]. The assumption is that the signal is composed of a deterministic and a stochastic part. The deterministic part represents the vibration response, and the stochastic part is assumed to be caused by noise, and it is further assumed, that this component can be eliminated when averaging the time signal over enough time segments. The signal of the free vibration response is then transformed into Hilbert space. The eigenfrequency ω_0 and damping D are obtained from

$$\omega(t) = \frac{d\varphi(t)}{dt} = \omega_d \tag{1}$$

$$ln(\hat{y}(t)) = -D\omega_0 t + ln(\hat{q}) \tag{2}$$

with the quasi eigenfrequency ω_d, $\hat{y} = \hat{q}e^{-D\omega_0 t}$, and $\varphi(t) = \omega_d t + \varphi_0$, where $\hat{q}$ is the amplitude and φ the phase of the signal. Usually a least squares fit algorithm is used to solve these equations. A flow chart of the procedure is illustrated in Fig. 1. The advantage of the HHT method over other techniques

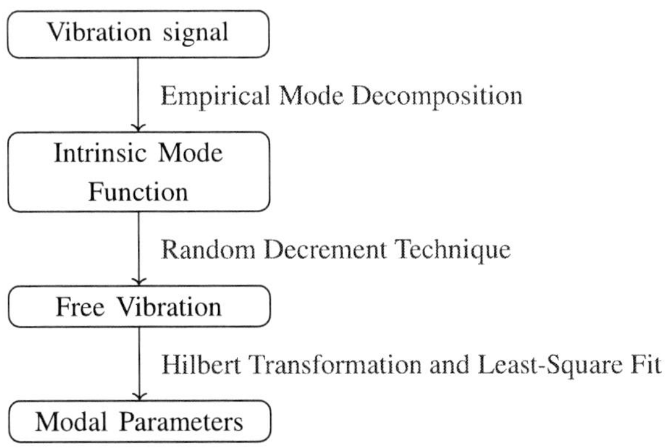

Figure 1: Process of Hilbert-Huang transform

is the possibility to process time variant data and even data which is captured from nonlinear systems. The implementation used in the presented work fits the signal to the vibration response of a system with a single degree of freedom (DOF), which does not cover nonlinearities, as nonlinear behavior of the structure was not observed, cf. [10]. This technique cannot be used to calculate eigenvectors, as only a single channel can be treated simultaneously for the analysis.

Bayesian OMA

The Bayesian OMA approach considers modal parameters as randomly distributed variables. The procedure intends to determine their probability distribution. It is based on the Bayes' theorem

$$P(\Phi|y_k) = \frac{P(y_k|\Phi)P(\Phi)}{P(y_k)} \tag{3}$$

with P the probability of Φ a set of modal parameters and y_k the measured vibration data. Equation (3) describes the probability of an event A ($\widehat{=}\Phi$) under the condition that the event B ($\widehat{=}y_k$) has occurred. $P(\Phi|y_k)$ can be estimated using a likelihood function. In our implementation, the Bayesian OMA algorithm is based on the fast Fourier transform (FFT) of the vibration data as described in the work of Au [13]. It enables the identification of a single mode in the selected frequency band by minimizing a simplified negative log-likelihood function (NLLF).

Stochastic Subspace Identification

The SSI is one of the broadly used methods to study the structural behavior from in-operation data. It is known as a robust method and performs the analysis in the time domain. This method is based on the state space representation of a dynamic system. The objective is to identify the system matrices **A** (state matrix) and **C** (output matrix), which contain the structural information on the dynamics of the underlying system. It is assumed to be observable according to the Kalman criterion. A subspace matrix $\mathscr{H}$ is constructed by means of the measured values. A singular value decomposition is applied to $\mathscr{H}$ in order to obtain the observability matrix $\mathbf{O}$. This in turn contains the system matrix $\mathbf{A}$ with the necessary information. A detailed description of the procedure can be found in [14].

Clustering Techniques
The application of the SSI, leads to a stabilization diagram with poles over the calculated model order, which can be selected by the user. A very simple, but unfortunately often not very satisfying, approach is to choose the stable poles which are obtained for the highest model order. These selected poles, however, are not necessarily the ones describing the real dynamics of the system. Often there are "artificial poles", which have a mathematical, but no physical meaning. In order to select only those poles, which do have a physical meaning, several automated techniques have been proposed, which choose the most appropriate poles from the stability diagram. Hence, a multistage clustering algorithm (MSC), and a fuzzy-c-means clustering scheme (FCM) were implemented and tested within the toolbox [15, 16]. Reynders et al. developed a fully automated OMA using a MSC technique, which is implemented in the following three steps [15].

1. Application of soft and hard validation criteria (SVC, HVC) to separate the modes in non-physical and potentially physical modes using k-means clustering.

2. Application of hierarchic clustering and definition of mode sets.

3. Division of mode sets into non-physical and physical mode-sets using k-means clustering and selection of physical modes.

In total, nine criteria were implemented for the first step. The SVC contain three dimensionless distances for frequency, damping and eigenvalue, as well as the modal assurance criterion (MAC), the mode phase complexity (MPC), and the mode phase deviation (MPD), which can have values between 0 and 1. The values for the HVC in turn can only be exactly 0 or 1 and include limitations for damping values ($D > 0/D < 0.2$), and the postulate of conjugate complex eigenvalues. The algorithm is adjusted so that only a single pair of the complex conjugate eigenvalues is identified as a physical mode. The k-means clustering divides a data set in k clusters. The objective is to minimize the sum of squared deviations from the cluster centers.
Another clustering method, the so-called fuzzy-c-means algorithm, was proposed by Scionti et. al. [16]. It is based on the division of the data set into a set of clusters. It further estimates stable poles according to a membership matrix $\mathbf{U}$, which describes the affiliation of the data points to a cluster, that is being constantly updated until a termination criteria is reached. The minimum affiliation u_{min} is set to 0.95. Modes, which have a lower value than u_{min} are eliminated. Only stable poles, which are determined by simple stability criteria applied to the stability diagram, are passed on to the algorithm. In this case, the stability criteria between two poles is set to $\Delta f = 1\%$ and $\Delta D = 30\%$. It is important to choose the right number of initializing clusters, as otherwise the algorithm can lead to an incorrect number of identified modes.

Harmonic Detection
As mentioned in the introduction, a major challenge for the modal parameter identification of rotating machinery is caused by the superposed harmonic excitation due to the rotation. Motte et al. suggested to divide possible procedures into four categories [5]:

1. statistically driven identification,

2. pre-processing techniques,

3. modification to existing identification techniques, and

4. input spectrum independent techniques.

One statistically driven approach is based on the calculation of the kurtosis k, which is the fourth statistical moment of the probability distribution of a random variable. Equivalently the excess can be calculated, which is defined as $k-3$. In the presence of harmonic modes, the excess equals -1.5. Another procedure is to use the probability density function (PDF) itself for the harmonic detection. The PDF for a structural mode has only one peak, whereas the PDF for a harmonic mode has two peaks. This can be explained by the fact that a stochastic load leads to a response with a PDF close to a Gaussian distribution. However, a harmonic response has a PDF of $p(x) = \frac{1}{\pi\sqrt{a^2-x^2}}, x \in [-a,a]$ with the amplitude a that goes to infinity for $x \to a$ and $x \to -a$ and therefore has two distinct peaks [17]. This technique can also identify mathematical modes by the shape of the PDF and works well as long as the modes are not too strongly damped. A modification to existing techniques, which consider the periodic excitation can be made for the SSI through matrix extension considering the additional harmonic excitation. In this paper the method by Dong et al. is implemented [18]. Another way to treat the periodic excitation is by pre-processing techniques, such as filters. Here, the periodic frequency needs to be known before the analysis. This is usually the case, but it has to be considered that filters can change the whole data set, so the user needs to take care that results are not modified in an undesired way [4].

3. RESULTS

The results presented in the following section are obtained from the high speed axial compressor test rig at TFD shown in Fig. 2. Figure 2 (a) depicts the 49 positions of the uniaxial acceleration sensors attached

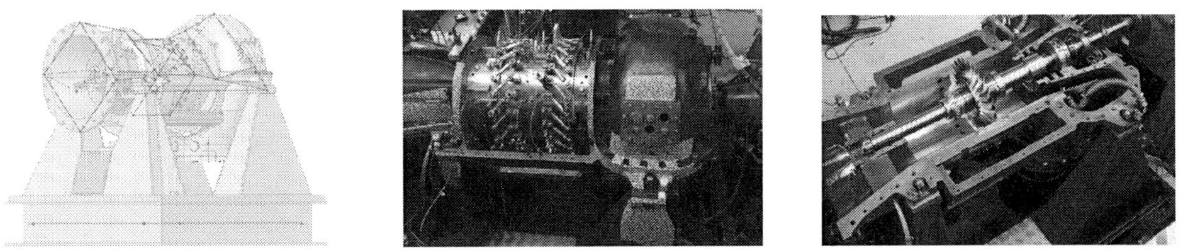

(a) (b) (c)

Figure 2: (**a**) Sensor positions on axial compressor (**b**) Instrumented axial compressor (**c**) Single stage rotor. Axial compressor test rig at TFD.

to the test rig for data acquisition. Figure 2 (b) illustrates the compressor with the casing components (inlet, stator housing, and outlet) each divided into two parts and assembled by screw connections, as well as the bearing support, where the components are mounted. Figure 2 (c) shows the single stage compressor in the fluid film bearings, which was used to conduct the experiments. From EMA of the

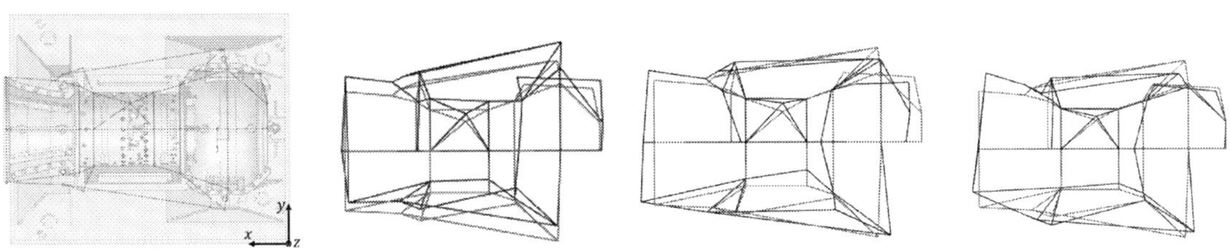

(a) (b) (c) (d)

Figure 3: (**a**) Compressor with grid lines from mode shape animation: (**b**) 65 Hz; (**c**) 111 Hz; (**d**) 132 Hz. First three mode shapes obtained from EMA of casing with rotor at rest.

test rig three characteristic modes were identified, namely the first rigid body mode at 65 Hz, where the whole structure moves in the y-direction, the second rigid body mode at 111 Hz where the structure moves in the x-direction, and the first bending mode at around 132 Hz, where a strong deflection of the inlet casing in the y-direction can be observed. A projection of the mode shapes into the horizontal x-y-plane is shown in Fig. 3. The objective in the following analysis is the identification of these three modes using the different OMA techniques.

Hilbert-Huang Transform

The knowledge of the frequency range of the sought-after eigenfrequency was used to choose the right limitation of the bandpass filter before the analysis. In Tab. 1 the results applying the HHT for different rotational speeds, as well as the results obtained from one measurement during a run down of the compressor are compared. Different frequency ranges were applied for the analysis between 50 and 150 Hz

Table 1: Comparison of results from HHT

rotational speed [rpm]	rotor state	filter range [Hz]	frequency [Hz]	damping [%]
3900	Ref	50-80 105-120 120-150	64.9 114.6 129.7	0.22 0.74 0.14
6600	Ref	60-80 100-120 130-140	61.4 110.1 134.8	1.89 0.01 1.12
7800	Ref	60-80 105-115 120-150	61.6 112.6 130.0	1.86 1.12 0.01
15390	Ref	50-80 105-115 125-140	58.8 108.0 137.6 142.1	0.41 2.19 0.78 1.20
17100	Ref	50-80 100-120 120-150	65.5 111.1 132.4	0.12 1,56 0.67
15390	U1	50-80 105-115 125-140	58.6 109.5 137.8	0.68 3.14 1.72
15390	U2	50-80 105-115 125-140	58.8 106.9 137.4	0.40 3.10 1.13
17100-3000	Run down	50-80 100-120 120-150	62.9 112.0 130.6	4.11 3.88 4.55

in order to find the three sought-after eigenfrequencies. The results for frequency and damping were calculated for different sensors, as well as different time segments as input for the RDT. The results shown in Tab. 1 are averaged over three sensors, one on the inlet casing, one on the loose bearing support, and one on the outlet casing, as well as for two different time segment numbers (1000, and 2000). A comparison of the results from sensors over all components of the axial compressor for a rotational speed of 3900 rpm showed, that the maximum deviation $\frac{f_{max}-f_{min}}{f_{max}}$ of the identified eigenfrequencies is around 0.3%. The estimates for the damping showed a large relative deviation among the individual results, but in general the estimated damping has a very small level. In Tab. 1 the rotation synchronous frequencies, which were identified for the datasets at 3900 rpm, 6600 rpm, and 7800 rpm are depicted. These are in case of 3900 rpm 64.9 Hz (first harmonic) and 129.7 Hz (second harmonic), 110.1 Hz in case of 6600 rpm and 130.0 Hz in case of 7800 rpm. These results show that the harmonic modes will be identified by the different algorithms, if no procedure for the elimination or detection is applied. These harmonic frequencies were identified with all three OMA techniques and will not be depicted in the following as they can clearly be identified due to the known rotational speed. In case of the 15390 rpm dataset two eigenfrequencies, which are close to each other, are identified in the same frequency range of the bandpass filter. The lower frequency at approx. 138 Hz was found for a time segment number of 1000 whereas the higher frequency at 142 Hz was found for 2000 time segments. The rotational speed of

15390 rpm (90% of the nominal speed) is chosen as a reference case for the investigation of the system under unbalance excitation. To this end, two levels of unbalance were intentionally introduced in the system, which are denoted by U1 and U2 in the following. U1 has an additional mass of 3.47 g in plane 1 and U2 has an additional mass of 3.49 g in plane 2. The unbalance masses decreased the balance quality by a factor of approximately 2.5. For the third sought-after eigenfrequency only the lower frequency at around 138 Hz will be considered in the comparison. As expected, the additional unbalance mass did not alter the extracted eigenfrequencies. Damping values for the time variant data are higher by a factor

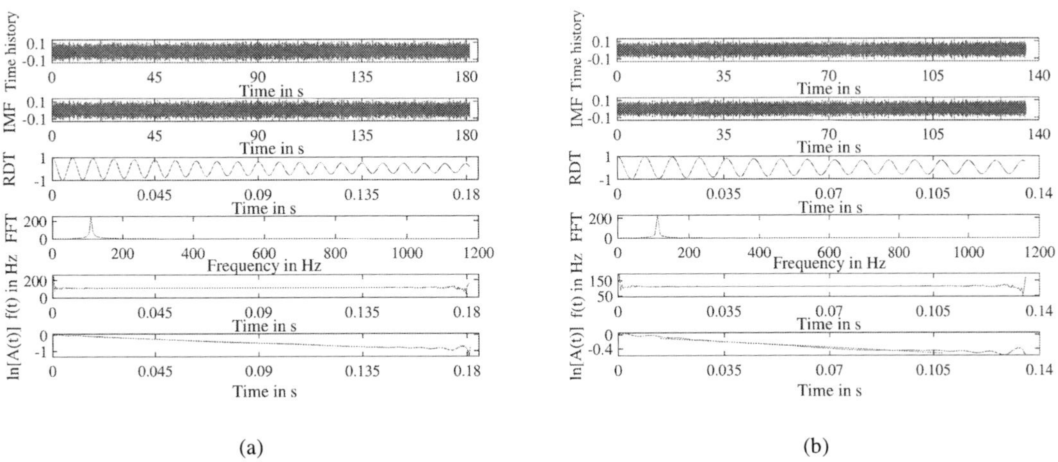

Figure 4: (**a**) HHT at 15390 rpm reference (**b**) HHT at 15390 rpm unbalance 1. HHT at 15390 rpm – comparison of the different steps for the reference and unbalance 1 case.

of approx. four compared to the stationary operating points, which can be explained by varying speed dependent friction and clearance conditions during the run down. The variation of the number of time segments has an insignificant impact on the frequencies identified. The filter order, which was set to two, is necessary as otherwise the speed synchronous frequency dominates the evaluation. Next to the three eigenfrequencies of interest, another frequency at around 90 Hz was identified for a different frequency range. Figure 4 shows the results for the different algorithm steps from two evaluations with the HHT.

Bayesian OMA

For the analysis with the Bayesian OMA, Welchs' method and a window length of 512 samples are selected. A variation of the downsampling factor, which was set to 40, and the window length did not alter the modal parameters. Table 2 shows the identified modal parameters for the different data sets, as well as their standard deviation calculated with this method. In Tab. 2 only the results corresponding to the three relevant frequencies are shown. For two datasets, 7800 rpm and 15390 rpm, again two frequencies, which are close to each other, are identified. For 7800 rpm frequencies at around 140 Hz and 145 Hz and for 15390 rpm frequencies at 138 Hz and 142 Hz are found. The frequency values obtained for the 17100 rpm dataset agree well with the values found for the EMA. Next to the results in Tab. 2, frequencies at approx. 80 Hz, 90 Hz, and 120 Hz are identified, which are not consistent with the frequencies in standstill condition. The reason for this will be explained in detail later. Figure 5 shows the selected frequency bands for the analysis of the 15390 rpm data set and the values received from the minimization of the NLLF.

Table 2: Comparison of results from Bayesian OMA

rot. speed [rpm]	rotor state	frequency [Hz]	freq. deviation [Hz]	damping [%]	damp. deviation [pp.]
3900	Ref	54.9	0.008	2.27	1.06
		108.4	0.009	0.66	1.05
		147.0	0.008	0.47	1.00
6600	Ref	61.3	0.008	0.14	0.98
		146.5	0.008	0.90	0.98
7800	Ref	61.3	0.009	1.01	1.12
		112.7	0.010	0.54	1.28
		139.9	0.009	0.78	1.05
		145.5	0.012	0.63	1.41
15390	Ref	58.9	0.007	0.17	0.84
		109.3	0.009	2.26	1.17
		138.2	0.128	0.26	1.45
		142.2	0.009	0.09	1.12
17100	Ref	65.3	0.006	0.18	0.70
		109.4	0.008	0.56	0.95
		132.3	0.007	0.91	0.90

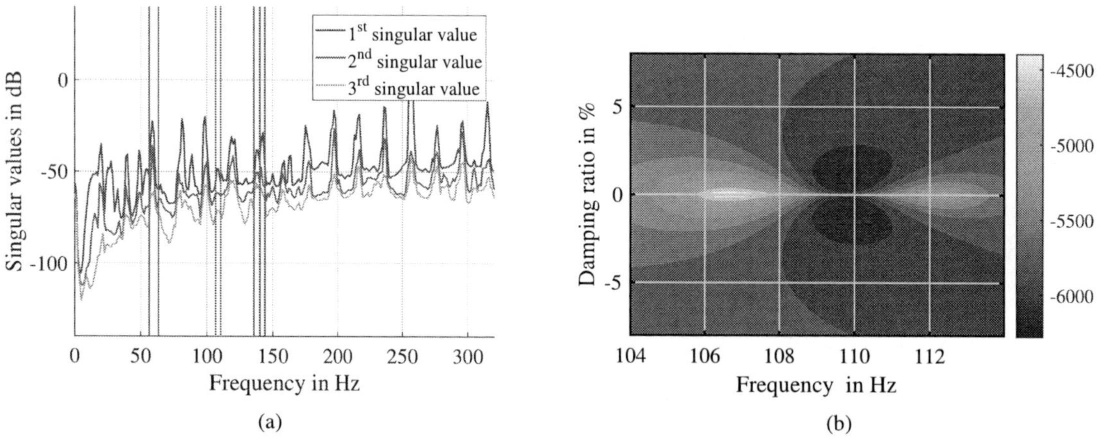

Figure 5: (**a**) Selected frequency ranges for analysis at 15390 rpm reference; (**b**) Contour plot of optimized modal parameters of 110 Hz at 15390 rpm reference. Analysis with Bayesian OMA for 15390 rpm reference.

SSI

In the toolbox, the covariance-driven, as well as the data-driven SSI approach are implemented. A comparison of the computational resources for the covariance-driven and the data-driven SSI approach has been performed in [10] showing that the covariance-driven method is less time-consuming. Thus, it is preferably used in the ongoing analysis. The results using the SSI technique are displayed in Tab. 3. The variation of the window length for the calculation of the power spectral density does not have an impact on the eigenfrequencies identified. Figure 6 depicts two stability diagrams for a rotational speed of 3900 rpm with the regular SSI and the extended SSI that can consider harmonic frequencies and should eliminate them as stable frequency line. Considering the harmonic excitation in the SSI algorithm did not change the stable frequency lines in the stability diagram. For this reason, the presented harmonic detection method does not seem to work well with the axial compressor data. The frequency results are equal using the usual and the extended SSI and the harmonic frequencies are identified as stable frequency lines in the extended SSI. For the SSI the same characteristics as for the Bayesian OMA are observed. The datasets for 7800 rpm and 15390 rpm show frequencies that are close to each other around 140 Hz and the identified frequency values at 17100 rpm match the standstill results well. Fig. 7 shows an example of the MAC matrix for the 7800 rpm dataset confirming that the frequencies at around 140 Hz and 145 Hz are representing different modes. Again the SSI identifies additional stable frequencies at around 80 Hz, 90 Hz, and 120 Hz. Lastly, the covariance-driven and the data-driven approach were

Table 3: Comparison of results from SSI

rotational speed [rpm]	rotor state	method	frequency [Hz]	damping [%]
3900	Ref	cov	56.2 108.6 146.4	1.13 0.16 0.08
3900	Ref	cov harmonics	56.1 108.6 146.4	1.24 0.17 0.09
6600	Ref	cov	61.3 146.8	0.06 0.07
7800	Ref	cov	61.6 112.6 140.3 145.8	0.92 0.28 0.11 0.35
15390	Ref	cov	58.9 107.9 138.1 142.3	0.17 0.33 0.09 0.01
17100	Ref	cov	64.9 109.5 134.3	0.02 0.38 0.03
15390	U1	cov	59.2 138.2 142.3	0.08 0.07 0.04
15390	U2	cov	58.8 138.2 142.2	0.2 0.07 0.06

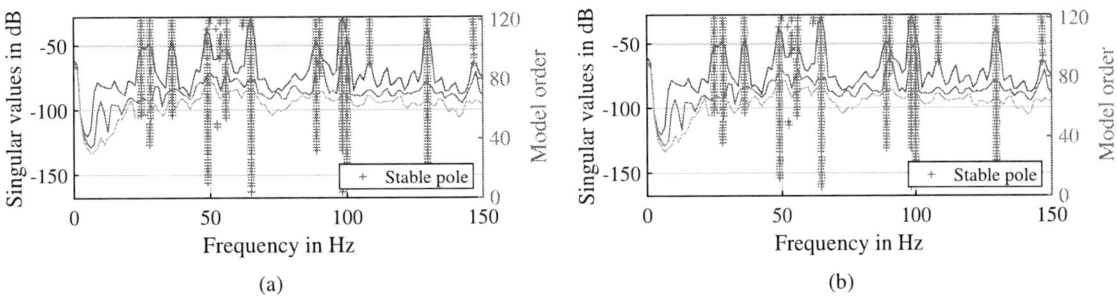

Figure 6: (**a**) Stability diagram at 3900 rpm; (**b**) Stability diagram at 3900 rpm using extended SSI for the elimination of harmonics. Stability diagrams at 3900 rpm SSI and extended SSI.

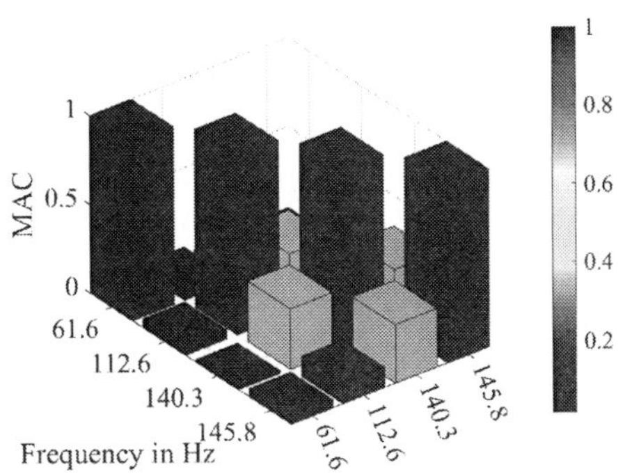

Figure 7: MAC matrix for eigenvectors identified from SSI at 7800 rpm

compared leading to a maximum deviation of 1% for the identified frequencies.

Clustering

Table 4 contains the results performing the SSI and selecting the poles with the two automated pole picking techniques MSC and FCM instead of choosing them manually as shown in Tab. 3. The initial

Table 4: Comparison of results from Clustering techniques

rotational speed [rpm]	method	MSC		FCM	
		f	D	f	D
6600	cov	61.3	0.06	61.3	0.06
7800	cov	61.6	0.97		
		112.5	0.29		
15390	cov	138.1	0.09		
		142.2	0.11	141.8	0.08
17100	cov	64.8	0.14	65.4	0.15
		109.5	0.43	109.3	0.40
17100	data	65.9	0.02	65.4	0.01
		109.6	0.02	109.4	0.02

cluster number for the FCM method is set to 30 after performing a parameter study. This number has shown to be most suitable in order to identify a reasonable number of clusters. The calculation time for both clustering methods is compared using a work memory of 100 GB. The FCM method requires 6.6 s, whereas the MSC procedure requires 14.2 s, averaged over ten analyses. For the data set at 17100 rpm

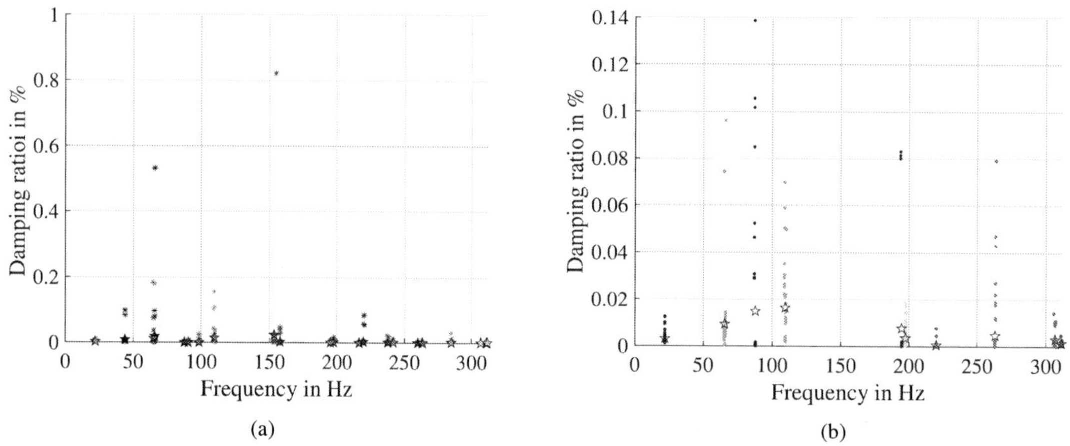

Figure 8: (**a**) Selected modes for MSC; (**b**) Selected modes for FCM. Different cluster results for dataset at 17100 rpm with data-driven SSI.

the data-driven SSI and covariance-driven SSI are compared. While the MSC method is robust and finds the same modal parameters for each run, the FCM method provides different results if performed repeatedly. This can be explained by the random initialization of the clusters in the beginning of the FCM algorithm. Additionally, the MSC identifies overall more of the sought-after frequencies and is thus preferred. Nevertheless, not all of the eigenfrequencies that were found with the different OMA methods are identified with the clustering techniques, thus their application for the identification of modes related to rotating machinery requires further research. Again the clustering techniques identify frequencies at around 80 Hz, 90 Hz and 120 Hz in some of the datasets. Figure 8 compares the selected modal parameters for the stable clusters obtained by the MSC and FCM using the data-driven SSI approach.

Harmonic Detection

Next to the SSI extension for the consideration of harmonic frequencies, the PDF and kurtosis criterion are applied to the results from the SSI to identify possible harmonic modes. Figure 9 (a) shows the PDF for two potential modes identified for the 3900 rpm data set. The frequency around 65 Hz belonging to the actual rotational speed can be clearly identified as a harmonic frequency by the shape of the PDF. The excess criterion depicted in Fig. 9 (b) shows harmonic frequencies for 50 Hz, 65 Hz, 100 Hz, and

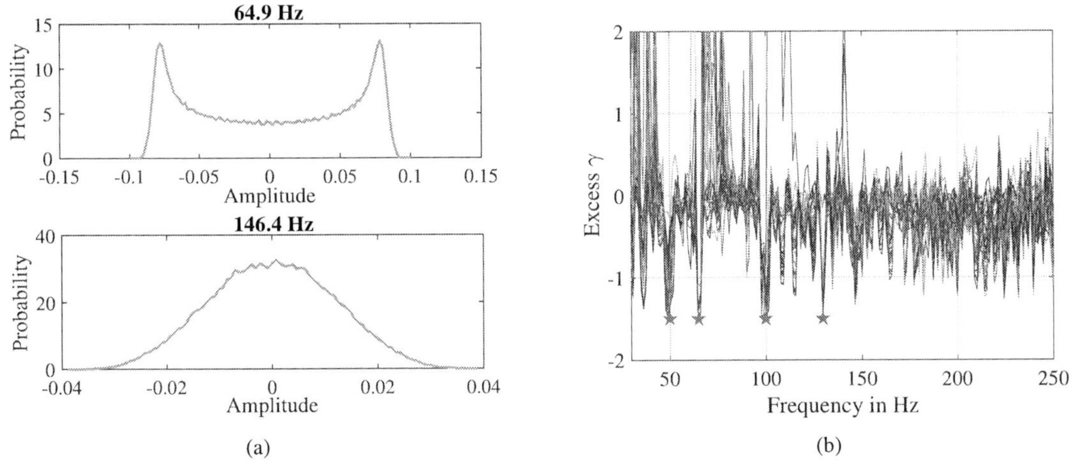

Figure 9: (**a**) PDF of harmonic mode at 65 Hz and structural mode at 146 Hz for 3900 rpm reference (channel 1); (**b**) Excess of all channels for 3900 rpm reference, harmonic modes are marked with a pink star. Harmonic detection using statistically driven identification.

130 Hz. 50 Hz and 100 Hz belong to the frequency of the power supply (first and second harmonic), whereas 65 Hz and 130 Hz belong to the first and second harmonic of the test rig's rotational speed. The different lines in Fig. 9 (b) represent each one sensor of the total 49 sensors attached to the structure. Another method to deal with the speed synchronous excitation is filtering the data. As described in the literature, this technique alters the complete data set. The power spectral density shows a sharp drop at the frequencies where the filter is applied. Additionally, new stable frequency lines are identified in the stability diagram, which might be mathematical modes.

4. DISCUSSION

The focus of the presented analysis was to identify the first three modes of the axial compressor, which were also found in standstill conditions (65 Hz, 111 Hz, 132 Hz). In operation more modes are identified compared to the standstill conditions. This can be explained by the influence of the motor and gearbox connected to the compressor. The total mass of motor and gearbox is approximately 8.1 t and thus these components play a significant role in the vibrational behavior of the compressor (total weight of compressor approx. 800 kg) and its modal parameters. The operation of the compressor induces vibrations of the motor and gearbox and the whole system (containing compressor, gearbox, and motor) has to be considered for the modal identification. In addition, the structural behavior of the test hall itself is not considered in these results as the floor was not instrumented. It is assumed that it contributes to the elastic behavior of the overall test rig. Table 5 compares the three identification processes presented in this paper and shows their advantages and disadvantages. The speed comparison was performed with a 100 GB working memory averaging ten analyses. The time measured for the HHT does not include the filter process. The speed for the execution of one HHT analysis is high and accelerates with an elevating number of time segments. The high speed can be explained as only one time signal of a single sensor is analyzed simultaneously. In contrast, the Bayesian OMA and SSI use all sensor signals for the analysis and therefore demand a higher computational time. Moreover, it needs to be considered that for the Bayesian OMA and HHT only one eigenfrequency can be evaluated simultaneously, whereas the SSI yields a stability diagram with all eigenfrequencies in the frequency range of interest. As a conclusion, the HHT does not seem suitable for the structural identification of rotating machinery. This is especially true in this case, as no strong nonlinear behavior could be observed. The possibility of using HHT for nonlinear data is clearly one of its strength. Nevertheless, it can be a good alternative if the frequencies are already identified and validated. This technique can be used to confirm and check a frequency, e.g. after a structural modification. However, the SSI has proven to be a reliable method. The clustering

Table 5: Comparison of analysis methods

	advantages	disadvantages	computational speed
HHT	• analysis of single sensors, ability to check data quality • fast technique	• no calculation of eigenvectors possible • knowledge of eigenfrequencies required • use of bandpass filter for certain frequency range	0.7 s
Bayesian OMA	standard deviation for frequency and damping is calculated	• simultaneous analysis of only one mode possible (fit of 1 DoF system) • modes need to be separate	65.4 s
SSI	• robust and exact method • can consider non-proportional damping (complex eigenvectors)	computationally intensive	175.0 s

schemes facilitate the parameter selection compared to the manual selection of poles from the stability diagram, where a high expertise of the user is required. However, since the initialization process of the FCM technique is random and can yield different results with each run, the MSC is preferred and still offers an acceptable time frame for the analysis. The investigation with the statistically driven techniques for the harmonic detection after performing the SSI showed that some of the identified frequencies are related to harmonic excitation and that therefore the rotational influence, especially when close to structural modes, has a strong influence. The PDF seems suitable for the identification of harmonic modes. Its strength is confirmed by its ability to also identify mathematical modes by the shape of the PDF. It calculates the PDF for each channel, so that misleading channels can be detected and eliminated. It is a simple and clear criterion, which can be applied to the data. Filters, however, are not recommended for the harmonic detection as it is not clear why the filtered data yields new stable poles and the data manipulation seems to be too strong. The SSI extension for consideration of harmonic effects did not work successfully as shown in the presented results.

5. CONCLUSIONS

An extensive study on various data sets from the operation of an axial compressor test rig has been performed in order to find a suitable method to handle this data and identify the modal parameters. Three identification methods, namely the stochastic subspace identification, the Hilbert-Huang transform and the Bayesian OMA have been tested. As already indicated by the literature, the stochastic subspace identification has proven to be the most robust method, although it is also the most time-consuming one. For the automatization of the pole picking process from the stability diagram, the multistage clustering, as well as the fuzzy-c-means clustering have been studied. The fuzzy-c-means clustering is a promising technique, but it also yields varying results with each run. For this reason, the multistage clustering based on pre-defined criteria is a more robust method. For the harmonic identification the investigation of the probability density function is recommended, as it is a clear method to separate structural from harmonic modes.

More frequencies beyond those three considered so far, have been identified throughout the process. These were presumably not found during the standstill measurements, as the motor was not specifically excited during these measurements, but plays a significant role in operation. More research will go into the characterization of these frequencies, which is associated with an extensive analysis of the mode shapes to confirm the current results and classify the new findings. Mastering the harmonic influence is still the biggest challenge, for this reason, more techniques for the harmonic detection will be studied in the future. Hence, input independent techniques such as the transmissibility based OMA shall be investigated. Currently, an approach to use the energy spectrum for the identification of structural modes is investigated. The identified structural behavior of the axial compressor, as well as the different techniques used in operation can be represented in a digital model. Hence, future changes or critical conditions can be monitored running new analyses with the tools presented. These updated results can be compared to the verified modal parameters to identify structural changes.

REFERENCES

[1] Goursat, M., Döhler, M., Mevel, L., and Andersen, P. (2011). Crystal clear SSI for operational modal analysis of aerospace vehicles. In: *Structural Dynamics, Volume 3*. Springer, pp. 1421–1430.

[2] Schwochow, J. and Jelicic, G. (2015). Automatic operational modal analysis for aeroelastic applications. In: *Proceedings of the 6th International Operational Modal Analysis Conference*.

[3] Peeters, B. and De Roeck, G. (2001). Stochastic system identification for operational modal analysis: a review. In: *Journal of Dynamic Systems, Measurement, and Control* 123.4, pp. 659–667.

[4] Mohanty, P. and Rixen, D. J. (2004). Operational modal analysis in the presence of harmonic excitation. In: *Journal of sound and vibration* 270.1-2, pp. 93–109.

[5] Motte, K., Weijtjens, W., Devriendt, C., and Guillaume, P. (2015). Operational modal analysis in the presence of harmonic excitations: a review. In: *Dynamics of Civil Structures, Volume 2*, pp. 379–395.

[6] Wilkes, J. C. et al. (2018). The Development and Application of an Operational Modal Analysis Method for Centrifugal Compressors. In: *Proceedings of Montreal 2018 Global Power and Propulsion Forum*.

[7] Arjmand, M. and Bratek, W. (2019). Operational modal analysis to identify modal parameters in reciprocating compressors. In: *GMRC Gas Machinery Conference*.

[8] Clarke, H., Stainsby, J., and Carden, E. P. (2011). Operational modal analysis of resiliently mounted marine diesel generator/alternator. In: *Rotating Machinery, Structural Health Monitoring, Shock and Vibration, Volume 5*. Springer, pp. 237–244.

[9] Amer, M. et al. (2021). Determining the Influence of Casing Vibrational Behaviour On Rotordynamics. In: *Journal of Engineering for Gas Turbines and Power*.

[10] Amer, M., Wallaschek, J., and Seume, J. R (2022). Operational Modal Analysis of an Axial Compressor Rotor and Casing System for the Online Identification of a Digital Twin. In: *Applied Mechanics* 3.1, pp. 244–258.

[11] Huang, N. E. et al. (1998). The empirical mode decomposition and the Hilbert spectrum for nonlinear and non-stationary time series analysis. In: *Proceedings of the Royal Society of London. Series A: mathematical, physical and engineering sciences* 454.1971, pp. 903–995.

[12] Cole Jr., H.A. (1968). On-the-line analysis of random vibrations. In: *9th structural dynamics and materials conference*, p. 288.

[13] Au, S. (2011). Fast Bayesian FFT method for ambient modal identification with separated modes. In: *Journal of Engineering Mechanics* 137.3, pp. 214–226.

[14] Peeters, B. and De Roeck, G. (1999). Reference-based stochastic subspace identification for output-only modal analysis. In: *Mechanical systems and signal processing* 13.6, pp. 855–878.

[15] Reynders, E., Houbrechts, J., and De Roeck, G. (2012). Fully automated (operational) modal analysis. In: *Mechanical systems and signal processing* 29, pp. 228–250.

[16] Scionti, M. and Lanslots, J.P. (2005). Stabilisation diagrams: Pole identification using fuzzy clustering techniques. In: *Advances in Engineering Software* 36.11-12, pp. 768–779.

[17] Brincker, Rune, Andersen, Palle, and Møller, Nis (2000). An indicator for separation of structural and harmonic modes in output-only modal testing. In: *Proceedings of the European COST F3 Conference on System Identification & Structural Health Monitoring, 6-9 June, 2000, Universidad Politécnica de Madrid, Spain*. Universidad Politécnica de Madrid, pp. 265–272.

[18] Dong, X., Lian, J., Yang, M., and Wang, H. (2014). Operational modal identification of offshore wind turbine structure based on modified stochastic subspace identification method considering harmonic interference. In: *Journal of Renewable and Sustainable Energy* 6.3, p. 033128.

9th International Operational Modal Analysis Conference
iomac
July 3 - 6, 2022
Vancouver, Canada

DYNAMIC DECOUPLING OF A BEARING SUPPORT STRUCTURE: COMPARISON OF FOUR DIFFERENT DECOUPLING METHODS BASED ON A DUAL APPROACH

Vitor Martini[1], Eduardo Okabe[2] and Katia Cavalca[3]

[1] Ph.D. student, School of Mechanical Engineering, University of Campinas, v265297@dac.unicamp.br.
[2] Assistant Professor, School of Applied Sciences, University of Campinas, okabe@unicamp.br.
[3] Full Professor, School of Mechanical Engineering, University of Campinas, katia@fem.unicamp.br.

ABSTRACT

Dynamic substructuring is an efficient tool in the analysis of large structures and is represented by coupling and decoupling techniques. This paper presents the decoupling of a bearing support structure from a rotating machine foundation with four decoupling methods based on a dual approach and the assembling of the complete foundation by dynamic coupling. The decoupled responses obtained by each method are analyzed as well as the influence of the number of excitation nodes. Frequency response functions are synthesized using modal parameters determined by experimental modal analysis and the least squares method for complex exponentials. An analytical system is also used for a preliminary substructuring analysis. The decoupling methods, named Standard, Extended Interface, Overdetermined and Internal, differ on the definition of the interface conditions and can present distinct behaviors depending on the experimental data. The study demonstrates that if the dynamic response of the bearing component is decoupled, it can be coupled to the foundation in any other number or positions in numerical simulations without the necessity to physically modify the test rig.

Keywords: Substructuring, Rotating Machines, Experimental Modal Analysis, Foundations

1. INTRODUCTION

Substructure decoupling techniques constitute a fundamental branch of dynamic substructuring (DS), which is a methodology initially proposed in 1963 for the static analysis of complex structures [1] by their subdivision in several components. Nevertheless, the lack of efficient methods back then when dealing with these dynamic systems demanded new paths to overcome the existing limitations of computers. Among the first and most well-known methods developed, one could refer to the frequency-based substructuring, formulated by [2] in 1988 and known for using frequency response functions (FRFs) to perform the necessary analyses [3]. Although the basic theoretical background of DS in the frequency domain was established at the end of the 20th century, new challenges arise everyday as experimental results become more relevant to understand complex systems. In the following years, two new concepts were proposed to reduce computational costs, namely the primal and dual approaches [3], which are responsible for satisfying interface conditions a priori and reducing the total amount of variables to be determined. The primal formulation defines a unique set of displacement degrees of freedom (DOF) for the interfaces, which satisfies the compatibility condition. On the other hand, the dual approach, presented by [4], satisfies the equilibrium condition by defining a unique set of interface forces whose amplitudes are commonly written as Lagrange multipliers, as shown in [5].

The main applications of dynamic substructuring are the coupling and decoupling of substructures, techniques that have been used to study several different structures [6,7,8]. When the dynamic behavior of every component in a global system is individually known, the total response due to their interaction when assembled can be determined by coupling. Alternatively, if one needs to extract the dynamic characteristics of a substructure that cannot be separately measured, decoupling techniques are able to numerically isolate that component [9]. In complex systems such as rotating machinery and their supporting structures, component-mode synthesis and substructuring techniques have been discussed [10,11]. Nonetheless, they still demand more investigation. These supporting structures, also named foundations, besides providing mechanical support for the machine, interact dynamically with the rotor and that interaction must be taken into account in the analysis of the complete system [12]. Therefore, dynamic characterization of each component of the foundation is necessary if one aims to scrutinize the measurement responses of the rotating machine and observe the exact influence of the foundation substructures.

In this paper, the applicability of dynamic substructuring in a rotating machinery foundation is investigated. The system considered in the analysis comprehends a metallic base and two bearing supports, also named pedestals. Experimental modal analysis (EMA) and synthesis of the frequency response functions of four different measurement configurations were performed. The dynamic decoupling of the bearing support was performed with four different decoupling methods, namely Standard, Extended Interface, Overdetermined and Internal. Finally, the decoupled pedestal is numerically coupled to the test rig and the results are compared to experimental data.

2. SUBSTRUCTURING FORMULATION

Each component of the foundation structure must respect two interface requirements in relation to its neighbouring substructures: the compatibility and equilibrium conditions [13]. These conditions assure that the corresponding interface DOF present the same displacements (compatibility) and forces (equilibrium) and that they have to be met regardless of the substructuring method. The compatibility condition can be expressed as in Eq. (1):

$$\boldsymbol{Bu} = \boldsymbol{0} \tag{1}$$

where $\boldsymbol{B}$ is a signed Boolean matrix if the interface nodes are in matching order and $\boldsymbol{u}$ is the global vector of displacements. This indicates that corresponding DOF pertaining to a same interface node have equal responses [13]. Secondly, the equilibrium condition is given by Eq. (2):

$$\boldsymbol{L}^T\boldsymbol{g} = \boldsymbol{0} \tag{2}$$

where $\boldsymbol{L}$ is a Boolean localization matrix and $\boldsymbol{g}$ is the vector of interface forces. This notation shows that for every pair of matching DOF, the connection forces have equal magnitudes and opposite directions and thus they sum to zero when assembled [14]. A useful relation is obtained when observing that $\boldsymbol{L}$ and $\boldsymbol{B}$ represent each other's null spaces.

By associating the interface conditions with the dynamic behavior of the structure written in the frequency domain, the resulting system of equations is presented in Eq. (3):

$$\begin{Bmatrix} Zu = f + g \\ Bu = 0 \\ L^T g = 0 \end{Bmatrix} \tag{3}$$

In Eq. (3), $\boldsymbol{Z}$ is the mechanical impedance block matrix of the foundation components and $\boldsymbol{f}$ is the vector of external forces acting on the entire system. The frequency dependency is omitted for brevity. Subsequently, the dual formulation is achieved by choosing coupling forces as Eq. (4):

$$\boldsymbol{g} = -\boldsymbol{B}^T\boldsymbol{\lambda} \tag{4}$$

where $\boldsymbol{\lambda}$ are Lagrange multipliers that correspond to the intensities of the coupling forces. The minus sign is used to obtain a symmetric system later. By substituting the interface forces in Eq. (3), one finds Eq. (5):

$$\begin{bmatrix} \boldsymbol{Z} & \boldsymbol{B}^T \\ \boldsymbol{B} & \boldsymbol{0} \end{bmatrix} \begin{Bmatrix} \boldsymbol{u} \\ \boldsymbol{\lambda} \end{Bmatrix} = \begin{Bmatrix} \boldsymbol{f} \\ \boldsymbol{0} \end{Bmatrix} \tag{5}$$

Since experimental measurements of the foudation result in FRFs, which are used to sythesize receptance matrices, it is common to rewrite Eq. (5) using $\boldsymbol{Y} = \boldsymbol{Z}^{-1}$, where $\boldsymbol{Y}$ is a receptance matrix, and solving it for the Lagrange multipliers first. Then, Eq. (6) can be written and therefore is called the dual interface problem in the frequency domain, suitable for substructuring with experimental data. The simplified notation with $\widetilde{\boldsymbol{Y}}$ is commonly used.

$$\boldsymbol{u} = \boldsymbol{Yf} - \boldsymbol{YB}^T(\boldsymbol{BYB}^T)^{-1}\boldsymbol{BYf} = (\boldsymbol{I} - \boldsymbol{YB}^T(\boldsymbol{BYB}^T)^{-1}\boldsymbol{B})\boldsymbol{Yf} = \widetilde{\boldsymbol{Y}}\boldsymbol{f} \tag{6}$$

Assuming the dynamic behavior of n_s coupled substructures of the foundation must be determined, Eq. (6) can be used after writing an appropriate Boolean matrix $\boldsymbol{B}$ acting on all interface DOF. Since the dual formulation maintains all DOF of the n_s substructures, the coupled receptance matrix $\widetilde{\boldsymbol{Y}}$ will have repeated rows and columns, which can be removed by using Eq. (7):

$$\widehat{\boldsymbol{Y}} = (\boldsymbol{L})^+\widetilde{\boldsymbol{Y}}(\boldsymbol{L}^T)^+ \tag{7}$$

where $(\boldsymbol{L})^+$ is the pseudoinverse of $\boldsymbol{L}$.

The inverse operation, i.e., dynamic decoupling, is easier to formulate if we consider two subsystems A and B and the assembled system AB. Subsystem B would be the bearing pedestal while subsystem A represents the metallic base.

We start by writing the equations of motion for the assembled system AB and the subsystem A in terms of their impedance matrices as Eq. (8):

$$\begin{aligned} \boldsymbol{Z}^{AB}\boldsymbol{u}^{AB} &= \boldsymbol{f}^{AB} + \boldsymbol{g}^{AB} \\ \boldsymbol{Z}^{A}\boldsymbol{u}^{A} &= \boldsymbol{f}^{A} - \boldsymbol{g}^{A} \end{aligned} \tag{8}$$

After substituting the interface forces for the Lagrange multipliers and associating the interface conditions, the equations are arranged in a matrix form, as shown in Eq. (9):

$$\begin{bmatrix} \boldsymbol{Z}^{AB} & \boldsymbol{0} & \boldsymbol{B}^{AB^T} \\ \boldsymbol{0} & -\boldsymbol{Z}^{A} & \boldsymbol{B}^{A^T} \\ \boldsymbol{B}^{AB} & \boldsymbol{B}^{A} & \boldsymbol{0} \end{bmatrix} \begin{Bmatrix} \boldsymbol{u}^{AB} \\ \boldsymbol{u}^{A} \\ \boldsymbol{\lambda} \end{Bmatrix} = \begin{Bmatrix} \boldsymbol{f}^{AB} \\ \boldsymbol{f}^{A} \\ \boldsymbol{0} \end{Bmatrix} \tag{9}$$

The similarity with Eq. (5) indicates that decoupling means determining interface forces that act in opposite direction on system AB, removing the influence of A on AB, leaving just the uncoupled response of B [14]. After solving the system for $\boldsymbol{u}^{AB}$ while considering $\boldsymbol{f}^{A} = 0$, the final expression is shown in Eq. (10), where the expression multiplying $\boldsymbol{f}^{AB}$ is the receptance matrix of the decoupled system.

$$\boldsymbol{u}^{AB} = \left(\boldsymbol{Y}^{AB} - \boldsymbol{Y}^{AB}\boldsymbol{B}^{AB^T}\left(\boldsymbol{B}^{AB}\boldsymbol{Y}^{AB}\boldsymbol{B}^{AB^T} - \boldsymbol{B}^{A}\boldsymbol{Y}^{A}\boldsymbol{B}^{A^T}\right)^{-1}\boldsymbol{B}^{AB}\boldsymbol{Y}^{AB}\right)\boldsymbol{f}^{AB} \quad (10)$$

Different solutions can be achieved for this expression and each one corresponds to a specific choice regarding the interface conditions. Four important decoupling methods can be derived: Standard, Extended Interface, Overdetermined and Internal. All of them require strong compatibility when combined with the interface conditions of Eq. (1) and Eq. (2) and will be addressed in the next section.

2.1. Decoupling methods

When both interface conditions are defined within the same set of DOF, the decoupling methods are said to be collocated. On the other hand, when they are written for different sets of DOF, the methods are non-collocated. Hence, it is useful to separate matrix $\boldsymbol{B}$ in matrix $\boldsymbol{C}$ for compatibility and matrix $\boldsymbol{E}$ for equilibrium [5].

The first collocated method is obtained by choosing only the interface DOF (or nodes) for both conditions, situation in which the connection forces are determined using the minimum information needed. This method is referred to as Standard and the Boolean matrices are expressed as:

$$\boldsymbol{C}^{A} = \boldsymbol{E}^{A} = [\boldsymbol{0}_{ca} - \boldsymbol{I}_{cc}], \boldsymbol{C}^{AB} = \boldsymbol{E}^{AB} = [\boldsymbol{0}_{ca}\ \boldsymbol{I}_{cc}\ \boldsymbol{0}_{cb}] \quad (11)$$

where a, b and c are the number of nodes internal to subsystem A, internal to subsystem B and from the interface, respectively. This notation implies that interface DOF are numbered in the same way in A and AB. The standard method may sometimes fail if measurement errors are too significant. In those situations, a second collocated method can be chosen by defining $\boldsymbol{C}^{A}$ and $\boldsymbol{C}^{AB}$ as in Eq. (12).

$$\boldsymbol{C}^{A} = \boldsymbol{E}^{A} = \begin{bmatrix} -\boldsymbol{I}_{aa} & \boldsymbol{0} \\ \boldsymbol{0} & -\boldsymbol{I}_{cc} \end{bmatrix}, \boldsymbol{C}^{AB} = \boldsymbol{E}^{AB} = \begin{bmatrix} \boldsymbol{I}_{aa} & \boldsymbol{0} & \boldsymbol{0} \\ \boldsymbol{0} & \boldsymbol{I}_{cc} & \boldsymbol{0} \end{bmatrix} \quad (12)$$

This is known as the Extended Interface method since a additional internal nodes from subsystem A are also considered. This extra information aims to minimize measurement errors since these points also respond to the connection forces between the substructures. Frequently, this method results in a bad conditioned matrix inversion if measurement errors are negligible. In that case, the Lagrange multipliers become redundant due to repeated terms in the receptance matrices [5]. In this paper, we try to circumvent this problem by using the Moore-Penrose pseudoinverse.

The first non-collocated method, named Overdetermined, uses only interface nodes for the equilibrium condition but both interface and internal nodes of A for compatibility. Hence, it results in $a + c$ compatibility conditions and only c Lagrange multipliers to be estimated in a least-squares sense. The corresponding Boolean matrices are written as:

$$\boldsymbol{C}^{A} = \begin{bmatrix} -\boldsymbol{I}_{aa} & \boldsymbol{0} \\ \boldsymbol{0} & -\boldsymbol{I}_{cc} \end{bmatrix}, \boldsymbol{C}^{AB} = \begin{bmatrix} \boldsymbol{I}_{aa} & \boldsymbol{0} & \boldsymbol{0} \\ \boldsymbol{0} & \boldsymbol{I}_{cc} & \boldsymbol{0} \end{bmatrix}, \boldsymbol{E}^{A} = [\boldsymbol{0}_{ca} - \boldsymbol{I}_{cc}], \boldsymbol{E}^{AB} = [\boldsymbol{0}_{ca}\ \boldsymbol{I}_{cc}\ \boldsymbol{0}_{cb}] \quad (13)$$

The second non-collocated method is called Internal and it uses interface DOF for compatibility and internal DOF of A for equilibrium. Great practical advantage is achieved since inversion of interface receptance matrices is avoided. Eq. (14) presents the Boolean matrices of the Internal method.

$$\boldsymbol{C}^{A} = [\boldsymbol{0}_{ca} - \boldsymbol{I}_{cc}], \boldsymbol{C}^{AB} = [\boldsymbol{0}_{ca}\ \boldsymbol{I}_{cc}\ \boldsymbol{0}_{cb}], \boldsymbol{E}^{A} = [-\boldsymbol{I}_{aa}\ \boldsymbol{0}_{ac}], \boldsymbol{E}^{AB} = [\boldsymbol{I}_{aa}\ \boldsymbol{0}_{ac}\ \boldsymbol{0}_{ab}] \quad (14)$$

Each method and its respective performance depends on the system characteristics. It is necessary to investigate whether a specific approach best suits an experimental setup and results in a well-represented decoupled substructure.

3. THEORETICAL AND EXPERIMENTAL SYSTEMS DESCRIPTION

3.1. Analytical system – a preliminary analysis

The preliminary analysis of the decoupling methods considers the mechanical system shown in Figure 1, which consists of three independent subsystems, A, B and C.

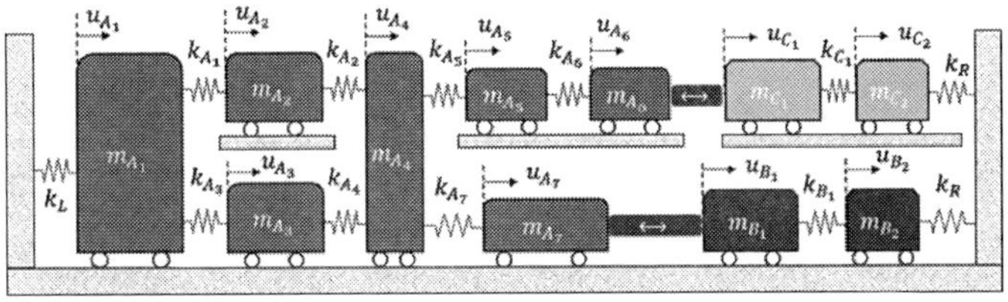

Figure 1. Analytical mechanical system.

Their respective displacement variables are indicated as u_A, u_B and u_C. Mass and stiffness coefficients are presented in Table 1 and the damping is proportional to the stiffness matrix with a factor of $2 \cdot 10^{-4}$. Frequency response functions were obtained from 0 to 50 Hz and white noise with amplitude of 1% the RMS value of the FRFs was added to the responses used in the substructuring processes to resemble real-life measurement situations. First, subsystem C was ignored. Hence, there is only system AB, from which B was decoupled with all four decoupling methods. Next, this decoupled subsystem B was duplicated and named subsystem C, explaining why their physical parameters in Table 1 are identical. Finally, subsystems A, B and C were all coupled and the responses were compared to the exact ones.

Table 1. Mass and stiffness coefficients of the analytical mechanical system.

Subsystem A				Subsystems B and C			
Mass [kg]		Stiffness [kN/m]		Mass [kg]		Stiffness [kN/m]	
m_{A_1}	6	k_{A_1}	3	m_{B_1}	5	k_{B_1}	1.5
m_{A_2}	2	k_{A_2}	2	m_{B_2}	2	k_R	2
m_{A_3}	2	k_{A_3}	3	m_{C_1}	5	k_{C_1}	1.5
m_{A_4}	5	k_{A_4}	1.5	m_{C_2}	2	k_L	0.8
m_{A_5}	1.5	k_{A_5}	0.7				
m_{A_6}	1.5	k_{A_6}	0.2				
m_{A_7}	3	k_{A_7}	2				

3.2. Rotating machinery foundation – experimental analysis

The rotating machinery foundation, shown in Figure 2, consists of a rectangular metal base (1) and two bearing support structures (2) attached to an inertial structure (3). The metallic base is made of steel and it is connected to the inertial block by four fixing columns placed each in one of the four edges. The first bearing pedestal is near the electric motor and it is located at 75 mm from the left extremity of the base whilst the second distances 400 mm from the first. Measurements were performed on the foundation [15] considering four different configurations:

i) Configuration 1: metallic base without pedestals in free-free condition;
ii) Configuration 2: metallic base (free-free) with one pedestal coupled;
iii) Configuration 3: metallic base fixed to the inertial block without pedestals;
iv) Configuration 4: metallic base fixed to the inertial block with two pedestals, as in Figure 2.

Figure 2. Rotating machinery test rig.

Seven accelerometers were used to acquire vibration data. A signal conditioner, an acquisition board and an impact hammer are also part of the measurement equipment. The frequency response functions range from 0 to 5 kHz (0.5 Hz step) and were obtained by St. Martin [15] with a sampling frequency of 10 kHz. Configurations 1 and 2 were measured in order to decouple the bearing support while evaluating the four methods presented earlier. Configurations 3 and 4, on the other hand, were measured for two reasons: synthesis of the complete receptance matrices of configuration 3 is required to perform the dynamic coupling between the previously decoupled pedestal and the metallic base; secondly, experimental results of configuration 4 can then be used to compare and validate the substructuring processes of assembling the complete foundation. Figure 3 shows the measurement grid for the base and Figure 4 shows the measurement grids for the pedestal [15].

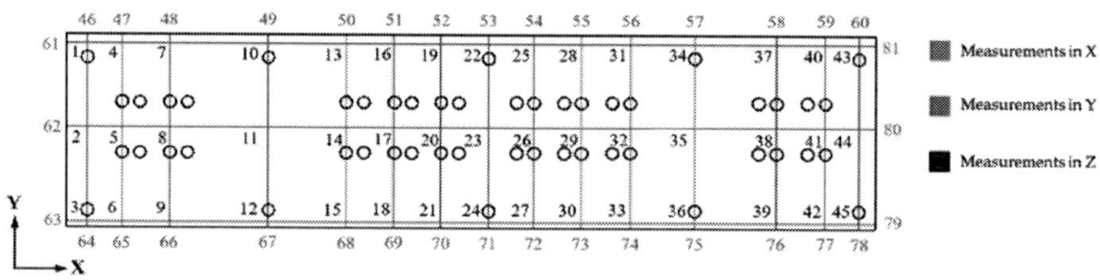

Figure 3. Measurement grid for the metallic base.

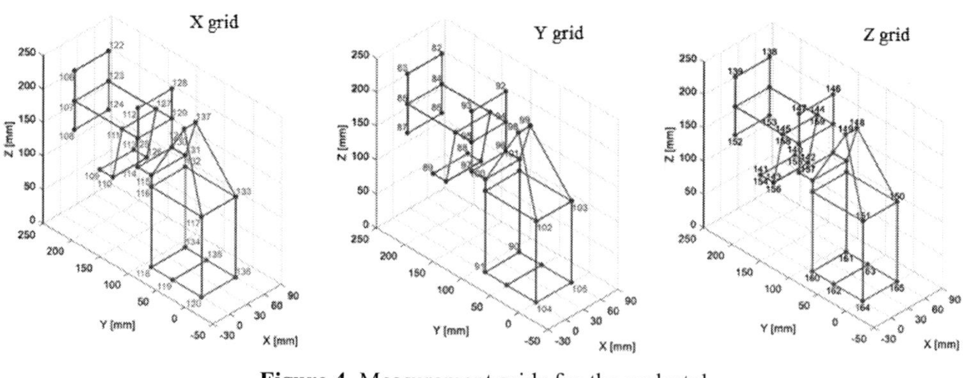

Figure 4. Measurement grids for the pedestal.

Measurement and excitation nodes for each configuration are exhibited in Table 1. The Least Squares Complex Exponential (LSCE) algorithm [16] is used to identify modal parameters from 5 to 250 Hz. This frequency range removes rigid body components and includes higher frequency modes. Furthermore, FRF reconstitution [17] is also applied to synthesize complete receptance matrices and the Modal Assurance Criterion (MAC) is used to compute mode similarity [18,19].

Table 2. Measurement and excitation nodes of each foundation configuration.

Configuration	Measurement nodes	Excitation nodes
1	5, 13, 24, 35, 65, 75,80	1 to 63
2	16, 94, 103, 113, 134, 147, 151	13 to 27, 50 to 54, 61 to 64, 84 to 165
3	5, 13, 24, 35, 65, 75, 80	1 to 63
4	12, 26, 72, 82, 85, 91, 94	1 to 64, 79 to 99

To investigate the influence of the number of excitation nodes upon the quality of the decoupled responses of the pedestal, three sets of nodes were defined, as presented in Table 3. Regarding the measurement data and driving points locations, a previous analysis showed that nodes 13 and 147 - of configurations 1 and 2, respectively - are good options since their responses adequately represent all the modes within the frequency range of interest. The pedestal nodes, 64 to 165, are only considered in the EMA of configuration 2.

Table 3. Sets of nodes used for the EMA of the first two configurations of the foundation.

Set	Measurement nodes	Excitation nodes
1	13 and 147	13, 20, 24, 51, 52, 54, 61, 62, 63, 92, 94, 98, 111, 112, 128, 134, 147, 149, 150, 151
2	13 and 147	13, 20, 52, 62, 94, 112, 147, 149
3	13 and 147	13, 19, 94, 98, 111, 112, 147, 149, 151

4. RESULTS

4.1. Analytical system

Two components of the decoupled subsystem B are shown in Figure 5 for the four decoupling methods. The FRF diagrams are truncated at 12 Hz for the sake of visualization.

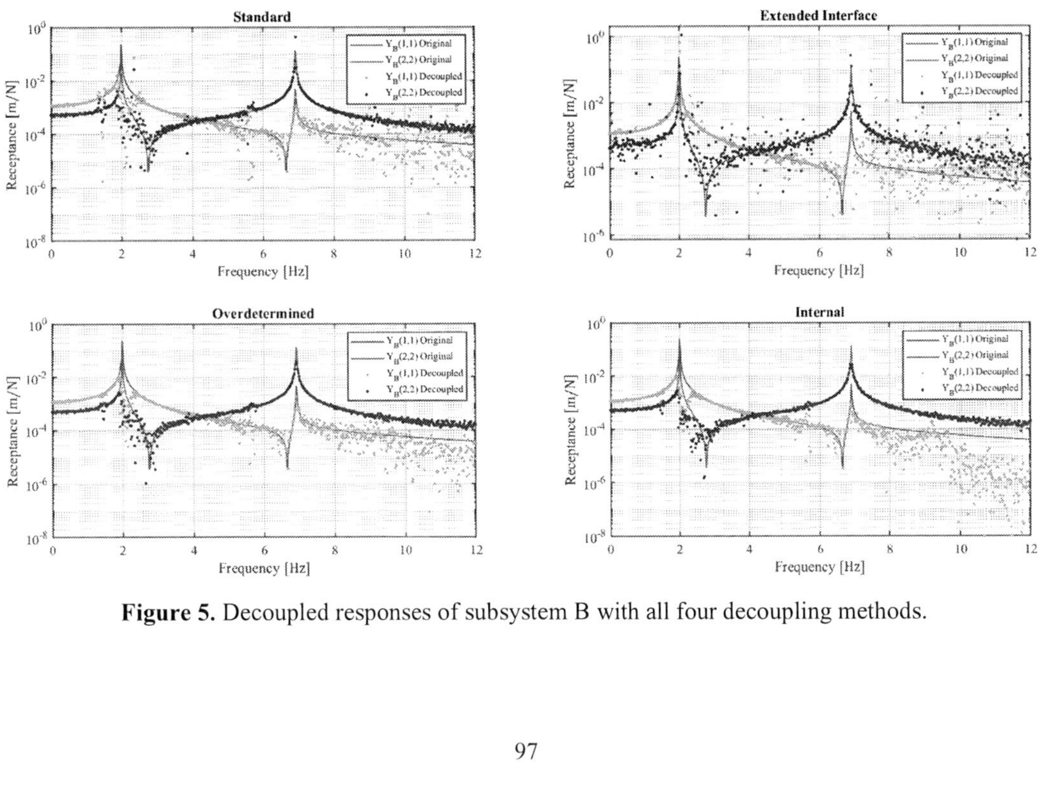

Figure 5. Decoupled responses of subsystem B with all four decoupling methods.

As one can see, the four decoupling methods perform with consistent results. The Gaussian noise added to the FRFs causes some disturbances on the decoupled subsystem B, more apparent with the Extended Interface method and around the resonances and at higher frequencies for the others. Nevertheless, the noise addition and the use of the pseudoinverse operation seem to avoid the singularities issue often observed with Extended Interface.

The decoupled responses of B were then duplicated, originating subsystem C. After coupling all three substructures, Figure 6 presents some of its FRF components for all four cases. The Overdetermined method seems to handle the noise influence better, which can be concluded by determining the relative errors between original and coupled/decoupled responses. Since the Lagrange multipliers are determined by a least-squares approach, they tend to estimate interface forces more adequately in the presence of noise.

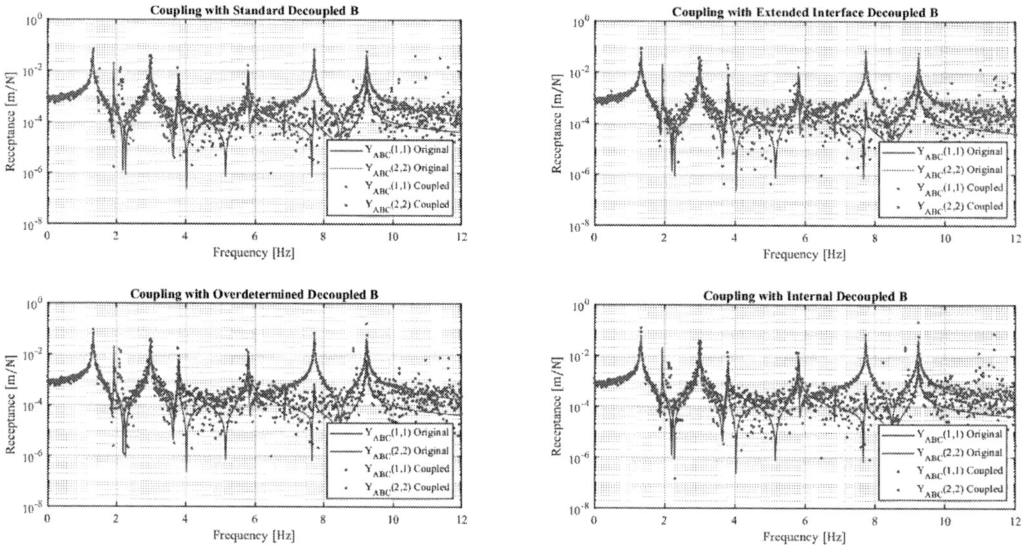

Figure 6. Coupled responses of the analytical substructures.

It is noted that, even though the noise certainly influences the coupling procedure, the system ABC can be similar to the original. In fact, modal parameters of the coupled system show that the dynamic data is actually retained. Considering the analogous behaviors observed with the four methods, a more thorough analysis is carried out with the experimental data of the rotating machinery foundation.

4.2. Experimental foundation

Since the metal base and the pedestal's measurement grids are defined separately, their interface points were approximated. Therefore, the interface region was delimited as shown in Figure 7 to best represent the actual physical coupling. In other words, nodes contained within the interface region are the ones that, possibly, best describe the coupling points between the two substructures.

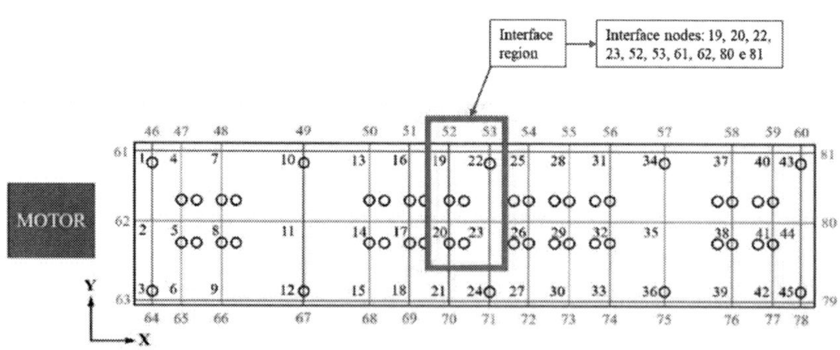

Figure 7. Interface region.

Stabilization diagrams of the first set of nodes from Table 3 were analyzed in order to select the best approximation order of the LSCE algorithm. It was possible to filter out spurious frequencies and manually select the stable ones corresponding to physical modes. Five modes were found for configuration 1 and ten for configuration 2. The corresponding natural frequencies are therefore used to guide the LSCE algorithm to seek for stable points near those values. Subsequently, the modal parameters were identified for configurations 1 and 2 with the three sets of nodes. Experimental modal analysis details were previously explored thoroughly since the main focus is to observe the variations on the decoupled responses in relation to the three sets of nodes. Table 4 presents the natural frequencies and damping coefficients obtained for configurations 1 and 2 with measurements from nodes 13 and 147, respectively. Mode shapes are omitted but are also computed. With the estimated modal parameters, the remaining lines of the receptance matrices could be satisfactorily synthesized.

Table 4. Natural frequencies and damping coefficients of configurations 1 and 2.

Configuration 1 (base free-free)		Configuration 2 (base and pedestal free-free)	
Natural frequencies [Hz]	Damping coefficients	Natural frequencies [Hz]	Damping coefficients
43,47	0,0093	39,92	0,0099
99,58	0,0069	59,32	0,0096
121,77	0,0036	98,06	0,0092
209,53	0,0025	113,95	0,0044
238,64	0,0024	131,06	0,0195
		150,63	0,0064
		170,81	0,0072
		185,19	0,0171
		217,10	0,0040
		226,66	0,0048

After writing the appropriate interface condition matrices, the solution of Eq. (10) with all four decoupling methods and all three sets of nodes was accomplished. The modal data of the decoupled pedestal responses is determined with the LSCE algorithm. Results show that the first set of nodes seems to contain more than necessary information and ends up disturbing the decoupled responses with excessive data and noise. Consequently, natural frequencies, damping coefficients and mode shapes of the bearings support vary notably regardless of the decoupling method applied. Moreover, some base modes are still present in the pedestal FRFs, which suggests that the interface nodes of set 1 are not good approximations of the real coupling points. The second set reduces base nodes to one and maintains the same three interface nodes. Again, frequencies that belong to the base appear in the pedestal FRFs. In addition, only four pedestal internal nodes are decoupled, which may poorly represent the support's mode shapes due to the lower number of physical points considered. Finally, the third set leads to better performances of all four decoupling methods, meaning that node 19 is, very likely, the best approximation to an interface point. Nevertheless, considerable differences are observed among the four decoupling methods. Table 5 displays nine natural frequencies found within 5 to 250 Hz for the pedestal. These frequencies represent the medium values obtained with thirty-two samples, i.e., for each decoupling method there are eight samples corresponding to a different driving point of the (set 3) decoupled pedestal.

A thorough analysis of all the thirty-two samples revealed a weak influence of the driving point on the estimation of the modal parameters.

Table 5. Natural frequencies estimated for the bearing support structure.

Natural frequencies [Hz]					
1st	39,87	4th	118,95	7th	173,03
2nd	57,47	5th	130,80	8th	208,87
3rd	100,01	6th	151,01	9th	225,57

The best results were obtained with the Overdetermined and Standard decoupling methods. Their responses contain less spurious modes, more consistency and precision. On the other hand, the Extended Interface and Internal methods generate decoupled responses that contain approximately less than half of the natural frequencies shown in Table 4 and several spurious and repeated frequencies. The Extended Interface method may require a weak formulation of the interface conditions, as already discussed by [5], since the coupling region is an approximation. For a similar reason, the Overdetermined method delivers good results because there is an intrinsic weakening of the interface conditions since the Lagrange multipliers are determined by least-squares.

An indirect evaluation of the four methods was attempted by coupling back the decoupled pedestal to node 19 of the base in free-free condition (configuration 1), so as to compare the mode shapes of this coupled system to those experimentally obtained from configuration 2. This comparison uses the MAC matrices, shown in Figure 8. All nodes of set 3 are used.

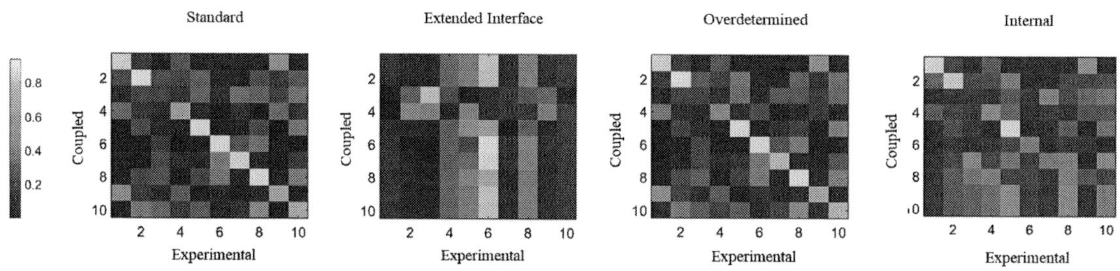

Figure 8. Comparison of the four decoupling methods by their influence in a simple coupling.

It is clear that the Standard and Overdetermined methods return a decoupled subsystem that actually represents the bearing support since the numerically coupled structure resembles its original equivalent. The MAC values show great similarity between experimental and the so-called coupled mode shapes for both methods. On the contrary, assembling the system with pedestals obtained with Extended Interface and Internal do not result in similar mode shapes. Nevertheless, since the main goal is to couple two pedestals to the inertial foundation and obtain the complete structure, some differences may still be perceived. For this last step, only the Overdetermined and Standard methods were considered. Hence, the decoupled pedestal was coupled to the foundation in configuration 3, whose FRFs were synthesized with internal nodes 9 and 13 and interface nodes 4 and 19. Figure 9 shows the positions where the pedestals are coupled and the corresponding coupling nodes.

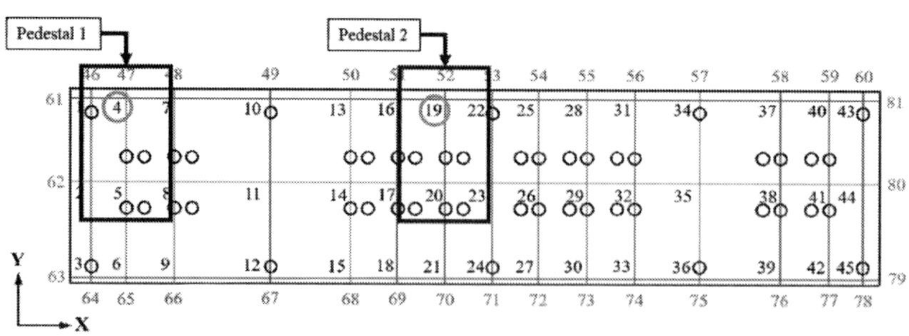

Figure 9. Coupling of two pedestals: nodes and positions.

Finally, Table 6 compares experimental and coupling-obtained modal parameters for the foundation.

Table 6. Comparison of experimental and coupling-obtained modal parameters.

Natural Frequencies [Hz]		Relative Error
Experimental	Coupling	
37,03	39,80	7,48%
58,71	59,22	0,88%
80,05	75,39	5,82%
95,16	93,47	1,77%
123,64	119,25	3,55%
132,67	132,57	0,07%
169,61	169,94	0,19%
186,33	183,92	1,29%
219,51	217,2	1,05%
241,06	242,57	0,62%

The relative errors are indicators that the natural frequencies of the foundation assembled by dynamic coupling are, in fact, equivalent to the frequencies experimentally determined. The same conclusion is obtained when damping factors are compared, showing that the substructuring model of the foundation is appropriate and therefore can be used to substitute the real structure in order to simulate the rotating machine response. Moreover, it becomes clear that the bearing pedestals can be coupled to other regions since their dynamic characteristics are known and therefore can be easily manipulated.

5. CONCLUSIONS

Both experimental coupling and decoupling techniques were presented in this paper for a rotating machine foundation. Four decoupling methods were analyzed and compared in the process of extracting a bearing support structure from a coupled subsystem of the foundation. The Overdetermined method, which computes interface loads in a least-squares sense, performed better and resulted in a bearing pedestal that represents the actual substructure. The subsequent coupling of this pedestal to the rest of the rotor foundation showed that the complete structure can be numerically assembled since all modal parameters resemble the experimental ones. Applications from this study comprise the possibility of simulating systems in different configurations whilst still using experimental data, optimization of structures and damage detection through modal parameters identification.

ACKNOWLEDGEMENTS

The authors acknowledge the funding received from CNPq – Conselho Nacional de Desenvolvimento Científico e Tecnológico, grants number 131848/2020-8 and 307941/2019-1.

REFERENCES

[1] Przemieniecki, J.S. (1963). Matrix structural analysis of substructures. *AIAA Journal*, 1(1), 138-147.

[2] Jetmundsen, B., Bielawa, R.L., & Flannelly, W.G. (1988). Generalized Frequency Domain Substructure Synthesis. *Journal of the American Helicopter Society*, 33(1), 55-64.

[3] Voormeeren, S.N. (2012). *Dynamic substructuring methodologies for integrated dynamic analysis of wind turbines*. PhD Thesis. Delft University of Technology, Delft.

[4] Rixen, D.J. (2004). A dual Craig–Bampton method for dynamic substructuring. *Journal of Computation and Applied Mathematics*, 168(1-2), 383-391.

[5] Voormeeren, S.N., & Rixen, D.J. (2012). A family of substructure decoupling techniques based on a dual assembly approach. *Mechanical Systems and Signal Processing*, 27, 379-396.

[6] Peeters, P., Tamarozzi, T., Vanhollebeke, F., & Desmet, W. (2014). A robust approach for substructure decoupling. In: *Proc. Int. Conf. on Noise and Vibration. Eng. ISMA* (pp. 3907-3921). Leuven, KU.

[7] D'Ambrogio, W., & Fregolent, A. (2009). Decoupling Procedures in the General Framework of Frequency Based Substructuring. In: *Proc. Int. Modal Analysis Conference XXVIII*. Jacksonville, Society of Experimental Mechanics.

[8] Sjövall, P., & Abrahamsson, T. (2008). Substructure system identification from coupled system test data. *Mechanical Systems and Signal Processing*, 22(1), 15-33.

[9] Voormeeren, S.N., & Rixen, D.J. (2011). A Dual Approach to Substructure Decoupling Techniques. In: *Proc. Int. Modal Analysis Conference XXVIII* (pp. 601-616). Jacksonville, Society of Experimental Mechanics.

[10] Seshu, P. (1997). Substructuring and Component Mode Synthesis. *Shock and Vibrations*, 4(3), 199-210.

[11] Glasgow, D.A., & Nelson, H.D. (1980). Stability Analysis or Rotor-Bearings Systems Using Component Mode Synthesis. *ASME Journal of Mechanical Design*, 102, 352-359.

[12] Cavalca, K. L., Cavalcante, P. F., & Okabe, E.P. (2005). An investigation on the influence of the supporting structure on the dynamics of the rotor system. *Mechanical Systems and Signal Processing*, 19(1), 157-174.

[13] Allen, M.S., Rixen, D.J., Van der Seijs, M., Tiso, P., Abrahamsson, T., & Mayes, R.L. (2020). *Substructuring in Engineering Dynamics: Emerging Numerical and Experimental Techniques*, 594, Cham: Springer International Publishing.

[14] Van der Seijs, M.V. (2016). *Experimental dynamic substructuring: Analysis and design strategies for vehicle development*. PhD Thesis. Delft University of Technology, Delft.

[15] St. Martin, L.B. (2020). *Interaction between rotor and flexible foundation subject to structural variations*. PhD Thesis. School of Mechanical Engineering, University of Campinas, Campinas.

[16] He, J., & Fu, Z.-F. (2001). *Modal Analysis*. Oxford, Butterworth-Heinemann.

[17] Ewins, D.J. (2000). *Modal testing: theory, practice, and application*, 2ed. Baldock, Research Studies Press.

[18] Pastor, M., Binda, M., & Harčarik, T. (2012). Modal Assurance Criterion. *Procedia Engineering*, 48, 543-548.

[19] Allemang, R.J. (2003). The Modal Assurance Criterion – Twenty Years of Use and Abuse. *Journal of Sound and Vibration*, 37(8), 14-23.

DAMAGE DETECTION UNDER CHANGING OPERATING CONDITION

9th International Operational Modal Analysis Conference
IOMAC
July 3 - 6, 2022
Vancouver, Canada

MONITORING INTERNAL STRAINS IN MARSHALL SPECIMEN UNDER DYNAMIC LOADS USING RAYLEIGH SCATTERING-BASED DISTRIBUTED FIBER SENSORS

Andreas Roth[1], *Mathias Leopold*[2], *Thomas Schmidt*[3], *Sascha Kayser*[4]

[1] M. Sc., Magdeburg-Stendal University of Applied Sciences, andreas.roth@h2.de.
[2] Dipl. -Ing., Magdeburg-Stendal University of Applied Sciences, mathias.leopold@h2.de.
[3] Prof. Dr.-Ing., Magdeburg-Stendal University of Applied Sciences, thomas.schmidt@h2.de.
[4] Prof. Dr.-Ing., Magdeburg-Stendal University of Applied Sciences, sascha.kayser@h2.de.

ABSTRACT

The aim of the investigations is to establish a non-destructive testing method for the condition of asphalt roads. For this purpose, a sensor system is inserted into the asphalt layers during construction. In the recent developments Rayleigh scattering-based distributed optical-fiber sensors (DOFS) have been used increasingly for measurements at barely accessible locations, for which the base layer of a road is an example. This paper explores the feasibility of embedded distributed optical-fiber sensors in asphalt roads to record the fatigue behavior. Comparative measurements are carried out to confirm the validity of the measurement results. Dynamic loads (cyclic indirect tensile test) have already been used to determine the fatigue behavior of asphalt. The DOFS allows to measure with a high spatial resolution, where the conventional method only acquires one value per time step. The horizontal strain function of the asphalt specimen in dependence of time and space in the CITT can be perfectly matched to a Gausian-sinusoidal-3D-fit, which subsequently can be applied to Young's-modulus calculations. Obvious deviations from the fit could be used for crack detection in asphalt structures. Furthermore, it is discussed how the lab-scale results can be used for the implementation of DOFS in asphalt roads.

Keywords: Rayleigh Scattering, Distributed Optical-Fiber Sensors (DOFS), Non-Destructive Testing, Asphalt, Strain Measurements, Dynamic Loads

1. INTRODUCTION

An asphalt road construction usually consists of a base layer and surface. While the asphalt base layer represents the foundation of the pavement, the surface is considered a wearing course. Thus, the requirements for the service life of different construction layers varies significantly (asphalt surface 10 - 20 years; asphalt base course 30 - 40 years), and failure to achieve these leads to economic losses.

The structural condition of asphalt pavement as well as its change over time have been measured for some time [1]. This information is then evaluated and used for planning maintenance measures. Maintenance measures serve to preserve the substance and utility value of traffic pavements, including the ancillary surfaces, as well as the environmental compatibility. This includes measures of operational as well as structural maintenance, which are usually carried out within the property serving.

Considering ecological and economic sustainability, maintenance measures need to achieve their intended service life. This applies most strongly for extensive measures, e.g., complete renewal of the asphalt surface layer. For that purpose, the asphalt base layer must be in a structural condition that results in a service life longer than the targeted service life of the maintenance measure carried out. It is therefore imperative that the structural condition of the asphalt base layer is known at the time of maintenance planning.

The assessment of the structural condition of asphalt base courses is of particular importance. Currently, there are only destructive methods available [2]. The basis of the corresponding guidelines for evaluating the condition of the asphalt base course is extensive material examinations, which can only be carried out by drilling core samples from the existing pavement. The data from the material examinations is then used within a computational model, deriving information about the remaining service life and thus structural substance.

An area-wide and/or continuous evaluation of the structural substance can barely be realized with the described methods due to high effort and additional damage, making this workflow not economically feasible. In addition to the high costs for the laboratory tests and the evaluation of the results, there are also high economic costs as a result of the necessary traffic restrictions during the sampling.

For the derivation of simulation models (FE models with realistic material laws), a better understanding of the time/load-dependent development of damage in the base courses is needed. Due to the rapid development of new measurement techniques (fiber optical methods), a comprehensive and continuous evaluation of the structural substance becomes possible.

2. MATERIALS AND METHODS

2.1. Measuring temperature and strain using OFDR

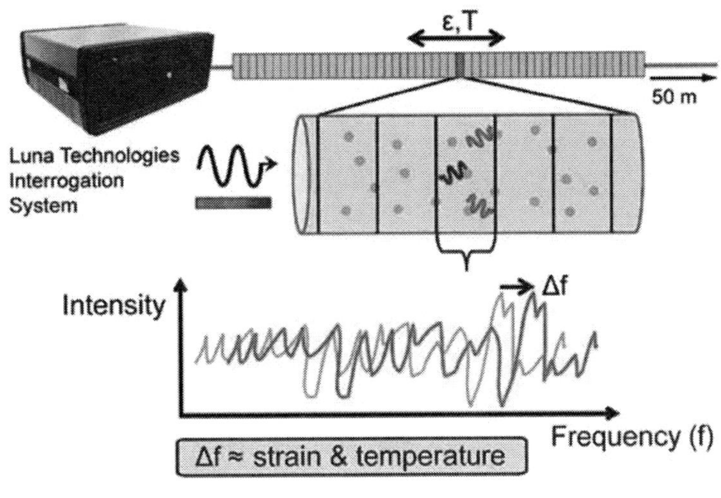

Figure 1. Effect of strain and temperature on Rayleigh backscatter for a particular frequency window [3].

Fiber optic sensors are commonly used for temperature measurements and the acquisition of mechanical properties. These systems consist of the connected passive fiber and a readout unit, with the latter emitting light from a tunable laser or broadband source into the fiber. In the fiber the properties are modified by the state of its temperature and strain. These modifications are detected by the readout unit and remapped in strain or temperature differences [4]. The measurement rate depends on sensor length, measurement mode, gage pitch, performance mode, and number of channels (Table 1). If there are multiple fibers the measurement rate is divided by the number of channels.

Table 1. Measurement rates of a Luna Odisi 6100 for a single channel [5].

Mode	Gage pitch			
	0.65 mm	1.3 mm	2.6 mm	5.2 mm
2.5 m	62.5 Hz	125 Hz	250 Hz	250 Hz
5 m	40Hz	80 Hz	160 Hz	160 Hz
10 m	25 Hz	50 Hz	100 Hz	100 Hz
20 m	12.5 Hz	25 Hz	50 Hz	50 Hz
50 m	-	10 Hz	20 Hz	20 Hz
100m	-	-	10 Hz	10 Hz

2.2. Preparing the data

Under certain circumstances, the measuring device may output no values or values with errors. For this reason, a filter was applied that first removes non-matching values and interpolates missing values through neighboring measurement points. The filter uses a sliding window and removes values that differ to far from the median. Often there is a lot of NaN (not a number) values at the end of the fiber. Under laboratory conditions the sample is not so close to the end, hence these values have no impact. In the case of fibers that are installed in the road, such values must not be included in the evaluation. Values that are missing or incorrect are then linearly interpolated.

2.3. Embedding sensor cables in Marshall specimen

For the determination of strains in asphalt using fiber optic cables, it is necessary to clarify which fibers are suitable. Due to the high mechanical stresses in the compaction process, it is required to use protected fiber structures. Simple glass fibers as in Figure 2a are unsuitable due to the shear forces that occur during application. Various alternative designs are available on the market for use in highly stressed environments (Figure 2b and Figure 2c), where the glass fiber is surrounded by a protective metal capillary and, in Figure 2c, additionally by a profiled plastic cladding. The different variants were tested to validate their mechanical suitability. It was shown that both the metal-coated and the metal- and plastic-coated glass fiber were functional after compaction of the asphalt. The main difference was, that in the case of the simple smooth metal capillary, it was not possible to establish a sufficient bond with the surrounding asphalt. Thus, there was only a limited transfer of strain to the fiber. In comparison, the glass fiber additionally equipped with a profiled plastic coating, a form-fit connection with the asphalt was observed, resulting in a transmission of the strain. Therefore, the glass fiber cable shown in Figure 2c was used for all further investigations (Solifos BRUsens V9).

a) b) c)

Figure 2. Different measurement fibers.

For the cyclic indirect tensile test (CITT), in accordance to [6], drilled test specimens made of rolled sector compacted samples or asphalt road pavements are commonly used. This possibility does not exist for integrated fiber optic cables, as they are destroyed by drilling and become unusable. An alternative method of specimen fabrication had to be chosen for the integration of these variants. A modified Marshall specimen, in accordance to [7], was chosen, where the basic difference is the percussive compaction in contrast to the rolling compaction. It is necessary to build up the specimens in two layers in order to integrate the fiber optic cable in a process-safe manner. The lower part of the specimen is compacted and cooled, then the fiber optic cable is placed in the modified specimen mold and the upper asphalt layer is placed and compacted (Figure 3). Investigations confirmed that the modified manufacturing methodology has a negligible influence on the measurement results. Comparative measurements were carried out with classically produced specimens and further modifications, which validate permissible use.

Figure 3. Lower half of the specimen with V9 cable (left) and full specimen with cable (right).

2.4. The evaluation of damage in asphalt

Miner's rule is one of the most used cumulative damage equations for failures caused by fatigue and researches suggest that Miner's rule can be applied for asphalt as a material [8]. Miner's hypothesis describes linear damage accumulation. Each load change consumes a small proportion of the total possible lifetime, not considering sequence and interaction effects. Undamaged materials have a damage $D = 0$ and failure occurs when the $D = 1$. The accumulated damage can be written as the sum of the damages on different stress levels, where the damage of each stress level D_i can be calculated with the respective number of loads on that stress level n_i and the total number of loads N_i that the material can survive (Eq. 1).

$$D = \sum_i D_i = \sum_i \frac{n_i}{N_i} \tag{1}$$

The cyclic indirect tensile test (CITT, in accordance to [7]) has been used to determine the fatigue behavior of asphalt.

In the CITT, a sinusoidal compressive swell load is introduced into a cylindrical specimen via two load application bars diametrically opposite each other on the lateral surface.

When the specimen is loaded, a vertically directed compressive stress is induced, which is variable along the vertical specimen axis. This results in a horizontally directed tensile stress, which is almost constant in the central area of the vertical specimen axis. In a fatigue test, the initial elastic strain and the fatigue load cycles are determined. From a test series consisting of several fatigue tests the material-specific fatigue function can be determined.

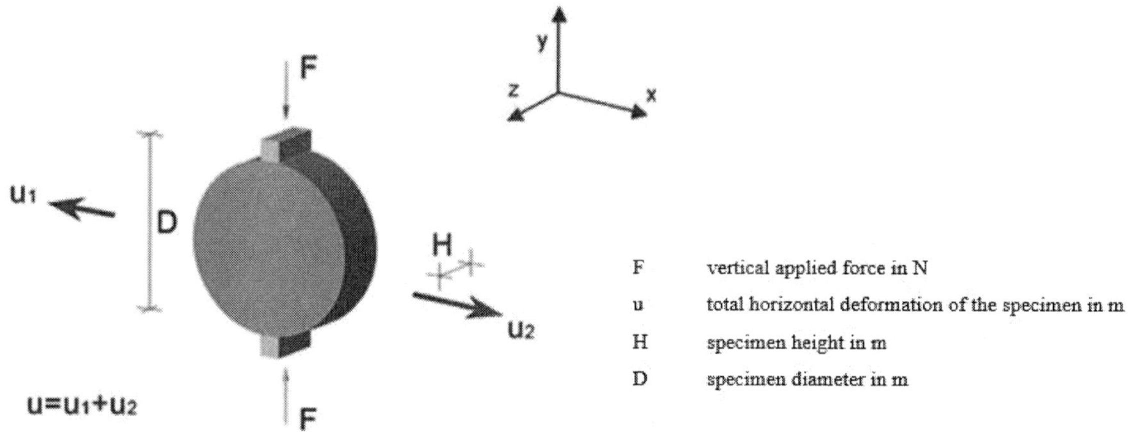

Figure 4. Principle of the CITT [7].

The load used in the CITT is a continuous, force-controlled, harmonic sinusoidal threshold load without load pauses. Therefore, horizontal deformation in response to the load is described with Eq. 2:

$$u(t) = a + b \cdot sin(2\pi \cdot f\ t + c) + d \cdot \mathrm{t} \tag{2}$$

$u(t)$ = total horizontal deformation in mm
f = frequency of the load function in Hz
t = time in s
a = absolute deformation in mm
b = sinusoidal amplitude of the deformation in mm
c = phase shift in rad
d = linear change of sine in mm/s

The absolute Young's Modulus, $|E|$, is calculated using the following formula:

$$|E| = \frac{\Delta F}{2 \cdot b \cdot H}\left(\frac{4}{\pi} - 1 + \nu\right) \tag{3}$$

ν is the Poisson's ratio, which depends on the temperature T, and is estimated using Eq. 4:

$$\nu = 0.15 + \frac{0.35}{1 + e^{1.83034 - 0.07619 \cdot T}} \tag{4}$$

The load cycle number N_{Makro} is defined at which macrocracks in the specimen can be observed during the fatigue test. Based on the concept of the dissipated energy ratio, ER is calculated as the product of the number of load cycles N and the stiffness modulus $|E|$:

$$ER = |E| \cdot N \tag{5}$$

N_{Makro} is now defined as the cycle where the energy ratio has its maximum. A polynomial fit of the 4th degree was applied in the vicinity of the maximum measured value to cancel out noise. The young modulus (thick red line) and the ER (thin red line) during a CITT can be seen in Figure 55.

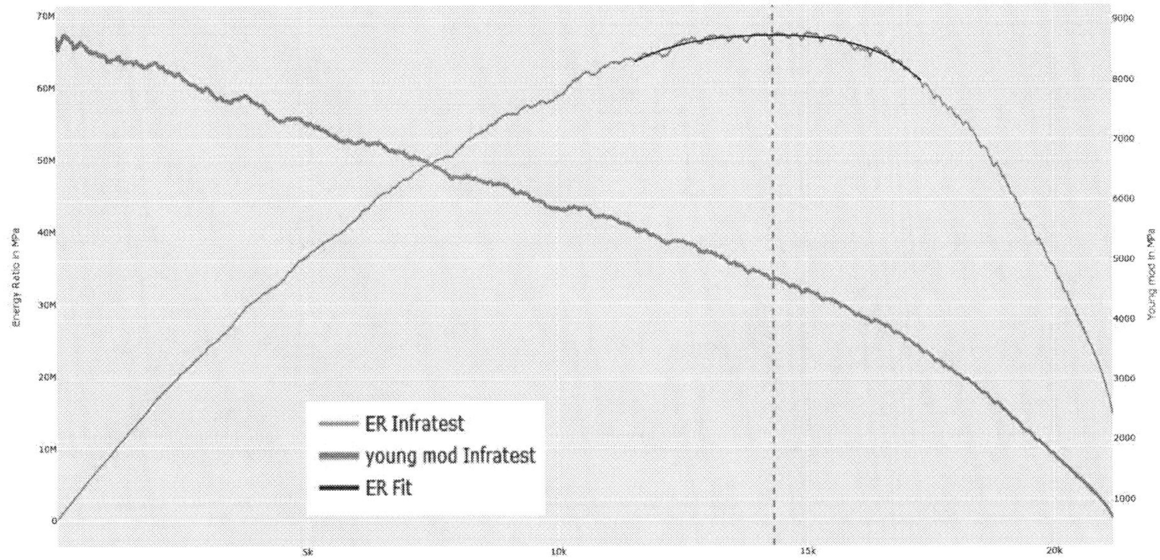

Figure 5. Young's modulus and ER during an CITT.

Applying Miner's rule damage at each point in the CITT can now be defined as:

$$D = \frac{N}{N_{Makro}} \tag{6}$$

The elastic horizontal strain ε_{el} generated by the force F at the specimen center is calculated according to the equation 7. The initial elastic strain $\varepsilon_{el,0}$ for each measurement is estimated from the cycles 98-102.

$$\varepsilon_{el} = \frac{2 \cdot \Delta u}{D} \cdot \frac{1 + 3 \cdot \nu}{4 + \pi \cdot \nu - \pi} \tag{7}$$

3. RESULTS

3.1. Description of the internal strains in Marshall specimens

The internal strain has been monitored during the CITT. At the beginning of the CITT the internal strain can almost perfectly be fitted by a Gausian-sinusoidal-3D function, similar to Eq. 8:

$$\varepsilon(x,t) = \left(\varepsilon_{\mathrm{abs}} + \frac{\varepsilon_{el}}{2} \cdot sin(2\pi \cdot f \cdot t + c) + \delta \cdot t\right)\left(exp\frac{-(x - x_0)^2}{2 \cdot \sigma^2}\right) \tag{8}$$

$\varepsilon(x,t)$ = strain of the fiber in $\mu\varepsilon$
f = frequency of the load function in Hz
t = time in s
$\varepsilon_{\mathrm{abs}}$ = strain from plastic deformations and from base stress in $\mu\varepsilon$
$\frac{\varepsilon_{el}}{2}$ = amplitude eps in $\mu\varepsilon$
c = phase shift in rad
δ = linear change of sine in $\mu\varepsilon/s$
x = location along the fiber in mm
x_0 = expected value in mm
σ^2 = variance in mm^2

The measured internal strains in the specimen in the beginning of the CITT for five load cycles (red) are shown in Fig. 5a, along with the fitted function (blue). More damaged specimens tend to derivate from the fit as seen in **Fehler! Verweisquelle konnte nicht gefunden werden.**b, suggesting the occurrence of cracks. A new variable, $\Delta\varepsilon$, has been introduced to take this derivation into account and is defined by the maximum difference between the fit and the measured value of a timestep. As the fit is applied for five load cycles, $\Delta\varepsilon$ is also averaged over the time.

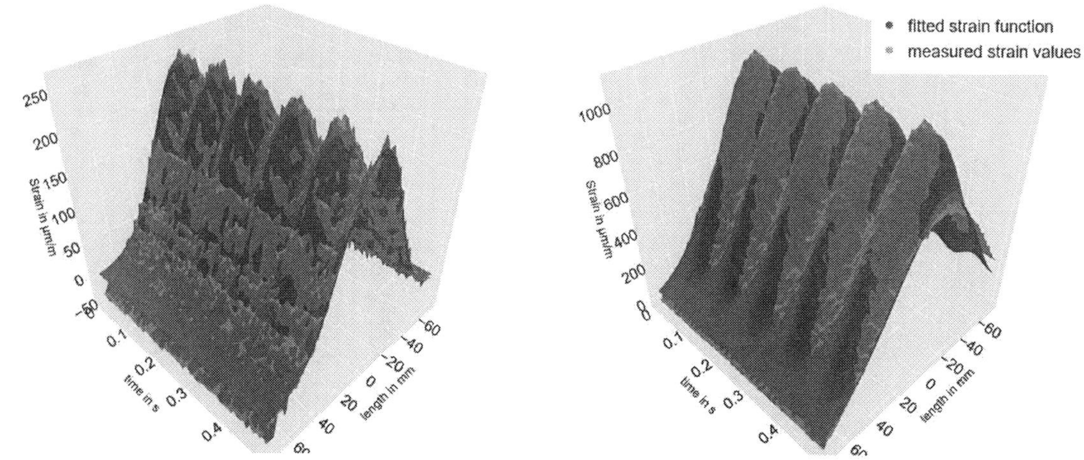

(a) (b)

Figure 6. Internal strain and fitted function over 5 cycles in the CITT. (a) at the beginning (b) in the end

3.2. Comparison of the results with conservative measurement methods

Similar to the calculation in formula (Eq. 3.), the Young's - modulus and the ER has been calculated during the CITT, where the following equation for the Young's - modulus has been used (Eq. 9).

$$|E| = \frac{\Delta F}{2 \cdot \varepsilon_{el} \cdot H}(1 + 3 \cdot \nu) \tag{9}$$

The curves of the Young's- moduli and energy ratios of the 3d fit (green) and the conservative measurement method (red, Fig. 6) are similar. However, the Young's modulus of the new method is always slightly higher than the Young's modulus of the conservative method, which was shown for all measurements. A reason for that could be the assumption that a plane stress state prevails in the slice, i.e. the stresses directed perpendicular to the slice disappear. Since the young modulus does not affect damage directly, the difference is neglected.

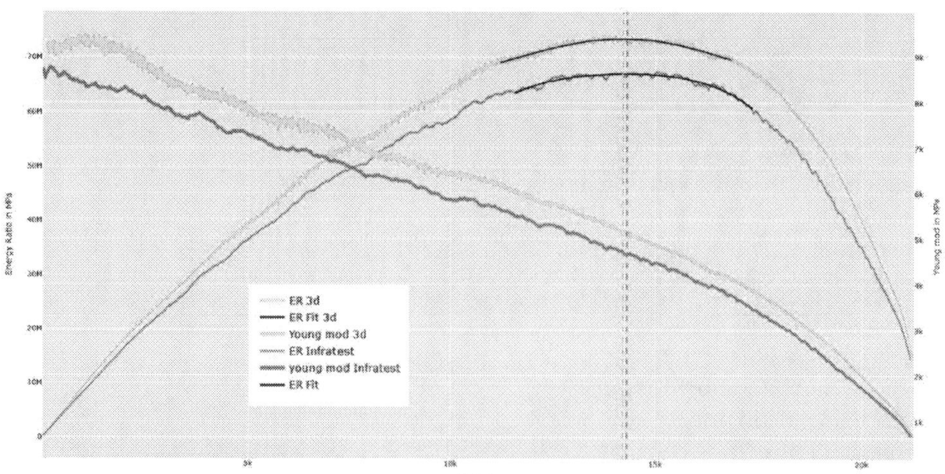

Figure 7. Young Modulus and ER of the 3d fit and the conventional measurement method.

3.3. Predicting the damage in lab scale

To predict the damage a shallow neural network (one hidden layer with 75 neurons) has been trained. The features on which the network where trained were $\Delta\varepsilon, \beta, \delta, x_0, \sigma^2$ and $\varepsilon_{el,0}$. 20 CITT's with five different level of top stress have been carried out. The data of 15 tests has been used to train the network, while the remaining five have been used for testing. Data with a damage higher than 1.1 has been discarded. The actual calculated damage and the prediction of the neural network is shown in Fig. 9. To evaluate the performance of the network. The mean squared error (MSE Eq 10: 0.013) and the mean absolute error (MAE Eq 11: 0.09) have been calculated.

$$MSE = \frac{1}{n}\sum_{i=1}^{n}\left(Y_i - \hat{Y}_i\right)^2 \tag{10}$$

$$MAE = \frac{1}{n}\sum_{i=1}^{n} Y_i - \hat{Y}_i \tag{11}$$

Where n is the number of data points, Y_i is the value of the data point, in this case damage accoring to Eq. 6, and $\hat{Y}_i$ is the predicted damage. As seen in Fig. 8 the predicted damage seems to be quite accurate for most of the measurements, but there are some values where the prediction is way off. This might be solved with more training data.

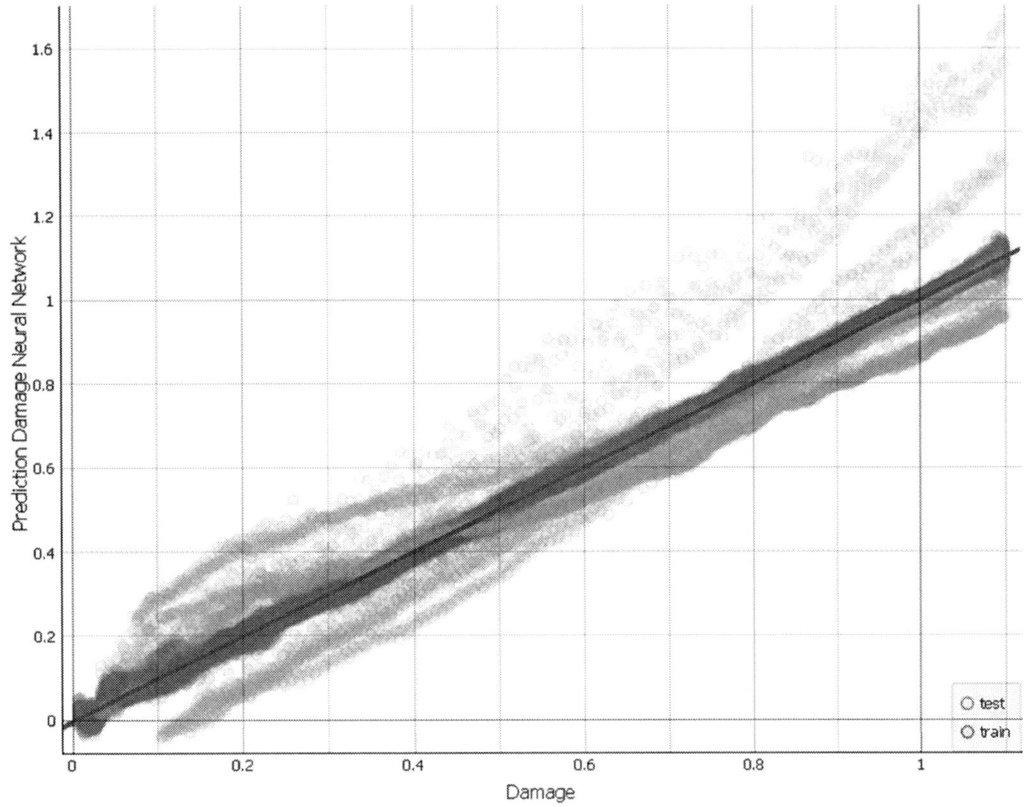

Figure 8. The predicted damage of the test data over the actual damage

ACKNOWLEDGEMENTS

This work is funded by the Federal Ministry for Economic Affairs and Climate Action within the project 'ODEsSA' under grant numbers 'KK5031201SY0' and 'KK5031202SY0' in the Central Innovation Programme for small and medium-sized enterprises (ZIM - Zentrales Innovationsprogramm Mittelstand). Also, a special thanks to the practice partners F. Winkler GmbH & Co. KG Bauunternehmen and Uhlig & Wehling GmbH - Ingenieurgesellschaft. We also would like to thank all the co-workers in the Magdeburg-Stendal University of Applied Sciences, who are supporting this project.

REFERENCES

[1] *Zusätzliche Technische Vertragsbedingungen und Richtlinien zur Zustandserfassung und -bewertung von Straßen.* (2018). Köln: Forschungsgesellschaft für Straßen- und Verkehrswesen e.V.

[2] *Richtlinien zur Bewertung der strukturellen Substanz des Oberbaus von Verkehrsflächen in Asphaltbauweise.* (2014). Köln: Forschungsgesellschaft für Straßen- und Verkehrswesen e.V

[3] Davis, C., Knowles, M., & Swanton, G. (2018). *Evaluation of a Distributed Fibre Optic Strain Sensing System for Full- Scale Fatigue Testing*

[4] Samiec, D. *Verteilte faseroptische Temperatur- und Dehnungsmessung mit sehr hoher Ortsauflösung.* From https://www.polytec.com/fileadmin/website/optical-systems/allgemein/pdf/fachartikel-photonik-verteilte-faseroptische-temperaturmessung.pdf accessed (12. 05 2022).

[5] LUNA. *ODiSI 6000 Series.* From https://lunainc.com/sites/default/files/assets/files/data-sheet/Luna%20ODiSI%206000%20Data%20Sheet.pdf accessed (12. 05 2022)

[6] *Asphalt-StB, TP Teil 24 Spaltzug-Schwellversuch - Beständigkeit gegen Ermüdung.* (2018). Köln: Forschungsgesellschaft für Straßen- und Verkehrswesen e.V.

[7] *Asphalt-StB, TP Teil 30 Herstellung von Asphalt-Probekörpern mit dem Marshall-Verdichtungsgerät (MWG).* (2007). Köln: Forschungsgesellschaft für Straßen- und Verkehrswesen e.V.

[8] Weise, C. (2009). Untersuchungen zur Gültigkeit der Hypothese von Miner. *Dresdner Asphalttage*, 149-160.

IDENTIFICATION TECHNIQUES

9th International Operational Modal Analysis Conference
iomac
July 3 - 6, 2022
Vancouver, Canada

ON THE INITIAL PERFORMANCE ASSESSMENT OF A FREQUENCY-DOMAIN MAXIMUM LIKELIHOOD FORMULATED IN Z-DOMAIN

Sandro D. R. Amador[1], *Simona Miraglia*[2], *Umberto Alibrandi*[3] *and Rune Brincker*[4]

[1] Assistant Professor, Technical University of Denmark (DTU), Denmark, sdio@byg.dtu.dk.
[2] Dr. Simona Miraglia, Bane Denmark, Denmark, smrl@bane.dk.
[3] Associate Professor, Aarhus University, Denmark, ua@cae.au.dk.
[4] Professor Rune Brincker, Brincker Monitoring ApS, rune@brincker-monitoring.com.

ABSTRACT
In frequency domain experimental modal identification, the main goal is to extract the modal properties from the measured transfer function or power spectral densities. The modal parameter estimation can be carried out in a Linear Least Squares (LLS) sense by means of parametric identification methods. When the accuracy of such estimates is not accurate enough, non-linear identification methods based on Maximum Likelihood (ML) can by employed to improve precision of the LLS estimates in an iterative manner. One the main advantages of the ML-based optimization techniques is that, apart from providing more accurate estimates, they are also capable of estimating the uncertainties on the optimized estimates if the noise information is also taken in account in the optimization process. In this paper, the performance of a new frequency-domain ML-based technique formulated in Z-domain modal is investigated by means of a simulated example.

Keywords: Maximum Likelihood, Non-Linear Least Squares, Modal Identification, Modal Parameter Estimation, Frequency Domain, Modal Analysis, Identification Technique

1. INTRODUCTION

When it comes to **E**xperimental and **O**perational **M**odal **A**nalysis (**EMA** and **OMA**) the main challenge is the extract the physical properties of the dynamic system being tested from the measured vibration data. The vibration properties' estimation can be carried either in time or in frequency domain using the so-called parametric identification based on **L**inear **L**east **S**quares model (**LLS**) fitting. Several identification methods exist for this purpose as, for instance, the **p**oly-reference **L**east **S**quares **C**omplex **F**requency

Domain (**pLSCF**) [1] formulated in frequency domain and the **S**tochastic **S**ystem **I**dentification (**SSI**) algorithms developed to estimate the modal parameters from the measured responses [2], the **I**brahim **T**ime **D**omain (**ITD**) [3, 4] and the **p**oly-reference **L**east **S**quares **C**omplex **E**xponential (**pLSCE**) (also known as **LSCE**-Prony) [5, 6].

It turns out that, in some circumstances, the accuracy of the **LLS** methods is not good enough due several sources of errors such as noise and estimation errors. In these circumstances, the **N**on-**L**inear **L**east **S**quares (**NLLS**) techniques such as those based in **M**aximum **L**ikelihood (**ML**) can be employed to iteratively improve the accuracy of **LLS** estimates for the modal properties. The underlying idea of the **NLLS** identification with the **ML**-based approaches is to use the estimates from a **LLS** technique as a starting guess to iteratively improve their accuracy by minimizing the cost function computed from the difference between the measure data and model synthesized from the estimates obtained in each iteration. In the case of **ML**-based methods, this is achieved by making use of the so-called Gaussian-Newton algorithm in combination with the Levenberg–Marquardt [7] approach to prevent the cost function to converge to local minima.

In [9–11] a frequency domain **ML** estimator is introduced to iteratively optimize the invariants of the Frequency Response Function (**FRF**) in Laplace-domain, i.e., the mode shape vectors, continuous time poles, modal participation factor vector and out-of-band residuals. The idea behind this approach is to use the estimates from a previous **LLS** Modal Parameter Estimation (**MPE**) as starting guess. Then, after performing some Gauss-Newton iterations, the **ML**-based approach yields the optimized estimates. Afterwards, the authors formulated another **ML**-based technique in Laplace-domain to optimize the **LLS** modal properties in the cases where reciprocity in considered [12]. One of the main advantages of the **ML**-based **MPE** algorithms is that it considers both the measured vibration data and the noise information in the optimization process. Therefore, apart from providing optimized estimates for the modal properties, they also compute the confidence bounds for these estimates.

In this paper, an initial performance assessment of a new **ML**-based estimator is presented. The **ML** estimator herein introduced is formulated in z-domain Modal Model, hence the acronym **ML-ZMM**. Differently from the **ML-MM** described in [9, 10], the **ML-ZMM** aims at improving the estimates for the discrete-time poles after some Gauss-Newton iterations, rather than the continuous-time poles. Apart from assessing the ability of providing optimized estimates for the natural frequencies and damping coefficients, the robustness in predicting confidence bounds for this properties is also evaluated in this paper.

2. DERIVATION OF THE ML-ZMM

Once the modal parameters are estimated with a **LLS** algorithm, they can be optimized by means of the Maximum Likelihood algorithm formulated using the modal model in z-domain. If displacement responses are measured during the vibration test, the **FRF** matrix $H(z) \in \mathbb{C}^{N_o \times N_i}$ with N_i inputs and N_o outputs is modeled in z-domain by

$$H(z) = \sum_{m=1}^{N_m} \frac{\phi_m l_m^T}{z - \mu_m} + \frac{\phi_m^* l_i^H}{z - \mu_m^*} \tag{1}$$

with N_m denoting the number of vibration modes, $\mu_m \in \mathbb{C}$, $\phi_m \in \mathbb{C}^{N_o \times 1}$, $l_m \in \mathbb{C}^{N_i \times 1}$ stand for the discrete-time poles, mode shape and the operational factor vectors corresponding to the mth vibration mode; $z = e^{j\omega\Delta t}$ is the z-domain variable, with $j = \sqrt{-1}$ denoting the imaginary unit and $\omega = 2\pi f$ is the angular frequency, where f designates the frequency in cycles per second (Hertz); and the operators $(\bullet)^*$ and $(\bullet)^H$ denote the conjugate and Hermitian of a complex matrix, respectively. The continuous-time poles, $\lambda_m \in \mathbb{C}$, are related to their discrete-time counterparts as $\mu_m = e^{\lambda_m \Delta t}$, with $\Delta t \in \mathbb{R}$ standing for the sampling interval. The poles λ_m occur in complex-conjugated pairs and are related to the eigenfrequencies ω_{n_m} and damping ratios ξ_{n_m} as:

$$\lambda_m, \lambda_m^* = -\omega_{n_m}\xi_{n_m} \pm j\sqrt{1-\xi_{n_m}^2}\,\omega_{n_m} \tag{2}$$

Compared to conventional **LLS**-based approaches, **ML**-based algorithms have the advantage of taking into account not only the measured **FRF**s, but also the noise information during the parametric identification process, and thus, apart from providing the optimized estimates of modal parameters, they also yield the confidence intervals of these estimates. The optimization of the starting parameters with the **ML-ZMM** is accomplished by minimizing the following (negative) log-like cost function

$$\sum_{o=1}^{N_o}\sum_{f=1}^{N_f} l(\Theta)_{ML-ZMM} = E_o(\Theta, z_f)E_o^H(\Theta, z_f) \tag{3}$$

with N_f the number of frequency lines, $z_f = e^{j\omega_f \Delta t}$ the z-domain variable evaluated at frequency line f and $E_o(\Theta, z_f)$ the row vector error between the measured and the estimated **FRF** for the oth measured output, which is calculated as:

$$E_o(\Theta, z_f) = \left(\frac{\hat{H}_{o1}(\Theta, z_f) - H_{o1}(z_f)}{\sigma_{H_{o1}(z_f)}} \cdots \frac{\hat{H}_{oN_i}(\Theta, z_f) - H_{oN_i}(z_f)}{\sigma_{H_{oN_i}(z_f)}} \right) \tag{4}$$

where $\hat{H}_o(\Theta, z_f) \in \mathbb{C}^{1\times N_i}$, $H_o(z_f) \in \mathbb{C}^{1\times N_i}$ and $\sigma_{H_o(z_f)} \in \mathbb{R}^{1\times N_i}$ are the oth row of the **FRF** in modal model formulation (1), and of the measured **FRF** and its corresponding standard deviation, respectively. The parameter Θ is a column vector with all the parameters to be optimized by means of the Gauss-Newton Newton algorithm and is given by:

$$\Theta = \begin{bmatrix} \theta_1 & \theta_2 & \cdots & \theta_{N_o} & \theta_{L\mu} \end{bmatrix}^T \in \mathbb{R}^{2N_m(N_i+N_o)} \tag{5}$$

with

$$\theta_{L\mu} = \begin{bmatrix} \theta_L & \theta_\mu \end{bmatrix} \in \mathbb{C}^{2N_m N_i} \tag{6}$$

The parameter $\theta_o \in \mathbb{C}^{2N_m}$ is a vector with the real and imaginary parts of the mode shape ordinates corresponding to the oth output, given by

$$\theta_o = \begin{bmatrix} \Re\mathfrak{e}(\phi_{o1}) & \Re\mathfrak{e}(\phi_{o2}) & \cdots & \Re\mathfrak{e}(\phi_{oN_m}) & \Im\mathfrak{m}(\phi_{o1}) & \Im\mathfrak{m}(\phi_{o2}) & \cdots & \Im\mathfrak{m}(\phi_{oN_m}) \end{bmatrix} \in \mathbb{R}^{2N_m} \tag{7}$$

where $\Re\mathfrak{e}(\bullet)$ and $\Im\mathfrak{m}(\bullet)$ stand for the real and imaginary parts of a complex number. The parameters $\theta_L \in \mathbb{R}^{2N_m(N_i-1)}$ and $\theta_\mu \in \mathbb{C}^{2N_m}$ in eq. (6) are columns vectors containing, respectively, the real and imaginary parts of all the operational factors elements, and the real and imaginary parts of the discrete-time poles. These parameters are defined, respectively, as:

$$\theta_L = \begin{bmatrix} \Re\mathfrak{e}(L_{11}) & \cdots & \Re\mathfrak{e}(L_{N_k 1}) & \Re\mathfrak{e}(L_{11}) & \cdots & \Im\mathfrak{m}(L_{N_k 1}) & \cdots \\ \cdots & \Re\mathfrak{e}(L_{1N_m}) & \cdots & \Re\mathfrak{e}(L_{N_k N_m}) & \Re\mathfrak{e}(L_{1N_m}) & \cdots & \Im\mathfrak{m}(L_{N_k N_m}) \end{bmatrix} \tag{8}$$

and

$$\theta_\mu = \left[\mathfrak{Re}(\mu_1) \quad \mathfrak{Re}(\mu_2) \quad \cdots \quad \mathfrak{Re}(\mu_{N_m}) \quad \mathfrak{Im}(\mu_1) \quad \mathfrak{Im}(\mu_2) \quad \cdots \quad \mathfrak{Im}(\mu_{N_m})\right] \in \mathbb{R}^{2N_m} \tag{9}$$

where $L_{km} \in \mathbb{C}$ is the kth element of the operational factor vector of the mth vibration mode $l_m \in \mathbb{C}^{N_i \times 1}$, with $k = 1,\ 2,\ \cdots,\ N_k$, and $N_k = N_i - 1$, which means that only the operational factors that differ from 1 are optimized by the algorithm during the performed iterations. As the identified operational factors are normalized with regard to the maximum element of each mode in the identification with the **pLSCF**, the derivatives of the elements that equals 1 are not evaluated and, therefore, are not included in the vector defined by eq. (8). In fact, this works like a constraint, since the operational factors elements that equal 1 are not updated during the minimization of the cost function (3). The maximum likelihood optimization of the parameters Θ is accomplished by minimizing the cost function (3) in a non-linear least squares sense. This is performed by means of the Gauss-Newton optimization algorithm combined with Levenberg–Marquardt approach [7], which forces the cost function to decrease with the performed iterations. The Gauss-Newton iteration is basically divided in two steps:

1. Solve the normal equations

$$J_i^H J_i \text{vec}(\Delta\Theta_i) = -J_i^H E_i \quad for \quad \text{vec}(\Delta\Theta_i). \tag{10}$$

2. Compute an update of the previous solution

$$\Theta_{i+1} = \Theta_i + \Delta\Theta_i \tag{11}$$

where $\text{vec}(\Delta\Theta_i) \in \mathbb{R}^{2N_m(N_o+N_i)}$ is the perturbation on the modal parameters, E_i is the error between the measured quantity and the parametric model (i.e. **FRF** equation in z-domain modal model formulation (1)), J_i is the Jacobian matrix evaluated at the ith iteration, and the $\text{vec}(\bullet)$ stands for the column stacking operator. The equation error calculated at the ith iteration $E_i = E(\Theta_i)$ is given by

$$E_i = \begin{Bmatrix} \text{vec}(E_1(\Theta_i)) \\ \text{vec}(E_2(\Theta_i)) \\ \vdots \\ \text{vec}(E_{N_o}(\Theta_i)) \end{Bmatrix} \in \mathbb{R}^{N_f N_o N_i \times 1}, \quad E_o(\Theta_i) = \begin{bmatrix} E_o(\omega_1, \Theta_i) \\ E_o(\omega_2, \Theta_i) \\ \vdots \\ E_o(\omega_{N_f}, \Theta_i) \end{bmatrix} \in \mathbb{R}^{N_f \times N_i} \tag{12}$$

and the corresponding Jacobian matrix by

$$J_i = \left[\frac{\partial E(\Theta_i)}{\partial \Theta_i}\right] \in \mathbb{R}^{N_f N_o N_i \times 2N_m(N_o+N_i)} \tag{13}$$

with Θ_i representing the parameters given by eq. (5) at the ith iteration. This matrix has the following structure:

$$J = \begin{bmatrix} Y_1 & 0 & \cdots & 0 & X_1 \\ 0 & Y_2 & \cdots & 0 & X_2 \\ \vdots & \vdots & \ddots & \vdots & \vdots \\ 0 & 0 & \cdots & Y_{N_o} & X_{N_o} \end{bmatrix} \tag{14}$$

where X_o is a matrix with the derivatives of the equation error (4) with regard to the discreet-time poles and operational factors, and Y_o is a matrix with the derivatives with respect to the mode shapes. The matrix X_o is computed as:

$$X_o = \begin{bmatrix} X_L & X_\mu \end{bmatrix} \tag{15}$$

where the entries X_L and X_μ are sub-matrices containing the derivatives of the equation error (4) with respect to the real and imaginary of the operational factors, real and imaginary parts of the discreet-time poles, respectively. The sub-matrix X_L is computed as:

$$X_L = \begin{bmatrix} X_{L_1} & X_{L_2} & \cdots & X_{L_{Nm}} \end{bmatrix} \tag{16}$$

with X_{L_m} containing the derivatives of the equation error with respect to the real and imaginary parts of the elements of the operational factor of the mth mode. The sub-matrix X_μ is calculated as:

$$X_\mu = \left[\text{vec}\left\{ \frac{\partial E_o(\Theta)}{\partial \mathfrak{Re}(\mu_1)} \right\} \quad \cdots \quad \text{vec}\left\{ \frac{\partial E_o(\Theta)}{\partial \mathfrak{Re}(\mu_{Nm})} \right\} \quad \text{vec}\left\{ \frac{\partial E_o(\Theta)}{\partial \mathfrak{Im}(\mu_1)} \right\} \quad \cdots \quad \text{vec}\left\{ \frac{\partial E_o(\Theta)}{\partial \mathfrak{Im}(\mu_{Nm})} \right\} \right] \tag{17}$$

The sub-matrices X_{L_m} in eq. (16) are defined by

$$X_{L_m} = \left[\text{vec}\left\{ \frac{\partial E_o(\Theta)}{\partial \mathfrak{Re}(L_{1m})} \right\} \quad \cdots \quad \text{vec}\left\{ \frac{\partial E_o(\Theta)}{\partial \mathfrak{Re}\left(L_{N_k m}\right)} \right\} \quad \text{vec}\left\{ \frac{\partial E_o(\Theta)}{\partial \mathfrak{Im}(L_{1m})} \right\} \quad \cdots \quad \text{vec}\left\{ \frac{\partial E_o(\Theta)}{\partial \mathfrak{Im}\left(L_{N_k m}\right)} \right\} \right] \tag{18}$$

with $N_k = N_i - 1$. It is worth noting that the same constraint strategy used in the definition of eq. (8) must be used to calculate the derivatives in eq. (18). Therefore, only the derivatives with respect to the operational factors elements which are different from 1 are included in this equation. In eq. (14), Y_o is a sub-matrix with the derivatives of the equation error with respect to the real and imaginary parts of the oth mode shape vector

$$Y_o = \left[\text{vec}\left\{ \frac{\partial E_o(\Theta)}{\partial \mathfrak{Re}(\phi_{o1})} \right\} \quad \cdots \quad \text{vec}\left\{ \frac{\partial E_o(\Theta)}{\partial \mathfrak{Re}(\phi_{oNm})} \right\} \quad \text{vec}\left\{ \frac{\partial E_o(\Theta)}{\partial \mathfrak{Im}(\phi_{o1})} \right\} \quad \cdots \quad \text{vec}\left\{ \frac{\partial E_o(\Theta)}{\partial \mathfrak{Im}(\phi_{oNm})} \right\} \right] \tag{19}$$

It is worth noting that, apart from the measured **FRF**s, the variance of the noise is also taken into account during the parametric identification with **ML**-based algorithms. In the context of **EMA**, the variance is estimated by means of the so-called $H1$ **FRF** estimator [7]. In case of single-input measurements (i.e **SISO** and **SIMO** systems), the variance can be calculated as:

$$\sigma^2_{H_{oi}} = \frac{1}{N_b} \left(\frac{1 - \gamma^2_{oi}}{\gamma^2_{oi}} \right) |H_{oi}|^2 \tag{20}$$

where N_b and γ^2_{oi} stand for the number of averaged data blocks used to estimate the **FRF** and the coherence function, respectively. Given the block structure of the Jacobian matrix, the normal equations (10) are rewritten as follows

$$\begin{bmatrix} R_1 & 0 & \cdots & 0 & S_1 \\ 0 & R_2 & \cdots & 0 & S_2 \\ \vdots & \vdots & \ddots & \vdots & \vdots \\ 0 & 0 & \cdots & R_{N_o} & S_{N_o} \\ S_1^T & S_1^T & \cdots & S_{N_o}^T & \sum_{o=1}^{N_o} T_o \end{bmatrix} \begin{Bmatrix} \text{vec}(\Delta\theta_1) \\ \text{vec}(\Delta\theta_2) \\ \vdots \\ \text{vec}(\Delta\theta_{N_o}) \\ \text{vec}(\Delta\theta_{L\mu}) \end{Bmatrix} = - \begin{Bmatrix} \mathfrak{Re}\left(Y_1^H E_1\right) \\ \mathfrak{Re}\left(Y_2^H E_2\right) \\ \vdots \\ \mathfrak{Re}\left(Y_{N_o}^H E_{N_o}\right) \\ \sum_{o=1}^{N_o} \mathfrak{Re}\left(X_o^H E_o\right) \end{Bmatrix} \tag{21}$$

with

$$
\begin{aligned}
R_o &= \mathfrak{Re}\left(Y_o^H Y_o\right) \in \mathbb{R}^{(2N_mN_i)\times(2N_mN_i)}\\
S_o &= \mathfrak{Re}\left(Y_o^H X_o\right) \in \mathbb{R}^{(2N_mN_i)\times(2N_mN_i)}\\
T_o &= \mathfrak{Re}\left(X_o^H X_o\right) \in \mathbb{R}^{(2N_mN_i)\times(2N_mN_i)}
\end{aligned}
$$

From eqs. (21), the perturbation on the coefficients $\mathrm{vec}(\Delta\theta_o)$ (i.e., the perturbations on the real and imaginary parts of the mode shape vectors) can be written as a function of the perturbation on the natural frequencies, damping ratios, operational factors, $\mathrm{vec}(\Delta\theta_{L\mu})$, as:

$$
\mathrm{vec}(\Delta\theta_o) = -R_o^{-1}(\mathfrak{Re}\left(Y_o^H E_o\right) + S_o\mathrm{vec}(\Delta\theta_{L\mu})) \tag{22}
$$

and the perturbations $\mathrm{vec}(\Delta\theta_o)$ can be eliminated from the last set of equations in (21) by means of eq. (22), yielding

$$
\sum_{o=1}^{N_o}(T_o - S_o^T R_o^{-1} S_o)\mathrm{vec}(\Delta\theta_{L\mu}) = -\sum_{o=1}^{N_o}(\mathfrak{Re}\left(X_o^H E_o\right) - S_o^T R_o^{-1}\mathfrak{Re}\left(Y_o^H E_o\right)) \tag{23}
$$

or in a more compact form

$$
M_1\mathrm{vec}(\Delta\theta_{L\mu}) = M_2 \tag{24}
$$

with

$$
M_1 = \left(T_o - S_o^T R_o^{-1} S_o\right), \quad M_2 = \sum_{o=1}^{N_o}\left(S_o^T R_o^{-1}\mathfrak{Re}\left(Y_o^H E_o\right) - \mathfrak{Re}\left(X_o^H E_o\right)\right) \tag{25}
$$

This elimination reduces the memory required to run the algorithm. An efficient implementation of the **ML-ZMM** is only possible if the variances are taken into account in the cost function (3). Once the perturbations on the discrete-time poles and operational factors are calculated in the last iteration by means of eq. (23), then perturbations on the mode shape vectors are computed using eq. (22).

2.1. Estimation of the uncertainty bounds

One of the main advantages of the **ML**-based algorithms is the possibility to estimate the confidence intervals for the identified modal parameters using the noise information measured together with the **FRF**s during the vibration tests. As shown in [7], a good approximation of the covariance of the **ML** parameters Θ_{ML-MM} is obtained by

$$
\mathrm{Cov}(\phi, L, \mu) \simeq \frac{1}{2}\mathfrak{Re}\left(\left[J_l^H J_l\right]\right)^{-1} \tag{26}
$$

with J_l the Jacobian matrix evaluated in the last iteration of the Gaussian-Newton algorithm. Taking advantage of the structure of the Jacobian matrix and using the matrix inversion lemma [8], the covariance of the natural frequencies, damping ratios and the operational factors can be estimated independently as follows

$$\mathrm{Cov}(L,\mu) \simeq \frac{1}{2}M_1^{-1} \tag{27}$$

Therefore, it is not necessary to invert the full matrix in eq. (21). Once the uncertainties on the discrete-time poles are found from (27), they can be propagated to the natural frequencies and damping ratios by means of the following linearization formulas [13]:

$$\begin{aligned} \mathrm{Var}(F_{n_m}) &\simeq \left[\frac{\partial f_{nm}\left(\theta_{\mu m}\right)}{\partial\hat{\theta}_{\mu m}}\right] \mathrm{Cov}(\hat{\theta}_{\mu_m}) \left[\frac{\partial f_{nm}\left(\theta_{\mu m}\right)}{\partial\hat{\theta}_{\mu m}}\right]^T \\ \mathrm{Var}(\xi_{n_m}) &\simeq \left[\frac{\partial \xi_{nm}\left(\theta_{\mu m}\right)}{\partial\hat{\theta}_{\mu m}}\right] \mathrm{Cov}(\hat{\theta}_{\mu_m}) \left[\frac{\partial \xi_{nm}\left(\theta_{\mu m}\right)}{\partial\hat{\theta}_{\mu m}}\right]^T \end{aligned} \tag{28}$$

Given the structure of the Jacobian matrix, it is straightforward to apply matrix inversion lemma [8] and derive the covariance of the mode shapes, yielding

$$\mathrm{Cov}(\phi_o) \simeq R_o^{-1} + R_o^{-1}S_oM_1^{-1}S_o^TR_o^{-1} \tag{29}$$

3. VALIDATION OF THE ML-ZMM IMPLEMENTATION

The example used to validate the **ML**-based approach discussed in Section 2. is illustrated in Fig. 1. This system was used by [14] to compare different modal parameter estimation techniques in terms of their sensitivity to statistical errors. It comprises five masses supported by cantilever beams which are connected among themselves by arch springs. The exact natural frequencies, damping ratios and modal masses of the system are given in Tab. 1, whereas the real modes are shown in Tab. 2. These properties were used to generate the **FRF**s used in simulated **EMA**.

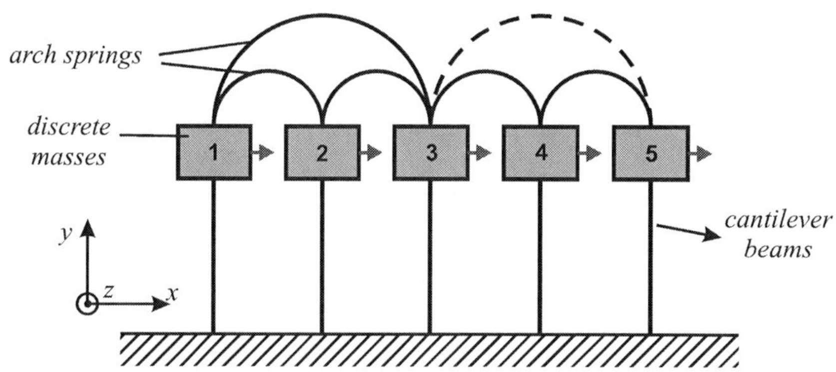

Figure 1: Five-**DOF** system connected with arch springs [14]

The system was excited by a white Gaussian noise at masses 1 and 2, and the responses were measured at all **DOF**s, resulting in **FRF** matrix with two columns and five rows. The **FRF** was calculated in the frequency range of 0-80 Hz with a resolution of 0.1 Hz. Afterwards, a colored noise was added to the **FRF** matrix with a standard deviation of 10%. The noise was added to the real and imaginary parts independently, and was calculated as a percentage of the absolute value of the **FRF** at each frequency line. This was achieved by adding a complex random number to the **FRF** at each frequency line. This number was computed so that its amplitude is a random number of a normal distribution and its phase is an uniform random number between 0 and 2π.

Table 1: Eigenfrequencies, damping ratios and modal masses of the five-**DOF** system

Mode	f_n [Hz]	ξ_n [%]	m_i [Kg]
1	26.06	2	2.52
2	36.84	2	2.97
3	51.47	2	0.90
4	56.21	2	1.09
5	62.60	2	1.05

Table 2: Real modes of the five-**DOF** system

DOF/Mode	1	2	3	4	5
1	0.7147	1.0000	-0.0911	-0.9230	-0.6083
2	0.7166	0.9999	-0.1493	1.0000	-0.1937
3	0.7981	0.2257	0.1554	-0.1518	1.0000
4	0.8518	-0.5166	1.0000	0.1231	-0.3936
5	1.0000	-0.8590	-0.5860	0.0196	-0.2041

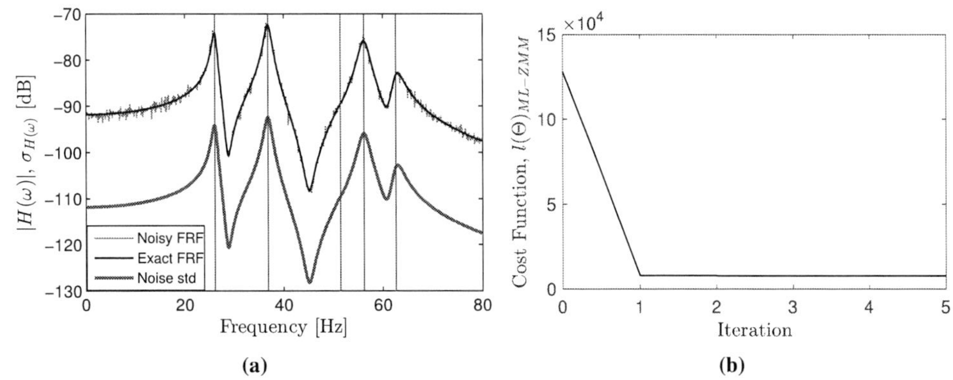

Figure 2: Element(1,1) of the **FRF** matrix contaminated with 10% noise: exact (black line) and noisy (red line) **FRF**, noise standard deviation (green line) and exact natural frequencies (vertical lines) (a); and cost function variation over the performed **ML-ZMM** iterations

The exact and noisy element(1,1) of the **FRF** matrix, and the corresponding "exact" standard deviation of the noise are shown in Fig. 2a. A set of 500 **FRF**s with 800 frequency lines contaminated with noise was generated to perform Monte Carlo simulations in order to assess the efficiency of the proposed **ML-ZMM**. The modal parameters of each dataset were identified with the **pLSCF** and **LSFD** estimators and then used as starting values to be optimized by the **ML-ZMM** algorithm. The identification of each dataset was performed using the full frequency band, i.e., with no upper and lower residual terms. In Fig. 2b, it is shown that variation of the cost function, $l(\Theta)_{ML-ZMM}$, over the five performed iterations in a typical Monte Carlo realization.

The variations of the **pLSCF** and **ML-ZMM** estimates for the 3rd natural frequency and damping ratio over the Monte Carlo simulations are shown in Figs. 3. These results show that the bias on the **pLSCF** estimates is removed after only 5 Gauss-Newton iterations of **ML-ZMM**. Apart from its optimization capabilities, the **ML**-based techniques have also the advantage of predicting the confidence bounds for the optimized estimates if the noise information is taken into account in the optimization process. In Figs. 4, the standard deviations of the 3rd natural frequency and damping ratio (estimated after 5 iterations of the **ML-ZMM** in each Monte Carlo realization) are compared to the respective sample standard deviation. It is clear from these figures that the **ML-ZMM** provides accurate estimates for the sample standard deviations of such modal properties.

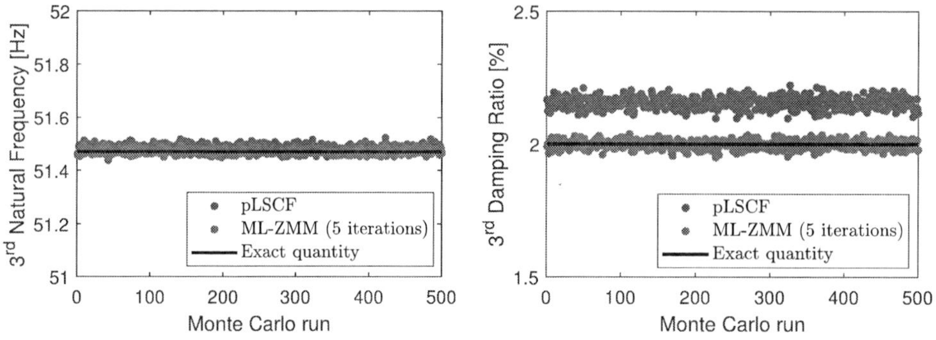

(a) (b)

Figure 3: Estimates for natural frequency (a) and damping ratio (b) of the 3rd vibration mode obtained with the **pLSCF** (blue dots) and **ML-ZMM** after 5 iterations (red dots)

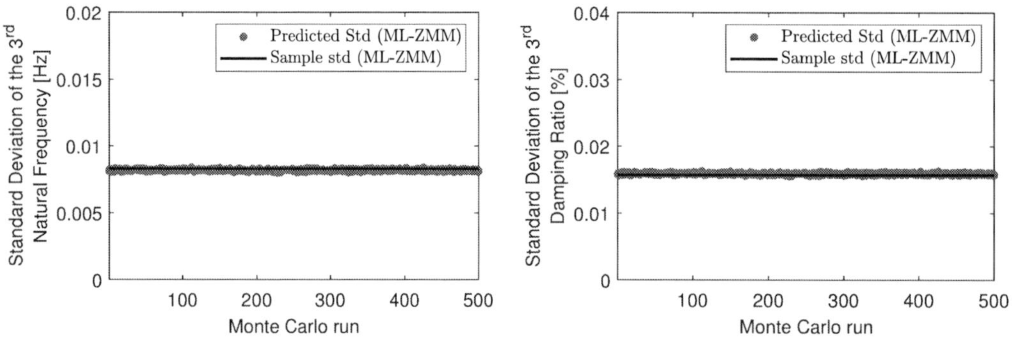

(a) (b)

Figure 4: Estimates for the standard deviation of the natural frequency (a) and damping ratio (b) of the 3rd vibration mode obtained after 5 **ML-ZMM** iterations (red dots) and sample standard deviation (solid black line)

4. CONCLUSIONS

In this paper, an initial performance assessment of a **ML**-based estimator formulated in z-domain modal model is presented. Just like any other **ML**-based approach, the **ML-ZMM** requires a good starting guess to assure convergence over the performed Gauss-Newton iterations. Despite the fact that any **LLS**-based identification technique can be used to provide the starting guess, the proposed **ML** approach is combined with the **pLSCF** estimator to retain the multi-reference information and improve the accuracy of the **LLS** estimates. The main difference of the **ML-ZMM** herein introduced with regards to the **ML-MM** described in [10] is that the former optimizes the discrete-time rather than the continuous-time poles. The efficiency of the **ML-ZMM** was assessed by means a simulated application example with no upper and lower residuals. The results obtained from such simulations show that not only did the **ML-ZMM** reduce the bias on the estimates for the natural frequencies and damping ratios, but it also provided accurate estimates for the confidence intervals of those estimates.

5. ACKNOWLEDGEMENTS

The authors acknowledge all the support received from Danish Offishore Center (**DOC**) at the **T**echnical **U**niversity of Denmark (**DTU**).

REFERENCES

[1] P. Guillaume, P. Verboven, S. Vanlanduit, H. Van-der-Auweraer and B. Peeters, "A Poly–reference Implementation of the Least-squares Complex Frequency–domain Estimator", *In Proceedings of the International Conference on Noise and Vibration Engineering*, Leuven, Belgium, 2003.

[2] B. Peeters, "System Identification and Damage Detection in Civil Engineering. Katholieke Universiteit Leuven, Belgium", *PhD thesis*, Katholieke Universiteit Leuven, Leuven, Belgium, 2000.

[3] Ibrahim, S. R., Milkulcik, E. C., A Method for Direct Identification of Vibration Parameters from Free Response. *Shock and Vibration Bulletin*, 47, (pp. 183–196) 1977.

[4] Brincker R, Olsen P, Amador S, Juul M, Malekjafarian A, Ashory M., Modal participation in multiple input Ibrahim time domain identification. *Mathematics and Mechanics of Solids, vol. 24, issue 1, (pp. 168–180)* 2019.

[5] Vold, H., Kundrat, J., Rocklin, G. T., Russel, R., A Multi-input Modal Estimation Algorithm for Mini-computers. *In SAE Technical Paper Number 820194.* 1982.

[6] Vold, H., Rocklin, G. T., The Numerical Implementation of a Multi-input Modal Estimation Algorithm for Mini-computers. *In proceedings of the 1st International Modal Analysis Conference*, Orlando, FL., USA, 1982.

[7] R. Pintelon and J. Schoukens, "System Identification: A Frequency Domain Approach". *IEEE Press*, vol. 1, ed. 1, Piscataway, 2001.

[8] T. Kailath, "Linear Systems". *Prentice–Hall*, vol. 1, ed. 1, 1998.

[9] M. El–Kafafy, T. De–Troyer, B. Peeters, and P. Guillaume, "Fast maximum-likelihood identification of modal parameters with uncertainty intervals: A modal model–based formulation". *Mechanical Systems and Signal Processing*, vol. 37, pp. 422–439, 2013.

[10] M. El–Kafafy, T. De–Troyer and P. Guillaume, "Fast maximum-likelihood identification of modal parameters with uncertainty intervals: A modal model formulation with enhanced residual term". *Mechanical Systems and Signal Processing*, vol. 48, pp. 49–66, 2014.

[11] Amador, S., El-Kafafy, M., Cunha, Á. and Brincker, R., "A New Maximum Likelihood Estimator Formulated in Pole-Residue Modal Model" *Applied Sciencies*, 9, 3120, 2019.

[12] M. El–Kafafy, B. Peeters, P. Guillaume and T. De–Troyer, "Constrained maximum likelihood modal parameter identification applied to structural dynamics". *Mechanical Systems and Signal Processing*, vol. 72–73, pp. 567–589, 2016.

[13] R. Pintelon, P. Guillaume and J. Schoukens, "Uncertainty calculation in (operational) modal analysis". *Mechanical Systems and Signal Processing*, vol. 21, pp. 2359–2373, 2007.

[14] M. Böswald, D. Göge, U. Füllekrug and Y. Govers, "A review of experimental modal analysis methods with respect to their applicability to test data of large aircraft", *In Proceedings of the International Conference on Noise and Vibration Engineering* Leuven, Belgium, 2006.

9th International Operational Modal Analysis Conference
iomac
July 3 - 6, 2022
Vancouver, Canada

ROBUST PROBABILISTIC CANONICAL CORRELATIONS FOR STOCHASTIC SUBSPACE IDENTIFICATION

B. J. O'Connell[1], *E. J. Cross*[1], *T. J. Rogers*[1]

[1]Dynamics Research Group, Department of Mechanical Engineering, University of Sheffield, Mappin Street, Sheffield, S1 3JD, United Kingdom - {bjoconnell1, e.j.cross, tim.rogers}@sheffield.ac.uk

ABSTRACT

Stochastic subspace identification (SSI) has become one of the key algorithms for the identification of linear structural dynamic systems. Commonly used in operational modal analysis, SSI is an efficient method for recovering the modal properties of a structure from measured data. When formed as "covariance-driven SSI" (Cov-SSI) the method relies on the computation of the canonical correlations and canonical directions between the past and future responses of the dynamic system, across a set of measured sensors. The mathematical tool that recovers this information is known as canonical correlation analysis (CCA). Using this knowledge, this paper presents two novel contributions. The first is a probabilistic interpretation of Cov-SSI, through the substitution of traditional CCA with its probabilistic interpretation. The second is an extension to the probabilistic SSI formulation, a robust form using the latent variable interpretation of the Students' T-distribution and robust CCA. This robust probabilistic SSI method is first benchmarked against Cov-SSI on a simple simulated dataset. Both identification procedures are then assessed on their resistance to noise and outliers in a corrupted dataset, typically caused by practically encountered scenarios such as sensor drop-out or partial detachment. Cov-SSI is shown to perform poorly, producing unrealistic results, whilst robust probabilistic SSI remains capable of confidently identifying the system in the presence of outliers. This evidence may lead to suggest that this new robust method could be more regularly used over classical Cov-SSI when the practitioner is worried about outliers in the measured response.

Key words: Probabilistic, Robust, Modal Analysis, System Identification, Stochastic Subspace

1 INTRODUCTION

The characterisation of structural dynamic systems remains a key feature of modern engineering analysis. Modal analysis is a common method of system identification used in industry and research to obtain the modal properties of linear dynamic systems, namely the natural frequencies (eigenfrequencies), damping ratios and mode shapes (eigenmodes). The availability of this modal information helps to facilitate more informed decisions throughout the entire lifecycle of an engineering structure. Subspace identification algorithms have gained increasing attention in the modal analysis community [1]. This is largely due to their inherent robustness and ability to deal with a large numbers of inputs and outputs. *Stochastic subspace identification* (SSI) is a prominent, time-domain method of experimental and operational modal analysis, operating in the state space, that frequently appears in the literature and continues to be a reliable means of modal analysis [2, 3, 4]. Subspace identification algorithms, such as SSI, are rarely used in isolation. In reality, these algorithms form an integral part of a much larger set of tools and processes used in the design, manufacture and maintenance of engineering structures. Such an example could be determining the modal properties of a bridge, during operation, for the purpose of damage detection and prevention [5].

Currently, the vast majority of SSI algorithms operate deterministically. That is to say the algorithms do not usually account for, or explicitly calculate, any uncertainty. However, a general shift to operate in more probabilistic frameworks within many engineering fields such as structural health monitoring (SHM) [5] and digital twins [6] has led to an increase in probabilistic methods. This increase is predominantly due to the significant value associated with quantifying and applying uncertainty through probabilistic analysis [7]. The inherent use of modal information in fields such as SHM and digital twins, coupled with their use of probabilistic frameworks, highlights an explicit need to develop probabilistic modal analysis tools. Recasting SSI as a probabilistic method would add more value to its inclusion as a component in broader probabilistic frameworks and open up avenues for future research. The construction and definition of the full framework, however, is beyond the scope of this paper.

An established mathematical concept, upon which covariance-driven SSI (Cov-SSI) fundamentally depends, is canonical correlation analysis (CCA) [8]. CCA is concerned with finding the canonical vectors or directions between two datasets such that they are maximally correlated with one another; thus diagonalising the cross-covariance matrix. The solution to CCA is typically recovered via the solution to a generalised eigenvalue problem which can be achieved via the singular value decomposition (SVD). In 2005, Bach and Jordan [9] proposed a probabilistic interpretation of CCA (PCCA) which followed the same latent approach taken by Tipping and Bishop in their development of probabilistic principal component analysis [10]. This probabilistic viewpoint on the algorithm deepened the understanding of CCA and could provide a deeper understanding of SSI and unlock its potential within probabilistic frameworks. Therefore, in an effort to formulate a probabilistic interpretation of SSI, this paper takes a logical approach and first reconstructs Cov-SSI using probabilistic CCA.

The ability to reformulate SSI as a probabilistic model also allows consideration of a statistically robust extension using standard probabilistic methods. A typical weakness with current SSI methods lies in their handling of outliers. Outliers and non-Gaussian noise may appear on time series data in practical measurement campaigns from sources such as electrical noise, or from unpredicted events that are often independent of the system being measured. In the case of OMA, these 'events' refer to practically encountered scenarios such as sensor drop-out or partial detachment. In typical data analysis, data will often be pre-processed to remove these outliers and 'clean' the dataset before use. However, this approach cannot be easily applied to SSI due to its dependency on sequential data, required to obtain the Hankel matrices used in the analysis. This presents a significant dilemma. During the application of standard SSI, these outliers remain present in the analysis, distorting the measurement of the response and result in a misidentification of the system. However, there is no simple mechanism to deal with such anomalies in SSI. Using a robust form of CCA, developed by Archambeau, Delannay and Verleysen [11], this paper exploits this extension and presents a robust version of Cov-SSI and demonstrates its capability on a simple dynamic system, with particular attention paid to the methods ability to combat outliers arising from sensor dropout.

2 COVARIANCE-DRIVEN STOCHASTIC SUBSPACE IDENTIFICATION (COV-SSI)

This section gives a brief overview of Cov-SSI for an output-only case, highlighting the presence of CCA in the method. This derivation is based on the descriptions given by Katayama [12], Van Overschee and De Moor [13] and Döhler and Mevel [14]. The reader is directed towards the aforementioned texts for a fuller derivation and specifics. Only the most important details are repeated here.

Consider a nth order state space model of a linear dynamic system, equivalent to a mechanical system with m degrees of freedom, such that $n = 2m$, in the form

$$\mathbf{x}_{k+1} = \mathbf{A}\mathbf{x}_k + w_k \tag{1a}$$

$$\mathbf{y}_k = \mathbf{C}\mathbf{x}_k + v_k \tag{1b}$$

where $\mathbf{y}_k \in \mathbb{R}^p$ is the output vector at time k, $\mathbf{x}_k \in \mathbb{R}^n$ is the internal state vector, $\mathbf{A}$ is the state matrix and $\mathbf{C}$ is the output matrix. $w_k \in \mathbb{R}^n$ and $v_k \in \mathbb{R}^p$ are samples of the process noise and measurement noise at time k, respectively. These are assumed to be stationary, white noise Gaussian with zero mean and covariance matrix

$$\mathbb{E}\left\{\begin{bmatrix} w_k \\ v_k \end{bmatrix} \begin{bmatrix} w_k^{\mathsf{T}} & v_k^{\mathsf{T}} \end{bmatrix}\right\} = \begin{bmatrix} \mathbf{Q} & \mathbf{S} \\ \mathbf{S}^{\mathsf{T}} & \mathbf{R} \end{bmatrix} \tag{2}$$

where $\mathbb{E}[\cdot]$ denotes the expectation.

Now consider a finite dataset, sampled from a stationary process, given by $\{\mathbf{y}_k, k = 0, 1, \ldots, N + 2j - 2\}$, where $j > 0$ and N is sufficiently large (i.e much larger than 2). Here $\mathbf{y}$ are response measurements of a dynamic system (e.g. accelerometer data) given some broadband excitation. As is common, the response, based on all measurement channels, p, can be arranged into a block Hankel Matrix using lags to give

$$\mathbf{Y}_{0|2j-1} \in \mathbb{R}^{2pj \times N} = \begin{bmatrix} \mathbf{Y}_{0|j-1} \\ \mathbf{Y}_{j|2j-1} \end{bmatrix} = \begin{bmatrix} \mathbf{Y}_p \\ \mathbf{Y}_f \end{bmatrix} \begin{matrix} \text{“Past”} \\ \text{“Future”} \end{matrix} \tag{3}$$

where $j > n$ and the number of columns of block matrices is N. The resultant cross-covariance matrix of the future with the past is therefore given by

$$\mathbf{\Sigma} = \frac{1}{N} \begin{bmatrix} \mathbf{Y}_p \\ \mathbf{Y}_f \end{bmatrix} \begin{bmatrix} \mathbf{Y}_p^{\mathsf{T}} & \mathbf{Y}_f^{\mathsf{T}} \end{bmatrix} = \begin{bmatrix} \mathbf{\Sigma}_{pp} & \mathbf{\Sigma}_{pf} \\ \mathbf{\Sigma}_{fp} & \mathbf{\Sigma}_{ff} \end{bmatrix} \tag{4}$$

where $\mathbf{\Sigma}_{pf}$ and $\mathbf{\Sigma}_{fp}$ are finite block Hankel matrices, and $\mathbf{\Sigma}_{ff}$, $\mathbf{\Sigma}_{pp}$ are finite block Toeplitz matrices. The canonical correlations $\mathbf{\Lambda} = \mathrm{diag}(\lambda_1, \cdots, \lambda_n)$ between the future and past covariance matrices are the singular values, obtained through the singular value decomposition (SVD), of the covariance matrix

$$\mathbf{\Sigma}_{ff}^{-1/2} \mathbf{\Sigma}_{fp} \mathbf{\Sigma}_{pp}^{-1/2} = \mathbf{U}\mathbf{\Lambda}\mathbf{V}^{\mathsf{T}} \backsimeq \hat{\mathbf{U}}\hat{\mathbf{\Lambda}}\hat{\mathbf{V}}^{\mathsf{T}} \tag{5}$$

such that,

$$\mathbf{\Sigma}_{fp} \backsimeq \mathbf{\Sigma}_{ff}^{1/2} \hat{\mathbf{U}}\hat{\mathbf{\Lambda}}\hat{\mathbf{V}}^{\mathsf{T}} \mathbf{\Sigma}_{pp}^{1/2} \tag{6}$$

where $\hat{\mathbf{\Lambda}}$ neglects sufficiently small singular values (canonical correlations) in $\mathbf{\Lambda}$, such that the resultant state vector has the dimension $n = \dim(\hat{\mathbf{\Lambda}})$. The block Hankel matrix, $\mathbf{\Sigma}_{fp}$, can be decomposed into the corresponding extended observability ($\mathcal{O}$) and controllability ($\mathcal{C}$) matrices using $\mathbf{\Sigma}_{fp} = \mathcal{O}\mathcal{C}$ where

$$\mathcal{O} = \mathbf{\Sigma}_{ff}^{1/2}\hat{\mathbf{U}}\hat{\mathbf{\Lambda}}^{1/2} \quad , \quad \mathcal{C} = \hat{\mathbf{\Lambda}}^{1/2}\hat{\mathbf{V}}^{\mathrm{T}}\mathbf{\Sigma}_{pp}^{1/2} \tag{7}$$

respectively and where rank($\mathcal{O}$) = rank($\mathcal{C}$) = n. The extended controllability and observability matrices can then be subsequently used to recover the state matrix $\mathbf{A}$ and output matrix $\mathbf{C}$ [1] and trivially, the modal properties in the usual manner for operational modal analysis. The reader is again directed towards [12, 13, 14].

3 PROBABILISTIC SSI

A probabilistic interpretation of CCA (PCCA) was developed by Bach and Jordan (2006) [9] using a latent variable model. This followed a similar approach taken by Tipping and Bishop (1999) [10] in their earlier development of probabilistic principal component analysis. The latent model presented by Bach and Jordan is shown graphically in Fig. 1 and given in Equations 8-10.

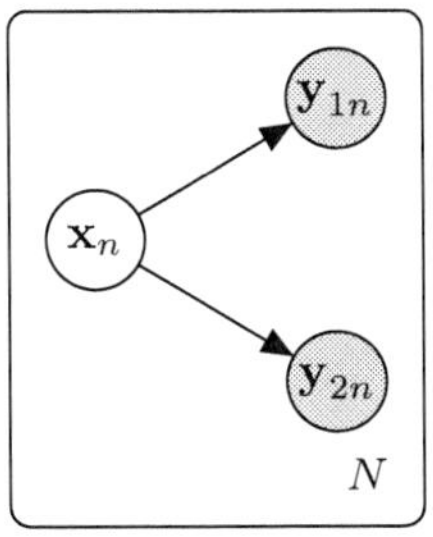

Fig. 1: Graphical latent model for Probabilistic Canonical Correlation Analysis (PCCA)

$$\mathbf{x}_n \sim \mathcal{N}(\mathbf{0}, \mathbb{I}_d) \tag{8}$$
$$\mathbf{y}_{1n}|\mathbf{x}_n \sim \mathcal{N}(\mathbf{W}_1\mathbf{x}_n + \boldsymbol{\mu}_1, \mathbf{\Sigma}_1) \tag{9}$$
$$\mathbf{y}_{2n}|\mathbf{x}_n \sim \mathcal{N}(\mathbf{W}_2\mathbf{x}_n + \boldsymbol{\mu}_2, \mathbf{\Sigma}_2) \tag{10}$$

where $\mathcal{N}(\boldsymbol{\mu}, \mathbf{\Sigma})$ represents a multivariate Gaussian with mean $\boldsymbol{\mu}$ and covariance $\mathbf{\Sigma}$, $\{\mathbf{x}_n\}_{n=1}^N$ is a set of lower dimensional latent variables, $\{\mathbf{y}_{1n}\}_{n=1}^N$ and $\{\mathbf{y}_{2n}\}_{n=1}^N$ are two sets of observations (with N being the total number of observations), $\mathbf{W}_1$ and $\mathbf{W}_2$ are the corresponding linear projections or 'weights', $\boldsymbol{\mu}_1$ and $\boldsymbol{\mu}_2$ the corresponding means, $\mathbf{\Sigma}_1$ and $\mathbf{\Sigma}_2$ the corresponding covariance matrices

Using this model, Bach and Jordan demonstrated that the MLE estimates of the transformations to the data space from the latent space, the weights ($\mathbf{W}$), contain all the necessary information obtained through the SVD. Furthermore, due to the nature of latent models, Bach and Jordan were also able to provide expectation-maximisation (EM) update equations as an alternative means of finding the MLE solution, negating the need for the SVD if required. Substituting this probabilistic method for traditional CCA in the SSI algorithm, it can be trivially shown that the MLE estimates for the weights $\widehat{\mathbf{W}}_1$ and $\widehat{\mathbf{W}}_2$ are equivalent to the observability

[1] The method described here for recovering the system matrices is one of many. See Stochastic Balanced Realisation Algorithm B, Chapter 8 in Katayama [12]

matrix and controllability matrix transposed, respectively, that are recovered in traditional SSI. Recall Equation 7. The MLE estimates for the weights are shown in Equations 11 and 12.

$$\widehat{\mathbf{W}}_1 = (\mathbf{\Sigma}_{ff})^{1/2}\mathbf{V}_{1d}\mathbf{M}_1 = \mathbf{\Sigma}_{ff}\mathbf{U}_{1d}\mathbf{M}_1 = \mathcal{O} \tag{11}$$

$$\widehat{\mathbf{W}}_2 = (\mathbf{\Sigma}_{pp})^{1/2}\mathbf{V}_{2d}\mathbf{M}_2 = \mathbf{\Sigma}_{pp}\mathbf{U}_{2d}\mathbf{M}_2 = \mathcal{C}^{\mathsf{T}} \tag{12}$$

where $\mathbf{M}_1, \mathbf{M}_2 \in \mathbb{R}^{d\times d}$ are arbitrary matrices such that $\mathbf{M}_1\mathbf{M}_2^{\mathsf{T}} = \mathbf{\Lambda}$, the columns of $\mathbf{U}_{1d}$ and $\mathbf{U}_{2d}$ are the first d canonical directions. Note U and V here are different from the left and right singular vectors defined previously. The reader should also note that throughout the rest of the paper, Cov-SSI and probabilistic SSI (solved using direct MLE estimation), will be synonymous with one another since Cov-SSI and the PCCA formulation are shown to be equivalent in the MLE case.

4 ROBUST PROBABILISTIC SSI

Following the probabilistic interpretation of CCA, Archambeau, Delannay and Verleysen [11] used a similar approach to construct a robust equivalent of PCCA. This alternative model relies on the assumption that the observed and latent variables can be modelled by a Students' T-distribution $\mathcal{S}(\boldsymbol{\mu}, \mathbf{\Sigma}, \nu)$ with mean $\boldsymbol{\mu}$ and covariance $\mathbf{\Sigma}$. The T-distribution has heavier tails than a Gaussian which are determined by the parameter, ν (degrees of freedom). The presence of heavier tails is preferable as it makes the T-distribution better equipped to handle outliers as it is more likely to capture them in the distribution. Using the T-distribution, Archambeau et. al. consequently defined the following probabilistic model:

$$p(\mathbf{x}_n) = \mathcal{S}(\mathbf{x}_n|\mathbf{0}, \mathbb{I}_d, \nu) \tag{13}$$

$$p(\mathbf{y}_{1n}|\mathbf{x}_n) = \mathcal{S}(\mathbf{y}_{1n}|\mathbf{W}_1\mathbf{x}_n + \boldsymbol{\mu}_1, \mathbf{\Sigma}_1, \nu) \tag{14}$$

$$p(\mathbf{y}_{2n}|\mathbf{x}_n) = \mathcal{S}(\mathbf{y}_{2n}|\mathbf{W}_2\mathbf{x}_n + \boldsymbol{\mu}_2, \mathbf{\Sigma}_2, \nu) \tag{15}$$

where $\{\mathbf{x}_n\}_{n=1}^N$ is a set of lower dimensional latent variables, $\{\mathbf{y}_{1n}\}_{n=1}^N$ and $\{\mathbf{y}_{2n}\}_{n=1}^N$ are two sets of observations (with N being the total number of observations), $\mathbf{W}_1$ and $\mathbf{W}_2$ are the corresponding linear projections or 'weights', $\boldsymbol{\mu}_1$ and $\boldsymbol{\mu}_2$ the corresponding means, $\mathbf{\Sigma}_1$ and $\mathbf{\Sigma}_2$ the corresponding covariance matrices and ν is the degrees of freedom. Making the set of latent variables explicit, the model can be reformulated into the following, more compact, form:

$$p(u_n) = \mathcal{G}\left(u_n|\tfrac{\nu}{2}, \tfrac{\nu}{2}\right) \tag{16}$$

$$p(\mathbf{x}_n|u_n) = \mathcal{N}\left(\mathbf{x}_n|\mathbf{0}, u_n^{-1}\mathbb{I}_d\right) \tag{17}$$

$$p(\mathbf{y}_n|\mathbf{x}_n, u_n) = \mathcal{N}\left(\mathbf{y}_n|\mathbf{W}\mathbf{x}_n + \boldsymbol{\mu}, u_n^{-1}\mathbf{\Sigma}\right) \tag{18}$$

where $\mathcal{G}(\cdot,\cdot)$ represents the Gamma distribution, $\mathbf{W} = [\mathbf{W}_1^{\mathsf{T}}, \mathbf{W}_2^{\mathsf{T}}]^{\mathsf{T}}$, $\boldsymbol{\mu} = [\boldsymbol{\mu}_1, \boldsymbol{\mu}_2]^{\mathsf{T}}$ and $\mathbf{\Sigma}$ a block covariance matrix containing $\mathbf{\Sigma}_1$ and $\mathbf{\Sigma}_2$ along the diagonal. The graphical model is shown in Figure 2.

Unlike the standard probabilistic result, in which the MLE can be obtained directly or using the EM algorithm, the MLE of the robust method can only be retrieved using EM. The intractability of the MLE comes as a result of the extra (Gamma) distribution present in the model. The robust CCA method, specifically the EM update equations for the parameters, is given and follows from the derivation in [11]. These equations are provided due to an error identified by the authors in the original derivation. The main variation can be seen in the definition of the covariance update in Equation 20c. The E-step is given by Equations 19a - 19d and the M-step by Equations 20a - 20d. In each iteration, the MLE estimate of ν is found by carrying out a line

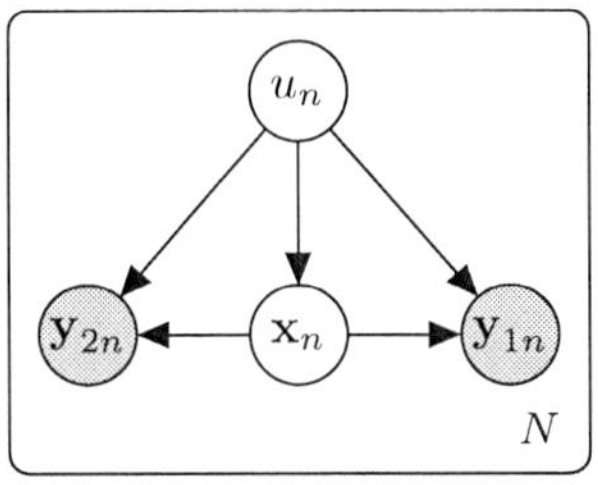

Fig. 2: Graphical model for latent interpretation of robust CCA

search on Equation 20d.

$$\bar{u}_n = \frac{D+\nu}{(\mathbf{y}_n-\boldsymbol{\mu})^{\mathsf{T}}\mathbf{A}(\mathbf{y}_n-\boldsymbol{\mu})+\nu} \tag{19a}$$

$$\log \tilde{u}_n = \psi(\tfrac{D+\nu}{2}) - \log\left(\frac{(\mathbf{y}_n-\boldsymbol{\mu})^{\mathsf{T}}\mathbf{A}(\mathbf{y}_n-\boldsymbol{\mu})+\nu}{2}\right) \tag{19b}$$

$$\bar{\mathbf{x}}_n = \mathbf{B}^{-1}\mathbf{W}^{\mathsf{T}}\Psi(\mathbf{y}_n-\boldsymbol{\mu}) \tag{19c}$$

$$\bar{\mathbf{S}}_n = \mathbf{B}^{-1} + \bar{u}_n\bar{\mathbf{x}}_n\bar{\mathbf{x}}_n^{\mathsf{T}} \tag{19d}$$

where $D = D_1 + D_2$, $\boldsymbol{\Psi} = \boldsymbol{\Sigma}^{-1}$, $\mathbf{A}^{-1} \equiv \mathbf{W}\mathbf{W}^{\mathsf{T}} + \boldsymbol{\Psi}^{-1}$, $\mathbf{B} \equiv \mathbf{W}\boldsymbol{\Psi}\mathbf{W}^{\mathsf{T}} + \mathbb{I}_d$, $\bar{u}_n \equiv \mathbb{E}\{u_n\}$, $\log\tilde{u}_n \equiv \mathbb{E}\{\log u_n\}$, $\bar{\mathbf{x}}_n \equiv \mathbb{E}\{\mathbf{x}_n\}$ and $\bar{\mathbf{S}}_n \equiv \mathbb{E}\{u_n\mathbf{x}_n\mathbf{x}_n^{\mathsf{T}}\}$. In (19b), $\psi(.)$ denotes the digamma function.

$$\boldsymbol{\mu} \leftarrow (\textstyle\sum_n \bar{u}_n(\mathbf{y}_n - \mathbf{W}\bar{\mathbf{x}}_n))(\sum_n \bar{u}_n)^{-1} \tag{20a}$$

$$\mathbf{W} \leftarrow (\textstyle\sum_n \bar{u}_n(\mathbf{y}_n - \boldsymbol{\mu})\bar{\mathbf{x}}_n^{\mathsf{T}})(\sum_n \bar{\mathbf{S}}_n)^{-1} \tag{20b}$$

$$\begin{aligned}\boldsymbol{\Sigma}_i \leftarrow (\tfrac{1}{N}\textstyle\sum_n\{&\bar{u}_n(\mathbf{y}_n-\boldsymbol{\mu})(\mathbf{y}_n-\boldsymbol{\mu})^{\mathsf{T}} - \bar{u}_n(\mathbf{y}_n-\boldsymbol{\mu})(\mathbf{W}\bar{\mathbf{x}}_n)^{\mathsf{T}} \\ &- \bar{u}_n(\mathbf{W}\bar{\mathbf{x}}_n)(\mathbf{y}_n-\boldsymbol{\mu})^{\mathsf{T}} + \mathbf{W}\bar{\mathbf{S}}_n\mathbf{W}^{\mathsf{T}}\})_{ii}\end{aligned} \tag{20c}$$

$$0 = 1 + \log(\tfrac{\nu}{2}) - \psi(\tfrac{\nu}{2}) + \tfrac{1}{N}\textstyle\sum_n\{\log\tilde{u}_n - \bar{u}_n\} \tag{20d}$$

where $i \in 1, 2$ such that $(\cdot)_{11}$ and $(\cdot)_{22}$ denote the matrix upper left block of size $D_1 \times D_1$ and the matrix lower right block of size $D_2 \times D_2$, respectively.

In a similar way to probabilistic SSI, robust CCA can be substituted for traditional CCA in Cov-SSI where the resultant estimates for the weights (obtained through EM) can be used to recover the observability matrix and controllability matrix transposed, respectively.

5 RESULTS AND DISCUSSION

To benchmark the identification performance of the new robust SSI method and compare it to Cov-SSI, response data was repeatedly generated using a generic 3 degree of freedom (DOF) linear dynamic system, with natural frequencies $\omega_n = \{24.2030, 44.7214, 58.4314\}$ and damping ratios $\zeta_n = \{0.0029, 0.0022, 0.0012\}$, due to a white noise excitation. The system was simulated 15 times at a sample rate of 1×10^3 Hz and generated 4086 samples.

To assess and compare the resistance of both methods to outlier influence during system identification, the same datasets were then artificially corrupted with outliers indicative of sensor drop out. The rate of sensor dropout was fixed at 0.1% per sensor channel, equivalent to 4 data points per channel, and were chosen at random. Dropout was simulated by setting the affected data point to some negative value which mimics a data acquisition system drifting to its lower supply rail.

Both methods were initially applied to the clean dataset and used to identify the system, assuming a model order of 6 (3 modes). The obtained natural frequencies can be seen in Figure 3a. It is evident, and was expected, that both methods perform comparably not only in their identification of the natural frequencies, but also in their overall variance. In the absence of any outliers the robust method should tend towards a Gaussian over the latent space recovering PCCA which is equivalent to Cov-SSI. The variation seen in the methods arises from the random realisations of the white noise forcing input.

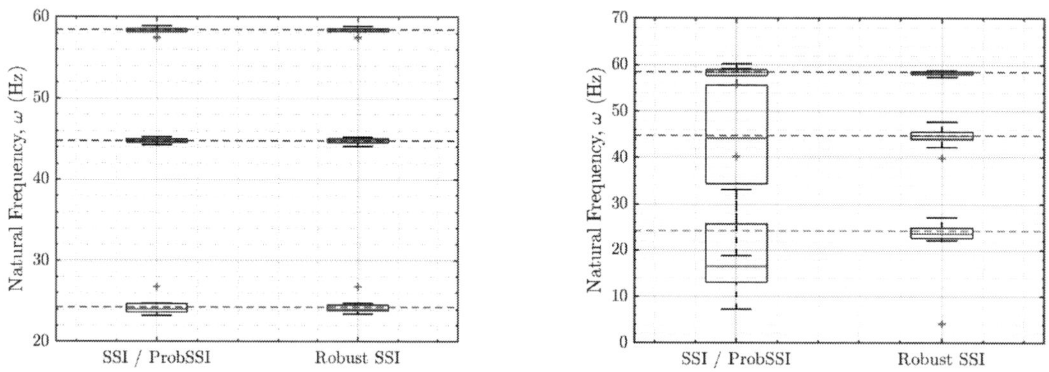

(a) (b)

Fig. 3: (a) Box and whisker plots of the natural frequency estimates identified from the clean dataset using Cov-SSI (left) and robust probabilistic SSI (right). (b) Box and whisker plots of the natural frequency estimates identified from the corrupted dataset using Cov-SSI (left) and robust probabilistic SSI (right).

The methods were then subsequently used on the corrupted dataset. The obtained natural frequencies are shown in Figure 3b. It is immediately apparent that the performance of standard SSI has dropped significantly. This has ultimately resulted in incorrect estimates of the natural frequency and a greater variance in the estimated poles of the state matrix A which defines the dynamics. In striking contrast, the robust method was still very capable of successfully identifying the system, albeit with a marginally increased variance in its results when directly compared to the clean case. A comparison of the two methods can be made in more detail when viewing the plot of identified identified continuous time complex system poles. This is shown in Figure 4.

For the results of standard SSI, the majority of the poles do not align with the true values. Several poles also have no corresponding conjugate and some would even imply unstable behaviour. It is known from the dynamics of the system that these results cannot be physically true as it is expected that poles should appear in conjugate pairs on the left hand half plane to ensure $\zeta < 0$. It is fair to conclude, therefore, that identification ability of standard SSI has been compromised due to the presence of outliers. Remembering that only 0.1% of the data has been distorted, this result is quite concerning when relying on SSI to perform operational identification. It is now also possible to contrast this result with that obtained by the robust method. It can be see that the poles identified by the robust algorithm, although still deviating in some cases, generally cluster close to the known true poles of the system. Additionally, all poles identified appear in conjugate pairs and in only one instance is non-physical damping found.

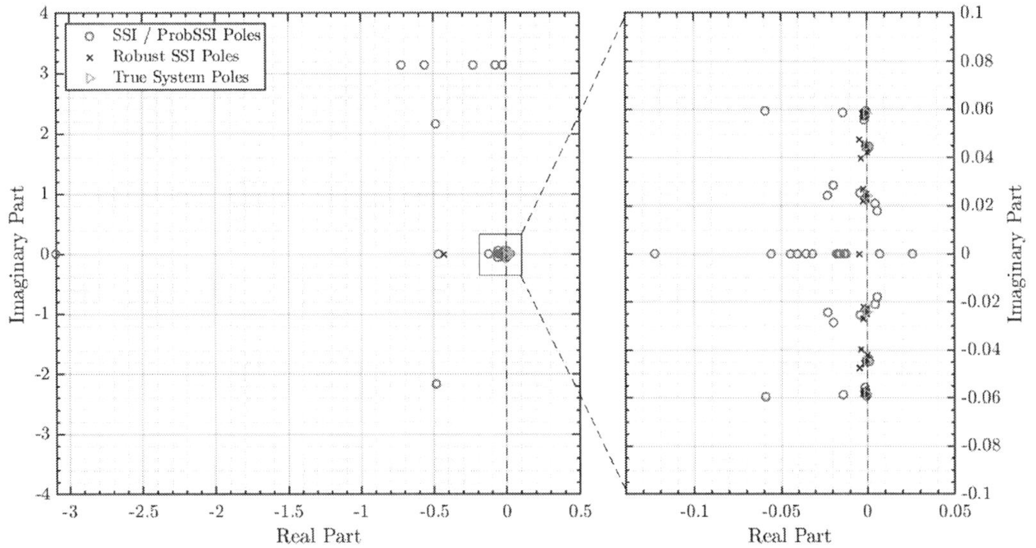

Fig. 4: A plot of the real and imaginary parts of the true complex system poles and the identified poles using standard SSI and Robust SSI.

6 CONCLUSIONS

In this paper, two novel methods have been presented. The first was a probabilistic interpretation of covariance-driven stochastic subspace identification (Cov-SSI) using probabilistic canonical correlations and the second was a robust interpretation of Cov-SSI using robust canonical correlations. This robust formulation was only made possible due to the probabilistic interpretation of SSI. The robust probabilistic SSI method was benchmarked against Cov-SSI and demonstrated to be a comparable standard of system identification on a clean dataset. The two methods were then tested on a corrupted version of the dataset, containing a subset of outliers. Whilst Cov-SSI performed poorly in its identification of the system, producing unrealistic results, the new robust method remained capable of confidently identifying the system. This evidence may lead to suggest that the robust method should be more regularly used over classical Cov-SSI.

Following this initial scope of work, future work will aim to apply this method to a selection of case studies, attempt to quantify its performance on different types of outliers seen in OMA, and conduct a rigorous exploration of the effect on the stabilisation diagram.

ACKNOWLEDGEMENTS

The authors gratefully acknowledge the support of the Engineering and Physical Sciences Research Council (EPSRC), UK through grant number EP/W002140/1. The authors also thank Ramboll Energy for their support in particular Ulf Tygesen with whom they work closely. For the purpose of open access, the author has applied a Creative Commons Attribution (CC BY) licence to any Author Accepted Manuscript version arising.

REFERENCES

[1] Peeters, B., & De Roeck, G. (2001). Stochastic system identification for operational modal analysis: A Review. *Journal of Dynamic Systems, Measurement and Control, Transactions of the ASME, 123*(4), 659–667.

[2] Reynders, E. P. B. (2012). System identification methods for (operational) modal analysis: Review and comparison. *Archives of Computational Methods in Engineering, 19*(1), 51–124.

[3] Reynders, E. P. B. (2021). Uncertainty quantification in data-driven stochastic subspace identification. *Mechanical Systems and Signal Processing, 151.*

[4] Nord, T. S., Petersen, Ø. W., & Hendrikse, H. (2019). Stochastic subspace identification of modal parameters during ice-structure interaction. *Philosophical Transactions of the Royal Society A: Mathematical, Physical and Engineering Sciences, 377*(2155).

[5] Farrar, C., & Worden, K. (2012). *Structural Health Monitoring: A Machine Learning Perspective.* John Wiley & Sons, Ltd.

[6] Worden, K., Cross, E. J., Barthorpe, R. J., Wagg, D. J., & Gardner, P. (2020). On digital twins, mirrors, and virtualizations: Frameworks for model verification and validation. *6.*

[7] Hughes, A. J., Barthorpe, R. J., Dervilis, N., Farrar, C. R., & Worden, K. (2021). A probabilistic risk-based decision framework for structural health monitoring. *Mechanical Systems and Signal Processing, 150.*

[8] Jolliffe, I. T. (1986). Principal component analysis and factor analysis. In *International encyclopaedia of education* (pp. 115–128).

[9] Bach, F. R., & Jordan, M. I. (2005). A probabilistic interpretation of canonical correlation analysis. *Dept. Statist., Univ. California, Berkeley, CA, Tech. Rep, 688,* 1–11.

[10] Tipping, M. E., & Bishop, C. M. (1999). Probabilistic principal component analysis. *Journal of the Royal Statistical Society: Series B (Statistical Methodology), 61*(3), 611–622.

[11] Archambeau, C., Delannay, N., & Verleysen, M. (2006). Robust probabilistic projections. *Proceedings of the 23rd International Conference on Machine Learning, 148,* 33–40.

[12] Katayama, T. (2005). *Subspace Methods for System Identification: A Realisation Approach.* Springer.

[13] Van Overschee, P., & De Moor, B. (1996). *Subspace Identification for Linear Systems.* Kluwer Academic.

[14] Döhler, M., & Mevel, L. (2013). Efficient multi-order uncertainty computation for stochastic subspace identification. *Mechanical Systems and Signal Processing, 38*(2), 346–366.

9th International Operational Modal Analysis Conference
iomac
July 3 - 6, 2022
Vancouver, Canada

ON THE ACCURACY OF THE MODAL PARAMETER ESTIMATES IN OMA

Thomas Thougaard Paulsen[1], Giuliano Coppotelli[2], and Ilmar Ferreira Santos [3]

[1] Ph.D. Student, Department of Civil and Mechanical Engineering at the Technical University of Denmark, ththpa@dtu.dk.
[2] Associate Professor, Department of Mechanical and Aerospace Engineering at the University of Rome "La Sapienza", giuliano.coppotelli@uniroma1.it.
[3] Professor, Department of Civil and Mechanical Engineering at the Technical University of Denmark, ifs@dtu.dk.

ABSTRACT

Modal identification procedures are used to evaluate the vibration properties of structures and can be divided into two branches, that is Input-Output and Output-Only analyses. Several methods are developed to assess the accuracy of the modal parameter estimates in the Input-Output framework, whereas deeper investigation is still needed to assess the confidence boundaries of Output-Only methods. Such accuracy of the estimates is generally given by comparing them with the expected set of modal parameters provided by a numerical model. In this paper, the accuracy of the modal parameters estimated using Output-Only techniques is investigated aided by the use of both time and frequency-based estimating methods coupled to a sensitivity analysis when varying data acquisition settings. Furthermore, insights into the robustness of the estimating process to the measuring chain is obtained from several independent tests and changes to the boundary conditions. Indeed, the experimental boundary conditions are altered by using materials with different elastic properties and different connection configurations. The uncertainties arising from the estimating process and the experimental setup mounting are evaluated for the natural frequencies, damping ratios, mode shapes through several modal assurance criterion formulations. The tests show that the accuracy of modal parameter estimates can be assessed and increased by weighting the similarity between multiple estimates of the same vibration mode. The accuracy depends on mounting configurations due to changes of structural properties. An evaluation of the overall accuracy of the modal parameter estimates finds that the accuracy is increased when information from multiple OMA algorithms is used.

Keywords: Operational Modal Analysis, Identification, Modal Parameters, Modal Assurance Criteria, Signal Processing

1. INTRODUCTION

Vibrations are present in all structures and in some cases the vibration amplitudes either deteriorate or damage the structure. Modal parameters are used to mathematically describe the vibration characteristics of a structure which can be used to assess if the vibrations have potential of causing damage to the structure. Therefore, it is desired to estimate the modal parameters for specific structures. Modal parameters can be estimated using numerous methodologies which assume different causes for measured vibrations to arise.

Experimental Modal Analysis (EMA) has been exploited for decades and often provides an indication of the expected accuracy for estimated modal parameters for example through an evaluation of the coherence function. In [1], an overview from Schwarz and Richardson describes different EMA testing and modal extraction techniques. The interest of estimating modal parameters from e.g., large scale structures, vehicles, rotating machines, etc., is continuously increasing and in many cases excitation forces that are not controllable nor measurable exist. These excitations are named ambient excitations and undermine the assumption of EMA methods that all input excitations are measurable. Reynders [2] provides a review and comparison of methods that are capable of extracting modal parameters both for inputs that are known and inputs that include or only consist of ambient excitations. When no measured input excitations exist, Operational Modal Analysis (OMA) techniques are used. OMA identification techniques are often tested on simulated responses for simple systems to grow confident with the accuracy of extracted modal estimates in experimental studies. As an example, Cara et al. [3] test an algorithm that calculates modal participation factors using simulated data of a spring, mass, and damper system before using the algorithm to calculate modal parameters and participation factors from a steel mast structure. In [4], Reynders uses data-driven stochastic subspace identification on a simulated response to estimate statistical uncertainties for the extracted modal parameters to navigate in the choice of input parameters to the algorithm. The algorithm is then applied to a concrete beam examined under destructive loading. The beam is found to have great changes in modal parameters as damage start to appear. Equivalent analyses on changing modal parameters for structures have spawned the idea of structural health monitoring. The monitoring requires use of automated methods in modal analysis which have been intensively tested. Automated OMA methods compare similarities between the modal parameter estimates obtained in a stabilization diagram to group modal parameters that describe the same vibration mode. In [5], Magalhães et al. use a structural health monitoring algorithm on a bridge. The algorithm calculates an Euclidian distance to define differences between modal parameter estimates. The modal parameters are grouped using a hierarchical cluster based on their similarities. A similar approach is presented in [6] with the addition of soft and hard validation criteria for modal parameter estimates to clear the stabilization diagram from certainly spurious poles. In [7], Covioli and Coppotelli test the use of gaussian mixture models for grouping modal parameters within a stabilization diagram and present the method to evaluate flight vibration test data.

In rotating machines, modal parameters depend on operational conditions in machine elements such as e.g., seals, bearings, impeller, etc. The dependency of operational conditions can be translated into a change of boundary conditions for a structure and has interesting prospects with the possibility of monitoring the changes made to modal parameters. The presented work aims to assess the accuracy of modal parameter estimates obtained from a simple and well-controlled experimental study. The evaluation of the accuracy is tested based on an assumption that independent of the method and acquisition settings used, extracted modal parameter estimates should be similar. To evaluate the similarity between the modal estimates, several formulations of modal assurance criteria are tested. The modal assurance criteria provide an estimate of the sensitivity for the modal parameters to the algorithm and number of samples used. The modal identification experiments are repeated to indicate the uncertainty of the modal parameter estimates with the possibility of calculating mean and standard deviations related to the identification routines. A comparison of the results to modal parameter extractions from EMA procedures is used to investigate if the obtained uncertainty can be related to the accuracy of the modal parameters from the OMA procedures. The estimated accuracy and uncertainty of the modal parameters are used to investigate if changing the boundary conditions of the beam can be detected through estimates of the modal parameters. Toward an automatic modal parameter extraction algorithm, the proposed investigation will be able to indicate the accuracy for modal parameters related to a specific vibration mode from the modal parameter estimates acquired in a stabilization diagram.

2. TEST FACILITY

The tests presented in this paper have been carried out at the Structural Dynamic Laboratory at the University of Rome "La Sapienza" as part of a collaboration between the University of Rome "La Sapienza" and the Technical University of Denmark. A cantilever beam made from aluminium is tested. In figure 1, the cantilever beam setup is presented including the positions of seven accelerometer measurement points. A total of four accelerometers are used, meaning that three accelerometers are rowing over two experiments. The accelerometers in positions two through four (Acc_{2-4}) in one experiment are moved to accelerometer positions five through seven (Acc_{5-7}) in a second experiment. A point mass equivalent to that of the accelerometer is positioned at the accelerometer locations which are not measured in that experiment. Seven different boundary conditions are tested. Of the seven boundary conditions, four configurations consist of a screw torque of 30 NM with the interface between a clamping device and beam being either **a**) steel - aluminium, **b**) rubber mat - aluminium, **c**) thin foam - aluminium, or **d**) thick foam - aluminium. One boundary condition with a screw torque of 10 NM for the interface type **e**) steel - aluminium is also tested along with two boundary conditions with a screw torque of 5 NM for the interfaces **f**) steel - aluminium and **g**) stiff foam - aluminium. The number of tests for each configuration are described in table 1.

Table 1. Summary of number of tests and experiments carried out for different clamping configurations.

	Clamping configurations						
Screw torque [NM]	30	30	30	30	10	5	5
Boundary vs. aluminium	Steel	Rubber mat	Thin foam	Thick foam	Steel	Steel	Stiff foam
Experiments	11	1	1	1	1	1	1
OMA Tests per experiment	76	76	76	76	76	76	76
EMA Tests per experiment	2	2	2	2	2	2	2

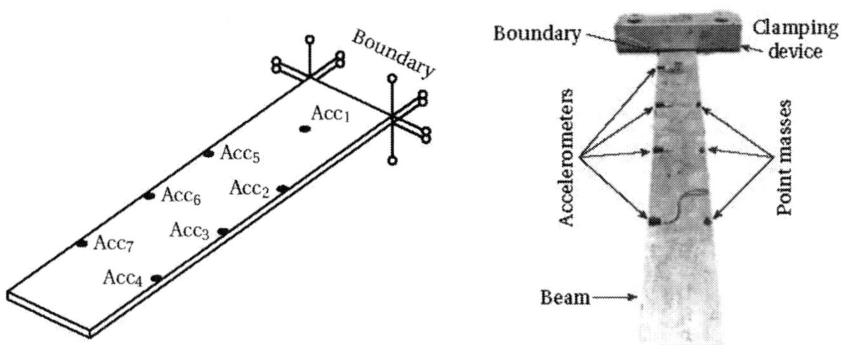

Figure 1. Presentation of the cantilever beam with accelerometer positions in schematic (left hand side) and a picture of the second rowing experimental configuration (right hand side).

The cantilever beam is tested under influence of two types of disturbances. The first type (i) of disturbance is an impact at the point Acc_5 and the second type of disturbance (ii) consists of multiple impacts distributed along the length and width of the beam, also at locations different from 1 to 7. When the first type of disturbance (i) is tested, both the impact force and the resulting accelerations are measured for 4 s with a sampling frequency of 1024 Hz. 8 impacts with high correlation are used in the data analyses. During the experiments with the second type of disturbance (ii), only the resulting accelerations are measured. The OMA identification experiments are carried out using 2^{17} (131,072) number of samples sampled at a sampling frequency of 1024 Hz. The consistency of the modal parameter estimates is tested by repeating the identification experiments and analyses 10 times under clamping configuration **a**).

3. ANALYSIS METHODOLOGIES

The two types of experiments (i) and (ii) require algorithms built on a different set of assumptions to obtain estimates of modal parameters. Experiments of type (i) require methods within the framework of Experimental Modal Analysis (EMA), while Operational Modal Analysis (OMA) methods are required to obtain estimates of modal parameters for the cantilever beam when experiments of type (ii) are used. The EMA algorithms considered in this analysis exist in the LMS Test.Lab Modal Analysis software package in the form of PolyMAX and Time MDOF. The software is described in a manual [8] and the idea behind PolyMAX is presented in [9]. The OMA algorithms used in this study are Frequency Domain Decomposition (FDD), Hilbert Transform Method (HTM), Stochastic Subspace Identification (SSI), and Balanced Realization (BR). The FDD and SSI methods are presented in [10] with the BR method being closely related to the SSI method. A description of the HTM method is available in [11].

3.1. Weighting methods

The resulting estimates of the modal parameters describing the vibrations of the cantilever beam are compared using different definitions of modal assurance criteria. Initially, the classical eigenvalue λ and an eigenvalue not considering the damping contribution of the modal parameter λ_{nD} are defined in Eq. (4). The vibration frequency ω_d and damping factor ζ are required for estimating the classical eigenvalue, while only the vibration frequency is used as the eigenvalue not considering damping.

$$\lambda = -\zeta \cdot \frac{\omega_d}{\sqrt{1-\zeta^2}} + i \cdot \omega_d, \qquad \lambda_{nD} = \omega_d \tag{1}$$

Vacher et al. [12] describe the use of different modal assurance criteria with its simplest form MAC in Eq. (5) able to define the collinearity between two monophase vectors $\mathbf{v}_1$ and $\mathbf{v}_2$.

$$\mathrm{MAC}(\mathbf{v}_1,\mathbf{v}_2) = \frac{|\mathbf{v}_1^*\mathbf{v}_2|^2}{\|\mathbf{v}_1\| \cdot \|\mathbf{v}_2\|} \tag{2}$$

Here, $\{\}^*$ denotes the conjugate transpose of a complex vector. The simplest form of the modal assurance criterium can be extended to compare vectors that are not monophase by adding a contribution that consider the collinearity between $(\mathbf{v}_1,\mathbf{v}_2)$ and $(\bar{\mathbf{v}}_1,\mathbf{v}_2)$ simultaneously, shown in Eq. (6).

$$\mathrm{MACX}(\mathbf{v}_1,\mathbf{v}_2) = \frac{\left(|\mathbf{v}_1^*\mathbf{v}_2| + |\mathbf{v}_1^{\mathrm{T}}\mathbf{v}_2|\right)^2}{\left(\mathbf{v}_1^*\mathbf{v}_1 + |\mathbf{v}_1^{\mathrm{T}}\mathbf{v}_1|\right) \cdot \left(\mathbf{v}_2^*\mathbf{v}_2 + |\mathbf{v}_2^{\mathrm{T}}\mathbf{v}_2|\right)} \tag{3}$$

$\{\}^{\mathrm{T}}$ denotes the transpose of a vector. If also the estimated eigenvalues are compared, an extension with the consideration of the free-decay responses can be written in Eq. (7). The eigenvalues to be compared can be the classical or the one that does not consider the damping contribution.

$$\mathrm{MACXP}(\mathbf{v}_1,\lambda_1,\mathbf{v}_2,\lambda_2) = \frac{\left(\frac{|\mathbf{v}_1^*\mathbf{v}_2|}{|\lambda_1^* + \lambda_2|} + \frac{|\mathbf{v}_1^{\mathrm{T}}\mathbf{v}_2|}{|\lambda_1 + \lambda_2|}\right)^2}{\left(\frac{\mathbf{v}_1^*\mathbf{v}_1}{2|\mathrm{Re}(\lambda_1)|} + \frac{|\mathbf{v}_1^{\mathrm{T}}\mathbf{v}_1|}{2|\lambda_1|}\right) \cdot \left(\frac{\mathbf{v}_2^*\mathbf{v}_2}{2|\mathrm{Re}(\lambda_2)|} + \frac{|\mathbf{v}_2^{\mathrm{T}}\mathbf{v}_2|}{2|\lambda_2|}\right)} \tag{4}$$

The modal assurance criterium using the eigenvalues that do not consider the damping contribution is denoted MACXPnD. The modal assurance criteria are used to compare estimates of the modal properties that describe the same vibration mode. In figure 2, a schematic of the use of the modal assurance criteria is presented. It includes a symmetric matrix that is obtained by comparing an estimated modal parameter set from multiple modal analysis algorithms. A resulting modal parameter estimate from one experiment is wished to be obtained using the information provided by all the tested methods. By a summation through the rows of the symmetric matrix and a normalization of the resulting vector, the modal parameter estimates can be weighted by a vector $\mathbf{w}$. The obtained weights describe how comparable a modal parameter set is to estimates from other methods. If the value of a method is close to one, the

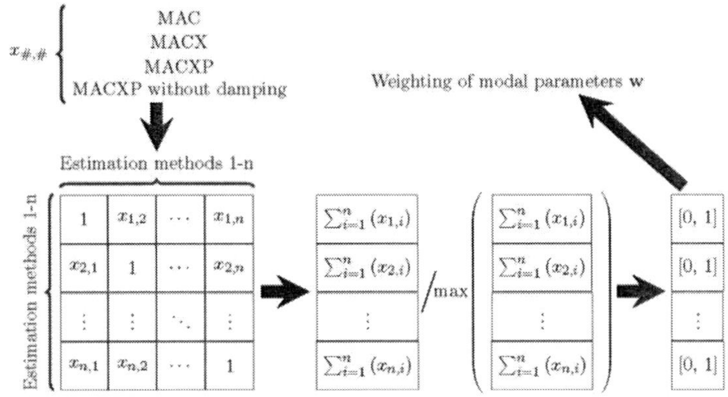

Figure 2. Schematic of modal parameter estimate comparison through modal assurance criteria to obtain a weighting vector.

results from this method compare well to other estimations and vice versa. The weights can then be used to reduce the influence on the resulting modal parameter set from modal parameter estimates that compare little to estimates from other estimation methods. Here, the weights are used in the calculation of statistical properties that estimate the resulting modal parameter set and help evaluate the uncertainty of the obtained estimates. Illustrated for the vibration frequency, the mean value μ and standard deviation σ can be calculated using the weighting vector as described in Eqs. (8) and (9), respectively. Regular mean μ and standard deviation σ can be obtained by assuming an equal weighting for all estimation methods [13].

$$\mu(\boldsymbol{\omega}_d) = \frac{1}{\sum_{i=1}^{n}(w_i)} \cdot \sum_{i=1}^{n} (\omega_{d,i} \cdot w_i) \tag{5}$$

$$\sigma(\boldsymbol{\omega}_d) = \sqrt{\frac{1}{\sum_{i=1}^{n}(w_i) - 1} \cdot \sum_{i=1}^{n} \left(\left(\omega_{d,i} - \mu(\boldsymbol{\omega}_d) \right)^2 \cdot w_i \right)} \tag{6}$$

4. RESULTS

Experimental acceleration signals are tested using multiple OMA methods to investigate if a comparison between estimated modal parameters provides insights on the accuracy of the results from that experimental test. Figure 3 presents modal estimates for vibration mode 1 from all OMA methods used on acceleration signals acquired from one experimental test. Signal block lengths varying from 2^0 s to 2^4 s with total signal lengths varying from 1 block length until 2^7 (128) s are evaluated for the FDD and HTM algorithms (for a signal block length of 1 s, total signal lengths of 1 s, 2 s, 4 s, 8 s, 16 s, 32 s, 64 s, and 128 s are used). Total signal lengths from 2^0 s to 2^7 s are evaluated for the BR and SSI algorithms. The modal estimates include the vibration frequency, damping factor, and mode shape.

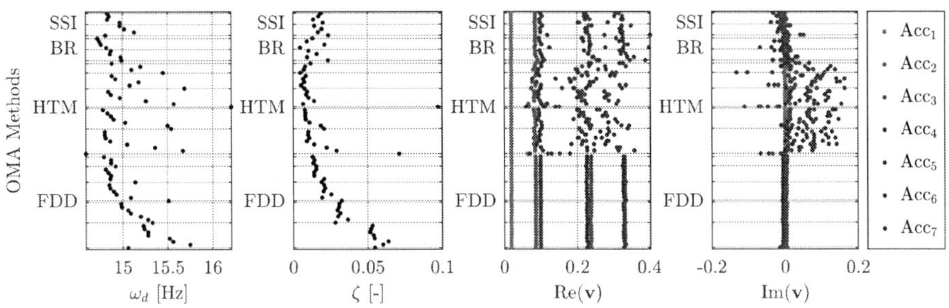

Figure 3. Modal parameter estimates for vibration mode 1 depending on method and data acquisition settings.

The vibration mode is normalized at Acc_1 and scaled by a factor of 0.02. This is done to ensure that the vibration mode is not phase-shifted by a change of the point with maximum deflection for the estimated mode shape. The resulting estimates of the modal parameters do show differences in the modal parameter estimates that are both dependent on the method and data acquisition settings used.

The similarities between the estimates of each vibration mode are evaluated using the modal assurance criteria described in section 3.3 to visualize differences between the modal parameters from the different OMA methods. The MACXP comparison of vibration modes 1 through 3 are presented in figure 4. As indicated by figure 3, the MACXP depicts that the estimated modal parameters for vibration mode 1 show differences between estimation methods and data acquisition parameters used. The MACXP also indicates that the vibration modes 1 through 3 are differently affected by the estimation methods and data acquisition settings. The visualization shows that the estimated modal parameters for vibration mode 3 has most differences depending on estimation methods and data acquisition parameters, the modal parameters for vibration mode 1 have slightly less differences, while the estimations for vibration mode 2 are least affected by the methods and acquisition parameters used.

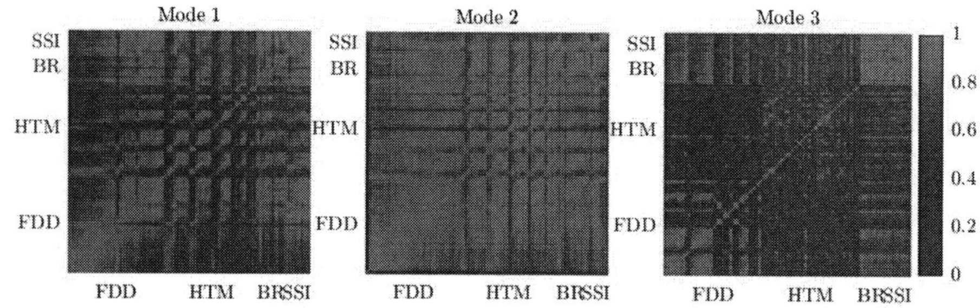

Figure 4. MACXP values for modal parameter estimates depending on algorithm and data acquisition settings for vibration modes 1 through 3.

The visual comparison of the modal parameter estimates is used to formulate a weighting vector to compensate for differences between the estimates when calculating statistical parameters. An analysis about which part of the estimates that introduce the differences is conducted by comparing the resulting weightings from the different modal assurance criteria in figure 5. The MACX and MACXPnD present high and similar weights for the estimated modal parameters describing vibration mode 1 which indicate that both the estimated mode shape and vibration frequency are quite similarly estimated between the estimation methods and data acquisition parameters used. The weights are slightly lower for the MAC results when the estimations contain a complex part in the mode shape vector which is mostly pronounced in the HTM algorithm. This illustrates that the MAC should be used with care as described in [12]. The MACXP presents significant differences between the resulting weights which is expected from the illustration of the compared methods from figure 4. The large difference between the MACXP weights and the weights from the other modal assurance criteria must be explained in the estimation of the damping coefficient. Partly because the damping coefficient estimates are known to carry a high uncertainty and partly because the contribution is provided with a larger weight in the $\frac{|v_1^* v_2|}{|\lambda_1^* + \lambda_2|}$ term of the MACXP expression due to smaller numbers in scale of the denominator. The comparisons between

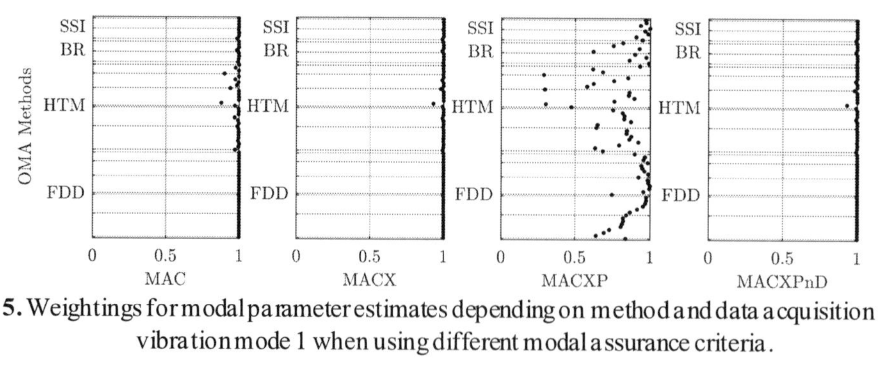

Figure 5. Weightings for modal parameter estimates depending on method and data acquisition settings for vibration mode 1 when using different modal assurance criteria.

the modal assurance criteria show the same tendency for vibration modes 2 and 3. However, the differences between the weights are not as pronounced for the MACXP of vibration mode 2.

The weighted mean and standard deviation are calculated from the MACXP for each repeated experiment to test the consistency between the estimations. The resulting weighted means of the estimations are used to generate a weighted mean and standard deviation for the estimations across all the repeated experiments using the MACXP. The two statistical evaluations allow one to focus on uncertainties in different parts of the investigation. The distributions calculated from the individual experiments primarily present the uncertainties from the methods and data acquisition parameters used to estimate the modal parameters while the distribution of the mean values primarily express uncertainties in the experimental setup and testing method. Additionally, the distributions are compared by subtracting the mean from each distribution and scaling the standard deviation by the mean value of the distribution to which it belongs. The scaled standard deviation provides an estimate of the precision for the modal parameter estimate through the relative error. Figure 6 visualizes the resulting probability density functions for the vibration frequency estimate of 10 repeated experiments. A visual comparison of the statistics for the individual experiments finds that for each vibration mode the probability density functions have very similar tendencies. The similarity of the statistical parameters indicates that the tendency found in one experiment provide statistical parameters that can describe the uncertainty of the estimated modal parameters from that experiment. The distribution for the mean estimates of the repeated experiments MACXP shows a much smaller scaled standard error which indicates that the differences in the estimations by repeating the experiment are smaller than the differences between the estimates obtained from changing the method or acquisition parameters used. The MACXP distributions indicate that the repeatability of the estimated vibration frequency is lowest for vibration mode 1 while the repeatability is similar for vibration modes 2 and 3. This is not exactly the conclusion that would be derived from evaluating the distribution for one experiment due to a higher uncertainty in the methods and data acquisition parameters used for vibration mode 3. It is observed that the uncertainty of the damping coefficient is substantially higher than for the estimations of the eigenfrequency.

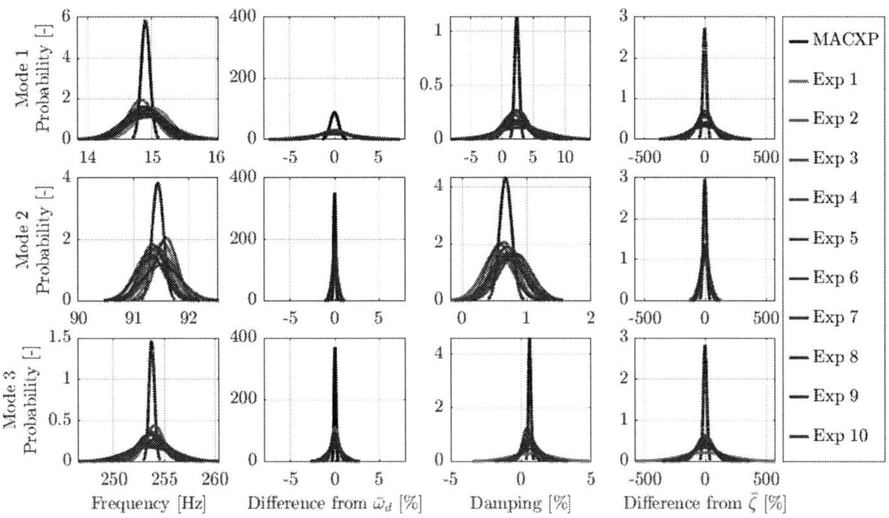

Figure 6. Comparison of probability density functions from MACXP weighting of modal parameter estimates for vibration modes 1 through 3 plotted with the MACXP weighting of the resulting mean values.

Distributions for the modal parameter estimates from the EMA are calculated with the weighting directly applied to the resulting estimations provided by the PolyMAX and Time MDOF algorithms since only two estimations are available for each repeated experiment. For the OMA, different weighting methods i.e., unitary (Mean), MAC, MACX, MACXP, and MACXPnD, are used to generate an estimation of the modal parameters for each repeated experiment. Distributions for the estimations from the repeated experiments are then calculated using the same weighting method as the one used in each repeated experiment. The influence on the distributions from the weighting methods is thereby analysed. Figure 7 illustrates that the use of a weighting method for statistical parameters reduces the uncertainties in the resulting estimation from an experiment when there are large differences in estimated modal parameters that are assumed to be similar. As the differences between the estimated modal parameters are largest for vibration modes 1 and 3 using the OMA methods, these are also observed to carry the greatest alteration of the resulting estimation by the weighting methods. Additionally, the alterations are observed to tend towards the estimates obtained from the EMA estimations. This can be explained by the tendency that the accuracy of the estimates from EMA in general is better than for the OMA methods tested in this paper. For vibration mode 1, it is indicated by the scaled standard deviation of the estimated vibration frequency that the uncertainties are substantially larger for the OMA methods than for the EMA methods and that the resulting estimations also differ. Therefore, the estimation accuracy must be assumed higher for the EMA results than for the OMA results when evaluating the vibration frequency for mode 1. On the other hand, the scaled standard deviation of the estimated damping factor for vibration mode 1 indicates that the accuracy is higher for the OMA methods than for the EMA methods. If a clamping configuration of an aluminium beam is appropriate, the damping factor will primarily consist of the damping factor for the material. In [14] (6.2.1), the clamping configuration of a steel beam is discussed. Here, it is indicated that the tests should present a damping coefficient of approximately 0.001 to 0.002. Following a Wicket plot in [14] (Fig. X2.1), it is presented that the damping coefficient estimate increases slightly if a stiff material is replaced by a slightly less stiff material. Since the steel is a stiff material and the stiffness of aluminium is slightly lower compared to that of steel, the damping coefficient is expected to be higher but still in the same order of magnitude. This indicates that the accuracy of the EMA methods is much higher than for the OMA methods. Therefore, an upper limit for the scaled standard deviation that provide a useful interpretation of the accuracy might exist.

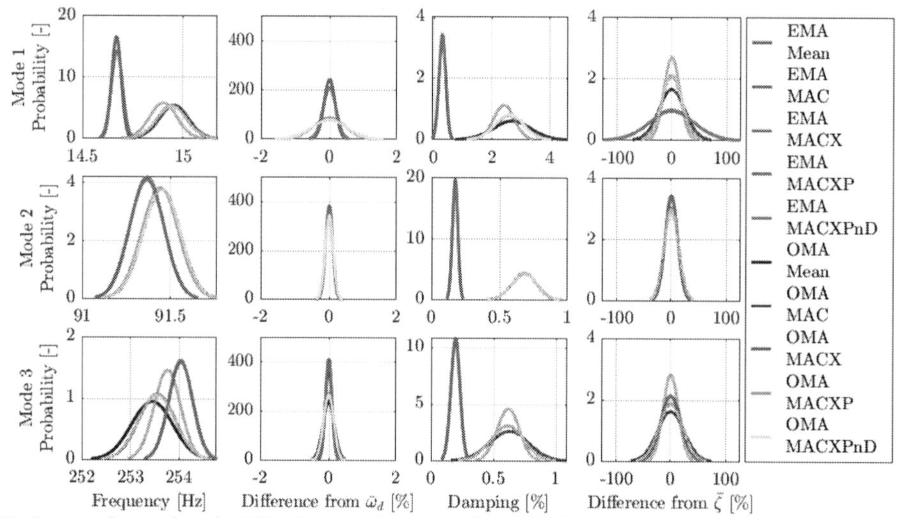

Figure 7. Comparison of probability density functions from different weightings used on modal parameter estimates from repeated experiments for modes 1 through 3.

The indications that the statistical tendencies found in one experiment can be used to describe the general uncertainties in a repeated set of experiments and that the MACXP weighting reduces the uncertainty are used to test the influence on the modal parameter estimates by changes to the boundary conditions for the cantilever beam. Figure 8 presents the general tendency that when the estimated vibration frequency is reduced the uncertainty of the estimation of the vibration frequency increases. The tendency is clearest for vibration modes 2 and 3 for which the uncertainty is visibly the smallest. The higher uncertainty for smaller eigenfrequency could be related to the scale of the acceleration signals. When the vibration frequency is lowered, the relative contribution of the modal mass for that vibration mode is increased which in turn will provide lower accelerations from the same disturbance force. This can harm the quality of the signal. However, the uncertainties indicate that a difference of the vibration frequency is visible in the data as a result of changing boundary conditions. The estimates of the damping factor have high uncertainties for all modes. This indicates that the accuracy of the damping factor from the estimations is that low that changes because of changing boundary conditions cannot be deemed significant.

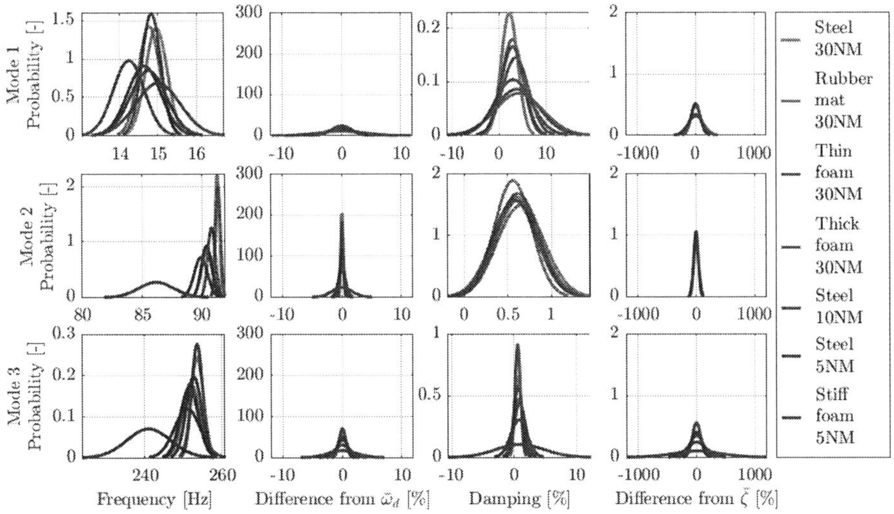

Figure 8. Comparison of probability density functions from MACXP weighting of modal parameter estimates for vibration modes 1 through 3 under different clamping conditions.

When estimations from OMA are tested, often a single method is used. It is therefore tested what the accuracy of the modal parameter estimates is compared to the estimate from all OMA methods when the mean value from the EMA methods is used as benchmark. The estimates from each method are individually weighted using the MACXP. From the experimental tests and the statistical analysis, the overall accuracy of the vibration frequency is 0.67 % for FDD, 1.00 % for HTM, 1.07 % for BR, 1.16 % for SSI, and 0.75 % for a combination of the methods. The damping ratio has the overall accuracy of 476 % for FDD, 591 % for HTM, 263 % for BR, 300 % for SSI, and 456 % combining the methods. A MACX comparison of the mode shapes yields 0.995 for FDD, 0.993 for HTM, 0.994 for BR, 0.995 for SSI, and 0.996 for a combination of all methods. It is observed that the combined estimate using information from all tested methods is enhanced by the methods which have more accurate predictions for each modal parameter. As indicated by figure 5, the evaluation of the overall accuracy presents very accurate estimates of the vibration frequency and mode shapes for both the individual and combined OMA methods, whereas the damping estimate is far from accurate for a cantilever beam. Table 2 presents comparisons of estimates for vibration mode 1 of one experiment with clamping configuration **a**).

Table 2. Comparison of estimates from different OMA methods to the overall OMA and EMA estimates for vibration mode 1. $\mathbf{Acc_1}$ is left out since this is used as reference for comparing the mode shapes.

Screw torque	30 NM							
Boundary	Steel vs. aluminium							
Methods	ω_d [Hz]	ζ [%]	Acc_2	Acc_3	Acc_4	Acc_5	Acc_6	Acc_7
FDD MACXP	15.01	2.798	0.07-0.00i	0.23-0.01i	0.34+0.00i	0.09-0.00i	0.25-0.01i	0.33+0.00i
HTM MACXP	14.95	2.151	0.07+0.00i	0.19+0.05i	0.24+0.09i	0.08+0.01i	0.19+0.06i	0.23+0.09i
BR MACXP	14.84	1.356	0.09+0.00i	0.24+0.01i	0.33-0.00i	0.10-0.00i	0.24+0.00i	0.34-0.01i
SSI MACXP	14.92	1.787	0.07-0.00i	0.23-0.00i	0.34-0.01i	0.09-0.00i	0.25+0.00i	0.33-0.01i
OMA MACXP	14.96	2.271	0.07-0.00i	0.22+0.01i	0.30+0.03i	0.09+0.00i	0.23+0.02i	0.30+0.03i
PolyMAX	14.64	0.236	0.12+0.10i	0.27+0.06i	0.30-0.06i	0.10+0.01i	0.22-0.08i	0.23-0.23i
Time MDOF	14.63	0.257	0.11+0.12i	0.27+0.10i	0.33-0.01i	0.10+0.02i	0.25-0.05i	0.29-0.20i

5. CONCLUSIONS

A method able to weigh modal parameter estimates to provide statistical parameters that indicate its accuracy has been tested for a cantilever beam with changing clamping configurations. The method compares modal parameter estimates to reduce the influence from differing estimates to achieve an increased accuracy which is demonstrated in a repeated experiment for a single clamping configuration.

The indicated uncertainty from the repeated experiments is found to be equivalently described by the uncertainty explained from a single experiment and consistent for each repetition of the experiment. The uncertainties are helpful when evaluating if an accurate estimation of the modal parameters is obtained.

The evaluation of the method indicates that the accuracy of modal estimates from the identification methods used in this work is affected by the clamping configuration. Structural dynamical properties being the stiffness, inertia, or dissipation impact the signal propagation through the structure in question. The method indicates for a specific mode that when the vibration frequency of a mode is reduced, the accuracy of the estimated vibration frequency is also reduced. The signal propagation from the same input is lowered when the modal stiffness is reduced and the modal mass is increased.

The accuracy of modal parameter estimates is found to benefit from information of multiple OMA methods compared to using a modal parameter estimate from one methodology only. The evaluation of the accuracy also presents far more accurate estimates of the vibration frequency and mode shapes compared to that of the damping ratio when a cantilever beam is examined.

In a stabilization diagram, the method can be used to weigh poles that possibly describe a vibration mode of interest. The weighting of a compared set of modal parameter estimates can thereby both indicate the uncertainty of the resulting modal parameter estimate and possibly provide a more accurate estimate. The weighting is also suitable for a validation criterion in an automated parameter selection for instance as to define the Euclidian distance in a hierarchical cluster algorithm.

ACKNOWLEDGEMENTS

Thanks to the research team of the Structural Dynamic Laboratory at the University of Rome "La Sapienza" for providing the opportunity to do a research exchange with the Technical University of Denmark. The funding received from Reinholdt W. Jorck og Hustrus Fond is also acknowledged.

REFERENCES

[1] Schwarz, B. J., & Richardson, M. H. (1999). Experimental modal analysis. *CSI Reliability week*, 35(1), 1-12.

[2] Reynders, E. (2012). System identification methods for (operational) modal analysis: review and comparison. *Archives of Computational Methods in Engineering*, 19(1), 51-124.

[3] Cara, F. J., Juan, J., Alarcón, E., Reynders, E., & De Roeck, G. (2013). Modal contribution and state space order selection in operational modal analysis. *Mechanical Systems and Signal Processing*, 38(2), 276-298.

[4] Reynders, E. P. (2021). Uncertainty quantification in data-driven stochastic subspace identification. *Mechanical Systems and Signal Processing*, 151, 107338.

[5] Magalhães, F., Cunha, Á., & Caetano, E. (2009). Online automatic identification of the modal parameters of a long span arch bridge. *Mechanical Systems and Signal Processing*, 23(2), 316-329.

[6] Reynders, E., Houbrechts, J., & De Roeck, G. (2012). Fully automated (operational) modal analysis. *Mechanical Systems and Signal Processing*, 29, 228-250.

[7] Covioli, J. V., & Coppotelli, G. (2021). On the use of Gaussian Mixture Models for Automated Modal Parameters Estimation. In: *AIAA Scitech 2021 Forum* (p. 1035).

[8] LMS Test.Lab (2012). *The LMS Test.Lab Modal Analysis manual*. Leuven, LMS International.

[9] Peeters, B., Van der Auweraer, H., Guillaume, P., & Leuridan, J. (2004). The PolyMAX frequency-domain method: a new standard for modal parameter estimation? *Shock and Vibration*, 11(3-4), 395-409.

[10] Brincker, R., & Ventura, C. (2015). Introduction to operational modal analysis. John Wiley & Sons.

[11] Agneni, A., Crema, L. B., & Coppotelli, G. (2010). Output-only analysis of structures with closely spaced poles. *Mechanical Systems and Signal Processing*, 24(5), 1240-1249.

[12] Vacher, P., Jacquier, B., & Bucharles, A. (2010, September). Extensions of the MAC criterion to complex modes. In: *Proceedings of the international conference on noise and vibration engineering* (pp. 2713-2726).

[13] Bendat, J. S., & Piersol, A. G. (2011). Random data: analysis and measurement procedures. John Wiley & Sons.

[14] American Society for Testing and Materials. (2010). *Standard test method for measuring vibration-damping properties of materials*. ASTM International.

MACHINE LEARNING APPLICATIONS IN OMA

9th International Operational Modal Analysis Conference
iomac
July 3 - 6, 2022
Vancouver, Canada

EVALUATION OF AN AUTOMATIC OMA IDENTIFICATION METHOD ON ROTATING MACHINERY

Gustavo Chaves Storti[I], Nathali Rolon Dreher[II], Tiago Henrique Machado[III]

[1] M.Sc., Ph.D. student, School of Mechanical Engineering, University of Campinas (UNICAMP), gucstorti@gmail.com.
[2] M.Sc., Ph.D. student, School of Mechanical Engineering, University of Campinas (UNICAMP), nathali.r.d@hotmail.com.br.
[3] Ph. D., Associate Professor at School of Mechanical Engineering, University of Campinas (UNICAMP), tiagomh@fem.unicamp.br

ABSTRACT

Classical input-output experimental modal analysis was focused on solving machine vibration problems. However, the improvement of techniques for analysis evolved to subsequent identification of modal parameters of structures under operational conditions, enabling the update of finite element models and structural modification to improve reliability, allowing a more integrated physical and mathematical approach. Meanwhile, large-scale industry applicability has led to the need for more efficient, robust, and lower-cost analysis. To meet new demands, rapid data analysis and verification of modal properties for health monitoring have become a powerful tool in the industry. The comprehensive use of rotating machinery, with notable application in wind generators, but also in more common components such as compressors, pumps, and turbines, requires efficient and fast ways of applying OMA. In this way, the objective of the paper is to propose the use of clustering techniques already known, such as k-means and hierarchical clustering, with the identification of relevant parameters extracted from the stabilization diagram of the stochastic subspaces identification (SSI) of experimental signals, treated to remove outliers using random forests for rapid identification of the modal parameters. Data from a test rig rotor with hydrodynamic bearings were used to evaluate the algorithm. The results show that modal identification parameters based on damping and vibration modes, without removing the influence of harmonics tend to be very biased and show a large standard deviation for the analysis of the extracted frequency, allowing only an indication of the mode location region in the spectrum.

Keywords: multi-stage clustering, automatic operational modal analysis, time-domain techniques.

1. INTRODUCTION

The modal study of equipment and systems has its foundations well discussed and documented, as shown in (Silva & Maia, 1999). Classical methods of modal analysis, in general, consist of analyzing the system through a transfer function, i.e., establishing a relationship between inputs and outputs, describing the system as a filter, and defining its parameters, as natural frequencies, damping factors, and vibration modes. However, a clear limitation of this approach is that necessarily all inputs and outputs must be known, or better said, the methods are deterministic. In practice, systems that cannot be correctly isolated present great difficulty to be tested by the methods known as experimental modal analysis (EMA) (Brincker & Ventura, 2015).

For this reason, different approaches from the deterministic method were proposed and the initial focus was on systems that could not have their behavior completely detached from the environment. The excitations to which the equipment is subjected in operation can have different sources and often do not have a defined behavior, making them difficult (or even impossible) to be measured and reproduced. One of the pioneering studies was done in (CLARKSON & MERCER, 1965), for aerospace application, but it was with the end of the 1990s that there was a rapid popularization, mainly through the NeXT (James et al., 1995) study, which made it possible for EMA identification methods to be extended to Operational Modal Analysis (OMA) as well. Thus, OMA is a method known as output-only, since the modal parameters are estimated only from the dynamic response of the structure, without necessarily knowing which excitation the system is subjected to. Using OMA, the modal parameters reflect the operating behavior of the structure, with all components assembled. For this reason, it has been widely applied in aerospace (Goursat et al., 2011), automotive (Guillaume et al., 2003), civil engineering (Rainieri & Fabbrocino, 2010), and others.

The requirement of a less controlled environment for modal analysis led to new applications being achieved. For example, nowadays, in addition to improving the accuracy of mathematical models, the application of machine health monitoring has gained strength. With this most popular application, the method capabilities have expanded, ranging from signal analysis techniques for identifying faults in rolling bearings, such as (Randall & Antoni, 2011), to Bayesian statistical methods (Brownjohn et al., 2019). Notably, several recent works have brought attention to emerging methods such as (Poddar & Shunmugam, 2019; Wu et al., 2020), advancing the study of SHM by combining OMA with automated algorithms for obtaining the modal parameters.

As is known, the study of rotating machines also has its separate chapter in several methods, mainly due to the dynamic characteristics which these machines present in operation. References such as (Brandt & Linderholt, 2012; R. Liu et al., 2018), already demonstrated the challenge of applying identification techniques and OMA in rotating machines and the challenge of automatic identification of physical modes. Aspects such as gyroscopic effects, critical speeds, frequencies proportional to the shaft's speed (harmonics), modes with large damping, foundation modes, and others, that involve the behavior of rotating machines tend to require adequate treatment to have an accurate identification of modes of interest.

As a result, both time and frequency domain techniques can be explored and analyzed in rotating machinery to provide as much information as possible. In OMA, the classical FDD (Brincker et al., 2001) technique based on spectral density is widely used as a preliminary signal reference. The stochastic subspace method, a reference for analyzing the system in the time domain, is applied in several works both in its covariance-driven (Brownjohn et al., 2010) and data-driven (Peeters & De Roeck, 1999) variants, due to its mathematical formulation and the ease of extracting system parameters, which later are used as features in several automatic identification algorithms (He et al., 2021).

Therefore, the objective of this work is to explore clustering techniques combined with statistical data to make a systematic extraction of modal parameters analyzing only the response, as fundamentals demonstrated in (Neu et al., 2017) for a highly damping composite cantilever beam in different signal to noise ratio conditions, but here exploring the proposed multi clustering technique and its parameters for a rotating machine supported by hydrodynamic bearings, and including a substantial step for outlier removal based on isolation forests (F. T. Liu et al., 2008), a promising method that tends to improve the values extracted from the stabilization diagram.

2. METHODOLOGY

In this section, a quick contextualization of the clustering methods and the adapted algorithm with the outlier analysis will be described. For a reference on OMA identification methods, it is suggested to consult references such as (Magalhães & Cunha, 2011; Storti, Carrer, et al., 2021).

2.1. Clustering Techniques

Machine learning is the ability of artificial intelligence to acquire knowledge by extracting patterns from raw data (Goodfellow et al., 2016), and unsupervised learning is one of machine learning's divisions. The data input space is structured in such a way that a certain pattern occurs more often than others and the aim of unsupervised learning is to find these regularities (Ethem Alpaydin, 2014). This task can be accomplished by clustering techniques, whose goal, considering a set of N unlabeled D-dimensional samples $\boldsymbol{X} = \{\boldsymbol{x}_1, \boldsymbol{x}_2, \ldots, \boldsymbol{x}_N\}$, is to group similar samples forming clusters.

K-means is one of the most popular clustering algorithms and is explained here based on (Bishop, 2006). Its goal is to separate a set of samples $\boldsymbol{X}$ into K clusters, assuming the value of K is given. One can see the cluster as a group of samples whose distances from each other are small compared to the distances with samples from other clusters, which is formalized by introducing a set of D-dimensional vectors $\boldsymbol{\mu}_k$, where $k = 1, \ldots, K$, being $\boldsymbol{\mu}_k$ a prototype associated with the kth cluster and representing its center, so that the quadratic sum of the distances of each sample to its nearest $\boldsymbol{\mu}_k$ vector is minimal.

For each sample $\boldsymbol{x}_n$, a set of binary indicator variables $r_{nk} \in \{0,1\}$ is introduced describing to which of the K clusters the sample $\boldsymbol{x}_n$ was assigned, so that if a sample $\boldsymbol{x}_n$ is assigned to cluster k then $r_{nk} = 1$ and $r_{nj} = 0 \; \forall \; j \neq k$. Therefore, it is possible to define an objective function, given by eq. (1), which represents the quadratic sum of the distances from each sample to the prototype $\boldsymbol{\mu}_k$ assigned to it.

$$J = \sum_{n=1}^{N} \sum_{k=1}^{K} r_{nk} \|\boldsymbol{x}_n - \boldsymbol{\mu}_k\|^2 \tag{1}$$

The goal is to find values for r_{nk} and $\boldsymbol{\mu}_k$ to minimize J, which can be accomplished through an iterative method. (Bishop, 2006) highlights that the convergence of the algorithm is guaranteed because at each iteration the value of the objective function is reduced, but it can converge to a local minimum instead of a global minimum. (Géron, 2017) points out that the K-means++ algorithm was proposed by introducing a smarter initialization step that tends to initialize centroids far from each other and claims that this improvement made the K-means algorithm far less likely to converge to a suboptimal solution.

Hierarchical clustering is another popular clustering algorithm and is solely based on similarity measures between samples. It can be divided into agglomerative and divisive. According to (Ethem Alpaydin, 2014), the first one starts with the number of clusters equal to the number of samples and continues merging similar clusters into larger clusters until there is only one cluster, while the second follows the opposite direction. To obtain the clusters from the hierarchical clustering algorithm, one can provide to the method the desired number of clusters or a threshold for the similarity measure, so that when the number of clusters or the specified threshold is reached, the hierarchical clustering returns the clusters to the user, described as sample sets.

2.2. Multi-stage clustering algorithm

The method applied in this paper is based on (Neu et al., 2017), making use of successive clustering techniques (respectively k-means and hierarchical clustering) together with a prior selection of eigenvalues output from SSI-data driven, chosen using hard validation criteria, to identify the predominant modes in the analysis of a rotating machine data set. The algorithm can be described as shown in Figure 1.

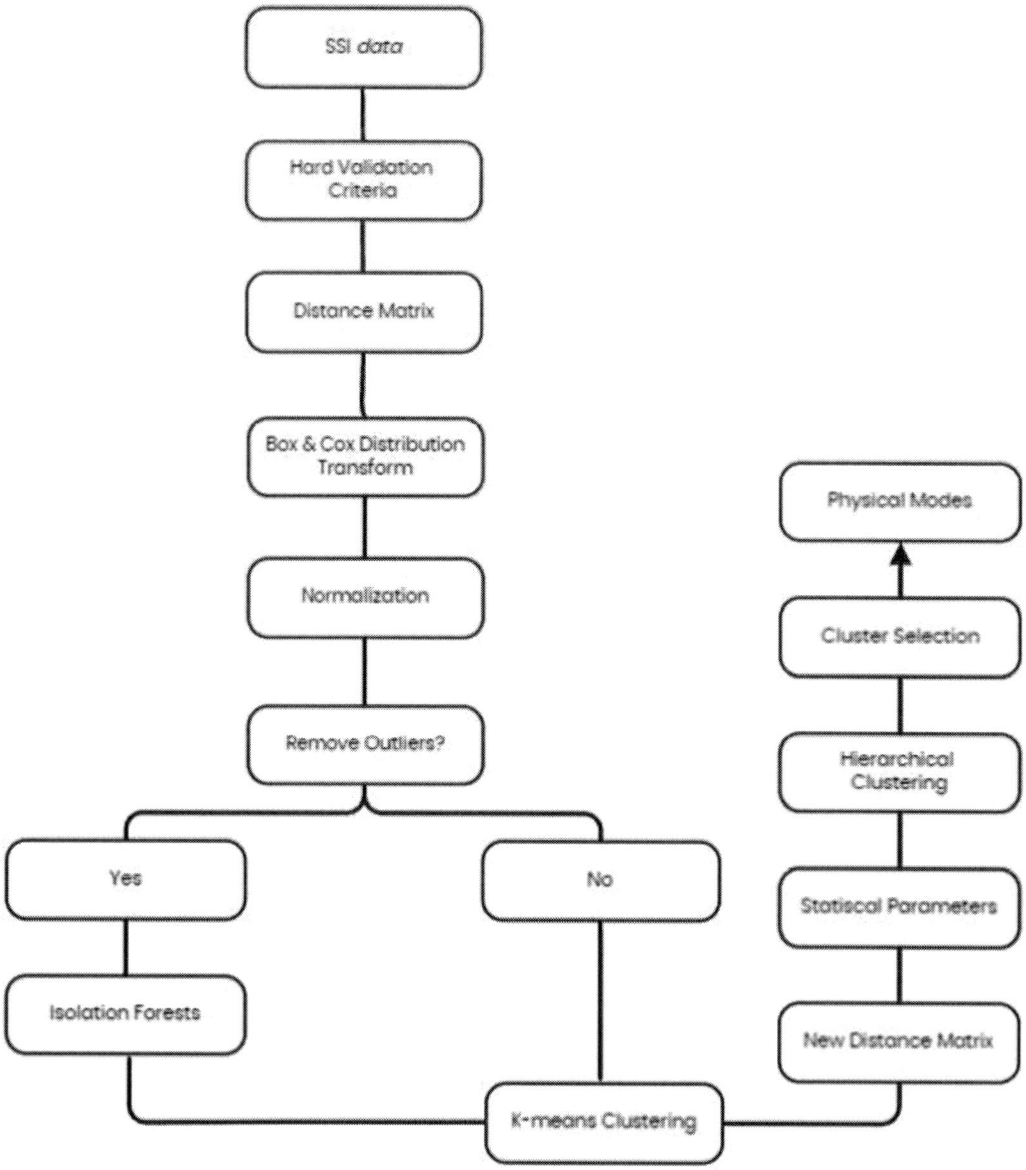

Figure 1. Block diagram showing the algorithm steps.

In this algorithm, initially, the eigenvalues extracted from the SSI algorithm are analyzed and those that have a positive imaginary part, a positive real part, and that do not have conjugate complex are removed in what is called Hard Validation Criteria (HVC). Then, a matrix of the distance between successive order modes is calculated using the following expression (2):

$$d_{i,j} = d\lambda_{i,j} = \frac{|\lambda_i - \lambda_j|}{\max(|\lambda_i|, |\lambda_j|)} \tag{2}$$

where i is the mode of one order and j each of the modes of a successive order of the stabilization diagram. This metric was adapted from (Neu et al., 2017) and from other researches, such as (de Almeida Cardoso et al., 2018; Reynders et al., 2012), since in experimental data from rotating machines, the repeatability of successive modes tends to have poor repeatability when considering the value of the Modal Assurance Criterion (MAC), generated mainly due to the complex modes of this type of system.

It can be shown that expression (2), together with the other features as applied in (Neu et al., 2017) have a distribution that does not favor the clustering algorithms. Therefore, the feature distributions are transformed using Box and Cox transform (Box & Cox, 1964). Then, the treatment of outliers by the isolation forests method will be shown and how its application facilitates the final average mode values obtained in the automatic identification of rotor response signals. The process continues by applying the k-means clustering labels and removing from the later steps the modes that were classified as certainly mathematical. A new distance matrix is then generated from the labels obtained and clusters are estimated based on the 92nd percentile of the distribution, which will be applied as a threshold for the hierarchical clustering, in the sequence.

Finally, considering the clusters generated in this last method, only those that have a significant amount of representation in the stabilization diagram are selected as modes of interest, namely, those that are repeated in great number and with stable features. This value is considered 2/3 of the largest cluster.

3. EXPERIMENTAL DATA

The test rig configuration is shown in Figure 2, and detailed information is also presented in (Storti, da Silva Tuckmantel, et al., 2021). It consists of a steel shaft, with a length of 620 mm and a diameter of 15 mm, connected to an electrical motor by a flexible coupling. A frequency inverter, connected to the data acquisition computer drives the motor. The shaft is supported by two identical hydrodynamic journal bearings, with 31 mm of diameter, 18 mm of axial length, and 90 μm of radial clearance. Bearings are lubricated with oil through a metering pump. Bearings 1 and 2 are placed at, approximately, 175 mm and 585 mm from the coupling, respectively. A steel disk with a diameter of 120 mm and length of 20 mm is placed, approximately, at 120 mm after the first bearing.

A magnetic actuator is used for applying an external force to the shaft in the first test, as a Gaussian white noise input. Hall-sensors, located at the coil poles, measure the produced magnetic field to control the force levels. It is worth mentioning that the actuator is experimentally calibrated for the assembled system, that is, a linear relationship is found between the 'control' electromagnetic field and the experimental forces generated in the system, measured through the load cells present in each one of the bearings. The measurements were obtained through accelerometers positioned on the bearings' shafts, measured separately in the vertical and horizontal direction of the test rig (z and y axes of Figure 2).

Figure 2. Test rig configuration.

4. RESULTS

As mentioned earlier, the algorithm was applied to data from four accelerometers for the rotor operating with a constant shaft speed of 75 Hz. The extracted acceleration values can be seen in Figure 3.

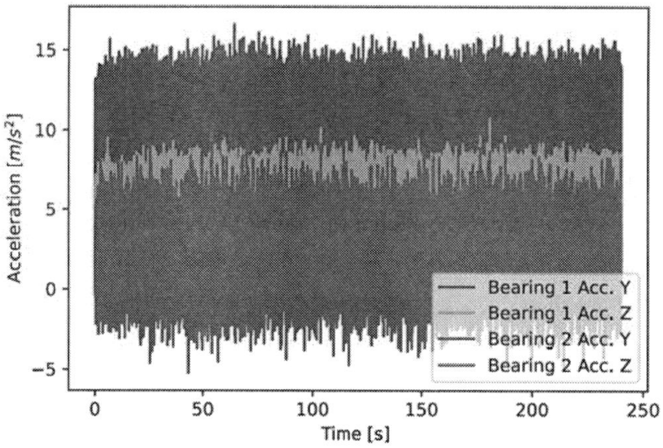

Figure 3. Accelerometer data is used in the results section.

From the data obtained, with processing to remove the mean of each one of the series, the stabilization diagram can be obtained from the SSI data-driven algorithm (Figure 4). In addition, spectral densities are plotted in the background of the graph to aid in the interpretation of results. The maximum number of eigenvalues to be estimated via SSI was fixed at 100 after a successive analysis over different model orders since in the analyzed frequency range, this parameter proved to be sufficient to indicate the repeatability of the modes of interest.

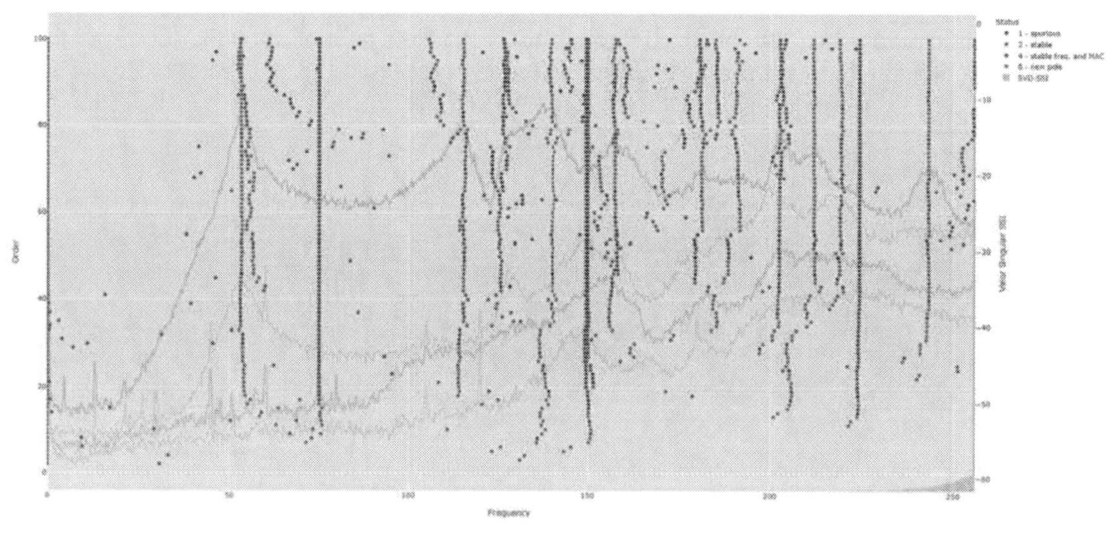

Figure 4. SSI data plot using conventional analysis.

In this conventional analysis, stabilization limits are previously defined, generally considering the frequency deviation between successive modes, the MAC, and damping coefficients to classify the modes as stable. However, this analysis is very particular, depending mainly on user knowledge and system characteristics. As can be seen in Figure 4, this analysis is possible and relatively simple, however, when a large amount of data need to be tested with almost no prior knowledge, or when the monitoring of modal factors is necessary to be done constantly, it is extremely valuable to have an algorithm able to interpret the information from the stabilization diagram in a similar way to the user and provide reliable results from the automatically extracted modal parameters.

In this way, clustering methods were added as described in the previous section. The first step is elimination by HVC, which results in the elimination of modes that are physically meaningless, i.e., mathematical modes that cannot represent actual physical modes of the rotor. Then, after calculating the distances between nearest neighbors' modes, the Box-Cox transformation is performed, resulting in a matrix of attributes that are evaluated by the k-means. For the problem investigated, there are only two clusters to be formed in this step: Probably Physical and Certainly Mathematical. The distribution of attributes according to the assigned labels and the correlation between the attributes can be analyzed in Figure 5. The correlation values, shown in the upper right part of Figure 5, show that the contribution of the distance from damping from neighbors' modes has a low correlation with the label assigned by k-means, which shows that damping values tend to have a greater dispersion and make the analysis of automatic identification algorithms difficult.

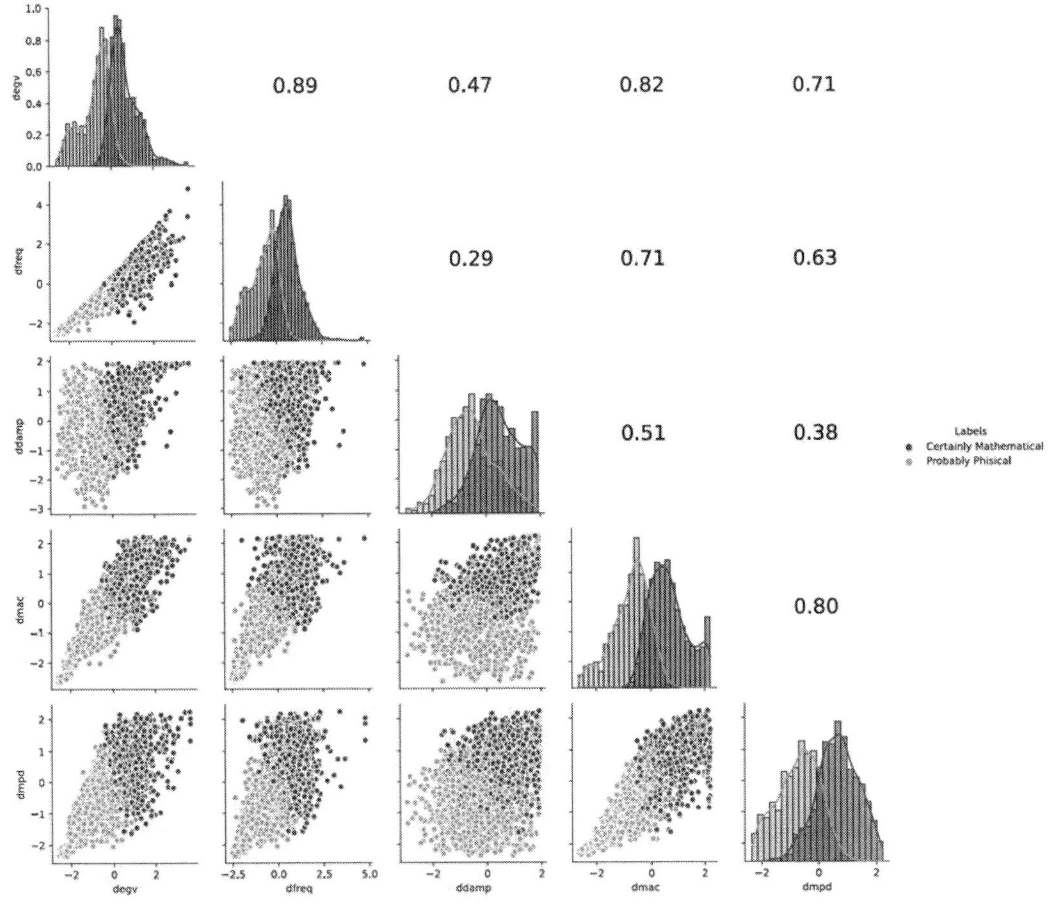

Figure 5. Features distribution based on labels after k-means clustering.

The removal of unexpected values, represented here as outliers, plays a key role in determining the final modes. Two conditions will be tested to illustrate this feature: the first one without any analysis by the isolation forests algorithm, and a second applying outlier removal considering 20 ensemble estimators. No other parameters are modified between these cases. The value is taken arbitrarily as respectively

1/10 of the number of modes grouped in the largest cluster of the first condition, however, the authors consider that a deeper analysis of this value still needs to be done. The results are presented respectively in Figure 6 and Figure 7.

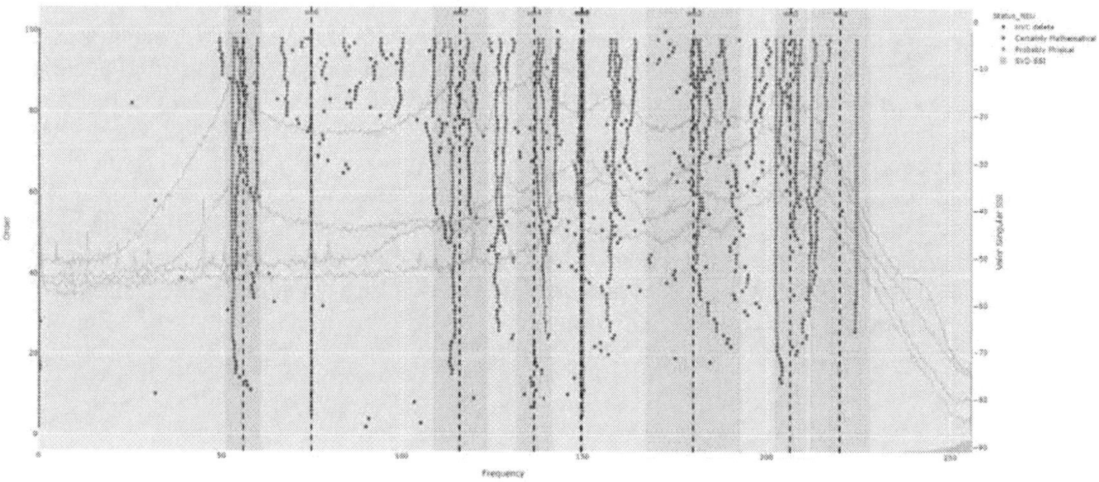

Figure 6. Automatic identification of physical modes without isolation forests.

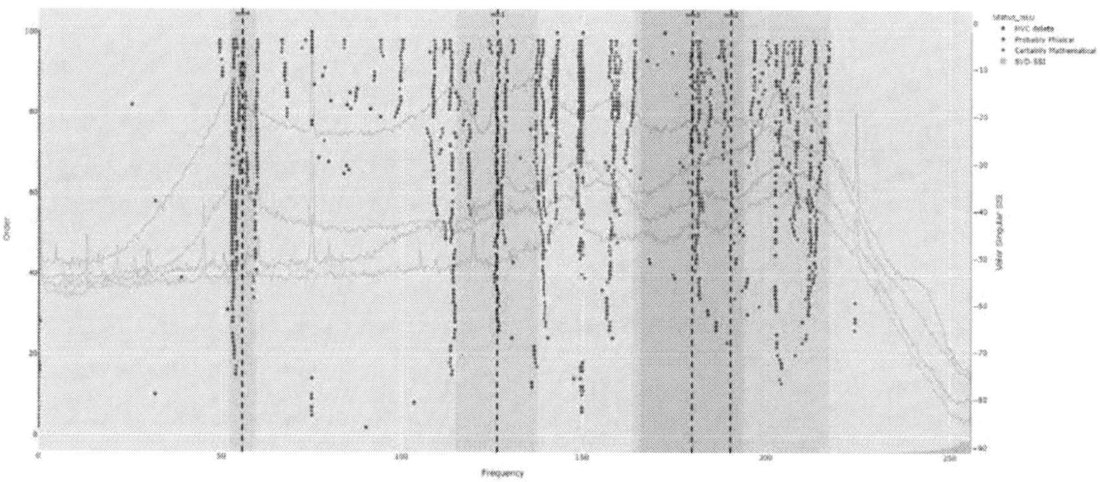

Figure 7. Automatic identification of physical modes with isolation forests and using an ensemble of 20 estimators.

The result obtained in the comparison of Figure 6 and Figure 7 can be quite challenging in the first analysis: visually, the algorithm seems to have decreased the precision of the final clusters. However, this is not what happens: if the mean frequency and standard deviation values for the first rotor mode are compared (the most prominent peak in frequency, determined in (Storti, da Silva Tuckmantel, et al., 2021) as 52.3 Hz through a numerical model), see Table 1, it is possible to notice that the precision for this mode has increased. Another fundamental observation of the results is that the method was able to remove the frequencies proportional to the rotational speed of the shaft (75 Hz, 150 Hz, and 225Hz), which are undesirable in the modal analysis of rotating machines, as these can be easily mistaken with rotor or foundation modes, for example, making it difficult to visualize the real modes of the system. Generally, harmonic removal must be based on some deterministic method, such as extracting kurtosis values (Brincker et al., 2000) across the spectrum or by orthogonal projections (Gres et al., 2019), which in practice can make the process numerically more expensive and make an automatic identification of the system modes even impossible, especially when in the presence of different signal to noise ratio conditions. Harmonics can be interpreted as an outlier when compared to physical modes for two very clear reasons: they tend to have a practically zero deviation (when the rotor is operated at constant rotation) and approximately zero damping, characteristics not observed in physical modes.

Table 1. Mean natural frequency and standard deviation for the first rotor mode automatically identified by the multi-stage clustering method.

	Mean Frequency [Hz]	Standard Deviation [Hz]
Case 1 wihout Isolation Forests	56.00	4.89
Case 2 with Isolation Forests	55.74	3.54

REFERENCES

Bishop, C. M. (2006). *Pattern Recognition and Machine Learning*. Springer.

Box, G. E. P., & Cox, D. R. (1964). An Analysis of Transformations. *Journal of the Royal Statistical Society: Series B (Methodological)*, *26*(2), 211–243. https://doi.org/10.1111/j.2517-6161.1964.tb00553.x

Brandt, A., & Linderholt, A. (2012). A periodogram-based method for removing harmonics in operational modal analysis. *International Conference on Noise and Vibration Engineering 2012, ISMA 2012, Including USD 2012: International Conference on Uncertainty in Structure Dynamics*, *4*, 2625–2633.

Brincker, R., Andersen, P., Møller, N. B., & Moller, N. (2000). An Indicator for Separation of Structural and Harmonic Modes in Output-Only Modal Testing. *Proceedings of the 18th International Modal Analysis Conference (IMAC)*, 1649–1654.

Brincker, R., & Ventura, C. E. (2015). *Introduction to Operational Modal Analysis*. John Wiley & Sons, Ltd. https://doi.org/10.1002/9781118535141

Brincker, R., Zhang, L., & Andersen, P. (2001). Modal identification of output-only systems using frequency domain decomposition. *Smart Materials and Structures*, *10*(3), 441–445. https://doi.org/10.1088/0964-1726/10/3/303

Brownjohn, J. M. W., Magalhaes, F., Caetano, E., & Cunha, A. (2010). Ambient vibration re-testing and operational modal analysis of the Humber Bridge. *Engineering Structures*, *32*(8), 2003–2018. https://doi.org/10.1016/j.engstruct.2010.02.034

Brownjohn, J. M. W., Raby, A., Au, S. K., Zhu, Z., Wang, X., Antonini, A., Pappas, A., & D'Ayala, D. (2019). Bayesian operational modal analysis of offshore rock lighthouses: Close modes, alignment, symmetry and uncertainty. *Mechanical Systems and Signal Processing*, *133*, 106306. https://doi.org/10.1016/j.ymssp.2019.106306

CLARKSON, B. L., & MERCER, C. A. (1965). Use of cross correlation in studying the response of lightly damped structures to random forces. *AIAA Journal*, *3*(12), 2287–2291. https://doi.org/10.2514/3.3358

de Almeida Cardoso, R., Cury, A., & Barbosa, F. (2018). A clustering-based strategy for automated structural modal identification. *Structural Health Monitoring*, *17*(2), 201–217. https://doi.org/10.1177/1475921716689239

Ethem Alpaydin. (2014). *Introduction to Machine Learning* (3rd Editio). MIT Press.

Géron, A. (2017). Hands-On Machine Learning with Scikit-Learn & TensorFlow. In *Hands-On Machine Learning with R* (1st ed.). O'Reilly.

Goodfellow, I., Bengio, Y., & Courville, A. (2016). *Deep Learning: Machine Learning Book*. 785. http://www.deeplearningbook.org/

Goursat, M., Döhler, M., Mevel, L., & Andersen, P. (2011). Crystal Clear SSI for Operational Modal Analysis of Aerospace Vehicles. In T. Proulx (Ed.), *Structural Dynamics, Volume 3* (pp. 1421–1430). Springer New York. http://link.springer.com/10.1007/978-1-4419-9834-7_125

Gres, S., Andersen, P., Hoen, C., & Damkilde, L. (2019). Orthogonal projection-based harmonic signal removal for operational modal analysis. *Conference Proceedings of the Society for Experimental Mechanics Series*, *6*, 9–21. https://doi.org/10.1007/978-3-319-74476-6_2

Guillaume, P., Verboven, P., Cauberghe, B., Vanlanduit, S., Parloo, E., & Sitter, G. de. (2003). Frequency-Domain_ System Identification for OMA and EMA.pdf. *IFAC*, 1609–1614.

He, M., Liang, P., Li, J., Zhang, Y., & Liu, Y. (2021). Fully automated precise operational modal identification. *Engineering Structures*, *234*(January), 111988. https://doi.org/10.1016/j.engstruct.2021.111988

James, G., Carne, T., & Lauffer, J. (1995). The natural excitation technique (NExT) for modal parameter extraction from operating structures. *Modal Analysis-the International Journal of Analytical and Experimental Modal Analysis*, *10*(4), 260.

Liu, F. T., Ting, K. M., & Zhou, Z. H. (2008). Isolation forest. *Proceedings - IEEE International Conference on Data Mining, ICDM*, 413–422. https://doi.org/10.1109/ICDM.2008.17

Liu, R., Yang, B., Zio, E., & Chen, X. (2018). Artificial intelligence for fault diagnosis of rotating machinery: A review. *Mechanical Systems and Signal Processing*, *108*, 33–47. https://doi.org/10.1016/j.ymssp.2018.02.016

Magalhães, F., & Cunha, Á. (2011). Explaining operational modal analysis with data from an arch bridge. *Mechanical Systems and Signal Processing*, *25*(5), 1431–1450. https://doi.org/10.1016/j.ymssp.2010.08.001

Neu, E., Janser, F., Khatibi, A. A., & Orifici, A. C. (2017). Fully Automated Operational Modal Analysis using multi-stage clustering. *Mechanical Systems and Signal Processing*, *84*, 308–323. https://doi.org/10.1016/j.ymssp.2016.07.031

Peeters, B., & De Roeck, G. (1999). Reference-based stochastic subspace identification for output-only modal analysis. *Mechanical Systems and Signal Processing*, *13*(6), 855–878. https://doi.org/10.1006/mssp.1999.1249

Poddar, D., & Shunmugam, M. S. (2019). Development of an automated modal extraction methodology through OMA by random cutting excitation of a legacy milling machine. *Mechanical Systems and Signal Processing*, *122*, 448–462. https://doi.org/10.1016/j.ymssp.2018.12.036

Rainieri, C., & Fabbrocino, G. (2010). Automated output-only dynamic identification of civil engineering structures. *Mechanical Systems and Signal Processing*, *24*(3), 678–695. https://doi.org/10.1016/j.ymssp.2009.10.003

Randall, R. B., & Antoni, J. (2011). Rolling element bearing diagnostics-A tutorial. In *Mechanical Systems and Signal Processing*. https://doi.org/10.1016/j.ymssp.2010.07.017

Reynders, E., Houbrechts, J., & De Roeck, G. (2012). Fully automated (operational) modal analysis. *Mechanical Systems and Signal Processing*, *29*, 228–250. https://doi.org/10.1016/j.ymssp.2012.01.007

Silva, J. M. M., & Maia, N. M. M. (1999). *Modal Analysis and Testing* (J. M. M. Silva & N. M. M. Maia (eds.)). Springer Netherlands. https://doi.org/10.1007/978-94-011-4503-9

Storti, G. C., Carrer, L., da Silva Tuckmantel, F. W., Machado, T. H., Cavalca, K. L., & Bachschmid, N. (2021). Simulating application of operational modal analysis to a test rig. *Mechanical Systems and Signal Processing*, *153*, 107529. https://doi.org/10.1016/j.ymssp.2020.107529

Storti, G. C., da Silva Tuckmantel, F. W., & Machado, T. H. (2021). Modal parameters identification of a rotor-journal bearing system using operational modal analysis. *Journal of the Brazilian Society of Mechanical Sciences and Engineering*, *43*(3). https://doi.org/10.1007/s40430-021-02887-9

Wu, G., He, M., Liang, P., Ye, C., & Xu, Y. (2020). Automated Modal Identification Based on Improved Clustering Method. *Mathematical Problems in Engineering*, *2020*. https://doi.org/10.1155/2020/5698609

9th International Operational Modal Analysis Conference
iomac
July 3 - 6, 2022
Vancouver, Canada

OUTPUT-ONLY BAYESIAN SEMI-PARAMETRIC IDENTIFICATION OF A NONLINEAR DYNAMIC SYSTEM

J. D. Longbottom[1], *E. J. Cross*[1], *T. J. Rogers*[1]

[1]Dynamics Research Group, Department of Mechanical Engineering, University of Sheffield, Mappin Street, Sheffield, S1 3JD, United Kingdom - {jdlongbottom1, e.j.cross, tim.rogers}@sheffield.ac.uk

ABSTRACT

This paper presents one possible solution for the identification of a nonlinear dynamic system with unknown linear model parameters and an unknown nonlinear function in the equation of motion. The task is to recover internal states of the nonlinear system (displacement and velocity), the parameters of the linear component of the system and the functional form of the nonlinearity. From only the output data and in the presence of measurement noise, the system is identified in a Bayesian manner. The identification is performed within a Gaussian process latent force model framework, in three stages. The first is to make a biased linear estimate of the system; the second to recover the displacement, velocity and latent restoring force; finally this recovered latent force is fit. The fitting of the latent restoring force is also achieved with a Gaussian process regression model which allows for the noise free restoring force function to be recovered, which eliminates the influence of the unmeasured input to the system under the assumption that the input is broadband. It is shown how this framework effectively recovers accurate estimates of the displacement and velocity of the system as well as very good fits over the nonlinear restoring force which defines the equations of motion.

Key words: Bayesian, Gaussian Process, Output-only, Nonlinear, System Identification

1 INTRODUCTION

The demand placed on modelling and identification of engineering structures has only increased over time and along with it the complexity of the structures being modelled. The prevalence of significant nonlinear behaviour in engineered dynamic systems has increased, as has the desire to understand and model that nonlinearity. Potential sources of nonlinearity, such as large deflections, non-linear-elastic materials and contact or friction between components, must now be understood if a practitioner seeks to construct an accurate model of the system.

The rise in demand for accurate models which replicate the behaviour of physical systems, the so-called *digital twin*, alongside increased availability of operational data leads engineers to ask if it is possible to model nonlinear dynamic effects. As in the linear case, when access to measurements the inputs/excitation given to the dynamic system are available, the identification is greatly simplified — although still a significant challenge. Moving to the output-only or operational case, the task of identification from data greatly increases in difficulty.

When the inputs are available a great deal of work has been done in the literature, for example, see the review papers Kerschen *et al.* [5] or more recently Noël and Kerschen [8]. A wide variety of methods in both the time and frequency domain have been explored with varying levels of success. In the output-only case the number of works in the literature reduce. However, work is still being carried out with promising results. For example, Friis *et al.* [2] propose a methodology based on determining an equivalent linear system. Vesterholm *et al.* [14] propose a technique for detecting nonlinearity based on a random decrement method combined with principal component analysis. This work was compared to previous attempts by Macıas *et al.* [6] where again principal component analysis is used in combination with a finite element model for detection of nonlinear dynamic behaviour.

In this work, a time domain approach is also taken to detect and subsequently identify the effect of a nonlinearity in a system where only output acceleration measurements are available. The developed method will be based upon results from a Gaussian process (GP) Latent Force Model (LFM), an emerging framework for structural identification based on original work in the computer science community [1, 3].

In [10] it is shown how for a linear system under narrowband loading (which coincides with the resonant modes of the system) it is possible to perform joint input-state-parameter identification of the system through the GPLFM framework. Shortly before this, [7] independently presented work on the use of the GPLFM for input estimation of a linear dynamic system, specifically for the learning of traffic loading on a structure where the modal properties were known *a priori*. Since these two publications, work on the application of GPLFM models has shown a great deal of promise in the structural dynamics community, notably Petersen *et al.* [9] demonstrate the use of this model structure for inferring wind loads on a long-span suspension bridge. On the theoretical side, development has also continued with the work being extended for input/load estimation of known nonlinear systems [12] and for identification of nonlinear systems with known inputs [11] (the experimental modal analysis case). This current paper will demonstrate how, under the assumptions of broadband excitation, a nonlinear system may be detected and subsequently identified from only its output measurements within the same framework — the operational modal analysis case.

2 GAUSSIAN PROCESS LATENT FORCE MODELS

Before introducing the GPLFM, it is worth briefly reviewing the GP for readers unfamiliar with the topic, this tool will also be used in the fitting of the unknown restoring force surface. The GP is a Bayesian machine learning tool which is predominantly used to solve regression problems, a good introductory text on the topic which goes beyond the information shown here is [15]. There are a number of ways to develop the GP as a tool for learning functional relationships between data, perhaps the most intuitive is to describe the GP as a "probability distribution over functions". This means that a sample from a GP, rather than being a single number or a vector of numbers is instead one possible function defined at any input on the real line. In practice, it is not possible to assess the GP at every point on this function, however, since the GP can be seen as an infinite collection of jointly Gaussian distributed random variables, it is possible to assess any finite subset of those exactly such that the function can be evaluated at any point of interest.

Moving towards a more substantial definition, imagine a set of training data $\mathcal{D} = \{\boldsymbol{x}_i, y_i\}_{i=1}^N$ where $\boldsymbol{x}_i$ is the ith training input (vector) and y_i the ith training target (scalar) such that,

$$y_i = f(\boldsymbol{x}_i) + \varepsilon, \qquad \varepsilon \sim \mathcal{N}\left(0,\ \sigma_n^2\right)$$

for some unknown function $f(\cdot)$ and additive zero-mean Gaussian measurement noise ε with variance σ_n^2. Two important mathematical concepts are used to develop the GP, the first is the *kernel trick*, without exhaustive detail, this allows the covariance between any two function values $f(\boldsymbol{x}_i)$ and $f(\boldsymbol{x}_j)$ to be expressed directly through a covariance kernel/function $k\left(\boldsymbol{x}_i, \boldsymbol{x}_j\right)$. Many choices exist and the reader is referred to [15] for details, importantly this covariance kernel is a function of only the inputs $\boldsymbol{x}$ to the function so may be assessed at new, as yet unseen, values for testing $\boldsymbol{x}^\star$. Secondly, given that every point in the function $f\left(\boldsymbol{x}\right)$ is jointly Gaussian distributed, one can construct the joint distribution between the training data $\mathcal{D}$ and the test data $\mathcal{D}^\star = \{\boldsymbol{x}_i^\star, y_i^\star\}$, remembering that the values of $y_i^\star$ are unknown. Collecting all the training inputs and outputs into a matrix $\boldsymbol{X}$ and vector $\boldsymbol{y}$, then similarly for the testing data $\boldsymbol{X}^\star$ and vector $\boldsymbol{y}\star$,

$$\begin{bmatrix} \boldsymbol{y} \\ \boldsymbol{y}^\star \end{bmatrix} \sim \mathcal{N}\left(\begin{bmatrix} m\left(\boldsymbol{X}\right) \\ m\left(\boldsymbol{X}^\star\right) \end{bmatrix},\ \begin{bmatrix} K(\boldsymbol{X},\boldsymbol{X}) + \sigma_n^2\mathbb{I} & K(\boldsymbol{X},\boldsymbol{X}^\star) \\ K(\boldsymbol{X}^\star,\boldsymbol{X}) & K(\boldsymbol{X}^\star,\boldsymbol{X}^\star) + \sigma_n^2\mathbb{I} \end{bmatrix}\right) \tag{1}$$

where $m(\cdot)$ is the mean function (often assumed to be zero, as is done in this work) and $K(\boldsymbol{X}, \boldsymbol{X})$ is the covariance matrix between all the pairs of inputs and equivalent for the testing data. By the well known identities for conditioning in multivariate Gaussian distributions a predictive distribution can be established over $\boldsymbol{y}^\star$ conditioned on $\mathcal{D}$,

$$\boldsymbol{y}^\star \sim \mathcal{N}\left(\mathbb{E}\left[\boldsymbol{y}^\star\right],\ \mathbb{V}\left[\boldsymbol{y}^\star\right]\right), \tag{2a}$$

$$\mathbb{E}\left[\boldsymbol{y}^\star\right] = m(\boldsymbol{X}^\star) + K(\boldsymbol{X}^\star,\boldsymbol{X})\left(K(\boldsymbol{X},\boldsymbol{X}) + \sigma_n^2\mathbb{I}\right)^{-1}\boldsymbol{y}, \tag{2b}$$

$$\mathbb{V}\left[\boldsymbol{y}^\star\right] = K(\boldsymbol{X}^\star,\boldsymbol{X}^\star) + K(\boldsymbol{X}^\star,\boldsymbol{X})\left(K(\boldsymbol{X},\boldsymbol{X}) + \sigma_n^2\mathbb{I}\right)^{-1}K(\boldsymbol{X},\boldsymbol{X}^\star) + \sigma_n^2\mathbb{I}. \tag{2c}$$

In possession of Eq. (2), it is possible to predict the distribution over possible unknown $\boldsymbol{y}^\star$ values at any new set of inputs $\boldsymbol{X}^\star$. Note, in order to develop the model fully, there are a handful of hyperparameters which must be determined, usually (as is the case in this work) this is done by minimising the negative log marginal likelihood of the process (see [15] for details). This model has proven both useful and flexible in a range of applications but is limited by the fact that it learns a *static map* from $\boldsymbol{x}$ to y.

One approach to overcome this limitation was presented in [1] where the authors imagined a set of data where the generating process was given by some ordinary differential equation (ODE) which was itself driven by a GP. In other words, choosing a second order system, a process which could be written as,

$$\ddot{y}_i + \alpha\dot{y}_i + \beta y_i = U(t), \qquad U(t) \sim \mathcal{GP}\left(0, k(\boldsymbol{x}, \boldsymbol{x}')\right) \tag{3}$$

where overdot is used to denote a derivative with respect to time, which those in the structural dynamics community will agree is a far more expressive model. The above model, shown in Eq. (3) is the GPLFM.

One major challenge when using GP models as a prediction tool is the computational complexity, which is $\mathcal{O}(N^3)$ for N training data points. This difficulty continues in the GPLFM. Owing to developments shown in [4], work in [3] shows how the GP component of Eq. (3) can can be rewritten as a linear Gaussian probabilistic state-space model. Once in this new form, it can be shown that the system is solvable with a Kalman filter and Rauch-Tung-Striebel (RTS) smoother [13] which reduces the computational complexity to $\mathcal{O}(N)$. Within this framework the number of data points is determined by the length of the time series which is being considered, therefore, $N \equiv T$ if a signal of length T points in time are observed. Under this framework it is also possible to extend the model to sets of differential equations so multiple time series can be inferred at once. For example, multiple unknown inputs $U_d(t)$ acting on different masses/modes from multiple acceleration sensors can be inferred if d indexes which force is being inferred [7, 9, 12].

This model form has been previously shown for joint input-state [7, 9] and joint input-state-parameter learning of *linear* structural dynamic systems. In these works, the unknown forces (potentially narrowband) which drive the linear systems to induce a response are inferred.

2.1 GPLFM for Nonlinear Systems

When considering an extension to nonlinear systems, the obvious line of approach is to consider what may happen when the left-hand side of the ODE in Eq. (3) is no longer linear. In other words a more general model where

$$\ddot{y}_i + f(y_i, \dot{y}_i) = U(t), \qquad U(t) \sim \mathcal{GP}\left(0, k(\boldsymbol{x}, \boldsymbol{x}')\right) \tag{4}$$

if $f(y_i, \dot{y}_i)$ is some nonlinear function in the displacement and the velocity. Under this setup, it is possible to recover unmeasured inputs to a nonlinear dynamic system, see [12] for details. However, there are a number of significant drawbacks. Firstly, [12] assumes that the form of the nonlinearity ($f(y_i, \dot{y}_i)$) is known *a priori* and its parameters are available to the modeller, such that just the forces are unknown.

Secondly, the equivalent state-space model of the the system is now nonlinear despite the component representing the GP remaining linear because of the nonlinearity in the ODE itself. To address this challenge, one must turn to nonlinear inference methods. Instead of the Kalman filter and RTS smoother giving the solution to the GPLFM, an alternative nonlinear filter and smoother must be used, e.g. the Extended Kalman Filter (EKF), Unscented Kalman Filter (UKF) or particle filter (PF) [13]. The user must then trade off between computational load in the case of the PF and potentially larger approximation errors in the case of the EKF/UKF.

However, the approach described above cannot be taken unless some prior knowledge can be incorporated regarding either $f(y_i, \dot{y}_i)$ or $U(t)$ since there is an inherent non-identifiability between the contribution of the unknown nonlinear restoring force $f(y_i, \dot{y}_i)$ and the unknown loading $U(t)$. It will be shown that, if the practitioner were interested in learning the unknown restoring force, $f(y_i, \dot{y}_i)$, a similar approach can still be taken which has an additional benefit of the state-space model remaining linear. In [11] it is suggested that, if the inputs $U(t)$ were known then one could imagine a situation where the unknown contribution of the missing nonlinear terms is modelled as some missing external input in time. In other words

$$\ddot{y}_i + 2\zeta\omega_n\dot{y}_i + \omega_n^2 y_i + R(t) = U(t), \qquad R(t) \sim \mathcal{GP}\left(0, k(t, t')\right) \tag{5}$$

for some natural frequency ω_n and damping ratio ζ and assuming $R(t) \approx f(y_i, \dot{y}_i) - 2\zeta\omega_n\dot{y}_i + \omega_n^2 y_i$. One important detail to notice in the model construction shown above is that the nonlinear component $R(t)$ is now modelled as a function of time t rather than the states y and $\dot{y}$. This change is what allows the latent force approach to be adopted but necessitates a further identification step after the smoother to infer $f(y, \dot{y})$. If $U(t)$ is known, i.e. the experimental modal analysis case, then the GPLFM can be used to infer the "missing" restoring force $R(t)$ (and linear parameters) again using the Kalman filter and RTS smoother. This gives a computationally efficient and powerful framework for recovering the nonlinear contribution to the ODE which, in a second stage, is then used to infer the nonlinearity itself.

3 OUTPUT-ONLY NONLINEAR SYSTEM IDENTIFICATION

Now attention can turn to the output-only case, i.e. when $U(t)$ is unmeasured in Eq. (5). As previously mentioned in the case where the loading $U(t)$ is unmeasured and could be any possible function it will prove very challenging to perform some identification as there can be an infinity of solutions where $R(t) + U(t)$ equals a constant. In other words, the contribution to the response of the system from the nonlinear dynamics and from the unknown input cannot be separated without further insight. This (as yet) unsolvable model could be considered to be written as,

$$\ddot{y}_i + 2\zeta\omega_n\dot{y}_i + \omega_n^2 y_i + R(t) = U(t), \qquad R(t) \sim \mathcal{GP}\left(0, k_r(t,t')\right), \; U(t) \sim \mathcal{GP}\left(0, k_u(t,t')\right) \tag{6}$$

where $k_u(t,t')$ is the kernel of the input process $U(t)$ and $k_r(t,t')$ of the unknown restoring force $R(t)$.

However, in this work, a case is imagined where, under some assumptions, it will be possible to recover a good estimation of $f(y_i, \dot{y}_i)$ from only response measurements. As is commonplace in many operation modal analysis procedures, it will be assumed that $U(t)$ is broadband and can be imagined to be generated by some white noise process. It can be shown that a GP can be constructed which generates functions which are simply realisations of white noise by choosing a particular form for the covariance kernel. Another useful property of the GP is that the sum of two GPs is available in closed form, such that,

$$U(t) + R(t) \sim \mathcal{GP}(0, k_u(t,t') + k_r(t,t')) \tag{7}$$

If the kernel $k_u(t,t')$ is chosen to be a white noise process, i.e. $k_u(t,t') = \sigma_f^2\,\delta(t-t')$ with δ being the delta function and σ_f^2 the variance of the white noise, this imposes the prior belief that $U(t)$ is simply white noise, i.e. the contribution of the mean of $U(t)$ to the expected value of $U(t) + R(t)$ will be zero.

Under this assumption it can be shown that the expectation of $U(t) + R(t)$ will be equal to the expectation of only $R(t)$, i.e. only the contribution of the nonlinear terms in the ODE. Therefore, if the assumption that $U(t)$ is white noise holds, then the nonlinearity in the system can be recovered by inspecting the relationship between the estimated displacement and velocity, and the expectation of the inferred restoring force $R(t)$. Owing to constraints on the space available in this conference paper the details of constructing the state-space model which allows this inference to take place are omitted. The constructed state-space model solves a model in the now familiar GPLFM form,

$$\ddot{y}_i + 2\zeta\omega_n\dot{y}_i + \omega_n^2 y_i = \hat{R}(t), \qquad \hat{R}(t) \sim \mathcal{GP}\left(0, k_r(t,t') + k_u(t,t')\right) \tag{8}$$

with $k_u(t,t')$ set as a white noise kernel.

Inference of the model shown in Eq. (8) is achieved by converting the system into an augmented state-space model which contains the linear system dynamics and the representation of $\hat{R}(t)$ as a linear state-space model. The linear system parameters, ω_n and ζ, are estimated by a linear identification of the system, which will be biased by the nonlinearity. This is not an issue as the identified "missing" force $R(t)$ is actually identified with a component correcting that linear bias, as was observed in [11]. Once the Kalman filter and RTS smoother have recovered the states, the practitioner is in possession of estimates for y_i, $\dot{y}_i$ and $\hat{R}(t)$. Given these estimates and the assumed linear parameters ω_n and ζ it is possible to estimate the expected total internal restoring force of the model $f(y,\dot{y})$. It remains to identify the functional form of the nonlinearity $f(y,\dot{y})$, unfortunately, the estimated restoring force will still contain the effect of the random excitation $U(t)$ in its estimate of $\hat{R}(t)$. However (and luckily for identification), the expectation over the input $U(t)$ remains zero because it is white noise. Therefore, one simply has to determine the expectation over the restoring force in the absence of noise. Recalling Eq. (2) it has already been seen how an unknown nonlinear function can be learnt non-parametrically from data and the expectation of that function at some new test point $\mathbb{E}[\boldsymbol{y}^\star]$ is available. It transpires that the expectation $\mathbb{E}[\boldsymbol{y}^\star]$ is the same as the expectation of the underlying noise free function $\mathbb{E}[\boldsymbol{f}^\star]$ which in the case being considered is the contribution of the internal restoring force $f(y,\dot{y})$ without the influence of $U(t)$. In this way, it is possible to use the estimated quantities from the filter/smoother to infer the internal restoring force of the nonlinear system if that system is under broadband excitation close to white Gaussian noise.

4 RESULTS

To demonstrate the proposed method a simulated Duffing oscillator is studied with the equation of motion,

$$m\ddot{y} + c\dot{y} + ky + k_3y^3 = v(t), \qquad v(t) \sim \mathcal{N}\left(0,\, \sigma_p^2\right) \tag{9}$$

with mass $m = 1$, viscous damping $c = 2$, linear stiffness $k = 1 \times 10^4$ and cubic stiffness $k_3 = 1 \times 10^9$ driven by a white noise $v(t)$ with variance σ_p. For the purposes of simulation this white noise is modelled as a multisine including every $0.2\,$Hz limited from $0.2\,$Hz to $1000\,$Hz. The dataset is simulated for five seconds with a sample rate $f_s = 2048\,$Hz with the measurements being acceleration which has a random Gaussian measurement noise added with a variance of one.

Initially, estimates of the linear system parameters are made as $\omega_n = 46.2\,$Hz and $\zeta = 0.021$ which are biased from the true values of $15.91\,$Hz and 0.01 respectively by the nonlinearity in the system. Using these biased linear estimates the states of the system are recovered along with the estimated contribution $\hat{R}(t)$ using the Kalman filter and RTS smoother. In Fig. 1 the displacement, velocity and $\hat{R}(t)$ states are shown, for the displacement and velocity the ground truth is also indicated. Despite the significant bias in the linear parameters of the model, it is seen that the displacement and velocity of the system are estimated with a high degree of accuracy (normalised mean squared error values of 0.19% and 0.11% respectively). This fit quality is sustained even when there is a substantial nonlinear contribution to the system, see right hand panes of Fig. 1 for a detailed view. Turing attention to the recovered $\hat{R}(t)$ which is the latent force in the system, it can be seen that the signal is definitely not Gaussian white noise, this is to be expected as $\hat{R}(t)$ contains both the unmeasured input $U(t)$ and the missing components of $f(y,\dot{y})$. This identification also serves as a detector for nonlinearity in the system, if the estimated $\hat{R}(t)$ is indistinguishable from white noise (and the assumption of broadband loading holds) then it may be assumed that inside the observed data no significant nonlinearity is active.

Given that a good estimate of y, $\dot{y}$ and $\hat{R}(t)$ is now in hand, one can consider identifying the nonlinearity. As discussed this will be done non-parametrically by fitting a GP from the estimated y and $\dot{y}$ to $\hat{R}(t)$. In Fig. 2 this fit is shown, Fig. 2a shows the result of fitting the GP to the recovered $\hat{R}(t)$ and predicting across displacement and velocity. It can be seen that the learnt surface does not align well with the known true restoring force in the model. Remember that the linear parameters used in the filter were biased, the mismatch between the surface and the true force is a result of the GP estimating $\hat{R}(t)$ correcting for this bias. However,

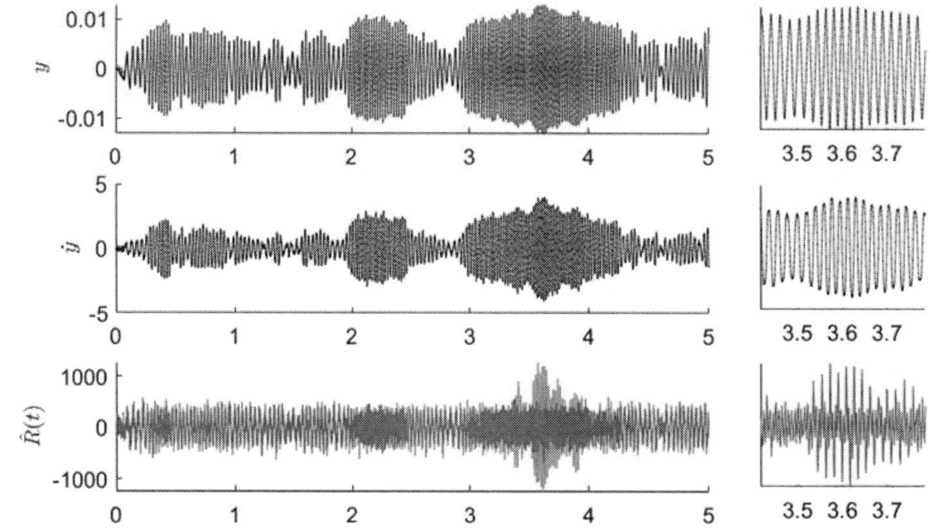

Fig. 1: State estimates recovered by the smoother, showing the expected values (in blue) against the ground truth (black dots). The ground truth is shown only for the displacement and velocity states. In the right hand panes a section of the time series, where the most nonlinear contribution is found, is shown in more detail.

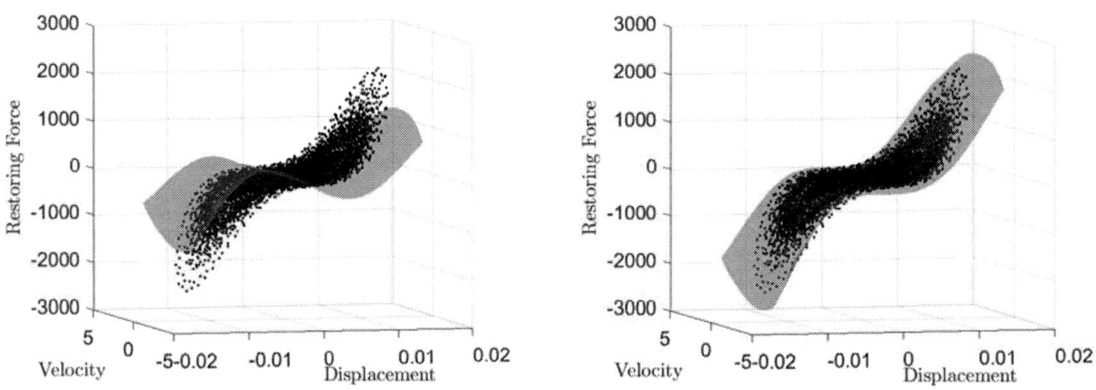

(a) Without linear contribution

(b) With linear contribution

Fig. 2: Recovered restoring force surfaces, the expected restoring force is shown in blue and the true restoring force in the training data as black dots.

it is still possible to use the biased parameters to determine the total restoring force (linear plus nonlinear components) which may be compared to the ground truth, this comparison is made in Fig. 2b. It is clear that the learnt restoring force surface now aligns very well with the ground truth, this learnt surface could be used in further simulation or could be interrogated by an engineer seeking to extract physical insight.

To highlight the fit of the nonlinear component in the system once this restoring force GP has been learnt, Fig. 3 shows a slice of the surfaces from Fig. 2 at the zero velocity point. In addition to the expected surface presented in Fig. 2, the 3σ confidence intervals on the learnt noise-free restoring force function are also shown. In Fig. 3a the linear bias in $\hat{R}(t)$ is shown far more clearly than before, the negative linear term can be

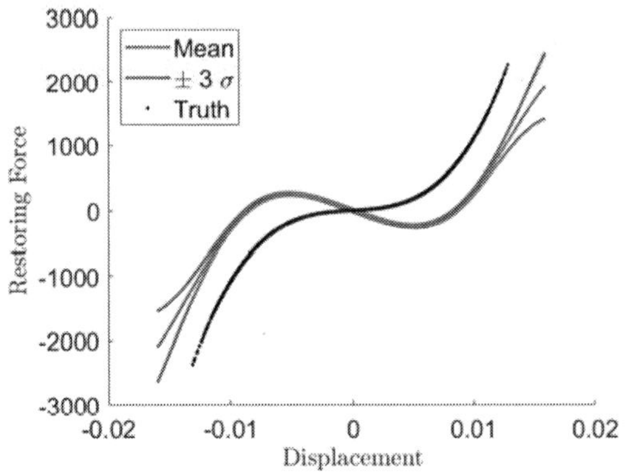

(a) Without linear contribution

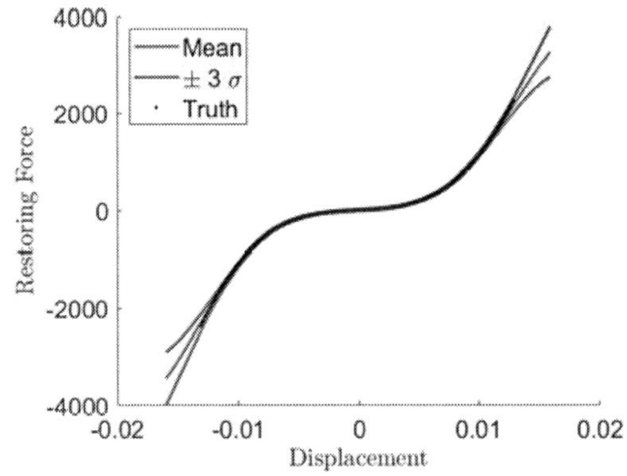

(b) With linear contribution

Fig. 3: Isolating only the stiffness component from the learnt restoring force. The true restoring force is shown in black, the expected restoring force in blue and the $\pm 3\sigma$ confidence bounds in red.

seen to align very well with the overestimation of ω_n, which was used in the filter. Again correcting for this inaccuracy in the linear parameters by investigating the total restoring force, Fig. 3b shows how the cubic behaviour in the Duffing oscillator is captured very well by the learnt GP model. The classic behaviour of the GP is also seen where, once extrapolating from the already observed data, the variance in the estimate increases. Encouragingly, it appears that (owing to the longer length scale learnt by the GP) the model is also able to extrapolate quite well the cubic behaviour of the stiffness nonlinearity.

5 CONCLUSIONS

This paper has shown how a Gaussian process latent force model framework might be applied to identification of a dynamic system with an unknown nonlinearity from only output (response) data. While the general case is highly non-identifiable, it has been seen that, if the input to the system can be assumed to be white Gaussian noise, the expectation over a recovered latent force contains the contribution of the nonlinear dynamic components of a system. It was shown that even when the estimates of the linear modal properties of a system are biased the GPLFM remains capable of recovering extremely accurate estimates of the displacement and velocity of the system. Alongside this, the recovered latent force contains the unmeasured input to the system, the contribution of the nonlinear terms in the equations of motion and a contribution which corrects the bias in the linear modal parameters. It is then possible, by considering the expected noise free function from the displacement and velocity to this recovered latent force to infer a good model for the nonlinearity in the system and correct the linear bias. The current work demonstrated this method only on a simulated single degree of freedom system, it is therefore reasonable to consider that the key point of future work will be proof of concept in an experimental study and extension to more complex dynamical systems with multiple degrees of freedom.

ACKNOWLEDGEMENTS

The authors gratefully acknowledge the support of the Engineering and Physical Sciences Research Council (EPSRC), UK through grant number EP/W002140/1 and support from Ramboll Energy for J. D. Longbottom.

REFERENCES

[1] Alvarez, M., Luengo, D., & Lawrence, N. D. (2009). Latent force models. *Artificial Intelligence and Statistics*, 9–16.

[2] Friis, T., Tarpø, M., Katsanos, E. I., & Brincker, R. (2020). Equivalent linear systems of nonlinear systems. *Journal of Sound and Vibration*, *469*, 115126.

[3] Hartikainen, J., & Sarkka, S. (2012). Sequential inference for latent force models. *arXiv preprint arXiv:1202.3730*.

[4] Hartikainen, J., & Särkkä, S. (2010). Kalman filtering and smoothing solutions to temporal Gaussian process regression models. *2010 IEEE international workshop on machine learning for signal processing*, 379–384.

[5] Kerschen, G., Worden, K., Vakakis, A. F., & Golinval, J.-C. (2006). Past, present and future of nonlinear system identification in structural dynamics. *Mechanical systems and signal processing*, *20*(3), 505–592.

[6] Macıas, E. G., Castro-Triguero, R., Gallego, R., Carretero, J., & Gómez-Casero, M. (2015). Operational modal analysis and detection of non-linear structural behavior of bowstring arch bridge. *International Operational Modal Analysis Conference*.

[7] Nayek, R., Chakraborty, S., & Narasimhan, S. (2019). A Gaussian process latent force model for joint input-state estimation in linear structural systems. *Mechanical Systems and Signal Processing*, *128*, 497–530.

[8] Noël, J.-P., & Kerschen, G. (2017). Nonlinear system identification in structural dynamics: 10 more years of progress. *Mechanical Systems and Signal Processing*, *83*, 2–35.

[9] Petersen, Ø., Øiseth, O., & Lourens, E. (2022). Wind load estimation and virtual sensing in long-span suspension bridges using physics-informed Gaussian process latent force models. *Mechanical Systems and Signal Processing*, *170*, 108742.

[10] Rogers, T. J., Worden, K., & Cross, E. (2020). On the application of Gaussian process latent force models for joint input-state-parameter estimation: With a view to Bayesian operational identification. *Mechanical Systems and Signal Processing*, *140*, 106580.

[11] Rogers, T. J., & Friis, T. (2021). A latent restoring force approach to nonlinear system identification. *arXiv preprint arXiv:2109.10681*.

[12] Rogers, T. J., Worden, K., & Cross, E. J. (2020). Bayesian joint input-state estimation for nonlinear systems. *Vibration*, *3*(3), 281–303.

[13] Särkkä, S. (2013). *Bayesian filtering and smoothing*. Cambridge university press.

[14] Vesterholm, K. K., Brincker, R., & Brandt, A. (2020). Random decrement technique for detection and characterization of nonlinear behavior. *Mechanical Systems and Signal Processing*, *143*, 106841.

[15] Williams, C. K., & Rasmussen, C. E. (2006). *Gaussian processes for machine learning*. MIT press Cambridge, MA.

9th International Operational Modal Analysis Conference
iomac
July 3 - 6, 2022
Vancouver, Canada

REAL-TIME LOCALIZATION OF DYNAMIC IMPACT LOAD ON PLATE STRUCTURE USING DEEP LEARNING

Yuxin Pan[1], Teng Li[2], Carlos E. Ventura[3], Shunduo Zhang[4], Xiaoxi Liang[5], and Xiaofan Song[6]

[1] Postdoctoral Fellow, Department of Civil Engineering, The University of British Columbia, ypan@civil.ubc.ca.
[2] Professor, School of Control Science and Engineering, Shandong University, li.teng@sdu.edu.cn.
[3] Professor, Department of Civil Engineering, The University of British Columbia, ventura@civil.ubc.ca.
[4] Research Assistant, School of Control Science and Engineering, Shandong University, zhangshunduo@mail.sdu.edu.cn.
[5] Research Assistant, School of Control Science and Engineering, Shandong University, 201900170043@mail.sdu.edu.cn.
[6] Research Assistant, School of Control Science and Engineering, Shandong University, 201900170106@mail.sdu.edu.cn.

ABSTRACT

Identification and localization of a dynamic impact load applied to a structure are crucial for monitoring its health and safety. Traditional methods based on inversion techniques, either in time-domain or frequency-domain, require large computational cost which cannot achieve real-time implementation. This study proposes a novel deep learning algorithm for accurately localizing a dynamic impact load applied to a structure by deploying a limited number of sensors. The development of the deep learning algorithm involves: 1) time history analysis of a structural finite element model subjected to random impact loading to generate training dataset; 2) development of a deep neural network model to extract and regress the inherent relationship in multivariate time series between input loading and output responses. The proposed approach is verified on a rectangular plate structure subjected to simulated impact loading at a total of 88 possible locations. A high accuracy rate of 96% achieved in 1 millisecond demonstrate the superiority of the proposed deep neural network in achieving real-time localization of structural impact load.

Keywords: Load localization, Real-time inference, Finite element model, Deep neural network

1. INTRODUCTION

Plates are essential components that have been widely used in many civil and mechanical engineering applications, such as bridges, aircrafts, ships, wind turbines [1]. During the life cycle of a plate or plate-like structure, it will experience various kinds of external load actions that may affect its health condition. Impact load is one of the most common types of loading that can cause damage to a plate structure [2]. Direct localization of the impact load is a challenging topic in the field of structural health monitoring (SHM) for two main reasons: 1) a force transducer directly placed on the structure may be damaged when measuring the applied force; 2) it is not possible to take measurement at each location due to limited accessibility.

Indirect approaches have been developed in both frequency domain [3-5] and time domain [6] through operational modal analysis (OMA) to overcome these problems in direct localization. These methods are also called inverse methods as they determine system inputs (e.g., location of impact load) based on given responses (e.g., recorded output signals), boundary conditions, and structural model [7]. Both methods involve placement of a finite number of sensors to measure output responses [8]. In the frequency domain, Fourier transformation is performed on the recorded responses and then multiplied by the inverse of the frequency response function (FRF) matrix to determine the input force. In the time domain, the input force is estimated by solving the convolution equation of the structural response as a function of its impulse response function (IRF). It has been reported that the time domain methods are more suitable to identify dynamic impact load as the frequency domain methods require long stationary condition [2]. However, even the time domain methods require rigorous mathematical derivation based on deconvolution theory, making their applications less practical. Another drawback of those methods is the real-time incapability, which is essential for fast and effective decision making to mitigate potential damage.

In recent years, deep learning (DL) methods have been widely used in SHM and deep neural network (DNN) models have been developed for sensor placement, structural response prediction, and damage detection [9]. DNN models allow computers to learn the relationship from a large amount of input-output data samples by extracting the certain features and use this trained model to automatically generate desired outputs based on the learned features for given inputs [10]. One of the biggest advantages of this method is that it can achieve real-time requirement. Liu and Zhang [11] developed a computationally efficient CNN model for crack detection in metal plates. Pan and Yang [12] proposed a real-time convolutional neural network (CNN) model to inspect rebar exposure in reinforced concrete structures and evaluate repair cost. Li et al. [13] trained an attention-based long-short term memory (LSTM) model DL to predict structural responses under future earthquake events in real-time manner. Pan et al. [14] developed a CNN model to determine the best instrumentation scheme for infrastructure and reconstruct the seismic responses at unmeasured locations in milliseconds.

Although DL methods have shown powerful capacity in SHM and Operationa, their applications in impact load identification, however, are very limited. Zhou et al. [15] and Chen et al. [16] proposed two different DNN models for load identification in plate structures, but the former did not consider load localization while the latter did not meet real-time requirement (i.e., time cost was above one minute). In this regard, an online impact load localization framework is developed based on a deep learning algorithm in this paper. As one of the four components of the project, this framework has two main parts: 1) a DNN model is developed and trained with input-output time series data obtained from structural FE model subjected to large volume of impact loading at random locations; 2) the trained model that learns the spatial and temporal features of dynamic responses among different locations is used to localize the source input load using measured responses from a limited number of sensors in real time. The other three components of the project include: impact load localization and damage localization using experimental data; extention of the DNN model to OMA using simulated data; and extention to OMA using experimental data. The widely used accelerometer sensor in SHM is adopted to measure the acceleration response. The proposed method is demonstrated on a numerical FE model of a thin aluminum plate which is gridded into 80 shell elements with a total of 88 nodes. A number of 4 accelerometer sensors are placed where the recorded responses are used as inputs to localize an unknown impact load. The localization accuracy and real-time performance of the proposed method are discussed.

2. PROPOSED METHOD

This section describes the proposed framework and the DNN model in detail.

2.1. Framework

The overview of the proposed framework is presented in Figure 1, which includes three components, namely, dataset generation, network training and testing, and real-time application. The first step is to generate reliable and sufficient dataset of a target plate structure that can cover as many impact scenarios as possible. Time history analyses on FE model of the structure are carried out by applying random impact load at any grid nodes. The impact load is characterized as a typical triangular impulse loading defined by loading duration and amplitude parameters. Large number of different loading pattern can be generated by adjusting the parameters. During each random loading case, the input loading pattern and the location are treated as inputs, while the dynamic acceleration time history responses at all grid nodes (except those at fixed boundary) are recorded as outputs. Next, the generated input-output dataset is used to train the DNN model to learn the multi-variate time-series hidden features of dynamic responses between different grid nodes on the plate as well as with input impact load. The final step is to apply the developed localization algorithm and an pre-defined instrumentation plan into the plate structure. With the continuously measured acceleration responses, the neural network can localize the impact load in real-time.

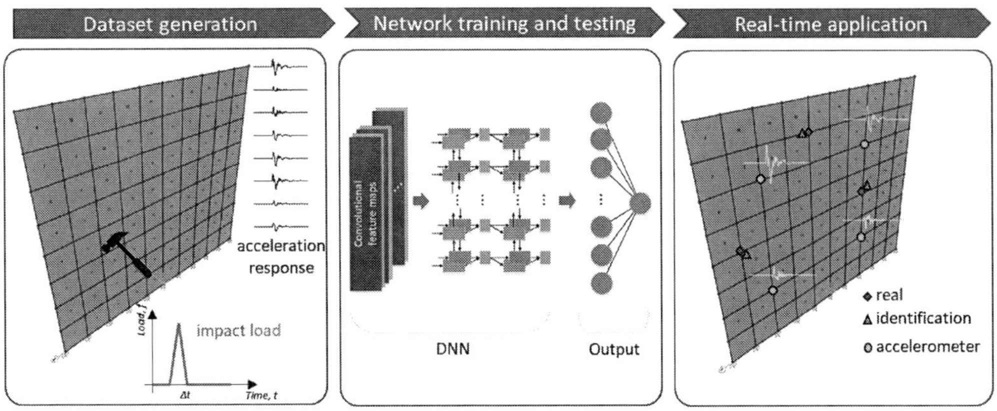

Figure 1. Proposed framework for impact load localization

2.2. CNN-BLSTM algorithm design

The task can be characterized as a multi-target regression problem since the goal is to localize the impact position based on the data sampled by instrumented sensors. A DNN model is designed to regress input signals and determine the location of the impact load. The core idea of the proposed DNN model is to extract spatial features of the input multi-variate time series through convolutional network layers, and to exploit the temporal relationship by recurrent network layers.

To properly exploit the multivariate input signals, first, CNN layers are embedded in the network model to learn the spatial data correlation. The general formulation of the CNN layers can be provided as $\mathbf{H} = CNN(\mathbf{X})$, where $\mathbf{H}$ represents the extracted features in terms of the input acceleration signal $\mathbf{X}$. Multiple convolutional layers are used in the model to extract high-level features.

CNN features consider the spatial correlation over multivariate time series. To capture the temporal correlation between sensor readings at different time steps, the sequential chracteristics within the learned convolutional features is learned using a recurrent neural network. A long-term time series input may lead to the problem of gradient disappearance or explosion in back-propagation. To extract the temporal features that exist among long-term time series, the proposed model splits the full-length time series into p slices and input them into recurrent layers. The split slices are given as $H_{1:p} = [H_1, H_2, \dots, H_p]$. These shorten slices can avoid the problem of gradient disappearance or explosion caused by the long-term time series inputs. LSTM generally operates in the direction of time flow. However, the variation of sensor readings is bidirectionally related. To extract the bidirectional connections between historical and future data, a bidirectional LSTM (BLSTM) structure is utilized in the proposed model, which is shown in Figure 2.

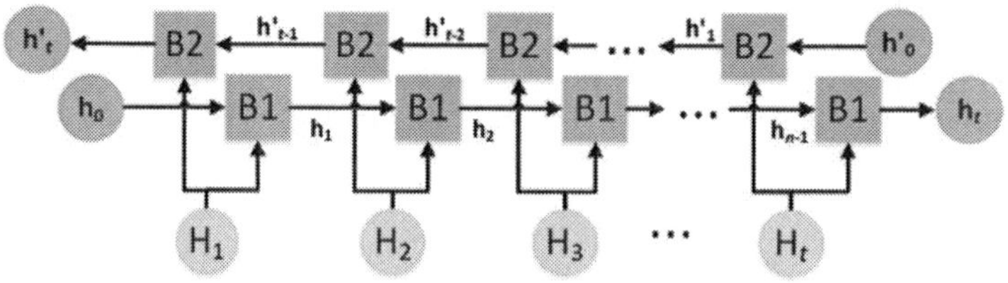

Figure 2. Bidirectional LSTM

In the figure, B1 represents forward operation in the BLSTM, and B2 represents backward operation. In the forward operation, the hidden state $\mathbf{h}_t$ is related to $\mathbf{h}_{t-1}$ while the hidden state $\mathbf{h}'_t$ of the hidden layer is related to $\mathbf{h}'_{t+1}$. Since it is a bidirectional network, each recurrent layer has two hidden states. After the two hidden states are merged through a concatenation and Relu activation at the last BLSTM module. Finally, a fully connected layer is embedded to output the final required position estimation. The final output is the position of an impact and is generated by a fully connected layer.

The overall architecture of the proposed neural network, named as CNN-BLSTM, is presented in Figure 3. The original data is the time-series signals of n acceleration sensors, which is input to the CNN layer for feature extraction, and then the data slices are combined into p sequences and sequentially fed into the BLSTM to exploit the temporal correlation. A fully connected (FC) layer completes the regression task and generate the impact location result.

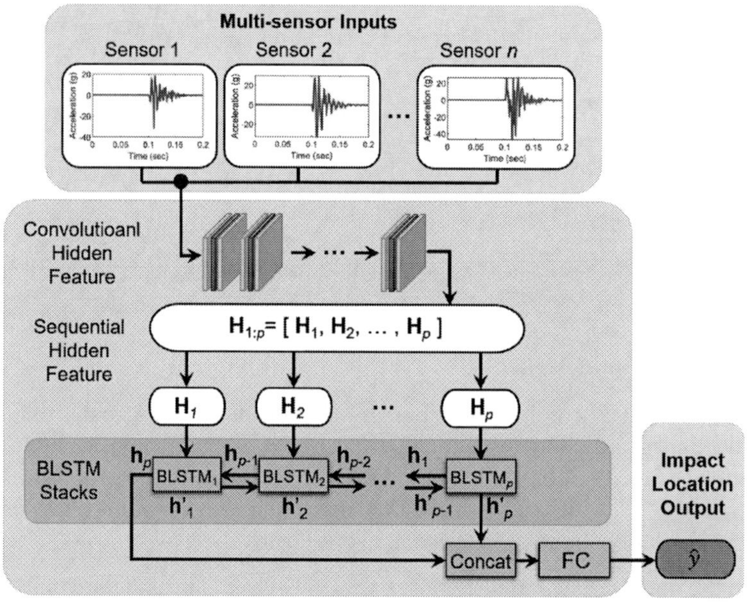

Figure 3. The overall architecture of the proposed DNN model

3. NUMERICAL STUDY

To validate the performance of the proposed method, a numerical study is conducted on a plate structure. The plate had a dimension of 640 mm by 800 mm with a thickness of 20 mm. A FE model of the plate was developed in SAP2000 using thin shell element, as seen in Figure 4a. The Young's modulus of the plate was 250,000 MPa with a Poisson's ratio of 0.3 and a density of 2,800 kg/m^3. The plate was meshed with 8 by 10 elements and a fixed bounday condition was assigned at the bottom edge. There are a total of 88 nodes that can be used for applying impact load in the out-of-plane direction.

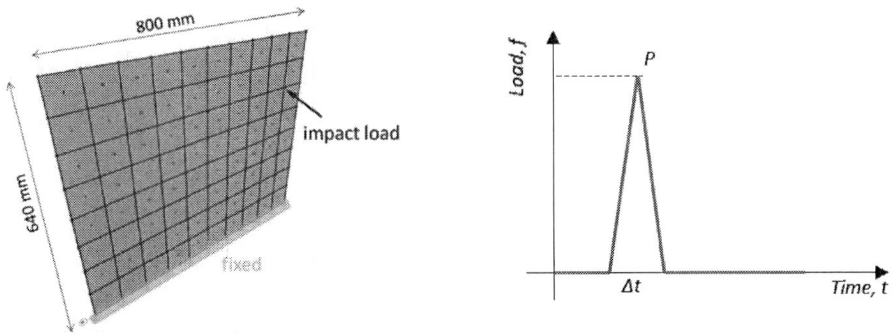

a) b)

Figure 4. a) FE model of the plate structure and b) impact load pattern

3.1. Generation of dataset

There are three datasets required in the case study: training set, validation set, and test set. All the datasests are generated by performing time history analysis on the developed FE model of the plate subjected to random impact loads at 88 grid nodes. An impact load can be numerically characterized as a triangular load pattern, as seen in Figure 4b. Two main parameters, amplitude *P* and duration time Δt, are used to define a impact load case. According to previous studies, a range of 0.002 sec to 0.02 sec was considered for Δt where the total duration was 0.5 sec. The peak load was in a range from 1kN to 5 kN. For each loading case, the impact load location, loading pattern, and the acceleration time histores at non-fixed grid nodes were recorded. In total, 1,000 loading scenarios were simulated and the datasets were collected at a sampling rate of 1,000 Hz for 0.5 sec. Figure 5 shows the accelearation responses at three selected locations during one impact load simulation. In this case study, four locations were assumed to place acceleraometer sensors.

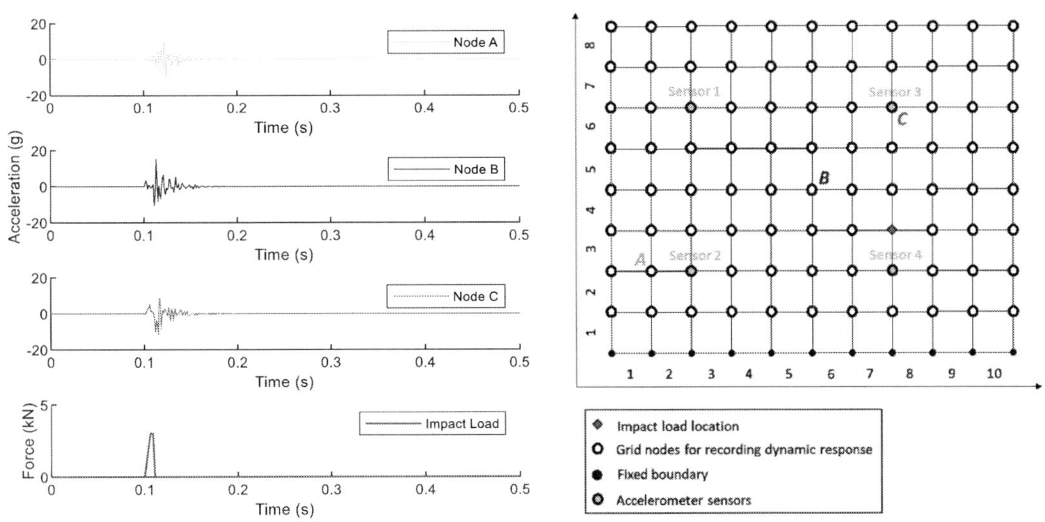

Figure 5. Illustrative dynamic responses at grid nodes during sample impact scenario.

3.2. Neural network training

To assess the accuracy of the proposed method, a mean absolute error (MAE) is calculated for each impact loading case in the test set according to Qiu et al. [2]:

$$e_{Error} = \sqrt{(x - \hat{x})^2 + (y - \hat{y})^2} \quad (1)$$

where x and y denote cooridnates of actual impact load, while $\hat{x}$ and $\hat{y}$ denote cooridnates of predicted impact load location. The cooridnate is a linear function of grid length, for example, in Figure 5, coordinate [1, 3] indicates a position of the third column of the first row in the plate. It marks as "True" if the distance between the estimated position and the label position is zero, otherwise, it marks as "False", indicating a misjudgement. It should be noted that the locations within an grid element was not considered. The final estimation accuracy is recorded as "Accuracy" rate, which is defined as:

$$Accuracy = \frac{True}{True + False} * 100\% \tag{2}$$

The analysis was performed using Python 3.7 and Pytorch 1.11 on a desktop PC with an Nvidia GeForce MX 150 GPU, an Intel i5-8250U CPU and 8 GB RAM. In the numerical example, the learning rate is set to 0.01; the number of training epochs is set to 350 , the training data ratio is set to 0.8 (i.e., 800 time history analyses).

The loss function is calculated by the MAE. There are three convolution layers embedded in the model (with kernel size 9, padding size 4, and stride 1). The number of hidden neurons in each layer is 128; the number of fully connected layer is set to 3; the number of neurons in the first layer is 256, the number of neurons in the second layer is 50 , and the number of the last layer is 2. During the training process, the model automatically updates the learnable weights. The loss value during training is shown in Figure 6. It can be observed that the loss value converges around 50 training epochs.

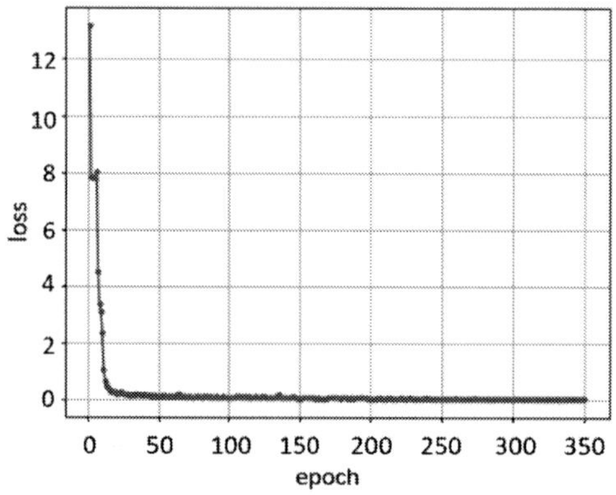

Figure 6. Loss value variation

3.3. Impact load localization performance

The final accuracy rate and the error distribution probability is shown in Figure 7. It can be found that the accuracy of the CNN-BLSTM model has reached as high as 96% of all 200 test scenarios, meaning only 8 misjudgments. It is worth to mention that the positional deviations of the misjudgment results are all within one unit length of the grid.

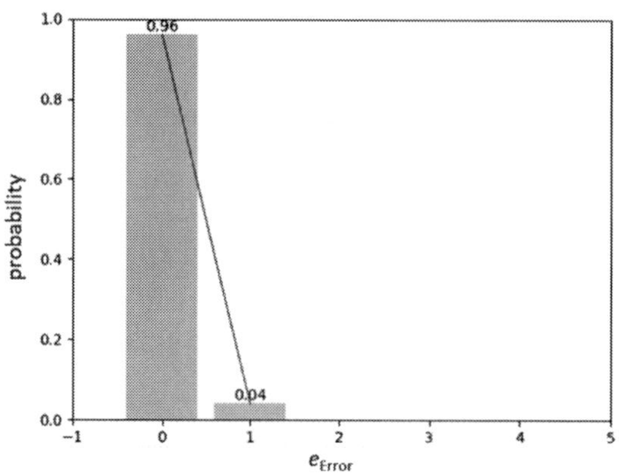

Figure 7. Accuracy rate and error distribution.

Figure 8 illustrates the location identification results of 5 testing points based on the CNN-BLSTM model. The real impact locations were marked as a red diamond, 3 of them are "True" identification which was marked as a blue triangle, and 2 of them are "False" identification which were marked as a grey triangle. It can be seen that the "True" identification location completely coincide with the real ones as the e_{Error} is 0, while those "False" identifications were at the most adjacent grid point with one unit length.

The training time for each epoch was 0.8 sec with a total training time of 4.7 mins. The average time cost for predicting the impact location in the test set was 1 ms, which satisfies the real-time requirement.

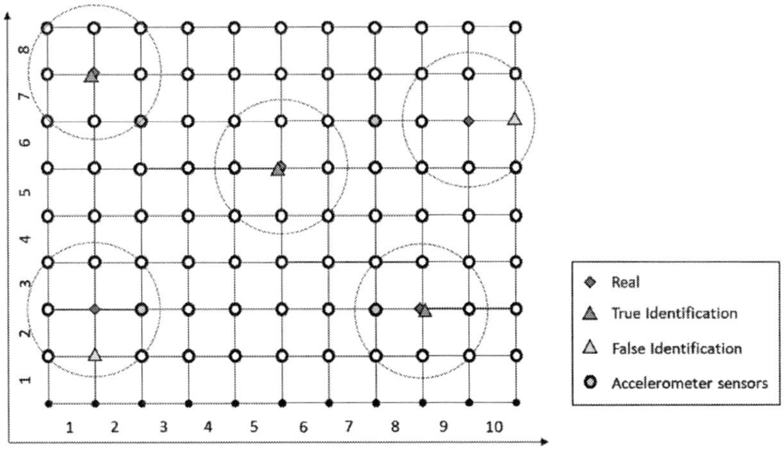

Figure 8. Real impact locations and predicted locations of 5 testing points.

4. CONCLUSIONS

This paper proposed a novel DNN model for localizing impact load on plate structures in real-time. The developed model is trained by using datasets generated from time history analysis on a structural finite element model to learn the inherent spatiotemporal relationship between input impact load and output acceleration dynamic responses among different locations. A numerical case study was performed on a thin plate to examine the effectiveness of the proposed method.

Based on the analysis, it was found for the case study plate with 4 accelerometer sensors deployed, real-time load localization can be achieved. The accuracy rate for impact load localization was 96%. The time cost of the localization was 1 millisecond, which fulfill the real-time requirement. Since the presented study was limited to numerical demonstration, future research needs to examine the real-world application with different materials and boundary conditions, as well as optimal sensor placement. Future work also includes the extension of this method to damage localization and OMA using both simulated data and experimental data as part of the project. Such experimental programs are underway at the Earthquake Engineering Research Facility lab at The University of British Columbia.

ACKNOWLEDGEMENTS

This work is supported in part by a Discovery Grant by the Natural Science and Engineering Research Council of Canada awarded to the last author (Grant No. RGPIN-2017-04988).

REFERENCES

[1] Huang, T., & Schröder, K.-U. (2021). A Bayesian probabilistic approach for damage identification in plate structures using responses at vibration nodes. *Mechanical Systems and Signal Processing, 146*, 106998.

[2] Qiu, B., Zhang, M., Li, X., Qu, X., & Tong, F. (2020). Unknown impact force localisation and reconstruction in experimental plate structure using time-series analysis and pattern recognition. *International Journal of Mechanical Sciences, 166*, 105231.

[3] Inoue, H., Harrigan and, J. J., & Reid, S. R. (2001). Review of inverse analysis for indirect measurement of impact force. *Applied Mechanics Reviews, 54*(6), 503-524.

[4] Liu, J., Sun, X., Han, X., Jiang, C., & Yu, D. (2015). Dynamic load identification for stochastic structures based on Gegenbauer polynomial approximation and regularization method. *Mechanical Systems and Signal Processing, 56*, 35-54.

[5] Movahedian, B., & Boroomand, B. (2016). Inverse identification of time-harmonic loads acting on thin plates using approximated Green's functions. *Inverse Problems in Science and Engineering, 24*(8), 1475-1493.

[6] Qiu, B., Zhang, M., Xie, Y., Qu, X., & Li, X. (2019). Localisation of unknown impact loads on a steel plate using a pattern recognition method combined with the similarity metric via structural stress responses in the time domain. *Mechanical Systems and Signal Processing, 128*, 429-445.

[7] Uhl, T. (2007). The inverse identification problem and its technical application. *Archive of Applied Mechanics, 77*(5), 325-337.

[8] Gupta, D. K. (2013). *Inverse methods for load identification augmented by optimal sensor placement and model order reduction.* The University of Wisconsin-Milwaukee.

[9] Malekloo, A., Ozer, E., AlHamaydeh, M., & Girolami, M. (2021). Machine learning and structural health monitoring overview with emerging technology and high-dimensional data source highlights. *Structural Health Monitoring*, 14759217211036880.

[10] Avci, O., Abdeljaber, O., Kiranyaz, S., Hussein, M., Gabbouj, M., & Inman, D. J. (2021). A review of vibration-based damage detection in civil structures: From traditional methods to Machine Learning and Deep Learning applications. *Mechanical Systems and Signal Processing, 147*, 107077.

[11] Liu, H., & Zhang, Y. (2019). Deep learning based crack damage detection technique for thin plate structures using guided lamb wave signals. *Smart Materials and Structures, 29*(1), 015032.

[12] Pan, X., & Yang, T. (2020). Postdisaster image-based damage detection and repair cost estimation of reinforced concrete buildings using dual convolutional neural networks. *Computer-Aided Civil and Infrastructure Engineering, 35*(5), 495-510.

[13] Li, T., Pan, Y., Tong, K., Ventura, C. E., & de Silva, C. W. (2021). Attention-Based Sequence-to-Sequence Learning for Online Structural Response Forecasting Under Seismic Excitation. *IEEE Transactions on Systems, Man, and Cybernetics: Systems.* doi:https://doi.org/10.1109/TSMC.2020.3048696

[14] Pan, Y., Ventura, C. E., & Li, T. (2022). Sensor placement and seismic response reconstruction for structural health monitoring using a deep neural network. *Bulletin of Earthquake Engineering*, 1-20.

[15] Zhou, J., Dong, L., Guan, W., & Yan, J. (2019). Impact load identification of nonlinear structures using deep Recurrent Neural Network. *Mechanical Systems and Signal Processing, 133*, 106292.

[16] Chen, T., Guo, L., Duan, A., Gao, H., Feng, T., & He, Y. (2021). A feature learning-based method for impact load reconstruction and localization of the plate-rib assembled structure. *Structural Health Monitoring*, 14759217211038065.

MODAL SCALING

FULL-SCALE DYNAMIC MEASUREMENT SYSTEM FOR FE-MODEL UPDATING OF MASONRY BUILDING AGGREGATES

Antonino Maria Marra[1], *Valerio Alecci*[2], *Dora Pugliese*[3], *Mario De Stefano*[4]

[1] Post-doctoral research fellow, Department of Civil and Environmental Engineering, University of Florence antoninomaria.marra@unifi.it
[2] Associate Professor, Department of Architecture, University of Florence, valerio.alecci@unifi.it
[3] PhD student, Department of Architecture, University of Florence, dora.pugliese@unifi.it
[4] Full Professor, Department of Architecture, University of Florence, mario.destefano@unifi.it

ABSTRACT

Masonry building aggregates represent a recurrent structural typology of historic centers, which has shown several damages during earthquake events. Thus, improving the seismic behavior of building aggregates takes on great importance not only to increase the safety of their occupants but also to reduce the losses on their cultural and artistic value. Unfortunately, the lack of information about their structural characteristics (material properties, connections between structural elements, etc.) prevents the set-up of suitable models without calibrations through the results of measurements on the real structure, as commonly done for other structural typologies. With the aim of improving the predictions of finite element (FE) models of masonry building aggregates, this study reports the results of a preliminary research activity developed within S-MoSES project (Smart Monitoring for Safety of Existing Structures and Infrastructures). A three-dimensional FE model with solid elements of a portion of a masonry building aggregate has been set-up to obtain valuable information for the design of a monitoring system. The sensor network, once installed on the building aggregate, will be used in subsequent research activities of S-MoSES project to develop a procedure for the FE model updating.

Keywords: Masonry building aggregates, Three-dimensional FE model, Monitoring system

1. INTRODUCTION

Historic centers mainly comprise masonry building aggregates, whose safeguarding and preservation are mandatory for modern societies. When hit by earthquakes, urban aggregates have shown significant structural damages together with several injuries and deaths. Thus, implementing appropriate retrofit strategies on existing building aggregates represents a priority for public administrations. Establishing the right retrofits for existing structures requires reliable finite element (FE) models, which still constitute a complex task.

A masonry aggregate is an assembly of connected structural units. An accurate definition of the single structural units and their mutual interactions requires a thorough knowledge of the whole building. Unfortunately, this task is commonly accomplished by accepting non-negligible uncertainties since acquiring information about these structures is complex. Documents of historic constructions erected in progressive steps are difficult to recover, and the definition of the geometry and construction details is not always achievable. In addition, a suitable definition of the boundary conditions of structural units can be attempted only through a complete FE analysis of masonry building aggregate based on in-situ tests to estimate the mechanical properties [1-3]. This task is mainly conducted for research scopes and strategic or monumental structures. For these reasons, the Italian building code suggests simplified analyses conducted through very simplified methods, not enough validated.

The scientific literature on seismic behavior of masonry aggregates has been growing in the recent years. Advanced numerical strategies have been applied in recent works [4-5], which are based on the coupling of nonlinear static and dynamic seismic analyses on three-dimensional FE models together with local analyses. The application of different analysis procedures allows catching the seismic behavior of building aggregates as accurate as possible. Nonlinear analysis procedures have been developed to study the structural units [6-8] for practical applications. A seismic fragility assessment has been conducted in [9] with reference to a case study. Shake table tests have been also employed to explore the seismic behavior of masonry aggregates [10-11]. Finally, numerical analyses have been used to evaluate various strengthening techniques [12].

An improvement in the definition of the FE model of a building aggregate may be obtained through full-scale measurements of the modal frequencies and shapes, which allow updating the model. With this aim, this paper refers to the first step of a more extensive study within the S-MoSES project (Smart Monitoring for Safety of Existing Structures and Infrastructures), financed by MUR (Italian Ministry for University and Research), which intends to update the FE model by taking advantage of the information provided by an ad hoc monitoring system installed on a building aggregate. The ambient vibrations registered by accelerometers placed on salient points will be used to define the system's dynamic behavior (e.g., main natural frequencies and modal shapes). This information will be used for updating the FE model of the entire aggregate or single units, in which the boundary conditions should be properly modeled (e.g., spring constants simulating the interaction with the neighboring structural units). The work reported in this paper is limited to the design of the monitoring system for a building aggregate of the historic center of Anghiari (Arezzo, Italy), selected as a case study. For this scope, a modal analysis of the three-dimensional FE model of the building aggregate has been carried out. The model's response has been used to define both number and positions of the measuring points.

The next section is dedicated to the description of the case study, in which information about the materials, the geometry and the structural units of the aggregate are reported. Section 3 refers to main characteristics of the FE model used in the dynamic analysis of the structure. The results of the modal analysis on the aggregate are reported in section 4 together with some indications about the positions of the accelerometers belonging to the monitoring system. Finally, some concluding remarks are reported at the end of the paper.

2. CASE STUDY

The building aggregate is in Baldaccio Square, which is a central place in the city of Anghiari (Arezzo, Italy), located just outside to the medieval walls. From the historic document denoted "Codice Corsi", date back to '700, the building presents a configuration very close to the current one. Other documents date back to '800 allow identifying some structural interventions, like the removal of the buttress from a lateral wall as well as the presence of ties. Figure 1 shows the buildings at the earlier of the twentieth century, which is practically unchanged a century later.

An important concern is that the building does not have independent structural behavior since it shares midwalls with adjacent buildings. This means that its seismic response should be studied at the level of the aggregate. Due to the limited information available during this preliminary research, the dynamic behavior of the buildings has been analyzed by considering a three-dimensional model with the plan shown in Figure 2. The area bounded by dashed lines represents a part of the aggregate which is structurally connected to the analyzed one but for which no information are available.

The geometry of the aggregate is irregular in height; Figure 3 shows a variation of the number of floors in the modeled structure. In particular, the highest building shows a ground floor, two elevated floors and an attic, while the other building presents the same floors except being characterized by only one elevated floor. Both buildings have a basement underneath all the plans.

A systematic use of wood was observed in structural elements of floors and roofing structures, while the bearing walls have been constituted by roughly hewn stone blocks.

Figure 1. Baldaccio Square in 1903 (left) and 2018 (right).

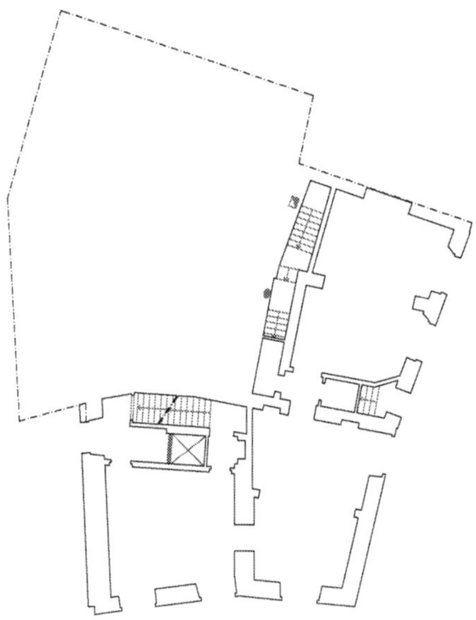

Figure 2. Plan view of the building aggregate at the ground level considered in the present study.

Figure 3. Front and lateral views of the building aggregate.

3. FE MODEL

The FE model of the building were made through Abaqus CAE software [13], which is characterized by quadratic tetrahedral elements namely C3D10. Some sensitivity analyses on the dimension of the mesh elements were carried out to check the convergence of the results.

Linear elastic behavior has been assumed for all the elements of the FE model. The material density, the Poisson coefficient and the elastic modulus of the masonry walls have been considered, respectively, equal to 2000 kg/m^3, 0.25 and 1230 MPa, in agreement with the values provided by IBC [14-15]. To compute the natural modal frequencies and shapes of the model structural and non-structural weights together with the 30% of the live loads for a residential building (2 kN/m^2) have been used. A view of the three-dimensional FE model is reported in Figure 4.

The basement has been modeled to account for its stiffness along the vertical direction. The basement walls have been simply supported at the base and restrained in the horizontal directions to consider the confinement provided by the adjacent soils.

Figure 4. FE model of the aggregate.

4. RESULTS

A modal analysis of the three-dimensional FE model has been carried out to identify the parts of the masonry aggregate mainly involved in the dynamic of the structure. Modal shapes up to the tenth mode have been estimated but just the first three modal shapes are shown in the following figures, the other modal shapes refer to local vibrations. It is worth noting that the results should be considered just preliminary outcomes since no information about the iteration between the analyzed structure and the neighboring buildings were available when the FE model was built. They are used just for the definition of the monitoring system that will be installed in the masonry aggregate.

The first natural mode can be considered as translational mode along the *y*-direction by considering the reference system reported in Figure 5. As expected, it is characterized by displacements that increase from the ground to the top floor, but it can be also seen that the main part of the horizontal displacements occur at the ceil of the ground floor. It is mainly due to the presence of the openings in the walls. A similar behavior is observed in the second mode, which mainly involves displacements in the *x*-direction (Figure 6). Similar considerations can be done also for this mode shape. Finally, the third mode can be classified as a torsional mode which shows a progressively increase of the modal rotations from the ground to the top floor (Figure 7). It is worth noting that the basement cannot shows horizontal oscillations in the external bearing walls due to horizontal restraints but can manifest vertical displacements. This means that the ground floor is supported by a "bed of springs" characterized by the stiffness of the walls.

The results of the modal analysis on the three-dimensional FE model of the portion of masonry building aggregate analyzed provide useful indications for the design of the monitoring system. First, preliminary information about the natural frequencies and modal shapes are useful to identify the modes of the structure under measurement. From a practical point of view, the indications gained by a preliminary modal analysis of the real structure helps to discern spectral peaks associated to the natural modes from those caused by environmental and electrical noises as well as secondary elements. Thus, subsequent analyses for the extraction of the modal shapes from the measured signals are facilitate. Second, a preliminary knowledge of the modal shapes gives valuable indications about the positions of the sensors. In the considered case study, the shapes of the first translational modal shapes suggest that the main variations in the horizontal displacements along the vertical faces are concentrated to the first floor. Therefore, for a proper identification of the first natural modes, sensors should be located at the top of the ground floor on both directions, other than at the classical sensor positions located at the top of the building where maxima modal displacements are shown. In addition, the identification of the first torsional mode requires the installation of the sensors on three of the four top edges of two orthogonal façades.

Figure 8 shows the sensor positions (red dots) suggested by the results of the modal analysis for the considered portion of masonry building aggregate. The positions of the sensors on the façades are also chosen to catch possible in-plane floor deformations.

Figure 5. First translational mode along x.

Figure 6. First translational mode along y.

Figure 7. First torsional mode.

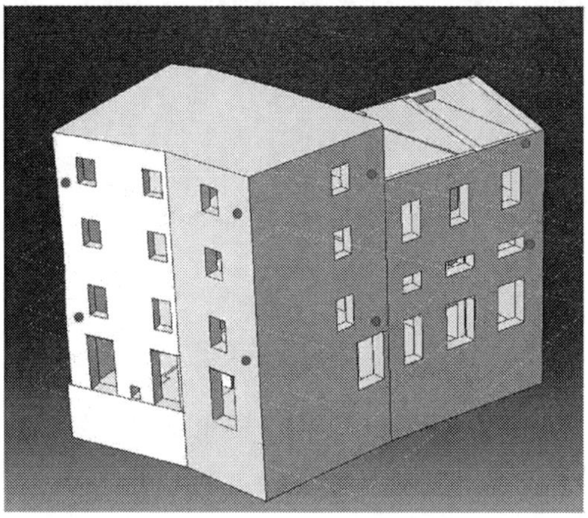

Figure 8. Sketch with sensor positions.

5. CONCLUSIONS

A three-dimensional FE model with solid elements of a portion of a masonry building aggregate, located in Tuscany, has been set-up with the aim of obtaining valuable information for the design of a monitoring system. The work represents a preliminary research activity within S-MoSES project (Smart Monitoring for Safety of Existing Structures and Infrastructures), which intends to update the FE model by taking advantage of the information provided by an ad hoc monitoring system installed on a building aggregate. In particular, the results of the modal analysis on the FE model of the aggregate have been used to gain important information for the definition of both the positions and number of sensors to be installed on the real structure. The sensor network, mainly composed by accelerometers, will be used for a proper identification of the structural interaction with the adjacent buildings belonging to the same aggregate, for which no detailed information are available.

ACKNOWLEDGEMENTS

The financial support provided through the S-MoSES (Smart Monitoring for Safety of Existing Structures and infrastructures) Project (Research Project of National Interest, PRIN 2020) by the MUR (Italian Ministry of University and Research) is gratefully acknowledged.

The Authors also wish to warmly thank Arch. Milton Riccardo Sperone, owner of the building, and Eng. Luca Romolini for providing the drawings and further information used to build the FE model.

REFERENCES

[1] Alecci V., Stipo G., La Brusco A., De Stefano M., Rovero L. (2021). Estimating elastic modulus of tuff and brick masonry: a comparison between on-site and laboratory tests, *Constr. Build. Mater.* 204, 828-838.

[2] Alecci V., De Stefano M., Luciano R., Marra A.M., Stipo G. (2020). Numerical investigation on the use of flat-jack test for detecting masonry deformability, *Journal of Testing and Evaluation*, 49, 1, 537-549.

[3] Alecci V., Ayala A.G., De Stefano M., Marra A.M., Nudo R., Stipo G. (2021). Influence of the masonry wall thickness on the outcomes of double flat-jack test: Experimental and numerical investigation, *Constr. Build. Mater*, 285.

[4] Grillanda, N., Valente, M., Milani, G., Chiozzi, A., Tralli, A. (2020). Advanced numerical strategies for seismic assessment of historical masonry aggregates. *Engineering Structures*, 212, 110441.

[5] Valente M., Milani G., Grande E., Formisano A. (2019). Historical masonry building aggregates: advanced numerical insight for an effective seismic assessment on two row housing compounds. *Engineering Structures* 190, 360-379.

[6] Bernardini C., Maio R., Boschi S., Ferreira T. M., Vicente R., Vignoli A. (2019). The seismic performance-based assessment of a masonry building enclosed in aggregate in Faro (Portugal) by means of a new target structural unit approach. *Engineering Structures*, 191, 386-400.

[7] Formisano A., Massimilla A. (2018). A Novel Procedure for Simplified Nonlinear Numerical Modeling of Structural Units in Masonry Aggregates. *International Journal of Architectural Heritage*, 12(7-8), 1162-1170.

[8] Fagundes C., Bento R., Cattari S. (2017). On the seismic response of buildings in aggregate: Analysis of a typical masonry building from Azores. *Structures*, 10, 184-196.

[9] Battaglia L., Ferreira T. M., Lourenço P.B. (2020). Seismic fragility assessment of masonry building aggregates: A case study in the old city Centre of Seixal, Portugal. *Earthquake Engng Struct Dyn.*, 1-20.

[10] Guerrini G., Senaldi I., Graziotti F., Magenes G., Beyer K., Penna A. (2019). Shake-Table Test of a Strengthened Stone Masonry Building Aggregate with Flexible Diaphragms. *International Journal of Architectural Heritage*, 13(7), 1078-1097.

[11] Senaldi I. E., Guerrini G., Comini P., Graziotti F., Penna A., Beyer K., Magenes G. (2020). Experimental seismic performance of a half-scale stone masonry building aggregate. *Bulletin of Earthquake Engineering*, 18, 609-643.

[12] Vicente R., Rodrigues H., Varum H., Mendes da Silva J. A. R. (2011). Evaluation of strengthening techniques of traditional masonry buildings: case study of a four-building aggregate. *Journal of Performance of Constructed Facilities*, 25, 202-216.

[13] Dassault Systemes, Simulia - ABAQUS/CAE user's guide 6.14.

[14] NTC2018, Aggiornamento delle “Norme tecniche per le costruzioni”. S.O. alla G.U. n. 42 del 20/02/2018. (in Italian)

[15] CIRC2019, Istruzioni per l’applicazione dell’Aggiornamento delle Norme tecniche per le costruzioni di cui al decreto ministeriale 17 gennaio 2018. (in Italian)

9th International Operational Modal Analysis Conference
iomac
July 3 - 6, 2022
Vancouver, Canada

LENGTH OF MODE SHAPES IN NUMERICAL AND EXPERIMENTAL MODELS

N. García-Fernández[1], *F. Pelayo*[2], *R. Brincker*[3], *M. Aenlle*[4],

[1] PhD Student, University of Oviedo, garciafnatalia@uniovi.es
[2] Professor, University of Oviedo, fernandezpelayo@uniovi.es
[3] Professor, Technical University of Denmark, runeb@byg.dtu.dk
[4] Professor, University of Oviedo, aenlle@uniovi.es

ABSTRACT

A new concept of length of a continuous mode shape has been recently defined by the authors, which depends on the mode shape and how the volume is distributed in the structure. This concept was then extended to discrete systems by introducing the concept of a volume matrix. However, finite element programs do not provide the lengths of the mode shapes according to this new definition. Moreover, the volume matrices cannot be exported from the finite element programs.

In this paper, an approximate approach is proposed to calculate the length of numerical mode shapes from the nodal components. It has been demonstrated that the length can be estimated with a reasonable accuracy if small finite elements are used. These new techniques are illustrated by several numerical models assembled in ABAQUS.

The length of numerical mode shapes can be used to estimate the length of experimental mode shapes using the structural dynamic modification, which is valuable information to validate the modal masses estimated with the existing techniques to determine the modal masses in operational modal analysis.

Keywords: Mode shapes, Conference, Operational, Modal, Analysis

1. INTRODUCTION

A mode shape is said to be normalized to the unit length if its length is unity. In one-dimensional continuous systems, the Euclidean length squared $L_{E\psi}^2$ of a function $\boldsymbol{\psi}(\boldsymbol{x})$, also known as Euclidean norm or $L^2 - norm$, is defined as [1]:

$$L_{E\psi}^2 = \int_0^L |\psi(x)|^2 dx \tag{1}$$

In discrete systems, the length squared of the mode shape vector $\boldsymbol{\psi}$ (length of a vector in an Euclidean space) is defined as [1]:

$$L_{E\psi}^2 = \boldsymbol{\psi}^T\boldsymbol{\psi} \tag{2}$$

The main inconvenience of Eq. (2) is that the length depends on the number of components of the vector.

In [2] the squared length L_ψ^2 of the mode shape $\boldsymbol{\psi}$ was defined as the average of the length squared $|\psi|^2$ of the mode shape over the volume $V$of the structure i.e.:

$$L_\psi^2 = \frac{1}{V_T}\int_V |\boldsymbol{\psi}|^2\, dV \tag{3}$$

where V_T is the total volume of the system.

Eq. (3) secures that the length definition has the same unit as the mode shape. Thus, if the mode shape is dimensionless, so is the length. Eq. (3) was naturally extended to discrete systems as:

$$L_\psi^2 = \frac{1}{V_T}\, \boldsymbol{\psi}^T\boldsymbol{V}\boldsymbol{\psi} \tag{4}$$

where $\boldsymbol{V}$ is the volume matrix of the system.

In continuous straight planar beams with length L, distributed mass density $\rho(x)$ and cross section with area $A(x)$, the modal mass (also denoted as generalized mass in some books of structural dynamics) corresponding to an arbitrary normalized continuous mode shape vector $\boldsymbol{\psi}(\boldsymbol{x})$, is given by [2,3,4]:

$$m_\psi = \int_0^L \rho(x)A(x)|\boldsymbol{\psi}(\boldsymbol{x})|^2 dx \tag{5}$$

A general equation to calculate the modal mass for the continuous case is given by [2]:

$$m_\psi = \int_V \rho|\boldsymbol{\psi}|^2 dV \tag{6}$$

wich can be easily extended to discrete systems as:

$$m = \boldsymbol{\psi}^T\boldsymbol{M}\boldsymbol{\psi} \tag{7}$$

where $\boldsymbol{M}$ is the mass matrix.

If the mass-density ρ of a system is constant, Eq. (7) can be expressed as:

$$m_\psi = \boldsymbol{\psi}^T\boldsymbol{M}\boldsymbol{\psi} = \rho\, \boldsymbol{\psi}^T\boldsymbol{V}\boldsymbol{\psi} \tag{8}$$

where $\boldsymbol{V}$ is the volume matrix. Eq. (8) can also be formulated as:

$$m_{\psi} = M_T \frac{\boldsymbol{\psi}^T \boldsymbol{V} \boldsymbol{\psi}}{V_T} = M_T L_{\psi}^2 \quad (9)$$

If the mass density ρ is not constant, Eq. (7) can be expressed as:

$$m_{\psi} = M_{ap} L_{\psi}^2 \quad (10)$$

where M_{ap} is an apparent mass.

One of the problems of the length defined by Eq. (4) is that finite element programs do not provide the lengths of the mode shapes. On the other hand, the volume matrices $\boldsymbol{V}$ cannot be exported from the finite element programs either.

If the numerical model is discretized with N_V small finite elements of equal volume ΔV Eq. (4) can be approximated as:

$$L_{\psi}^2 \cong \frac{\Delta V \sum_{k=1}^{N_V} \psi_k^2}{N_V \Delta V} = \frac{\sum_{k=1}^{N_V} \psi_k^2}{N_V} = \frac{\boldsymbol{\psi}^T \boldsymbol{\psi}}{N_V} \quad (11)$$

However, in numerical models, the components of the mode shapes are commonly known at the nodes of the elements, and Eq. (11) can also be approximated by means of the expression:

$$L_{\psi}^2 \cong \frac{\boldsymbol{\psi}^T \boldsymbol{\psi}}{N} \quad (12)$$

where N is the number of nodes in the model.

According to the structural dynamic modification (SDM), the experimental mode shapes can be expressed as a linear combination of the numerical mode shapes [5,6], i.e.:

$$\boldsymbol{\psi}_{\boldsymbol{X}} = \boldsymbol{\psi}_{\boldsymbol{FE}} \boldsymbol{T} \quad (13)$$

where $\boldsymbol{T}$ is a transformation matrix.

Due to the fact that the experimental mode shapes are only known at the measured DOF's, an approximation of matrix $\boldsymbol{T}$ can be obtained by means of the expression [5]:

$$\boldsymbol{T} = \boldsymbol{\psi}_{\boldsymbol{FE}_a}^{+} \boldsymbol{\psi}_{\boldsymbol{X}_a} \quad (14)$$

where '+' indicates pseudoinverse and subindex 'a' indicates active or measured DOF's. The experimental mode shapes can then be expanded to the unmeasured DOF's by:

$$\boldsymbol{\psi}_{\boldsymbol{X}_d} = \boldsymbol{\psi}_{\boldsymbol{FE}_d} \boldsymbol{T} \quad (15)$$

where subindex 'd' indicates deleted or unmeasured.

Finally, an approximation of the squared length of the experimental mode shapes can be obtained using the expanded experimental shapes with the expression:

$$L_{\psi X}^2 \cong \frac{\boldsymbol{\psi}_{\boldsymbol{X}}^T \boldsymbol{\psi}_{\boldsymbol{X}}}{N} \quad (16)$$

where it is assumed that the number of elements is the same in both the numerical and the experimental models.

2. A CANTILEVER BEAM WITH CONSTANT MASS-DENSITY

2.1. 3D numerical model

A steel cantilever beam with rectangular cross-section (4cm×5cm) and 1 meter long, was assembled in the finite element software ABAQUS [7] (see Figure 1-a). The steel was considered linear -elastic and the following material properties were assumed: mass-density $\varrho = 7850\ kg/m^3$, Young's modulus $E = 210\ GPa$, and Poisson ratio $\nu = 0.3$. The total mass of the system is $M_T = 15.7\ kg$.

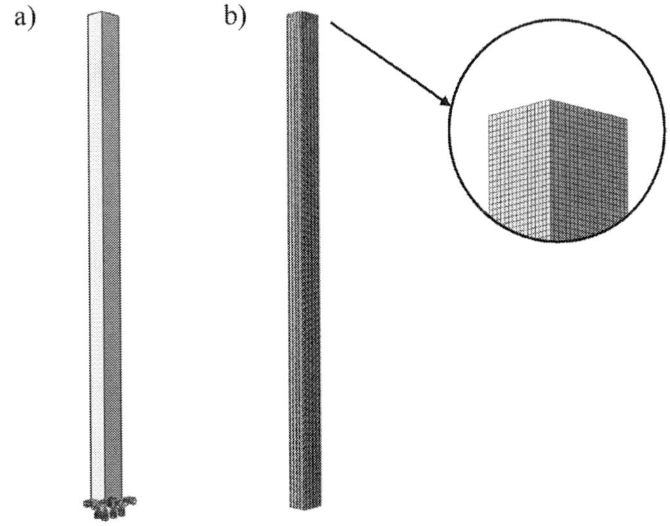

Figure 1. a) 3D steel numerical model; b) mesh with element size of 0.0025 m

Particularizing Eq. (3) to a beam with constant cross-section, the analytical length of the mode shapes can be obtained with:

$$L_\psi^2 = \frac{1}{L}\int_0^L |\boldsymbol{\psi}(\boldsymbol{x})|^2\, dx \tag{17}$$

The analytical expressions of the bending mode shapes $\boldsymbol{\psi}(\boldsymbol{x})$ corresponding to beams with constant mass-density and constant cross-section, are reported in the literature [1,8], and for a cantilever beam are given as:

$$\psi_k = C_1\left(cosh(\beta_k x) - cos(\beta_k x) - \frac{cosh(\beta_k L) + cos(\beta_k L)}{sinh(\beta_k L) + sin(\beta_k L)}\left(sinh(\beta_k x) - sin(\beta_k x)\right)\right) \tag{18}$$

where 'k' indicates the order of the mode and the values of β_k are shown in Table 1.

Table 1. Values of $\boldsymbol{\beta_k L}$ for bending modes of a cantilever beam [1,8]

	k				
	1	2	3	4	$k > 4$
$\beta_k L$	1.8751	4.6941	7.8548	10.996	$(2k-1)\frac{\pi}{2}$

In this particular case the squared length results $L_\psi^2 = 0.25$ for all the bending modes.

The beam was meshed with quadratic twenty-node hexahedral elements (C3D20R) and with different size of the elements. The natural frequencies corresponding to the first eight modes, using an element size of 2.5 mm, are presented in Table 2, whereas the mode shapes are shown in Figures 2. The modal masses, corresponding to mode shapes normalized to the largest component equal to unity, are presented in Table 3. Where it can be observed that approximately the same modal masses are obtained for sizes less than 20 mm.

Table 2. Natural frequencies of the cantilever beam.

	Mode	Finite element model C3D20R (Element size 2.5 mm)	Beam model B32 (Element size 2.5 mm)
1	1st Bending Y	33.452	33.379
2	1st Bending X	41.774	41.694
3	2nd Bending Y	208.090	207.630
4	2nd Bending X	258.800	258.290
5	3rd Bending Y	575.950	574.610
6	3rd Bending X	711.860	710.370
7	1st Torsion	720.160	719.400
8	4rd Bending Y	1110.400	1107.600

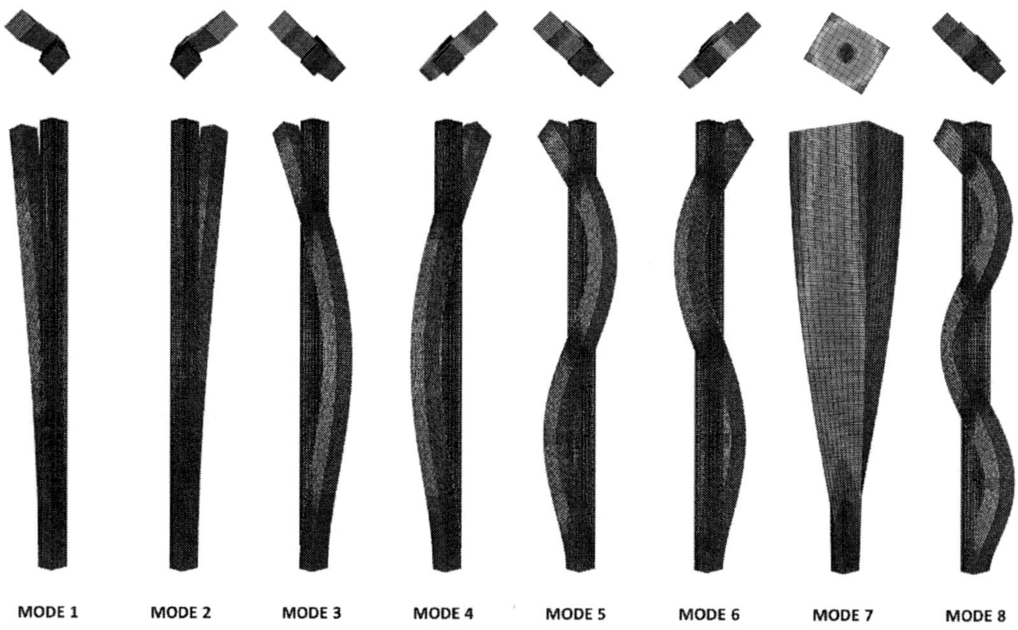

Figure 2. First 8 mode shapes.

The length of the mode shapes was calculated with Eq. (12) and they are presented in Table 4. As expected, the accuracy obtained with Eq. (12) increases as increasing the number of the elements in the model. Moreover, the error is larger for the higher modes. All the lengths obtained with the numerical model approaches the analytical values as decreasing the size of the elements, but the rate of convergence is slower for the torsional mode.

Table 3. Modal masses obtained from the numerical model.

	Mode	Element size (mm)					Analytical
		2.5	5	10	20	30	
1	1st Bending Y	3.9267	3.9265	3.9262	3.9253	3.9221	3.925
2	1st Bending X	3.9305	3.9304	3.9301	3.9294	3.9285	3.925
3	2nd Bending Y	3.9667	3.9665	3.9661	3.9650	3.9592	3.925
4	2nd Bending X	3.9927	3.9925	3.9922	3.9914	3.9902	3.925
5	3rd Bending Y	4.0317	4.0315	4.0311	4.0296	4.0200	3.925
6	3rd Bending X	4.0927	4.0925	4.0921	4.0912	4.0897	3.925
7	1st Torsion	4.2839	4.2838	4.2835	4.2884	4.2819	3.925
8	4rd Bending Y	4.1246	4.1244	4.1239	4.1211	4.1073	3.925

Table 4. Values $\boldsymbol{L_\psi^2}$ using Eq. (12).

	Mode	Element size (mm)					Analytical
		2.5	5	10	20	30	
1	1st Bending Y	0.2506	0.2510	0.2519	0.2537	0.2552	0.25
2	1st Bending X	0.2508	0.2513	0.2522	0.2539	0.2556	0.25
3	2nd Bending Y	0.2532	0.2538	0.2549	0.2570	0.2592	0.25
4	2nd Bending X	0.2549	0.2555	0.2566	0.2587	0.2609	0.25
5	3rd Bending Y	0.2575	0.2582	0.2596	0.2623	0.2654	0.25
6	3rd Bending X	0.2614	0.2622	0.2636	0.2662	0.2692	0.25
7	1st Torsion	0.2953	0.3177	0.3626	0.4354	0.5568	---
8	4rd Bending Y	0.2636	0.2645	0.2664	0.2699	0.2741	0.25

Due to the fact that the mass-density of the system is constant, the ratio $\boldsymbol{m_\psi/L_\psi^2}$ is the same for all the modes and equal to the total mass, i.e. $\frac{m_\psi}{L_\psi^2} = M_T = 15.7\ kg$. This ratio is shown in Table 5 and as expected, the numerical ratios $\frac{m_\psi}{L_\psi^2}$ approaches the analytical values for small size of the elements.

Table 5. Ratio $\boldsymbol{m_\psi/L_\psi^2}$.

	Mode	Element size (mm)					Analytical
		2.5	5	10	20	30	
1	1st Bending Y	15.669	15.643	15.586	15.472	15.369	15.7
2	1st Bending X	15.672	15.640	15.583	15.476	15.370	15.7
3	2nd Bending Y	15.666	15.628	15.559	15.428	15.275	15.7
4	2nd Bending X	15.664	15.626	15.558	15.429	15.294	15.7
5	3rd Bending Y	15.657	15.614	15.528	15.363	15.147	15.7
6	3rd Bending X	15.657	15.608	15.524	15.369	15.192	15.7
7	1st Torsion	14.507	13.484	11.813	9.849	7.690	15.7
8	4rd Bending Y	15.647	15.593	15.480	15.269	14.985	15.7

A better estimation of the lengths can be obtained with a linear extrapolation of the results obtained with two different sizes or fitting the results corresponding to several models meshed with different size of elements. If the lengths of Table 4 obtained with sizes 5 and 10 mm are extrapolated with a straight line to zero size, the results presented in Table 6 are obtained, where it can be observed that the total mass M_T is estimated with an error less than 0.05%. The results obtained fitting all the results of Table 6 with a straight line are also shown in the same table, achieving again a good accuracy. The extrapolation of the results corresponding to the torsional mode are shown in Figure 3.

Table 6. Length L_ψ^2 and ratio m_ψ/L_ψ^2 by extrapolation.

	Mode	Sizes 5 mm and 10 mm		Linear fit of all values in Table 4	
		L_ψ^2	m_ψ/L_ψ^2	L_ψ^2	m_ψ/L_ψ^2
1	1st Bending Y	0.2501	15.7005	0.2502	15.6927
2	1st Bending X	0.2504	15.6969	0.2504	15.6941
3	2nd Bending Y	0.2527	15.6973	0.2527	15.6952
4	2nd Bending X	0.2544	15.6946	0.2544	15.6929
5	3rd Bending Y	0.2568	15.6998	0.2568	15.7004
6	3rd Bending X	0.2608	15.6929	0.2607	15.6939
7	1st Torsion	0.2728	15.7034	0.2690	15.9262
8	4rd Bending Y	0.2626	15.7068	0.2626	15.7046

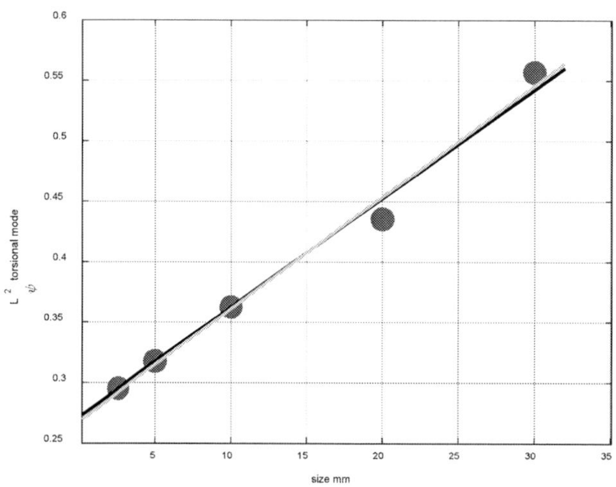

Figure 3. Calculation of the squared length of the torsional mode. Red circles: data from Table 4. Black line: fit using data of 5 and 10 mm. Green line: Linear fit using all the results.

2.2. A 3D beam model

The cantilever beam was also meshed with quadratic beam elements B32 with a length of 2.5 mm (801 nodes) and 1.25 mm (1601 nodes), obtaining very similar modal parameters. The natural frequencies are shown in Table 2 and the modal masses (mode shapes normalized to the largest translational component equal to unity) are shown in Table 7. The length of the mode shapes was estimated with Eq. (12) using only the translational components. The ratio m_ψ/L_ψ^2 is obtained with an error less than 1.6% for all the modes. Thus, beam models can be used successfully to estimate the length of the mode shapes with low computational cost.

With this model, all the translational components of the torsional mode are zero, and ABAQUS normalize this mode shape to the largest rotation equal to unity. This means that the squared length of the torsional mode (L_θ^2) is dimensionless and the modal mass is given in units of $kg \cdot m^2$, which can also be obtained analytically with the expression:

$$m_\theta = I_M L_\theta^2 \tag{19}$$

Where I_M is the mass moment inertia of the structure with respect to the longitudinal axes of the beam, which for a rectangular section of dimensions $a \times b$ is given by:

$$I_M = M_T \frac{(a^2 + b^2)}{12} \tag{20}$$

For this beam, Eq. (20) gives I_M=0.0054 kgm^2

From the finite element model, it has been obtained that $L_\theta^2 = 0.5$ and $m_\theta = 2.682 \times 10^{-3}\ kgm^2$, which gives a ratio $\frac{m_\theta}{L_\theta^2} = 0.0054\ kgm^2$.

The modal masses and the squared lengths of the torsional mode, obtained with the 3D model and with the beam model, are related by the expression:

$$M_T = \frac{m}{L^2} = \frac{m_\theta}{L_\theta^2} \frac{1}{\frac{(a^2 + b^2)}{12}} \tag{21}$$

Table 7. Length L_ψ^2, modal mass m_ψ and ratio m_ψ/L_ψ^2 for the bending modes of the beam model.

	Mode	Beam model B32 2.5 mm (801 nodes)			Beam model B32 1.25 mm (1601 nodes)		
		L_ψ^2 [−]	m_ψ [kg]	m_ψ/L_ψ^2 [kg]	L_ψ^2 [−]	m_ψ [kg]	m_ψ/L_ψ^2 [kg]
1	1st Bending Y	0.2505	3.9309	15.6922	0.2504	3.9309	15.6985
2	1st Bending X	0.2507	3.9342	15.6929	0.2505	3.9342	15.7054
3	2nd Bending Y	0.2522	3.9710	15.7454	0.2520	3.9710	15.7579
4	2nd Bending X	0.2532	3.9967	15.7848	0.2531	3.9967	15.7910
5	3rd Bending Y	0.2549	4.0369	15.8372	0.2548	4.0369	15.8434
6	3rd Bending X	0.2575	4.0978	15.9138	0.2573	4.0978	15.9262
7	1st Torsion	--	--	---	---	---	---
8	4rd Bending Y	0.2590	4.1317	15.9525	0.2588	4.1317	15.9648

3. A CANTILEVER BEAM MADE OF STEEL AND CONCRETE

A three-dimensional cantilever beam with the same dimensions as those used in section 2, and made of steel and concrete is considered in this section (see Figure 4a). The encastre boundary condition is placed at the end of the steel part. The following material properties were assumed for the steel: mass-density $\varrho = 7850\ kg/m^3$, Young's modulus $E = 210\ GPa$, and Poisson ratio $\nu = 0.3$. The material properties assumed for the concrete were following: mass-density $\varrho = 2400\ kg/m^3$, Young's modulus $E = 20\ GPa$, and Poisson ratio $\nu = 0.18$.

The beam was meshed with twenty-node hexahedral elements (C3D20R) with an approximate global size of 0.0025m (see Fig. 4b). The natural frequencies and modal masses (mode shapes normalized to the largest component equal to unity) corresponding to the first eight modes are presented in Table 8. The total mass of the beam is $M_T = 10.25\ kg$, distributed as $M_s = 7.85\ kg$ and $M_c = 2.4\ kg$, where subindexes 's' and 'c' indicate steel and concrete respectively.

The partial and the total squared lengths estimated with Eq. (12) are shown in Table 8. The partial lengths and the total length are related by the equation [2]:

$$L_\psi^2 = \frac{V_s L_{\psi_s}^2 + V_c L_{\psi_c}^2}{V_T} \tag{1}$$

In this case $V_s = V_c = V_T/2$ and Eq. (22) leads to:

$$L_\psi^2 = \frac{L_{\psi_s}^2 + L_{\psi_c}^2}{2} \tag{2}$$

The lengths of the mode shapes were calculated with models using size elements of 5 and 10 mm, and then extrapolated to zero size (see Table 8).

On the other hand the apparent mass is given by:

$$M_{ap} = V_T \frac{\rho_s L_{\psi_s}^2 + \rho_c L_{\psi_c}^2}{L_{\psi_s}^2 + L_{\psi_c}^2} \tag{3}$$

With respect to the modal masses of the structure, they can be calculated as the sum of the contributions of the steel and the concrete parts by:

$$m = M_s L_{\psi_s}^2 + M_c L_{\psi_c}^2 \tag{4}$$

The modal masses and the apparent masses calculated with Eqs. (25) and (24) are shown in Table 9.

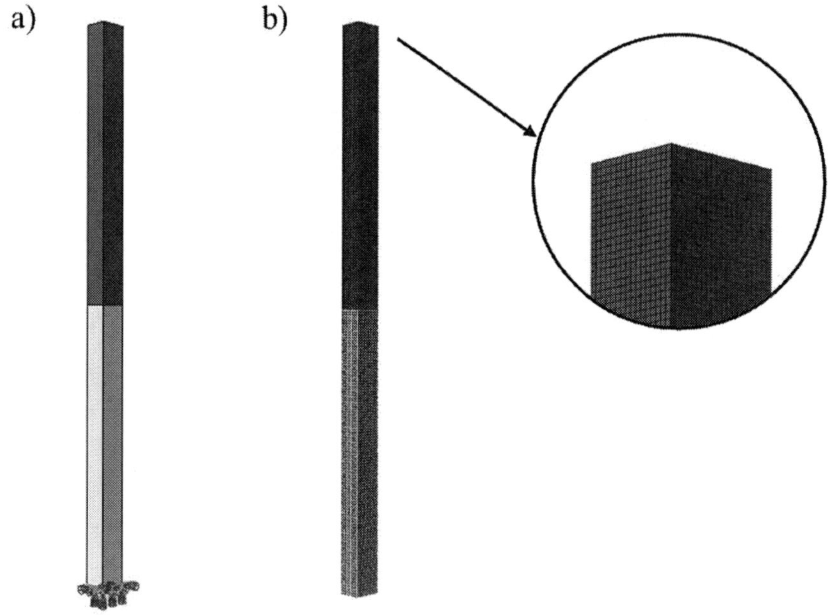

Figure 4. a) 3D concrete-steel model; b) mesh with element size of 0.0025 m

Table 8. Natural frequencies, modal masses and length of the concrete-steel the cantilever beam.

	Mode	Natural frequencies [Hz]	Modal mass	Length		
				Steel $L^2_{\psi_S}$	Concrete $L^2_{\psi_C}$	Total L^2_{ψ}
1	1st Bending Y	47.81	0.93	0.0089	0.3583	0.1836
2	1st Bending X	59.66	0.93	0.0089	0.3583	0.1836
3	2nd Bending Y	148.44	1.32	0.0879	0.2625	0.1752
4	2nd Bending X	184.83	1.32	0.0892	0.2625	0.1758
5	3rd Bending Y	440.37	0.90	0.0382	0.2542	0.1462
6	3rd Bending X	542.98	0.91	0.0382	0.2583	0.1483
7	1st Torsion	743.98	0.79	0.0073	0.3076	0.1705
8	3rd Bending Y	798.21	1.56	0.1108	0.2917	0.2012

Table 9. Contribution of the steel and concrete parts to the modal mass. Apparent mass.

	Mode	Modal mass			Apparent mass
		Steel $M_{Ts}L_s^2$	**Concrete** $M_{Tc}L_c^2$	$M_{Ts}L_s^2 + M_{Tc}L_c^2$	
1	1st Bending Y	0.066	0.863	0.929	5.05
2	1st Bending X	0.066	0.864	0.930	5.05
3	2nd Bending Y	0.692	0.630	1.322	7.54
4	2nd Bending X	0.697	0.633	1.330	7.54
5	3rd Bending Y	0.295	0.606	0.901	6.21
6	3rd Bending X	0.300	0.617	0.917	6.21
7	1st Torsion	0.057	0.74	0.796	5.04
8	3rd Bending Y	0.865	0.698	1.564	7.79

4. CONCLUSIONS

In constant mass-density systems, the modal mass is equal to the product between the total mass of the structure and the length squared. If the mass-density is not constant, the modal mass is equal to the product between an apparent mass (different for each mode) and the length squared. The length of the mode shapes can be useful to validate experimental modal masses and to know how the mass is distributed in the structure. The experimental mode shapes can be expanded to the unmeasured DOF's using a numerical model, and the length can be estimated using eq.(16). Alternatively, the length of the experimental mode shapes can be estimated using the transformation matrix **T** and the length of the numerical mode shapes,.

In this paper, the accuracy obtained in the length of the numerical mode shapes of two cantilever structures, one with constant mass-density and the second one made of steel and concrete, is analyzed. The length of numerical mode shapes can be estimated with a good accuracy using eq.(12) if small 3D elements of equal size are used to mesh the model.

Both cantilever models were meshed with 3D elements C3D20R, and the lengths of the mode shapes were estimated with eq. (12). The results corresponding to models of different size, were linearly extrapolated to zero size, allowing to estimate the length of all the modes with a very good accuracy.

The structures were also meshed with beam elements B32 and the length of the mode shapes were calculated with eq.(12) considering only the translational DOF's (the contribution of the rotations can be neglected if the elements are small). It has been demonstrated that beam models can be used successfully to estimate the length of the mode shapes with low computational cost. Beam elements can also be used to calculate the length of the torsional modes, considering only the rotational DOF's.

ACKNOWLEDGEMENTS

The financing support given by the Spanish Ministry of Education through the project MCI-20-PID2019-105593GB-I00/AEI/10.13039/501100011033 is gratefully appreciated.

REFERENCES

[1] Dianat, S. A., & Saber, E. (2009). *Advanced Linear Algebra for Engineers with MATLAB.* CRC Press.

[2] Aenlle, M., Juul, M., & Brincker, R. (2020). Modal Mass and Length of Mode Shapes in Structural Dynamics. *Shock and Vibration, 2020*, 1-16. https://doi.org/10.1155/2020/8648769

[3] Leissa, A. W., & Qatu, M. S. (2011). *Vibrations of Continuous Systems*. McGraw-Hill

[4] Rao, S. S. (2007). *Vibration of Continuous Systems*. John Wiley & Sons.

[5] Brincker, R., Skafte, A., López-Aenlle, M., Sestieri, A., D'Ambrogio, W., & Canteli, A. (2014). A local correspondence principle for mode shapes in structural dynamics. *Mechanical Systems and Signal Processing,* 45(1), 91–104. https://doi.org/10.1016/j.ymssp.2013.10.025

[6] Sestieri, A. (2000). Structural dynamic modification. *Sadhana*, *25*(3), 247-259.

[7] *ABAQUS UNIFIED FEA*. Dassault Systems.

[8] Clough R.W. and Penzien J. (1993) *Dynamics of structures*. New York: McGraw-Hill

9th International Operational Modal Analysis Conference
iomac
July 3 - 6, 2022
Vancouver, Canada

PRECISE AZIMUTH AND ANGULAR SPEED ESTIMATION FOR WIND TURBINE SHAFTS BY MEANS OF IMU

Miroslav Zivanovic[1], *Xabier Iriarte*[2], *and Aitor Plaza*[3], *and Alfonso Carlosena*[4]

[1] Dr. Zivanovic, Public University of Navarre, miro@unavarra.es.
[2] Dr. Iriarte, Public University of Navarre, xabier.iriarte@unavarra.es.
[3] Dr. Plaza, Public University of Navarre, aitor.plaza@unavarra.es.
[4] Dr. Carlosena, Public University of Navarre, alfonso.carlosena@unavarra.es

ABSTRACT

This paper presents the design of a recursive filter based on the kinematic model of a wind turbine to estimate with a high degree of accuracy its azimuth (angular position of the main shaft). The design of the filter is conditioned by two requirements to be fulfilled. On the one hand, the integrity of the machine must be preserved, and its original design must not be modified, and, on the other hand, the design must be valid for any type of horizontal axis machine regardless of its geometrical properties and where the sensor is placed. The designed filter estimates the azimuth from the data measured by an accelerometer located on the same axis. In addition, the filter is able to estimate other variables such as the angular speed and acceleration, radius and tilt of the shaft. Due to the nonlinear nature of the equations describing the wind turbine kinematics, the so-called Extended Kalman Filter has been implemented. This procedure has been validated by means of both simulated and experimental data.

Keywords: *Conference, Operational, Modal, Analysis*

1. INTRODUCTION

Wind turbines that were installed in Europe in the 1990s are reaching the end of their lifetime, but instead of repowering them, developers are opting to extend the life of these machines to maximize the benefits they provide. This decision is strongly conditioned by the trade-off between maintenance costs and energy production benefits. In this context, the choice of an appropriate maintenance strategy is crucial to be able to predict in advance the remaining lifetime of the components in order to facilitate the scheduling of maintenance tasks and reduce the non-production time associated with them. Thus, condition-based monitoring [1] is postulated as the best strategy, monitoring the machines to know their condition and foresee well in advance any maintenance operation.

When a predictive maintenance strategy for a machine or component is proposed, it will be necessary to determine a periodic measurement procedure to get information on the state of the machine or component. Therefore, depending on the components to be monitored and the types of failure to be detected, it will be necessary to install additional sensors to those that were included in the design of the machine and were installed at the time of its construction. The possibility to take certain measurements will sometimes be conditioned to the design of the machine itself. In some situations, it will not be possible to use sensors that, if their installation had been decided at the time of design, would have been optimal for the measurement of certain variables. In these circumstances, the engineer performing the experiments for predictive maintenance will need tools that make it possible to perform the measurements quickly, easily and robustly, without having to dedicate specific sensors and acquisition equipment to each machine and without having to abandon sensors and measurement systems once the measurement campaign has been carried out.

The measurement of the Low Speed Shaft (LSS) azimuth is an important variable in wind turbine monitoring since many types of faults correlate with a specific phase of this angle. For example, in [2] wind turbine component loads are calculated in order to improve their life forecasting and all relevant variables are analysed versus the azimuth. This way, the engineer can identify the type of fault knowing the phase of the signals measured in other sensors such as accelerometers and strain gauges. In addition, knowledge of this variable is essential to be able to calculate loads on a basis fixed to the nacelle when measurements are made on a fixed basis to the LSS, which is required by the current standard for load calculation IEC 61400-13 2015 [3]. Although new wind turbines usually include a sensor that provides a measurement of this angle, in wind turbines that are reaching the end of their useful life, the measurement of the LSS rotation angle is not one of the variables that is monitored by a SCADA system. There are several ways in which this angle can be estimated based on other measurements, but all of them present implementation difficulties or lack sufficient accuracy.

One possible method to estimate the azimuth is based on using the gear ratio of the gearbox and the speed measurement of the High Speed Shaft (HSS). This solution has the disadvantage that the integration error amplifies linearly with time, and that this must be eliminated by using an external sensor that gives information of each zero crossing of the LSS. This could be an inductive sensor using some metallic element characteristic of the machine to consistently detect a phase value of the azimuth. A drawback of this method is that the integration error will propagate equally over an entire lap from the inductive sensor signal, giving larger and larger errors until it is suddenly corrected when it passes through 0 again, resulting in a notoriously discontinuous azimuth estimate at zero crossings. This solution may not be accurate enough for some applications. Another major drawback of the method is its difficult installation. On the one hand, metallic elements of the wind turbine (hub joint bolts) will be used as reference elements, so the installation will depend on the structure of the machine. In addition, external elements will have to be attached to the machine. When the measurement campaign is over and these sensors are removed, they may not be useful in the sensing of another machine. On the other hand, the need to use SCADA measurements of the machine would greatly complicate the acquisition of the measurements, since the SCADA measurements would have to be synchronized with those of the additional sensors placed to monitor the machine.

Extensive research has been conducted to investigate full 3-degree-of-freedom orientation tracking using inertial/magnetic sensor modules. Common application, very far from wind turbine azimuth estimation, are head-tracking [4, 5] and aircraft attitude-determination [6]. In [7], for example, a real-time estimation of projectile roll angle and roll rate are performed. These algorithms use not only acceleration data but usually gyroscopic and geomagnetic signals too. Although some of these approaches could be used for a single rotation angle estimation, they would not perform optimally for the estimation of a single degree-of-freedom problem and some sensor signals might be unnecessary. Moreover, the applications of these algorithms are very little related to the estimation of the angle of rotation of the LSS of a wind turbine.

Numerous papers related to wind turbine applications have been published in which the angular speed of the LSS is estimated. In [8], the instantaneous angular speed of the LSS is estimated using vibration signals for tacho-less order tracking under speed variation operating conditions. In [9], acceleration vibration signals are also used to estimate the instantaneous angular speed of every single shaft of the gearbox. In [10] a two-step method for instantaneous angular speed estimation is proposed which accounts for large speed fluctuations and is also based on vibration signals. These articles manage to estimate the angular speed of the LSS but there does not appear to be many works in which the azimuth is estimated based on signals other than tachometer or directly from an encoder.

2. METHODOLGY

Figure 1 shows the scheme of a triaxial accelerometer placed on the periphery of the LSS. The sensor primarily measures the acceleration of gravity on a base fixed to the axis, which rotates precisely the angle to be estimated. In addition to gravity, the accelerometers will also measure the normal and tangential acceleration components of the point where the sensor is placed, including the components related to the translation of the nacelle caused by tower deflection.

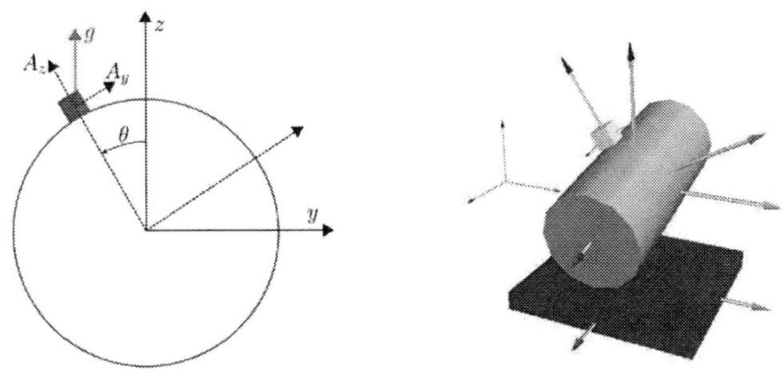

Figure 1. Scheme of the LSS and accelerometer

The objective of this paper is to design an algorithm that estimates the azimuth of the LSS based on these acceleration signals. Moreover, this algorithm must be robust to accelerometer placement errors, it does not need to know the geometry of the shaft (particularly its radius) and must not be affected by the tilt of the shaft itself. Following the standard wind turbine signal measurement, 600 seconds signals will be used to estimate the azimuth off-line. Finally, since it is intended to measure the acceleration of gravity, the accelerometer must be capable of measuring acceleration down to 0 Hz. With these requirements, the design of an extended state observer of the turbine based on Kalman filters will be proposed [11].

2.1. Signal model

Under these conditions the signals of the accelerometer will be calculated based on a kinematic model of the shaft. The only degree of freedom of the model will be the rotation of the shaft with respect to its own axis (θ), *i.e.* the so-called azimuth. However, the measured signal will depend on two more parameters: the radius of the shaft (R) and the tilt angle of the shaft (α). The signal for the three axes of the accelerometer at the nth time instant will thus be:

$$A_{x,n} = -g\sin\alpha_n + \gamma_{x,n} \tag{1a}$$

$$A_{y,n} = g\cos\alpha_n \sin\theta_n - R\ddot{\theta}_n + \gamma_{y,n} \tag{1b}$$

$$A_{z,n} = g\cos\alpha_n \cos\theta_n - R\dot{\theta}_n^2 + \gamma_{z,n} \tag{1c}$$

where g is the acceleration of the gravity and A_x, A_y and A_z are the accelerations measured by the sensor in its own base. Moreover, $\gamma_{i,n}$ will be the random variables that take into account the measuring noise and the translational accelerations of the nacelle. As these expressions are nonlinear with respect to the azimuth an Extended Kalman Filter (EKF) approach will be used [12].

2.2. System model

In order to obtain the process equations for the EKF, we must determine which variables will form the state vector and how they are going to evolve with respect to time. In this paper the state variables will be θ, $\dot{\theta}$, $\ddot{\theta}$, R, and α. The evolution of the first two will be modelled as a uniformly accelerated movement while the last three of them will be modelled as an autoregressive process of order 1, i.e. AR(1). Thus, the equations representing such system are:

$$\theta_{n+1} = \theta_n + \dot{\theta}_n \Delta t + \frac{1}{2}\ddot{\theta}_n \Delta t^2 + \gamma_{\theta,n} \tag{2a}$$

$$\dot{\theta}_{n+1} = \theta_n + \ddot{\theta}_n \Delta t + \gamma_{\dot{\theta},n} \tag{2b}$$

$$\ddot{\theta}_{n+1} = k\,\ddot{\theta}_n + \gamma_{\ddot{\theta},n} \tag{2c}$$

$$R_{n+1} = k\,R_n + \gamma_{R,n} \tag{2d}$$

$$\alpha_{n+1} = k\,\alpha_n + \gamma_{\alpha,n} \tag{2e}$$

where $\gamma_{i,n}$ are random variables following Gaussian probability distributions with 0 mean. On the other hand, the model parameter $|k| < 1$ controls the smoothness in the output of a stable filter. Note that, in this case, the process equations are linear with respect to the state variables.

2.3. Estimation of the azimuth and angular velocity

Using sets of Equations (1) and (2), we have everything we need to create an EKF that iteratively estimates the state variables.

Although variable R is a certain constant in the system, for the robustness of the model it has been considered into the state vector. This way, the user does not need to know precisely the radius of the shaft as the filter will estimate it. This makes the filter robust with respect to this kind of uncertainties.

On the contrary, the α variable will be unknown and will experience significant variations with respect to its mean value. These variations will be taken into account by the model and will make it more robust so that the problem can be addressed without the need to know its value a priori.

3. RESULTS AND DISCUSSION

In this section the performance of the developed algorithm is evaluated using data from two very different sources. On the one hand, acceleration data from a simulated wind turbine model is used. In this way the true values of the azimuth and angular speed will be available while the acceleration data while the signal from the virtual accelerometers will have all the richness that will be found in the experimental measurements. On the other hand, the algorithm is evaluated using accelerations measured experimentally in the LSS of an actual 3MW wind turbine. Although in this second system it will not be possible to validate the accuracy of the algorithm (since the true value of the azimuth will not be available) it will be possible to verify that the algorithm behaves qualitatively as well as in the simulated case.

3.1. Wind turbine simulation in OpenFAST

In order to evaluate the algorithm with realistic simulation data, the OpenFAST software [13] has been used. This is a free software developed by National Renewable Energy Laboratory (NREL) which is certified for the design of on-shore as well as off-shore wind turbines. This software is a standard for the design of aerodynamic, aeroelastic, structural and control system components and simulations and allows very realistic simulations under different wind turbine operating conditions. It can determine the position, velocity and acceleration at various points of the machine.

The generic OpenFAST wind turbine model consists of 24 degrees of freedom (DOF). The model allows specifying the structural properties (stiffness, damping, inertias) of the tower, drive train and blades, as well as the geometrical and aerodynamic properties of the tower and blades. In addition, it allows the placement of virtual sensors (accelerometers, IMU-s and deformation sensors) at arbitrary locations on the tower, powertrain and blades. This allows obtaining information of these variables in the simulation for off-line post-processing.

The specific 5 MW onshore wind turbine [14] is simulated in this work consists of a 3-bladed 126 m diameter wind rotor on an 87.6 m high tower. This wind turbine model, also developed by NREL, has been widely used in many research projects.

3.2. Results for the OpenFAST model

As a virtual experiment, a 600 s simulation has been performed, for $6\,m/s$ turbulent wind where the rotation speed oscillates between 0.75 and $0.95\,rad/s$. The actual values for the whole simulation are shown on Figure 2.

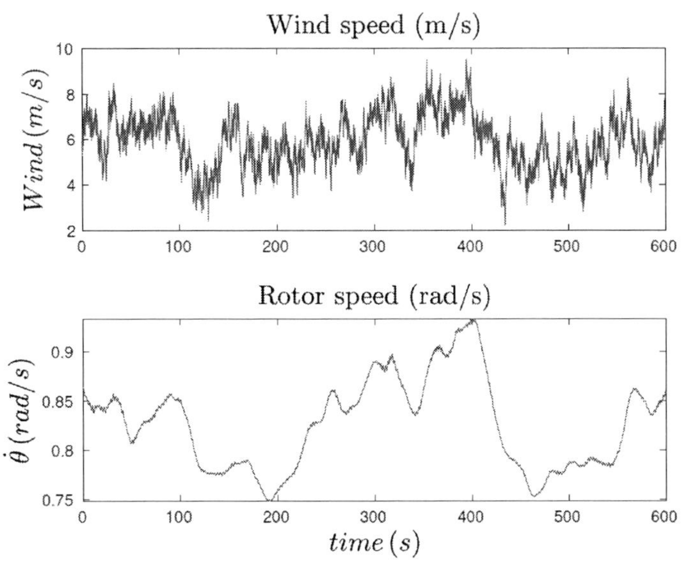

Figure 2. Operation conditions in the simulation

Once the OpenFAST simulation results are available, the different parameters of the EKF are set as follows: the constant for the autoregressive model has been set to $k = 1 - 10^{-6}$ and the process variance matrix is determined accordingly; the synthetic accelerations signals were corrupted with Gaussian noise (γ_x,γ_y,γ_z) of mean 0 and standard deviation of $0.25\,m/s^2$; the measuring variance matrix was determined accordingly and all data was collected at a constant rate of $\Delta t = 1/160\,s$. The acceleration measurements for this case study are shown in Figure 3.

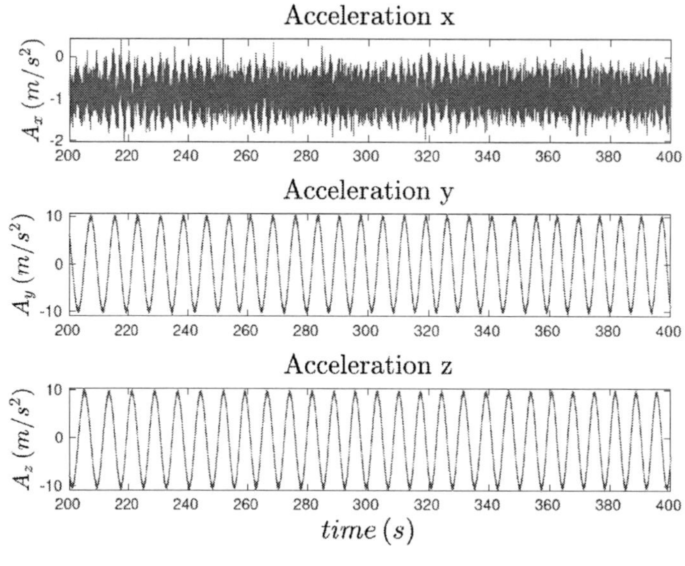

Figure 3. Virtual acceleration measurements

As shown in Figure 2, the wind speed varies significantly along the analised period of time (due to its turbulent nature) and the rotor speed varies up to 20%. Despite these difficult conditions, the algorithm behaves adequately and is able to capture the angular speed variations, as shown in Figure 4. Likewise, the error of the Kalman filter in the azimuth estimation remains around 0.5^o. Compared to the direct application of the arctangent function to the acceleration data ($\hat{\theta} = atan(A_z, A_y)$) the developed filter performs much better with an error around 10 times smaller.

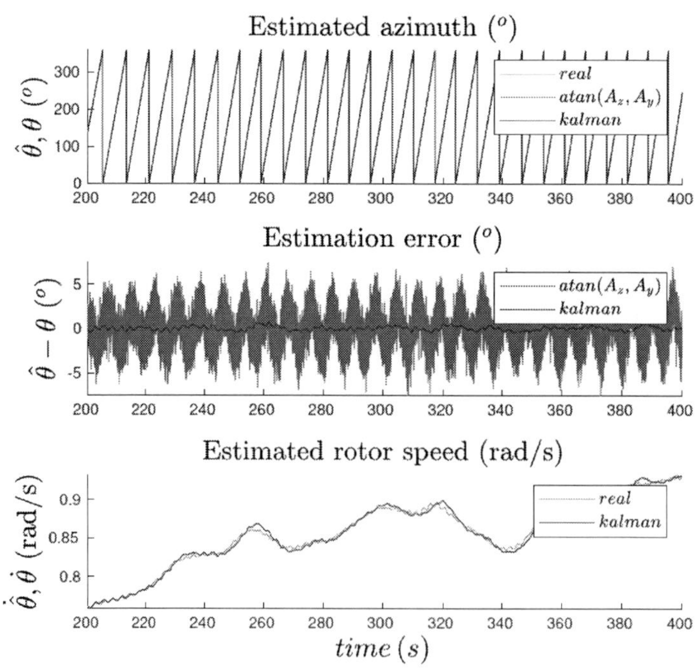

Figure 4. From top to bottom: azimuth estimations and real value, difference between the estimations and real azimuth, estimated and real rotor speed.

Finally, Figure 5 shows the estimated α and R. The results show that the estimation of these variables is consistent with the assumptions made in the modeling process behaving nearly as constants.

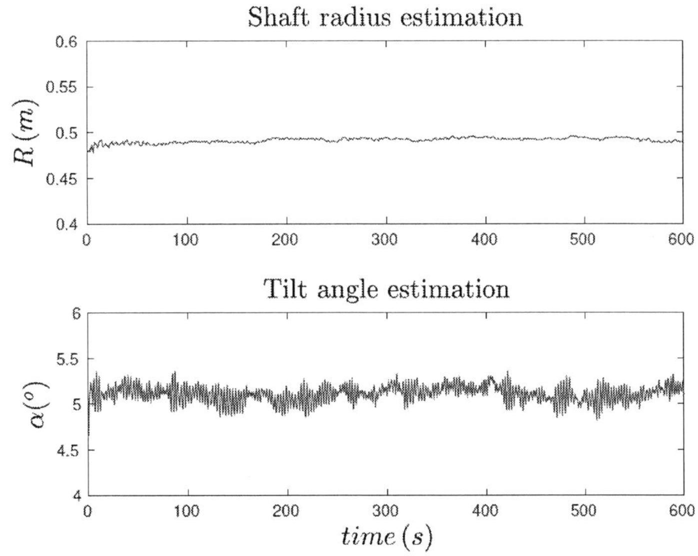

Figure 5. Estimation of the shaft radius ***R*** and the tilt angle **α**

3.3. Results for the actual wind turbine

The set of real-world data used to validate the proposed method corresponds to accelerations measured in the LSS of a 3MW wind turbine. It contains standard 600 *s* records, sampled at 20 milliseconds. The approximate characteristics of the 3-bladed turbine are 126 m diameter rotor and 120 m high tower. The acceleration signals measured are shown in Figure 6. It can be appreciated that the signals are very similar to those of the simulated case.

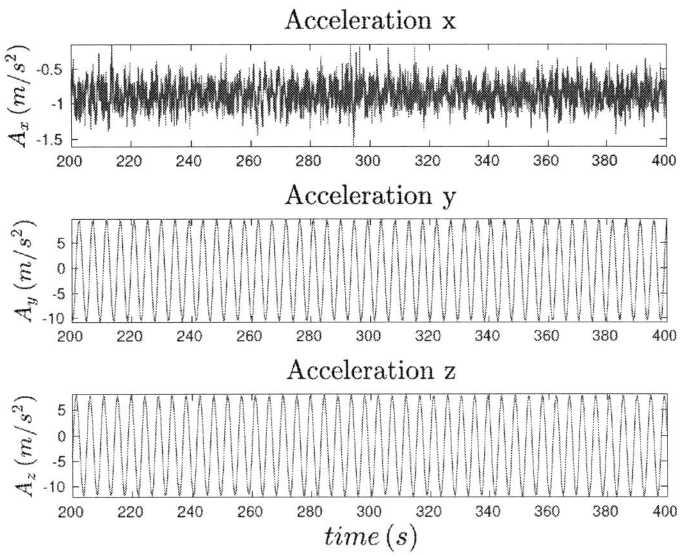

Figure 6. Experimental acceleration measurements

In Figure 7 the estimations of the azimuth and the rotor speed are shown. The characteristic bumps of the arctangent method are evident while the filter provides a smoother estimation. These bumps are due to the significant contribution of the normal acceleration to the calculation of the azimuth as the arctangent of the ratio of accelerations. The rotor speed estimation shows a nearly constant value with an additional contribution of the first harmonic of the rotor rotation.

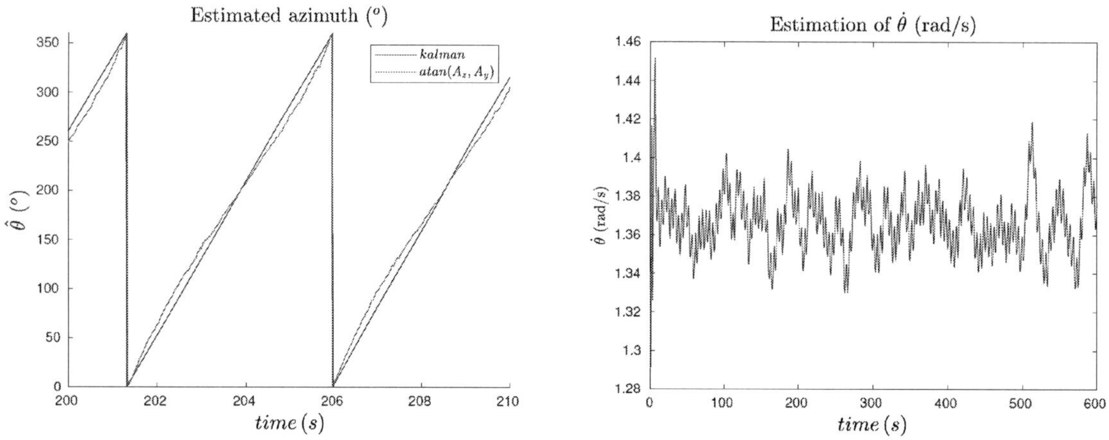

Figure 7. Estimation of the azimuth for *atan* method and for the kalman filter

Finally, Figure 8 shows the estimated radius and tilt of the shaft. The first one shows a clear tendency to a stationary value while the second one shows oscillations of greater amplitude that could be due to actual tilt variations. The higher frequency content of the tilt signal also contains a significant contribution of the first harmonic of the rotor rotation.

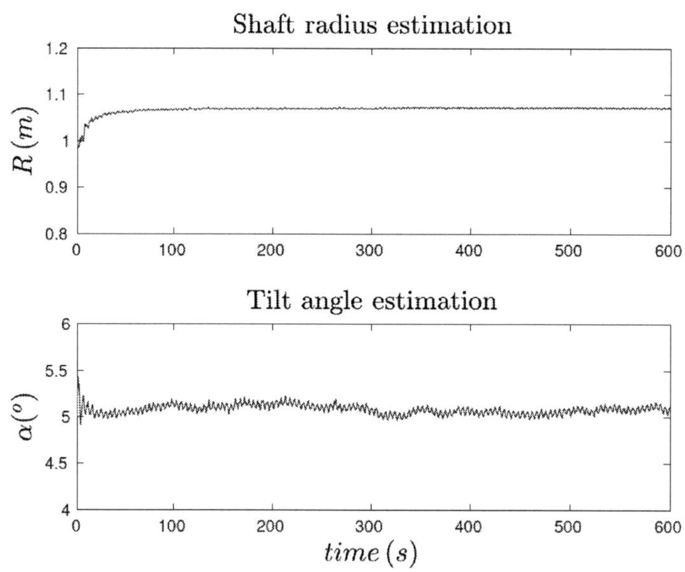

Figure 8. Estimation of the shaft radius ***R*** and the tilt angle **α**

4. CONCLUSIONS

A simple and efficient Kalman filter has been developed for the accurate estimation of the azimuth and rotor speed of the LSS of a wind turbine. In the simulation case study with OpenFAST, the algorithm has demonstrated its ability to estimate with relative accuracy both variables, comparing the results with the real value of the simulation and obtaining errors below 0.5^o in the estimation of the azimuth and around 1% in the estimation of the rotor speed. The Kalman filter parameters have been adjusted satisfactorily since the tracking of both variables is relatively smooth.

Regarding the results obtained for the estimation with experimental data, it is not possible to make a reliable comparison due to the lack of real values of the variables to be estimated. Comparing the estimations of the azimuth by the filter and the direct calculation by means of the arctangent, the shortcomings of the latter can be appreciated and it can be seen that the estimation of the azimuth is much more accurate using the filter presented in this article.

Finally, it should be noted that the designed filter can estimate azimuth and rotor speed in real time due to its recursive character and its low computational cost. In addition, it is robust to the unknown radius at which the accelerometer is placed and is able to take into account variations of the tilt angle of the axis. These characteristics make it very suitable for use in predictive maintenance operations where azimuth and rotor speed estimations are desired without the need to access SCADA measurements.

5. REFERENCES

[1] Márquez, F. P. G., Tobias, A. M., Pérez, J. M. P., & Papaelias, M. (2012). Condition monitoring of wind turbines: Techniques and methods. *Renewable energy*, *46*, 169-178.

[2] Rommel, D. P., Di Maio, D., & Tinga, T. (2020). Calculating wind turbine component loads for improved life prediction. *Renewable energy*, *146*, 223-241.

[3] International-Electrotechnical-Commission. (2015). IEC 61400-13: Wind turbines-Part 13: Measurement of mechanical loads. *International Electro-technical Commission (IEC), Geneva.*

[4] Foxlin, E. (1996, March). Inertial head-tracker sensor fusion by a complementary separate-bias Kalman filter. In *Proceedings of the IEEE 1996 Virtual Reality Annual International Symposium* (pp. 185-194). IEEE.

[5] Foxlin, E., Harrington, M., & Alshuler, Y. Miniature 6DOF inertial for track HMDs. *Proc. SPIE Helmet, Head-Mounted Displays III*, 214-228.

[6] Gebre-Egziabher, D., Elkaim, G. H., Powell, J. D., & Parkinson, B. W. (2000, March). A gyro-free quaternion-based attitude determination system suitable for implementation using low cost sensors. In *IEEE 2000. Position Location and Navigation Symposium (Cat. No. 00CH37062)* (pp. 185-192). IEEE.

[7] Gao, L., Zhang, Y., Zhang, X., & Xue, Y. (2020). A real-time estimation method of roll angle and angular rate based on geomagnetic information. *Mathematical Problems in Engineering*, *2020*.

[8] Wang, Y. I., Tang, B., Meng, L., & Hou, B. (2019). Adaptive estimation of instantaneous angular speed for wind turbine planetary gearbox fault detection. *IEEE Access*, *7*, 49974-49984.

[9] Peeters, C., Leclere, Q., Antoni, J., Guillaume, P., & Helsen, J. (2017, May). Vibration-based angular speed estimation for multi-stage wind turbine gearboxes. In *Journal of Physics: Conference Series* (Vol. 842, No. 1, p. 012053). IOP Publishing.

[10] Urbanek, J., Barszcz, T., & Antoni, J. (2013). A two-step procedure for estimation of instantaneous rotational speed with large fluctuations. *Mechanical Systems and Signal Processing*, *38*(1), 96-102.

[11] Ritter, B. A. S. T. I. A. N., Schild, A. X. E. L., Feldt, M. A. T. T. H. I. A. S., & Konigorski, U. L. R. I. C. H. (2016, September). The design of nonlinear observers for wind turbine dynamic state and parameter estimation. In *Journal of Physics: Conference Series* (Vol. 753, No. 5, p. 052029). IOP Publishing.

[12] Grewal, M. S., & Andrews, A. P. (2014). *Kalman filtering: Theory and Practice with MATLAB*. John Wiley & Sons.

[13] OpenFAST. Open-source wind turbine simulation tool, available at http://github.com/OpenFAST/OpenFAST/ (2022).

[14] Jonkman, J., Butterfield, S., Musial, W., & Scott, G. (2009). *Definition of a 5-MW reference wind turbine for offshore system development* (No. NREL/TP-500-38060). National Renewable Energy Lab.(NREL), Golden, CO (United States).

MODAL SCALING/NEW APPLICATIONS IN OMA

9th International Operational Modal Analysis Conference
iomac
July 3 - 6, 2022
Vancouver, Canada

A PHYSICAL INTERPRETATION OF THE MODAL MASS IN STRUCTURAL DYNAMICS

M. Aenlle[1], R. Brincker [2], N. García-Fernández[3], F. Pelayo[4]

[1] PhD, University of Oviedo, Spain, aenlle@uniovi.es
[2] PhD, Technical University of Denmark, runeb@byg.dtu.dk
[3] PhD Student, University of Oviedo, garciafnatalia@uniovi.es
[4] Professor, University of Oviedo, fernandezpelayo@uniovi.es

ABSTRACT

The magnitude and the units of the modal mass of a mode shape is not unique but it depends on the normalization method used to define the mode shape. Moreover, the magnitude can also depend depends on the number of degrees of freedom (DOFs) used to discretize the model. Recently, a new definition of the length of a mode shape, which depends on the mode shape and how the volume is distributed in the structure, has been proposed by the authors. This definition allows a better definition of the modal mass, which is physically meaningful and does not depend on the number of DOFs of a discrete model. With this new definition, the modal mass in constant mass-density systems is equal to the product between the total mass of the structure and the length squared. This property can be used advantageously to validate the modal masses estimated with the techniques proposed by different authors to determine the modal masses in operational modal analysis.

In this paper, these new concepts are explained by analytical, numerical, and experimental examples. The model masses of an experimental steel beam structure were estimated by experimental modal analysis and validated with the equations proposed in this paper. Moreover, the modal masses and lengths of a rigid beam supported on two springs, were calculated using different sets of DOF's and different types of normalization, demonstrating that the same mass normalized mode shapes are obtained.

Keywords: Modal mass, Normalization of mode shapes, apparent mass

1. INTRODUCTION

A mode shape contains information of both the deflection shape and the length of the vector. The length (also denoted in algebra as Euclidean norm, Euclidean length or L^2norm) of an arbitrary normalized mode shape $\boldsymbol{\psi}$ is given by [1]:

$$L_{E\psi} = \sqrt{\boldsymbol{\psi}^T \cdot \boldsymbol{\psi}} \tag{1}$$

A mode shape is said to be normalized to the unit length when its length L_{ψ_L} is unity. The mode shape normalized to the unit length, hereafter denoted $\boldsymbol{\psi}_{\boldsymbol{L}}$, is related to the mode shape $\boldsymbol{\psi}$ by:

$$\boldsymbol{\psi}_{\boldsymbol{L}} = \frac{\boldsymbol{\psi}}{\sqrt{\boldsymbol{\psi}^T \cdot \boldsymbol{\psi}}} = \frac{\boldsymbol{\psi}}{L_{E\psi}} \tag{2}$$

In structural dynamics the modal mass of a mode shape $\boldsymbol{\psi}$ is defined as [2,3]:

$$m_\psi = \boldsymbol{\psi}^{\boldsymbol{T}} \boldsymbol{M} \boldsymbol{\psi} \tag{3}$$

Where $\boldsymbol{M}$ is the mass matrix.

A mode shape is said to be mass normalized, hereafter denoted $\boldsymbol{\phi}$, if the modal mass is dimensionless unity [2,5], i..e:

$$m_\phi = \boldsymbol{\phi}^{\boldsymbol{T}} \boldsymbol{M} \boldsymbol{\phi} = 1 \tag{4}$$

The mass normalized mode shape $\boldsymbol{\phi}$ is related with the mode shapes $\boldsymbol{\psi}$ and $\boldsymbol{\psi}_{\boldsymbol{L}}$ as:

$$\boldsymbol{\phi} = \boldsymbol{\psi} \frac{1}{\sqrt{m}} = \boldsymbol{\psi}_{\boldsymbol{L}} \frac{1}{\sqrt{m_L}} \tag{5}$$

Where m and m_L are the modal masses of $\boldsymbol{\psi}$ and $\boldsymbol{\psi}_{\boldsymbol{L}}$, respectively.

Eq. (5) can also be expressed as:

$$\boldsymbol{\phi} = \boldsymbol{\psi} \alpha = \boldsymbol{\psi}_{\boldsymbol{L}} \alpha_L \tag{6}$$

Where α and α_L are scaling factors, related to the modal masses as:

$$\alpha = \frac{1}{\sqrt{m}} \tag{7}$$

$$\alpha_L = \frac{1}{\sqrt{m_L}} \tag{8}$$

The modal masses and the lengths of the mode shapes are related by:

$$\frac{m_\phi = 1}{L_{E\phi}^2} = \frac{m_{\psi_L}}{L_{E\psi_L}^2 = 1} = \frac{m_\psi}{L_{E\psi}^2} \tag{9}$$

whereas the scaling factors are related to the lengths as:

$$L_{E\phi}^2 = \alpha_L^2 = \alpha L_{E\psi}^2 \tag{10}$$

A mode shape is commonly defined with the deflection shape and the modal mass. However, from eqs. (7) to (9) it is inferred that the length of the mode shapes and the scaling factors can be used as an alternative to the modal masses.

The modal mass m_ϕ corresponding to the mass normalized mode shape $\boldsymbol{\phi}$ is dimensionless unity. From eq. (4) it is easily inferred that the translational components $\boldsymbol{\phi_T}$ of the mode shape $\boldsymbol{\phi}$ have the units $1/\sqrt{kg}$ in the international system, whereas the units of the rotational components $\boldsymbol{\phi_R}$ are $1/\left(m\sqrt{kg}\right)$. On the other hand, the translational components $\boldsymbol{\psi_{LT}}$ of the mode shape $\boldsymbol{\psi_L}$ are dimensionless and the modal mass m_{ψ_L} has the unit of kg. With respect to the length of mode shapes, $L_{E\psi}^2$ is dimensionless whereas $L_{E\phi}^2$ has units of $1/kg$ [6,7].

2. CONSTANT MASS DENSITY SYSTEMS

If the mass-density ρ of a system is constant, eq. (3) can be expressed as [6]:

$$m_\psi = \boldsymbol{\psi}^T \boldsymbol{M} \boldsymbol{\psi} = \rho\, \boldsymbol{\psi}^T \boldsymbol{V} \boldsymbol{\psi} \tag{11}$$

Where **V** is the volume matrix. If the total volume of the system is denoted as V_T, eq. (11) can also be formulated as [6]:

$$m_\psi = M_T \frac{\boldsymbol{\psi}^T \boldsymbol{V} \boldsymbol{\psi}}{V_T} = M_T L_\psi^2 \tag{12}$$

Where the term [6]:

$$L_\psi^2 = \frac{\boldsymbol{\psi}^T\, \boldsymbol{V} \boldsymbol{\psi}}{V_T} \tag{13}$$

is the length of the mode shape, which depends on the volume of the structure and on the mode shape. This new definition of length secures that the length has the same unit as the mode shape. Thus, if the mode shape is dimensionless, so is the length.

Eq. (13) involves the volume matrix $\boldsymbol{V}$ and it is different to the usual concept of Euclidean length. If a structure is discretized with small finite elements of equal volume ΔV eq. (13) can be approximated as:

$$L_\psi^2 \cong \frac{\Delta V \sum_{k=1}^{N_V} \boldsymbol{\psi}_k^2}{N_V \Delta V} = \frac{\sum_{k=1}^{N_V} \boldsymbol{\psi}_k^2}{N_V} = \frac{\boldsymbol{\psi}^T \boldsymbol{\psi}}{N_V} \tag{14}$$

And the length L_ψ^2 can be related to the euclidean length $L_{E\psi}^2$ as:

$$L_\psi^2 \cong \frac{L_{E\psi}^2}{N_V} \tag{15}$$

In finite element models, the components of the mode shapes are commonly known at the nodes of the elements, and eq. (14) can also be approximated by means of the expression:

$$L_\psi^2 \cong \frac{\boldsymbol{\psi}^T \boldsymbol{\psi}}{N} \tag{16}$$

Where N is the number of nodes in the model.

3. NON-CONSTANT MASS DENSITY SYSTEMS

If the structure is constituted by two parts with the two volumes, V_1 with the mass density ρ_1 , and , V_2 with the mass density ρ_2, from eq. (3) is inferred that the modal mass is given by:

$$m_\psi = M_1 \frac{\psi^T V_1 \psi}{V_1} + M_2 \frac{\psi^T V_2 \psi}{V_2} = M_1 L_{\psi_1}^2 + M_2 L_{\psi_2}^2 \quad (17)$$

Where

$$L_{\psi_1} = \frac{\psi^T V_1 \psi}{V_1};\ L_{\psi_2} \frac{\psi^T V_2 \psi}{V_2} \quad (18)$$

are the partial lengths defined over the partial volumes, $V_1$and , V_2, respectively, which are related to the total length by:

$$V_T L_\psi^2 = V_1 L_{\psi_1}^2 + V_2 L_{\psi_2}^2 \quad (19)$$

Eq.(17) can also be expressed as:

$$m_\psi = M_{ap} L_\psi^2 \quad (20)$$

Where M_{ap} is an apparent mass given by:

$$M_{ap} = \frac{M_1 L_{\psi_1}^2 + M_2 L_{\psi_2}^2}{L_\psi^2} = V_T \frac{M_1 L_{\psi_1}^2 + M_2 L_{\psi_2}^2}{V_1 L_{\psi_1}^2 + V L_{\psi_2}^2} \quad (21)$$

Eqs. (17) and (21) can be generalized to systems constituted by n parts as:

$$m_\psi = \sum_{k=1}^{n} M_k L_{\psi_k}^2 \quad (22)$$

And

$$M_{ap} = \frac{\sum_{k=1}^{n} M_k L_{\psi_k}^2}{\sum_{k=1}^{n} V_k L_{\psi_k}^2} \quad (23)$$

4. A STEEL STRUCTURE

The structure consists of a vertical column (length 1.45 m) and a horizontal beam (0.615 m), both with a rectangular hollow steel section 8cm×4cm and thickness 4mm, which is fixed at the bottom of the column (see Fig. 1). The structure was weighed the total mass being $M_{T_X} = 13.24$ kg. The modal parameters were estimated with experimental modal analysis and the test setup is also shown in Fig. 1.

The structure was excited with an impact hammer applying forces in DOF's 10, 11 and 12, respectively, and the responses were measured in fifteen points using twelve accelerometers (two data sets) with a sensitivity of 100 mV/g, , using a sampling frequency of 2132 Hz. The responses were recorded with a National Instruments Compact DAQ acquisition system equipped with NI9234 acceleration modules. The modal parameters were estimated with the with the Complex Mode Indication Function (CMIF) technique [4] technique.

A model of the structure was assembled in ABAQUS [8] and meshed with shell elements S8R (8 nodes with reduced integration) using a global size of 0.005m. The following mechanical properties were considered for the steel: mass density $\varrho = 7850\ kg/m3$, Young's modulus $E = 210 \cdot 10^9\ N/m2$ and

Poisson ratio $\nu = 0.3$. The total mass of the model is $M_{T_{FE}} = 14.59\ kg$. The length of the numerical mode shapes was estimated with eq. (16).

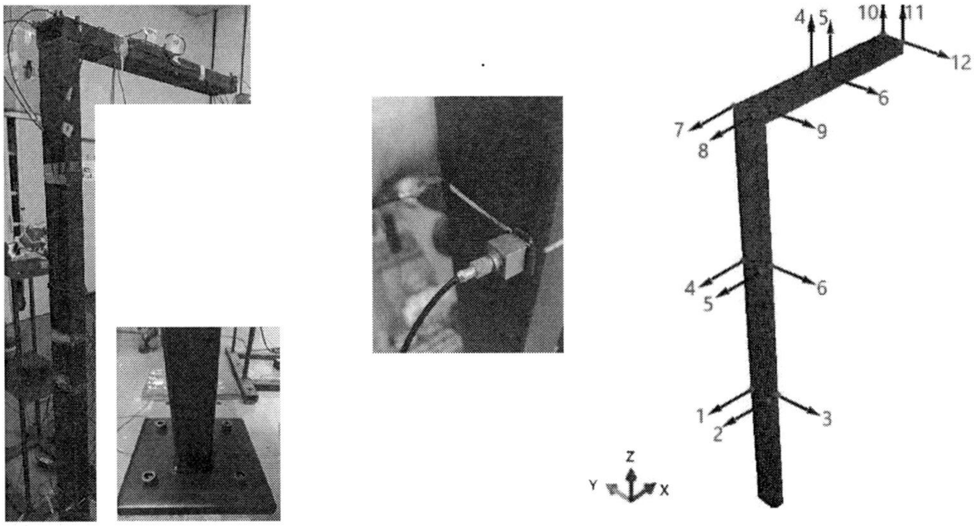

Figure 1. Steel structure and test setup

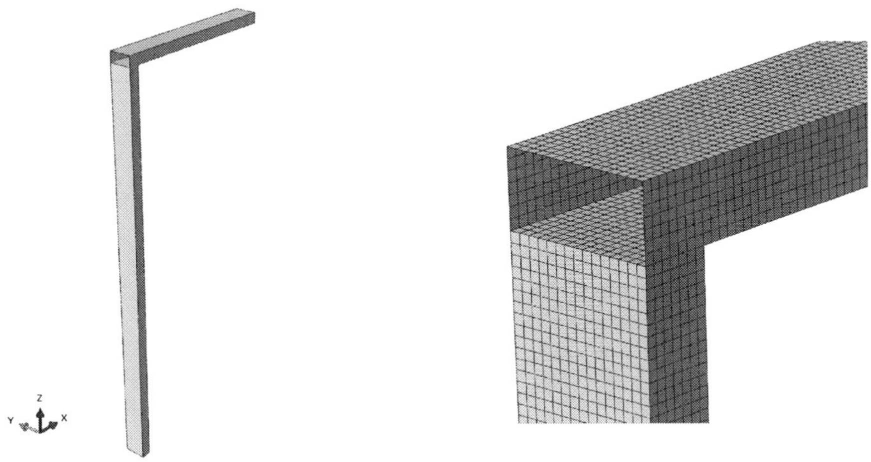

Figure 2. Numerical model meshed with shell elements.

The natural frequencies and the modal masses (mode shapes normalized to the largest component equal to unity) corresponding to the first 8 modes are shown in Table 1. The mode shapes are presented in Table 2.

An approximate transformation matrix $\boldsymbol{T}$ was obtained with the equation:

$$\boldsymbol{T} = \boldsymbol{\Phi}_{FEa}^{+} \cdot \boldsymbol{\Psi}_{Xa} \tag{24}$$

Where the subindex 'a' indicates active or measured DOF's. Then, the experimental mode shapes were expanded to the unmeasured DOF's using the numerical mode shapes, i.e:

$$\boldsymbol{\Psi}_{Xd} = \boldsymbol{\Phi}_{FEd} \cdot \boldsymbol{T} \quad (25)$$

Where subindex 'd' indicates unmeasured DOF's.

The length of the experimental mode shapes was also estimated with eq. (16) using the expanded mode shapes.

The ratio modal mass-square length is presented in Table 2. In this structure the mass-density is constant, and it can be observed that the ratio m_{FE}/L_{FE}^2 is equal for all the modes and equal to the total mass of the system ($M_{T_{FE}} = 14.59\ kg$).

Similar ratio m_X/L_X^2 has been obtained for all the experimental modes. As this ratio must be the same for all the modes, the results presented in Table 2 indicates that the modal masses have been estimated with a good accuracy. Morevoer, the ratio m_X/L_X^2 is, as expected, very close to the mass of the system $M_{T_X} = 13.24$ kg. The results of the ratio m_ψ/L_ψ^2 (Table 2) show that the modal masses were estimated with a good accuracy (error less than 1.5%), whereas modes 3 and 6 were estimated with errors of 5.5% and 8.25%, respectively.

Table 1. Numerical and experimental natural frequencies and modal masses.

Mode	Natural frequency [Hz]		Modal mass [kg]	
	Experimental	Numerical	Experimental	Numerical
1	12.53	10.938	6.25	6.90
2	20.85	18.75	3.74	3.66
3	55.74	50.781	1.47	1.71
4	55.31	54.688	1.87	2.04
5	131.98	115.625	6.57	7.12
6	198.10	180.469	5.51	5.63
7	324.78	284.572	4.93	5.42
8	502.56	465.35	4.18	5.63

Table 2. Comparison between experimental and numerical results.

Mode	**Ratio modal mass-square length**		**Error** $\frac{m_X}{L_X^2}/M_{TX}$ **(%)**
	m_X/L_X^2	m_{FE}/L_{FE}^2	
1	13.1607	14.5815	0.599
2	13.4442	14.5658	-1.542
3	12.5100	14.5152	5.513
4	13.3107	14.4991	-0.534
5	13.4068	14.5855	-1.260
6	14.3328	14.6002	-8.254
7	13.6395	14.6066	-3.017
8	13.0553	14.5295	1.395

5. A RIGID BEAM ON SPRINGS. CONSTANT MASS-DENSITY

In this section the modal masses and mode shape lengths of a rigid beam supported on two springs (see Tables 3, 4 and 5) vibrating in the x-y plane (bouncing mode and pitch mode) have been calculated.

The beam has constant density ρ, length a, total mass M, total volume $V = V/\rho$, and inertia $J = Ma^2/12$ with respect to de center of gravity of the beam.

In Table 3 the system is modelled with two translational DOF's and the mode shapes are normalized to the largest component equal to unity. All the components of the mode shapes are dimensionless and the lengths of the mode shapes are also dimensionless. The modal masses of both modes are given in kg. As the density is constant, the modal mass is equal to the product between the total mass of the structure and the length squared.

Table 3. Rigid beam on two springs. Two traslational DOF's. Mode shapes normalized to the largest traslational component equal to unity.

	MODE 1	MODE 2
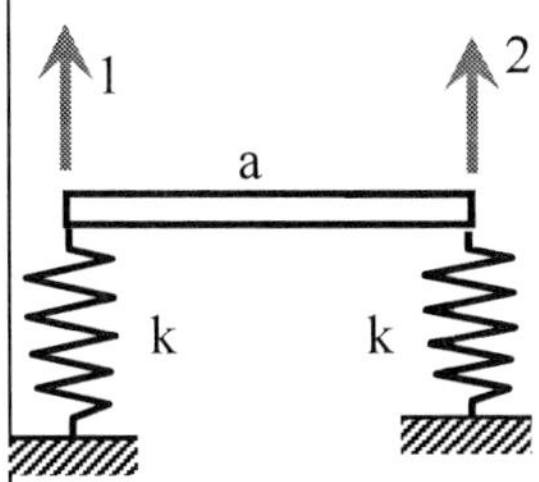		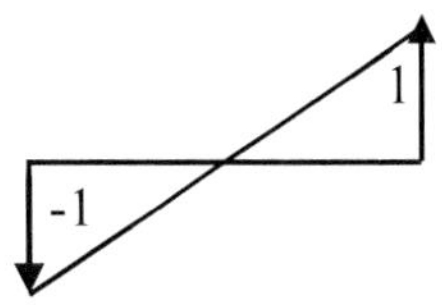
NORMALIZATION	Largest component equal to unity	Largest component equal to unity
MODE SHAPES	$\boldsymbol{\psi}_1 = \begin{Bmatrix} \mathbf{1} \\ \mathbf{1} \end{Bmatrix} \begin{bmatrix} m/m \\ m/m \end{bmatrix}$	$\boldsymbol{\psi}_2 = \begin{Bmatrix} \mathbf{-1} \\ \mathbf{1} \end{Bmatrix} \begin{bmatrix} m/m \\ m/m \end{bmatrix}$
MASS MATRIX $\boldsymbol{M}$	$\begin{bmatrix} \frac{M}{3} & \frac{M}{6} \\ \frac{M}{6} & \frac{M}{3} \end{bmatrix}$	
VOLUME MATRIX $\boldsymbol{V}$	$\begin{bmatrix} \frac{V}{3} & \frac{V}{6} \\ \frac{V}{6} & \frac{V}{3} \end{bmatrix}$	
LENGTH OF MODE SHAPES $L^2 = \frac{1}{V}\boldsymbol{\psi}^T\boldsymbol{V}\boldsymbol{\psi}$	$L_1^2 = 1$	$L_2^2 = \frac{1}{3}$
MODAL MASS $m = \boldsymbol{\psi}^T\boldsymbol{M}\boldsymbol{\psi}$	$m_1 = M\ (kg)$	$m_2 = \frac{M}{3}\ (kg)$

In Table 4 the system is modelled with a translational and a rotational DOF's, The first mode is normalized to the largest translational component equal to unity, and the second mode with largest rotational component equat to unity. The length of the first mode shape is dimensionless and that corresponding to the second mode has the units of m^2. The modal mass of the first mode is a mass (kg) and that of the second mode is a modal inertia (kgm^2) .

Table 4. Rigid beam on two springs. Two traslational DOF's. Mode shapes normalized to the largest traslational component equal to unity.

	MODE 1	MODE 2
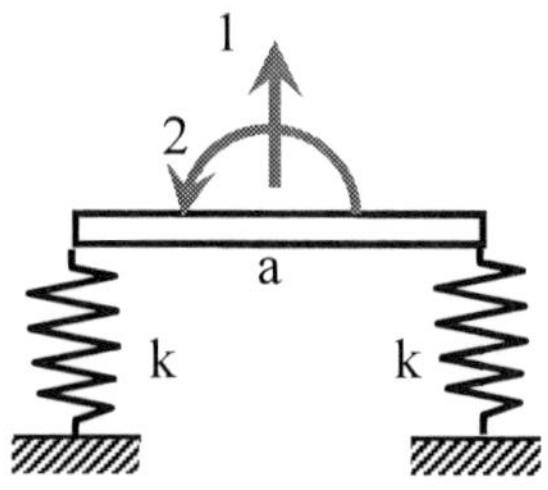	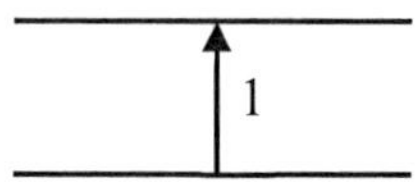	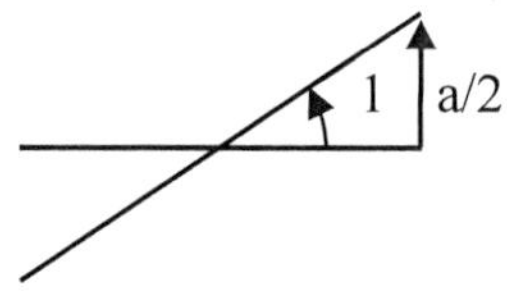
NORMALIZATION	Largest traslational component equal to unity	Largest rotational component equal to unity
MODE SHAPES	$\psi_1 = \begin{Bmatrix}1\\0\end{Bmatrix}\begin{bmatrix}m/m\\rd/m\end{bmatrix}$	$\psi_2 = \begin{Bmatrix}0\\1\end{Bmatrix}\begin{bmatrix}m/rd\\rd/rd\end{bmatrix}$
MASS MATRIX $\boldsymbol{M}$	$\begin{bmatrix}M & 0\\0 & J\end{bmatrix}$	$J = \frac{Ma^2}{12}$
VOLUME MATRIX $\boldsymbol{V}$	$\begin{bmatrix}V & 0\\0 & \frac{Va^2}{12}\end{bmatrix}$	
LENGTH OF MODE SHAPES $L^2 = \frac{1}{V}\boldsymbol{\psi}^T\boldsymbol{V}\boldsymbol{\psi}$	$L_1^2 = 1$	$L_2^2 = \frac{a^2}{12}\ (m^2)$
MODAL MASS $m = \boldsymbol{\psi}^T\boldsymbol{M}\boldsymbol{\psi}$	$m_1 = M\ (kg)$	$m_2 = J = \frac{Ma^2}{12}\,(kgm^2)$

In Table 5 the system is also modelled with a translational and a rotational DOF's. Both modes are normalized to the largest translational component equal to unity so the rotational components have the units $\frac{rd}{m}$. The lengths are dimensionless and the modal masses are given in kg and they are equal to those obtained Table 3.

It can be checked that multiplying the mode shapes by the term $\frac{1}{\sqrt{m}}$, the same mass normalized mode shapes are obtained with the results presented in Tables 3 to 5.

Table 5. Rigid beam on two springs. Two traslational DOF's. Mode shapes normalized to the largest traslational component equal to unity.

	MODE 1	MODE 2
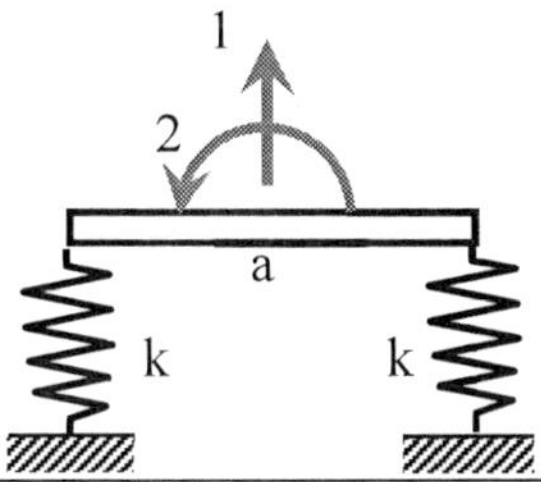	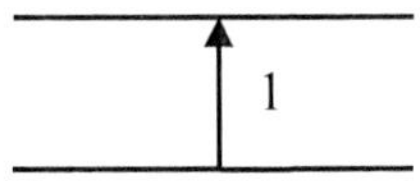	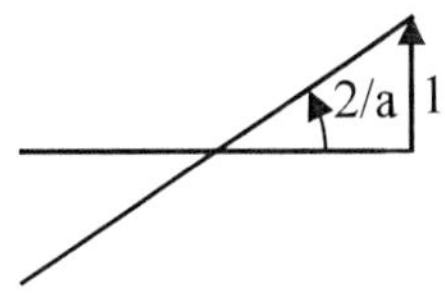
NORMALIZATION	Largest traslational component equal to unity	Largest traslational component equat to unity
MODE SHAPES	$\boldsymbol{\psi}_1 = \begin{Bmatrix} 1 \\ 0 \end{Bmatrix} \begin{bmatrix} m/m \\ rd/m \end{bmatrix}$	$\boldsymbol{\psi}_2 = \begin{Bmatrix} 0 \\ 2/a \end{Bmatrix} \begin{bmatrix} m/m \\ rd/m \end{bmatrix}$
MASS MATRIX $\boldsymbol{M}$	$\begin{bmatrix} M & 0 \\ 0 & J \end{bmatrix} \quad J = \frac{Ma^2}{12}$	
VOLUME MATRIX $\boldsymbol{V}$	$\begin{bmatrix} V & 0 \\ 0 & \frac{Va^2}{12} \end{bmatrix}$	
LENGTH OF MODE SHAPES $L^2 = \frac{1}{V} \boldsymbol{\psi}^T \boldsymbol{V} \boldsymbol{\psi}$	$L_1^2 = 1$	$L_2^2 = \frac{1}{3}$
MODAL MASS $m = \boldsymbol{\psi}^T \boldsymbol{M} \boldsymbol{\psi}$	$m_1 = M\ (kg)$	$m_2 = \frac{M}{3}\ (kg)$

6. A RIGID BEAM ON SPRINGS. TWO DIFFERENT MATERIALS

The system shown in Table 6 also consists of a rigid beam supported on two springs, but the beam is made of steel (left half) and concrete (right half), i.e. the mass-density is not constant. The following geometrical and mechanical properties were considered: $total\ length\ of\ the\ beam\ a = 1m$, $square\ section\ 0.1 \times 0.1\ m^2$, $k = \frac{10^6 N}{m}, E_s = 210\ Gpa, \nu_s = 0.3, \rho_s = 7850 \frac{kg}{m^3}, E_c = 25\ Gpa$, $\nu_c = 0.2, \rho_c = 2400 \frac{kg}{m^3}$, where subindexes 's' and 'c' indicate steel and concrete, respectively.

The system is modelled with two translational DOF's and the mode shapes were mass normalized, i.e. the components have the units $1/\sqrt{kg}$, and the modal masses are dimensionless unity. The lengths and the partial lengths of the mode shapes were calculated with eqs. (13) and (18). In this case, an apparent mass, different for each mode, is obtained.

Table 6. Rigid beam on two springs. Two traslational DOF's. Mode shapes normalized to the largest traslational component equal to unity.

<table>
<tr><td></td><td>MODE 1</td><td>MODE 2</td></tr>
<tr><td>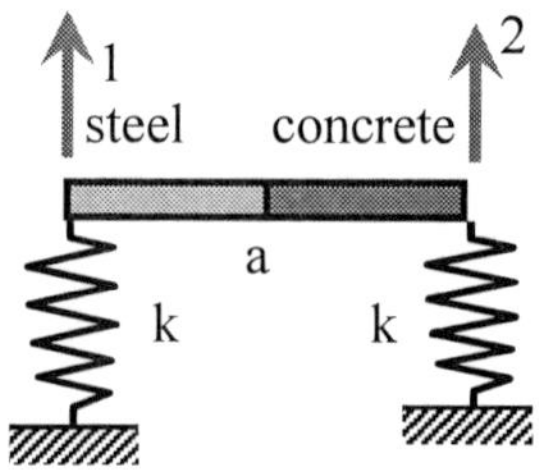
</td><td>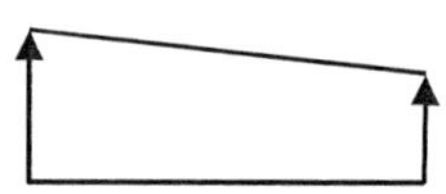</td><td>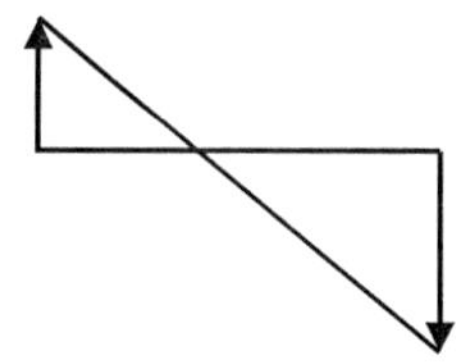</td></tr>
<tr><td>NORMALIZATION</td><td>Mass normalization
$m_\phi = 1$</td><td>Mass normalization
$m_\phi = 1$</td></tr>
<tr><td>MODE SHAPES</td><td>$\boldsymbol{\phi_1} = \begin{Bmatrix} 0.1829 \\ 0.05421 \end{Bmatrix} \begin{bmatrix} 1/\sqrt{kg} \\ 1/\sqrt{kg} \end{bmatrix}$</td><td>$\boldsymbol{\phi_2} = \begin{Bmatrix} 0.1599 \\ -0.3662 \end{Bmatrix} \begin{bmatrix} 1/\sqrt{kg} \\ 1/\sqrt{kg} \end{bmatrix}$</td></tr>
<tr><td>MASS MATRIX $\boldsymbol{M}\ (\boldsymbol{kg})$</td><td colspan="2">$\begin{bmatrix} \frac{7}{12}M_s + \frac{1}{12}M_c & \frac{1}{6}M_s + \frac{1}{6}M_c \\ \frac{1}{6}M_s + \frac{1}{6}M_c & \frac{1}{12}M_s + \frac{7}{12}M_c \end{bmatrix} = \begin{bmatrix} 23.8958 & 8.5417 \\ 8.5417 & 10.2708 \end{bmatrix}$
$M_s = 39.25\ kg, M_c = 12\ kg$</td></tr>
<tr><td>VOLUME MATRIX
$\boldsymbol{V}\ (\boldsymbol{m^3})$</td><td colspan="2">$\begin{bmatrix} \frac{7}{12}V_s + \frac{1}{12}V_c & \frac{1}{6}V_s + \frac{1}{6}V_c \\ \frac{1}{6}V_s + \frac{1}{6}V_c & \frac{1}{12}V_s + \frac{7}{12}V_c \end{bmatrix} = \begin{bmatrix} 0.0033 & 0.0017 \\ 0.0017 & 0.0033 \end{bmatrix}$</td></tr>
<tr><td>LENGTH OF MODE SHAPES
$L^2 = \frac{1}{V}\ \boldsymbol{\psi}^T\boldsymbol{V}\boldsymbol{\psi}\ \left(\frac{1}{kg}\right)$
$L_s^2 = \frac{1}{V_s}\ \boldsymbol{\psi}_s^T\boldsymbol{V}_s\boldsymbol{\psi}_s\left(\frac{1}{kg}\right)$
$L_c^2 = \frac{1}{V_c}\ \boldsymbol{\psi}_c^T\boldsymbol{V}_c\boldsymbol{\psi}_c\ \left(\frac{1}{kg}\right)$</td><td>$L_1^2 = 0.0154$
$L_{1s}^2 = 0.0231$
$L_{1c}^2 = 0.0078$</td><td>$L_2^2 = 0.0337$
$L_{2s}^2 = 0.0066$
$L_{2c}^2 = 0.0608$</td></tr>
<tr><td>APPARENT MASS
$M_{ap} = \frac{M_s L_{\psi_s}^2 + M_c L_{\psi_c}^2}{L_\psi^2}$</td><td>$M_{ap1} = 64.717\ (kg)$</td><td>$M_{ap1} = 29.315(kg)$</td></tr>
<tr><td>MODAL MASS
$m = \boldsymbol{\psi}^T\boldsymbol{M}\boldsymbol{\psi}$
$m = M_s L_{\psi_s}^2 + M_c L_{\psi_c}^2$</td><td>$m_1 = 1$</td><td>$m_2 = 1$</td></tr>
</table>

7. CONCLUSIONS

When the mass density of a structure is constant, the modal mass is always equal to the product between the total mass of the structure and the length squared ($m_\psi = M_T L_\psi^2$). If the mass density is not constant, the modal mass is equal to the product between an apparent mass (which is different for each mode) and the length squared. The modal mass of a mode shape normalized to a displacement equal to unity, is given in kg. On the other hand, if the normalization is to a rotation equal to unity, then the modal mass is given in kgm^2, i.e. it is a modal inertia.

In constant mass density systems, the ratio m_ψ / L_ψ^2 is constant for all the modes and equal to the total mass of the system. This property has been used in an experimental steel beam structure, to validate the modal masses estimated by experimental modal analysis. The experimental mode shapes were expanded to the unmeasured DOF's using a numerical model and the squared lengths estimated with eq. (16). The results of the ratio m_ψ / L_ψ^2 (Table 2) show that the modal masses were estimated with a good accuracy (error less than 1.5%), except modes 3 and 6, which were obtained with errors of 5.5% and 8.25%, respectively.

The modal masses and lengths of a rigid beam supported on two springs, vibrating in the x-y plane, were calculated using different sets of DOF's and different types of normalization. It has been demonstrated that all the models provide the same mass normalized mode shapes, independently of the type of normalization and the set of DOF's considered to define the system.

ACKNOWLEDGEMENTS

The authors would like to express their gratitude to the Spanish Ministry of Science and Innovation for the financial support through the project MCI-20-PID2019-105593GB-I00/AEI/10.13039/501100011033.

REFERENCES

[1] Dianat S.A and Saber E. (2009) *Advanced Linear Algebra for Engineers wiht MATLAB*, New York: CRC Press.

[2] Clough RW and Penzien J (1993) *Dynamics of structur*es, 2nd edition. New York: McGraw-Hill-

[3] Chopra AK (1995) *Dynamics of Structures*. New Jersey: Prentice Hall.

[4] Heylen W, Lammens S and Sas P (2007) *Modal Analysis theory and testing*. Belgium: Katholieke Universiteit Leuven, Faculty of Engineering.

[5] Brincker R., Ventura C. (2015). *Introduction to Operational Modal Analysis*. Chichester: John Wiley & Sons Ltd.

[6] Aenlle M, Juul M, Brincker R. Modal Mass and Length of Mode Shapes in Structural Dynamics. Shock Vib 2020;2020:1–16.

[7] M. Aenlle and R. Brincker, "Basic Concepts of Modal Scaling," 8th Int. Oper. Modal Anal. Conf., 2019.

[8] ABAQUS UNIFIED FEA. Dassault Systems.

9th International Operational Modal Analysis Conference
iomac
July 3 - 6, 2022
Vancouver, Canada

F.E. STRUCTURAL UPDATING OF AN ULTRALIGHT HELICOPTER COMPONENT USING OMA METHODS

Luca Conti[1], *and Giuliano Coppotelli*[2]

[1] Ph.D Student, University of Rome "La Sapienza", lu.conti@uniroma1.it
[2] Associate Professor, University of Rome "La Sapienza, giuliano.coppotelli@uniroma1.it

ABSTRACT

In this paper, a structural update method based on modal analysis is introduced to define an updated FEM model for use in the digital-twin model simulation. A component of an ultralight helicopter is tested with different experimental techniques to identify the dynamic parameters. The use of Operational Modal Analysis (OMA) allows the acquisition of different experimental data sets, both of which can be used in the structural upgrade phases. In this paper, such experimental data are used to estimate the modal parameters and then correlated with the numerical predictions. The structural updating algorithm allows the correlation of numerical and experimental data using different benchmark variables, such as FRF and modal parameters. Here natural frequencies and mode shapes are used to update the structural model by selecting appropriate updating variables related to the truss structure representing a fuselage component of the ultralight helicopter. Results showed that the OMA techniques can be successfully used to obtain an accurate structural model of an operating structure, thus constituting a valuable tool for analysis engineers and credible support of the certification process.

Keywords: Operational Modal Analysis, Structural Updating, Structural dynamics.

1. INTRODUCTION

The dynamic analysis of rotating wing aircraft is mandatory to receive flight clearance. With reference to an ultra-light helicopter and to the European regulation EASA-VLR, manufacturers have to demonstrate that such an aircraft is capable to guarantee specific flight characteristics in all the operating conditions, including a sudden performance reduction, with an acceptable increase in the pilot's effort and without exceeding the load safety limits. **[1]**. To be compliant with these regulations, manufacturers define a test plan aimed at characterizing the dynamic behavior of every structural subcomponent. In this paper, a portion of the truss structure of an ultra-light helicopter fuselage is considered. By dynamic testing such a truss structure when subjected to an equivalent operational loading condition an updated finite element model will be derived to support the manufacturer in predicting the helicopter's responses at different flight conditions. In this framework, the paper investigates the possibility to use modal parameters estimated with operational modal analysis (OMA) methods as the experimental basis for the finite element model updating. The relevance of using the modal parameters estimated in operating conditions relies on the possibility to develop a procedure for the continuous monitoring of the structure besides the increase of the representativeness of the modal base since it is relative to an operating system instead of a system subjected to laboratory boundary conditions, **[3-4]**. At the prototype aircraft development phase a dynamically tuned finite element model is vital for industries to guarantee the expected dynamic performance when applying structural modifications, verifying airframe upgrades, or when installing new equipment, and/or changing the overall layout such as when adding external stores. A well-matched finite element model will dramatically reduce the number of tests. Also, the dependency on the costly trial and error approach could be reduced for a systematic process of development. Thanks to the availability of the prototype model, data measurements could be used to improve the dynamic finite element model. Furthermore, validating the finite element model at the subsystem level will allow to dramatically reduce the efforts to obtain a validated numerical model of the whole aircraft structure. Each sub-system will be characterized by its own validated finite element model and it could receive the flight certification separately from the other sub-systems, thus accelerating the development time of new helicopter designs. The global finite element representation of the whole helicopter structure is then achieved by assembling each subsystem finite element that is, in turn, validated through the corresponding experimental data. In this paper, the modal properties of the truss component of a helicopter structure have been identified by using the so-called Hilbert Transform Method (HTM), **[5]**, operational modal analysis method that operates in the frequency domain and is based on the application of the Hilbert transform to the output power spectral densities to estimated the biased frequency response functions (FRFs). Then an iterative sensitivity-based method called Predictor-Corrector, also available in the FEM-Tools commercial software is applied to improve the correlation between the experimental and numerical model this identifying the structural properties requiring updating, **[6]**. It will be shown how the error in the natural frequencies and the correlation between the mode shapes are greatly improved thus confirming the accuracy of the numerical predictions and opening new opportunities for operational modal analysis as a support methodology in the field of flight certification process. Indeed, such a validated numerical model could be considered as an important tool for the prediction of the helicopter structural performances under different flight conditions, also during the developing phase with a great reduction of the development costs.

2. METHODOLOGY

In this paper, the actual capabilities of an OMA-based structural updating approach are assessed through the dynamic analysis of a truss component of a lightweight helicopter fuselage. Both the Frequency Domain Decomposition, FDD, **[3]** and the Hilbert Transform Method, HTM, Ref. **[5]** were used to estimate the modal parameters. The excitation is a broadband uncorrelated random excitation provided by finger tapping the whole structure. Details on these methods are omitted for the sake of brevity, but they could be found in the previously specified references. Furthermore, the identified modal parameters have been successfully compared with those estimated using the traditional Input-Output-based modal analysis. Indeed, both the natural frequencies and mode shapes compare well between the approaches, whereas a larger discrepancy has been found when the estimate of the damping ratios is considered. However, such a discrepancy is within the typical uncertainty characterizing the identification of the damping. For this reason, the paper is referring to the experimental modal basis, without specifying the approach used to estimate it and it represents the reference dynamic behavior for the considered structural updating method. Having a dynamically tuned finite element model of the structure is of paramount importance for industries to guarantee the expected dynamic performance when applying structural modifications, verifying airframe upgrades, or when installing new equipment, and/or changing the overall layout such as when adding external stores. And that is particularly true when referring to the certification process, for which the availability of an accurate mathematical model is the key point to the prediction of the amplitude of the vibration levels, **[5]**, at the relevant flight condition. In this paper, a sensitivity-based structural updating method has been applied to improve the dynamic finite element model of a truss component of a helicopter fuselage that uses the modal base estimated by the operational modal analysis methods previously described. Such an updating method evaluates the sensitivities of the natural frequencies and mode shapes to the changes of some selected structural properties, **[6-7]**, such as the thickness distribution and the Young modulus of the alloy used to manufacture the structure. These structural parameters have been selected because of the higher uncertainties associated with them during the whole investigation process since they were not disclosed to the authors. The structural sensitivities are numerically evaluated by using the reference finite element model providing the actual changes that minimize the difference, also known as error function, between the numerical and the experimental models. The error minimization procedure is therefore iterated until the convergence of the numerical modal parameters to the experimental ones is reached within a given tolerance.

3. OPERATIONAL MODAL ANALYSIS

The considered truss component of the helicopter fuselage, shown in Fig.1 (left), is developed to support the tail and the main rotor shaft, thus carrying both bending and torsional loadings. The structure has been cantilevered in the Structural dynamics laboratory of the University of Rome "La Sapienza" for the experimental characterization, Fig.1 (right). The output response accelerations (both in the vertical and in the horizontal directions) have been recorded at 24 measuring points, see Fig. 2, whereas the random input loading was provided by finger tapping the truss so that the excitation could be considered as a broadband random excitation and uncorrelated in the space domain. The tested truss weight is 4.701 Kg.

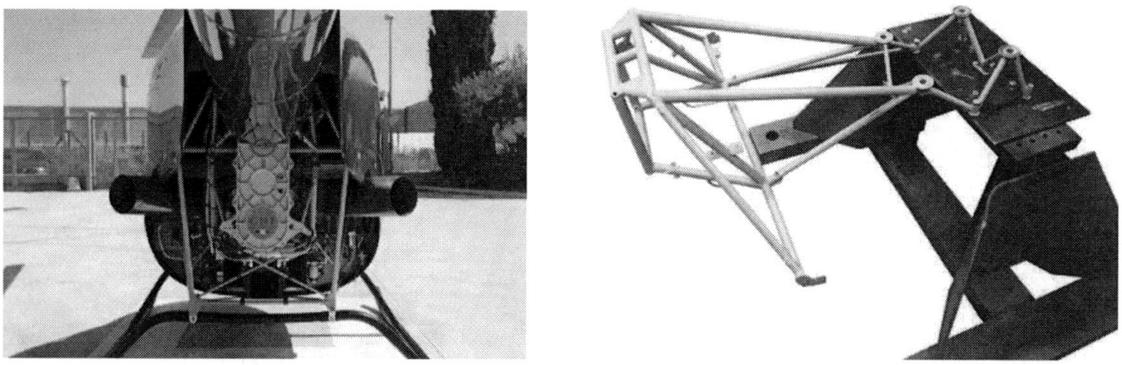

Figure 1: General view of the truss component of the helicopter fuselage (left); laboratory test stup (right)

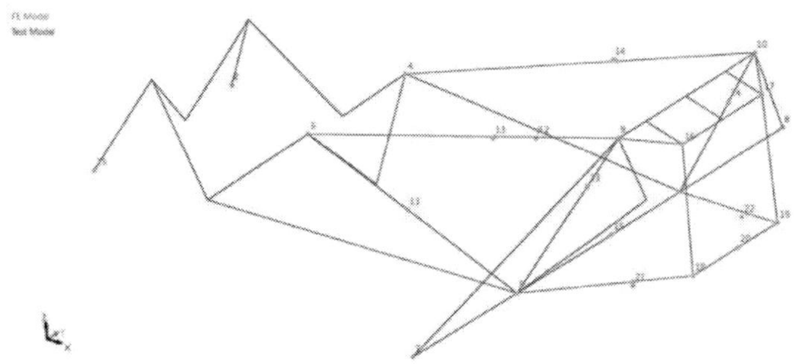

Figure 2: Location of the measuring points

The modal parameters estimated using the HTM method are consistent not only with those estimated with other OMA methods, here the FDD method has been considered for comparison but also with the estimates from the traditional LMS PolyMax EMA method. For this reason, the paper will refer to OMA modal parameters only, without clearing the approach used for the estimate. The experimental investigation has been carried out in the [0 – 50] Hz frequency range, using 4096 spectral lines, and filtering the output signal with the Hanning windowing function to reduce the leakage. The resulting modal parameters are reported in Tab. 1 in which B stands for a coupled vertical-horizontal bending mode, whereas T for a torsional mode.

Table 1. OMA estimated modal parameters.

Mode #	Mode Type	f_n (Hz)	ζ (%)
1	B + T	11.81	0.92
2	B + T	24.14	1.30
3	T	33.53	0.32

4. INITIAL F.E. MODEL AND CORRELATION OF THE TRUSS STRUCTURE

From the actual geometrical measurements and the material properties of the truss component, it has been possible to develop the corresponding F.E. model composed of bar elements, for a total of 3430 elements with 4231 nodes, see Fig. 3. The overall mass estimated by the finite element code is 3.410 Kg.

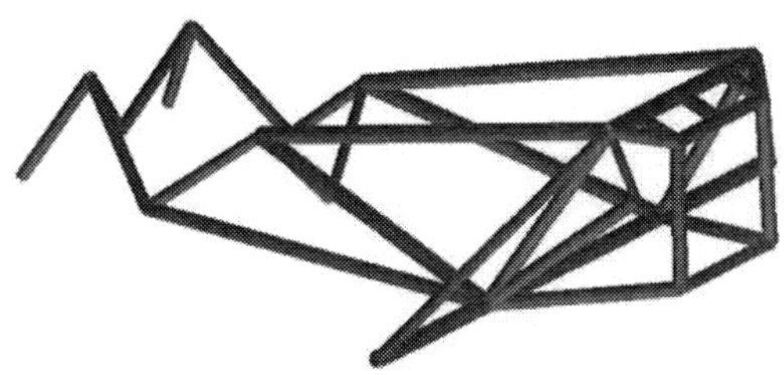

Figure 3: F.E. model representation of the truss component of the helicopter fuselage

In Tab. 2 the numerical evaluated natural frequencies and mode type are reported, whereas the mode shapes are reported in Figures from 4 to 6.

Table 2. Numerically (FE) evaluated modal parameters.

Mode #	Mode Type	f_n (Hz)
1	B + T	14.23
2	B + T	24.75
3	T	33.72

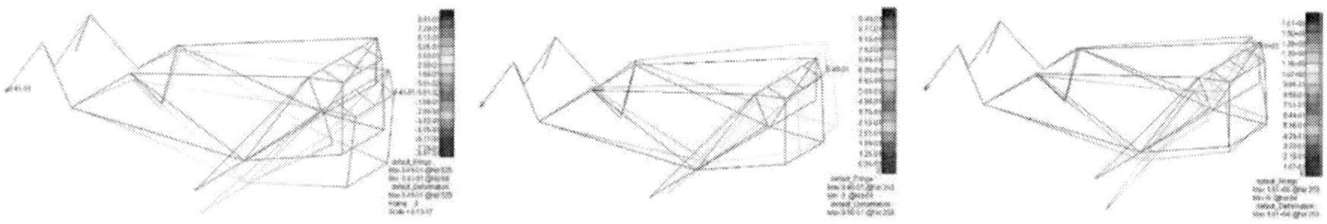

Figure 4: Numerical mode shapes of the truss component of the helicopter fuselage (Mode 1 – left; Mode 2 – center; Mode 3 – right).

The numerically predicted mass of the truss component is clearly underestimating the actual structural mass. This is probably due to the simplified F.E .modeling that is not taking into account the extra mass the manufacturing process introduces when welding together the bar components. The relative difference in the masses of about 27% is the main reason for the differences among the natural frequencies, as reported in Tab. 3 where Δf_n is the relative error between the natural frequencies, being the experimental finding the reference quantity, and MAC is the correlation between corresponding mode shapes, expressed by the Modal Assurance Criterium. Such a correlation is very encouraging because it is evidence of the relatively high representativeness of the numerical model with respect to the experimental one, despite the large errors in the correlation between the natural frequencies. Indeed, the numerical underestimate of the structural mass is responsible for the overall overestimation of the natural frequencies. However, it seems that mass distribution is, on the contrary, acceptable since the high value of the correlation between modes. In Fig. 5, the graphical representation of the whole correlation between the mode shapes is depicted from which it can be seen that the identified modes do represent a modal base for the considered truss structure.

Table 3 Initial comparison between numerical and experimental modal parameters.

Mode #	Δf_n (%)	MAC (%)
1	-20.76	85.0
2	-2.50	80.2
3	-0.57	67.3

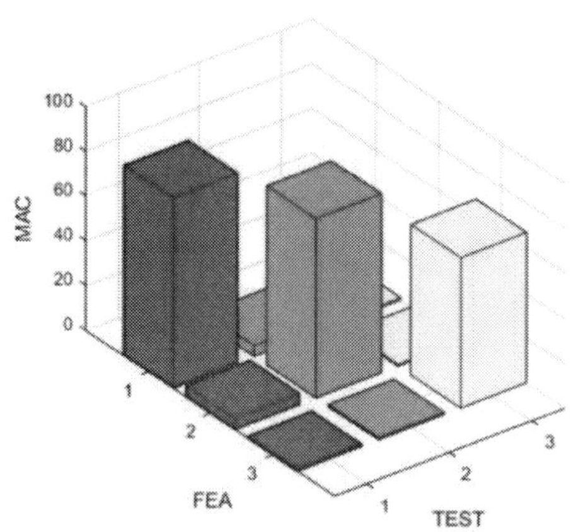

Figure 5: Initial correlation between mode shapes.

5. STRUCTURAL UPDATING

From the analysis of the correlation between the numerical model and experimental findings, it was clear the role played by the mass distribution was found to be underestimated in the numerical model. For this reason and also because the finite element model has been previously assessed from the static behavior point of view, not reported for the sake of brevity, the authors chose the mass distribution as the design variable for the structural updating process. However, before performing the structural updating, lumped masses have been added to the finite element model to introduce the missing mass caused by the welding of the connecting bars forming the truss. These non-structural masses have been added to the connecting points highlighted in Fig. 6 with circles.

Figure 6: Detailed view of the points with added lumped mass (circled).

As a result, the difference between the numerical and the experimental masses was noticeably reduced from an error of 27% to 12% since this increased the numerical mass to the value of 4.152 Kg. The new modal parameters also exhibited an increased correlation with the experimental ones, as reported in Tab. 4, thus demonstrating the beneficial effect of the considered mass change.

Table 4. Numerical-Experimental correlation after adding the lumped mass of the connecting truss points.

Mode #	Num. f_n (Hz)	Δf_n (%)	MAC (%)
1	12.63	6.94	85.1
2	24.57	1.80	85.8
3	33.98	1.34	66.5

The corresponding finite element model has been considered as the starting point for the updating process. The minimized error function is represented by the error in the natural frequencies and by the increase of the correlation between modes, whereas the updating variables are the non-structural mass distribution of the bars. These updating variables are collected together when referring to bars belonging to the same geometrical set to speed up the solution process. As one can see from Fig. 7 and Fig. 8, the iterative process led to an acceptable error after less than 20 iteration steps, to which corresponded a local increase of the mass associated with the bar of about 3%

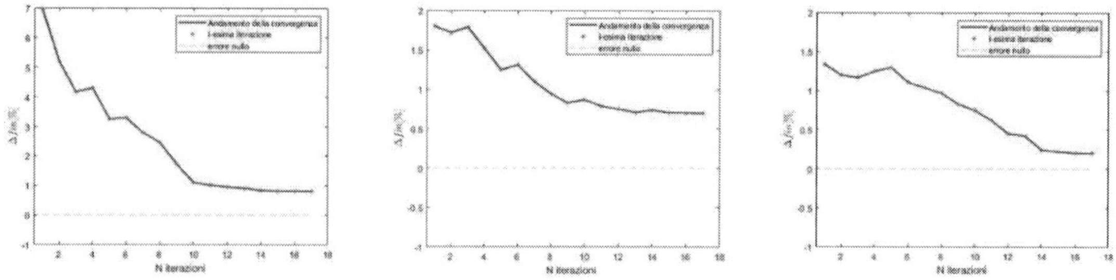

Figure 7: Convergence history for the natural frequencies. Mode #1 left – Mode#2 center – Mode #3 right.

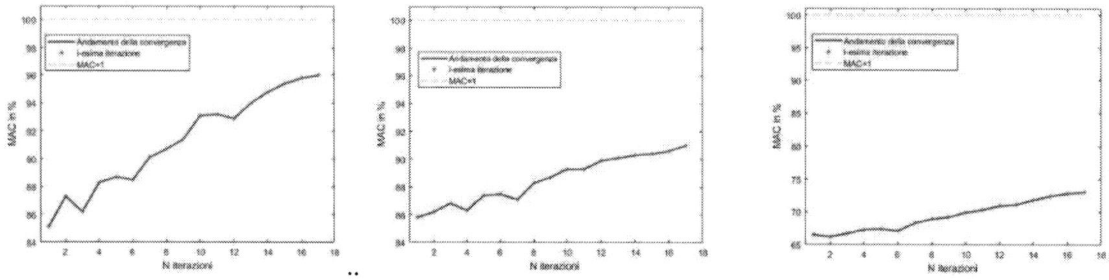

Figure 8: Convergence history for the mode correlation. Mode #1 left – Mode#2 center – Mode #3 right.

The final (updated) correlation is reported in Tab. 5. The natural frequency shifts are now all less than 1 % and the correlation between the mode shapes is higher than 90% for the first two modes and higher than 70% for the third mode.

Table 5. Numerical-Experimental correlation at the end of the updating process.

Mode #	Exp. f_n (Hz)	Num. f_n (Hz)	Δf_n (%)	MAC (%)
1	11.81	11.90	-0.76	96
2	24.14	23.97	0.70	91
3	33.53	33.59	-0.18	73

In Fig. 9, the graphical representation of the whole correlation between the mode shapes after the updating process is shown.

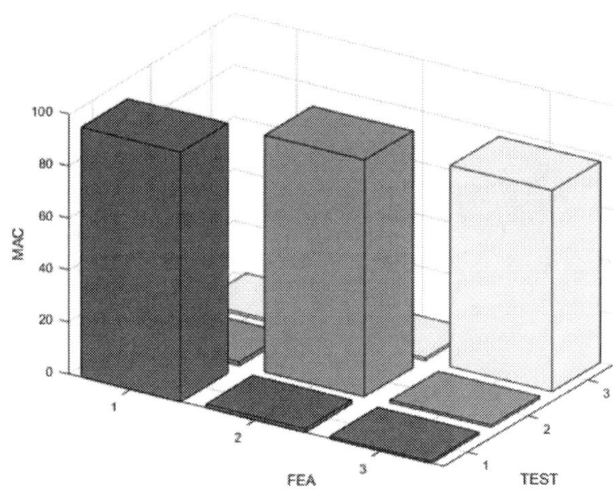

Figure 9: Final (updated) correlation between mode shapes.

6. CONCLUSIONS

In this paper, a structural update method based on modal analysis has been proposed. The approach combines the operational modal analysis method (OMA) called HTM and the sensitivity-based iterative method and has been applied to an actual truss component of a helicopter fuselage. The effectiveness of the use of the OMA estimated modal parameters and the updating method for such a class of dynamic problems have been successfully demonstrated as a perfectly correlated numerical model has been achieved. The presented application could be considered important real-life support to the flight certification process since it is capable to take into account the experimental behavior as characterizing the flying structure. Therefore, the proposed approach could help the development of new helicopter configurations taking into account possibly ongoing structural modifications thus dramatically reducing the efforts to obtain a validated numerical model of the whole aircraft structure.

ACKNOWLEDGEMENTS

This work has been granted by the University of Rome ''La Sapienza'', year 2020, ''Identification of damping mechanism in a sloshing wing-like system''.

REFERENCES

[1] EASA (2003). Certification Specifications for Very Light Rotorcraft. Decision no. 2003/17/RM of *The Executive Director of the Agency.*

[2] L. Herman s , H. Van der Auweraer , *Modal Testing and Analysis of Structures under Operational Conditions: Industrial Applications* , Mechanical Systems & Signal Processing, Vol . 13, No. 2, p p 193- 216, (1999)

[3] R. Brincker, L. Zhang, P. Andersen, *Modal Identification from Ambient Responses Using Frequency Domain Decomposition*, XVIII IMAC, S. Antonio, TX, (USA), (2000)

[4] Brincker, R. & Ventura, C. (2021). *Introduction to Operational Modal Analysis.* Wiley.

[5] Agneni, A. & Balis Crema, L. & Coppotelli, G. (2013). *Modal Parameters Directly Estimated from Power Spectral Densities or Correlation Functions in Output-Only Analysis.* In: *Experimental Techniques (2013), Society for Experimental Mechanics.* Experimental. Techniques (2016) 40: 331-321.

[6] Friswell, M.I. & Mottershead, J.E. (1996). *Finite Element Model Updating in Structural Dynamics.* Kluwer Academic Publishers.

[7] M. Arras, G. Coppotelli (2015). *Finite element structural updating using frequency response functions.* Journal of Aircraft, vol. 52, p. 1454-1468, ISSN: 0021-8669, doi: 10.2514/1.C032964.

9th International Operational Modal Analysis Conference
iomac
July 3 - 6, 2022
Vancouver, Canada

DIRECTIONAL COORDINATES FOR THE IDENTIFICATION OF BACKWARD AND FORWARD FREQUENCIES OF ROTATING MACHINES VIA OMA

Nathali Dreher[1], Gustavo Storti [2], and Tiago Machado [3]

[1] PhD Student, University of Campinas, School of Mechanical Engineering, nathalidreher@gmail.com.
[2] PhD Student, University of Campinas, School of Mechanical Engineering, gucstorti@gmail.com.
[3] Associate Professor, University of Campinas, School of Mechanical Engineering, tiagomh@fem.unicamp.br.

ABSTRACT

Operational Modal Analysis has been widely used to extract and monitor modal parameters of systems in operation. There is a great number of research in which OMA was successfully implemented, the majority encompassing civil structures, such as beams, bridges, and buildings. However, applying OMA to rotating machines can be a real challenge. These systems are usually subjected to non-stationarity, caused, for example, by changes in rotational speed. In addition, they can be installed in areas without the influence of excitation conditions that agree with OMA's main premise. However, even when the operating conditions are favorable, the identification of the rotor's modes is still a challenge. Due to the gyroscopic effect, the backward and the forward frequencies of each vibration mode may move away or towards each other, appearing sometimes as closely spaced frequencies that are difficult to identify and differentiate via OMA techniques. The transformation of the rotor's response from the physical coordinates to directional coordinates have been widely used to separate the forward and backward components of the rotor's response. The purpose of this paper is to employ this transformation and apply OMA to each directional coordinate, enabling the identification of both forward and backward frequencies of the rotor's modes and improving the results of OMA in rotating machines. The methodology was applied to a dataset of a test rig with a rotor supported by hydrodynamic bearings, and the results showed that directional coordinates are a promising tool to improve the identification of rotor modes.

Keywords: Operational Modal Analysis, Directional Coordinates, Rotating Machines

1. INTRODUCTION

Rotating machines are components of great importance in the most diverse branches of industry, requiring attention for their operation and maintenance. Defects and failures in these machines can lead to undesired expenses and unscheduled stops, delaying production and increasing company costs. In more serious cases, failures can lead to catastrophes that compromise the environment and risk the processes' security. With the purpose of preventing critical problems such as these, the constant monitoring of rotating machines can be employed.

The monitoring of rotating machines can be carried out through several different techniques that encompass the monitoring of the machine's parameters, such as electrical signals, noise, vibration levels, and modal parameters, the last being usually extracted from vibration signals using classical modal analysis. However, the application of classical modal analysis in the constant monitoring of systems is a counterproductive task, since it demands more time and the use of additional devices coupled to the system. Operational Modal Analysis (OMA) brings some advantages in comparison to classical modal analysis, such as not requiring equipment to excite the system and not taking it out of operation to extract the modal parameters, reducing costs and allowing the constant monitoring. Thus, OMA has been a focus of research to extract modal parameters of systems in operation through the past decades, and, as already stated, have been successfully applied to several civil structures. This prominent success is associated to two main factors. First, the loads acting upon these structures are provided by elements such as the wind and the pedestrian or vehicle traffic, that altogether can be modeled as white noise inputs and agree with OMA's main premise. Moreover, OMA requires the system under analysis to be linear and time-invariant, as is the case with most civil structures. However, applying OMA to more complex systems, like rotating machines, is still a great challenge to be overcome.

In the special case of rotating machines, non-linearities in the system, excitation conditions that do not satisfy OMA's main premise, and closely spaced frequencies difficult to differentiate pose challenges to the modal identification. Although some research [1] already demonstrated that, under adequate excitation conditions, the rotor's modal parameters can be extracted through OMA's techniques with results really close to the ones extracted by classical modal analysis techniques, non-linearities and closely spaced modes are still challenges to OMA. Focusing on the last, some remarks about the rotor dynamics must be made. It is worth mentioning that the modes of a rotor usually appear in pairs, the forward and backward modes, and that one of the consequences of the gyroscopic effect on the dynamics of the rotor is the approximation or diversion of these two modes, which can originate closely spaced modes that are difficult to identify and differentiate via OMA techniques.

In 1991, Lee [2] developed the basic theory of the directional modal analysis of rotating machines, comparing it with the classical modal analysis. The author stated that the application of classical modal testing to rotating machinery has resulted in the heavy overlapping of the backward and forward modes in the frequency domain. Therefore, Lee [2] proposed the use of the complex notation and enabled not only a clear distinction of the forward and backward modes, but also the separation of those modes in the frequency domain, so that effective modal parameter identification was possible [2].

This methodology was further investigated and employed, as can be seen in the works of [3], [4], [5], [6] and [7], becoming an essential tool in the study of rotor dynamics.

In order to enable the identification of the rotor's forward and backward frequencies via OMA techniques, this work proposes the use of directional coordinates before applying OMA to vibration signals of a rotating machine. The proposed methodology was applied to vibration signals of a rotor supported by hydrodynamic bearings and under different excitation conditions. Stochastic Subspace Identification (SSI-DATA) method was employed as the OMA technique.

2. METHODOLOGY

2.1. Directional Coordinates

Figure 1 illustrates the motion of a rotor in the Y and Z directions, from which it is possible to identify two rotations, the rotor spin (Ω) and the rotor precession (ω), that is, its rotation around itself and the rotation of the deflected axis around its undeflected configuration. The precession motion has two components: the forward one, that occurs in the same direction of the rotor spin (Figure 1 (a)), and the backward one, that occurs in the opposite direction of the rotor spin (Figure 1 (b)).

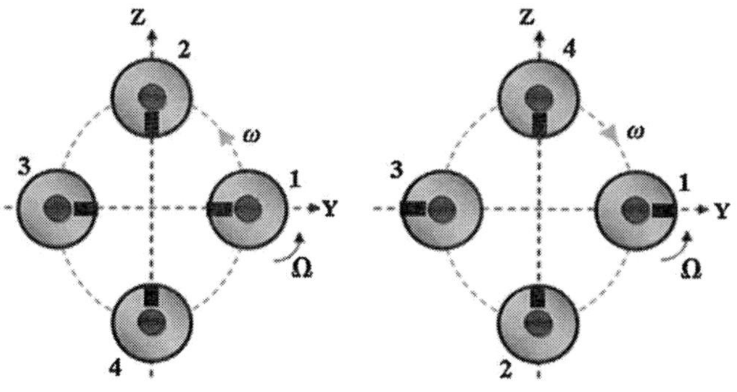

Figure 1. Forward (a) and backward (b) motions [7].

According to [7], for an external excitation force of frequency ω, the cartesian coordinates can be written in the complex plane as rotating vectors:

$$\boldsymbol{y} = \{\boldsymbol{y}_{re} + j\boldsymbol{y}_{im}\}e^{j\omega t} = (\boldsymbol{y}_{re}\cos\omega t - \boldsymbol{y}_{im}\sin\omega t) + j(\boldsymbol{y}_{im}\cos\omega t + \boldsymbol{y}_{re}\sin\omega t) \quad (1)$$

$$\boldsymbol{z} = \{\boldsymbol{z}_{re} + j\boldsymbol{z}_{im}\}e^{j\omega t} = (\boldsymbol{z}_{re}\cos\omega t - \boldsymbol{z}_{im}\sin\omega t) + j(\boldsymbol{z}_{im}\cos\omega t + \boldsymbol{z}_{re}\sin\omega t) \quad (2)$$

It is important to note that the imaginary parts in Eq. (1) and Eq. (2) are related to the rotation of the vectors $\boldsymbol{y}$ and $\boldsymbol{z}$, and the real parts correspond to the physical coordinates which can be measured. Therefore, the system response $\boldsymbol{q}$ can also be represented in the complex plane:

$$\boldsymbol{q} = (\boldsymbol{y}_{re}\cos\omega t - \boldsymbol{y}_{im}\sin\omega t) + j(\boldsymbol{z}_{re}\cos\omega t - \boldsymbol{z}_{im}\sin\omega t) \quad (3)$$

The same system response in Eq. (1) and Eq. (2) can be described by two rotating vectors, being one forward and one backward:

$$\boldsymbol{f} = \{\boldsymbol{f}_{re} + j\boldsymbol{f}_{im}\}e^{j\omega t} = (\boldsymbol{f}_{re}\cos\omega t - \boldsymbol{f}_{im}\sin\omega t) + j(\boldsymbol{f}_{im}\cos\omega t + \boldsymbol{f}_{re}\sin\omega t) \quad (4)$$

$$\boldsymbol{b} = \{\boldsymbol{b}_{re} + j\boldsymbol{b}_{im}\}e^{j\omega t} = (\boldsymbol{b}_{re}\cos\omega t + \boldsymbol{b}_{im}\sin\omega t) + j(\boldsymbol{b}_{im}\cos\omega t - \boldsymbol{b}_{re}\sin\omega t) \quad (5)$$

Comparing both representations and making que equality $\boldsymbol{p} = \boldsymbol{f} + \boldsymbol{b} = \boldsymbol{q}$, the following relation between physical and directional coordinates is obtained:

$$\begin{Bmatrix}\boldsymbol{y}\\\boldsymbol{z}\end{Bmatrix} = \boldsymbol{A}.\begin{Bmatrix}\boldsymbol{f}\\\overline{\boldsymbol{b}}\end{Bmatrix};\ \begin{Bmatrix}\boldsymbol{f}\\\overline{\boldsymbol{b}}\end{Bmatrix} = \boldsymbol{A}^{-1}.\begin{Bmatrix}\boldsymbol{y}\\\boldsymbol{z}\end{Bmatrix} \quad (6)$$

where $\overline{\boldsymbol{b}}$ is the complex conjugate of $\boldsymbol{b}$.

The transformation matrix $\boldsymbol{A}$ and its inverse $\boldsymbol{A}^{-1}$ are expressed as:

$$\boldsymbol{A} = \begin{bmatrix}\frac{1}{2} & \frac{j}{2}\\ \frac{1}{2} & -\frac{j}{2}\end{bmatrix};\ \boldsymbol{A}^{-1} = \begin{bmatrix}\frac{1}{2} & \frac{j}{2}\\ \frac{1}{2} & -\frac{j}{2}\end{bmatrix} \quad (7)$$

Thereby, the system of Eq. (6) allows the transformation of physical coordinates in the y and z directions to the forward (f) and backward (b) directional coordinates.

2.2. Description of Dataset

The dataset used in this work was taken from a test rig with a rotor supported by hydrodynamic bearings, displayed on Figure 2. The system is basically composed of a rotating steel shaft (15 mm in diameter and 719 mm in length) supported by two hydrodynamic bearings (31 mm diameter, 18 mm length, 90 μm of radial clearance and ISO VG32 oil at ambient temperature as working fluid) connected to an electric motor through a flexible coupling. In addition, the system has a hard disk and an electromagnetic actuator. The experiments were carried out with the rotor operating with an angular shaft velocity of 75 Hz and four accelerometers installed in both bearings (two accelerometers for each bearing) were used to collect the vibration on the Y and Z directions.

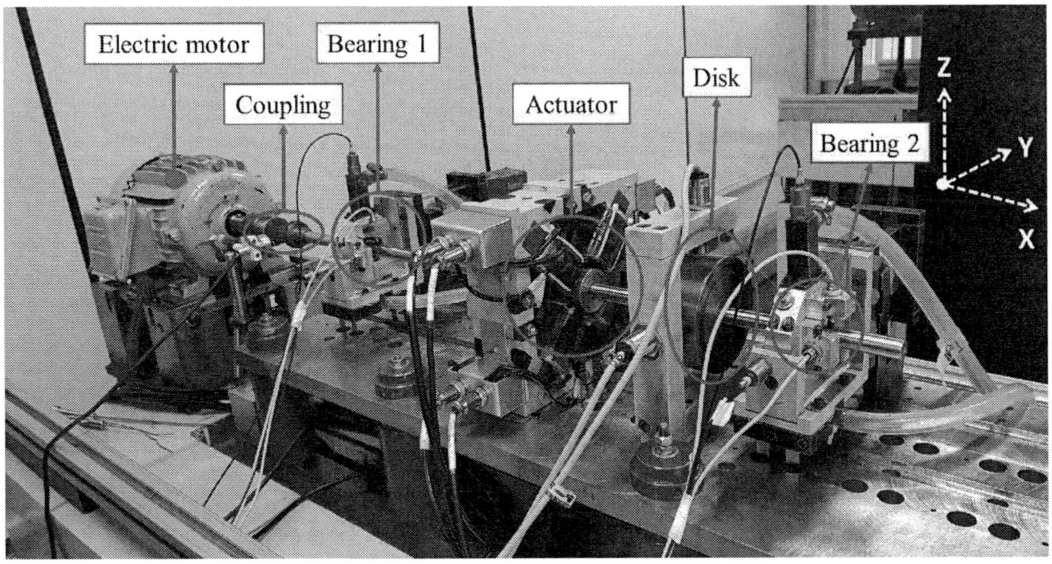

Figure 2. Dataset test rig.

As already mentioned, rotating machines can be subjected to different types of excitation conditions that can facilitate or hinder OMA's application. Hence, more than one test condition was used, with variation of inputs, excitation directions, sampling frequencies, and periods of time, resulting on the tests displayed in Table 1. Altogether, 106 measurements were collected.

Table 1. Test conditions.

Test	f_s [Hz]	Time [s]	Excitation Direction	Excitation
1	2048	240	Y	White noise – medium intensity
2	2048	240	Y	White noise – low intensity
3	2048	240	Z	White noise and tapping
4	2048	240	Y	Blue noise
5	1024	240	Y	White noise – medium intensity
6	2048	480	Y	White noise – medium intensity

An Experimental Modal Analysis (EMA) was also carried out to determine the modal parameters of the analysed rotor, so that reference values were known for further validation of the OMA's results. First, the analysis of the Frequency Response Functions (FRF) from white noise excitation over a wide frequency range was performed in order to identify frequency regions of the modes of interest. Then, the Stepped Sine and the Predicted Error Method (PEM) were employed to extract the rotor's modal parameters. Five measurements were collected to compute mean values and diminish random errors. The results are displayed in Table 2. It is important to emphasize that two pairs of natural frequencies were identified, each one containing the forward and the backward frequencies of the rotor.

Table 2. Modal parameters of the rotor.

Mode	Backward		Forward	
	Freq. [Hz]	Damp. [%]	Freq. [Hz]	Damp. [%]
First	52.8	4.26	53.1	4.25
Second	212.6	2.45	212.2	2.48

2.3. Proposed Methodology

With the acceleration signals of y and z directions of bearings 1 and 2 ($\boldsymbol{y_1}, \boldsymbol{z_1}, \boldsymbol{y_2}, \boldsymbol{z_2}$), the Fast Fourier Transform (FFT) is applied, and values of amplitude ($|\boldsymbol{X}|$) and phase ($\angle \boldsymbol{X}$) are extracted to create the following complex signal:

$$x_c = |X|.e^{-j\angle X} \tag{8}$$

Then, the transform to directional coordinates is performed following the equations:

$$\begin{Bmatrix} f_1 \\ b_1 \end{Bmatrix} = A^{-1}.\begin{Bmatrix} y_{c_1} \\ z_{c_1} \end{Bmatrix} \tag{9}$$

$$\begin{Bmatrix} f_2 \\ b_2 \end{Bmatrix} = A^{-1}.\begin{Bmatrix} y_{c_2} \\ z_{c_2} \end{Bmatrix} \tag{10}$$

The Inverse Fast Fourier Transform (IFFT) is then applied to signals $\boldsymbol{f_i}$ and $\boldsymbol{b_i}$ and the results of this operation are grouped in the forward ($\boldsymbol{f_1}$ e $\boldsymbol{f_2}$) and backward ($\boldsymbol{b_1}$ e $\boldsymbol{b_2}$) signals. OMA is applied using the SSI-DATA method, from which it is possible to obtain stabilization diagrams to the forward and backward signals. The diagrams are interpreted by an automatic algorithm that extracts global modes that represent physical modes of the system. This automatic algorithm was developed by the authors based on the research of [8], [9], and [10].

3. RESULTS

The methodology was applied to the signals of Table 1 and the resulting global modes of the rotor are displayed on Figure 3, together with the rotor modes extracted via traditional OMA and EMA (Table 2). From Figure 3, one can see that traditional OMA is unable to identify both forward and backward frequencies of the rotor in all tests, while the use of directional coordinates as a previous step of OMA enabled the identification of all pairs of rotor modes. For both modes, the frequencies extracted through the proposed methodology and through traditional OMA presented values close to the ones extracted via EMA, however, the values extracted through the proposed methodology were closer to the reference for most tests. Moreover, the differences between the forward and backward frequencies extracted through the proposed methodology were close to the differences observed on the frequencies extracted through EMA for most results, as expected from the system under analysis.

The damping ratios of the first mode (Figure 3 (b)) extracted through the proposed methodology also presented values closer to the EMA reference. On the other hand, the damping ratios of the second mode (Figure 3 (d)) extracted through the proposed methodology presented significantly different values for tests 1, 3, and 6. However, it is worth mentioning that it is difficult to estimate damping ratios even when well consolidated EMA tests are employed in the modal identification.

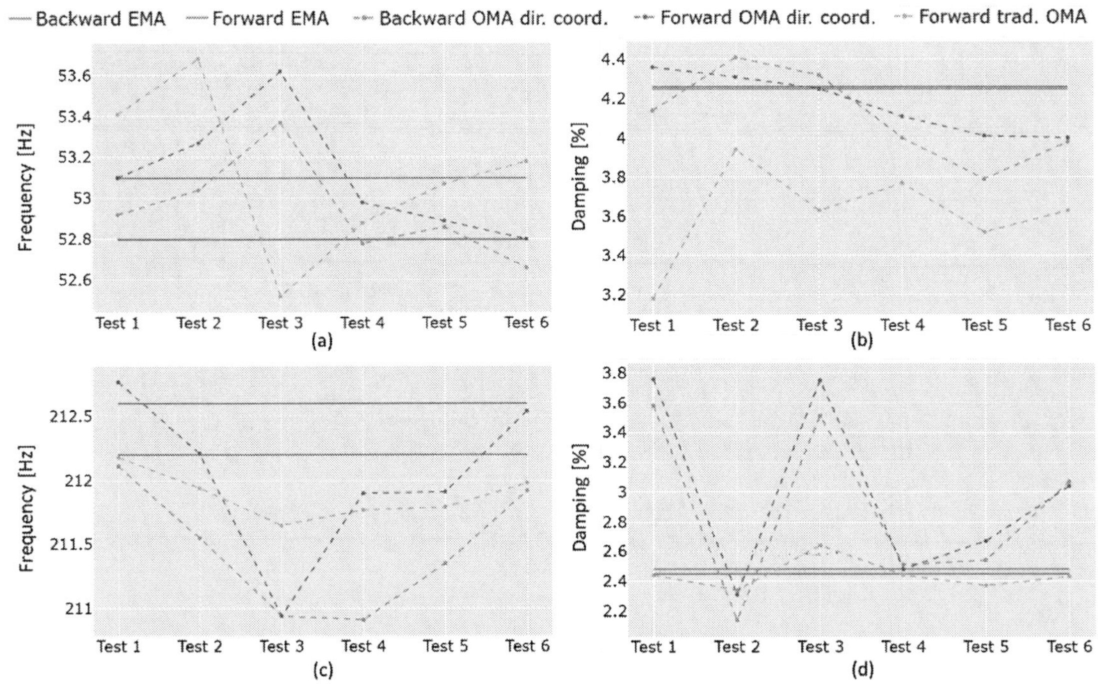

Figure 3. First (a and b) and second (c and d) rotor's global modes extracted using EMA, traditional OMA, and OMA with directional coordinates.

Figure 4 displays the stabilization diagrams of test 1 obtained with the raw data, that is, based on the traditional OMA (Figure 4 (a)), with the forward data (Figure 4 (b)), and with the backward data (Figure 4 (c)) of Eq. (9) and (10). All stabilization diagrams of Figure 4 have similar characteristics, although the diagrams obtained from the directional coordinates data altered the frequencies of the modes related to other components of the test rig. Since the directional coordinates are used to separate the forward and backward components of the rotor modes, this alteration is an expected result. Moreover, one can identify two alignments of poles near the first rotor mode (52.8 Hz) in all stabilization diagrams, which could lead to the idea that both forward and backward frequencies were identified in all of them. However, the poles on the right side of each order are mostly identified with high damping ratio (>7%), being inadequate to represent any rotor frequency. As for the second rotor mode (212.6 Hz), only one alignment of stable poles was identified in each stabilization diagram. The alignments of Figure 4 (b) and Figure 4 (c) have different frequencies, indicating that the directional coordinate transformation was able to separate modes that were once combined in Figure 4 (a).

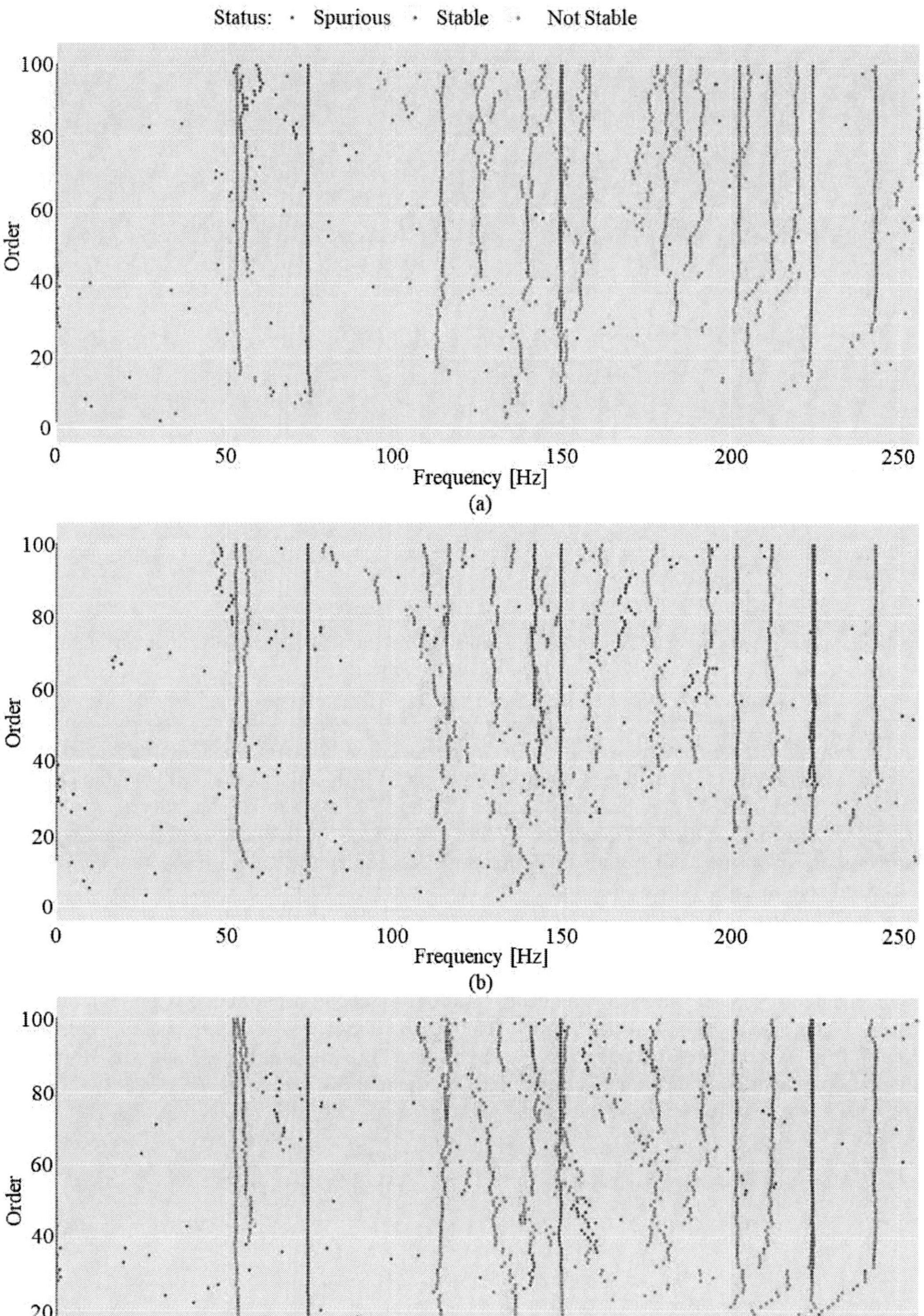

Figure 4. Stabilization diagrams of traditional OMA (a), and with the forward (b) and backward (c) directional coordinates.

4. CONCLUSIONS

This study proposes the use of the transformation of the rotor's response from physical coordinates to directional coordinates as a previous step of OMA to enable the identification of both forward and backward modes of the rotor. The methodology was applied on vibration signals from a test rig with a rotor supported by hydrodynamic bearings under different excitation conditions, so that different scenarios, that are common on the operation of rotating machines, would be tested. The results revealed that the use of directional coordinates as a previous step of OMA not only enabled the identification of both forward and backward modes, but also enhanced the values precision when compared to the EMA references. Therefore, the methodology proved to be a promising tool for the identification of closely spaced modes of forward and backward precessions of rotating machines. Nevertheless, additional studies are in progress to assess the methodology's robustness to other datasets with different characteristics and excitation conditions.

ACKNOWLEDGEMENTS

The authors would like to thank São Paulo Research Foundation (FAPESP), grant 2019/00974–1, for the financial support to this research.

REFERENCES

[1] Storti, G., & Machado, T. (2021). The use of operational modal analysis in the process of modal parameters identification in a rotating machine supported by roller bearings. *Journal of Mechanical Science and Technology*, 35(13), 1-10.

[2] Lee, C. W. (1991). A complex modal testing theory for rotating machinery. *Mechanical Systems and Signal Processing*, 5(2), 119-137.

[3] Kessler, C., & Kim, J. (1998). Complex Modal Analysis and Interpretation for Rotating Machinery. In: *Proc. of SPIE - The International Society for Optical Engineering* (pp. 782-787).

[4] Mesquita, A. L. A. (2004). Identificação de Modos Operacionais e Naturais de Vibração em Máquinas Rotativas Utilizando Coordenadas Complexas [Identification of Operational and Natural Modes of Vibration in Rotating Machines using Complex Coordinates]. [Unpublished doctoral dissertation]. Campinas, Brazil: *State University of Campinas*.

[5] Cavalca, K. L., & Okabe, E. P. (2011). On the analysis of rotor-bearing-foundation systems. In: Gupta, K. (Ed.). *IUTAM Bookseries - Symposium on Emerging trends in rotor dynamics: IUTAM Bookseries* (pp. 89-101). Dordrecht: Springer. https://doi.org/10.1007/978-94-007-0020-8_8

[6] Santana, P. M. F., Cavalca, K. L., Okabe, E. P., & Machado, T. H. (2010). Complex Response of a Rotor-Bearing-Foundation System. In: *Proc. of IFToMM – 8th International Conference on Rotor Dynamics* (pp. 231-238). Seoul, Korea.

[7] Machado, T. H., Mendes, R. U., & Cavalca, K. L. (2016). Directional frequency response applied to wear identification in hydrodynamic bearings. *Mechanics Research Communications*, 74, 60-71.

[8] Magalhães, F., Cunha, A., & Caetano, E. (2009). Online automatic identification of the modal parameters of a long span arch bridge. *Mechanical Systems and Signal Processing*, 23, 316-329.

[9] Reynders, E., Houbrechts, J., & De Roeck G. (2012) Fully automated (operational) modal analysis. *Mechanical Systems and Signal Processing*, 29, 228-250.

[10] Neu, E., Janser, F., Khatibi, A. A., & Orifici, A. C. (2017) Fully Automated Operational Modal Analysis using multi-stage clustering. *Mechanical Systems and Signal Processing*, 84, 308–323.

MODAL VALIDATION AND UPDATING

9th International Operational Modal Analysis Conference
iomac
July 3 - 6, 2022
Vancouver, Canada

FINITE ELEMENT MODELLING AND OMA OF THE "LABORAL CITY OF CULTURE" TOWER

F. Pelayo[1], *N. García-Fernández*[2], *M. Aenlle*[3],

[1] *Asociate Professor, University of Oviedo, fernandezpelayo@uniovi.es*
[2] *PhD Student, University of Oviedo, garciafnatalia@uniovi.es*
[3] *Professor, University of Oviedo, aenlle@uniovi.es*

ABSTRACT

The building of the Laboral City of Culture is located in the city of Gijón (Spain) and it was built in the 1950s. The tower of this building is reminiscent of the famous Giralda tower in Seville and the Lighthouse in Alexandria. The tower has a height of 130 m and a square shape 12 x 12 m. In order to have data about the dynamic behaviour of the tower at a present state, operational modal analysis (OMA) was applied in order to identify its modal parameters (natural frequencies, mode shapes and damping ratios). However, due to the difficulty of measuring the response of steel cross 25 meters height located at the top of the structure, the modal identification is quite an intricate task. With the aim of improving the understanding of the dynamic behaviour of the tower, a detailed 3D finite element model (FEM) was assembled in ABAQUS. The correlation between the experimental and the numerical modal parameters are presented in this paper and it is concluded that the FEM model leads to a satisfactory identification of all the mode shapes of the structure.

Keywords: Heritage buildings, Finite element model, OMA. Model-updating

1. INTRODUCTION

The Laboral City of Culture is a building located in the city of Gijón (Spain) and it was built between 1946 and 1956. It is the most important architectural work constructed in the twentieth century in
Asturias. The origin of the building was a serious accident occurred in an Asturian mine in the mid1940s due to a firedamp explosion [1, 2]. The government of the time decided to construct an orphanage to attend around 1000 orphaned students whose parents were victims of accidents in mining. The building was transformed during its construction into a Technical College under the name of "Universidad Laboral de Gijón" [1, 2].

Figure 1. "Laboral City of Culture" Building (Gijón-Spain)

In 2001, the regional government of the Principality of Asturias decided to transform the building in order to give it a new life. The project became a reality in 2007 and the building was then renamed as "Laboral City of Culture" [2]. The Tower (Figure 2) is perhaps the most characteristic building of the Laboral City of Culture, as it serves to identify the City of Culture at first sight.

In this work, a detailed finite element (FE) 3D model of the structure, which was correlated with the OMA tests performed in the tower, is presented. Moreover, the FEM was used to improve the understanding of the dynamic behaviour of the tower, which was necessary to identify local and global modes of the structure.

Figure 2. Views of the Tower (from https://jenaroartirusuarezprendes.webs.tl)

2. FINITE ELEMENT MODEL OF THE TOWER

2.1. The structure

With a heigh of 130 mn, the tower is a 3D concrete frame structure and it has 21 floors (Figure 3). Up to 4th floor the vertical elements are 4 concrete big columns located at the corners and a central reinforced concrete column (Figure 3). From 5th floor to 17th floor all the columns are made of reinforced concrete and there are 4 columns at the corners, 8 columns at the sides (2 in each side) and a central column. From 17th floor to the top; the structure consists only of 4 reinforced concrete columns (Figure 3). Its marvellous vantage points on the 14th, 17th and 18th floors provide tourists and visitors with magnificent views of La Laboral's surroundings. A Steel cross structure 25 meters long is located on the top of the tower.

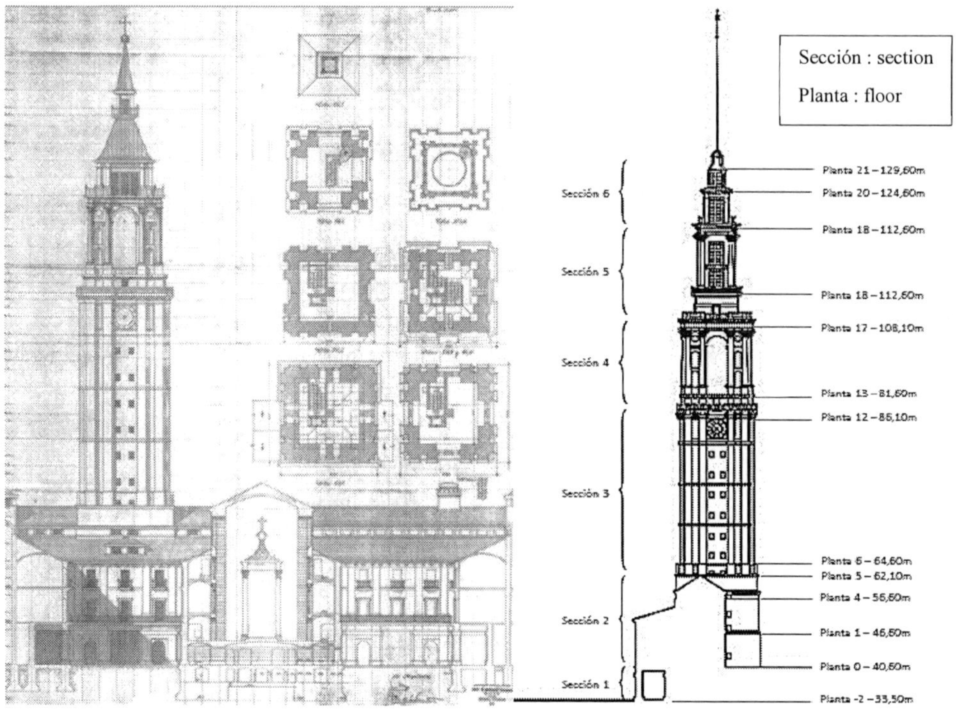

Figure 3. Original design and skecth of the different sections of the tower (from repository of Fernando González Verdesoto)

To modelling of the tower structure was quite complex due to the impossibility of obtaining the drawings used in the building process. The drawings of original design (see Figure 3) were available but they underwent several modifications before and during the construction process. Only the AUTOCAD drawings based on recent measurements in the structure, together with some photos corresponding to the construction of the structure, were used to assemble the finite element model. However, some important details were still missing and many assumptions about dimensions, materials, mechanical properties, etc., were considered. Some details of the different sections are presented in Figure 4.

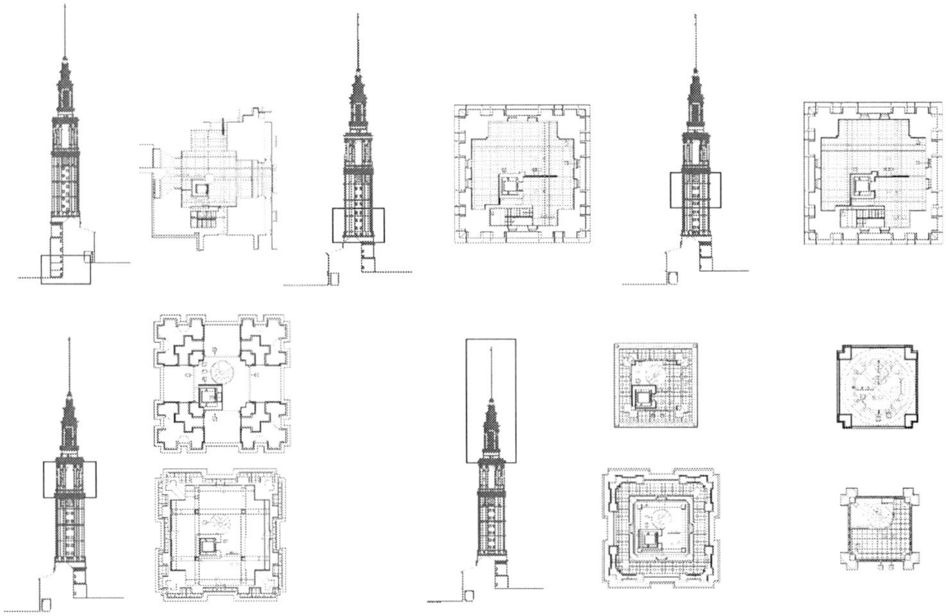

Figure 4. Different sections of the tower strcuture

2.2. The FE Model

Due to the complex geometry of several structural elements (columns, floors, walls, steel cross, etc.), a 3D finite element modellization was selected for this structure. The different sections presented in Figure 3 were modelled in different parts, in order to take easier control of the geometry and the mechanical properties of the materials), and then assembled in ABAQUS CAE []. 3D brick elements were used to mesh the sections 1 to 5 of the tower, whereas section 6 and the steel cross were meshed with 3D wegde elements. In order to get a good quality mesh, a large number of carefully partitions were made. The finite element model is presented in Figure 5

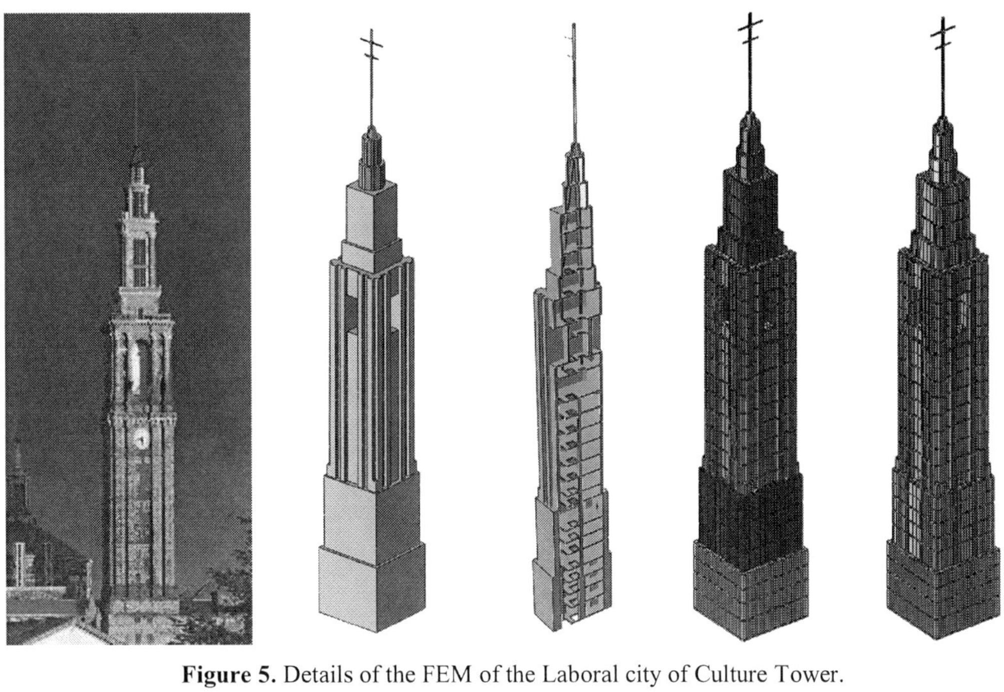

Figure 5. Details of the FEM of the Laboral city of Culture Tower.

The natural frequencies and mode shapes extracted from the finite element model are presented in in Table 1 and in Figs. 10 to 12 (Section 4).

3. OMA OF THE TOWER

In the OMA tests, the response of 21 DOF's in floors 8,12, 17 and 10 (see Figure 3) were measured with uniaxial and triaxial Guralp acceleration sensors. Two Guralp digital acquisition systems, synchronized via an internal cable, and with a total of 24 channels, were used to acquire the experimental responses using the Scream software. (see Figure 3). An skecth of the measurement layout and the location of accelerometers are presented in Figure 6. The sampling frequency was 25 Hz and the acceleration responses were recordered for approximately 24 hours.

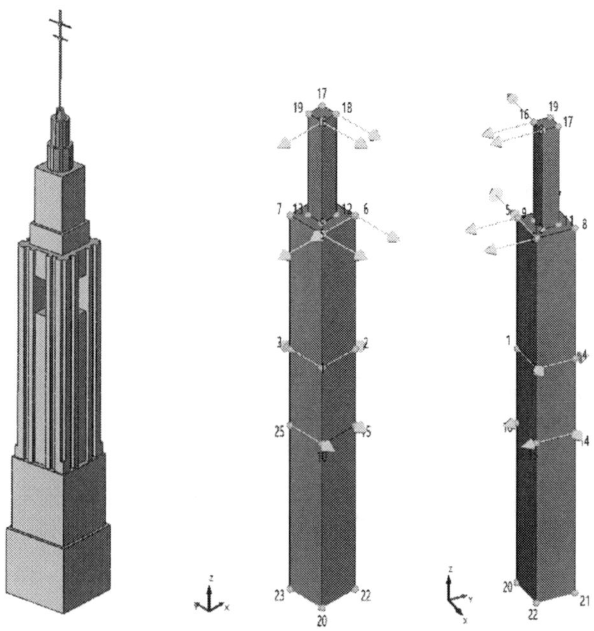

Figure 6. Test setup.

During the OMA tests, the temperature changed in the range 7º-19ºC (see Figure 8). The wind speed (slower during evening and night) during the OMA tests is also presented in Fig. 8, where 0 hours corresponds with the start of the data acquisition: 12:00 PM.

In order to analyze the effect of temperature in natural frequencies of the tower, the Short Time Fourier Transform were applied to the data, the results being presented in Figure 8. Yellow dashed lines correspond to constant frequency. It can be observed that natural frequencies decreases slightly with decreasing temperature. The results presented in Table 1 were estimated with the first 4 hours of testing. This period also coincide with the higher wind speeds.

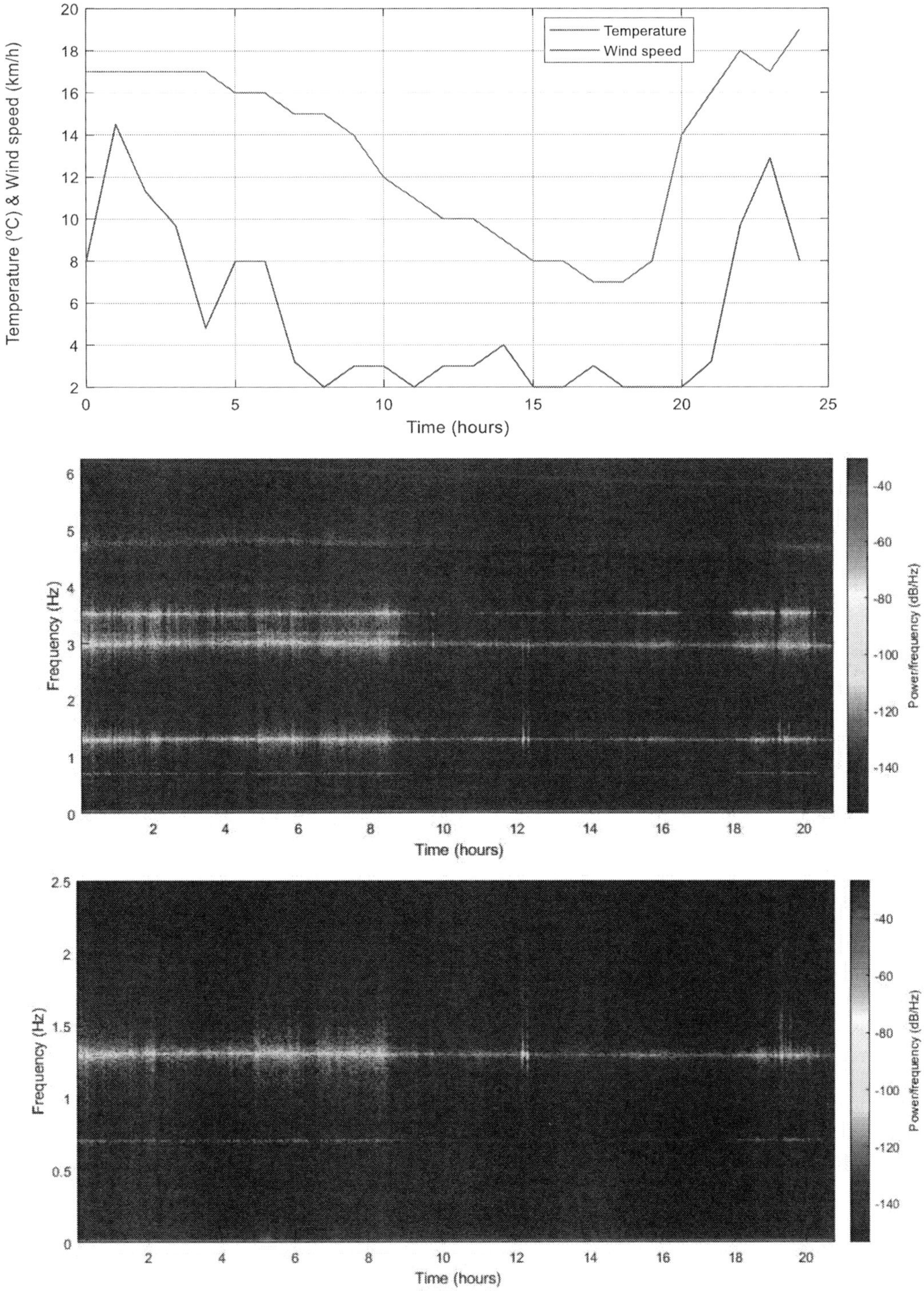

Figure 7. Temperature and wind speed during recording and STFT of the data.

The OMA identification was performed with the ARTEMIS Modal Pro software using the Frequency Domain Decomposition (FDD) technique. The singular value decomposition (SVD) of the responses is presented in Figure 7 with the modes identified in the range 0 – 5 Hz.

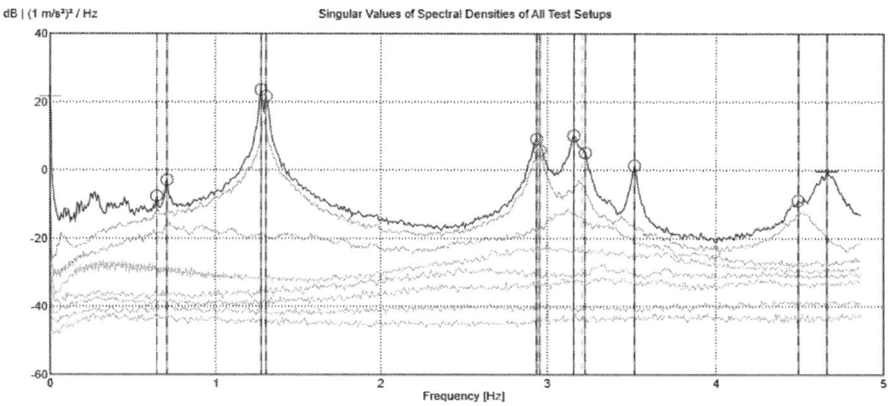

Figure 8. SVD of the registered signals.

The natural frequencies and the mode shapes estimated with OMA are presented Table 1 and in Figs. 10 to 12 (Section 4).

4. NUMERICAL AND EXPERIMENTAL RESULTS

The main drawbacks of the OMA identification in this structure, are the local mode shapes of the top steel cross, as well as the symmetry of the structure which implies closely or even repeated modes. In both cases, the FEM model was a valuable tool for improving the understanding of the dynamic behaviour of the tower.

In the operational modal analysis, the MAC between the modes at approximately 0.7 Hz and 1.3 Hz, is very close to unity. From the finite element model was inferred that the experimental modes at 0.657 Hz and 0.704 Hz (see Figure 9) correspond to the first bending modes of the top steel cross. On the other hand, the modes at 1.302 Hz and 1.341Hz corrrespond the first bending modes of the tower. Due to the fact that no sensors were located at the steel cross, the local bending modes of the steel cross and first bending modes of the tower look similar (spatial aliasing) due to the insufficient number of DOFs used in the measurements.

Five modes were identified in the range 2.8-3.6 Hz. It can be observed in Figure 9 that the local second bending modes of the steel cross are mixed with thesecond bending and the first torsional modes of the tower.

Finally the the modes identified in the range 4-6 Hz correspond to the 3rd bending modes and the second torsional mode of the tower.

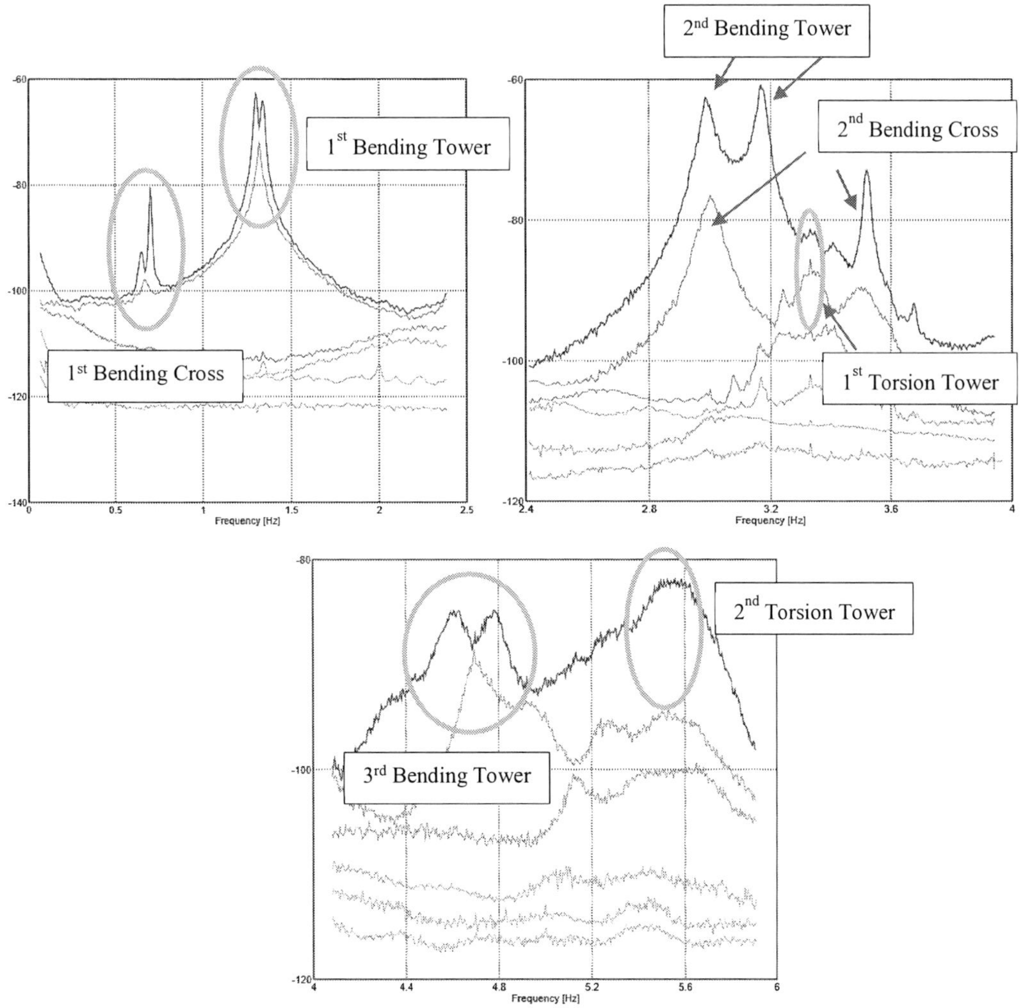

Figure 9. Details of the OMA identification modes of the tower.

The experimental and the numerical natural frequecies, together with the MAC between the numerical and the OMA mode shapes, are presented in Table 1. It can be inferred that a good correlation exists between the experimental and the numerical global bending modes, the maximum error being 10%.

A larger error exists in the torsional modes of the tower and the local modes of the steel cross, which indicates that the numerical model has to be modified in order to get a better correlation.

Table 1. Natural frequencies, error and MAC between the OMA and the FE model.

	Mode	Frequency OMA [Hz[	Frequency FEM [Hz]	Error [%]	MAC
1	1st bending Y (cross)	0.657	0.626	4.72	0.914
2	1st bending X (cross)	0.704	0.608	13.64	0.978
3	1st bending X	1.302	1.187	8.83	0.962
4	1st bending Y	1.341	1.212	9.61	0.975
5	2nd bending Y (cross)	2.991	3.571	19.39	–
6	2nd bending X	3	2.795	6.83	0.975
7	2nd bending Y	3.173	2.857	9.96	0.96
8	1st torsion	3.334	3.903	17.07	0.504
9	2nd bending X (cross)	3.52	3.602	2.27	–
10	3rd bending Y	4.613	5.147	11.58	0.639
11	3rd bending X	4.772	4.783	0.23	0.876
12	2nd torsion	5.551	ND	–	–

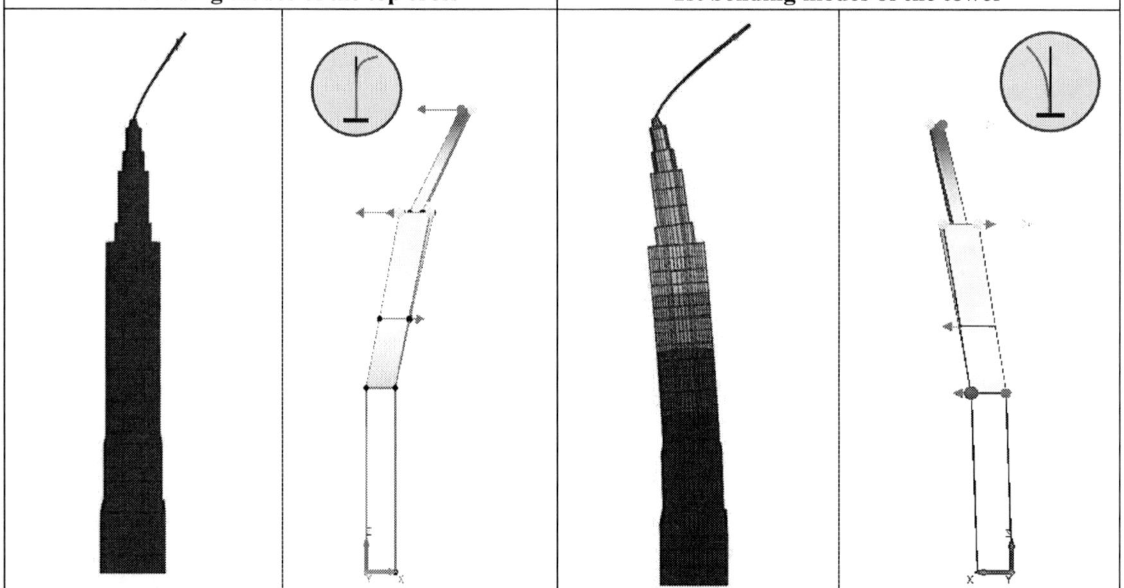

1st bending modes of the top cross		**1st bending modes of the tower**	
FEM	Experimental	FEM	Experimental
X – 0.626 Hz	X – 0.651 Hz	X – 1.187 Hz	X – 1.302 Hz
Y – 0.608 Hz	Y – 0.704 Hz	Y – 1.122 Hz	Y – 1.340 Hz

Figure 10. Mode shapes in the range 0-1.5 Hz.

2nd bending modes of the tower		1st torsional mode of the tower	
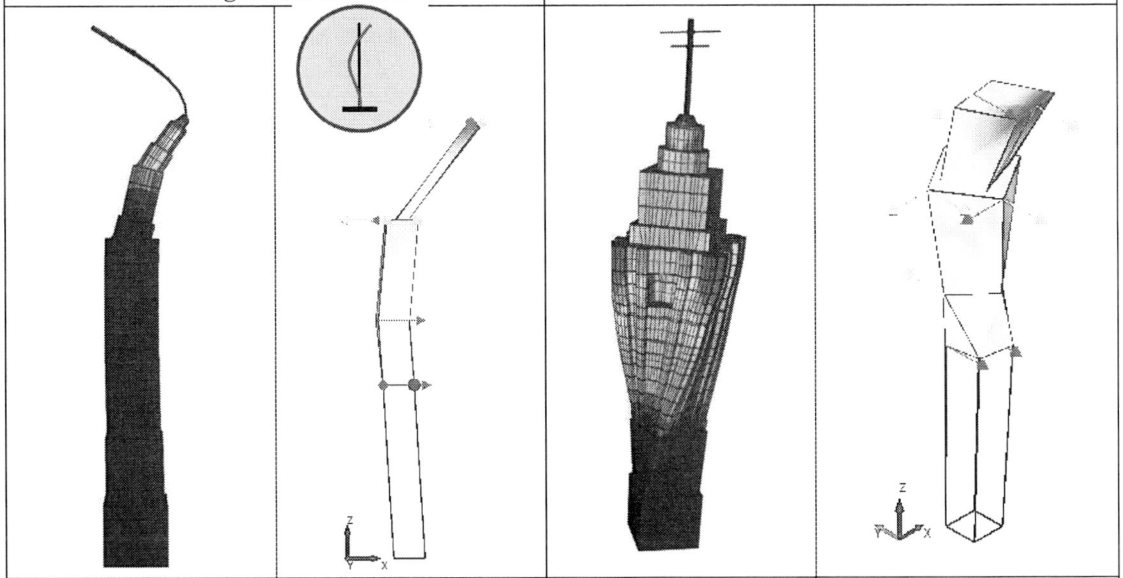			
FEM	Experimental	FEM	Experimental
X – 2.795 Hz	X – 2.991 Hz	3.903 Hz	3.340 Hz
Y – 2.857 Hz	Y – 3.173 Hz		

Figure 11. Mode shapes of the tower in the range 2-4 Hz.

3rd bending mode of the tower	
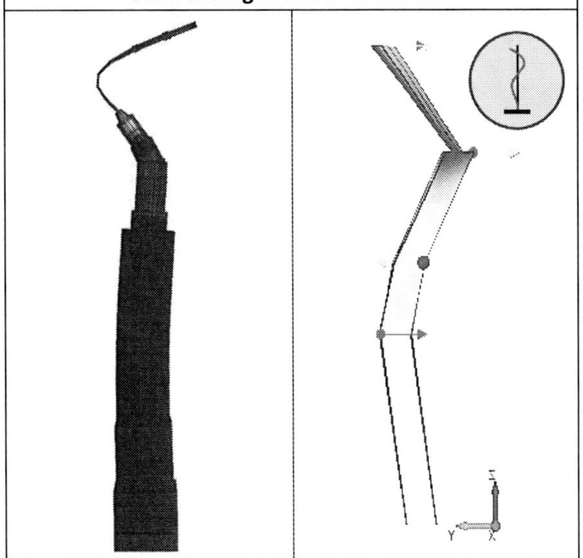	
FEM	Experimental
X – 4.783 Hz	X – 4.772 Hz

Figure 12. Third mode shape of the tower.

CONCLUSIONS

- A symmetric finite element model of the tower was assembled in ABAQUS using 3D elements. This model provided valuable information to understand the dynamic behaviour of the tower, in particular, to identify the local bending modes of the top part of the tower and the global modes of the tower.
- Operational modal analysis has been applied to the tower of "Laboral City of Culture" in order to determine its dynamic behaviour under ambient working conditions.
- Within the frequency range 0-6 Hz, 10 bending modes and 2 torsional modes were identified by OMA.
- The FE model presents a quite reasonable correlation between the numerical and the experimental identifiy modes.

ACKNOWLEDGEMENTS

The financing support given by the Spanish Ministry of Education through the project MCI-20-PID2019-105593GB-I00/AEI/10.13039/501100011033 is gratefully appreciated.

REFERENCES

[1] J. Zatón, J.C. Alvárez (1993). *Guía Histórico-Artística del C.E.I. de Gijón* –Antigua Universidad Laboral. Ediciones Júcar.

[2] (n.d). Retrieved from http://www.laboralciudaddelacultura.com/

[3] Brincker, R., Zhang, L. and Andersen, P. (2001). Output-Only Modal Analysis by Frequency Domain Decomposition. *Smart Materials and Structures* 10, 441-445.

[4] Van Overschee, P. and De Moor, B.(1996). *Subspace identification for linear systems:* Theory, implementation, applications. Kluwer Academic Publishers

9th International Operational Modal Analysis Conference
iomac
July 3 - 6, 2022
Vancouver, Canada

EXAMPLES OF MODEL CORRELATION WITH CLOSELY SPACED MODES

N. García-Fernández[1], *F. Pelayo*[2] *and M. Aenlle*[2]

[1] PhD Student, University of Oviedo, garciafnatalia@uniovi.es
[2] Professor, University of Oviedo, fernandezpelayo@uniovi.es
[3] Professor, University of Oviedo, aenlle@uniovi.es

ABSTRACT

In structural dynamics, two modes with natural frequencies ω_1 and ω_2, respectively, are closely spaced if the frequency separation $\Delta\omega = \omega_2 - \omega_1$ is very small. If $\Delta\omega = 0$, the modes are repeated. On the other hand, it is well known that closely spaced modes are highly sensitive to small perturbations of mass and stiffness.

When a system with closely spaced eigenvalues is perturbed, the associated mode shapes are mainly rotating in their initial subspace. This means that we can have a good correlation in terms of mass and stiffness between the models, but low values of modal assurance criteria (MAC) can be obtained because of this rotation. In this case, the individual mode shapes should not be used for correlation using the modal assurance criteria (MAC), but the subspaces spanned by the unperturbed and the perturbed mode shapes should be correlated.

If we still want to measure the correlation using MAC, the experimental mode shapes must be previously rotated in the subspace in order to get the best correlation between the experimental and the numerical mode shapes.

In this paper, three models with closely spaced modes are studied. Firstly, an analytical model with 4 DOF's and two repeated eigenvalues is perturbed with small mass changes. The other two models are experimental models with closely spaced modes which are correlated with two numerical models assembled in ABAQUS and ANSYS. The experimental mode shapes were rotated in the subspace to get the best correlation between the models in terms of MAC.

Keywords: Model correlation, closely spaced modes, Operational Modal Analysis, Rotation matrix

1. INTRODUCTION

1.1. General information

In structural dynamics, closely spaced modes are defined as modes which are close in frequency [1-3]. A rule of thumb to define a set of mode shapes as closely spaced was proposed in [3]. If we consider two modes with close natural frequencies ω_1 and ω_2, and frequency distance $\Delta\omega = \omega_2 - \omega_1$, they can be considered closely spaced if:

$$\frac{\Delta\omega}{\omega} < \frac{1}{1000} \qquad (1)$$

where $\omega = \omega_1$

The Modal Assurance Criterion (MAC) [4-5] is by far the most widely used technique to compare mode shapes. If two vectors $\boldsymbol{\phi_{FEi}}$ and $\boldsymbol{\phi_{Xj}}$, corresponding to a numerical and an experimental model, respectively, are compared, the MAC is given by:

$$MAC(\phi_{FEi}, \phi_{Xj}) = \frac{\left|\phi_{FEi}^H \cdot \phi_{Xj}\right|^2}{(\phi_{FEi}^H \cdot \phi_{FEi})(\phi_{Xj}^H \cdot \phi_{Xj})} \qquad (2)$$

where the subindex 'H' indicates complex conjugate.

If a set of mode shapes are compared, a MAC matrix is obtained, which can be presented in different formats: matrix, table, 2D or 3D plot.

Closely spaced modes are highly sensitive to small mass and stiffness perturbations of the system, and they mainly rotate in their subspace [1,2,3]. Thus, we can have a good correlation in terms of mass and stiffness between the compared models, but low values of MAC can be obtained because of this rotation. This means that for closely spaced modes, correlation between different identification estimates or between a numerical model and an experimental model, should be calculated between subspaces and not between the individual mode shape vectors [2,3].

According to the structural dynamic modification (SDM) [6], the experimental mode shapes can be expressed as a linear combination of the numerical mode shapes, i.e.:

$$\boldsymbol{\phi_X} = \boldsymbol{\phi_{FE}}\boldsymbol{T} \qquad (3)$$

where $\boldsymbol{T}$ is a transformation matrix.

If mass normalized mode shapes are used in eq. (3) to estimate the matrix $\boldsymbol{T}$, it was demonstrated in [2] that, in case of closely spaced modes, matrix $\boldsymbol{T}$ is related to the rotation matrix $\mathbf{R}$ as:

$$\boldsymbol{T} = \boldsymbol{R^T} \qquad (4)$$

In closely spaced modes the mode shapes mainly rotate in a subspace, a measure of the correlation can be obtained by means of the maximum angle θ between the subspaces defined by the experimental $\boldsymbol{\phi_X}$ and the numerical $\boldsymbol{\phi_{FE}}$ closely spaced mode shapes. This angle can be expressed as a MAC value [4,5] by:

$$MAC = \cos^2(\theta) \qquad (5)$$

If the correlation is measured using MAC, the experimental mode shapes must be previously rotated in the subspace in order to get the best correlation between the experimental and the numerical mode shapes [2,3].

D'ambrogio and Fregolent [7] proposed the concept of S2MAC, similar to the MAC between two modal vectors, to correlate an experimental mode shape ϕ_X with a linear combination of two numerical closely spaced mode shapes $\boldsymbol{\phi}_{FE1}$ and $\boldsymbol{\phi}_{FE2}$, which is expressed as:

$$S2MAC = \max_{\alpha,\beta}\left(\frac{\left|\phi_X^H(\alpha\boldsymbol{\phi}_{FE1} + \beta\boldsymbol{\phi}_{FE2})\right|^2}{\phi_X^H\phi_X(\alpha\boldsymbol{\phi}_{FE1} + \beta\boldsymbol{\phi}_{FE2})^H(\alpha\boldsymbol{\phi}_{FE1} + \beta\boldsymbol{\phi}_{FE2})}\right) \tag{6}$$

If case of normal modes, eq. (6) leads to:

$$S2MAC = \frac{\left(\phi_X^T\phi_{FE1}\right)^2 - 2\left(\phi_X^T\phi_{FE1}\right)\left(\phi_{FE1}^T\phi_{FE2}\right)\left(\phi_X^T\phi_{FE2}\right) + \left(\phi_X^T\phi_{FE2}\right)^2}{1 - \left(\phi_{FE1}^T\phi_{FE2}\right)^2} \tag{7}$$

In this paper, three cases with closely spaced modes are studied. Firstly, a 4 DOF system with two repeated modes is perturbed with small mass changes. Then, the experimental modal parameters of a square laminated glass plate are used for correlating the results of a numerical model assembled in ANSYS [8]. Finally, the experimental modal parameters of a symmetric lab-scaled two-floor steel frame are compared with those extracted from a numerical model also assembled in ABAQUS [9].

2. A SIMULATION CASE

A 4 DOF system (system U) with two repeated eigenvalues was simulated with MATLAB [10]. The natural frequencies and the mode shapes are shown in Tables 1 and 2, respectively. The mass and the stiffness matrices were calculated from the eigenvalues and the eigenvectors. However, the solution of the eigenvalue problem gives same eigenvalues but a different set of mode shapes (see Table 3). Nevertheless, the mode shapes in Table 3 are linear combinations of those shown in Table 2.

Table 1. Natural frequencies of the two simulated systems.

Frequencies [Hz]		
System U	System P	Error [%]
0.4502	0.4408	4.12
0.4502	0.4479	1.03
0.5513	0.5409	3.74
0.6164	0.6060	3.34

Table 2. Mode shapes of system U (original)

0.3000	0.5000	1.0000	1.0000
0.8000	1.2000	0.0000	-1.0000
1.1000	0.1000	-1.0000	1.0000
1.5000	-1.0000	1.0000	-0.8000

Table 3. Mode shapes of system U (after solution of the eigenvalue problem)

-0.4507	0.3700	1.0000	-1.0000
-1.1569	0.8611	0.0000	1.0000
-1.0696	-0.2757	-1.0000	-1.0000
-1.0764	-1.4462	1.0000	0.8000

This system U was perturbed with small mass changes, the mass change matrix being presented in Table 4. The natural frequencies of the perturbed system (system P) are shown in Table 1.

Table 4. Mass change matrix (kg)

0.0170	0	0	0
0	0	0	0
0	0	0.0120	0
0	0	0	0.0100

The MAC matrix between the mode shapes of both systems (perturbed and unperturbed from Table 3) presented in Table 5. As it can be observed, the correlation between the first two modes is very poor.

Table 5. MAC

0.6979	0.3807	0.0135	0.0233
0.4990	0.4177	0.0620	0.0082
0.0660	0.0128	0.9993	0.0509
0.0272	0.0002	0.0631	0.9985

The rotation matrix presented in Table 7 was estimated from the transformation matrix ***T*** obtained with eq. (3), and which is shown in Table 6. Mass normalized numerical and experimental mode shapes were used to estimate the matrix ***T***.

Table 6. ***T*** matrix

0.7390	-0.6522	0.0152	-0.0257
0.6421	0.7506	0.0141	0.0310
-0.0138	-0.0001	0.9809	-0.0139
-0.0007	-0.0217	0.0111	0.9826

Table 7. Rotation matrix

0.7549	0.6559
-0.6559	0.7548

This rotation matrix (Table 7) was used to rotate 40.98° the perturbed closely spaced mode shapes by:

$$\boldsymbol{\phi}_R = \boldsymbol{\phi}\, \boldsymbol{R}^T \qquad (8)$$

in order to obtain the best fit between the unperturbed and the perturbed mode shapes.

The new MAC obtained after the rotation of the mode shapes is shown in Table 8, where it can be observed that a very good correlation exists between both systems, which confirms that the discrepancies in terms of mass and stiffness are very low. The angle between the subspaces spanned by the closely spaced modes is 1.4727° (MAC=0.9993), which confirms the slight discrepancies between the two models. The angle between the first and the second unperturbed mode shapes is 78.4°, whereas that between the corresponding perturbed mode shapes is 79.05 °.

Table 8. MAC after rotation

0.9998	0.0383	0.0135	0.0233
0.0382	0.9995	0.0620	0.0082
0.0194	0.0764	0.9993	0.0509
0.0147	0.0186	0.0631	0.9985

3. A SQUARE LAMINATED GLASS PLATE

In this section, a square laminated glass plate with dimmensions 1400 x 1400 mm, and consisting of two glass layers with thickness 4 mm, and one polymeric interlayer with thickness 1.14 mm, is studied. The plate was fixed to a steel frame at the four corners (see Fig. 1).

A 3D finite element model was assembled in ANSYS using 20 node structural solid elements of type SOLID186 (see Fig. 2). The finite element model was meshed with 19200 elements and 97767 nodes. The numerical natural frequencies are shown in Table 9, and as it can be observed, modes 2 and 3 have repeated frequencies. The modes shapes are presented in Fig. 3.

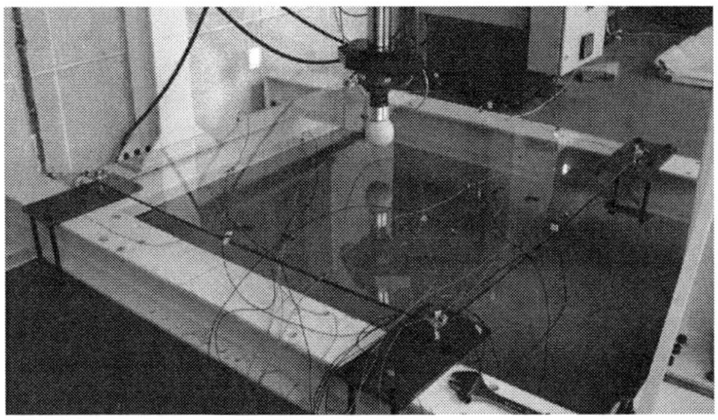

Figure 1. Data set used in the experiments.

The natural frequencies and the mode shapes were also estimated with operational modal analysis, The responses were measured with 16 accelerometers with a sensitivity of 100mV/g and registered with a TEAC LX-120 data recorder with 16 input channels. The plate was excited applying many randon small hits across the surface. The natural frequencies estimated with the EFDD (frequency domain decomposition) technique are shown in Table 9.

Table 9. Natural frequencies of the laminated glass plate.

Mode Shapes	Experimental [Hz]	Numerical [Hz]	Error [%]
Mode 1	9.35	9.72	3.80
Mode 2	19.62	21.10	7.01
Mode 3	19.83	21.12	6.10
Mode 4	22.53	24.82	9.22
Mode 5	55.76	56.11	0.62

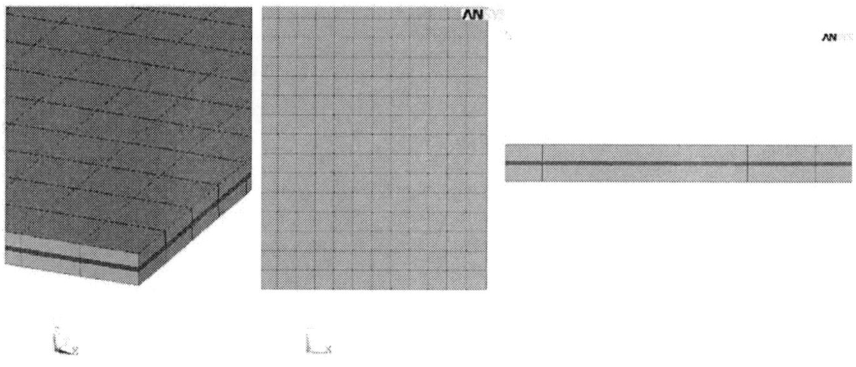

Figure 2. Numerical model.

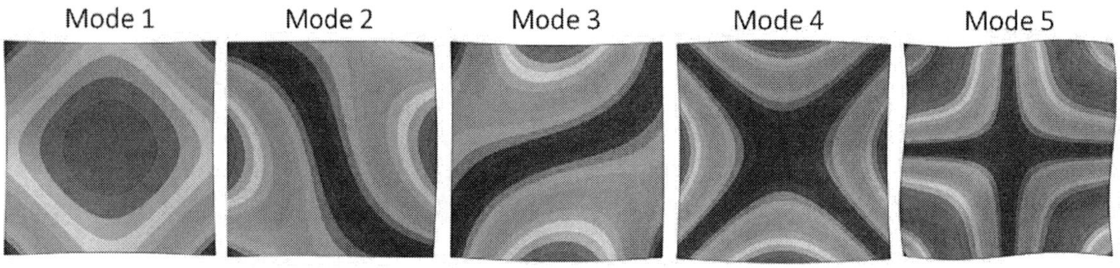

Figure 3. Numerical mode shapes

The MAC between the experimental and the numerical mode shapes is presented Table 10. As it can be observed there is no good correlation between the experimental and numerical models for the second the third modes.

Table 10. MAC.

0.9971	0.0000	0.0000	0.0000	0.0661
0.0000	0.5990	0.5099	0.0001	0.0002
0.0001	0.3965	0.4896	0.0000	0.0007
0.0000	0.0000	0.0002	0.9996	0.0000
0.0976	0.0001	0.0000	0.0000	0.9862

It can be seen Figure 4 that modes 2 and 3 are physically rotated, which explains the bad correlation between these two modes.

From the transformation matrix $\boldsymbol{T}$ (see Table 11), the rotation matrix shown in Table 12 was obtained using the same procedure presented in section 2. Mass normalized numerical mode shapes and experimental mode shapes normalized to the largest component equal to unity were used to estimate the matrix $\boldsymbol{T}$. From Table 12 it is inferred that the rotation angle is approximately 42.5°.

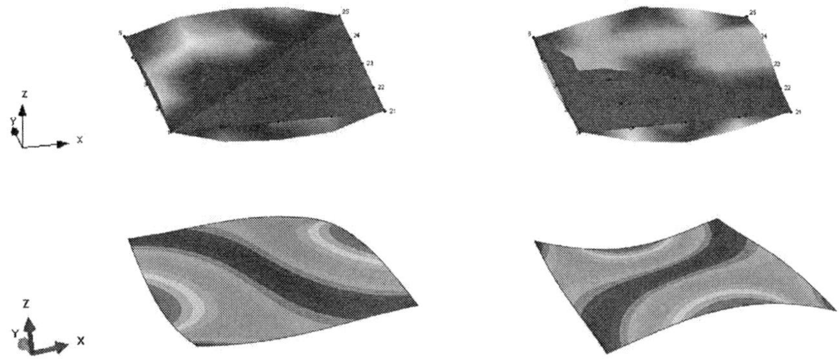

Figure 4. Numerical and experimental mode shapes 2 and 3

Table 11. ***T*** matrix.

1.4818	0.0063	-0.0065	-0.0006	0.0414
0.0018	0.9253	-0.8563	0.0111	0.0178
-0.0107	0.7523	0.8395	-0.0039	0.0313
-0.0011	0.0064	-0.0140	-0.9801	0.0005
-0.0327	0.0101	-0.0041	0.0011	1.0582

Table 12. Rotation matrix.

0.7379	0.6479
-0.6479	0.7379

Finally, the MAC between the rotated experimental mode shapes and the numerical mode shapes (Table 13) show a very good correlation between the two models.

An alternative to MAC is to calculate the angle between the subspaces spanned by the closely spaced modes. It is also interested to know if there is a relative deviation between the closely spaced eigenvectors (perfect rotation means no deviation). For this example, the angle between the subspaces spanned by the second and the third modes is 3.8203° (MAC= 0.9956). With respect to the angle between the second and the third numerical mode shapes, they are perfectly orthogonal (angle 90°), whereas in the experimental system the angle is 89.158°. These values confirm the good correlation between the two models in terms of mode shapes.

Table 13. MAC after rotation.

0.9971	0.0000	0.0000	0.0000	0.0661
0.0000	0.9965	0.0000	0.0001	0.0002
0.0001	0.0001	0.9974	0.0000	0.0007
0.0000	0.0002	0.0001	0.9996	0.0000
0.0976	0.0000	0.0000	0.0000	0.9862

4. A LAB-SCALED TWO-FLOOR STEEL FRAME

In this section a small symmetric lab scaled steel frame is studied (see Fig.5). The structure consists of four columns with square section 5 x 5 mm^2 and length 80 mm, and two square steel floors with thickness 5 mm and dimensions 30mm x 30mm.

Figure 5. Two-floor steel frame structure.

A model of the structure was assembled in ABAQUS and meshed with beam elements B33 (columns) and quadrilateral shell elements S4R (floors). The numerical natural frequencies are shown in Table 14 and the mode shapes in Fig 6.

The experimental modal parameters were estimated with operational modal analysis. The response of the structure was measured with 6 accelerometers with a sensitivity of 100mV/g and registered with a TEAC LX-120 data recorder. The natural frequencies estimated with the EFDD technique are also shown in Table 14.

Table 14. Experimental and natural frequencies

Mode Shapes	Experimental [Hz]	Numerical [Hz]	Error [%]
Mode 1- 1st bending	4.2200	4.2490	0.69
Mode 2- 1st bending	4.4280	4.2490	4.04
Mode 3-torsion	7.6735	7.8572	2.39
Mode 4-2nd bending	11.1262	11.680	4.98
Mode 5-2nd bending	11.3784	11.680	2.65
Mode 6-torsion	20.2675	21.401	5.59

Table 15. MAC.

0.9968	0.0026	0.0017	0.0004	0.0003	0.0000
0.0042	0.9773	0.3618	0.0001	0.0003	0.0066
0.0019	0.3708	0.9963	0.0001	0.0000	0.0003
0.0002	0.0000	0.0001	0.9013	0.0985	0.0346
0.0000	0.0006	0.0012	0.3132	0.6827	0.2030
0.0001	0.0022	0.0001	0.0002	0.3515	0.9992

Due to the symmetry of the structure, all the bending modes are repeated (see Fig. 6), i.e. modes 1 and 2 has repeated frequencies, and the same for modes 4 and 5. MAC between the numerical and experimental mode shapes are presented in Table 15.

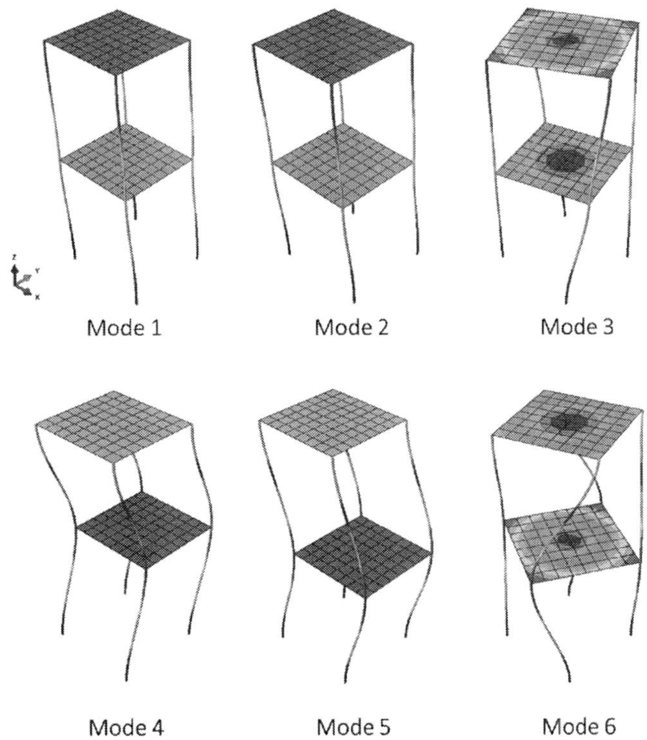

Figure 6. Numerical mode shapes.

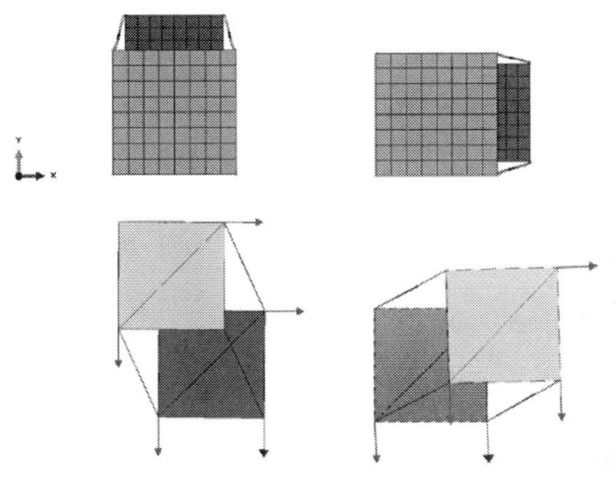

Figure 7. Numerical and experimental mode shapes 4 and 5.

Table 16. ***T*** matrix.

-0.0697	0.0026	-0.0011	0.0001	0.0000	-0.0001
-0.0040	-0.0610	-0.0020	-0.0001	-0.0002	0.0000
0.0005	0.0012	0.0196	-0.0001	-0.0002	0.0000
0.0002	-0.0004	0.0002	-0.0095	-0.0021	-0.0001
-0.0013	-0.0037	0.0004	0.0044	-0.0045	-0.0002
0.0002	0.0039	-0.0001	0.0001	0.0001	-0.0043

Mass normalized numerical mode shapes and experimental mode shapes normalized to the unit length were used to estimate the matrix ***T*** (see Table 16), from which the rotation matrix shown in Table 17 was obtained using the same procedure presented in section 2. From Table 17 itis inferred that the first bending modes were rotated 3.5° and the second bending modes were rotated approximately 24.7°.

Table 17. Rotation matrix

-0.9981	-0.0580	0.0000	0.0000	0.0000	0.0000
0.0580	-0.9981	0.0000	0.0000	0.0000	0.0000
0.0000	0.0000	1.0000	0.0000	0.0000	0.0000
0.0000	0.0000	0.0000	-0.9082	0.4183	0.0000
0.0000	0.0000	0.0000	-0.4183	-0.9082	0.0000
0.0000	0.0000	0.0000	0.0000	0.0000	1.0000

It can be seen in Table 18 that the MAC has improved for both the first and the second bending modes. The angles between the subspaces spanned by the closely spaced modes are 7.8436° (MAC = 0.9814). for modes 1 and 2 and 3.7228° (MAC = 0.9958) for modes 4 and 5. In the numerical model, all the bending modes are orthogonal (angle 90°), whereas in the experimental system the angle between the first bending modes is 87.65°, and 75.96° between the fourth and fifth modes.

A relatively low MAC has been obtained between the mode shapes of the fifth modes. On the other hand, the fourth and fifth experimental mode shapes are far from orthogonal, as it is the case in the numerical model. This can be attributed to discrepancies between the models or to errors in the estimation of the mode shapes.

Table 18. MAC after rotation.

0.9997	0.0001	0.0001	0.0004	0.0001	0.0000
0.0011	0.9864	0.3652	0.0001	0.0001	0.0030
0.0013	0.3710	0.9970	0.0001	0.0000	0.0003
0.0002	0.0000	0.0002	0.9737	0.0259	0.0103
0.0001	0.0006	0.0004	0.1984	0.8001	0.2510
0.0001	0.0022	0.0001	0.0002	0.3515	0.9992

5. CONCLUSIONS

According to the structural dynamic modification, an experimental system can be considered as a perturbation of a numerical model. When a numerical system with closely spaced eigenvalues is perturbed, the associated mode shapes are mainly rotating in their initial subspace [1,2,3]. This means that low MAC values can be obtained although a good correlation can exist in terms of mass and stiffness.

In order to obtain the best correlation in terms of MAC, the mode shapes have to be previously rotated. In this paper, the mode shapes of three models with closely eigenvalues have been successfully rotated to obtain the best correlation in terms of MAC. The first model was a simulated case with two repeated eigenvalues, which was perturbed with small mass changes. The other two models are experimental models with closely spaced modes which are correlated with two numerical models assembled in ANSYS and ABAQUS. The results have demonstrated that a good correlation exist between the numerical and the experimental models.

ACKNOWLEDGEMENTS

The financing support given by the Spanish Ministry of Education through the project MCI-20-PID2019-105593GB-I00/AEI/10.13039/501100011033 is gratefully appreciated.

REFERENCES

[1] Brincker, R., & Ventura, C. E. (2015). *Introduction to Operational Modal Analysis.* John Wiley & Sons, Ltd. https://doi.org/10.1002/9781118535141

[2] Brincker, R., & Lopez-Aenlle, M. (2015). Mode shape sensitivity of two closely spaced eigenvalues. *Journal of Sound and Vibration, 334,* 377–387. https://doi.org/10.1016/j.jsv.2014.08.015

[3] Brincker, R. Implications of Closely Spaced Modes In OMA. *International Operational Modal Analysis Conference*, Gijón (Spain), 2015.

[4] Allemang RJ, Brown D. Correlation Coefficient for Modal Vector Analysis. *Proc. Int. Modal Anal. Conf. Exhib.,* 1982.

[5] Allemang RJ. The modal assurance criterion - Twenty years of use and abuse. *Sound Vib* 2003.

[6] Sestieri, A., & D'Ambrogio, W. (2001). Structural dynamic modifications. In *Encyclopedia of Vibration* (pp. 1253–1264). Elsevier. https://doi.org/10.1006/rwvb.2001.0100

[7] D'Ambrogio, W., & Fregolent, A. (2002). Correlation of close modes using S2MAC. *Proceedings of the 2002 International Conference on Noise and Vibration Engineering, ISMA.*

[8] ANSYS, Inc. ANSYS *Contact Technology Guide*. Release 9.0, 2004.

[9] ABAQUS UNIFIED FEA. Dassault Systems.

[10] MATLA*B*, The MathWorks, Inc.

STRUCTURAL HEALTH MONITORING

9th International Operational Modal Analysis Conference
iomac
July 3 - 6, 2022
Vancouver, Canada

A GENERAL FRAMEWORK FOR DAMAGE DETECTION WITH STATISTICAL DISTANCE MEASURES: APPLICATION TO CIVIL ENGINEERING STRUCTURES

Niels-Jørgen Jacobsen[1], Palle Andersen[2], Alexander Mendler[3], Szymon Greś[4]

[1] Product Manager – Structural Dynamics Solutions, Hottinger Brüel & Kjær A/S, 2830 Virum, Denmark
[2] Managing Director, Structural Vibration Solutions A/S, NOVI Science Park, 9220 Aalborg, Denmark
[3] Postdoctoral Fellow, Technical University of Munich, TUM School of Engineering and Design, 80333 Munich, Germany
[4] Postdoc, Institute of Structural Engineering (IBK), SMM team, ETH Zürich, 8093 Zürich, Switzerland

ABSTRACT

Detecting damage in structural systems is often achieved by a statistical comparison of damage-sensitive characteristics of a structure evaluated on baseline data, against the corresponding characteristics obtained using data collected from a potentially defective structure. While several vibration-based methods have been proposed and successfully applied to detect damage in both mechanical and civil structures over the past years, the general framework describing their common properties and unifying the statistical decision about damage has mainly been elaborated in the control community. In this paper, we revise this framework in the context of detecting damage in structural systems. The statistical properties of three commonly used damage detection methods are recalled, and it is shown that their evaluation for damage boils down to a simple statistical distance. The framework is adopted to a commercial structural health monitoring software suite and its practical merit is illustrated on damage detection of two full-scale highway bridges.

Keywords: Damage detection, squared Mahalanobis distance, subspace methods, mode tracking, control chart, Structural Health Monitoring, Operational Modal Analysis

1. INTRODUCTION

Vibration-based damage detection refers to detecting damage through changes in a set of features extracted from the vibration signals collected from structural health monitoring (SHM) systems. Over the past decade, it became an effective methodology in triggering on-demand inspections after damaging events in large-scale civil and mechanical structures, e.g., wind turbines [1,2], offshore structures [3,4], and bridges [5,6]. It remains the sole aspect of the SHM triad, i.e., damage detection, localization, and quantification, that has been implemented in commercial software such as ARTeMIS Modal Pro [7] and PULSE™ Operational Modal Analysis [8].

In the field of fault diagnosis of mechanical systems, myriads of different vibration-based damage detection methods exist; see [9] for a review of early developments. Commercially available methods often use the modal approach, which presumes that the damage is manifested through a change in the modal parameters, i.e., the natural frequencies, damping ratios and mode shapes. The modal parameters are typically identified from measured data and compared to baseline values using statistical distance measures. However, some field work questions the use of the modal parameters as damage-sensitive features, arguing that they are not sensitive enough to identify local faults [1,2], especially if the structure is only excited by low-frequency inputs. One bypass to the modal framework employed in the commercial software, is to use the statistical fault detection and isolation methods [10,11], where the damage-sensitive features of the system are derived directly from measured data and comprise, e.g., angles between dynamic signal spaces, and are evaluated for damage in statistical hypothesis tests. While efficient in detecting damage, the practical use and interpretation of the latter methodology is often hindered by its complex mathematical formulation.

The goal of this paper is to illustrate that the current commercial practice for the vibration-based damage detection boils down to a simple statistical distance obtained from a residual evaluated between some baseline (reference) features of the system and the features from the currently tested data. In this context, three damage detection residuals are investigated, namely, the classic subspace-based residual [12], the robust subspace-based residual [10], and the modal parameter-based residual [13]. Each metric is calculated based on vibration data collected during normal operating conditions, and the damage is denoted as deviations of the distance measure from the reference state. The considered methods are implemented in the modal analysis and structural health monitoring software packages ARTeMIS Modal and PULSE Operational Modal Analysis, in which their joint features are concluded in a control chart to enhance the resolution of the damage detection. Methods are evaluated based on the ambient vibration signals from two benchmark structures, that is, the Z24 bridge in Switzerland and the S101 bridge in Austria. The results reveal that the performance of the damage detection methods is similar and the fusion of the damage indicators in the control chart provides the most accurate view on the progressively damaged systems. The paper is organized as follows: Section 2 recaps the statistical tests for damage detection, Section 3 contains two cases studies and Section 4 discusses the results.

2. METHODOLOGY

In this section, the background on output-only vibration analysis of mechanical systems is recalled, the definition of three different damage detection residuals is outlined and the general framework for the statistical decision-making about damage is stated.

2.1. Background

A fundamental step in damage detection is the evaluation of the dynamic features of the system from monitoring data, so that their changes can be related to the occurrence of damage. To this end, many classical features used for damage detection originate from system identification and comprise, e.g., subspace characteristics of data matrices, or modal parameters, where both can be obtained from the response measurements, e.g., accelerations, velocities, displacements, inclinations, or strains.

Consider N acceleration measurements $y = [y_1 \dots y_N]^T \in \mathrm{R}^{r x N}$ collected using r sensors sampling the dynamic response of the monitored linear time-invariant (LTI) dynamic system with a sampling frequency f_s. The covariance matrix of the output measurements $R_i = \mathrm{E}(y_{k+i}\mathrm{y}_\mathrm{k}^\mathrm{T}) \in \mathrm{R}^{r x r}$ can be structured in the block-Hankel matrix $H \in \mathrm{R}^{(p+1)r \; x \; qr}$ as follows:

$$H = \begin{bmatrix} R_1 & R_2 & \cdots & R_q \\ R_2 & R_3 & \cdots & R_{q+1} \\ \vdots & \vdots & \ddots & \vdots \\ R_{p+1} & R_{p+2} & \cdots & R_{p+q} \end{bmatrix}, \qquad (1)$$

where p and $q = p + 1$ are the parameters that denote the memory of the system. The factorization of H to some low-rank matrices fully describing the dynamics of the underlying LTI mechanical system is the cornerstone for obtaining the damage-sensitive features in the SHM methods considered in this paper. Assume that the order of the system n=2m is known, where m is the number of modal parameters observed in the considered frequency band. The singular value decomposition (SVD) of H writes:

$$H = [U_1 \quad U_2] \begin{bmatrix} D_1 & 0 \\ 0 & D_2 \end{bmatrix} \begin{bmatrix} V_1^T \\ V_2^T \end{bmatrix}, \tag{2}$$

where $U_1 \in \mathrm{R}^{(p+1)r \times n}$ and $V_1 \in \mathrm{R}^{qr \times n}$ are called the image and the co-image of a matrix, respectively, and correspond to a collection of n left and right singular vectors related to n singular values $D_1 \in \mathrm{R}^{n \times n}$. The matrices $U_2 \in \mathrm{R}^{(p+1)r \times (p+1)r-n}$ and $V_2 \in \mathrm{R}^{qr \times qr-n}$ are called the left and right nullspace of a matrix, respectively. They contain the left and right singular vectors that correspond to the singular values in $D_2 \in \mathrm{R}^{(p+1)r-n \times qr-n}$ which approximate zero. Their use in the context of the considered damage detection methodology is elaborated in Sections 2.2.1 - 2.2.3.

2.2. Damage detection residuals

Let ζ denote a damage detection residual obtained from some damage-sensitive features extracted from the measurement data in the reference and in the currently tested state and let Σ_ζ be its asymptotic covariance matrix. To compare the measurements from the healthy and the tested states, the residual is expressed to follow a Gaussian distribution, whose mean value is zero if the features of the currently tested system statistically correspond to the baseline features and is different from zero otherwise. The definition of the residual depends on the chosen damage detection method. A brief description of the damage detection residuals used in this paper is enclosed below. For brevity, only the definition of residuals is outlined and not their statistical characteristics, e.g., covariance computation. Regarding this, the interested reader is encouraged to refer to the references enclosed in the respective sections.

2.2.1. Classic subspace-based residual

The classic subspace-based damage detection residual is defined as a product of a Hankel matrix evaluated from the test data H^{test} and the left nullspace of the Hankel matrix obtained from the baseline data U_2^{ref} [12]. The resultant residual can be written as:

$$\zeta = \sqrt{N}\, {U_2^{ref}}^T H^{test}. \tag{3}$$

After the left nullspace property, i.e., ${U_2^{\mathrm{ref}}}^T H^{\mathrm{test}} \rightarrow 0$, when the test data statistically corresponds to the baseline data, the mean value of the residual (3) is zero when the currently tested data set is classified healthy, and it is different from zero when the currently tested data is collected from a damaged structure.

2.2.2. Robust subspace-based residual

The robust subspace-based residual is defined from a product of images of a Hankel matrix evaluated from the test data $U^{\mathrm{test}} = U_1^{\mathrm{test}}(U_1^{\mathrm{test}})^T$ and the left nullspace of the Hankel matrix obtained from the baseline data U_2^{ref} [10]. The resultant residual can be written as:

$$\zeta = \sqrt{N}\, {U_2^{\mathrm{ref}}}^T U^{\mathrm{test}}. \tag{4}$$

Like the classic residual, the mean value of the robust residual is zero when the features obtained from the currently tested data corresponds to the baseline features and it is different from zero otherwise. The benefit of using the image product U^{test} in (4) compared to H^{test} in (3) is that U^{test} is not heavily affected by the noise properties of the singular values and the right singular vectors; a clear drawback is its additional computational complexity related to the computation of the covariance matrix.

2.2.3. *Modal parameter-based residual*

The modal parameter-based residual is defined as the difference between currently estimated modal parameters and their reference values obtained from data in a baseline state [13]. Let x^{ref} and x^{test} contain a stacked and vectorized collection of the modal parameter estimates, e.g., the natural frequencies and the mode shapes, obtained from the baseline and the test data using SSI. The modal parameter-based residual is defined as:

$$\zeta = \sqrt{N}(x^{\text{ref}} - x^{\text{test}}), \tag{5}$$

The expected value of the residual is zero when the modal parameter estimates obtained from the currently tested data and the baseline modal parameter estimates converge to the same expected value. Otherwise, the expected value of the residual (5) is different from zero, which signifies the occurrence of damage. The computation of the consistent estimates of the joint covariance of the natural frequencies and the mode shapes can be found, e.g., in [14, 15], and case studies confirming the Gaussian characteristics of modal parameter estimates can be found, e.g., in [16].

2.3. General framework for damage detection

Based on the features extracted from the measurement data in the reference and in the currently tested state, the goal of damage detection is to decide whether there is a significant change between the two states, i.e., whether the expected value of the residual is statistically zero, or not. This decision can be achieved through statistical hypothesis tests, e.g., with Generalized Likelihood Ratio (GLR) test [11], or with some statistical distance measures, e.g., squared Mahalanobis distance [17]. For the residuals considered in this work, the likelihood ratio statistics boils down to the squared Mahalanobis distance, which is used for damage detection in the remainder of this paper.

The squared Mahalanobis distance describes a squared distance between a point and a distribution. The distance is zero if the investigated point is at the mean of the reference distribution, and it is not zero otherwise. As such, the metric:

$$d = \zeta^T \Sigma_\zeta^{-1} \zeta, \tag{6}$$

can be considered as a dissimilarity measure. When the residual follows an asymptotically Gaussian distribution with zero mean:

$$\zeta \to \mathrm{N}(0, \Sigma_\zeta), \tag{7}$$

the currently tested data set is classified healthy, since the expected value of the dissimilarity between the baseline features and the tested features is null, and then it is well-known that d follows a central χ^2 distribution [17]. When the system has undergone a change and the expected value of the residual is not zero but δ, then

$$\zeta \to \mathrm{N}(\delta, \Sigma_\zeta), \tag{8}$$

the currently tested data set is classified as damaged, and d follows a noncentral χ^2 distribution [17].

Residuals (3 - 5) satisfy properties (7 - 8) and consequently can be used for statistical damage diagnosis with the squared Mahalanobis distance (6). To decide about the damage, the value of the distance statistics is compared to a quantile of the distribution of the test derived from the baseline data. This quantile is evaluated for some confidence level α, where 1- α denotes the statistical significance level, i.e., the probability of false alarms to occur. The general premise of this statistical framework is illustrated in Figure 1.

To simplify the decision about damage, the squared Mahalanobis distance statistics obtained from different damage detection residuals are combined in a Hotelling T2 control chart [6]. The control chart statistics are computed from the sample mean and the sample covariance obtained from the test statistics of each damage detection residual.

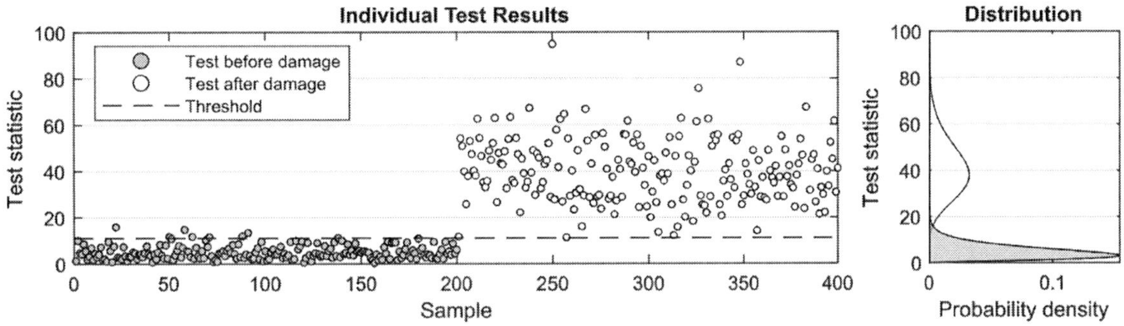

Figure 1. Decision framework for damage detection

3. CASE STUDIES

Below, two case studies on highway bridges are presented.

3.1. Z24 bridge

The Z24 bridge is a benchmark for many studies involving system identification and damage diagnosis [5]. Before its demolition in 1998, a progressive damage campaign was carried out and consisted of a series of ambient and forced vibration tests conducted while inducing different kinds of damage on the bridge. The vibration tests were conducted with 28 moving and 5 fixed sensors measuring vertical, transverse, and lateral accelerations of the bridge. For this study, only the measurements from 5 fixed sensors are analysed. The data acquisition was performed with a sampling frequency of 100 Hz and the length of each measurement was 655 seconds. A total number of 54 data sets were analysed, from which the first 18 measurements were under healthy conditions. Among the first 18 healthy data sets, 6 data sets were selected for the reference state computation. For data sets 19 to 36, measurements were collected after lowering one of the bridge piers by 20 mm. Data sets 37 to 54 were obtained after lowering the same pier by another 20 mm. The view on the bridge with positions and directions of the sensors is shown in Figure 2.

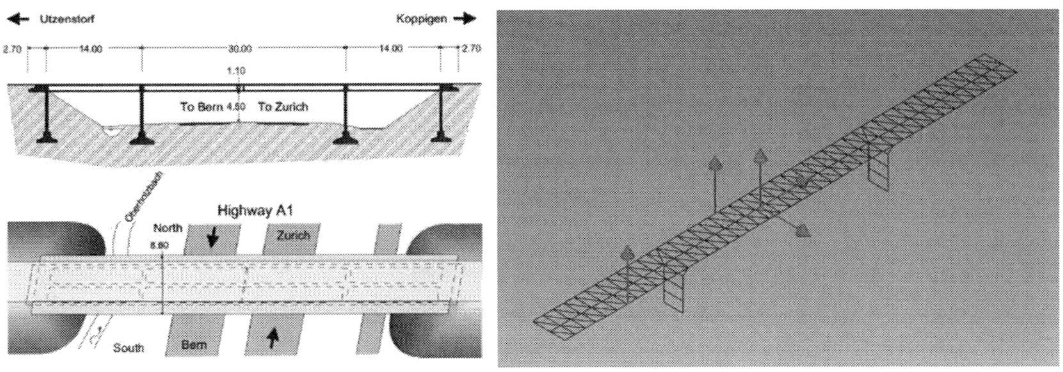

Figure 2. Front and top views of the Z24 bridge (left). Geometry with 5 fixed sensors (right)

The first 9 modes obtained with the Stochastic Subspace Identification – Extended Unweighted Principal Components (SSI–UPCX) method and tracked across the 54 data sets are shown in Figure 3.

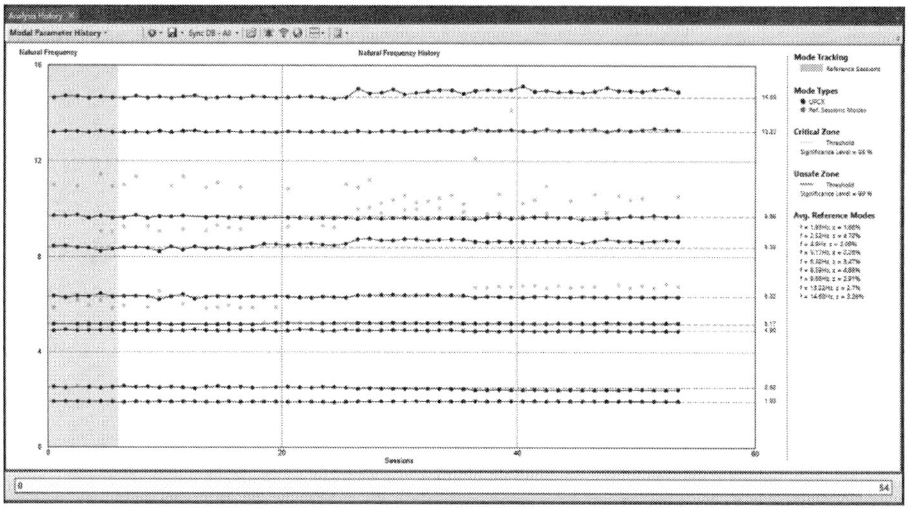

Figure 3. Modal parameters of the Z24 bridge tracked across the 54 data sets. Natural frequencies shown

The mean values of the corresponding natural frequencies and the mode shape estimates obtained over the first 6 data sets are used to establish a baseline (reference) for the modal parameter-based damage detection (5). The remaining 48 data sets are used for damage testing with the squared Mahalanobis distance (6). The resultant damage indicators are presented in Figure 4. Three decision zones are shown. The 'safe zone' is shown with green colour and indicates that the corresponding test values lie within the 95% quantile of the reference distribution statistics, the 'critical zone' shown with yellow colour indicates that the test values lie between the 95% quantile and the 99% quantile of the reference distribution, and the 'unsafe zone' shown with red colour indicates that the corresponding test values exceed the 99% quantile of the reference distribution.

Figure 4 illustrates that one test value corresponding to data collected from the bridge in an undamaged state has exceeded the 99% quantile threshold, falsely alarming damage. This is most likely caused by a missing tracked mode of the fourth and the seventh modes. Overall, however, the damage, after its inception, is well detected.

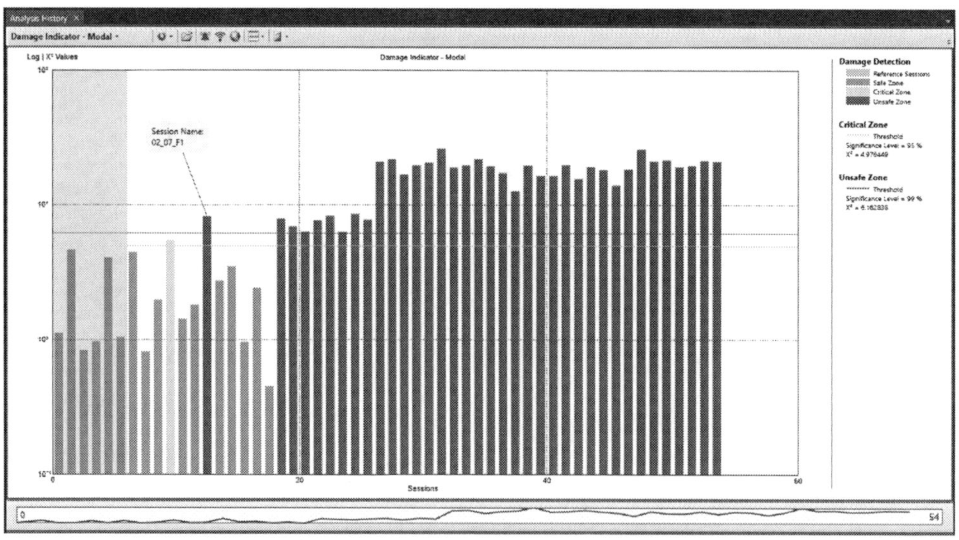

Figure 4. Damage detection with modal parameters (5) using Z24 bridge data

The results of damage diagnosis with the classic subspace residual are studied next. The first 6 data sets are used to obtain the baseline features. The output covariance Hankel matrix of both the reference and the test data set is obtained with $p = 7$ and the reference left nullspace is estimated with $n = 20$. The covariance of the residual is obtained after the first-order perturbation analysis of the residual, and the sample covariance of the Hankel matrix is computed by splitting data to 200 independent segments. The resultant damage indicators are illustrated in Figure 5. Despite few healthy data sets are classified to critical regions no false alarms occur, and all damage scenarios are detected.

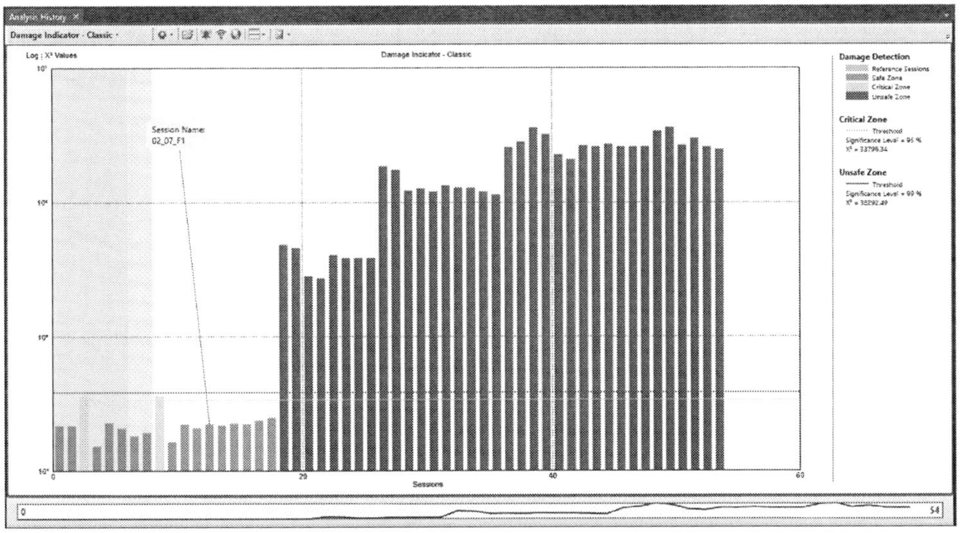

Figure 5. Damage detection with the classic residual (6) using Z24 bridge data

Lastly, the performance of the robust damage detection residual is studied. In this context, the parameters to obtain the baseline and the test features remain the same as in the classic subspace residual. The resultant damage indicators are illustrated in Figure 6. One can observe that while the damage indicators corresponding to the healthy data are classified to the safe region, damage in data sets 21 and 22 is undetected.

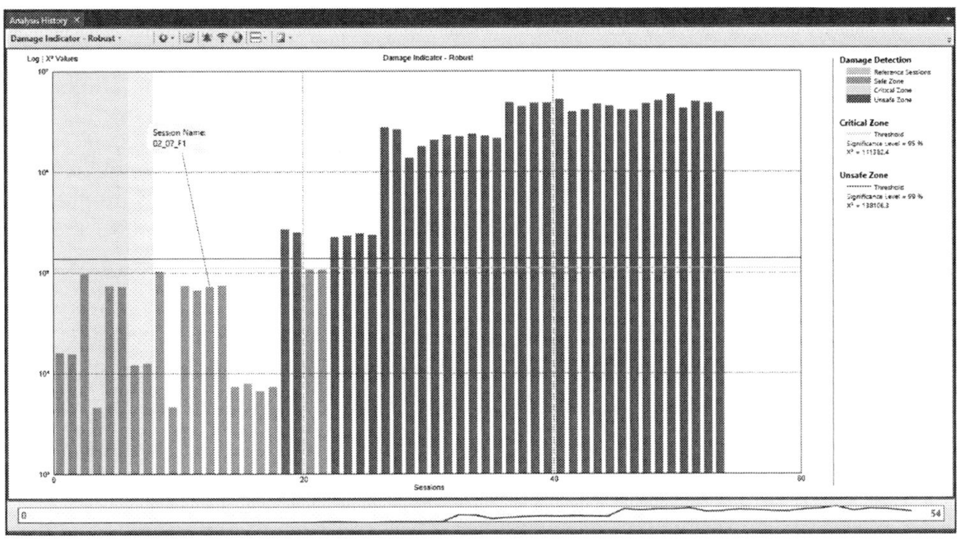

Figure 6. Damage detection with the robust residual (7) using Z24 bridge data

As the studied residuals have different statistical properties, the results also differ. To simplify the decision making about damage and to enhance the performance of the damage detection, the indicators from all the residuals are joined in a Hotelling T2 control chart, which is illustrated in Figure 7. The fusion of the methods in a control chart results in an increased resolution of the damage detection, allowing to distinguish different types of damage, while retaining no false alarms in the healthy state.

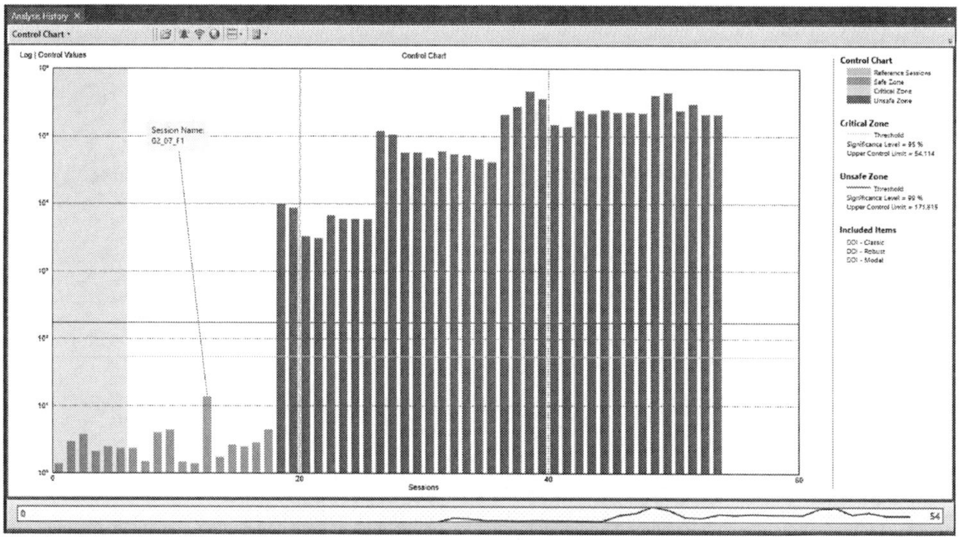

Figure 7. Fusion of damage indicators in a Hotelling T2 control chart, Z24 bridge

3.2. S101 bridge

The S101 was a prestressed concrete bridge located in Reibersdorf, Austria. With the main span of 32 m, side spans of 12 m, and a width of 6.6 m, it crossed the national highway A1 Westautobahn. Built in 1960, it had to be demolished due to structural problems and to allow space for additional lanes on the highway underneath. That created an opportunity for conducting progressive structural damage tests. The bridge was artificially damaged and monitored within the Integrated European Industrial Risk Reduction System research project [18].

The measurement campaign was conducted by Vienna Consulting Engineers ZT GmbH (VCE) [19] and the University of Tokyo. The purpose of the campaign was to demonstrate the impact of scientific insight and findings with regards to the rehabilitation measures and cost planning of the transportation infrastructure. Acceleration responses were recorded using 15 triaxial sensors mounted on the bridge deck. The bridge was monitored continuously from the 10th to the 13th of December 2008. A sampling frequency of 500 Hz was used and a total of 714 data sets with 165k samples in each were acquired.

The bridge was closed for any traffic during the progressive damage testing. As a result, the main source of ambient excitation was wind and the vibrations from traffic on the highway beneath the bridge. The structural damages introduced in the bridge were of several types and locations. Two major damage scenarios can be distinguished, as outlined in Table 1.

Table 1. Damage scenarios during the progressive damage test of the S101 bridge

Case 1	Damages	Sets	Case 2	Damages	Sets
A	First cut through the left pier	5	G	Inserting steel plates	45
B	Second cut through the left pier	15	H	2nd tendon cut	178
C	Settlement of the left pier (1st) – 1cm	10	I	2nd tendon cut	178
D	Settlement of the left pier (2nd) – 2cm	21	J	3rd tendon cut	23
E	Settlement of the left pier (3rd) – 3cm	9	K	4th tendon partly intersected	6
F	Lifting the left pier – 6mm	186			

Figure 8. The S101 bridge. Locations of introduced damage are marked in the figure around the north side pier (www.vce.at/iris/)

The first 4 modes obtained with the SSI–UPCX method and tracked across the 681 data sets are shown in Figure 9.

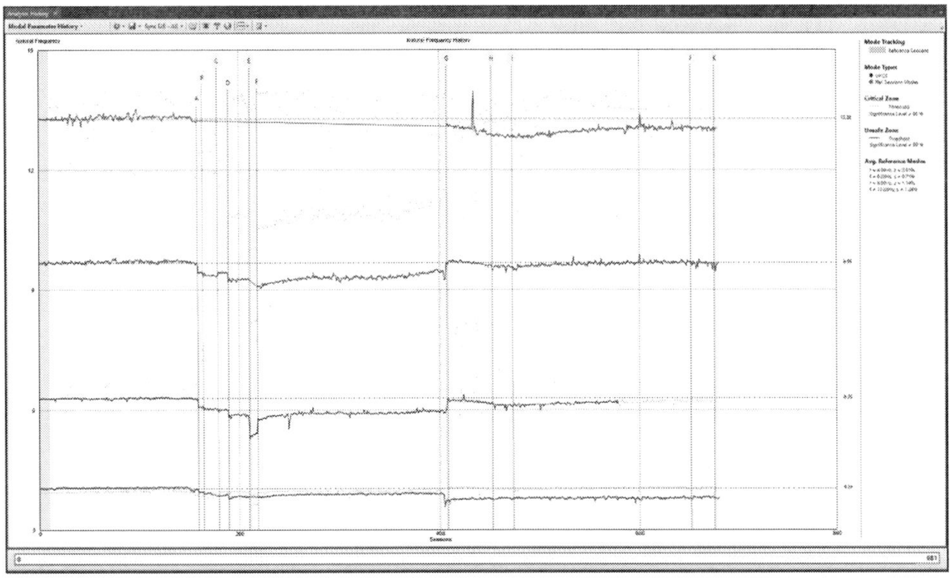

Figure 9. Modal parameters of the S101 bridge tracked across the 681 data sets. Natural frequencies shown

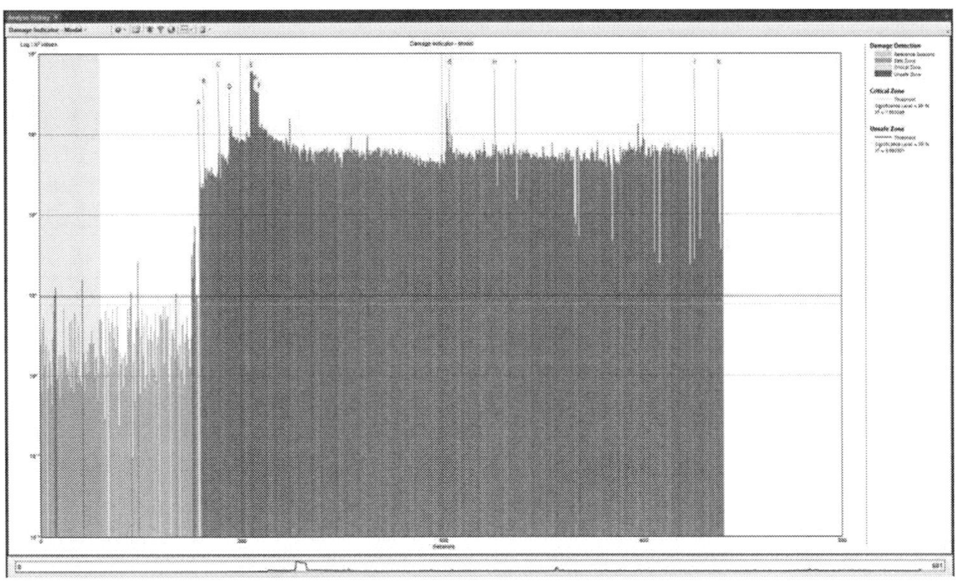

Figure 10. Damage detection with modal parameters (5) using S101 bridge data

The mean values of the corresponding natural frequencies and the mode shape estimates obtained over the first 60 data sets are used to establish a baseline (reference) for the modal parameter-based damage detection (5). The remaining 621 data sets are used for damage testing with the squared Mahalanobis distance (6). The resultant damage indicators are presented in Figure 10. There are a few false alarms in the reference part of the data sets, but there is a significant increase in the damage indicators when damage scenario A is introduced. The damage indicators stay high throughout the remaining data sets.

The results of damage diagnosis with the classic subspace residual are studied next. The first 100 data sets are used to obtain the baseline features. The output covariance Hankel matrix of both the reference and the test data set is obtained with $p = 8$ and the reference left nullspace is estimated with $n = 30$. The covariance of the residual is obtained after the first-order perturbation analysis of the residual, and the sample covariance of the Hankel matrix is computed by splitting data to 200 independent segments.

The resultant damage indicators are illustrated in Figure 11. Despite several false alarms in the reference state, the classic subspace damage indicator reacts heavily when damage is introduced. The results exceed the 99% quantile of the reference distribution for most of the damage cases. However, a small drop between damage cases I and J can be observed. This might be caused by insufficient excitation of the bridge at night.

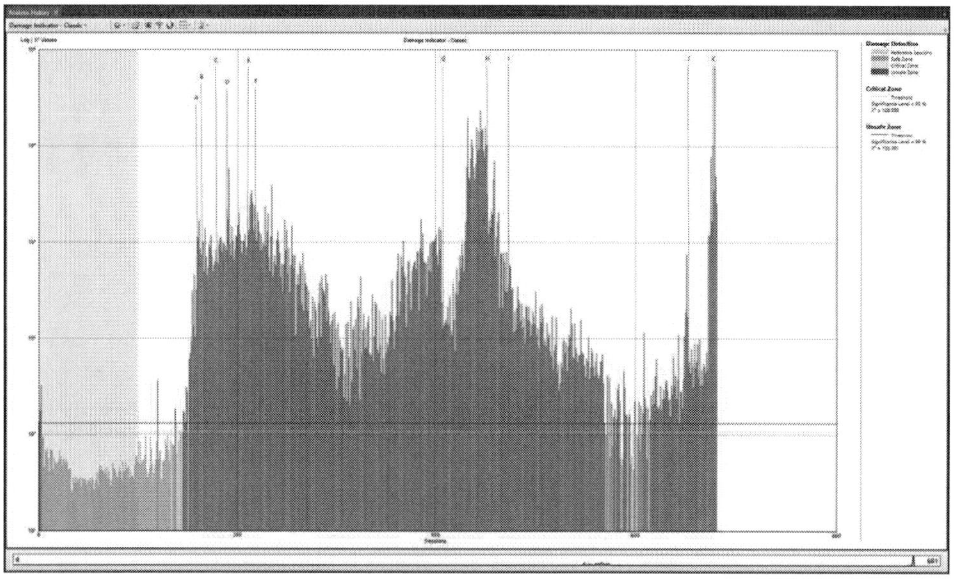

Figure 11. Damage detection with the classic residual (6) using S101 bridge data

The modal parameter-based and classic subspace damage indicators are fused in the control chart shown in Figure 12. The control chart compensates for the drawbacks of each of the two individual damage indicators. There are few false alarms in the reference data sets. However, there is a clear reaction to the damage introduced.

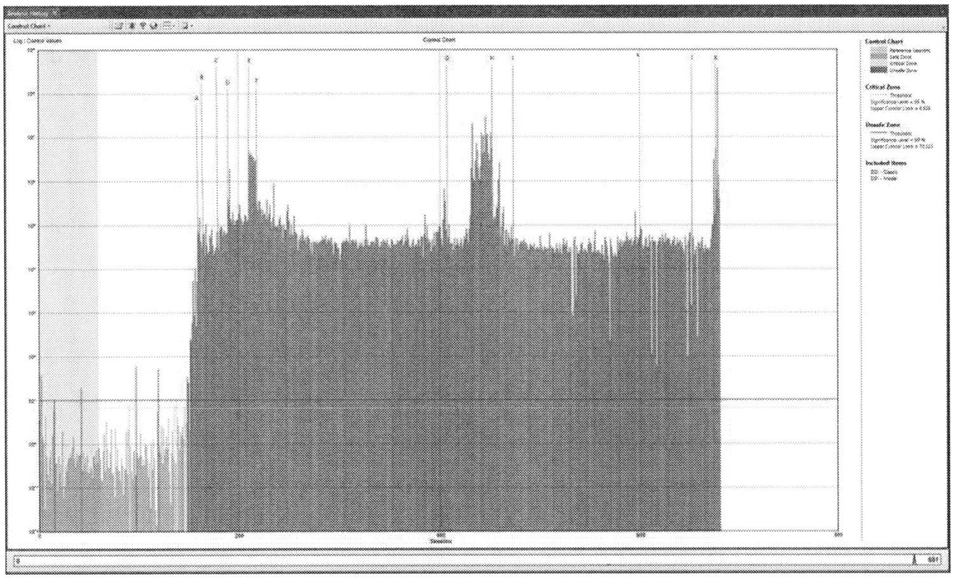

Figure 12. Fusion of damage indicators in a Hotelling T2 control chart, S101 bridge

4. DISCUSSION

The case studies clearly reason for a parallel analysis of multiple damage indicators. Each indicator has its shortcomings, directly related to the statistical properties of the underlying damage diagnosis residual [20]. Consequently, the choice of the method for an SHM system, before the actual analysis is performed, is not trivial. To enhance the reliability of the damage detection and simplify the decision about damage, the fusion of damage indicators in a control chart is beneficial, as demonstrated by the case studies. Additionally, some practical strategies to interpret false alarms can be developed, e.g., by using the fact that false alarms typically do not happen in consecutive data sets. Hence, an alert can be delayed until the next data set is processed, and the alarm occurs again. Furthermore, signal processing techniques exist to remove varying disturbances from the system dynamics by denoising Hankel matrices [21].

5. CONCLUSION

This paper presents a comparative study on three different damage detection residuals, i.e. the classic subspace-based residual, the robust subspace-based residual, and the modal parameter-based residual. To determine the health of structural systems, all three residuals are evaluated in a simple statistical test, which boils down to the squared Mahalanobis distance. The performance of each damage detection residual is compared using data from the Z24 and S101 highway bridges, where the capability of each method to detect the damages and to be ready to deploy in online SHM systems is shown. The fusion of the methods in a Hotelling T2 control chart resulted in the most effective detection of damage. In addition, it was discussed how to interpret and avoid false alarms in SHM systems.

ACKNOWLEDGEMENTS

We thank VCE for providing data from the S101 bridge.

REFERENCES

[1] Ulriksen, M. D., Tcherniak, D., Kirkegaard, P. H., & Damkilde, L. (2016). Operational modal analysis and wavelet transformation for damage identification in wind turbine blades. *Structural Health Monitoring*, *15*(4), 381-388.

[2] Tatsis, K., Ntertimanis, V. K., & Chatzi, E. (2018). On damage localization in wind turbine blades: a critical comparison and assessment of modal-based criteria. In *7th World Conference on Structural Control and Monitoring (7WCSCM)*.

[3] Viefhues, E., Döhler, M., Hille, F., & Mevel, L. (2022). Statistical subspace-based damage detection with estimated reference. *Mechanical Systems and Signal Processing*, *164*, 108241.

[4] Greś, S., Döhler, M., Andersen, P., & Mevel, L. (2021). Subspace-based Mahalanobis damage detection robust to changes in excitation covariance. *Structural Control and Health Monitoring*, *28*(8), e2760.

[5] Teughels, A., & De Roeck, G. (2004). Structural damage identification of the highway bridge Z24 by FE model updating. *Journal of Sound and Vibration*, *278*(3), 589-610.

[6] Kullaa, J. (2003). Damage detection of the Z24 bridge using control charts. *Mechanical Systems and Signal Processing*, *17*(1), 163-170.

[7] ARTeMIS Modal Pro (2022). Structural Vibration Solutions A/S. NOVI Science Park, 9220 Aalborg East, Denmark. www.svibs.com

[8] PULSE Operational Modal Analysis (2022). Hottinger Brüel & Kjær A/S, 2830 Virum, Denmark. www.bksv.com/structuraldynamics

[9] Carden, E. P., & Fanning, P. (2004). Vibration based condition monitoring: a review. *Structural health monitoring*, *3*(4), 355-377.

[10] Döhler, M., & Mevel, L. (2013). Subspace-based fault detection robust to changes in the noise covariances. *Automatica*, *49*(9), 2734-2743.

[11] Basseville, M., Abdelghani, M., & Benveniste, A. (2000). Subspace-based fault detection algorithms for vibration monitoring. *Automatica*, *36*(1), 101-109.

[12] Döhler, M., Mevel, L., & Hille, F. (2014). Subspace-based damage detection under changes in the ambient excitation statistics. *Mechanical Systems and Signal Processing*, *45*(1), 207-224.

[13] Greś, S., Mendler, A., Jacobsen, N. J., Andersen, P., & Döhler, M. (2022, July). Statistical damage detection and localization with Mahalanobis distance applied to modal parameters. In *IOMAC 2022-9th International Operational Modal Analysis Conference*.

[14] Döhler, M., & Mevel, L. (2013). Efficient multi-order uncertainty computation for stochastic subspace identification. *Mechanical Systems and Signal Processing*, *38*(2), 346-366.

[15] Reynders, E., Pintelon, R., & De Roeck, G. (2008). Uncertainty bounds on modal parameters obtained from stochastic subspace identification. *Mechanical systems and signal processing*, *22*(4), 948-969.

[16] Greś, S., Riva, R., Süleyman, C. Y., Andersen, P., & Łuczak, M. (2022). Uncertainty quantification of modal parameter estimates obtained from subspace identification: An experimental validation on a laboratory test of a large-scale wind turbine blade. *Engineering Structures*, *256*, 114001.

[17] Mahalanobis, P. C. (1936). On the generalized distance in statistics. National Institute of Science

[18] Döhler, M., Hille, F., Mevel, L., & Rücker, W. (2014). Structural health monitoring with statistical methods during progressive damage test of S101 Bridge. *Engineering Structures*, *69*, 183-193.

[19] VCE. Progressive Damage Test S101 Flyover Reibersdorf (draft), *Tech. Report 08/2308; 2009*

[20] Mendler, A., Döhler, M. (2022, July). Selection of damage-sensitive features based on probability of detection curves. In *IOMAC 2022-9th International Operational Modal Analysis Conference.*

[21] Greś, S., Tatsis, K., Ntertimanis, V. K., & Chatzi, E. (2022, July). Hankel matrix-based Denoising for Statistical Damage Diagnosis, In *IOMAC 2022-9th International Operational Modal Analysis Conference*.

AN EXPEDITIVE APPROACH FOR STRUCTURAL IDENTIFICATION THROUGH AMBIENT VIBRATIONS

Giacomo Imposa[1], Salvatore Russo[2]

1 Ph.D. student, IUAV University of Venice, Italy, gimposa@iuav.it
2. Full Professor of Structural Engineering, IUAV University of Venice, Italy, russo@iuav.it

ABSTRACT

Structural control monitoring is by now widely used in engineering structural field as safety's control approach and is also employed in procedure's assessment for conservation of Cultural Heritage as well as historic constructions and monuments. By the way, the research proposes an optimization procedure through OMA approach and specific sensors (tromograph velocimeters) which transform ambient vibrations (wind, traffic, pedestrian noise, ground's microseismic effects, common urban sounds, etc etc.) in term of sensitive information. In detail, the results of a structural survey of an Italian UNESCO Baroque church are showed. The results, through experimental modal analysis, frequency peak, fundamental frequency and mode shapes, obtained by means Operational Modal Analysis approach, are discussed. The obtained information appear partially critical from the completion point of view, but very useful in presence of the need of a rapid assessment and a speditive analysis. Particularly, outcomes allow to understand the identification of macro-structural elements, with a focus regarding the Façade.

Keywords: SCM, OMA, heritage, AVMs, microtremor, ambient vibrations

1. INTRODUCTION

The structural control of any construction, and particularly of historic ones, has been always strategic and has become a highly significant topic over the last forty years [1]. Nowadays, non-destructive (ND) tests are of fundamental importance in structural health monitoring (SHM) practices, since they can provide valuable information about material and structural properties such as resonance frequency, modal shapes and damping of the historical building [2].

The aim of this work is to evaluate the different positioning of one or more sensors, synchronized or not, for a rapid structural diagnosis in existing historic construction with an OMA approach. The frequency peaks are defined to assess if the control scheme is optimal to obtain the correct information with the less number of sensors. For each measurement is possible to evaluate the value and the amplitude of the related peak, and correlate this information to the structural features of the building. In particular, the micro tremors are considered constant, this hypothesis accounts for the signal synchronization and allows for the recording of the correct relative displacements along the measuring points.

The case of study is the San Giorgio Church in Ragusa (Italy) (**Figure 1**), a UNESCO Cultural World Heritage site. The building investigated is one of the most important examples of Sicilian Baroque architecture, built by Rosario Gagliardi in XVIII century. It is located on the Hyblean Plateu, famous for one of the most powerful and destructive earthquakes in Italian history [3], which occurred in 1693[4] (Mw 7). The high seismicity of the area where the structure is located highlights the need to perform studies aimed at the dynamic characterization of the structure and the subsoil on which it is built [5]. In the present study, the horizontal to vertical spectral ratio (HVSR) and the standard spectral ratio (SSR) techniques have been used to identify the site and the building's fundamental frequencies respectively [6]. In particular, the masonry macro elements investigated with ambient vibration measurements (AVMs) in the current study are the Dome, the right lateral Nave and the Façade. Fundamental frequencies of each macro element were obtained to highlight the mutual interaction between them, following the typical features of masonry structure behaviour. Also, an in-depth analysis regarding the Façade is discussed to compare the results obtained through SSR technique with two of the most common dynamic identification algorithms (e.g. EFDD, SSI).

2. DESCRIPTION OF THE CASE STUDY

Figure 1. View of the Church of San Giorgio

The interior of the Basilica has a Latin cross layout and consists of three aisles divided by two rows of ten pillars each with a transept and a semi-circular apse. The main dimensions are approximatively 27x68m, and the highest point is located on the dome, which is 43m high (see **Figure2**). The dome has a diameter of almost 12m and is founded on 4 pillars with an octagonal plan. It culminates with a lantern on the top and has uniquely distinctive blue stained-glass. The Façade (**see Figure 2**) is of the "tower" type and consists of 3 levels separated by three orders of columns, with the central one slightly convex. The bell tower is incorporated, and ends at the top with a bulb cusp, typical of Capuchin churches.

3. ANALYTICAL APPROACH

In literature, OMA approaches provide many algorithms to identify the modal parameters, applied to masonry historic buildings [7]. Firstly, the eigenvalue problem need to be solved (Eq.1):

$$([K] - \omega^2[M])\{\phi\} = 0 \tag{1}$$

Where *[K]* and *[M]* are matrix of stiffness and mass of the system, ω is the circular natural frequency and $\{\phi\}$ is the eigenvector or mode shape. Basically, output-only identification methods to resolve the eigenequation work with an unknown input through a process of inversion, deriving the properties of the structure from experimental output.

Given the matrix $H(\omega)$ as the representation of the dynamic system and equivalent to the ratio between the system's response and the stress the excites (Eq.2):

$$[H(\omega)] = \sum_{i=1}^{n} \frac{(v_i)\langle l_i^t\rangle}{j\omega - \lambda_i} + \frac{(v_i^*)\langle l_i^H\rangle}{j\omega - \lambda_i} \tag{2}$$

The response of the system itself to a dynamic stress is represented in the domain of frequencies by the well-known matrix S_{yy} (Eq.3)

$$[S_{yy}(j\omega)] = [H(\omega)][S_{uu}(\omega)][H(\omega)]^H \tag{3}$$

and in operative conditions where the input spectrum is of unknown entity, the central term of Eq.3 is actually constant and is thus independent from the frequency (Eq.4):

$$[S_{yy}(j\omega)] = [H(\omega)][S_{uu}][H(\omega)]^H \tag{4}$$

The last equation allows for analytical definition of the relationship between the system's response spectrum and its modal parameters [8]. To solve these problems, a large number of algorithms have been developed such as Peak-Picking (PP), Enhanced Frequency Domain Decomposition (EFDD) [9], Stochastic Subspace Identification (SSI) [10]. Following the expeditious way of the entire method used in this work, PP algorithm has been performed to identify the frequency peaks present in the acceleration spectra. In addition, to validate the expeditive approach results, a comparison in term of peak frequency and mode shapes with the other two algorithms mentioned is present (e.g. EFDD, SSI).
The investigative technique adopted in this work is passive seismic single station, based on micro tremor recordings performed with a Tromino device in a range of frequency from 0.1 Hz to 1024 Hz [11]. As is currently performed in the OMA approaches, the signal's source is Ambient Vibration or Micro tremor. This type of noise is a combination of Rayleigh and body waves and its displacements are in the order of 10^{-4} – 10^{-3} cm [9]. The environmental noise may be caused by natural (e.g. microseisms, wind, marine waves) or anthropic origins (e.g. human activities, car, pedestrian traffic, industrial machinery): in the first case the value is less than 1 Hz, while in the second case one his value is above 1 Hz. This approach is used also to determine site effects, employs the Fast Fourier Transform (FFT) to obtain the spectrum [12], whose the mathematical function is expressed as follows (Eq.5,6) where *f* is frequency and *t* is time:

$$h(t) = \int_{-\infty}^{\infty} H(f)\, exp(i2\pi ft)\, df = F[H(f)] \tag{5}$$

With h(t): (t) variable function; (F) Fourier Transform Function and H (f):

$$H(f) = \int_{-\infty}^{\infty} h(t')\, exp(-i2\pi ft')\, dt' \tag{6}$$

Note that *h(t)* and *H(f)* represent a pair of particular variables, whose product is 1. This allows the Fourier Transform to be expressed as follows (Eq.7):

$$h(t) = \sum_{n=-\infty}^{\infty} c_n\, exp(i2\pi n f_0 t) \tag{7}$$

If the period *T* of such a function tends to infinity, this causes the frequency f_0 to zero and that the integral form of the Fourier series also applies to non-periodic functions. We can calculate, thus, the Fourier spectra of horizontal H and vertical V components of the signal and then the spectral ratio H/V, which gives us information about the site resonance frequency [13]. Basically, the H/V technique allows to eliminate the effect of noise from the recordings as to obtain a stable curve with the resonance frequencies of the ground. The Horizontal to Vertical Spectra Ratio (HVSR) is one of the most common approaches to study the relationship between the amplification of seismic waves and site effects, linked to the structural damage caused by earthquakes [14]. This method was proposed first by Nakamura [15] after preliminary studies by Nogoshi and Igarashi [16] and it uses the ratio of the geometric averaged horizontal-to vertical frequency spectrum to identify soil fundamental frequency [17]. The test was performed with a tromograph and Fast Fourier Transform (FFT) software, which allows for the evaluation of site effects and analysis of related spectra [18]. Recently, this technique, named Standard Spectra Ratio (SSR), has been used to obtain the fundamental frequency of buildings and identify different modal shapes [19]. The modal frequency response analysis of the structure was carried out using deconvolution, a process of subtracting from the motion occurring at the roof level. In SSR analysis the spectral ratio was computed between the ambient vibrations (Fourier spectra) of horizontal components, recorded at points located on the same vertical at both roof and floor levels, as well as the same components recorded at a reference or standard station (EXT1) located outside the church [20]. In this regard, it is noted that this procedure is only reliable over a long period [21] or if the noise source is the same for the stations in question, including reference (or standard) ones.

4. AMBIENT VIBRATION TEST DESIGN – OMA APPROACH

During the experimental campaign, a total of 18 measurements inside the building and 1 external measurement (EXT1) were performed to characterize the site by n.6 three-component velocimeter, known as tromographs (TROMINO®) (**Figure 2d**). Among the six devices, each one of them is a stand-alone portable unit (~10×14×7 cm) but only two of them can be linked each other through the built-in radio (red version). The first step is to designing the monitoring scheme and it is consisting of positioning through the most optimal way all the devices inside the building due the macro element to be investigated (**Figure 2a,b,c**) and the number of sensors for each typology (e.g. presence of radio channel). This last factor is considered to perform different expeditive approaches for each macro element. The sampling frequency adopted to characterize the macro elements and the site was 512 Hz, for a time length about 16 minutes. In particular, the internal recordings were carried out by positioning the instruments with the instrumental axis parallel to the longer dimension of the church. Grilla® software was used to process the acquired signal during a 20s window and 1% triangular smoothing, and to apply the FFT.

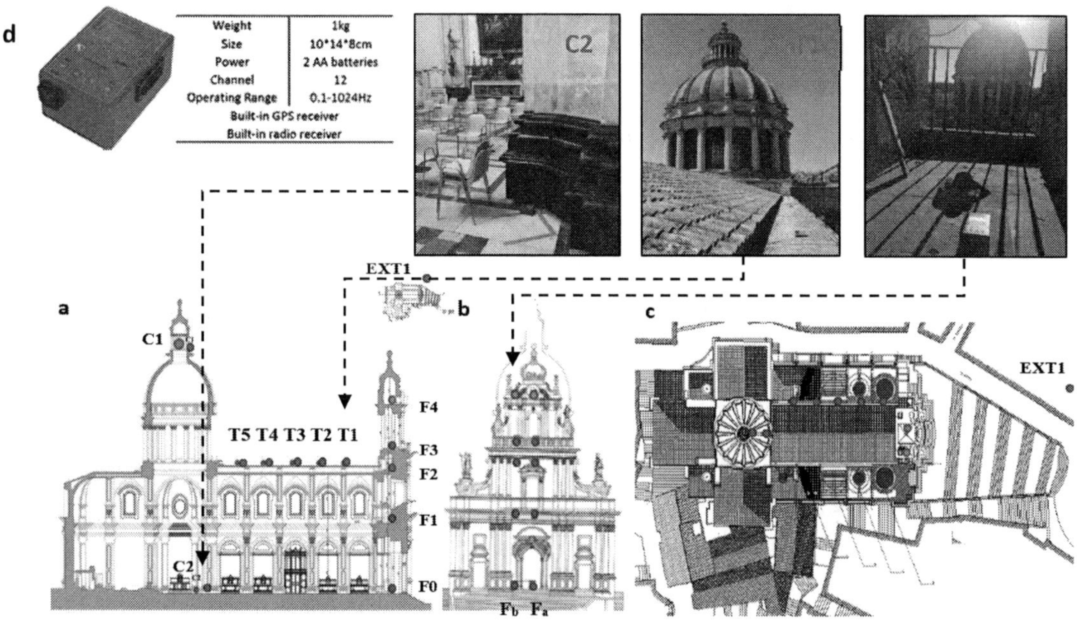

Figure 2. Monitoring scheme with combo Master (blue) and Rover (red) in longitudinal section a), in the facade b), on the roof c); TROMINO d) in location C_2, T_1, F_4.

As is shown in the monitoring scheme in **Figure 2**, the Right Nave has been characterized with n.5 measurements (T1,T2,T3,T4,T5) not synchronized. However, all the five devices started to recording almost simultaneously by manual setting. Otherwise, in the Dome and in the Façade, a synchronized set-up of two instruments, named Master (on the Top) and Rover (at the bottom/correspondent level) is used to characterize the macro elements. In the first case the instruments with the radio option were aligned in the same vertical, and in particular, the Master was located on the Top (C1, blue) and the Rover (C2, red) also near the corresponding pillar at the ground level. Lastly, into the Façade, the couple Master and Rover was located at five levels (0m, 11m, 19m, 22m, 30m) and ten measurements distributed on two vertical alignments, one located in the centre and the second one in the left part, were carried out to obtain the modal parameters of the macro element.

5. EXPERIMENTAL RESULTS

The results are divided into two horizontal components, showing the different peaks for each axis, but regarding to the Nave, only graphs related to the point T1 and T5 are shown (**Figure 3**). Four different peaks are identified for each positioning and reported with the relative average values for each component in **Table 1.** In addition, interesting aspects are visible in the spectra of the Lateral Nave: all measuring points show one peak related to the N-S component (f_1=2,34Hz) and two peaks related to the E-W component (f_1=3,18 Hz and f_2=3,75 Hz). The macro element vibrates at higher frequency along the E-W axis because this is parallel to the axis of minor inertia [22]. Furthermore, in the spectra relative to the point T5, the nearest to the Dome, there are the same values of the peaks of the Dome (f_1= 1,86 Hz in N-S and f_1=1,94 Hz in E-W) because the Nave is affected by the influence of the cupola. In the same way, in T1, the nearest to the Façade, the amplitude of the peak in the E-W spectra at f= 4,74 Hz is larger than other points, this is probably due to the vibration effect of the façade to the aisle.

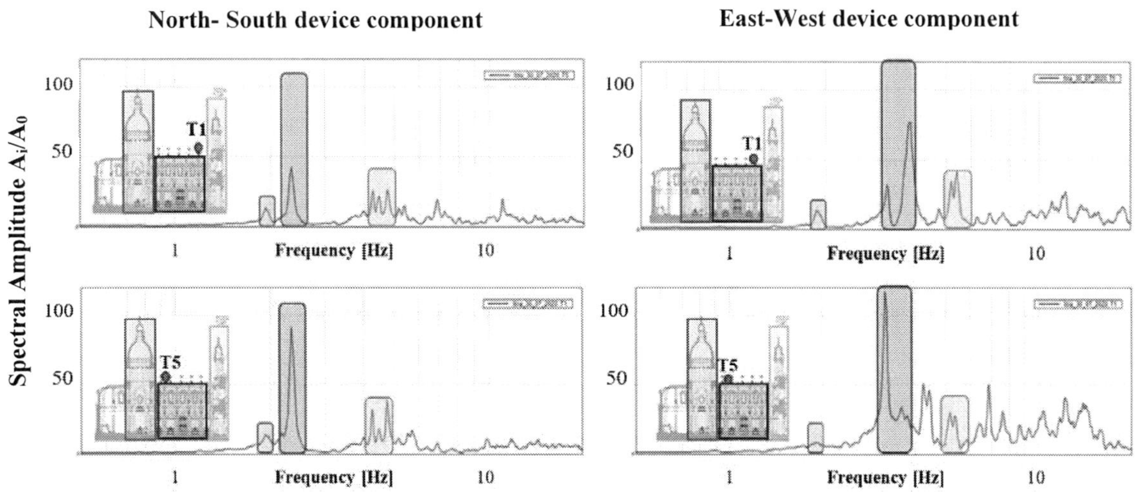

Figure 3. SSR analysis of Right Nave in point T1 and T5, and related spectra of N-S and E-W components

Peak	Macro Element	f_{N-S} [Hz]	f_{E-W} [Hz]
No.1	Dome	1,93	1,86
No.2	Nave	2,34	3,18
No.3	Façade/Dome	4,24	3,75
No.4	Facade	4,74	4,43

Table 1. Average frequencies of macro-elements in N-S and E-W direction

In the spectra related to the Dome (**Figure 4**) there are two main vibration modes. The first value is 1,90 Hz in both directions. The second value is 2,50 Hz, and it is shown clearly in the E-W spectra. However, the amplification of the first mode is higher in the N-S axis with respect to the other direction because the Dome is constrained to the short arm of the Latin Cross.

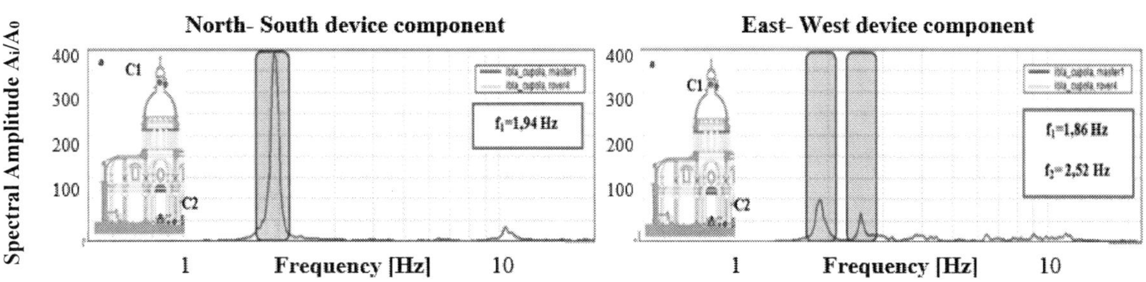

Figure 4. SSR analysis of Dome in point C1 (top) and C2 (base ground floor) and related spectra

Regarding the Façade, we obtained five couple of synchronized measurements (F1 - F5), for each alignment. Then, as an example, only results with centred vertical are shown in **Figure 5.**

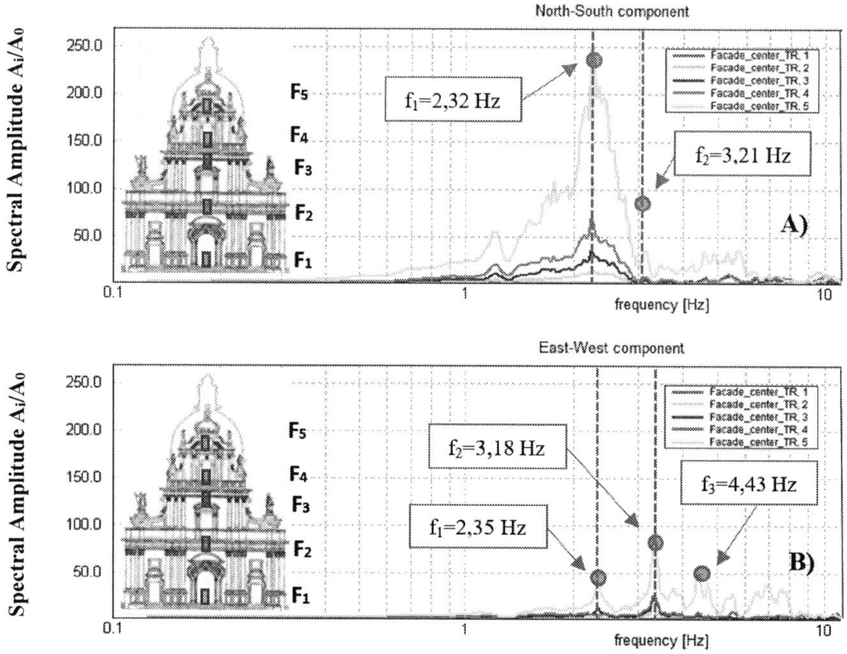

Figure 5. SSR analysis of Façade with the centred alignment, in N-S (a), E-W (b)

In the Façade, analysing E-W spectra, there are three fundamental frequencies values well-defined: f_1 =2,35 Hz, f_2 =3,18 Hz and f_3= 4,43 Hz. Otherwise, in the perpendicular direction, the frequencies obtained are f_1= 2,32 Hz and f_2=3,21 Hz. In both directions, the peak related to f_1 confirms the presence of the first flexional mode.

In addition, in **Figure 6**, through SSR technique, the mode shapes relative to the first flexional mode in both directions are clearly defined. Moreover, the displacements relative to pt. 4 and 5 are higher in respect to the previous, because from pt. 3 the macro element is not constrained to the Church, in particular to the Central Nave. In this regard, three locations could be named "vital" to define an optimal configuration and describe the modal features of the element with the less number of sensors as possible; i.e. one located at the bottom (TR1), the second one on the top (TR5) and the last in correspondence of the linking with the Nave (TR3). The experimental mode shapes are also compared with them obtained by SSI technique elaborated with ARTeMIS Modal pro software.

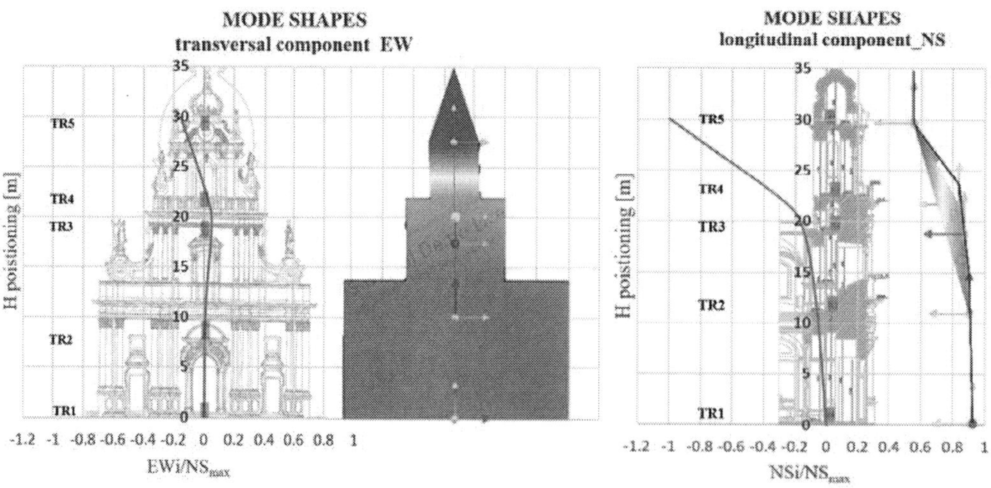

Figure 6. Modal Shapes of Facade in N-S a) and E-W b) direction regarding first mode

6. DISCUSSION

During the experimental survey, basically, three different type of set-up were performed: 1) Multiple-Single station along the Lateral Nave; 2) Single couple (Master and Rover synchronized by radio) into the Dome; 3) Multi-Single couple into the Façade.
The easiest set-up is made using only one device and two recordings, one located in the point of interest (T1-T5) and the second one external near the Church (EXT1). The device used is not provided of the built-in radio and the synchronization in not allowed. However, with the SSR procedure, it has been possible obtain the frequency peaks of the macro-elements, changing the position of the instrument along the Lateral Nave, for five different positions. As is notable in both T1 and T5 points, the proximity to the Façade (T1) or the Dome (T5) is confirmed by the presence of peaks related with interactive effects.
The Master and Rover combo has been essential to a rapid and correct evaluation of the main modes of the Dome. The synchronized recordings show clearly the first flexional mode and, as like the previous case, the influence of the transept in term of displacements. However, only one couple is not enough to consider the possible presence of torsional modes. In symmetric structures like the present one, torsion modes are characterized by having the same spectral amplitude in two measurements at the opposite corners but with opposite phase [23]. Unfortunately, the shape of the elements and his collocation inside the Church does not allow to positioning the instrument to produce this additional consideration.
The last set-up provides as many couple of synchronized recordings as many positions at different levels are available. The rapid mode shapes obtained shows that the number of points available is enough to produce satisfactory results and the matching between the expeditive results and the numerical ones can be easily observed. However, more detailed analyses should be made, including the whole masonry complex to assess the dynamic behaviour of the other macro elements, since the facade in the reality is not isolated.
It is also noteworthy that the OMA approach used in this work even if it is expeditive, is not lacking in precision. SSI and EFDD algorithms were performed to validating the experimental peaks defined with SSR technique. The first mode is correctly identified with the other two analyses (**Figure 7**), and they match with the previous one**,** but using a larger computational borden.

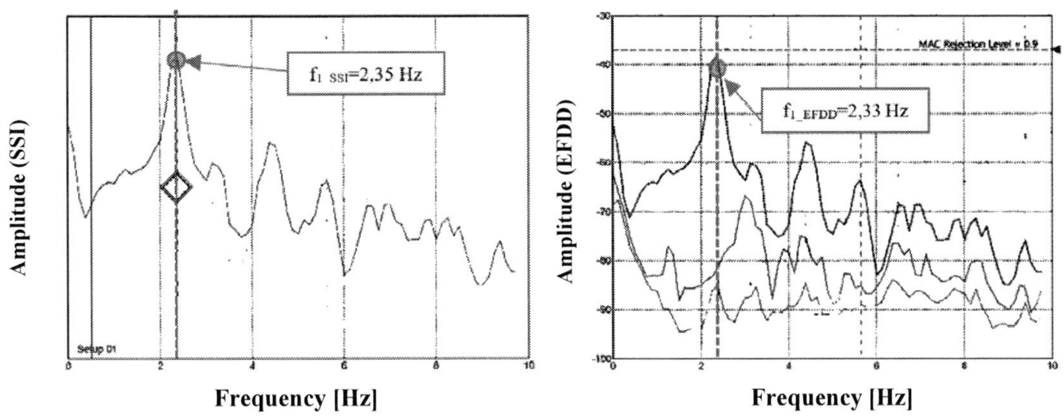

Figure 7. Peak Frequency Identification with SSI and EFDD

Regarding the possible presence of torsional modes, although the instruments were located along two alignments 3 meters apart, this distance is not enough to obtain satisfactory results. Further analyses with different tools will be performed to analyse the phase of the signal and the possible existence of torsional effects.

7. CONCLUSION

The object of this work was to performing an expeditive dynamic characterization in operative conditions of a UNESCO world heritage site through AVMs.
The following results were obtained:

- the fundamental frequencies of the Dome are: 1,90Hz and 2,50 Hz. Regarding the Nave, the values are: 2,34 Hz in longitudinal N-S direction and 3,18 Hz, 3,75 Hz in the transversal E-W component;
- The different set ups show that the synchro option is essential to do not miss the phase of the signal and to obtain the correct mode shapes of the element investigated. However, the SSR technique allows to identify the frequency peaks even with only one instrument.
- For a rapid structural identification of the buildings, the information regarding the modal parameters provided by two points for each macro element and the external one among eighteen (C1,C2, F1,F3, T1,T5, EXT1) are satisfactory.
- Indeed, if we consider just 30 minutes of recording for each couple of measurements the total length of the recordings is less 2 hours, including the instrumental placing.
- The eigenvalues calculation can be guaranteed by four positioning, (EXT1,C1,T5,F5). It should be noted that this is allowed by just one sensor located on the top of the macro element investigated, without any synchronization mode and it provides a huge gain in term of time and costs.

ACKNOWLEDGEMENTS

The authors are grateful to Prof. S. Imposa and Dr.ssa S. Grassi, members of the research group of the Applied Geophysics Laboratory of the University of Catania, for having supported them during the experimental survey and the post-processing step. In addition, thanks go to the architect Giorgio Battaglia, Superintendent of the Cultural Heritage of Ragusa and to Mons. Floridia, parish priest of the Cathedral.

REFERENCES

[1] R. Ceravolo, G. de Lucia, E. Lenticchia, e G. Miraglia, «Seismic Structural Health Monitoring of Cultural Heritage Structures», in *Seismic Structural Health Monitoring*, M. P. Limongelli e M. Çelebi, A c. di Cham: Springer International Publishing, 2019, pagg. 51–85. doi: 10.1007/978-3-030-13976-6_3.

[2] E. Spoldi, I. Ippolito, A. Stella, e S. Russo, «Non-destructive techniques for structural characterization of cultural heritage: A pilot case study», *Struct. Control Health Monit.*, vol. 28, n. 12, dic. 2021, doi: 10.1002/stc.2820.

[3] A. Greco, G. Lombardo, B. Pantò, e A. Famà, «Seismic Vulnerability of Historical Masonry Aggregate Buildings in Oriental Sicily», *Int. J. Archit. Herit.*, vol. 14, n. 4, pagg. 517–540, apr. 2020, doi: 10.1080/15583058.2018.1553075.

[4] S. Imposa, S., Motta, E., Capilleri, P., Imposa, G. HVSR and MASW seismic survey for characterizing the local seismic response: A case study in Catania area (Italy) (2016) 1st IMEKO TC4 International Workshop on Metrology for Geotechnics, MetroGeotechnics 2016, pp. 97-102.

[5] S. Grassi, S. Imposa, G. Patti, D. Boso, G. Lombardo, e F. Panzera, «Geophysical surveys for the dynamic characterization of a cultural heritage building and its subsoil: The S. Michele Arcangelo Church (Acireale, eastern Sicily)», *J. Cult. Herit.*, vol. 36, pagg. 72–84, mar. 2019, doi: 10.1016/j.culher.2018.09.015.

[6] R. Salvatore e S. Eleonora, «Damage assessment of Nepal heritage through ambient vibration analysis and visual inspection», *Struct. Control Health Monit.*, vol. 27, n. 5, mag. 2020, doi: 10.1002/stc.2493.

[7] E. Reynders, «System Identification Methods for (Operational) Modal Analysis: Review and Comparison», *Arch. Comput. Methods Eng.*, vol. 19, n. 1, pagg. 51–124, mar. 2012, doi: 10.1007/s11831-012-9069-x.
[8] S. Russo, «Using Experimental Dynamic Modal Analysis in Assessing Structural Integrity in Historic Buildings», *Open Constr. Build. Technol. J.*, vol. 8, n. 1, pagg. 357–368, dic. 2014, doi: 10.2174/1874836801408010357.
[9] R. Brincker, P. Andersen, e N.-J. Jacobsen, «Automated Frequency Domain Decomposition for Operational Modal Analysis», pag. 7.
[10] R. Brincker, «Understanding Stochastic Subspace Identification», pag. 7.
[11] S. Castellaro, L. A. Padrón, e F. Mulargia, «The different response of apparently identical structures: a far-field lesson from the Mirandola 20th May 2012 earthquake», *Bull. Earthq. Eng.*, vol. 12, n. 5, pagg. 2481–2493, ott. 2014, doi: 10.1007/s10518-013-9505-9.
[12] A.K. Chopra, Dynamic of Structures, Theory and Applications to Earthquake engineering, Prentice Hall: 3rd ed 2007.
[13] G. Dal Moro, «On the Identification of Industrial Components in the Horizontal-to-Vertical Spectral Ratio (HVSR) from Microtremors», *Pure Appl. Geophys.*, vol. 177, n. 8, pagg. 3831–3849, ago. 2020, doi: 10.1007/s00024-020-02424-0.
[14] S. Imposa, G. Lombardo, F. Panzera, e S. Grassi, «Ambient Vibrations Measurements and 1D Site Response Modelling as a Tool for Soil and Building Properties Investigation», *Geosciences*, vol. 8, n. 3, pag. 87, mar. 2018, doi: 10.3390/geosciences8030087.
[15] Nakamura Y., 1989. A method for dynamic characteristics estimation of subsurface using microtremor on the ground surface. Quaterly Report Railway Tech. Res. Inst., 30-1, 25- 30..
[16] Nogoshi M. and T. Igarashi, 1971. On the amplitude characteristics of microtremor (part 2) (in japanese with english abstract). Jour. Seism. Soc. Japan, 24, 26-40.
[17] S. Bonnefoy-Claudet, F. Cotton, e P.-Y. Bard, «The nature of noise wavefield and its applications for site effects studies», *Earth-Sci. Rev.*, vol. 79, n. 3–4, pagg. 205–227, dic. 2006, doi: 10.1016/j.earscirev.2006.07.004.
[18] E. Spoldi e S. Russo, «Damage Assessment and Dynamic Characteristics of Temples in Nepal Post Gorkha 2015 Earthquake», *Int. J. Archit. Herit.*, vol. 15, n. 3, pagg. 479–493, mar. 2021, doi: 10.1080/15583058.2019.1628322.
[19] S. Castellaro, «Dynamic characterization of the Eiffel tower», *Eng. Struct.*, pag. 13, 2016.
[20] S. Russo, E. Spoldi, I. Ippolito, G. Imposa, e A. Bretini, «Detection of 2009 L'Aquila's Earthquake Effects on Collemaggio Church through Experimental Surveys», *J. Archit. Eng.*, vol. 28, n. 1, pag. 05021017, mar. 2022, doi: 10.1061/(ASCE)AE.1943-5568.0000495.
[21] SESAME European project, 2004. J-SESAME User Manual, Version 1.08.
[22] S. Russo, D. Liberatore, e L. Sorrentino, «Combined ND Techniques for Structural Assessment: The Case of Historic Nepali Constructions after the 2015 Gorkha Earthquake», in *The 18th International Conference on Experimental Mechanics*, mag. 2018, pag. 421. doi: 10.3390/ICEM18-05271.
[23] S. Castellaro e S. Russo, «Dynamic characterization of an all-FRP pultruded construction», *Compos. Struct.*, vol. 218, pagg. 1–14, giu. 2019, doi: 10.1016/j.compstruct.2019.03.032.

9th International Operational Modal Analysis Conference
IOMAC
July 3 - 6, 2022
Vancouver, Canada

IDENTIFICATION OF CHANGES IN THE DYNAMICS OF A REINFORCED CONCRETE BUILDING THROUGH A MACHINE LEARNING APPROACH FOR DATA NORMALIZATION

Davide Arezzo [1], *Simone Quarchioni* [2], *Vanni Nicoletti* [3], *Sandro Carbonari* [4], *Fabrizio Gara* [5]

[1] Postdoc Researcher, Università Politecnica delle Marche, d.arezzo@pm.univpm.it.
[2] Scolarship Researcher, Università Politecnica delle Marche, simone96.quarchioni@hotmail.it.
[2] Postdoc Researcher, Università Politecnica delle Marche, v.nicoletti@staff.univpm.it.
[3] Associate Professor, Università Politecnica delle Marche, s.carbonari@staff.univpm.it.
[4] Full Professor, Università Politecnica delle Marche, f.gara@staff.univpm.it.

ABSTRACT

In recent years there has been a growing number of Structural Health Monitoring (SHM) applications based on environmental vibration measurements and Operational Modal Analysis techniques. It is nowadays widely recognised in the scientific literature the need of normalizing data (e.g. modal properties) of vibration-based monitoring systems from variations related to the effects of environmental conditions (e.g. temperature, wind speed, intensity of human activities).

In this paper, the results of the dynamic monitoring of a 10-storey reinforced concrete building in central Italy are presented. The building, which is monitored since 2017, hosts the Faculty of Engineering of the Università Politecnica delle Marche and can be considered of strategic importance. During 2021, retrofit works on the structural joints separating the building from adjacent bodies were carried out. This led to a slight modification of its dynamic behaviour; in detail, variations of the modal properties due to the interventions on joints hide beyond those due to environmental conditions and cannot be clearly detected with traditional multivariate statistics techniques for data cleansing. On the contrary, a data cleansing procedure based on the application of an artificial neural network revealed effective to detect the variation of the building dynamic behaviour.

Keywords: structural health monitoring, operational modal analysis, dynamic identification, environmental conditions, artificial neural networks.

1. INTRODUCTION

Vibration Based Structural Health Monitoring (VB-SHM) systems may not be effective when modal properties vary significantly with environmental parameters, especially under severe temperature changes [1]. Some studies have found that changes in structural vibration properties produced by temperature variations could be more significant than those caused by a medium degree of structural damage or under normal operational loads [2]. Thus, a lack of understanding of temperature effects can lead to an erroneous identification of the structural health.

To date, many experimental and field studies have observed the importance of temperature variations on modal parameters and different conclusions have been drawn depending on the structural typology. With reference to bridges, experimental tests on the Z24 bridge are certainly among the most impactful in this topic; interesting results in this sense can be found in the work of Peeters et al. [3]. For buildings, it is more difficult to find monitoring report in which dependencies between dynamic properties and temperature have been observed. One of the first works addressing the effects of environmental conditions on buildings is the study by Clinton et al [4], where monitoring results of the Millikan Library building of the Caltech Campus, are presented. Also, it is worth mentioning the work by Mikael et al. [5], who analysed the wandering of long-term frequency and damping values of three reinforced concrete buildings. In their work, the authors observed an interesting behaviour of the buildings for temperature values below the freezing temperature; while in general the correlation of frequencies with temperature seems to be positive, when the temperature drops below zero the trend reverses and the buildings become stiffer (as observed for the Z24 bridge [3]). Regarding the effects of temperature on the modal parameters of buildings, other interesting results can be found in Regni et al. [6].

Numerous studies have also been conducted on historical masonry buildings. Saisi et al. [7] present the main results of a recent post-earthquake evaluation of a masonry tower in Mantua (Italy) observing that the natural frequency of global modes tends to increase with the temperature increment. This behaviour has also been observed in other long-term studies of masonry towers [8, 9] and, in the work of Saisi et al. [7], it has been explained through the closure of surface cracks, minor masonry discontinuities or mortar voids induced by the thermal expansion of the materials. Thus, the temporary "compaction" of the materials induces a temporary increase in stiffness and thus in modal frequencies [7].

When measurements of the environmental parameters influencing the modal parameter estimates are not available, statistical methods must be adopted to eliminate the effects of environmental and operational factors. Such as an example, Rainieri et al. [10] explored the potential of Blind Source Separation Techniques (BSS) methods.

It should be noted that the period relative to the changes in environmental conditions are higher than the lowest fundamental period of the monitored structure. When monitored for a short period of time (seconds, minutes), the hypothesis of considering the structure as a time-invariant dynamic system is realistic. As the observation period increases (hours, days, months, years) changes of modal parameters often become non-linear, as they are due to non-linear temperature-stiffness relationships of the structural materials or in the boundary conditions of the structure [11]. For this reason, simple linear regression models are often not sufficient. To overcome this problem Reynders et al. [11] propose the application of the kernel PCA technique. Recently, researchers facing this problem have increasingly relied on machine learning techniques [12].

In this paper, the monitoring results of the Engineering Tower of the Università Politecnica delle Marche in Ancona are reported. The Tower has been monitored since 2017 and, although with some interruptions, the monitoring period allows the identification of a marked dependence of its vibration frequencies on environmental parameters, especially temperature and wind. These effects have been normalized through the implementation of an artificial neural network. Section 2 describes the case study and the monitoring system. Finally, in Section 3, the normalisation procedure and the results obtained are presented.

2. PRESENTATION OF THE CASE STUDY

The Tower at hand is located in Ancona (Central Italy), in the campus of the Faculty of Engineering of the Università Politecnica delle Marche. The building was designed and constructed between 1980 and 1983 according to standards that accounts for seismic actions. The structure, having a square floor plan, is composed by reinforced concrete (r.c.) frames with 3 columns 9 m spaced in the main building orthogonal directions. Detailed information about the building can be found in the work of Regni et al. [6] and Arezzo et al. [13], while in Figure 1 some pictures of the building are shown.

2.1. Preliminary identification tests

Over the years, several complete dynamic identifications of the Tower have been carried out to calibrate a Finite Element Model (FEM) and to control the evolution of the frequencies and mode shapes over time. These dynamic identifications allowed to deepen investigate the interaction between the main body and the staircase-elevator body. In this work, results of tests carried out in September 2020 are reported. Ambient vibration tests were performed with the aim of identifying the dynamic behaviour of the Tower, expressed in terms of modal parameters, i.e. eigenfrequencies, damping ratios and modal shapes. The tests consisted in placing six accelerometers per floor, three in the stairwell and three in the Tower, starting from level 155 to the roof at elevation 200 (i.e., 10 monitored storeys). The sensors layout is reported in Figure 2. The identification was carried out through the SSI-PC algorithm and Figure 3 shows the identification results in terms of frequencies, damping ratios and modal shapes of the first three modes.

(a) (b)

Figure 1. View of the tower: b) South c) and North-West views.

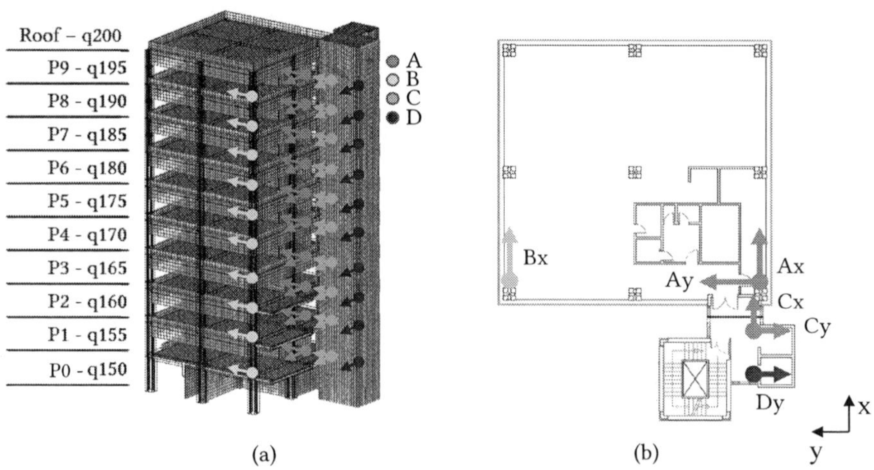

(a) (b)

Figure 2. Layout of the sensors adopted for the ambient vibration tests.

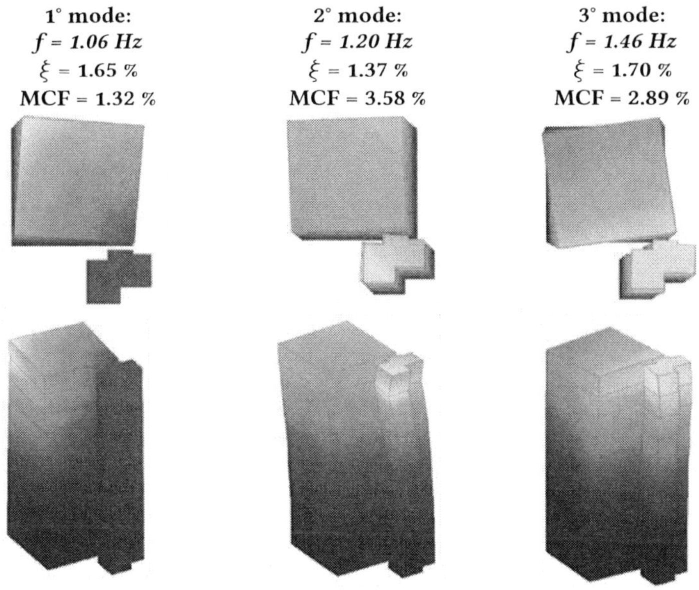

Figure 3. Dynamic identification results in terms of modal parameters of the first three vibration modes.

2.2. Description of the monitoring system

In 2017 a continuous monitoring system was installed on the Tower to monitor the evolution of its modal parameters and to measure its structural response to possible earthquakes. Initially, the monitoring system relied on the measurements of three accelerometers placed on the top floor (points A and B in Figure 2). In June 2018, the monitoring system was integrated with a Davis Vantage pro2 wireless weather station used to collect recordings on environmental parameters, mainly indoor and outdoor temperature, and wind, in order to more accurately control the variation of modal parameters of the structure with environmental changes. Since April 2021, the monitoring system has been extended with three additional accelerometers placed on the top floor of the stairwell in order to monitor the interaction of the two buildings. In addition, two thermocouples were installed to measure the temperature of the aluminium window frames, and a triaxial velocimeter was positioned at the foundation level for measuring the seismic input. Figure 4 shows a layout of the actual monitoring system, while Figure 5 shows the overall monitoring results obtained since 2017. Data relevant to 2020 are missing because of the difficulty due to the lock-down caused by Covid-19 pandemic.

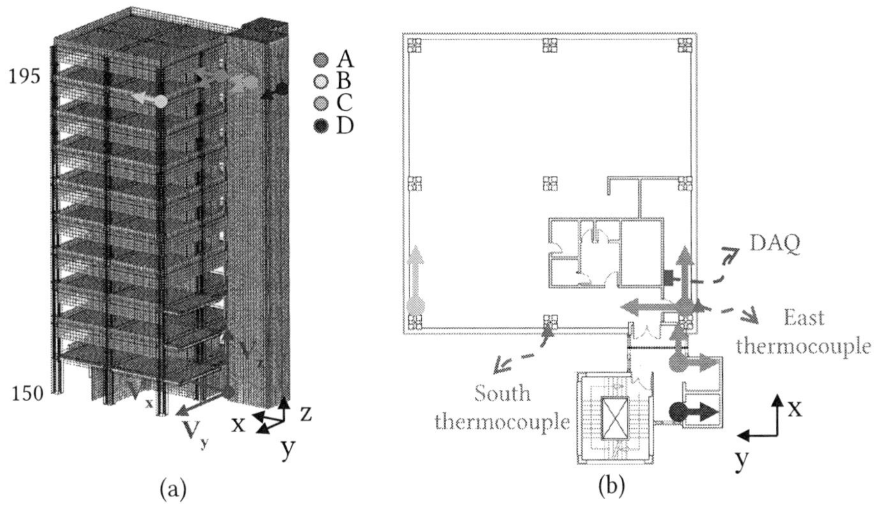

Figure 4. Actual layout of the monitoring system.

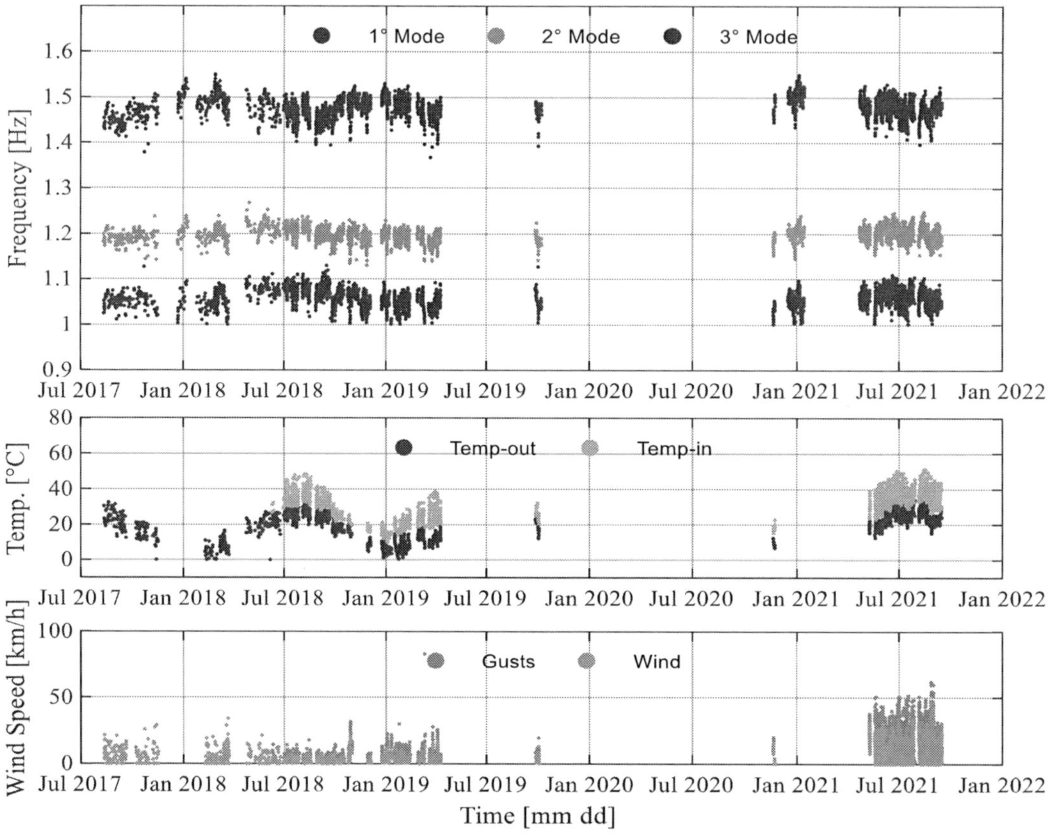

Figure 5. Global monitoring results from 2017 to date.

3. DATA NORMALIZATION THROUGH A MACHINE LEARNING APPROACH

3.1. Nonlinear autoregressive neural network with external input (NARX)

Traditional multivariate statistical analysis techniques cannot always efficiently normalize the data due to the non-linearity of the phenomena governing the dependency of the structural response with ambient parameters. More advanced numerical techniques, such as machine learning, may therefore be necessary. In particular, this work explores the capability of artificial neural networks to carry out this task.

A technical neural network is made up of simple processing units, the neurons, and of direct weighted connections between these neurons. An interesting introduction to the method can be found in the work of Markova [14]. Usually, neural networks have multiple connected layers. A layer whose output is the network output is called an output layer. The other layers are called hidden layers. The tasks of selecting the number of hidden layers, the number of neurons in the hidden layers and the number of output neurons, as well as the transfer functions, are not trivial. Hidden layers give the network its ability to generalize. As the number of hidden layers increases, it also increases computation time and the danger of overfitting, which in turn leads to bad out-of-sample prediction performance. In the case of neural networks, the number of weights, which is related to the number of hidden layers and neurons, and the dimension of the training set determine the probability of overfitting [15]. According to Baily and Thompson [16], for a three-layer network with n input neurons and m output neurons, the hidden layer would have $\sqrt{n \cdot m}$ neurons. Other criteria are mentioned in the review available in the work by Markova [14]. Most actual neural network models use the sigmoid transfer function, but it is possible to find other proposals, such as the hyperbolic tangent, the arctangent and linear transfer functions [14, 17].

Neural networks can be divided into dynamic and static categories. In dynamic networks, the output not only depends on the current input to the network, but also on the current or previous inputs, outputs, or states of the network. The non-linear autoregressive network with exogenous inputs [18] is a recurrent dynamic network with feedback connections enclosing different layers of the network. The NARX model is popularly used in time series modelling. The equation that defines the NARX model is:

$$y(t) = f(y(t-1), y(t-2), \dots, y(t-n_y), u(t-1), u(t-2), \dots u(t-n_a)) \tag{1}$$

wherein the next value of the dependent output signal *y*(t) is regressed on the past values of the output signal and the past values of an independent (exogenous) input signal. The output of the NARX network could be an estimate of the output of some non-linear dynamical system that is intended to be modelled.

There is a toolbox function in MATLAB that facilitates the preparation of data for dynamic (time series) networks. The general practice in training multilayer networks is to first divide the data into three subsets. The first subset is the training set, which is used to compute the gradient and update the weights and biases of the network. The second subset is the validation set. The error on the validation set is monitored during the training process. The input vectors and destination vectors are randomly split into three groups as follows:

- 70% used for training;
- 15% used to assess that the network is generalizing and to stop training before overfitting;
- 15% used as a completely independent test of network generalization.

When the weights and biases of the network are initialized, the network is ready for training. The training process of a neural network implies adjusting the values of the weights and biases of the network to optimize the performance of the network. The default performance function for feedforward networks is the mean square error (*mse*) between network outputs and target outputs.

$$F = mse = \frac{1}{N}\sum_{i=1}^{N}(e_i)^2 = \frac{1}{N}\sum_{i=1}^{N}(t_i - a_i)^2 \tag{2}$$

In order to train multilayer feedforward networks, any of the standard numerical optimization algorithms [18] can be employed to optimize the performance function;. One of the most widely used, thanks to its excellent performance for training neural network, is the Bayesian Regularization (BR) algorithm [18] which has been used in this work. It is a network training algorithm that updates the weight and bias values according to Levenberg-Marquardt optimization. It works by minimizing a combination of square errors and weights and then determines the correct combination to produce a network that generalizes well. This algorithm typically takes more time, but can result in good generalization for difficult, or noisy datasets. Figure 6 shows the adopted neural network implemented with the aid of machine learning toolbox provided by MATLAB. Output y(t) contain the time history of eigenfrequencies relative to the first three modes of vibration while, predictor x(t), contains the relative environmental parameters, i.e., external temperature, internal temperature, wind velocity and the root mean square of the acceleration measurements.

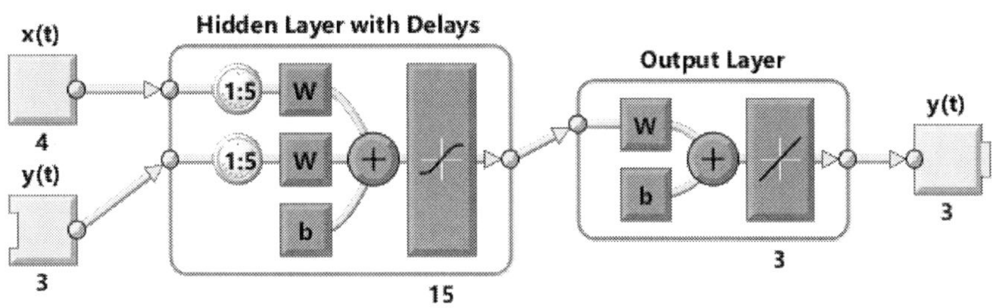

Figure 6. Neural network adopted for the data normalization.

3.2. Results of normalization procedure

The neural network has been trained on data recorded from July 2018 to January 2019 since indoor temperature measurements were not available in the previous period. Figure 7 shows the normalized dataset overlaid on the original dataset. It is useful to introduce the Gaussian Mixture Model (GMM), which allows to synthesize the information related to the three monitored frequencies by defining a statistical model composed of three averages, one for each variable, and a 3 x 3 covariance matrix Σ, where the element (i,j) is the variance between variable i and variable j, capable of representing the variation of the first three frequencies. Analyzing the training period, it is worth to note that the components of the covariance matrix of the GMM relative to the normalized dataset (Figure 8), are much smaller than those of the raw dataset.

Looking at the normalized dataset, it can be seen an increase in data dispersion starting from March 2021 revealing that the neural network predicts results of the monitoring system with increasing uncertainty. This could indicate a change in the dynamic behavior of the Tower. A possible reason for this change could be the retrofit work carried out on the structural joints, which started exactly in March 2021. Figure 9 shows some photos of the work done on all the structural joints separating the tower from the adjacent buildings. A slight variation in dynamics may be due to a different interaction between the Tower and the adjacent buildings, especially with the stairwell-elevator body since, as can be seen from Figure 9, joints were completely filled with debris. Because of this high dispersion, it could be necessary to train again the neural network in order to normalize the data with respect to this new dynamic behavior (different boundary conditions caused by the interactions between the Tower and the adjacent buildings).

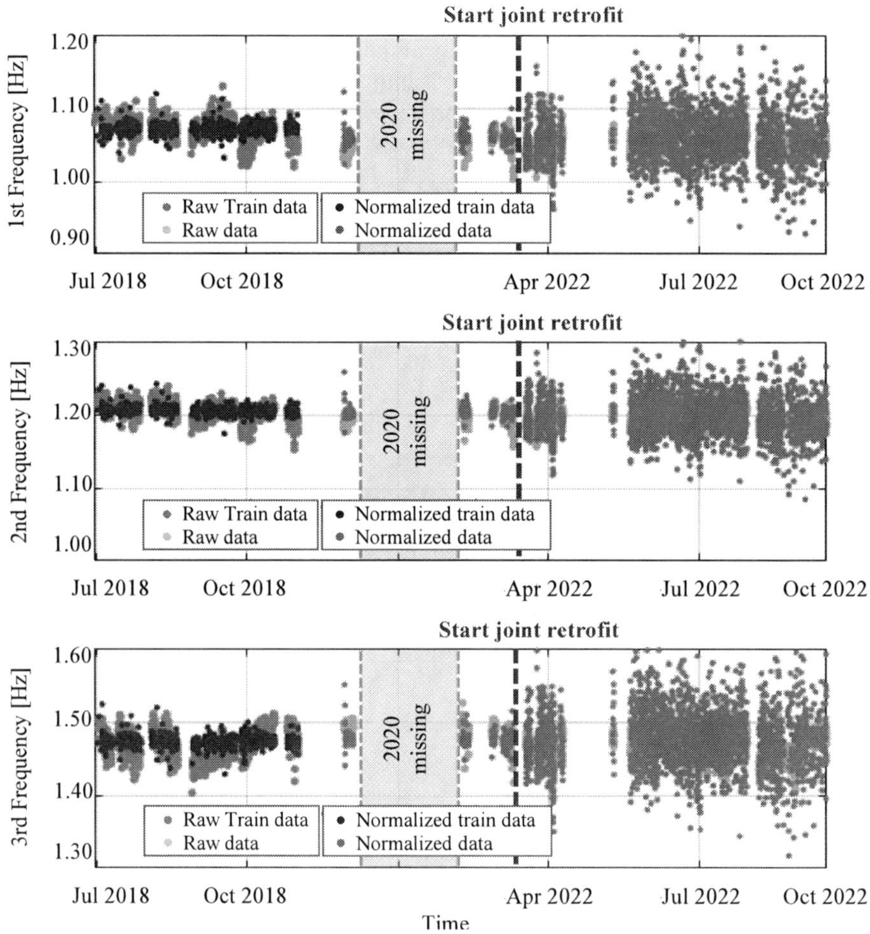

Figure 7. Original dataset superimposed on data predicted by statistical model via NARX.

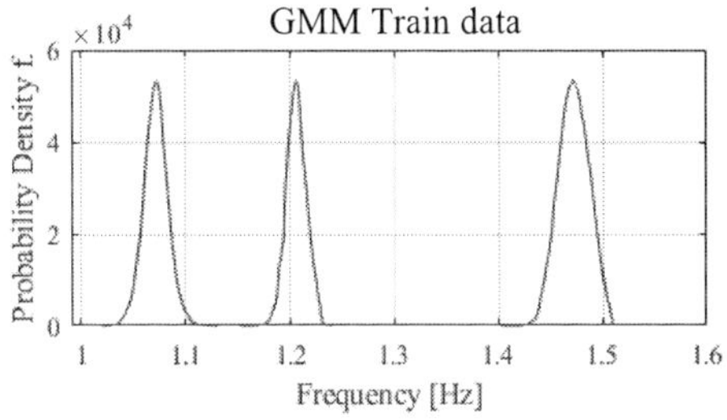

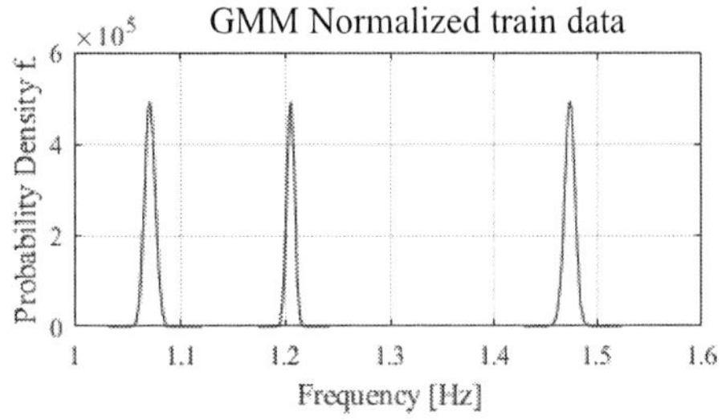

$$\Sigma = 1.00E{+}05 \begin{vmatrix} 19.62 & 14.51 & 9.05 \\ 14.51 & 13.77 & 11.42 \\ 9.05 & 11.42 & 35.34 \end{vmatrix} \qquad \Sigma = 1.00E{+}05 \begin{vmatrix} 3.71 & 1.50 & 1.55 \\ 1.50 & 2.15 & 1.64 \\ 1.55 & 1.64 & 4.23 \end{vmatrix}$$

Figure 8. Gaussian Mixture Model of the original dataset and the normalized data via NARX.

(b) (c)

Figure 9. Some photos of the retrofit works carried out on the tower structural joints.

4. CONCLUSIONS

Structural properties used in damage detection techniques because of their sensitivity to damage are usually also sensitive to changes in the environmental and operational conditions of structures. As evident from a literature review, the influence of temperature on the vibration frequencies of a structure was extensively studied in recent years and it is now well known that temperature can have important effects on the modal parameters of structures. In some cases, the frequency variations induced by temperature changes may be greater than those caused by damage. Furthermore, especially in the case of buildings, understanding the interaction between structural and non-structural elements may require a very advanced level of engineering analysis that can lead to unsustainable timing and economic resources. In this context, the use of machine learning techniques may be very useful to correctly remove the effects of temperature and promptly and effectively assess changes in structural dynamics.

In this work it was decided to implement an artificial neural network for the normalization of monitoring data from a real structure. In detail, the effectiveness of this approach has been demonstrated by analyzing data from the monitoring of a 10-storeys r.c. building; the adopted methodology permitted to detect changes in eigenfrequencies induced by minor retrofit works carried out on the building structural joints. For the case at hand, the retrofit works contributed to increasing its structural performance and the slight variation in the structural dynamics is not cause of concern. However, it is important to note that, if there had been a variation of the same magnitude due to the occurrence of structural damage or material degradation, without an effective data normalization strategy, the variation could not have been detected by the VB-SHM system.

REFERENCES

[1] Jin, C., Jang, S., Sun, X., Li, J., & Christenson. R. (2016). Damage Detection of a Highway Bridge under Severe Temperature Changes Using Extended Kalman Filter Trained Neural Network. *Journal of Civil Structural Health Monitoring 6 (July): 545–60.* https://doi.org/10.1007/s13349-016-0173-8.

[2] Xia, Y., Chen, B., Weng, S., Ni, Y. Q., & Xu. Y. L. (2012). Temperature Effect on Vibration Properties of Civil Structures: A Literature Review and Case Studies. *Journal of Civil Structural Health Monitoring 2 (May).* https://doi.org/10.1007/s13349-011-0015-7.

[3] Peeters, Bart, & Guido De Roeck. (2001). One-Year Monitoring of the Z24-Bridge: Environmental Effects versus Damage Events. *Earthquake Engineering & Structural Dynamics - EARTHQUAKE ENG STRUC DYNAM 30 (February): 149–71.* https://doi.org/10.1002/1096-9845(200102)30:23.0.CO;2-Z.

[4] Clinton, J., S. B., Heaton, T., & Favela. J., (2006). The Observed Wander of the Natural Frequencies in a Structure. *Bulletin of the Seismological Society of America 96 (March): 237–57.*

[5] Mikael, A., Gueguen, P., Bard, P. Y., Roux, P., & Langlais. M. (2013). The Analysis of Long-Term Frequency and Damping Wandering in Buildings Using the Random Decrement Technique. *Bulletin of the Seismological Society of America 103 (March).* https://doi.org/10.1785/0120120048.

[6] Arezzo, D., Regni, M., Carbonari, S., Gara F. & Daniele Zonta, "Effect of Environmental Conditions on the Modal Response of a 10-Story Reinforced Concrete Tower", Shock and Vibration, vol. 2018, Article ID 9476146, 16 pages, 2018. https://doi.org/10.1155/2018/9476146.

[7] Saisi, A., Gentile, C., & Guidobaldi. M., (2015). Post-Earthquake Continuous Dynamic Monitoring of the Gabbia Tower in Mantua, Italy. *Construction and Building Materials 81 (April): 101–12.* https://doi.org/10.1016/j.conbuildmat.2015.02.010.

[8] Giordano, Pier Francesco, Filippo Ubertini, Nicola Cavalagli, Alban Kita, & Maria Masciotta. (2020). Four Years of Structural Health Monitoring of the San Pietro Bell Tower in Perugia, Italy: Two Years before the Earthquake versus Two Years After. *International Journal of Masonry Research and Innovation 5 (December): 445–67.* https://doi.org/10.1504/IJMRI.2020.111797.

[9] Ramos, L.F., L. Marques, P.B. Lourenço, G. De Roeck, A. Campos-Costa, & J. Roque. (2010). Monitoring Historical Masonry Structures with Operational Modal Analysis: Two Case Studies. *Special Issue: Operational Modal Analysis 24 (5): 1291–1305.* https://doi.org/10.1016/j.ymssp.2010.01.011.

[10] Rainieri, C., Gargaro, D., & Fabbrocino, G. (2015). Statistical Tools for the Characterization of Environmental and Operational Factors in Vibration-Based SHM. *Conference Proceedings of the Society for Experimental Mechanics Series 7 (January): 175–84.* https://doi.org/10.1007/978-3-319-15230-1_16.

[11] Reynders E, Wursten G, & De Roeck G. Output-only structural health monitoring in changing environmental conditions by means of nonlinear system identification. *Structural Health Monitoring. 2014;13(1):82-93.* https://doi.org/10.1177/1475921713502836.

[12] Avendaño-Valencia, Luis David, & Eleni N. Chatzi. 2020. "Multivariate GP-VAR Models for Robust Structural Identification under Operational Variability." *Probabilistic Engineering Mechanics 60 (April): 103035.* https://doi.org/10.1016/j.probengmech.2020.103035.

[13] Arezzo, D., Regni, M., Carbonari, S., & Gara F. (2019). An integrated permanent dynamic monitoring system of a tall building in central Italy. *In: 8th IOMAC - International Operational Modal Analysis Conference, Proceedings. p. 663-669, International Operational Modal Analysis Conference (IOMAC), ISBN: 978-840904900-4, Copenhagen, Denmark, 13-15 May 2019.*

[14] Markova, M. (2019). Foreign Exchange Rate Forecasting by Artificial Neural Networks. *AIP Conference Proceedings. Vol. 2164.* https://doi.org/10.1063/1.5130812.

[15] Baum, Eric B., & David Haussler. (1989). What Size Net Gives Valid Generalization? *Neural Computation 1 (1): 151–60.* https://doi.org/10.1162/neco.1989.1.1.151.

[16] Bailey, David L., & Donna Thompson. (1990). Developing Neural-Network Applications. *AI Expert 5 (9): 34–41.*

[17] Haykin, Simon. (1998). Neural Networks: A Comprehensive Foundation. *2nd ed. USA: Prentice Hall PTR.*

[18] Beagle, M., Hagan, M., & Demuth, H. (2016). Neural Network Toolbox: User's Guide. *The MathWorks, Inc., Natick, MA.*

9th International Operational Modal Analysis Conference
iomac
July 3 - 6, 2022
Vancouver, Canada

INITIAL RESULTS FROM THE CONTINUOUS MONITORING CAMPAIGN OF A WOODEN FRAME SPECIMEN

Liga Gaile[1], Sandro Amador[2], Rune Brincker[3]

[1] Associate Professor, Riga Technical University, Institute of Structural Engineering, Liga.gaile_1@rtu.lv.

[2] Assistant Professor, Technical University of Denmark, Department of Civil and Mechanical Engineering, sdio@byg.dtu.dk.

[3] Rune Brincker, Brincker Monitoring, rune@brincker-monitoring.com.

ABSTRACT

Robust elimination of the environmental and operational variability from monitored vibration properties is essential for accurate vibration-based damage detection in civil engineering structures. This study uses the two-story wooden frame model of a shear building placed in real ambient conditions to extract natural frequencies of the structure by means of automated operational modal analysis. Further, input-output and output-only environmental models based on multiple linear regression and principal component analysis are developed to remove environmental influences from the identified frequency time series. This study aims to assess the robustness and performance of those methods in detecting damage and structural changes in civil structures exposed to highly variable environmental and operational conditions. The initial results show the superiority of the principal component analysis for modelling environmental effects and damage detection under challenging environments.

Keywords: Vibration-based monitoring, Operational and environmental factors, Damage detection

1. INTRODUCTION

The community of specialists in Structural Health Monitoring (SHM) still seeks an optimal and robust solution to remove variable operational and environmental factors (EOV) on modal parameter estimates [1]. It is well known that these factors can mask changes in modal parameters when they are used as damage indicators in a vibration-based SHM campaign and, therefore, mislead the condition assessment of the monitored structure. This is especially relevant for the civil engineering structures like buildings and bridges, which are generally exposed to varying environmental conditions.

Various environmental and operational factors influence the variability of the frequencies. Among those, the temperature is usually the dominant cause, as verified, for instance, in [2]. Different input-output [3] and output-only [4] environmental models are proposed and tested already on large-scale structures [5]. Nevertheless, most studies on frequency variability are performed in temperatures predominantly above and slightly below 0° C.

This paper continues the study on the performance of the Multiple Linear Regression models (MLR) and the Principal Component Analysis (PCA) in damage detection, which was previously investigated using the experimental specimen - a wooden pole placed in ambient conditions [6]. This study aims to assess the sensitivity of these methods in terms of modelling the varying ambient and operational conditions and detecting damages – which were deliberately added as simulated frequency variation.

This was conducted with a 2-storey timber frame that has been chosen as the object of the study. Although the monitoring campaign is planned to be carried out over a complete seasonal cycle (1 year), the initial results show the superiority of the PCA model over the MLR model in modelling environmental effects and damage detection under challenging environments.

The experimental model is located on the outskirts of the capital of Latvia, Riga. Its location and dimensions were chosen to approximate the study object to real conditions and modal parameters typical for medium-height buildings while allowing the addition of damages with increasing severity levels in a controlled manner. Experimental data is gathered during the autumn and winter of the temperate climate zone 4.5km from the Baltic seacoast, ensuring a challenging environment, including temperatures well below 0° C.

2. METHODOLOGY

2.1. Frequency identification, quality assessment of measurements and damage simulation

For frequency identification is used a robustified version of the Eigensystem Realization Algorithm (ERA), which is adapted for Operational Modal Analysis (OMA) purposes [7]. This algorithm is a time-domain approach and is included in the Matlab OMA toolbox developed by R. Brincker [8] that was used for this study.

Since the test model has a finite number of degrees of freedom and the approximate natural frequencies of the vibrations are known in advance (two sets of three rather closely spaced modes), the singular values in the reduced SVD matrix are adjusted accordingly.

The chosen strategy is to use all the measurements regarding its quality for identification purposes. Nevertheless, only those time series where all of the six modes were identified successfully were used for further analysis and included in the building of environmental models. It constitutes 77% of the total possible continuous data, including technical interruption periods (see section 3 for more information).

The model is planned to monitor for a full year before structural modifications are introduced in order to assess the effectiveness of damage detection models. Therefore, in initial investigations, time-dependent damage processes are simulated as additional changes in the first lateral bending mode and first torsional mode frequency. Damage approximately simulates the degradation effect in a lateral direction of one of the frame haunch elements. Then changes in the frequency are expected in the lateral direction and torsional one. The longitudinal frequency will not be considerably affected.

2.2. Environmental models

In this study, two environmental models were built using the data for the six identified frequencies of the wooden specimen. i) Multiple linear regression model, and ii) Principal component analysis.

Frequency data are split in the proportion of 70/30 between the training and test set. Therefore, the model is built on data from 10.11.2021 - 06.02.2022. This is a winter period with highly variable climatic conditions comprising sharp temperature fluctuations, small temperature fluctuations in some periods, both positive and negative temperatures, snow and rain precipitation, as well as dry periods and wind gusts up to 20 m/s and windless periods.

2.2.1. MLR model

Multiple linear regression is used to explain the relationship between dependent variables, in this case, frequencies, and several independent variables, e.g. ambient metrological variables, that do not have too high a mutual correlation. In practice, Pearson's correlation coefficient should be less than 0.6 [9] between independent variables. MLR model is an input-output model that considers only one frequency at a time, and it is defined as:

$$\boldsymbol{Y_n} = \boldsymbol{X_n \beta_n} + \boldsymbol{\varepsilon_n} \tag{1}$$

$$\boldsymbol{Y_n} = \begin{bmatrix} y_1 \\ y_2 \\ \vdots \\ y_m \end{bmatrix}, \boldsymbol{X_n} = \begin{bmatrix} 1 & x_{11} & \cdots & x_{1k} \\ 1 & x_{21} & \cdots & x_{2k} \\ \vdots & \vdots & \vdots & \vdots \\ 1 & x_{m1} & \cdots & x_{mk} \end{bmatrix}, \boldsymbol{\beta_n} = \begin{bmatrix} \beta_0 \\ \beta_1 \\ \vdots \\ \beta_k \end{bmatrix}, \boldsymbol{\varepsilon_n} = \begin{bmatrix} \varepsilon_1 \\ \varepsilon_2 \\ \vdots \\ \varepsilon_m \end{bmatrix}.$$

where $\boldsymbol{Y}$ denotes the time series vector of a dependent variable (frequencies), n the number of the vibration modes under consideration, m the total number of measurements, $\boldsymbol{X}$ the matrix of meteorological variables (time series as column vectors), $\boldsymbol{\beta}$ the regression coefficient vector, $\boldsymbol{\varepsilon}$ – residuals vector and k the number of independent predictors.

2.2.2. PCA model

PCA method converts a set of correlated variables into a set of uncorrelated variables through an orthogonal transformation [10]. In this study, each of the frequency-time series f_1 to f_6 is mean-centred, then calculated covariance matrix and performed its eigendecomposition on the frequency training set. Obtained eigenvalues and eigenvectors are often known as variances, and component loadings or PC components allow the original time series to be reconstructed using the full set of data. PCA produces the same number of principal components (PC) as there are features - time series in the training dataset. Reconstruction can be done utilizing a different number of principal components. The variance of the residuals between identified data and PCA fitted data considerably changes if structural damage occurs at some point in the test data. This approach was successfully applied to wooden pole short period testing [6].

In this study error between fitted and actual data is given as Root Mean Squared Error (RMSE) time series across all the frequencies for a relevant number of PC components used:

$$E_{RMS}^{m} = \sqrt{\frac{\sum_{i=1}^{N}(\boldsymbol{f}_i - \widehat{\boldsymbol{f}_i})^2}{N}} \tag{2}$$

where m is the number of PC components considered, N is the number of frequency time series, $\boldsymbol{f}_i$ denotes identified frequency time series and $\widehat{\boldsymbol{f}_i}$ designates fitted time series using PCA model.

3. MONITORING CAMPAIGN AND TEST SET-UP

The monitoring campaign was initiated in late autumn on 10.11.2021. It is planned to perform continuous monitoring for at least one year. The initial assessment is done for the time period of 10.11.2021. to 16.03.2022 covers the specimen's dynamic response to ambient conditions through the whole winter and the beginning of the spring.

The monitored structure is a two-storey shear frame building model with a plan dimension of 705 mm x 584 mm and an overall height of 1.2m placed in natural ambient environmental conditions (see Figure 1). The primary materials used for the model are 15 mm x 15 mm timber slats for the columns and haunches and 4 mm thick fibreboard for slab imitation. Materials and structure are chosen in a way that expected fundamental frequencies coincide with the typical frequencies of medium-rise buildings. Typical frequencies are summarized in the [11]. Therefore, it is ensured not only real environmental conditions for the experiment like temperature or humidity but also the characteristic response to vibration sources like traffic and wind. The model is placed 10 m from the village's access road. A detachable roof shields it in the winter season, ensuring that no extra mass due to snow is added to the frame slabs. However, the roof did not prevent snow concentration on the slabs after heavy snowfalls. The added snow was removed as soon as possible. This action is illustrated in Figure 1.

The sensors used for the measurements are six Dytran IEPE piezoelectric accelerometers with a built-in Faraday shield for electrostatic noise immunity. The sensors are hermetically sealed (model DY 3191A1) with a sensitivity of 10V/g. Operation range -51°C to 121°C. Dynamic signal analyzer DT9857E with an output range of ±10 V to the sensors is connected by 15m polyurethane, 2-pin(F) signal cables. Sensors are placed at the corners of the three joints in two horizontal directions. As each sensor's weight is approximately 800g, a balancing mass of 1.6kg was attached to the specimen corners without sensors to confer more stability to the structural system.

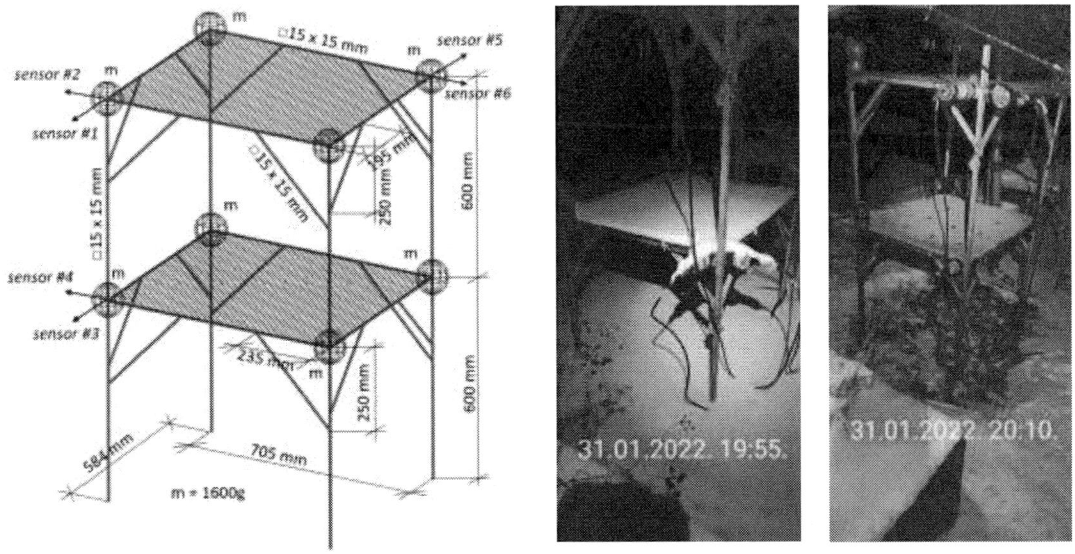

Figure 1. Left: Scheme of the model. Middle: Photo of the experimental model after snowfall with winds. Right: Photo of the experimental model after extra snow load is removed

Measurements are performed continuously with a sampling frequency of f_s = 400Hz. A few short-term interruptions of measurements have occurred during the monitoring campaign so far. It was mainly due to the failures of the system's robustness, e.g. software error or power shortage. Meteorological data (hourly mean), e.g. temperature, snow layer thickness on the ground, precipitation in mm and wind direction in degrees, are obtained from a nearby meteorological station. The test specimen is generally sheltered from the wind in a direction range of approximately 315 to 10 degrees.

The recorded accelerations were divided into time series containing 30min of vibration response data. These time series were subsequently detrended, bandpass filtered, and then passed as primary data to the ERA algorithm to identify the first 6 vibration modes of the wooden frame specimen. Identification is carried out in two steps. First, the band passed the first three closely spaced modes, performed identification and then repeated filtering and identification for the second set of closely spaced modes.

4. RESULTS

4.1. Environmental conditions and identified frequencies

During the observation period from November to March, air temperature fluctuated from the -20.8 C° to the +9.72 C°. Different temperature fluctuation regimes were observed: 1) mainly positive temperatures, 2) mainly negative temperatures, 3) temperatures close to 0 degrees, and 4) abrupt changes between positive temperatures during the day and negative temperatures at night. Prolonged periods of snow precipitation were observed three times throughout the monitoring campaign. Together with successfully identified six frequencies, the temperature time series are illustrated in Figure 2.

As expected from the assessment prior to this experiment, two sets of the closely spaced frequencies were identified: lateral f_1, longitudinal f_2 and torsional f_3 frequencies for the first bending and torsional mode, as well as lateral f_4, longitudinal f_5 and torsional f_6 frequencies for the second bending and torsional mode, respectively.

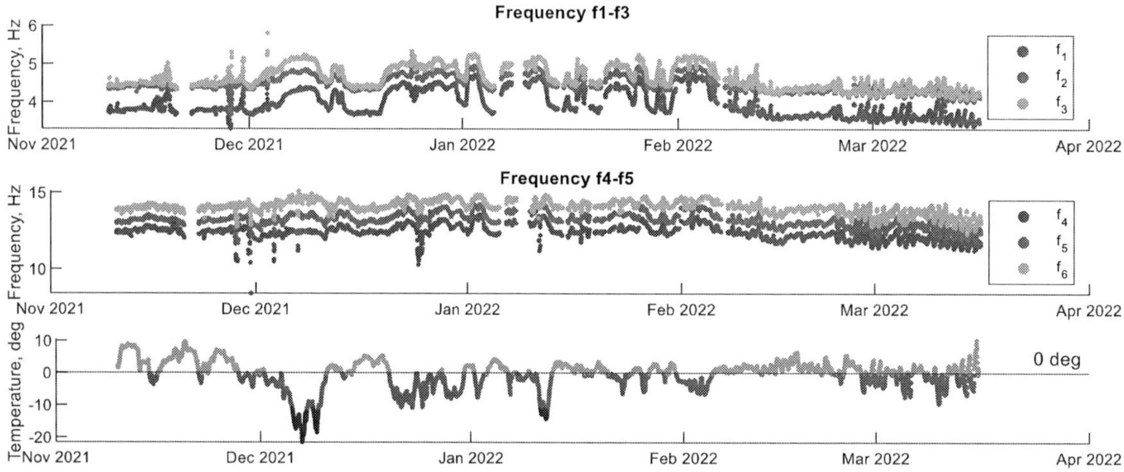

Figure 2. Time evolution of the identified frequencies every 30min and half-hourly mean temperature data.

The visually identifiable outliers in frequencies time series are explained by a change of the modal mass due to the snow on the platforms. When the platform was cleaned from snow, the frequencies returned to the normal regime. These outliers are left in the data for further analysis to evaluate different environmental model effectivity when noisy data are passed to the model creation.

In order to analyze the dependence between ambient condition variation and identified frequencies as well as to examine the possible multicollinearity of independent variables for MLR model, Pearson's correlation coefficients are computed. This measures the linear correlation between two variables [10]. Results are presented in Table 1. Data split between temperatures <-2 C°/ -2 ≤ 0 ≤2 C°/ >2 C° are respectively 23.1/ 45.3% / 31.69% of total data.

Table 1. Pearson's correlation coefficients between ambient variables and frequencies

Mode/ Ambient variable	Temperature			Humidity	Snow thickness on the ground	Precipitation	Wind direction
	<-2 C°	-2 ≤ 0 ≤2 C°	>2 C°				
f_1	-0.23	-0.39	+0.01	+0.13	+0.33	+0.01	+0.18
f_2	-0.37	-0.42	-0.01	+0.15	+0.45	+0.01	-0.23
f_3	-0.42	-0.41	-0.02	+0.17	+0.52	+0.02	-0.25
f_4	-0.06	-0.31	+0.16	+0.32	+0.08	-0.02	-0.10
f_5	-0.23	-0.36	+0.04	+0.27	+0.22	-0.02	-0.15
f_6	-0.32	-0.30	-0.02	+0.32	+0.39	+0.03	-0.17

Table 1 reveals complex relationships between frequencies and ambient variables and shows different dynamic responses at positive, negative and around 0 temperatures for different frequencies. This indicates the potential difficulties in successful modelling of frequencies with the MLR model only by considering ambient variables as independent variables. Examination of frequency distribution histograms also indicated at least two different behaviours under the ambient temperature changes. Especially it is prominent in the first bending and torsional modes.

Frequencies time series amongst themselves are highly correlated. Normalized linear correlations between identified frequencies were found to be in ranges from +0.69 (for f_3 and f_4) to the +0.96 (between f_1 and f_2; f_2 and f_3; f_1 and f_3).

4.1.1. *MLR model results*

The correlations summarized in Table 1 do not show pronounced multicollinearity of any ambient parameters. Therefore, for MLR model creation, the independent variables used are temperature, humidity, snow thickness on the ground, and wind direction. Precipitation data does not have any linear correlation with frequencies; therefore, it is left out. Due to the signs of frequency nonlinear behaviour under the ambient temperature, as expected, MLR model just using those parameters is not suitable as an environmental model for this case.

The removal or damage in one of the frame haunch elements mainly reduces global stiffness in one direction, and the perpendicular vibration mode will not be significantly affected, as verified by finite element calculations. Therefore, the solution proposed is to add one more predictor, namely, the frequency of perpendicular direction compared to the mode under consideration. This potentially allows for identifying damage from the growth of the amplitudes of errors between predicted and actual frequency data (Figure 3). The damage of the frame haunch is simulated as an addition of a non-periodic function to the first mode frequency f_1 time-series after the measurement point 4200. This damage was in the form of a coefficient multiplied by the cube-root of time as well as added normally distributed noise. Simulated change due to damage amounts to a maximum of 3% of the f_1 mean value. For the following sets: training, test and after the damage occurred set, is calculated the percentage of the outliers I_0. The threshold is set as three standard deviations of residual square error between true and fitted data in the test set between measurement points 3251 and 4200.

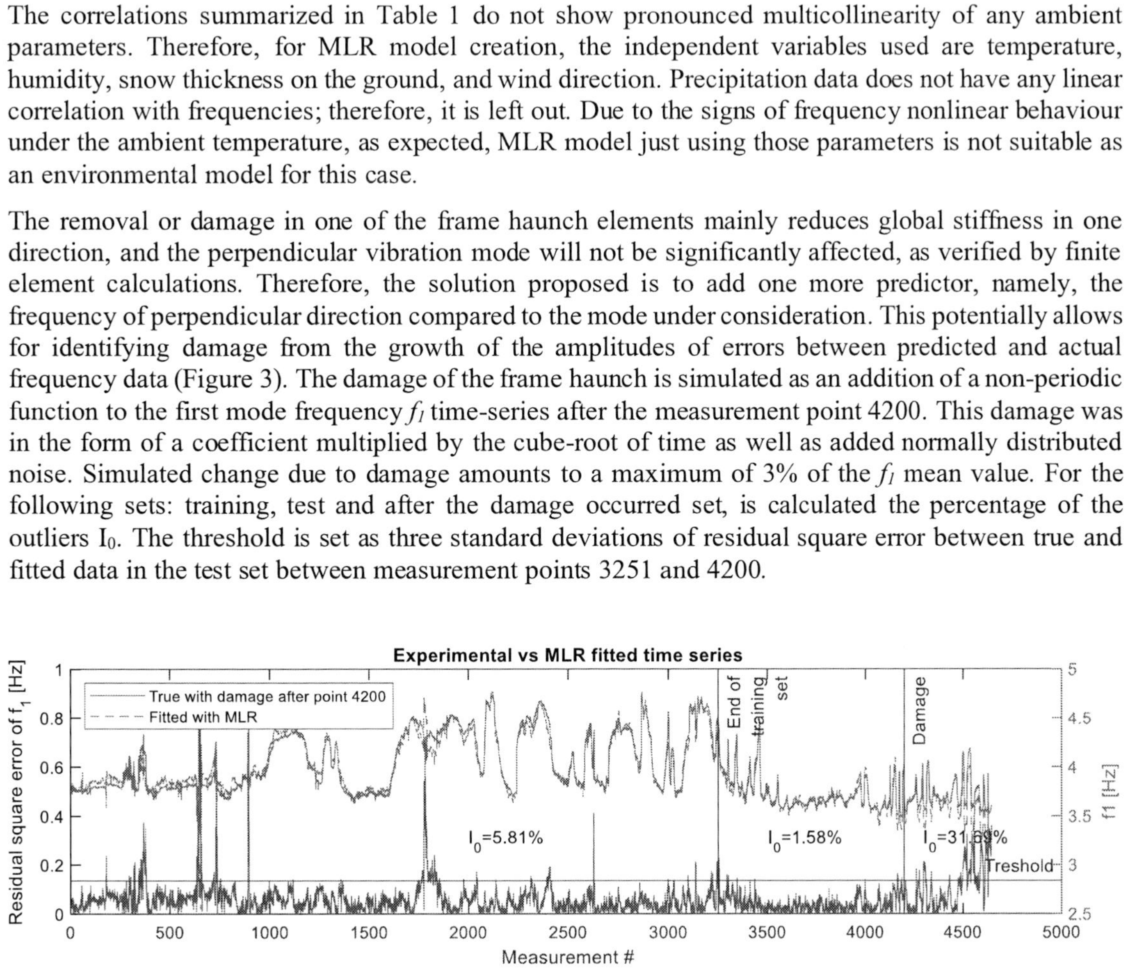

Figure 3. Frequency and residual square error between true data and MLR model fitted data

4.1.2. *PCA model results*

As a purely data-driven method, PCA does not require collecting ambient condition data such as temperature or humidity. When using this technique, it is assumed that the obtained time series that have maximal variances by the orthogonal transformation of the covariance matrix of frequency data are the principal components (PC). These components are mutually orthogonal. All six PC components explain 100% of the data, including the noise in the data and outliers due to the snow on the specimen platforms. In this case, the first component already explains 82.7% of the data variability, but the three components explain 97.9%.

Usually, overfitting by using all the PC's can be seen as a negative effect on time series analysis. Overfitted model does not perform well when new frequency changes in data after some measurement point occurs, like a new gradual function, step function or different character of noise on one or several frequencies. Nevertheless, if only some of the PC's are used, this change is an indication of possible structural damage and, therefore, damage sensitive feature. Figure 4 presents RMSE of the error between measured and PCA estimates across all six frequencies considering a different number of PC components. Threshold lines in plots are set as a value of RMSE three standard deviations in the test set. For each of the cases and data sets percentage of the outliers, I_0 is given in the plots. In this particular case overfitted model works perfectly also on the test set between measurement points 3251 and 4200. However, also five PC components show 100% outliers in the damage simulated region.

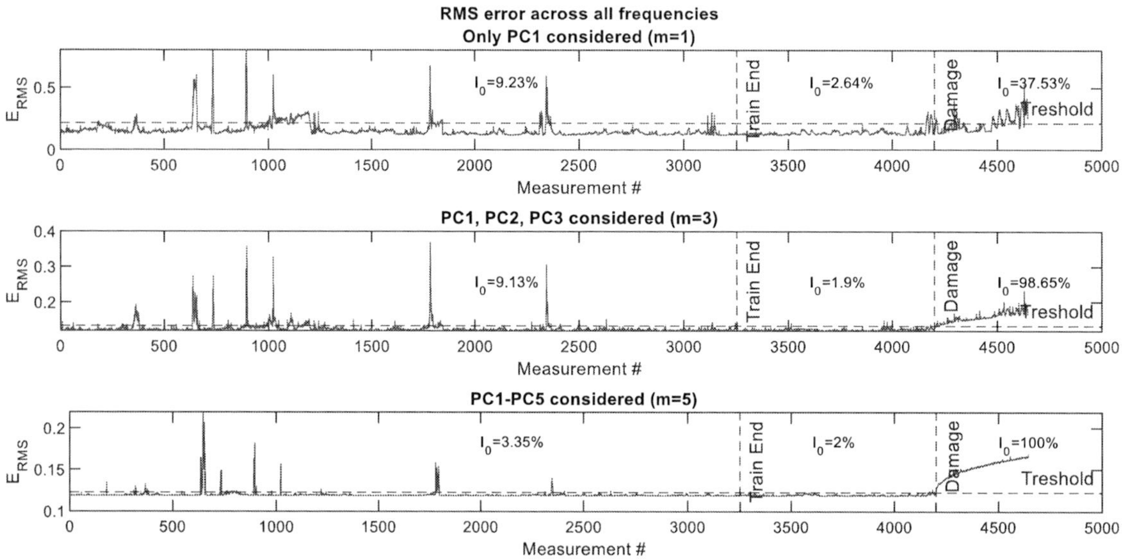

Figure 4. RMS error across all six frequencies between true data and PCA model fitted

Despite the fact that the frequency data has been noisy and not evenly sampled and applied small amplitude of frequency variation due to damage, PCA model using all six PC components perfectly discovered the start of the damage simulation point. Also, considering five or even four PC components, damage can be clearly identified, and outliers due to the platform's mass change can be recognized. Yet more, the use of only the first PC component gives a better outlier index I_0 than MLR approach.

5. CONCLUSIONS

This experimental study reveals the initial results of the planned long term SHM campaign by monitoring a two-storey shear frame wooden specimen that undergoes challenging environmental conditions, including different temperatures regimes i) sharp daily temperature fluctuations from positive to negative temperature ii) gradual daily temperature fluctuations in both negative and positive regions and iii) temperature fluctuations close to zero degrees.

Two methods, namely, MLR and PCA are chosen to model environmental and operational effects in this study because of their low level of man-made decision input.

The different temperature regimes are found to have an effect on the frequency-temperature relationship. The negative temperatures promote signs of non-linearities that could be related to different physical processes due to freezing and thawing, as well as snow precipitation.

For this reason, MLR does not perform as good as PCA for modelling the environmental effects. PCA relies on the relation between modes, and it is noticed that due to environmental condition changes, frequencies have high positive correlations between them. Despite the operational condition changes - mass on the platform due to short term snow load, simulation of the structural changes is shown as a distinguishable outlier in the PCA model. Nevertheless, PCA does not give information on which exactly frequencies damaged occurred as opposite to MLR approach.

Environmental and frequency data gathering of the specimen continues, and more refined investigations are expected.

ACKNOWLEDGEMENTS

This work has been supported by the European Regional Development Fund within the Activity 1.1.1.2 "Post-doctoral Research Aid" of the Specific Aid Objective 1.1.1 "To increase the research and innovative capacity of scientific institutions of Latvia and the ability to attract external financing, investing in human resources and infrastructure" of the Operational Programme "Growth and Employment" (No.1.1.1.2/VIAA/3/19/393).

REFERENCES

[1] Rainieri, C., & Magalhaes, F. (2017). Challenging aspects in removing the influence of environmental factors on modal parameter estimates. *Procedia Engineering*, *199*, 2244–2249. https://doi.org/10.1016/J.PROENG.2017.09.210

[2] Cornwell, P., Farrar, C. R., Doebling, S. W., & Sohn, H. (1999). Environmental variability of modal properties. *Experimental Techniques*, *23*(6), 45–48. https://doi.org/10.1111/J.1747-1567.1999.TB01320.X

[3] Laory, I., Trinh, T. N., Smith, I. F. C., & Brownjohn, J. M. W. (2014). Methodologies for predicting natural frequency variation of a suspension bridge. *Engineering Structures*, *80*, 211–221. https://doi.org/10.1016/J.ENGSTRUCT.2014.09.001

[4] Deraemaeker, A., Reynders, E., De Roeck, G., & Kullaa, J. (2008). Vibration-based structural health monitoring using output-only measurements under changing environment. *Mechanical Systems and Signal Processing*, *22*(1), 34–56. https://doi.org/10.1016/J.YMSSP.2007.07.004

[5] Diord, S., Magalhães, F., Cunha, Á., Caetano, E., & Martins, N. (2017). Automated modal tracking in a football stadium suspension roof for detection of structural changes. *Structural Control and Health Monitoring*, *24*(11), e2006. https://doi.org/10.1002/STC.2006

[6] Lysgaard, P., Amador, S. D. R., Nielsen, S. T., Katsanos, E., & Brincker, R. (2021). Vibration-based damage detection using input-output and output-only environmental models: A comparison. In *Conference Proceedings of the Society for Experimental Mechanics Series*. https://doi.org/10.1007/978-3-030-47634-2_5

[7] Pappa, R., Elliott, K. B., & Schenk, A. (1992). A consistent-mode indicator for the eigensystem realization algorithm. In *NASA Technical Memorandum 107607*. Dallas: American Institute of Aeronautics and Astronautics (AIAA). https://doi.org/10.2514/6.1992-2136

[8] Brincker, R., & Ventura, C. E. (2015). *Introduction to Operational Modal Analysis*. *Introduction to Operational Modal Analysis*. https://doi.org/10.1002/9781118535141

[9] Hair Jr, J. F., Black, W. C., Babin, B. J., & Anderson, R. E. (2019). *Multivariate Data Analysis Eight Edition*. *Cengage* (Vol. 49).

[10] Wei, W. W. S. (2019). *Multivariate time series analysis and applications*. John Wiley & Sons.

[11] Gaile, L., Sliseris, J., & Ratnika, L. (2020). Towards SHM of medium-rise buildings in non-seismic areas. In Cunha. A & Caetano E. (Eds.), *In Proceedings of the 10th International Conference on Structural Health Monitoring of Intelligent Infrastructure, SHMII*. Porto.

9th International Operational Modal Analysis Conference
iomac
July 3 - 6, 2022
Vancouver, Canada

OMA TESTS AND SETUP OF THE MODAL BASED SHM SYSTEM OF THE CIVITACAMPOMARANO BELFRY

Luigi Cieri[1], Ilenia Rosati[2], Giovanni Fabbrocino[3] and Carlo Rainieri [4]

[1] *Department of Biosciences and Territory, University of Molise, Campobasso, Italy, luigi.cieri@unimol.it.*
[2] *Department of Biosciences and Territory, University of Molise, Campobasso, Italy, ilenia.rosati@unimol.it.*
[3] *Department of Biosciences and Territory, University of Molise, Campobasso, Italy, giovanni.fabbrocino@unimol.it.*
[4] *Construction Technologies Institute, National Research Council of Italy, Naples, Italy; rainieri@itc.cnr.it.*

ABSTRACT

Protection and conservation of cultural and architectural heritage represent key problems worldwide and require advanced tools for structural assessment and monitoring under operational conditions as well as extreme loads. Vibration-based Structural Health Monitoring represents an attractive solution thanks to its little invasiveness and the ability to detect damage onset from the analysis of the global response of the structure without any prior information about the damage itself.

The present paper illustrates the results of preliminary OMA tests aimed at setting up the continuous modal-based Structural Health Monitoring (SHM) of the Civitacampomarano belfry. The tower is located close to a landslide which might affect its structural safety, so timely assessment of possible damage plays a critical role for its conservation and maintenance. The architecture of the SHM system and the technological solutions adopted for continuous monitoring of the vibration response of the tower under operational conditions are described in this paper, pointing out the role of Operational Modal Analysis for the remote assessment of the health state of the structure.

Keywords: Operational Modal Analysis, Structural Health Monitoring, Model Updating.

1. INTRODUCTION

Masonry towers are a very common structural typology in the Italian architectural heritage, and they mark the landscape of many historical city centers. Significant attention has been paid over the years about their dynamic and seismic behavior: in fact, masonry towers are often characterized by high seismic vulnerability, as also demonstrated by the heavy damage or collapses occurred after seismic events in the past [1].

Structural Health Monitoring (SHM) in combination with advanced automated Operational Modal Analysis (OMA) techniques [2] represents an attractive technological solution for timely and remote assessment of the health state and performance of civil structures under operational conditions [3]. When applied to historical masonry buildings and towers, it can also provide essential information for the optimization of structural interventions or to support setting up of appropriate maintenance programs [4]. Modal-based SHM is a global monitoring strategy which exploits acceleration data related to the operational response of the monitored structure to experimentally estimate and track the evolution over time of its modal properties (natural frequencies, damping, modal shapes). The basic idea behind modal-based SHM is that modal properties can be used as damage sensitive features, since damage is assumed to affect the mass and/or stiffness properties of the structure. In addition, the global nature of the approach allows to use even a limited number of sensors to estimate natural frequencies with sufficient accuracy and assess the structural condition from their variations. However, a relevant drawback of this approach is the sensitivity of modal properties and, in particular, natural frequencies to environmental factors, such as temperature or humidity, so that damage is often masked by daily or seasonal fluctuations of damage sensitive features due to environmental variables. As a consequence, long-term monitoring of modal parameters becomes essential to harness the full potential of modal-based SHM [5]. Setting up an effective modal-based SHM strategy is a challenging task, which requires an insight in the dynamic behavior of the monitored structures and appropriate consideration of technological aspects concerning sensor and measurement system selection to collect accurate raw data, effective data storage, and data processing aimed at tracking the patterns of the selected damage sensitive features in order to automatically detect anomalies in the structural response and issue appropriate warnings.

The present paper illustrates the results of preliminary OMA tests aimed at the implementation of a modal-based SHM system for the Civitacampomarano belfry. The tower is located close to a landslide which might affect its structural safety, so timely damage assessment is critical role for its conservation and maintenance. The architecture of the SHM system and the technological solutions adopted for continuous monitoring of the vibration response of the tower under operational conditions are also herein described, pointing out the role of Operational Modal Analysis for the remote assessment of the health state of the structure.

2. THE CIVITACAMPOMARANO BELFRY AND ITS MODAL-BASED SHM SYSTEM

Civitacampomarano is a small town located in the Molise region in Southern Italy. The bell tower (**Figure 1**) of the ruined church of Santa Maria Maggiore is located in front of the access staircase to the castle, on Largo Vincenzo Cuoco; its erection dates back to the end of the Eighteenth Century [6]. The bell tower is the only part of the ancient religious building that did not suffered significant damage after the earthquake occurred in the region in 1903.

The bell tower is built on a round arch in limestone and it is characterized by a quadrangular section. The structure has three levels with a terminal pyramidal cusp with a maximum height of 24.33 meters. Squared as irregular stone blocks characterize the outside masonry texture. The structure was accurately surveyed and no cracking pattern were identified. It is worth mentioning that in 1988 the bell tower underwent some structural interventions and extensive restoration works after the occurrence of damage affecting the bearing structure of the bell and the roof slab.

After the preliminary visual inspection and survey, the sensor layout for continuous modal-based SHM of the tower was defined. This operation was particularly complex because the preliminary visual inspection and survey revealed the presence of a number of signal polluting sources, such as the pathways of electrical cables powering the clock and the bells. Thus, sensor cable paths were defined in a way to avoid to cross those noise sources; moreover, special care was paid to ensure appropriate shielding to the sensor cables. The outcomes of preliminary inspections were also exploited to define the most appropriate locations of the accelerometers and the measurement equipment of the SHM system.

Figure 1. The Civitacampomarano bell tower.

In order to properly resolve the low-amplitude vibration response of the tower under operational conditions, high-sensitivity piezoelectric mono-axial accelerometers were installed. They were characterized by 10 V/g sensitivity, ± 0.5 g full scale range, and 0.1 to 200 Hz frequency bandwidth. The data acquisition system was characterized by 24-bit resolution, 102-dB dynamic range and on-board anti-aliasing filter.

The dynamic response of the bell tower is measured at three different levels (**Figure 2**) by ten accelerometers installed in bidirectional configuration in a way able to ensure observability of the fundamental bending and torsion modes of the belfry. In particular, a couple of accelerometers were installed at an elevation of 11.84 m in one corner of the plan section of the tower; other two couples of accelerometers were placed at an elevation 16.43 m in two opposite corners; the remaining sensors were placed also at opposite corners of the base of the cusp at an elevation of 18.77 m. All data were simultaneously acquired by the measurement system located at the base of the tower and acting as a server for local data processing and storage.

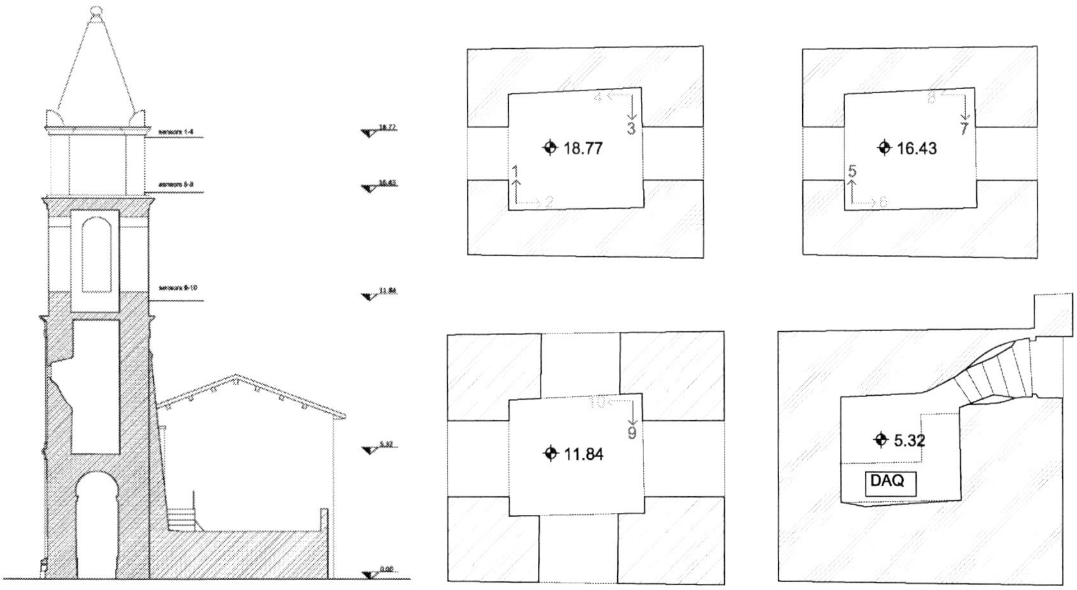

Figure 2. Section of the bell tower and sensors layout.

Sensors were screwed to steel plates mechanically anchored to the masonry walls. The sensor cables converge to the first level of the tower at an elevation of 5.32 m, where they are plugged to the PC-based data acquisition system (**Figure 3**). Acceleration signal are acquired at a sampling frequency of 100 Hz. Raw acceleration data are stored in a MySQL relational database to simplify interrogation and data transmission in case of seismic events or for the estimation of the fundamental modal parameters based on 3600 sec long time series of the ambient vibration response of the structure.

Figure 3. Data acquisition system (left) and installed sensors (right).

A number of records of the operational response of the tower have been collected and processed in order to check the functionality of the system and to carry out a preliminary estimation of the fundamental modal parameters. The main excitation sources were wind and bell swinging. Under such excitations, three fundamental modes could be identified, as discussed in the next section.

The continuously estimated modal parameters are going to be used for data-driven anomaly detection based on advanced statistical pattern recognition approaches [7], after output-only compensation of environmental influence [8]. In addition, the experimentally estimated natural frequencies and mode shapes will be used to update a numerical model of the belfry. The updated model will be in turn used to indirectly monitor relevant mechanical properties of masonry.

The modular nature of the SHM system makes easy the integration of additional sensors. If it will be deemed useful for model refinement or anomaly detection, the SHM system can be complemented with additional accelerometers, as well as with sensors of different type, such as temperature sensors, tiltmeters and displacement sensors.

In the current stage of implementation of the SHM system, vibration measurements are continuously collected and they can be automatically processed in order to estimate the fundamental modal parameters of the tower. Automatic OMA will be carried out by means of an algorithm previously developed by some of the Authors [9]. In addition, a procedure for continuous, automated model updating is going to be developed and integrated into the SHM system in order to indirectly track the evolution over time of the elastic modulus of masonry and detect possible damage.

The automatic and continuous model updating might also provide additional information about possible damage location and magnitude. The integration of model updating into vibration-based SHM system has been the object of significant research efforts. Particular attention has been paid in recent years to the possibility of using simplified models or meta-models to reduce the computational efforts associated with model updating. For instance, the suitability of this approach for the indirect monitoring of inherent properties of the monitored structure at varying temperature is discussed in [10]. In the context of the present application, an approach for continuous model updating based on meta-models is under investigation. If successful, it will be integrated into the SHM system, so that its data processing architecture can be schematically illustrated as shown in **Figure 4**. The resulting modal based SHM system will therefore be able to track the evolution over time of the modal parameters and, based on those estimates, continuously update the numerical model of the structure in order to indirectly monitor selected elastic uncertain parameters. The integration of advanced data-driven as well as model-based damage detection strategies in the same SHM system is expected to significantly enhance its reliability and robustness.

3. PRELIMINARY OMA RESULTS

The fundamental modal parameters of the tower were estimated by means of well-established OMA techniques operating in the frequency as well as time domain. Cross-correlation of the results provided by the different methods allowed to check their reliability

The applied OMA techniques [11] are the Frequency Domain Decomposition (FDD) [12], the Covariance Driven Stochastic Subspace Identification (Cov-SSI) [13], and the Second Order Blind Identification (SOBI) [14].

FDD is a non-parametric frequency domain OMA method based on the Singular Value Decomposition (SVD) of the Power Spectral Density (PSD) matrix. The resonance peaks are identified from the singular value plots through peak picking; the corresponding singular vector represent good estimates of the associated mode shapes.

Cov-SSI is a parametric time domain OMA method based on a state space description of the dynamic problem. The modal parameters are extracted from the state matrix and the output matrix of the structure estimated from measurements of the ambient vibration response of the structure.

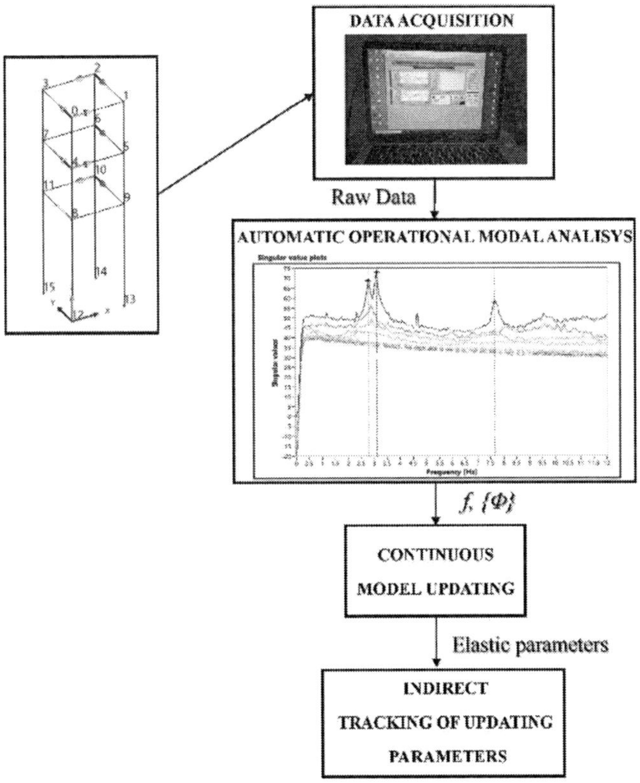

Figure 4. Illustration of the data processing scheme of the modal-based SHM system.

SOBI is a non-parametric time domain OMA method. It is a two-stage method, since it first provides an estimate of the mode shapes; natural frequencies and damping ratios are estimated afterwards, based on the estimated mode shape vectors.

Before estimating the modal parameters, a pre-treatment of the raw data was carried out to check the collected acceleration time series for validity [15]. After having verified the absence of anomalies in the data, PSDs were computed according to the Welch procedure by applying the Hanning window and a 66% overlap, and obtaining a frequency resolution of 0.01 Hz. The singular value plots obtained from SVD of the output PSD matrix are shown in **Figure 5**; **Figure 6** shows the complexity plots associated with the identified modes, which are normal. The first two modes are diagonal bending modes, while the third is a torsion mode (**Figure 7**).

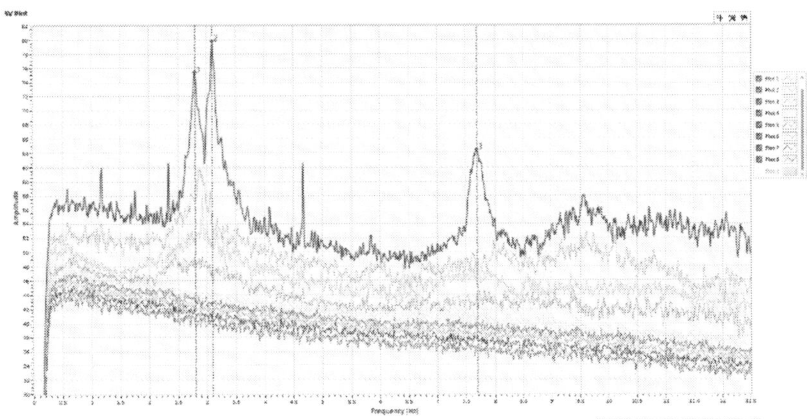

Figure 5. Singular value plots.

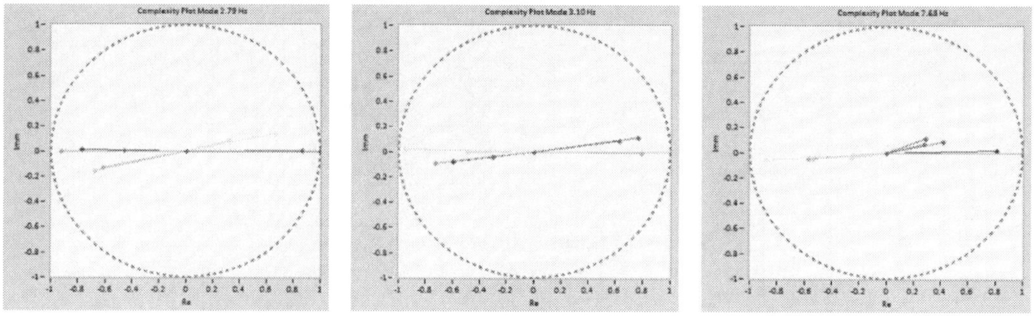

Figure 6. Complexity plots of modes I, II and III (from left to right).

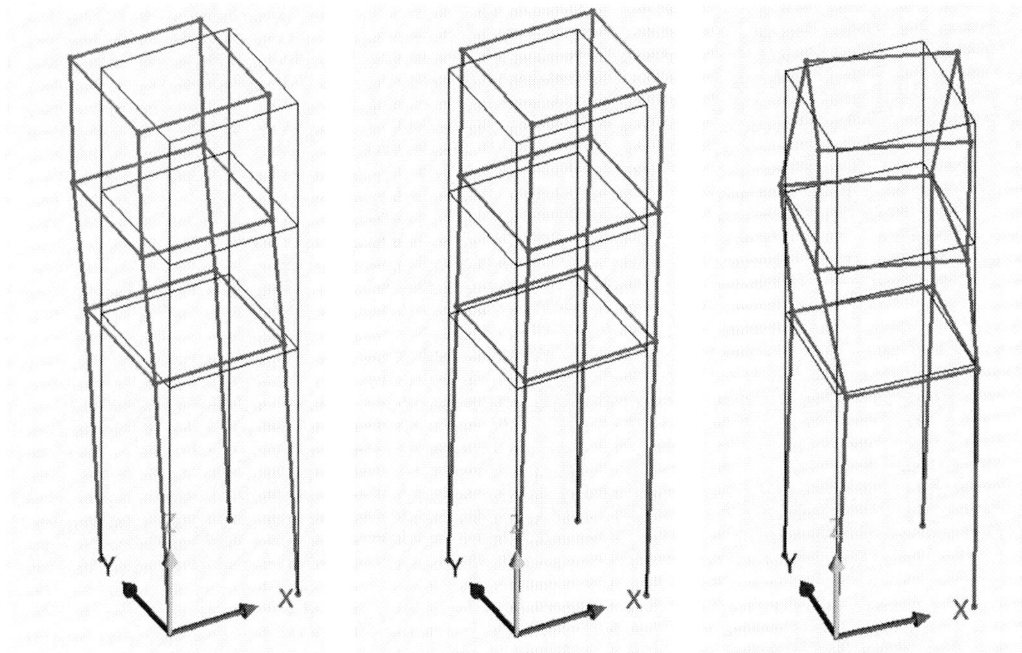

Figure 7. 3D plots of the identified mode shapes: mode I, II and III (from left to right).

The modal identification results obtained by the FDD method were confirmed by Cov-SSI and SOBI. The corresponding estimates are reported in **Table 1**, which confirms the reliability and accuracy of the obtained modal parameter estimates.

Table 1. OMA results.

Mode	Type	FDD	Cov-SSI		SOBI	
		f (Hz)	f (Hz)	ξ (%)	f (Hz)	ξ (%)
I	Transl.	2.79	2.79	1.27	2.79	0.95
II	Transl.	3.10	3.10	0.94	3.11	0.74
III	Torsional	7.69	7.68	0.96	7.70	1.33

4. CONCLUSIONS

The present paper illustrated the results of preliminary OMA tests aimed at setting up the continuous modal-based Structural Health Monitoring (SHM) of the Civitacampomarano belfry. The tower is located close to a landslide which might affect its structural safety, so timely assessment of possible damage plays a critical role for its conservation and maintenance. The architecture of the SHM system and the technological solutions adopted for continuous monitoring of the vibration response of the tower under operational conditions have been described, pointing out the primary role of Operational Modal Analysis in the process. The fundamental modes of the structure have been identified from measurements of its ambient vibration response, demonstrating the feasibility of a modal-based SHM approach for the structure. Automated OMA and finite element model updating procedures are going to be integrated to enhance the data processing capabilities of the system and to remotely identify possible damage under varying environmental and operational conditions. Those aspects are out of the scope of the present paper and they will be discussed in future publications.

ACKNOWLEDGEMENTS

The Authors gratefully acknowledge the financial support provided by the PRIN 2017 "SURMOUNT - Innovative Systems for the UpgRade of MasOnry structUres and Non sTructural elements" research project (n. 20173SJJF8) for the present research activities. The Authors also gratefully acknowledge the contribution of S2X s.r.l., which provided the software for dynamic data acquisition (http://www.s2x.it/en/s2-dda/) and OMA (http://www.s2x.it/en/s2-oma/) and technical support.

REFERENCES

[1] Gentile, C., & Saisi, A. (2018). Assessment of Environmental Effects for Vibration-Based Damage Detection of Historic Masonry Towers. *Proceedings*, 2(8).

[2] Rainieri, C., & Fabbrocino, G. (2010). Automated output-only dynamic identification of civil engineering structures. *Mechanical Systems and Signal Processing*, 24(3), 678-695.

[3] Cavalagli, N., Comanducci, G., Gentile, C., Guidobaldi, M., Saisi, A., & Ubertini, F. (2017). Detecting earthquake-induced damage in historic masonry towers using continuously monitored dynamic response-only data. *Procedia Engineering,* 199, 3416-3421.

[4] Saisi, A., Gentile, C., & Guidobaldi, M. (2015). Post-earthquake continuous dynamic monitoring of the Gabbia Tower in Mantua, Italy. *Construction and Building Materials*, 81, 101-112.

[5] Kita, A., Cavalagli, N., & Ubertini F. (2019). Temperature effects on static and dynamic behavior of Consoli Palace in Gubbio, Italy. *Mechanical Systems and Signal Processing*, 120, 180-202.

[6] Civerra, C., De Benedittis, G., Mustillo, I., & Tubito C. (2007). *Il Castello di Civitacampomarano.* Poligrafica Terenzi Editrice, Venafro, Italy (in Italian).

[7] Farrar, C.R., & Worden, K. (2012). *Structural Health Monitoring: a machine learning perspective*, John Wiley and Sons, Chichester, UK.

[8] Rainieri, C., Magalhaes, F., Gargaro, D., Fabbrocino, G., Cunha, A. (2019). Predicting the variability of natural frequencies and its causes by Second-Order Blind Identification. *Structural Health Monitoring*, 18(2), 486-507.

[9] Rainieri, C., & Fabbrocino, G. (2015). Development and validation of an automated operational modal analysis algorithm for vibration-based monitoring and tensile load estimation. *Mechanical Systems and Signal Processing*, 60-61, 512–534.

[10] Cabboi, A., Gentile, C., & Saisi A. (2017). From continuous vibration monitoring to FEM-based damage assessment: Application on a stone-masonry tower. *Construction and Building Materials*, 156, 252–265.

[11] Rainieri, C., & Fabbrocino, G. (2014). *Operational Modal Analysis of Civil Engineering Structures - An Introduction and Guide for Applications*. Springer, New York, USA.

[12] Brincker, R., Zhang, L., & Andersen, P. (2001). Modal identification of output-only systems using frequency domain decomposition. *Smart Materials and Structures*, 10, 441-445.

[13] Van Overschee, P., & De Moor, B. (1996). *Subspace identification for linear systems: Theory - Implementation – Applications*. Kluwer Academic Publishers, Dordrecht, The Netherlands.

[14] Rainieri, C. (2014). Perspectives of Second-Order Blind Identification for Operational Modal Analysis of Civil Structures. *Shock and Vibration*, Article ID 845106.

[15] Bendat, J.S., & Piersol, A.G. (1986). *Random Data: Analysis and Measurement Procedures*. John Wiley & Sons, New York, USA.

9th International Operational Modal Analysis Conference
iomac
July 3 - 6, 2022
Vancouver, Canada

ON LOCALIZED SENSORS IN A WIND TURBINE TOWER

Rune Brincker[1], Sandro Amador[2] and Johan Gjoedvad[3]

[1] Brincker Monitoring ApS, rune@brincker-monitoring.com.
[2] Assistant Professor, Technical University of Denmark, sdio@byg.dtu.dk.
[3] Sigicom AB, johan.gjodvad@sigicom.com.

ABSTRACT

In structural health monitoring (SHM) placement of the sensors is often a problem and the more we can do to simplify this the better. In this paper, we will consider the case where displacement, angle and curvature is measured in the transition piece of an offshore wind turbine instead of the traditional solution where sensors are distributed over different heights of the tower. The two cases are investigated with respect to estimation of the modal parameters in an SHM application.

Keywords: Structural health monitoring, localized sensors, wind turbine tower, modal parameters

1. INTRODUCTION

Structural health monitoring (SHM) of wind turbines are important for at least two reasons. First, it is important for optimization of the structures in the green energy production, and secondly, most of them will be offshore, and thus, difficult to reach.

It is not the scope of this paper to give a covering overview of the literature, but just to point to some main principles in SHM of wind turbines, let us mention Luengo et al 2016, [1] where SHM of wind turbines are treated from a statistical pattern recognition point of view, and Oliveira et al 2018, [2], where the problem is treated from an operational modal analysis (OMA) point of view.

In this paper, we will follow the ideas of reference [2], and discuss how a measurement system can be designed for offshore wind turbines obtaining maximum value for minimum investment.

The problem of obtaining information from wind turbine data is well illustrated in Tarpø et al 2021, [3] where a wind turbine has been equipped with a measurement system of the localized type that is to be considered in this paper.

Both in reference [2] and [3], OMA is used to extract information about the wind turbine from the operating response data. However, in these two cases, good results have been reached using OMA as described for instance in Brincker and Ventura, [10], but two different approaches are being used for the measurement system.

In [2] the classical wisdom has been followed where it is good practice to distribute the sensors over the structure, see for instance [10]. It makes sense to follow this principle, because if sensors are sitting closely around the same point, they tend to measure more or less the same signal, but if they are more distributed over the structure, we have more information about the mode shapes.

On the other hand, if SHM is going to be widely used on wind turbines, only the most effective systems that provide optimum information for a minimum investment will be used, because competition will be strong in this growing market.

The idea of the measurement system used in [3] is a so-called localized system where all sensors are placed in the transition piece. The reason why this is a good position for a measurement system is mainly that it is simple to mount and simple to maintain because you don't have to climb to higher levels inside the wind turbine tower in order to reach the sensors, and you minimize the amount of cables. The considered localized system has been developed by Sigicom, see [11], where the principal sensors are geophones. In this case the geophones has to be calibrated so that the influence of the natural frequency of the geophones can be removed, see Brincker et al [6], and signals can be integrated and/or differentiated to obtain both displacement, velocity and acceleration with quite low noise floors like described in Brandt and Brincker [9].

The scope of this paper is to consider if and why it is indeed a good idea to consider a localized measurement system instead of a more distributed measurement system following the conventional practice.

2. MEASUREMENT SYSTEMS

We are considering two measurement systems to acquire the operational response of wind turbine towers, a conventional system with distributed sensors, and a localized system where all sensors are mounted at the same section.

The conventional system is shown to the left in Figure 1. We are here assuming sensors in three levels, the lowest level assumed to be in the transition piece between the tower and the foundation, relative height at 0.4, and the next two systems is the relative heights 0.65 and 0.90. We assume that we need two sensors in the x-direction to measure torsion movements. We do that even though torsion modes are often not observed for wind turbines, because it is good practice to obtain the bending displacement in the x-direction as an average of the two sensors to get rid of possible mechanical torsion noise and to be able to check to what extend torsion is present.

With the conventional measurement system, we can define the following DOF's

(1) $$\mathbf{d}_1 = \{u_{x1}, u_{x2}, u_{x3}, u_{y1}, u_{y2}, u_{y3}\}^T$$

where u_{xn} and u_{yn} are the horizontal deflections in the x- and y- directions at the three levels n starting from the bottom. The corresponding signals are

(2) $$\mathbf{s}_1 = \{s_{x1}, s_{x2}, s_{y1}, s_{x3}, s_{x4}, s_{y3}, s_{x5}, s_{x6}, s_{y5}\}^T$$

and the relation between the signals and the DOF's can then be defined as

(3) $$\mathbf{s}_1 = \mathbf{T}_1\mathbf{d}_1$$

where $\mathbf{T}_1$ is a transformation matrix with rank 6.

The localized system is shown in Figure 1 to the right where four 3D sensors are mounted in the same section, normally at the transition piece between the tower and the foundation. The three components T (horizontal and perpendicular to the surface) , L (horizontal tangential to the surface), and V (vertical) are also defined in the Figure 1 for the sensor mounted in point 1. In this case we are also adding a vertical strain gauge at each 3D sensor with the component S. The corresponding signals are

$$\mathbf{s}_2 = \{s_{1T}, s_{1L}, s_{1V}, s_{1S}, s_{2T}, s_{2L}, s_{2V}, s_{2S}, s_{3T}, s_{3L}, s_{3V}, s_{3S}, s_{4T}, s_{4L}, s_{4V}, s_{4S}\}^T \quad (4)$$

The good question is now how we should define the DOF's. One way to do this is simply to say, that the section where the sensors are mounted is moving as a rigid body, and as result has only 6 DOF's, the three displacement components, and the three angles. But since in the case, we will only consider tower bending where we have no vertical displacement, we will not follow this approach. We will instead only use the four DOF's of the rigid body movement, the two x- and y-displacement and their corresponding angles. In order to achieve the same number of DOF's as for the conventional system, we also add in the bending curvature measured by the strain gauges. Thus, our 6 DOF's can be defined as

$$\mathbf{d} = \{u_x, u'_x, u''_x, u_y, u'_y, u''_y\}^T \quad (5)$$

where the quantities u' (angle) and u''_x (curvature) are defined by classical beam theory

$$u'_x = \frac{du_x(z)}{dz}; \quad u''_x = \frac{d^2u_x(z)}{dz^2} \quad (6)$$

and similar for the y-direction. Here is it important to note, that these DOF's will have different units, which is not allowed in case we will do OMA, because mode shapes must be dimensionless. One way to deal with the problem is to multiply by a length D so that all DOF's has the same unit

$$\mathbf{d}_2 = \{u_x, u'_xD, u''_xD^2, u_y, u'_yD, u''_yD^2\}^T \quad (7)$$

If we define D as the diameter of the tower and assume a slenderness ratio of the tower of 20, then the dimensionless diameter is 0.05. We can then define the relation between the signals and DOF's

$$\mathbf{s}_2 = \mathbf{T}_2\mathbf{d}_2 \quad (8)$$

where $\mathbf{T}_2$ as before is a dimensionless transformation matrix of rank 6.

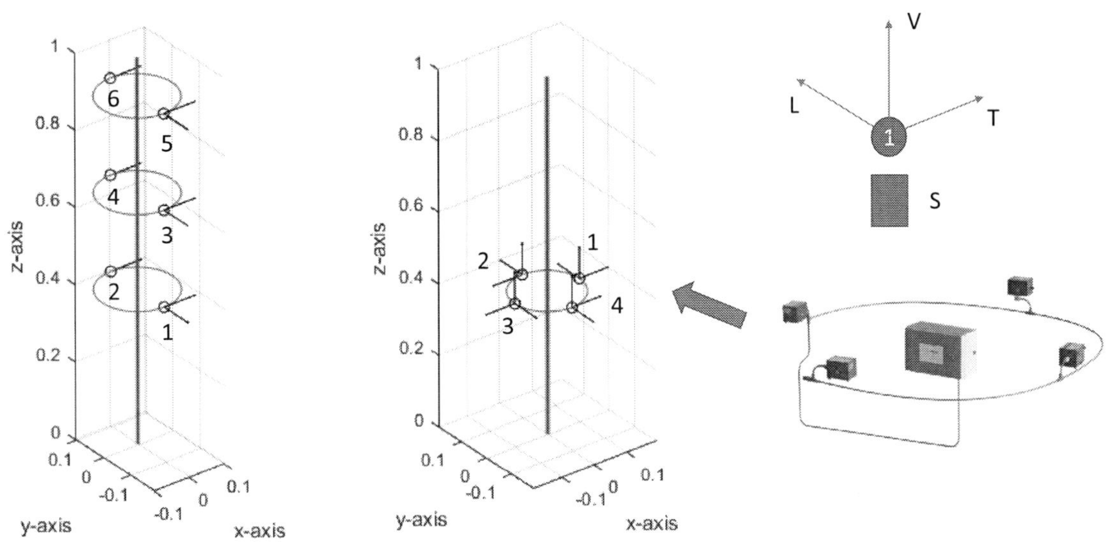

Figure 1. The two considered measurement systems. Left: The conventional system with sensors distributed over the height of the wind turbine tower. Middle: The localized sensor system mounted in the transition piece between the tower and the foundation. Right: The Sigicom SHM01 sensor system, see reference [11], developed for this kind of applications.

Before we leave this section it is worth considering one of the important reasons for using the localized system instead of the more conventional one.

If we had used a conventional system with only two sensors at each level like in [2], then if we loose a sensor, we also loose a DOF. Loosing a DOF might significant reduce the quality of the subsequent OMA, and this might be crucial for the SHM application.

Now our conventional system has a little more sensors than what is required to obtain the 6 DOF's in case all sensors are working. Mathematically this can be expressed by the fact that we can remove some rows in the transformation matrix $\mathbf{T}_2$ without loosing rank. We can loose any of the sensors in the x-direction because we have two sensors in this direction. But if we loose a sensor in the y-direction, then we loose rank, we loose a DOF, and obtain less accurate OMA results.

The special quality of the localized system is that we can loose any of the 16 sensors, and still be able to obtain the full number of DOF's. Mathematically this means, that we can remove any row in the transformation matrix $\mathbf{T}_2$ without loosing rank. The rank will remain 6 no matter what sensor we loose. We can simply continue our high quality SHM analysis, and replace the faulty sensor whenever we make a service visit for other reasons.

This is extremely important, because in future SHM applications, where the SHM system is a part of the design base that guaranties the reliability of the structure, the robustness of the measurement system is essential.

3. TOWER MODES

As we have just seen in the previous section, the information that we pick up in the DOF's are information about how the structure moves – mode shape information – and then also about the natural frequencies and the damping as it is well-known from general OMA principles, [10].

In this investigation we will concentrate on the first four bending modes of the tower, that is the first and the second fore-alt and side-side modes. Normally we would have to take the orientation of the rotor into account, because the fore-aft and the side-side modes are defined by the direction of the nacelle, so that fore-aft modes are moving the rotor back and fourth in the wind direction, and the side-side modes are moving the nacelle perpendicular to the wind.

However, it is not the scope of this paper to consider how the dominant modes are turning around with direction of the nacelle, like it has been done for instance in Tarpø et al [3], but just to investigate if we can estimate modal information from a localized measurement with the similar accuracy as when using a classically distributed measurement system.

Therefore, we will just assume a simple model for the four first tower modes, where we will use that these modes are mainly determined by the stiffness of the tower, and top mass. Neglecting the mass distribution in the tower, and assuming constant stiffness of the tower over the height, it means that the tower modes are just third order polynomials.

We assume a fixed support at the bottom of the tower, which introduce the conditions for the both the first order and the second order modes

$$z = 0: \quad \begin{cases} u = 0 \\ u' = 0 \end{cases} \tag{9}$$

For the first and second order modes we have the top conditions

$$z = 1: \quad \begin{cases} \text{First mode} & : u'' = 0 \\ \text{Second mode} & : u = 0 \end{cases} \tag{10}$$

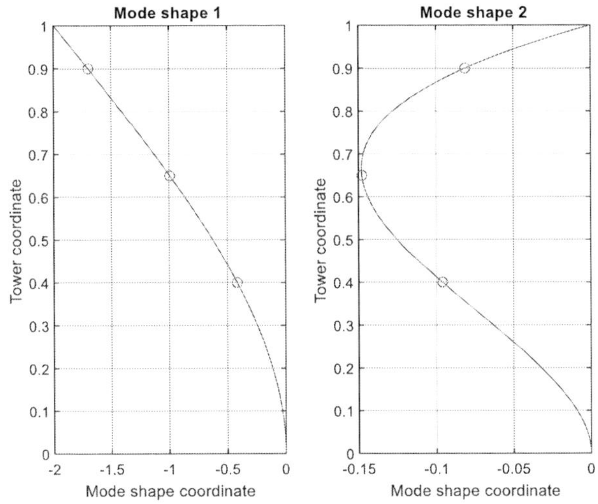

Figure 2. First and second order bending modes of a wind turbine tower modelled as a third order polynomial.

Table 1. Model parameters for the tower modes

Mode	1	2	3	4
Frequency [Hz]	0.33	0.4	2.1	2.7
Damping ratio	0.06	0.01	0.03	0.02

and we then achieve the mode estimates as shown in Figure 2 that correspond well with the mode shapes shown in [2].

Natural frequencies and damping ratios for the four modes are given in Table 1. Mode 1 is the first fore-aft mode which is know to have a relatively high damping, and mode 2 is relatively close to mode 1. Mode 3 is a fore-aft mode with somewhat lower frequency than the corresponding side-side mode which is often the cases due to difference in the nacelle inertial moments in the fore-aft and side-side directions.

4. SIMULATOIN

The responses for both systems are obtained using the following procedure

- Mode shapes for the DOF's as given by Eqs. (1) and (7)
- Mode shapes normalized to unit length
- The random DOF response simulated using the fftsim function in the OMA toolbox, [12] with white noise input
- Sensor signals obtained using Eqs. (3) and (8)
- Signals integrated 2 times to achieve acceleration signals using the principles in Brandt and Brincker [9].
- Noise added with an average (over the signals) signal-to-noise ratio of 60 dB

The signals were sampled with a sampling frequency of 7 Hz, and the total time length of the simulated data sets was about 3 quarters of an hour.

We have here used the scaling as defined by Eq. (7). We could have used some dimensionless additional scaling to the signals of the localized system, but since both the classical distributed system and the

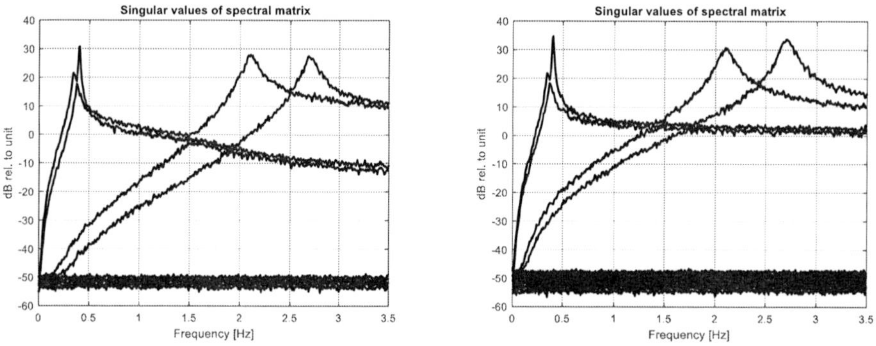

Figure 3. FDD plots according to Brincker et al [7] for the two cases. Left: distributed measurement system. Right: localized measurement system.

localized have around 7 to 8 in ratio between the largest and smallest standard deviations of the DOF's, nothing more was done concerning scaling.

The results of the simulated responses are shown in Figure 3. As we can see, there is a surprisingly little difference between the two plots. We can see that the main difference is that the conventional system gives us a bit more participation of the fore-aft modes.

5. IDENTIFICATION

The identification is performed using the enhanced frequency domain decomposition by Brincker et al [7,8] using a data segment size of 512.

One singular vectors were picked from each of the peaks representing the mode shapes, and the frequency and damping was then identified from the modal correlation functions in the time domain like described in Brincker et al [8]. The identified modes were then fitted to the empirical PSD's using the energy principle in Brincker et al [5] and the results are shown in Figure 4. Some of the modal fits show an underestimated energy, this is due to an underestimated modal coordinate using the FDD.

MAC values between theoretical mode shapes and estimated made shapes are shown in Figure 5. Results of frequency and damping are given in Table 2.

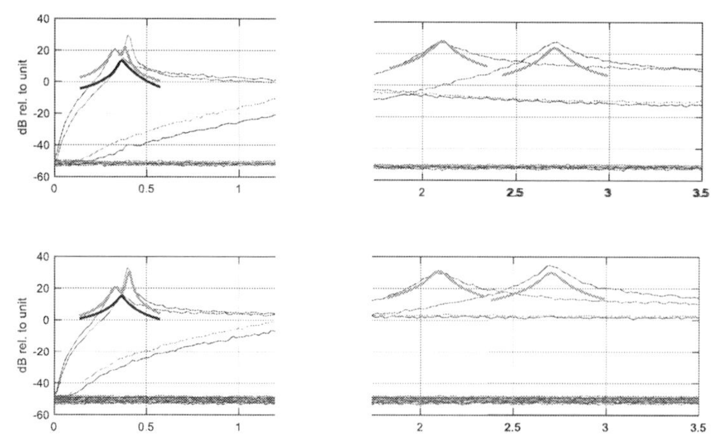

Figure 4. Identification of the four modes using the enhanced FDD. left: The first two tower modes. Right: the last two tower modes. Top: Results of using the distributed measurement system. Bottom: Results of using the localized measurement system.

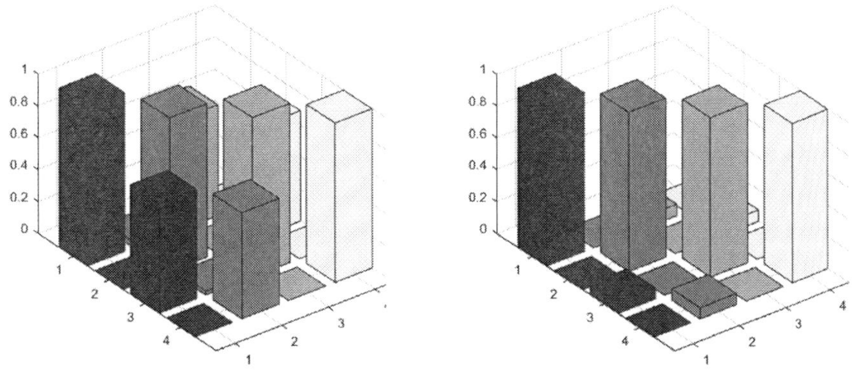

Figure 5. *MAC matrices for the two considered system. Left: MAC matrix for the distributed measurement system. Right: MAC matrix for the localized measurement system.*

Table 2. *Estimated modal parameters for the tower modes.*

Mode	1	2	3	4
Frequency [Hz], distributed system	0.3287	0.3817	2.1064	2.7028
Damping ratio, distributed system	0.0686	0.0292	0.0189	0.0145
Frequency [Hz], localized system	0.3335	0.4054	2.0991	2.7027
Damping ratio, localized system	0.0666	0.0160	0.0191	0.0164

6. DISCUSSION AND CONCLUSION

As it appears from the results, the OMA identification is more or less the same for the two systems. If we should declare a winner, the localized system is doing a bit better, that is accuracy of frequencies and damping ratios for mode 2, and MAC values due to larger off-diagonal elements for the distributed system.

In order to summarize the advantages of using the localized system we can conclude:

- Identificatoin uncertainty seem to be the same for the two systems
- Localized system is easier to mount and maintain
- Localized system can lose sensors and continue working, and any sensor can get lost – and replaced during scheduled service

One more very important advantage should be mentioned. That is the influence of tilt. Whenever a horizontal sensor is being tilted, its signal is getting disturbed by the gravity, and the influence can only be removed if the dynamic tilt, i.e. the angle given by the DOF u', is known, see Taarpø et el, [4]. The localized measurement system estimates this quantity, and thus, provides opportunity to remove the tilt. The conventional distributed system does not.

Finally we might ask: What if we compare a distributed system with two levels of sensors to a localized system where we have skipped the strain? In this case we will again have the same number of DOF's in the two measurement systems. Four displacement DOF's in the distributed system, and four DOF's in the localized system. What we learned from the present analyses indicate, that we will achieve similar results, but it is be further investigated.

REFERENCES

[1] Maria Martinez-Luengo, Athanasios Kolios, Lin Wang: Structural health monitoring of offshore wind turbines: A review through the Statistical Pattern Recognition Paradigm. Renewable and Sustainable Energy Reviews, Volume 64, October 2016, Pages 91-105.

[2] Gustavo Oliveira∗ , Filipe Magalhães, Álvaro Cunha, Elsa Caetano: Continuous dynamic monitoring of an onshore wind turbine. Engineering Structures, Vol 164, 1 June 2018, Pages 22-39.

[3] Marius Tarpø, Sandro Amador, Evangelos Katsanos, Mattias Skog, Johan Gjødvad and Rune Brincker: Virtual sensing and strain estimation on an offshore wind turbine using supervised learning. In Proceeding of COMPDYN 2021, Athens, Greece, 27—30 June 2021.

[4] Marius Tarpø, Bruna Nabuco, Ruben Boroschek, Rune Brincker: Tilt errors of translational accelerometers attached to dynamic systems with tilt motion caused by the system response. Journal of Sound and Vibration · January 2021.

[5] Rune Brincker, Sandro D. R. Amador, Martin Juul, and Manuel Lopez-Aenelle: Modal Participation Estimated from the Response Correlation Matrix. Shock and Vibration, Volume 2019.

[6] Rune Brincker, Thomas L. Lagö, Palle Andersen, Carlos Ventura: Improving the Classical Geophone Sensor Element by Digital Correction. In Conference Proceedings: IMAC-XXIII, 2005.

[7] Rune Brincker, Lingmi Zhang, Palle Andersen: Modal Identification from Ambient Responses using Frequency Domain Decomposition. Proceedings of the International Modal Analysis Conference (IMAC), San Antonio, Texas, USA, February 7-10, 2000.

[8] Rune Brincker, Carlos Ventura, Palle Andersen: Damping Estimation by Frequency Domain Decomposition. Brincker, R., Ventura, C. E., & Andersen, P. (2001). Damping Estimation by Frequency Domain Decomposition. In Proceedings of IMAC 19 februar 5-8, 2001, Hyatt Orlando, Kissimmee, Florida, 2001 (pp. 698-703).

[9] Anders Brandt, Rune Brincker: Integrating time signals in frequency domain – Comparison with time domain integration. Measurement, Volume 58, December 2014, Pages 511-519.

[10] Brincker and Ventura: Introduction to operational modal analysis. Wiley 2015.

[11] The Sigicom SHM01 sensor system, announced on the Sigicom webpage:
http://www.sigicom.com/shm/SHM01

[12] OMAtools, a Matlab toolbox by Rune Brincker. Available for download at:
http://www.brinckerdynamics.com/

9th International Operational Modal Analysis Conference
iomac
July 3 - 6, 2022
Vancouver, Canada

OPTIMAL SENSOR PLACEMENT FOR THE DYNAMIC MONITORING OF A HISTORICAL MASONRY CHURCH IN CENTRAL ITALY

Davide Arezzo [1], *Vanni Nicoletti* [2], *Sandro Carbonari* [3], *Fabrizio Gara* [4]

[1] Postdoc Researcher, Università Politecnica delle Marche, d.arezzo@pm.univpm.it.
[2] Postdoc Researcher, Università Politecnica delle Marche, v.nicoletti@staff.univpm.it.
[3] Associate Professor, Università Politecnica delle Marche, s.carbonari@staff.univpm.it.
[4] Full Professor, Università Politecnica delle Marche, f.gara@staff.univpm.it.

ABSTRACT

Italy is a seismic prone country with a great heritage of churches and historic masonry buildings that often suffer damage due to earthquakes. For buildings of high cultural value, the damaged structural systems are usually secured through immediate interventions, with the need of monitoring the evolution of damage in time up to the final restoration.

This paper presents some of the results of the research activities carried out on the church of Santa Maria in Via in Camerino, (central Italy), severely damaged by the 2016 Central Italy seismic sequence and secured through various interventions. In particular, a massive external retaining steel structure was built to prevent the collapse of the façade and, in the subsequent years, a static and dynamic monitoring system has been installed with the aim of monitoring the health status of the church and preventing the evolution of the kinematics triggered by the 2016 earthquake.

Ambient vibration tests have been performed on the church and its global dynamics has been identified by means of Operational Modal Analysis techniques. Also, a finite element model of the church has been developed, whose parameters have been optimised through the Particle Swarm Optimisation algorithm. Finally, starting from the results of the updated model, the sensor placement was optimised by employing the Effective Independence algorithm, in order to increase the efficiency of the monitoring system in tracking all the preliminarily identified modes.

Keywords: structural health monitoring, operational modal analysis, dynamic identification, cultural heritage, optimal sensors placement, particle swarm optimization.

1. INTRODUCTION

The key part of a Vibration Based Structural Health Monitoring (VB-SHM) system are sensors, and costs are largely influenced by the type and number of sensors to be installed, as well as the amount of data to be processed. Therefore, sensor number and position optimization are crucial in the design and implementation of an effective VB-SHM system [1]. Moreover, it is usually unnecessary to monitor all Degrees Of Freedom (DOF) of a structure because of the large amount of data to be acquired and processed. In this way, the Optimal Sensor Placement (OSP) can help to take decisions on how many and which DOF of a structure need to be monitored. Indeed, the OSP objective in a dynamic monitoring framework is that of finding the minimum number of DOF to be monitored to get enough information to describe the dynamic behaviour of the structure with good accuracy [2]. One of the first OSP applications was presented by Kammer in 1991 [3], where the optimization of the monitoring system for an orbiting space station is performed using the Effective Independence (EI) method. Successively, OSP has received considerable attention and, to date, several applications can be found in the literature. Heo et al [4] presented a kinetic energy optimization technique to obtain a higher signal-to-noise ratio to better identify modal shapes. In the work of Guo et al [5], a OSP performance index based on a genetic algorithm is presented. Flynn et al [6] proposed a Bayesian approach to minimize the type I and II error in measurements. Worden [7] and Li [1] presented review papers focusing on OSP in SHM, comparing many different algorithms; however, EI has proven to be a robust and simple method to apply. Moreover, differently from genetic algorithms, EI method does not rely on computationally intensive search techniques. In the work of Jiang et al. [8] a very useful numerical example is provided for the implementation of the EI algorithm.

The design of a VB-SHM system requires an in-depth knowledge of the dynamics of the structure to be monitored, but, usually, dynamic identification tests are carried out with a limited number of sensors, and the identified modal shapes may suffer from spatial aliasing. Performing a study to optimize the number and position of sensors based only on the identified modal components may not be effective. Finite Element Models (FEM) can substantially contribute to this preliminary phase, especially in the case of complex structures for which uncertainties on material characteristics and boundary conditions may be significant. Performing a Model Updating (MU) procedure in order to obtain a FEM that accurately represent the dynamics of the structure to be monitored is thus particularly important for the optimal positioning of sensors.

One of the main difficulties in the application of MU in the field of civil engineering is undoubtedly found in facing historical structures, which are characterized by an enormous complexity in terms of geometry, material properties, loads and boundary conditions, resulting in complex FEM that are difficult to validate. Some interesting works can be found in the literature dealing with the MU of historical masonry buildings [9-13]. MU of FEM is essentially based on the minimization of an error function that summarizes the distance between the dynamic behaviour of the model and that of the real structure. Also, the role of artificial intelligence algorithms in this field begun to emerge in recent years. In particular, a family of artificial intelligence algorithms, namely Swarm Intelligence (SI), seems to be very promising. SI is a family of population-based meta-heuristic algorithms inspired by the collective behaviours of insects, such as ants, termites, bees, wasps and other animals capable of performing certain intrinsic social actions [14]. The most common algorithm belonging to SI is the Particle Swarm Optimization (PSO) [15], and some interesting applications of its use for the MU of civil engineering FEM can be found in [16,17]. Anyway, a critical discussion of the effectiveness and performance of individual methods and a comparison of them is beyond the scope of this work.

This paper presents an application of the OSP technique for developing a VB-SHM system of an historical church severely damaged after the seismic sequence that stroke the Central Italy in 2016. The OSP analyses are carried out based on a FEM updated with the support of the PSO algorithm. At first, a description of the church case study is provided, together with a brief description of the dynamic tests performed on the church. Then, the FEM of the church is described, and the application of the optimisation algorithm for its updating is presented. Finally, after a brief description of the adopted EI algorithm, OSP application is presented and the obtained results are discussed.

2. PRESENTATION OF THE CASE STUDY

2.1. Overview of the church of Santa Maria in Via in Camerino

The church of Santa Maria in Via (Figure 1a) is located in the center of Camerino town in Central Italy. The first evidence of the existence of the church dates back to the 13th century, and up to the 16th century the church was a poor and irregular building [18]. The actual building was built between 1639 and 1642 and it is characterized by an irregular trapezoidal plan resulting from the combination of the pre-existing buildings; the latter were characterized by a wall fabric with a particularly incoherent core so that the external cladding was added to regularize the perimeter. The church is composed by many constructive elements typical of this type of buildings: the tiburium, which rises more than 8 m above the inner frame, the bell tower, that has an octagonal plan with a rather slender belfry, and a façade, which consists of two levels, the lower one incorporated into the main body of the church, and the upper one that rises next to the tiburium, to a maximum height of approximately 23 meters above the ground.

Following the seismic events that struck the Central Italy in 2016, in conjunction with the adverse environmental conditions of the winter months of 2017, the church suffered many damage that affected the bell tower, which underwent a partial collapse, the wooden roof and the camorcanna fake dome (both suffering a partial collapse), and the façade, with scattered cracks on both internal and external walls. In Figure 1b, photos of the damage suffered by the church are shown. The greatest collapse occurred in the rear part of the tiburium, which collapsed mainly inside the nave as a consequence of the progressive damage caused by the seismic activity of 26th October 2016 and the heavy snowfall of January 2017. Both the interior and exterior walls of the nave and apse are not affected by significant collapses or cracks, except for the two side altars adjacent to the façade section, which suffered significant damage to the arches and vault. At the south-west corner, under the shaft of the bell tower, there are diagonal cracks, which are concentrated on the floor bands between openings. The lower level of the façade underwent an out-of-plane rotation, while the upper part underwent a rigid translational motion that also affected the portion of the tiburium adjacent to the façade.

After the seismic sequence that produced many damage, the structure was secured with several interventions (Figure 1c). At first, a massive external retaining steel structure designed to prevent the front body collapse was built. The structure covers the front side and the two lateral sides of the anterior façade body for the whole height. To ensure the system stability in case of extreme events and to confine the base body of the church, fourteen steel strand cables connected to the steel structure and surrounding the whole church, are used. The collapsed portions of masonry on the lateral walls of the façade, produced by the overturning mechanism, were filled with steel latticed systems to restore gravitational loading paths. Moreover, a provisional roof was built to protect the interior of the church, together with a latticed structure built to prevent the out of plane collapse of the tiburium walls.

2.2. Preliminary dynamic identification tests

Once the securing systems were completely mounted, it was decided in 2020 to develop a combined static and dynamic monitoring system to control the health status of the church over time; the adopted dynamic system consists of a VB-SHM system. As already discussed, identifying the global dynamics of the building is the first step to design and develop a monitoring system. The identification of the church global dynamics was carried out through ambient vibration tests, employing sixteen accelerometers and two sensor configurations, as shown in Figure 2a and 2b. To get information on the overall dynamic behaviour of the church, it was decided to monitor eight points located around the ellipse of the tiburium, at two different heights from the ground level. At each point (from A to H) two uniaxial accelerometers were placed with measurement directions along the main axes of the church hall (called x and y directions). As for the instrumentation, PCB 393B31 accelerometers with sensitivity of 10V/g, NI 9234 analog-to-digital conversion modules, a 9045 cRIO and three 9185 cDAQs, were used. A distributed sensor network was set up by placing one cRIO for the measuring station close to the reference point 1B and three mobile cDAQs near the remaining measuring points. Synchronization was achieved through Time Sensitive Networking (TSN) technology providing distributed time synchronization and deterministic communication using standard ethernet networks.

The identification of modal parameters was carried out through OMAs, using the Principal Component - Subspace Stochastic Identification (SSI-PC) technique. Because acquisitions relevant to the two configurations are asynchronous, a data merging operation through scaling techniques was used in order to obtain correct mode shapes; in this case, global results were obtained applying the PoSER (Post Separate Estimation Re-scaling) technique. The global results in terms of frequencies, damping ratios and modal shapes are shown in Figure 3a, while in Figure 3b the relative AutoMAC matrix is shown. Globally, five vibration modes that mobilize the whole building, were identified. It is interesting to note that, despite the complex crack pattern, the dynamics of the structure presents very well decoupled modes, which could be expected for the undamaged system.

(a) (b) (c)

Figure 1. The Santa Maria in Via church: (a) pictures before the 2016 earthquakes; (b) damage suffered after the seismic sequence, (c) securing systems.

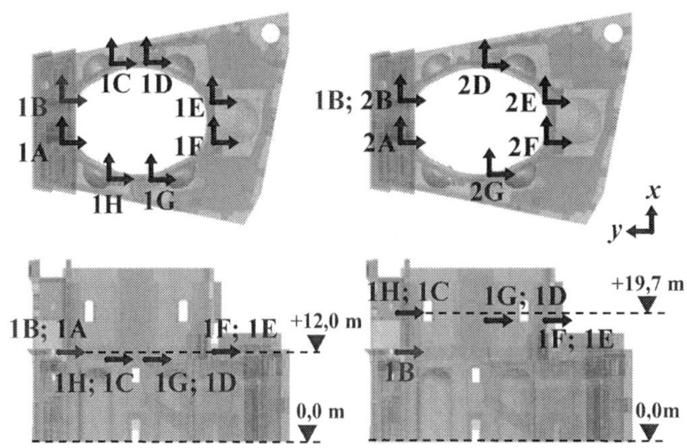

(a) (b)

Figure 2. Sensor layout for test configurations: (a) Configuration P1 and (b) P2.

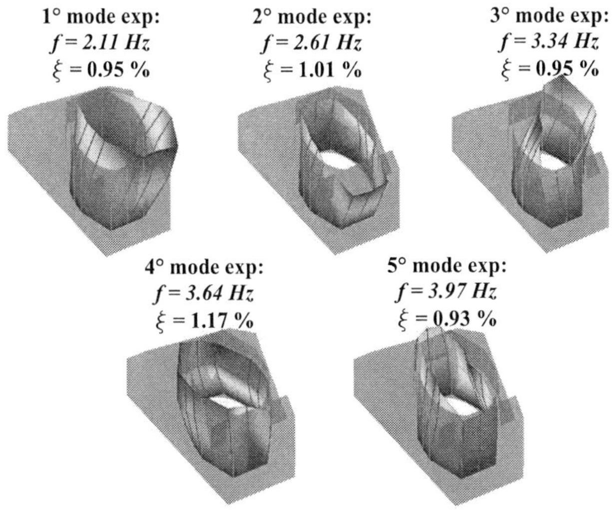

(a)

AutoMAC matrix

[Hz]	2.11	2.61	3.34	3.64	3.97
2.11	1.00	0.00	0.06	0.06	0.00
2.61	0.00	1.00	0.00	0.00	0.02
3.34	0.06	0.00	1.00	0.29	0.02
3.64	0.06	0.00	0.29	1.00	0.00
3.97	0.00	0.02	0.02	0.00	1.00

(b)

Figure 3. Global dynamics of the church: (a) modal parameters relevant to the five identified global modes, (b) AutoMAC matrix.

3. FINITE ELEMENT MODELLING AND MODEL UPDATING

The geometry of the church has been surveyed, and the technical drawings have been updated considering the structural damage. With regard to the construction materials, the church has a regular texture brick exterior cladding, made to make the wall fabric homogeneous, remediating to the numerous aggregations undergone by the building over the years. In-situ or laboratory mechanical tests on masonry have not been carried out, but a careful visual inspection has made it possible to classify the different types of masonry. A total of four different masonry typologies (M1, ..., M4) can be recognized, as illustrated in Figure 4. M1 masonry is composed of two outer layers of regular-textured brickwork, which are not connected to each other, and which contain a rubble infill. This type of masonry is used to construct the perimeter walls of the façade. M2 masonry is a multi-layer stone masonry with irregular courses and is used to build the inner walls of the façade and few walls of the church body, mainly those with high thickness. The M3 masonry is a double layer brickwork with rubble filling and, as for M1, the connection between the different layers is almost absent. This typology is adopted for most of the walls of the church and, as a consequence, presents diffused thicknesses due to the variation of the thickness of the rubble infill. Finally, the M4 masonry is composed of two layers: the inner one is made of masonry bricks, while the outer one is constituted by rough stone blocks with irregular courses. This typology is used for the walls of the tiburium. The parts of the church that collapses (rear part of the tiburium and lateral sides of the façade) are now filled with steel latticed systems, indicated as Braced-up regions in Figure 4, which are considered as additional material to be added to those previously described. Within the lateral volumes of the church and at different heights, there are many wooden floors which are localized in Figure 4 . Starting from this material survey, an initial estimate of the material mechanical characteristics has been done, and a FEM is developed.

The FEM is developed with the ANSYS software, and includes the whole body of the church, modelled with tetrahedral solid elements. The numerical model is composed by five different materials based on the definitions given in detail in the previous section. The geometric model has been divided into further sections to facilitate the control of the meshing operations. The wooden floors inside the church are modelled with shell elements, namely isotropic plates, because they contribute to the development of the box-like behaviour of the building, while the roof is not modelled and only its mass is taken into account, because the main part of it collapsed after the earthquakes. Moreover, the external steel securing system is modelled as well, since it is in contact with the church façade and, therefore, can contribute to the whole structural dynamic response; beam elements are adopted to model both the steel trusses and the steel cables surrounding the whole church. As far as restrains, the fixed condition is assumed. All modelled elements are automatically meshed by the software, resulting in a FEM consisting of 538275 nodes. All construction materials are assumed homogeneous, elastic and isotropic. Some pictures of the model and an initial estimate of the elastic moduli are shown in Figure 5.

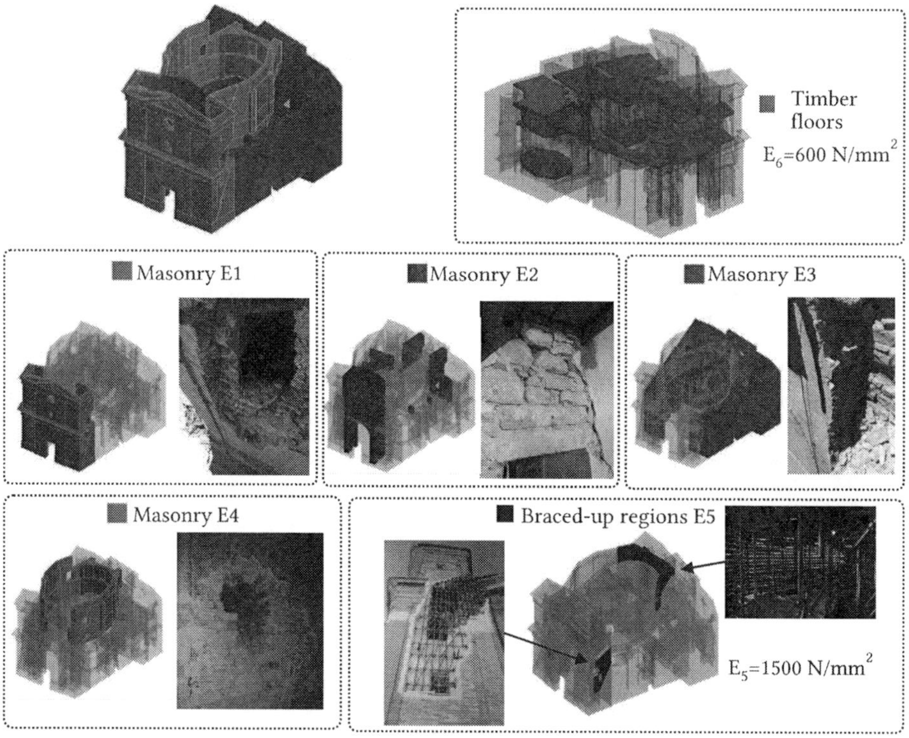

Figure 4. Different types of masonry recognized during the visual inspection and localization of wooden floors and repaired regions (braced-up regions).

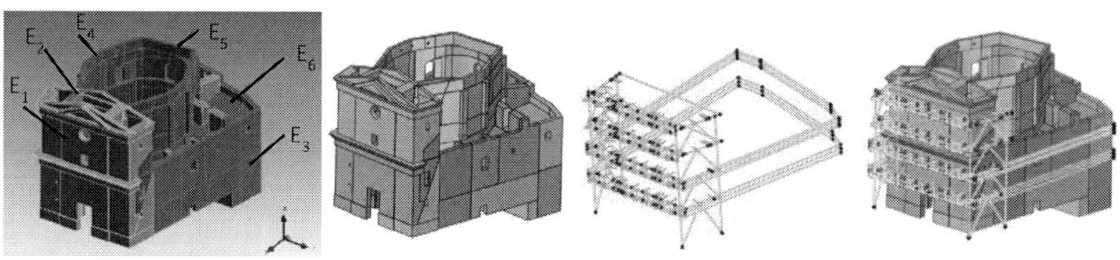

Mesh:
Sizing 0.5 m
538275 nodes
309541 tetrahedral elements

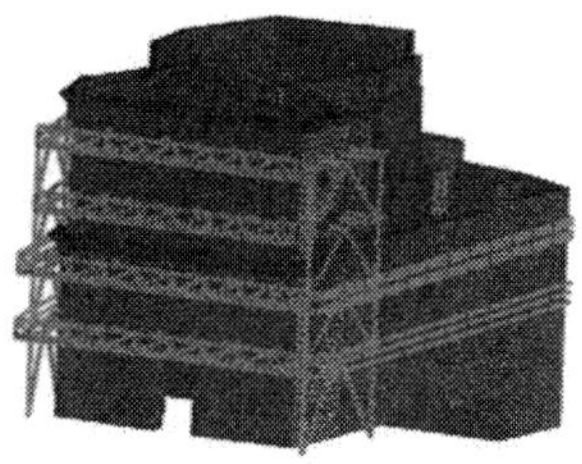

Materials:	E [N/mm2]	∂ [Kg/m3]	v [-]
Masonry E1	1092	1937.4	0.25
Masonry E2	1230	1937.4	0.25
Masonry E3	1200	1937.4	0.25
Masonry E4	1365	1937.4	0.25
Braced up region E5	1500	1000	0.25
Timber E6	600	800	0.25
Lattice beam	210000	7850	0.3
Bracing	210000	7850	0.3
Strands	110000	7850	0.3

Figure 5. Pictures of the model, details of the created mesh and an initial estimate of the mechanical characteristics of the construction materials.

3.1. Modal updating through Particle Swarm Optimization algorithm

The aim of Model Updating (MU) of FEM is to numerically reproduce the dynamic behaviour of the structure experimentally identified through OMA procedures. In this work, a matlab routine was implemented to automatically calibrate the model parameters via the Particle Swarm Optimization (PSO) algorithm. PSO is a stochastic optimization technique inspired by the social behaviour of a population of birds and applied in many research areas. In PSO, a number of particles are placed in the search domain of some objective function, and, for each position assumed by the particles, this function is calculated. Each particle then determines its movement through the search domain by combining some aspect of its own position and the best-fit position found with those of one or more members of the swarm. The aim of this algorithm is to find the global minimum of the chosen objective function. Each individual in the particle swarm is composed of three n-dimensional vectors, where n is the dimension of the search space. At the beginning, the particles are distributed randomly in the search space and a random velocity vector is defined, which is why PSO is called a stochastic algorithm. During the iterations the velocity of each particle is accelerated towards its previously found best position and towards the best solution found by the particle group. Therefore, this velocity is governed by the two best values found so far (personal and group) and by the inertia the particle is subjected to.

$$\mathbf{p}^{t+1} = \mathbf{p}^{t} + \mathbf{v}^{t+1} \tag{1}$$

$$\mathbf{v}^{t+1} = w\mathbf{v}^{t} + c_1 r_1 (\mathbf{p}^{t}_{best} - \mathbf{p}^{t}) + c_2 r_2 (\mathbf{p}^{t}_{bestglobal} - \mathbf{p}^{t}) \tag{2}$$

where **p** is the position and **v** the velocity at time *t*. The three vectors that allow to evaluate the velocity at each iteration are calibrated and weighted through three coefficients w, c_1, c_2 that are defined as hyperparameters; moreover, the contribution of the position of the single particle and the position of the group of particles are weighted through two coefficients r_1 and r_2. The hyperparameter w is used to define the ability of the swarm to change its direction. For the sake of brevity, the meaning of these parameters can be found in literature [14].

The variables considered for the analysis are the masonry elastic moduli E1, E2, E3 and E4 introduced in the previous paragraph and the elastic modulus E5 of the material used in the repaired regions. The objective function is shown in eq. 3.

$$err(\mathbf{e}) = \ln\left(1 + \left|\frac{f_{num}(\mathbf{e}) - f_{exp}}{f_{exp}}\right| + \left(1 - MAC_{num,exp.}(\mathbf{e})\right)\right) \qquad \text{where: } \mathbf{e} = \begin{bmatrix} E_1 \\ E_2 \\ E_3 \\ E_4 \\ E_5 \end{bmatrix} \tag{3}$$

where *err*(**e**) represents the objective function and returns a scalar value. The comparison is made between the experimental (*exp*) modal parameters identified though OMA, and the relevant numerical (*num*) ones obtained from FE analysis. In detail, natural frequencies and mode shapes of the 5 vibration modes are considered in the updating procedure, assuming that the algorithm converges below an error threshold of 5%. Table 2 synthetizes the results of the updating process. The masonry stiffness values for the church façade and the main body turned out to be much lower than the initial estimates shown in Figure 5, which is consistent with the severe crack pattern of the church. On the other hand, the tiburium requires much higher values of the modulus of elasticity to match the experimental results. The latter aspect might be explained by the presence of the latticed structure to prevent the out of plane collapse of the tiburium walls. The material for braced-up regions also needs much higher modulus of elasticity values of around 15000 MPa. These calibrated elastic moduli allow the dynamics of the structure to be well represented under operational conditions, i.e. with low vibration levels. The results of the modal analysis at the end of the optimization process are shown in Figure 6, where the numerical modes are represented together with the corresponding experimental ones. Table 1 shows the MAC values between the optimized and experimental modes and a comparison in terms of frequency. As can be seen from the terms on the diagonal, a very good match has been achieved for the first 5 modes.

Table 1. Comparison between experimental and numerical results

Mode	Frequency			
	Experimetal [Hz]	Numerical [Hz]	Error [%]	MAC
1	2.11	2.08	1	0.95
2	2.61	2.76	2	0.86
3	3.34	2.92	3	0.89
4	3.64	3.30	4	0.78
5	3.97	3.86	5	0.94

Table 2. Preliminar results of the updating procedure

Material	Young modules	
	E [MPa]	$E_{upd.}$ [MPa]
E1	1092	605
E2	1230	415
E3	1200	401
E4	1365	1542
E5	1500	16100

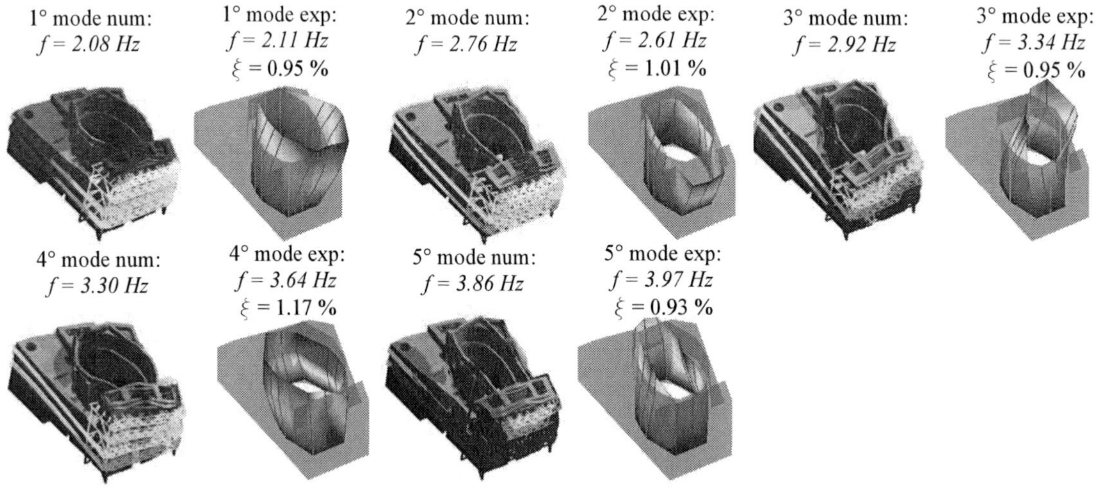

Figure 6. Optimized numerical modes with the corresponding experimental ones.

4. OPTIMAL SENSORS PLACEMENT

The method EI is an iterative method: the set of candidate positions is quickly reduced to the number of available sensors. The vector $\boldsymbol{E_D}$ represents the distribution of "Effective Independence" of a set of candidate positions and it is defined as the diagonal of the matrix [7],

$$\boldsymbol{E} = \boldsymbol{\psi}^T \boldsymbol{\psi} \{\boldsymbol{\psi}^T \boldsymbol{\psi}\}^{-1} \boldsymbol{\psi}^T \tag{4}$$

where $\boldsymbol{\psi}$ is a matrix of FE target modes partitioned according to a given sensor distribution. The i-*th* term of $\boldsymbol{E_D}$ represents the contribution of the sensor at the i-*th* position to the linear independence of the modes. If E_{Di} is equal to 0, the sensor at that position does not contribute; if E_{Di} is equal to 1, that position must be maintained in the final sensor configuration. Different sensor positions are classified iteratively and those that do not contribute are identified and eliminated. The best approximation of the optimal configuration is achieved by deleting one position at a time. In this work, EI has been implemented in a MATLAB routine and the analysis has been carried out taking into account 5 modes of vibration considering only the DOFs on the external surfaces of the model (they must be accessible for the installation of a sensor), more than 250,000 translational degrees of freedom are possible. To make the analysis faster, the points to be analyzed were randomly sampled to 25,000. After that, each iteration eliminates the position that less contributes to the system's Effective Independence, i.e., the position with the lowest E_D coefficient. The iterations end when only 5 positions remain, which possess ED=1. With the aim of limiting the number of sensors as much as possible, 2 of the 5 points identified were selected manually. Figure 7 shows the results of the OSP analysis carried out on the updated model of the church.

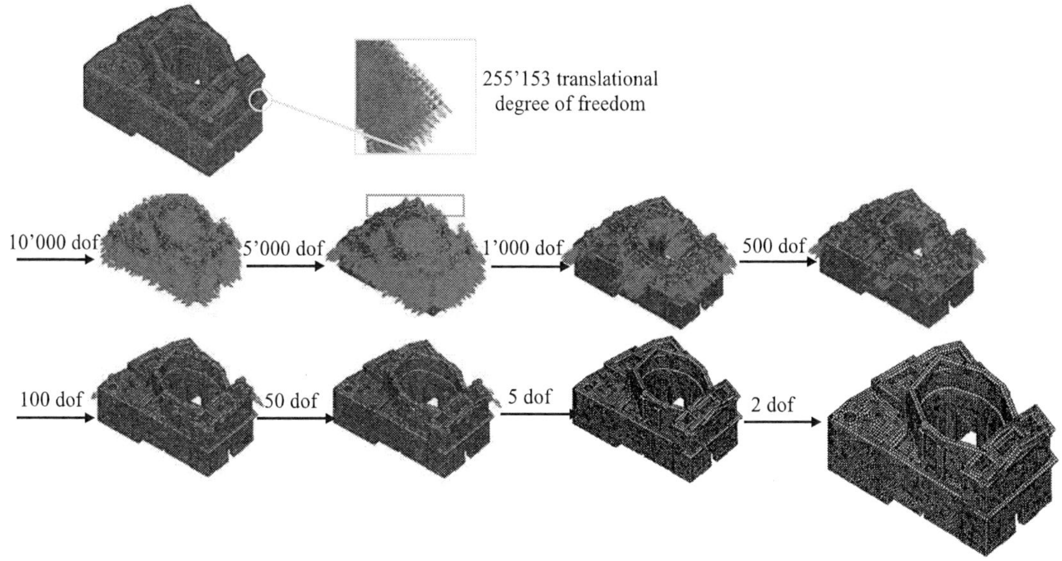

Figure 7. Results of the OSP analysis carried out on the updated model.

5. CONCLUSIONS

The design of a vibration-based structural health monitoring system requires a complete understanding of the dynamics of the structure to be monitored. Finite element modelling can substantially contribute to this preliminary phase, especially in the case of complex dynamic structures where uncertainty about material characteristics and boundary conditions may be significant. The modelling of the church of Santa Maria in Via has proved to be particularly challenging and, in this case, the Particle Swarm Optimization algorithm has been particularly suitable. The family of Swarm Intelligence is composed of several algorithms; furthermore, also the class of Genetic algorithms is becoming more and more popular in dealing with this type of problem. Furthermore, dynamic identification tests are carried out with a limited number of sensors, and the identified modal shapes may suffer from spatial aliasing, especially in those cases where it is difficult to make simplifying hypotheses (e.g. presence of rigid floors). Performing a study to optimize the number and position of sensors from only the identified modal components may not be effective. On the other hand, a finite element model has many degrees of freedom and manually choosing which is the most interesting to monitor can be a non-trivial challenge. It is therefore necessary to implement algorithms for optimal sensor placement and in this work Effective Independence method has been used due to its easiness of interpretation and implementation. Again, this is an actual problem with the increasing adoption of artificial intelligence algorithms, and it will be interesting as a future development to study which methodology is the most effective.

REFERENCES

[1] Li, Binbin, Dongsheng Li, Xuefeng Zhao, & Jinping Ou. (2012). Optimal sensor placement in health monitoring of suspension bridge. *Science China Technological Sciences* 55 (luglio). https://doi.org/10.1007/s11431-012-4815-8.

[2] Meo, M., & Zumpano. G. (2005). On the optimal sensor placement techniques for a bridge structure. *Engineering Structures* 27 (10) : 1488–97. https://doi.org/10.1016/j.engstruct.2005.03.015.

[3] Kammer, D. (1991). Sensor Placement for On-Orbit Modal Identification and Correlation of Large Space Structures. *Journal of Guidance, Control, and Dynamics*. 14. 251 - 259. 10.2514/3.20635.

[4] Heo, G., M.L. Wang, & D. Satpathi. (1997). Optimal transducer placement for health monitoring of long span bridge. *Soil Dynamics and Earthquake Engineering 16 (7): 495–502.* https://doi.org/10.1016/S0267-7261(97)00010-9.

[5] Guo, H Y, L Zhang, L L Zhang, & J X Zhou. (2004). Optimal placement of sensors for structural health monitoring using improved genetic algorithms. *Smart Materials and Structures* 13 (3): 528–34. https://doi.org/10.1088/0964-1726/13/3/011.

[6] Flynn, Eric B., & Michael D. Todd. (2010). A Bayesian approach to optimal sensor placement for structural health monitoring with application to active sensing. *Mechanical Systems and Signal Processing 24 (4): 891–903.* https://doi.org/10.1016/j.ymssp.2009.09.003.

[7] Worden, K, & A.P Burrows. (2001). Optimal Sensor Placement for Fault Detection. *Engineering Structures 23 (8): 885–901.* https://doi.org/10.1016/S0141-0296(00)00118-8.

[8] Jiang, Y., Li, D., & Song. G., (2017). On the physical significance of the Effective Independence method for sensor placement. *Journal of Physics: Conference Series 842*: 012030. https://doi.org/10.1088/1742-6596/842/1/012030.

[9] Roca, P., Cervera, M., Gariup, G., & Pela'. L., (2010). Structural Analysis of Masonry Historical Constructions. Classical and Advanced Approaches. *Archives of Computational Methods in Engineering 17 (3): 299–325.* https://doi.org/10.1007/s11831-010-9046-1.

[10] Castellazzi, G., D'Altri, A. M., de Miranda, S., & Ubertini F. (2017). An Innovative Numerical Modeling Strategy for the Structural Analysis of Historical Monumental Buildings. *Engineering Structures 132 (February): 229–48.* https://doi.org/10.1016/j.engstruct.2016.11.032.

[11] Ramos, L., Alaboz, M., Aguilar, R., & Lourenco. P. (2011). Dynamic Identification and FE Updating of S. Torcato Church, Portugal. *In Conference Proceedings of the Society for Experimental Mechanics Series*, 4:71–80. https://doi.org/10.1007/978-1-4419-9831-6_9.

[12] Torres, W., Almazán, J. L., Sandoval, C., & Boroschek. R. (2017). Operational Modal Analysis and FE Model Updating of the Metropolitan Cathedral of Santiago, Chile. *Engineering Structures 143 (July): 169–88.* https://doi.org/10.1016/j.engstruct.2017.04.008.

[13] Sabbatini, V., Carlo B., & Santini. S. (2019). Model updating of a masonry historical church based on operational modal analysis: the case study of San Filippo Neri in Macerata. *COMPDYN 2019.* https://doi.org/10.7712/120119.7186.18559.

[14] Blum, Christian, & Xiaodong Li. (2008). Swarm Intelligence in Optimization. *In Swarm Intelligence: Introduction and Applications, 43–85.* https://doi.org/10.1007/978-3-540-74089-6_2.

[15] J. Kennedy & R. Eberhart. (1995). Particle Swarm Optimization. *In Proceedings of ICNN'95 - International Conference on Neural Networks, 4:1942–48 vol.4.* https://doi.org/10.1109/ICNN.1995.488968.

[16] Tran-Ngoc, H., S. Khatir, G. De Roeck, T. Bui-Tien, L. Nguyen-Ngoc, & M. Abdel Wahab. (2018). Model Updating for Nam O Bridge Using Particle Swarm Optimization Algorithm and Genetic Algorithm. *Sensors 18 (12).* https://doi.org/10.3390/s18124131.

[17] Saada, Mohamed M., Mustafa H. Arafa, & Ashraf O. Nassef. (2013). Finite Element Model Updating Approach to Damage Identification in Beams Using Particle Swarm Optimization. *Engineering Optimization 45 (6): 677–96.* https://doi.org/10.1080/0305215X.2012.704026.

[18] Arezzo, D., Nicoletti, V., Cipriani, L., Carbonari, S., Leoni, G., & Gara, F. (2021). First results of the monitoring of the façade damage mechanism of the "Santa Maria in Via" Church in Camerino following the 2016 Central Italy Earthquake. *In: SHMII proceedings10. p. 1-7, Porto, Portugal, 30 June - 2 July 2021*

Optimization of a vibro-impact bistable energy harvester for structural health monitoring sensors

Mostafa Shahsavar[1*a], Mohammad-Reza Ashory[a], Mohammad Mahdi Khatibi[a]

[a] Modal Analysis (MA) Research Laboratory, Faculty of Mechanical Engineering, Semnan University, Semnan, Iran

Keywords: Broadband energy harvesting, Piezoelectric beam, Vibro-impact harvester, Cantilever beam, Bistable system

Abstract

Recently, health monitoring of civil infrastructure systems has attracted a lot of attention. Monitoring systems such as acoustic emission sensors used in bridge damage detection need to be empowered in the range of micro watt. Ambient ubiquitous vibration energy can be converted to electrical energy and used as a suitable resource of energy for this purpose. This paper focuses on frequency bandwidth optimization of a vibro-impact bistable piezoelectric energy harvester device for supplying power to embedded structural health monitoring self-powered sensors of highway bridges. The narrow band operating frequency bandwidth makes the majority of typical harvesters. However, these harvesters are inefficient due to this fact that in real life the external excitation frequencies have broadband spectrum. Therefore, increasing the frequency bandwidth of a vibration energy harvester improves the performance of the energy conversion. By broadening the operating frequency of a harvester, the obtained power will be increased over a range of working frequencies. A new design is proposed in which a cantilever beam containing a pair of permanent magnets and a motion limiting barriers are used for harvesting the energy The frequency bandwidth of the system is broaden by adding nonlinearity to the harvester comes from two sources: permanent magnets and vibro-impact motion. The optimum physical characteristic values of vibro-impact motion, such as initial gap, location and stiffness of the barrier aiming to increase the frequency bandwidth are investigated. Both analytical method of perturbation and numerical method of ode45 Matlab are implemented.

1. Introduction

In recent years, by extending new technologies, the importance of supplying low power consumption devices such as wireless sensors has become more obvious[1], [2]. These devices, need to be

[1] Correspomding author: m.shahsavar_iust@yahoo.com (M. shahsavar(M_shahsavar@semnan.ac.ir)) mashoori@semnan.ac.ir (M. R. Ashory), mmkhatibi@semnan.ac.ir (M. M. Khatibi)

empowered in the range of micro watt depending on their applications such as health monitoring. Converting ambient vibration or waste energies into electrical energy is the main subject of this field of study[3]–[5]. In particular, vibration energy harvesters has attracted many attentions, because ambient vibration sources are a long-lasting and ubiquitous source of energy that exist in the natural environment amply. Various methods such as, electromagnetic, electrostatic and piezoelectric transducers are implemented to convert vibration energies into electrical energies[6], [7]. Piezoelectric materials are one of the most effective ways of energy harvesting and supplying power to micro electrical component. Exploiting a cantilever beam equipped to a piezoelectric layer as a vibration energy harvester has been found a lot of attention, because of simplicity in manufacturing and showing high level of performance[8]. Due to inherent mechanical properties, linear vibration energy harvester (VEH) shows good efficacy in generating power only in a narrow working frequency bandwidth. So VEH produces maximum power if its oscillator works in resonant state. Such VEHs need some manipulation to make them suitable for harvesting energies from natural environment[7], [9]. To dominate this problem, various techniques are used to widening the working frequency bandwidth of a VEH. One of the most important method for increasing the efficiency of a VEH is adding nonlinearity to the system. This nonlinearity can be added by using bistability with a magnetic coupling or using frequency up-conversion techniques such as vibro-impact phenomenon[10], [11]. Typical bistable piezoelectric energy harvesters (TBPEH) are built with a pair of permanent magnets which are added to a piezoelectric cantilever beam. One permanent magnet is attached on the tip of the beam and the other one is fixed on the excitation frame. Adding a pair of magnets with opposed polarity to a cantilever beam energy harvester will make a bistable energy harvester[12]. Many researchers have focused on the TBPEH to improve the amount of harvested power. A. Erturk and D. Inman analyzed a piezo-magnetoelastic device for remarkable improvement of piezoelectric power generation in vibration energy harvesting[13]. Their proposed energy harvester amended the generated voltage about %200 respect to a simple energy harvester. Z. Zhou et al. worked on the bi-stable characteristics produced by the magnetic interaction were exploited to improve the performance of energy harvesting from a bridge under the excitation of moving vehicles. Their results showed that the BPEH can significantly improve the energy harvesting performance[14]. Non-smoothness behavior of impact process causes sudden change in amount and direction of oscillator velocity[15].This process leads to including the nonlinearity to a vibro-impact system. Several papers investigate the effects of vibro-impact methods on performance of VEH. M. M. Soliman and his colleagues proposed a new design for widening the operating frequency bandwidth of a VEH utilizing a namely piecewise-linear oscillator, instead of traditional linear energy harvester. In fact, they introduced a vibro-impact energy harvester by imposing a barrier to a cantilever beam system to confine the vibration amplitude. They found that the new architecture increased the operating frequency bandwidth of the harvester, significantly[16]. Abedini et al. studied a piezoelectric cantilever energy harvester by using a vibro-impact mechanism to convert low ambient vibration frequency to resonant frequency of the energy harvester to improve its performance. They used a single degree of freedom model to analyze the piezoelectric cantilever beam energy harvester. According to their conclusions, the energy harvesting efficiency drastically improved with using the vibro-impact process[17]. K. Vijayan et al studied a coupled vibro-impacting beams energy harvester that was under base excitation at different parameters[18]. They investigated the effects of contact stiffness, damping ratio and initial gap between beams on the generated power and frequency bandwidth of the system. They found, by appropriate optimization of contact stiffness impacting bodies, the VEH can generate more power rather than a linear system. Huicong Liu et al.[19] have examined the operating frequency bandwidth of a piezoelectric energy harvester system which is equipped with two symmetric mechanical stoppers. They found that the operating frequency bandwidth of the system is increased about 18 Hz.

This study represent a novel vibro-impact energy harvester by adding a stopping barrier to a typical bistable piezoelectric unimorph cantilever beam energy harvester. The tip beam transverse motion has been limited by a barrier limiting stop. Therefore, when the tip motion amplitude of the harvester exceeds the initial gap distance, the impact will occur. By using Euler-Lagrange equations, the governing equations of motion are derived. Finally, the working frequency bandwidth of the considered system will be investigated by solving the governing equations both with perturbation methods and numerically with Matlab ode45 function. The rest of this paper is organized as follows. In section. 2 the mechanical and electromechanical parameters and governing equations of the vibro-impact bistable energy harvester are introduced. Then the effects of vibro-impact phenomenon on the working frequency bandwidth and the amount of extracted power of the proposed harvester are analyzed in section. 3. Finally, in section. 4 the conclusions of the results are discussed.

2. Mathematical modeling

In present research a vibro-impact bistable energy harvester is considered. Figure. 1 illustrates the schematic of the proposed unimorph vibro-impact cantilever beam energy harvester.

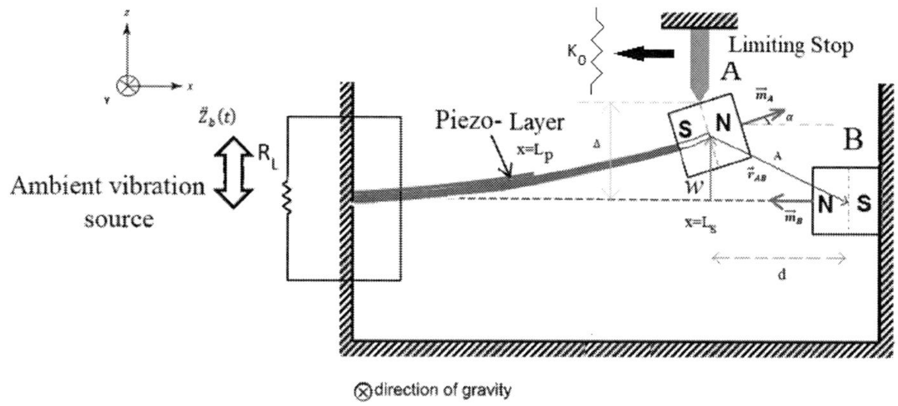

Fig. 1

The system is composed of a pair of permanent magnets, a limiting stop barrier and an electrical load R_L using to extract the generated power. The permanent magnets are deployed with same polarity and placed facing each other. One of them is attached to the free end of the beam as tip mass to reduce the natural frequency of the harvester and the other one is fixed on the harvester frame. The system has been excited by harmonic base motion. The barrier is modeled as a linear spring. The considered energy harvester is driven by external harmonic base excitation known as $\ddot{Z}_b(t) = Y_0 cos(\omega t)$ which Y_0 and ω are acceleration amplitude and frequency, respectively. The initial gap between piezoelectric beam and limiting stop is considered by Δ. In the following section, the governing equation of motion is be derived by extended general Hamilton theory and Euler-Bernoulli assumption. The total kinetic energy of the system is,

$$T_{tot} = \frac{1}{2}\rho_s A_s \int_0^{L_s} [\frac{\partial w_0(x,t)}{\partial t}]^2 dx + \frac{1}{2}\rho_p A_p \int_0^{L_p} [\frac{\partial w_0(x,t)}{\partial t}]^2 dx + \frac{1}{2} M_t [\frac{\partial w_0(L_s,t)}{\partial t}]^2 \quad \textbf{(1)}$$

Where ρ_s, ρ_p are mass density, A_s, A_p are cross-section area and L_s, L_p are length of substrate and piezoelectric layers respectively. The cross-sectional area of the substrate and piezoelectric harvester is defined as,

$$A_s = bh_s \quad \textbf{(2)}$$

$$A_p = bh_p \quad \textbf{(3)}$$

Where b is the width of the harvester and h_s, h_p is the thickness of the substrate and piezoelectric layer respectively. Also, M_t is considered as permanent magnet tip mass and w_0 is the relative displacement of the transverse motion of the neutral axis of harvester relative to the base motion. Now, the total potential energies of the harvester in non-impacting phase will be presented.

$$U_{tot} = U_{st} + U_{em} + U_{el} + U_{mag} + U_{Collision} \quad \textbf{(4)}$$

The total potential energy of the harvester is composed of structural, electromechanical, electrical potential energy, magnetic potential energy and potential energy of impact, respectively as follows,

$$U_{st} = \frac{1}{2} E_s I_s \int_0^{L_s} (\frac{\partial^2 w_0(x,t)}{\partial x^2})^2 dx + \frac{1}{2} C_{11}^E I_p \int_0^{L_p} (\frac{\partial^2 w_0(x,t)}{\partial x^2})^2 dx \quad \textbf{(5)}$$

$$U_{em} = -\frac{e_{31}\bar{y}_b A_p v(t)}{h_p} \int_0^{L_p} \frac{\partial^2 w_0(x,t)}{\partial x^2} dx \quad \textbf{(6)}$$

$$U_{el} = -\frac{A_p L_p \varepsilon_{33}^S}{2h_p^2} v(t)^2 \quad \textbf{(7)}$$

Where E_s, C_{11}^E and I_s, I_p are Young's modulus and second moment of area of substrate and piezoelectric layer about cross section neutral axis ($\bar{y}_b$) of harvester, respectively. In addition, e_{31}, $v(t)$ and ε_{33}^S, represent piezoelectric constant, permittivity constant and the generated voltage of piezoelectric layer. In electromechanical references, the term $\frac{A_p L_p \varepsilon_{33}^S}{h_p^2}$ in **Eq. 7** is known as piezoelectric capacitance and in this work is represented by C_p. As was said before, the limiting stop is modeled as a linear spring that is included if the amplitude of motion of the energy harvester is exceeds than the initial gap distance. If it does, the potential energy of the impact is,

$$U_{Collision} = \frac{1}{2} K_0 (w_0(x_i, t) - \Delta)^2 H(w_0(x_i, t) - \Delta) \quad \textbf{(8)}$$

Which $H(w_0(x_i, t) - \Delta)$ is Heaviside function and x_i is the location of the barrier. By considering a single mode assumption, the transverse motion of the harvester is,

$$w_0(x, t) = \phi(x)\eta(t) \quad \textbf{(9)}$$

Which $\phi(x)$ and $\eta(t)$ are fundamental mode shape and generalized coordinate, respectively. Based on assumed mode approximation, the first mode shape function for this of harvester is,

$$\phi(x) = 1 - \cos(\frac{\pi x}{2L_s}) \quad \textbf{(10)}$$

Now, the electromagnetic potential energy is derived by dipole theory.

So, the magnetic dipole moment vectors of installed permanent magnets $\overrightarrow{\boldsymbol{m}}_A$ and $\overrightarrow{\boldsymbol{m}}_B$ which are oriented as Fig. 1 are written as,

$$\overrightarrow{\boldsymbol{m}}_A = M_A V_A \cos(\alpha)\,\widehat{\boldsymbol{e}_x} + M_A V_A \sin(\alpha)\,\widehat{\boldsymbol{e}_z} \quad \textbf{(11)}$$

$$\overrightarrow{\boldsymbol{m}_B} = -M_B V_B \cos(\alpha)\,\widehat{\boldsymbol{e}_x} \tag{12}$$

M_A, M_B and V_A, V_B represent magnetization vectors and volumes of magnet A and B, respectively. Beside, $M = {}^{B_r}/_{\mu_0}$, which B_r and μ_0 are considered as magnet's residual flux density and permeability of free space, respectively. According to Fig. 1, "α" is the slope of the beam tip and is considered equal to $\tan^{-1}(\acute{w}_0(L_s,t))$ which, "´" represents special derivative. According to Fig. 1, the distance vector between magnets is presented as $\vec{\boldsymbol{r}}_{AB}$. The vector $\vec{\boldsymbol{r}}_{AB}$ is defined as follows,

$$\vec{\boldsymbol{r}}_{AB} = d\,\widehat{\boldsymbol{e}_x} - w_0(L_s,t)\widehat{\boldsymbol{e}_z} \tag{13}$$

Which "d" is the separation distance between two magnets. The magnetic potential energy of the harvester can be written as,

$$U_{mag} = \frac{\mu_0}{4\pi}\left[\frac{\overrightarrow{m}_A}{\|\vec{r}_{AB}\|^3} - \frac{3\vec{r}_{AB}(\overrightarrow{m}_A \cdot \vec{r}_{AB})}{\|\vec{r}_{AB}\|^5}\right] \cdot \overrightarrow{\boldsymbol{m}}_B \tag{14}$$

With substitution of **Eq. 9-10** in **Eq.14** the magnetic potential energy is obtained. According to extended Hamilton principle, the governing electromechanical motion for one mode approximation will be,

$$\frac{d}{dt}\left(\frac{\partial T}{\partial \dot{q}_i}\right) - \frac{\partial T}{\partial q_i} + \frac{\partial U}{\partial q_i} - \frac{\partial W_{ie}}{\partial q_i} = Q_i \qquad i = 1,2 \tag{15}$$

Which Q_i are related to non-conservative work of the system that is done by generated electrical charges. Finally, by non-dimensional techniques, the final equations of the motion are,

$$\frac{d^2X}{d\tau^2} + 2\epsilon\zeta\frac{dX}{d\tau} + \gamma^2 X + \epsilon\alpha_3 X^3 - \epsilon V = \epsilon f\cos(\Omega\tau) \tag{16}$$

$$\frac{dV}{d\tau} + \kappa^2\frac{dX}{d\tau} + \nu V = 0 \tag{17}$$

Which the dimensionless parameters are listed as,

$$\eta(t) = L_0 X(\tau),\ \tau = \omega_n t,\ \omega_n^2 = \frac{K}{M},\ \gamma^2 = 1 + \alpha_1 + \alpha_2,\ \kappa^2 = \frac{\theta^2}{C_p K},\ \nu = \frac{1}{C_p\omega_n R},\ v(t) = \frac{KL_0}{\theta}V(\tau),$$

$$K = E_s I_s \int_0^{L_s} \acute{\acute{\phi}}^2 dx + C_{11}^E I_p \int_0^{L_p} \acute{\acute{\phi}}^2 dx,\ M = \rho_s A_s \int_0^{L_s} \phi(x)^2 dx + \rho_p A_p \int_0^{L_p} \phi(x)^2 dx + M_t \phi(L_s)^2,\ \Omega = \frac{\omega}{\omega_n}$$

α_1 is activate when impact occurs and α_2, α_3 are coming from potential energy of magnets. α_2, α_3 are obtained from applying McLaren series to result of **Eq.14**. with the aid of Maple software.

2.1 Analytical solution based on perturbation techniques

In this section, the analytical solution of the **Eq. 16-17** is presented based on multiple scale perturbation techniques. The solution is derived in primary resonance around ω_n. In order to solve the equations time scale is defined as,

$$T_0 = \tau,\ T_1 = \epsilon\tau \tag{18}$$

And response expressions are,

$$X(\tau;\epsilon) = X_0(T_0,T_1) + \epsilon X_1(T_0,T_1) \tag{19}$$

$$V(\tau;\epsilon) = V_0(T_0,T_1) + \epsilon V_1(T_0,T_1) \tag{20}$$

The derivative operators respect to time scales are,

$$\frac{d}{d\tau} = D_0 + \epsilon D_1 \tag{21}$$

$$\frac{d^2}{d\tau^2} = D_0^2 + 2\epsilon D_0 D_1 \tag{22}$$

After substitution of **Eq.18-22** in **Eq. 16-17** and equate the coefficient of ϵ^0 and ϵ,

$$D_0^2 X_0 + \gamma^2 X_0 = 0 \tag{23}$$

$$D_0V_0 + 1 = -\kappa^2 D_0X_0 \quad \textbf{(24)}$$

and

$$D_0^2X_1 + \gamma^2X_1 = -2D_0D_1X_0 - 2\zeta D_0X_0 - \alpha_3X_0^3 + V_0 + f\cos(\omega_nT_0 + \sigma T_1) \quad \textbf{(25)}$$

$$D_1V_1 + V_1 = -D_1V_0 - \kappa^2(D_0X_1 + D_1X_0) \quad \textbf{(26)}$$

From ... the X_0 and V_0 are,

$$X_0 = A(T_1)e^{i\gamma T_0} + CC \quad \textbf{(27)}$$

$$V_0 = B(T_1)e^{-\nu T_0} - \frac{i\gamma\kappa^2A(T_1)e^{i\gamma T_0}}{1+i\gamma} + CC \quad \textbf{(28)}$$

$i = \sqrt{-1}$

Where CC refers to complex conjugate of previous terms. By substitution of **Eq. 27-28** in **Eq.25-26** with eliminating secular terms, and after some manipulations in Maple software the unknown function $A(T_1)$ and $B(T_1)$ are found. Then the final results of the **Eq. 16-17** will be obtained. In the following section, the effect of initial gap distance and barrier stiffness is analyzed both numerically and analytically. After finding the voltage expression, one can find the extracted power as,

$$P_{ex} = \frac{v^2}{R_L} \quad \textbf{(29)}$$

And finally the average extracted power is,

$$P_{ave} = \frac{1}{t}\int_0^t \frac{v^2}{R_L}dt \quad \textbf{(30)}$$

For optimization process, it is enough to take derivative of **Eq. 30** respect to stiffness barrier and initial gap as follows,

$$K_{0(opt)} = \frac{\partial P_{ave}}{\partial K_0} = 0 \quad \textbf{(31)}$$

$$\Delta_{opt} = \frac{\partial P_{ave}}{\partial \Delta} = 0 \quad \textbf{(32)}$$

All of the mathematical calculations is done in Maple software.

3. Results

This section investigates the numerical results of the proposed energy harvester. The physical parameters of the considered energy harvester of Fig. 1(a) are presented in the Table. 1.

Beam properties and symbol	value	Unit
Length ($\boldsymbol{L_s}$)	55.15	mm
Density ($\boldsymbol{\rho_s}$)	7900	Kg/m^3
Young's Modulus ($\boldsymbol{E_s}$)	92	GPa
Thickness ($\boldsymbol{h_s}$)	0.2	mm
Width ($\boldsymbol{b}$)	10	mm
Damping ratio (ζ)	0.02	-
Barrier initial gap ($\boldsymbol{\Delta}$)	4	mm
Barrier stiffness ($\boldsymbol{K_0}$)	13000	N/m
Base acceleration magnitude ($\boldsymbol{Y_0}$)	1g	m/s^2

Gravity acceleration (g)	9.81	m/s^2
Barrier location (x_i)	45	mm
Piezoelectric properties		
Length (L_p)	36	mm
Density (ρ_p)	7600	Kg/m^3
Young's Modulus (C_{11}^E)	62	GPa
thickness (h_p)	0.25	mm
Width (b)	10	mm
Piezoelectric constant (e_{31})	-21.08	C/m^2
Permittivity constant (ε_{33}^s)	44.27	nF/m
Electrical load (R_L)	5000	Ω
Magnet properties		
Separation distance (d)	24	mm
Magnets volume (V_A, V_B)	360	mm^3
Magnet mass (M_t)	4.5	gr
Residual flux density (B_r)	1.25	T
Permeability of free space (μ_0)	$4\pi \times 10^{-7}$	N/A^2

The harvester is driven by base acceleration that is defined as $\ddot{Z}(t) = Y_0 cos(\omega t)$, which Y_0 is the amplitude of the base acceleration and $\omega = 2\pi f$ is the external excitation frequency in which f varies from 0 up to 100 Hz. These plots are obtained while all transient results have passed. Fig. 2(a) illustrates the maximum minis minimum motion amplitude of the system in every period of external excitation at the absence of the limiting stop. Both analytical results and numerical results have a good consistency. According to Fig. 2a the operating frequency bandwidth in non-impacting motion is about 1-24.9 Hz. In Fig. 2b, after 24.9 Hz, the amount of produced voltage has been dropped drastically. According to Fig. 2c the generated power has a significant value until frequency 24.9 Hz. The maximum average power is about 15 Watt which occurred at 18.07 Hz. This value belongs to first natural frequency of the non-impacting system.

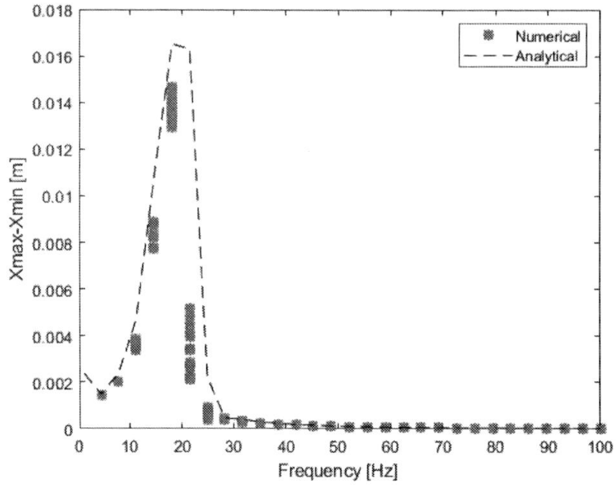
Xmax-Xmin [m]
Frequency [Hz]
Numerical
Analytical

a

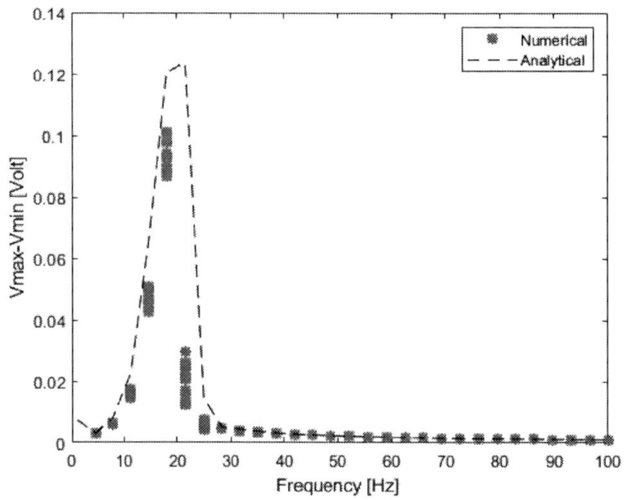
Vmax-Vmin [Volt]
Frequency [Hz]
Numerical
Analytical

b

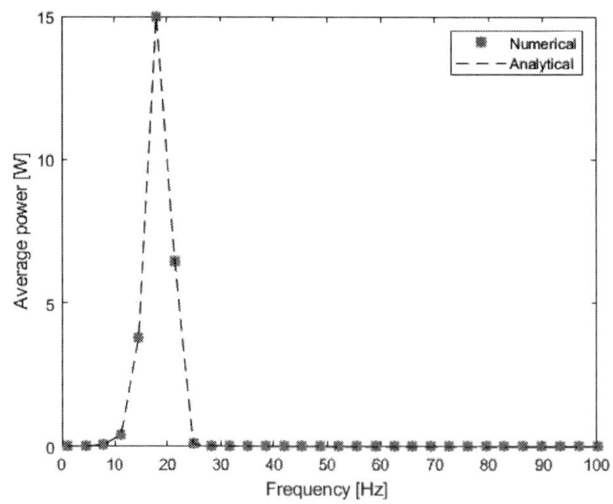
Average power [W]
Frequency [Hz]
Numerical
Analytical

c

Fig. 2. Frequency response diagram of the bistable unimorph piezoelectric energy harvester without impact

Fig. 3 shows the frequency response diagram of the harvester in impacting motion. According to the obtained results, the operating frequency bandwidth of the system is until 41.97 Hz. In impacting motion, the maximum average power is about 31 Watt. After the frequency 41.97 Hz, the amount of harvested power plummet drastically. So the operating frequency bandwidth in non-impacting motion is about 1-41.97 Hz

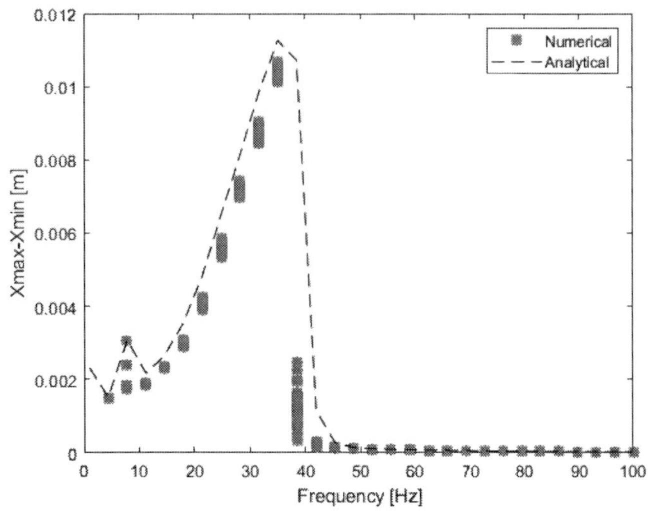

a

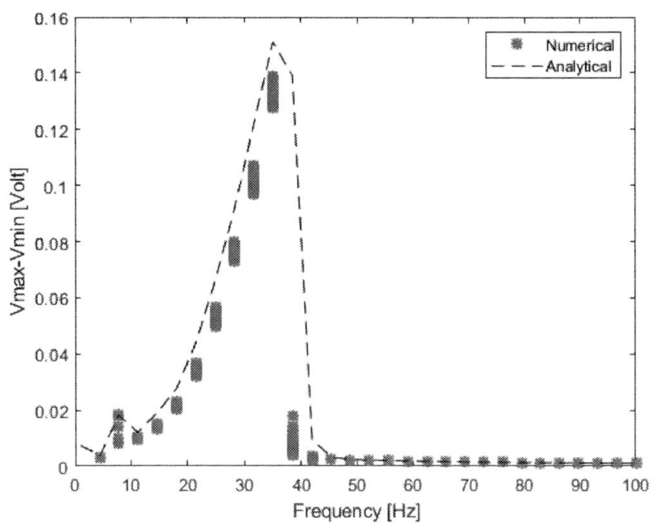

b

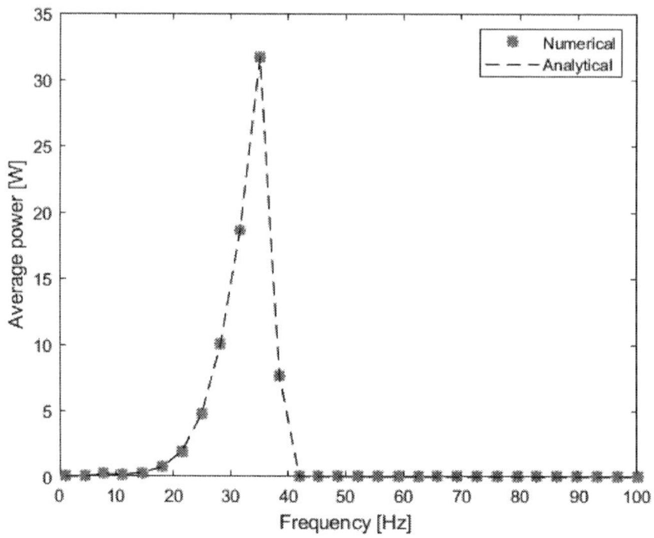

c

Fig. 3. Frequency response diagram of the vibro-impact bistable unimorph piezoelectric energy harvester

Fig. 4 represent the effect of stiffness barrier to the harvested power. According to Fig. 4 by increasing the barrier stiffness, the average of the harvested power decreased. So the best stiffness barrier option for optimizing the harvested power is the minimum one. But in future works it is demonstrated that decreasing the barrier stiffness will result in obtaining less operating frequency bandwidth.

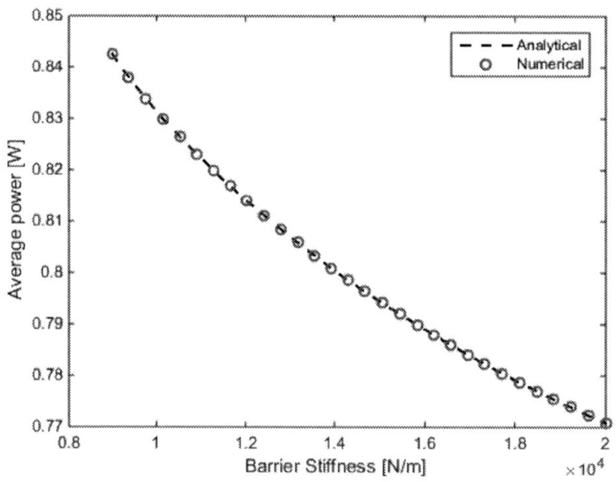

Fig. 4. Effect of barrier stiffness on level of harvested power at 18.3 Hz

Fig. 5 shows the effect of initial gap of the barrier on the frequency bandwidth and the harvested power of the system. As can be seen, by increasing the initial gap, amount of extracted power has increased noticeably. But after about the gap value of 3.3mm the maximum harvested power is obtained. This value is the gazing gap value that the harvester just touched the barrier.

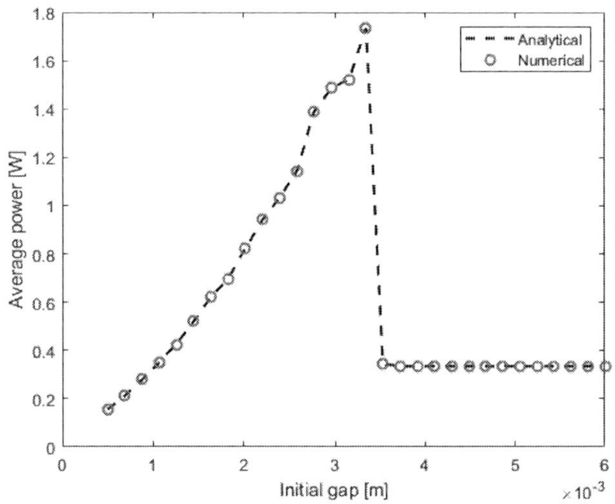

Fig. 5 effect of gap barrier on harvested power at 18.3 Hz

4. Conclusion

This work, present a novel vibro-impact energy harvester by adding a stopping barrier to a typical bistable piezoelectric unimorph cantilever beam for increasing the frequency bandwidth and the level of harvested power of the system. The operating frequency bandwidth and extracted power of the bistable energy harvester was examined in non-impacting and impacting motions via frequency response diagrams. It was shown that the impact phenomenon increases the working frequency bandwidth of the bistable harvesting system about 68.5 percent. Besides, the amount of harvested power is increased about 100.6 percent. According to the results, by increasing the barrier stiffness, the average of the harvested power decreased. Then, the optimum values of stiffness barrier and initial gap value is gained. As was shown, after about the gap value of 3.3mm the maximum harvested power is obtained. This value is the gazing gap value that the harvester just touched the barrier. This results can be used to simulate an optimum vibro-impact energy harvester.

Refferences

[1] M. Lu, G. Fu, N. B. Osman, and U. Konbr, "Green energy harvesting strategies on edge-based urban computing in sustainable internet of things," *Sustain. Cities Soc.*, vol. 75, p. 103349, 2021, doi: https://doi.org/10.1016/j.scs.2021.103349.

[2] S. Madruga, "Modeling of enhanced micro-energy harvesting of thermal ambient fluctuations with metallic foams embedded in Phase Change Materials," *Renew. Energy*, vol. 168, pp. 424–437, 2021, doi: https://doi.org/10.1016/j.renene.2020.12.041.

[3] T. Yang, S. Zhou, S. Fang, W. Qin, and D. J. Inman, "Nonlinear vibration energy harvesting and vibration suppression technologies: Designs, analysis, and applications," *Appl. Phys. Rev.*, vol. 8, no. 3, p. 31317, Sep. 2021, doi: 10.1063/5.0051432.

[4] A. Hosseinkhani, D. Younesian, P. Eghbali, A. Moayedizadeh, and A. Fassih, "Sound and vibration energy harvesting for railway applications: A review on linear and nonlinear techniques," *Energy Reports*, vol. 7, pp. 852–874, 2021, doi: https://doi.org/10.1016/j.egyr.2021.01.087.

[5] I. Ahmad, L. M. Hee, A. M. Abdelrhman, S. A. Imam, and M. S. Leong, "Scopes, challenges and approaches of energy harvesting for wireless sensor nodes in machine condition monitoring systems: A review," *Measurement*, vol. 183, p. 109856, 2021, doi: https://doi.org/10.1016/j.measurement.2021.109856.

[6] K. A. Cook-Chennault, N. Thambi, and A. M. Sastry, "Powering {MEMS} portable devices: a review of non-regenerative and regenerative power supply systems with special emphasis on piezoelectric energy harvesting systems," *Smart Mater. Struct.*, vol. 17, no. 4, p. 43001, Jun. 2008, doi: 10.1088/0964-1726/17/4/043001.

[7] J. Jiang, S. Liu, L. Feng, and D. Zhao, "A Review of Piezoelectric Vibration Energy Harvesting with Magnetic Coupling Based on Different Structural Characteristics," *Micromachines* , vol. 12, no. 4. 2021, doi: 10.3390/mi12040436.

[8] S. Bae and P. Kim, "Load Resistance Optimization of Bi-Stable Electromagnetic Energy Harvester Based on Harmonic Balance," *Sensors* , vol. 21, no. 4. 2021, doi: 10.3390/s21041505.

[9] A. Erturk and D. J. Inman, "Broadband piezoelectric power generation on high-energy orbits of the bistable Duffing oscillator with electromechanical coupling," *J. Sound Vib.*, vol. 330, no. 10, pp. 2339–2353, 2011.

[10] K. Aouali, N. Kacem, N. Bouhaddi, E. Mrabet, and M. Haddar, "Efficient broadband vibration energy harvesting based on tuned non-linearity and energy localization," *Smart Mater. Struct.*, vol. 29, no. 10, p. 10LT01, 2020, doi: 10.1088/1361-665x/abaa95.

[11] S. Onsorynezhad, A. Abedini, and F. Wang, "Parametric optimization of a frequency-up-conversion piezoelectric harvester via discontinuous analysis," *J. Vib. Control*, vol. 26, no. 15–16, pp. 1241–1252, 2020.

[12] S. Farhangdoust, A. Mehrabi, and D. Younesian, "Bistable wind-induced vibration energy harvester for self-powered wireless sensors in smart bridge monitoring systems," in *Nondestructive characterization and monitoring of advanced materials, aerospace, civil infrastructure, and transportation XIII*, 2019, vol. 10971, p. 109710C.

[13] A. Erturk, J. Hoffmann, and D. J. Inman, "A piezomagnetoelastic structure for broadband vibration energy harvesting," *Appl. Phys. Lett.*, vol. 94, no. 25, p. 254102, Jun. 2009, doi: 10.1063/1.3159815.

[14] Z. Zhou, H. Zhang, W. Qin, P. Zhu, and W. Du, "Improving Energy Harvesting from Bridge Vibration Excited by Moving Vehicles with a Bi-Stable Harvester," *Materials* , vol. 15, no. 6. 2022, doi: 10.3390/ma15062237.

[15] J. Marzbanrad, M. Shahsavar, and B. Beyranvand, "Analysis of force and energy density transferred to barrier in a single degree of freedom vibro-impact system," *J. Cent. South Univ.*, vol. 24, no. 6, pp. 1351–1359, 2017, doi: 10.1007/s11771-017-3539-0.

[16] M. S. M. Soliman, E. M. Abdel-Rahman, E. F. El-Saadany, and R. R. Mansour, "A wideband vibration-based energy harvester," *J. Micromechanics Microengineering*, vol. 18, no. 11, p. 115021, 2008.

[17] A. Abedini and F. Wang, "Energy harvesting of a frequency up-conversion piezoelectric harvester with controlled impact," *Eur. Phys. J. Spec. Top.*, vol. 228, no. 6, pp. 1459–1474, 2019.

[18] K. Vijayan, M. I. Friswell, H. H. Khodaparast, and S. Adhikari, "Non-linear energy harvesting from coupled impacting beams," *Int. J. Mech. Sci.*, vol. 96–97, pp. 101–109, 2015, doi: https://doi.org/10.1016/j.ijmecsci.2015.03.001.

[19] H. Liu, C. Lee, T. Kobayashi, C. J. Tay, and C. Quan, "Investigation of a MEMS piezoelectric energy harvester system with a frequency-widened-bandwidth mechanism introduced by mechanical stoppers," *Smart Mater. Struct.*, vol. 21, no. 3, p. 35005, 2012, doi: 10.1088/0964-1726/21/3/035005.

9th International Operational Modal Analysis Conference
iomac
July 3 - 6, 2022
Vancouver, Canada

PREDOMINANT FREQUENCY OF VIBRATION OF BUILDINGS DURING AN EARTHQUAKE FROM MEASURED GROUND WAVE PROPAGATION TIME

Leila Katebi[1], *and Carlos Ventura*[2]

[1] PhD student, Civil Engineering Department, University of British Columbia, leilaktb@mail.ubc.ca.
[2] Professor, Civil Engineering Department, University of British Columbia, ventura@civil.ubc.ca.

ABSTRACT

The vibration of a structure during an earthquake results from waves travelling through the soil from the source of the earthquake that reach the foundation of the structure and propagate through the structure. These waves can propagate in different directions, causing different structural responses. A critical aspect of these propagating waves is the travel time it takes a wave to go from one part of the structure (or the vicinity of the structure) to another part of the structure. In this paper, a waveform-based technique is introduced, which permits extracting the predominant frequency of ground motion propagating through the structure and could also potentially be used for damage estimation due to severe ground shaking. This technique is referred to as the "C method" and was originally introduced in Japan by Y. Nakamura in 2017. This method uses the measured vibration at roof level to estimate the dominant frequency of motions from the wave travel time throughout the structure by minimizing the difference between measured and estimated signal values at specific points. The validity of this output-only method is determined by comparing the results of frequencies obtained from actual recorded data in instrumented buildings during an earthquake. A case study using the data from a fifty two-story instrumented building in California was obtained during the 1994 Northridge Earthquake. The results of this study indicate the predominant frequencies that control the response of the building during the earthquake and can be used to estimate the damage potential of the waves propagating throughout the structure.

Keywords: Wave propagation, Structural health monitoring, Earthquake

1. INTRODUCTION

Earthquakes are one of the most catastrophic natural disasters, causing devastating effects, such as fatalities and massive loss of property. When earthquakes happen, the elastic energy accumulated in faults becomes released in waves that travel through the crust of the earth and result in the shaking of structures (Villaverde, 2009). From an engineering point of view, the destructive potential of earthquakes can be increased by design faults, poor material and construction quality, or a lack of proper maintenance of structures. Therefore, it proves necessary to regularly assess and monitor the health condition of structures.

When damage happens in a structure, its physical properties change, consequently altering its dynamic characteristics – such as frequency, damping ratio and mode shapes. During the last decades, several methods have been developed for identifying dynamic characteristics from the seismic response of structures. Some of the developed methods are categorized as output-only, meaning that they do not require the record of input excitation (Ghahari et al., 2013). These methods are of remarkable interest in civil engineering, for which the input excitation of structures might be unavailable.

Once a vibration or an excitation occurs in any medium, like soil, rock, or any other material, it will not be immediately felt within the entire space. In other words, it takes time for those waves to travel from the source point, where the disturbance has originated, to another point in the medium. To interpret the characteristics of earthquake waves carried through the media, d'Alembert developed the one-dimensional wave equation, describing the velocity of the media as a parameter relating the time and space domains (Tipler, 2003). Thereafter, some other researchers also conducted various studies to estimate the wave propagation velocity (Barkat et al., 2020; Clavero et al., 2014; Ikuta et al., 2002; Zhu & Harris, 2015).

Nakamura recently proposed an efficient method based on wave travel time that can be applied for the evaluation of the degradation in structures in a real-time manner (Nakamura et al., 2019). The suggested method, called the CERS method, includes a set of four methods – C, E, R, and S. The C technique can compute the wave propagation time and damping between a free end and a point in the medium in real-time, assuming a one-dimensional wave field. The E method can do the same between a free field and the reflecting plane. Furthermore, the R and S approaches can typically determine the time difference of waveforms between two spatially distant locations in real-time using the maximum cross-correlation and the minimal simple error, respectively.

The CERS method can also be applied in structures to detect the change of wave velocity, as well as damping and dynamic characteristics of buildings during vibrations (Nakamura et al., 2020). In 2020, the results of the method were validated using the Kalman filter technique and the recorded seismic responses of the Research Building in Tohoku (Nakamura, 2020). The travel time concept of the methods is calculated upon the waveform synthesis and cross-correlation between waveforms in two points of structures.

A fifty two-story office building in Los Angeles, California is one of the stations that has experienced more than ten strong earthquakes. Since 1989 seismic records from this building are available from the Center for Engineering Strong Motion Database (CESMD) (*Center for Engineering Strong Motion Data*, n.d.). The researchers have studied this building to calculate the dynamic characteristics of the structure. Ventura has calibrated the computer model of the structure to estimate the linear and nonlinear response of 3-D model during severe earthquakes(Ventura & Ding, 2000). Farahani et al. have identified the wave velocity variation of waveforms propagating vertically through the structure. By using the wave inversion algorithm, they were able to detect permanent stiffness changes of the structure during the severe shaking (Rahmani & Todorovska, 2015). Both studies reported no building damage has been observed.

The building is used as a case study to illustrate how the CERS method works. At first, the method is implemented and verified with the results of the recorded data of the research building of Tohoku University. Then, it is applied to vibrations observed on different floors of the Los Angeles steel-frame building excited by the Northridge earthquake.

The rest of the paper is organized as follows. A detailed outline of the C method and formulations are provided in Section 2. The validation of the method and obtained numerical results are presented in Section 3. Finally, the concluding remarks are included in Section 4.

2. DESCRIPTION OF THE C METHOD

In this section, the formulations of the C method are presented. The method calculates wave propagation time between two points in a medium – a free endpoint and another point inside the medium – using the observed waveforms at those points. The E method can also calculate the time propagates between a free field and reflecting plane. The R and S methods can generally calculate the time difference of waveforms between two points separated spatially based on the maximum cross-correlation basis and minimum simple error basis (Nakamura, 2020). Considering the available data from the case study, the goal of the paper is to calculate the changes in travel time measured between two points using the C method.

The vibration of a point in the surface layer is assumed as a sum of upward and downward waves. Therefore, the observed waveform in the ground at a distance x from the free end is expressed as:

$$G(x,t) = \frac{T\left(t+\frac{x}{V}\right)+T\left(t-\frac{x}{V}\right)}{2} \tag{1}$$

where T is the observed waveform at an endpoint; V stands for the distribution velocity; and $\frac{x}{V}$ shows the travel time. As defined in Eq. (2), based on Nakamura's method, the travel time is estimated as the product of a constant value (k) and the sampling rate (Δt). The unknown value k varies through the time.

$$\frac{x}{V} = k.\Delta t \tag{2}$$

By substituting the Eq. (2) in Eq. (1), the waveform G is reformulated as Eq. (3):

$$G(x,t) = \frac{T(t+k.\Delta t)+T(t-k.\Delta t)}{2} \tag{3}$$

When $t = j.\Delta t$, the estimated waveform at another point, with a distance of y from the free end, is expressed as Eq. (4):

$$H(y,j) = \frac{T\left(j.\Delta t+\frac{y}{V}\right)+T\left(j.\Delta t-\frac{y}{V}\right)}{2} \tag{4}$$

In Eq. (5), the distance y is defined as $y = i.\Delta t.V$, where i is a counter, expressing the time lag in terms of the sampling time interval Δt. Hence, Eq. (4) can be represented as:

$$H(i,j) = \frac{T(j.\Delta t+i.\Delta t)+T(j.\Delta t-i.\Delta t)}{2} = \frac{T((j+i)\Delta t)+T((j-i)\Delta t)}{2} \tag{5}$$

The error function is defined as the square of the difference between the estimated and the observed waveforms as below:

$$Err(i,j) = [H(i,j) - G(x,t)]^2 \tag{6}$$

The value of i can be derived through an optimization problem through which the error for each j changing in time is minimized, as shown in Eq. (7).

$$Err(j) = min[Err(i,j)] \tag{7}$$

Thus, it is possible to estimate the travel time based on the sampling time interval. When $y = x$, the estimated waveform complies with the observed one, leading to the fact that by considering i equal to k (i.e., $i = k$), the error for each time step is minimized.

According to Nakamura's article (Nakamura, 2020) ,applying the C method, the predominant frequency is derived as the inverse of quadrupled travel time between two points on the wave propagation direction from the end face to the reflecting plane.

$$f = \frac{V}{4H} = \frac{1}{4\frac{H}{V}} = \frac{1}{4\hat{t}} \tag{8}$$

where the parameter H is the wave travel distance and equals the height of the structure and $\hat{t}$ is the the value discribing thhe time travel between two points.

3. ESTIMATED RESULTS AND DISCUSSION

In this section, the C method is used to estimate the wave propagation time between the points on the roof (as the point at the free end) and on the ground level (as the point inside the medium) of the Milpitas building. In order to check that the method works properly and accurately estimates the change in travel time and frequency, the code is firstly verified with the same building studied in the reference article (Nakamura, 2020).

3.1. Research Building of Tohoku University

In this subsection, the Civil Engineering and Architecture Research Building of Tohoku University is studied, and the waveforms belong to the Pacific coast of the Tohoku Earthquake in 2011. Figure 1 shows photo of the THU building, its vertical cross section, and plans of the instrumented levels. According to the figure 1, the east-west (EW) and north-south (NS) directions refer to the longitudinal and transverse orientations. The responses are recorded on the 9th and 1st floor of the building and are averaged by exponential smoothing, setting the half-life period of 5 seconds (Nishiyama et al., 2011).

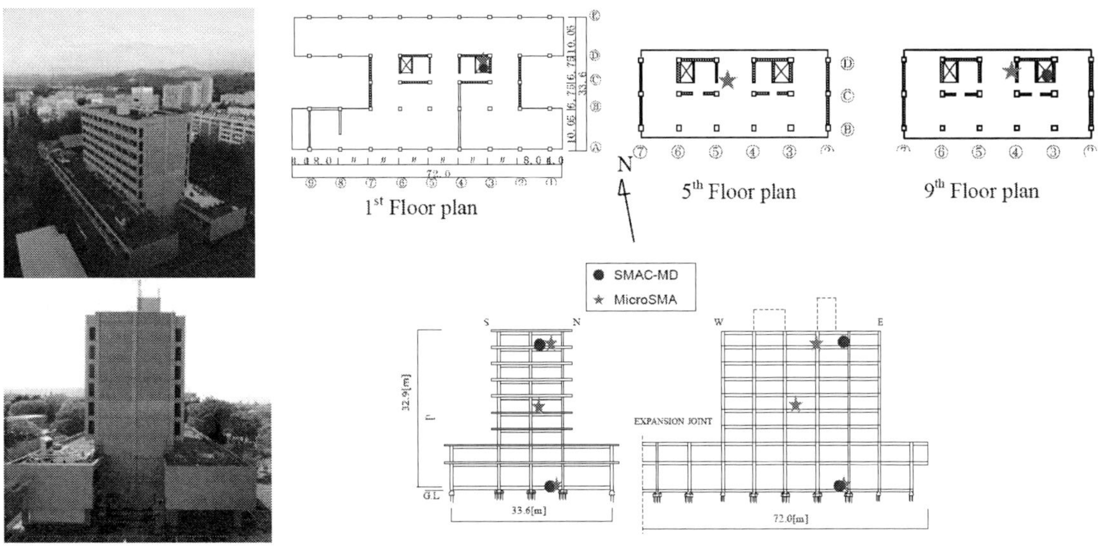

Figure 1: overview of the THU building with sensor locations(Motosaka et al., 2012)

The measurement on the 9th floor (U9) is considered as a measurement point at the free end, and U1 recorded on the 1st floor is assumed as a measurement point in the medium. Following Eq. (4), the waveform on the 1st floor is obtained by averaging the upward and downward waveforms on the 9th floor.

To better capture the difference, the seismic responses between the time 80 and 100 seconds of the observed and estimated waveforms on the first floor are represented in Figure 2. In the selected 20-second interval, there is a jump in the acceleration amplitude, and the numerical method should be robust enough to estimate the response with a minor error. As can be seen, there is a negligible error between the estimated and the observed acceleration.

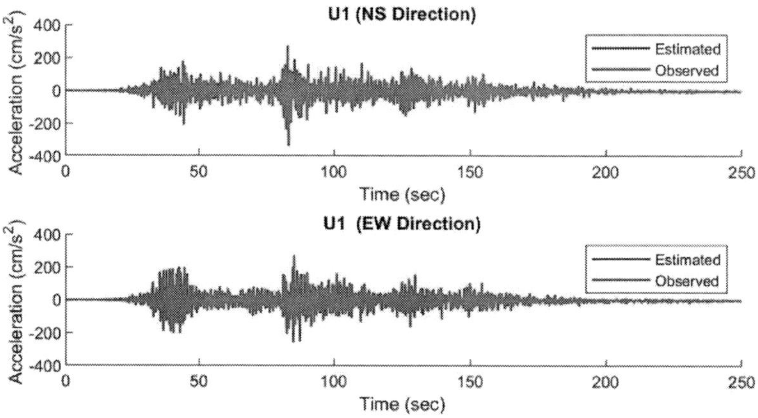

(a)

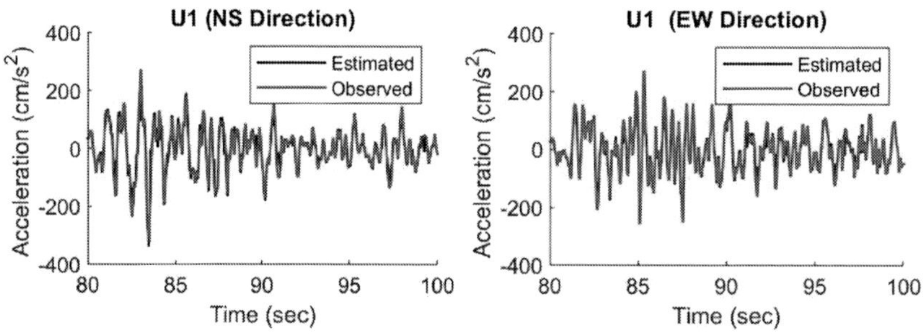

(b)

Figure 2: comparison between the observed and estimated waveform one at the first floor in both directions a) whole time history, and b) partial portion of the record (from 80 sec to 100 sec)

Figure 3 illustrates the comparioson of travel times versus time from Nakamura's article - colourful curves - as well as our obtained time travel - drawn in black and named as P. As can be seen, the obtained travel time using our codes fits well with those of(Nakamura, 2020). By applying a smoothing filter, such as a moving average, the results can closely align with those from the resource.

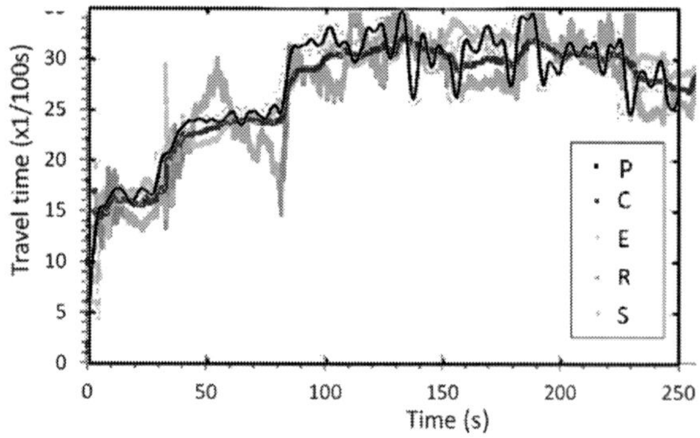

(a)

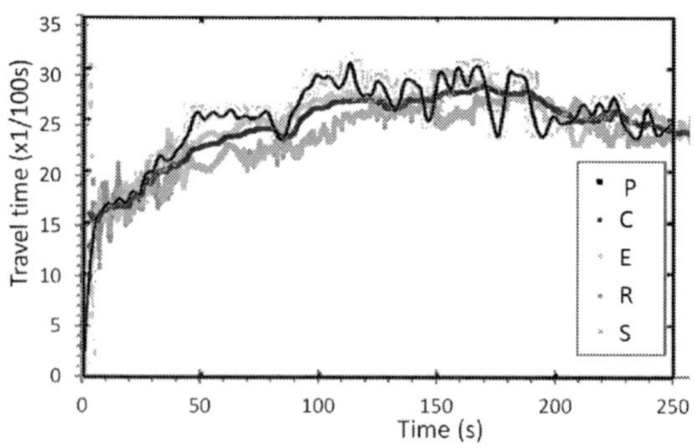

(b)

Figure 3: Comparison between the travel times estimated by Nakamura and the programmed Matlab code in a) transverse direction b)longitudinal direction

Since the result of the method agrees well with the result of ref. (Nakamura, 2020), it confirms that the implementation of the method was performed correctly and can be employed for other structures.

According to Figure 3, it is also evident that the structure has faced two major shocks. The primary shock has happened at around 40 second, and the secondary shock has occured at around 80 seconds. Interestingly, the travel time has considerably shifted around these times. For instance, in Figure 2 (a), the travel time was around $16\Delta t$ ($\Delta t = \frac{1}{100} sec$) at the beginning of the waveform, and after the first shock, it reached about $22\Delta t$. After experiencing the second shock, the travel time converged to $30\Delta t$. In the longitudinal direction, shown in Figure 2 (b), the first shock gradually shifted the travel time from $15\Delta t$ to $25\Delta t$, but the second one did not change the time lag. Nakamura and Mostaka seperately concluded that the structure has faced higher damage in the transverse-direction compared to the longitudinal-direction(Motosaka et al., 2012).

The predominant frequency derived from the C method is assumed as the fourfold increase in the travel time. Figure 4 illustrates the time history of the predominant frequency during the Tohoku Earthquake. The fluctuation in the NS-direction is much more evident than in the other direction. Similar jumps corresponding to the shocks can be observed in the NS-direction at 40 secs and 80 secs in Figure 4.

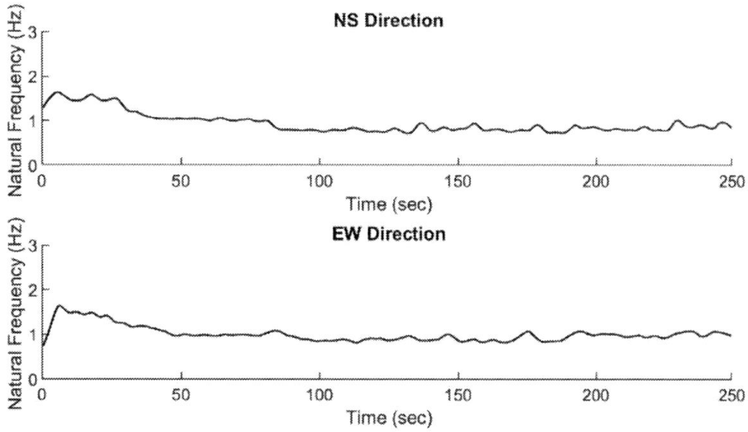

Figure 4: The estimated predominant frequency of Tohoku University in both directions

3.2. Los Angeles office Building

The structure studied in this section is the 52-story steel frame building shown in Figure 5. It is located in the City of Los Angeles, California, and was designed in 1988, constructed in 1988-90 and instrumented by the California Strong Motion Instrumentation Program (CSMIP) in 1990. The structureis the concentrically braced steel frames at the core with outrigger moment frames in both directions. The vertical load carrying system is concrete slabs on steel deck supported by steel frames.To improve the performance of the high rise buiding due to wind forces, the tip of every corner is clipped and the middle third of each side is notched. The foundation is concrete spread fittings founded on site class D Alluvium over rock. The building uses a total of 20 accelerometers on 7 levels to measure seismic motions.(*Center for Engineering Strong Motion Data(CESMD)*, n.d.) The figure below summarizes the locations of the accelerometers in the building.

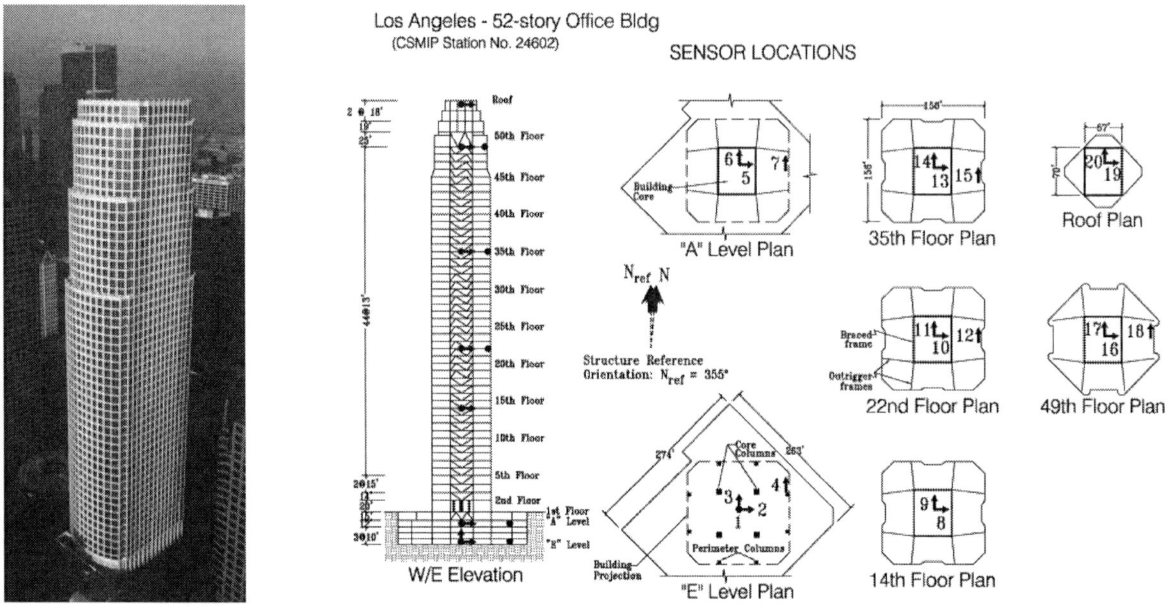

(a) (b)

Figure 5: The 52-storey building a) view(***777 Tower | Los Angeles Conservancy*, n.d.**) b) plan with sensor locations (Center for Engineering Strong Motion Data (CESMD), n.d.)

In this study, the Northridge earthquake with the magnitude of 6.4 and the epicenter depth of approximately 30 km from the building is considered. According to the C method, two measurement points along the vertical line are selected to present 1D wave propagation. Seismic acceleration responses of the roof of the structure recorded via sensor channels 20 and 19 during the Northridge earthquake were used as the observed waveforms at the endpoint for the N-S and E-W directions, respectively. Similarly, data from channels 6 and 5 of the "A" level of the building were used as the observed waveforms in the medium. Figure 6 shows the time history record data with a sampling rate of 100 samples per second on the "A level" floor, corresponding to Ground level, and roof of the building recorded in N-S and E-W directions.

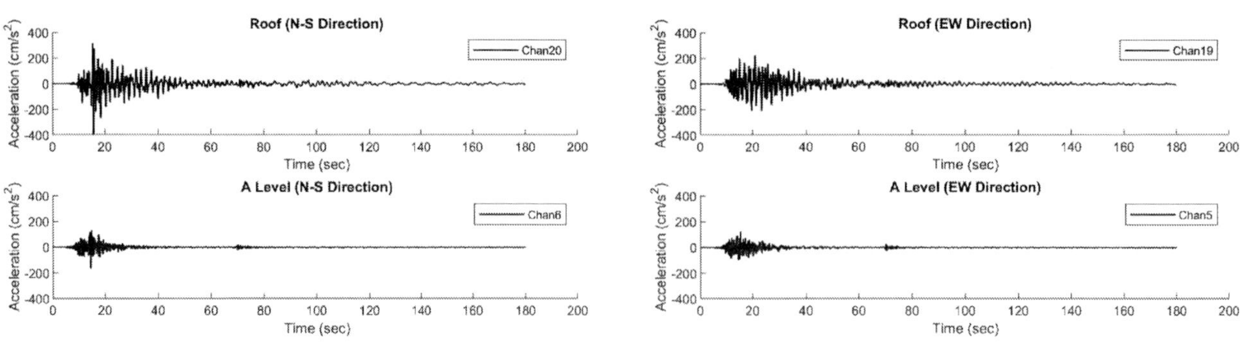

(a) (b)

Figure 6: The acceleration response of the Los Angeles building on roof and "A" level a) N-S direction b) E-W direction

The waveform at ground level is estimated from the waveform observed at roof level using the C method. The results of the estimated waveform as well as the observed response are presented in the Figure 7. The input data were averaged by using the moving average filter with half period of 2 seconds.

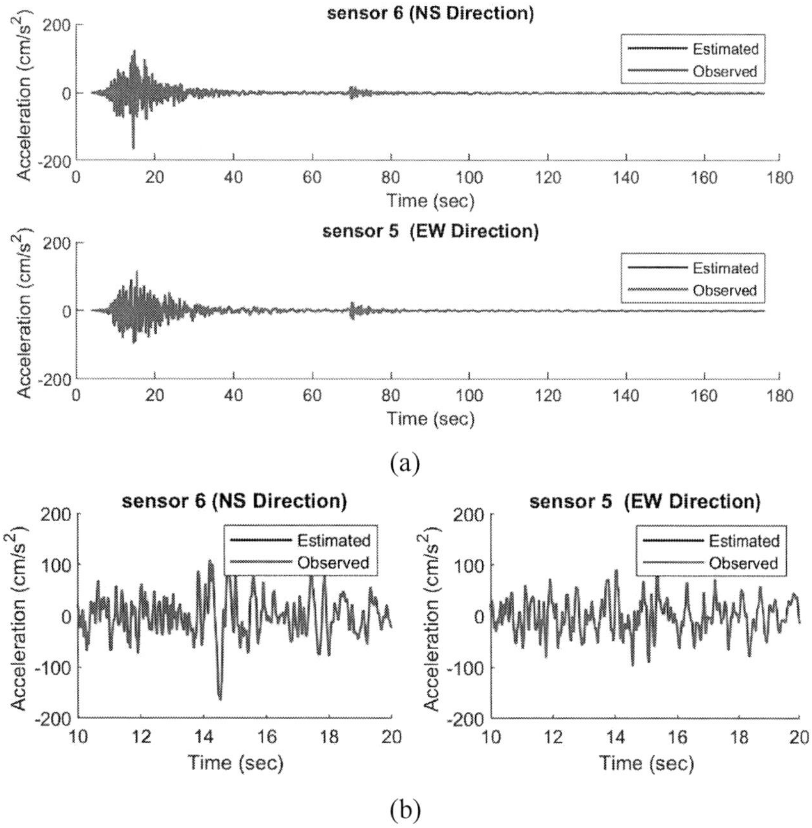

Figure 7: The comparison between the observed waveform and estimated one applying the C method to the observed waveform at roof level in both directions a) whole time history b) partial part of time history (from 10 sec to 20 sec)

Figure 7 presents the ground-level waveform estimated from the observed data at roof level and compared with the corresponding observed record on the ground floor. In other words, both observed and estimated waveforms agree well which indicates this method has successfully find the optimum travel time value at each time steps. Figure 7 compares the travel time change derived from the study method for north-south and east-west directions. As can be seen in Fig. 8, the travel time was around $200\Delta t$ ($\Delta t = 1/100$ seconds). The oscillation of the travel time is tangible, which reports no damages occured in the structure.

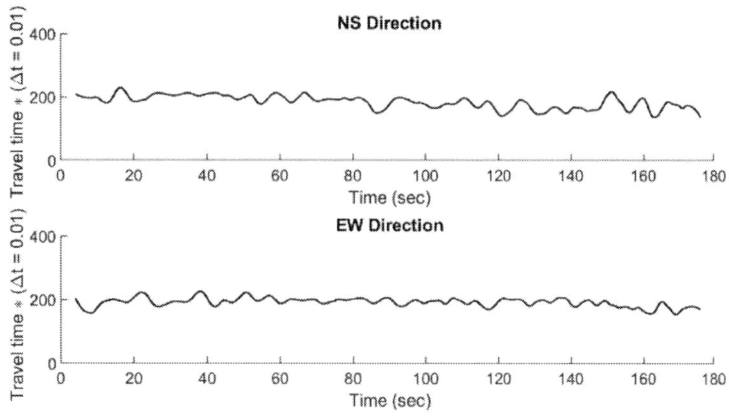

Figure 8: The estimated traveltime of the building in N-S and E-W directions

The natural frequency of the steel frame building is estimated from the inverse of the time of wave propagating between two points. As shown in figure 9, the fundamental natural frequency with the value of 0.16 Hz remains constant within the structure. The frequency results demonstrate the same value in the other direction. Ventura has reported the dominant period of 6.06 seconds, corresponding to 0.165 Hz, as the first mode of vibration in the EW direction (Ventura & Ding, 2000). The frequency results of figure 9 show no evidence jump occurred during the earthquake, which confirms the previous reports related to no severe damage to the building.

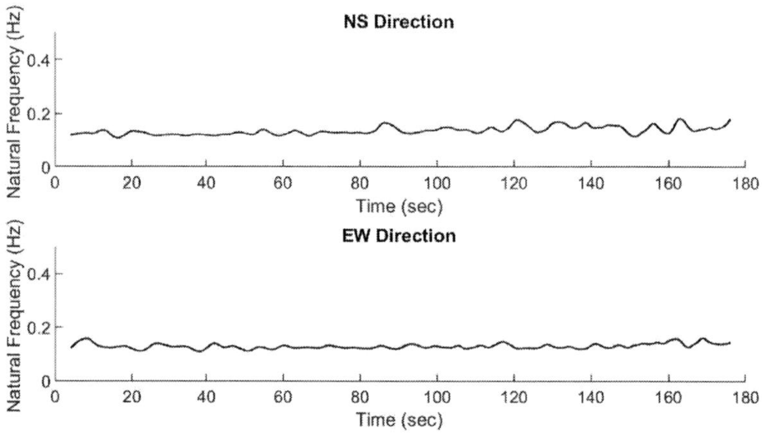

Figure 9: The Natural frequency of the building in N-S and E-W directions

4. CONCLUSION

In conclusion, this article applied the C method to extract the wave travel time by minimizing the differences between observed and the estimated waveforms. The frequency change of two buildings was examined for this research. In the first stage, the waveforms of the research building at Tohoku University were utilized for verifying and comparing the results of our MATLAB code with those of the original paper. In the second step, the 52-story Los Angeles steel frame building was used to study the wave propagation time between two points in the structure during the Northridge earthquake. The changes in the predominant frequency of the structure correlate with the shifts in travel time that does not occur during the shock waves and thereby indicating no damages induced in the structure.

The method can be utilized for real-time structural health monitoring of real-world structures during earthquakes, but the relationship between the structural elements and the result of the method needs to be further studied. As a future direction of this research, the authors intend to combine the output of the method with the stat-of-the-art modal identification techniques to establish an accurate and efficient damage detection method.

REFERENCES

777 Tower | Los Angeles Conservancy. (n.d.). Retrieved May 30, 2022, from https://www.laconservancy.org/locations/777-tower

Barkat, B., Ali, M. Y., Simeunović, M., & Djurović, I. (2020). A configuration with several linear subarrays for the joint estimation of the apparent velocity & direction of propagation of a seismic wave. *Journal of Petroleum Science and Engineering, 184,* 106472. https://doi.org/10.1016/J.PETROL.2019.106472

Center for Engineering Strong Motion Data. (n.d.). Retrieved May 24, 2022, from https://www.strongmotioncenter.org/

Center for Engineering Strong Motion Data(CESMD). (n.d.). Retrieved May 30, 2022, from https://www.strongmotioncenter.org/cgi-bin/CESMD/stationhtml.pl?stationID=CE24602&network=CGS

Clavero, D., Rosa-Cintas, S., López-Casado, C., Delgado, J., & Galiana-Merino, J. J. (2014). Shear wave velocity estimation in the metropolitan area of Málaga (S Spain). *Journal of Applied Geophysics*, *109*, 175–185. https://doi.org/10.1016/J.JAPPGEO.2014.07.025

Ghahari, S. F., Abazarsa, F., Ghannad, M. A., & Taciroglu, E. (2013). Response-only modal identification of structures using strong motion data. *Earthquake Engineering & Structural Dynamics*, *42*(8), 1221–1242. https://doi.org/10.1002/EQE.2268

Ikuta, R., Yamaoka, K., Miyakawa, K., Kunitomo, T., & Kumazawa, M. (2002). Continuous monitoring of propagation velocity of seismic wave using ACROSS. *Geophysical Research Letters*, *29*(13), 5–1. https://doi.org/10.1029/2001GL013974

Motosaka, M., Tsamba, T., Yoshida, K., & Mitsuji, K. (2012). Long-term Monitoring of Amplitude Dependent Dynamic Characteristics of a Damaged Building during the 2011 Tohoku Earthquake. *Journal of Japan Association for Earthquake Engineering*, *12*(5), 5_117-5_132. https://doi.org/10.5610/JAEE.12.5_117

Nakamura, Y. (2020). ON THE CERS METHODS FOR REALTIME EVALUATION ON A TRAVEL TIME AND DAMPING. *The 17th World Conference on Earthquake Engineering*.

Nakamura, Y., Saita, J., & Sato, T. (2020). THE DYNAMIC CHARACTERISTIC CHANGE OF A SKYSCRAPER SKS BUILDING DURING EARTHQUAKES APPLYING THE CERS METHODS. *The 17th World Conference on Earthquake Engineering*.

Nakamura, Y., Saita, J., Sato, T., Nakamura, Y., Saita, J., & Sato, T. (2019). *Assessing the Wave Propagation Velocity and Damping at Commodus Passage of Colosseum Using Microtremor Applying the CERS methods*.

Nishiyama, I., Ando, S., Nagasaki, T., Ishii, N., Ootake (NILIM), R., Shibata (NILIM), Y., Mori (NILIM), M., Arikawa (NILIM), S., & Takeya (NILIM), S. (2011). *Summary of the Field Survey and Research on "The 2011 off the Pacific coast of Tohoku Earthquake" (the Great East Japan Earthquake)*.

Paul A. Tipler, G. M. (2003). *Physics for Scientists and Engineers, Volume 1: Mechanics, Oscillations, and Waves; Thermodynamics* (illustrated, Vol. 1). W. H. Freeman.

Rahmani, M., & Todorovska, M. I. (2015). Structural health monitoring of a 54-story steel-frame building using a wave method and earthquake records. *Earthquake Spectra*, *31*(1), 501–525. https://doi.org/10.1193/112912EQS339M

Tipler, P. A. (2003). *Physics for Scientists and Engineers, Volume 1: Mechanics, Oscillations, and Waves; Thermodynamics* (illustrated, Vol. 1). W. H. Freeman.

Ventura, C. E., & Ding, Y. (2000). *LINEAR AND NONLINEAR SEISMIC RESPONSE OF A 52-STOREY STEEL FRAME BUILDING*.

Villaverde, Roberto. (2009). *Fundamental concepts of earthquake engineering*. https://books.google.com/books/about/Fundamental_Concepts_of_Earthquake_Engin.html?id=613NBQAAQBAJ

Zhu, T., & Harris, J. M. (2015). Improved estimation of P-wave velocity, S-wave velocity, and attenuation factor by iterative structural joint inversion of crosswell seismic data. *Journal of Applied Geophysics*, *123*, 71–80. https://doi.org/10.1016/J.JAPPGEO.2015.09.005

9th International Operational Modal Analysis Conference
iomac
July 3 - 6, 2022
Vancouver, Canada

STATISTICAL DAMAGE DETECTION AND LOCALIZATION WITH MAHALANOBIS DISTANCE APPLIED TO MODAL PARAMETERS

Szymon Greś[1], Alexander Mendler[2], Niels-Jørgen Jacobsen[3], Palle Andersen[4], Michael Döhler[5]

[1]Institute of Structural Engineering (IBK), SMM team, ETH Zürich, 8093 Zürich, Switzerland
[2]Technical University of Munich, TUM School of Engineering and Design, 80333 Munich, Germany
[3]Hottinger Brüel & Kjær A/S, 2830 Virum, Denmark
[4]Structural Vibration Solutions A/S, NOVI Science Park, 9220 Aalborg, Denmark
[4]Univ. Gustave Eiffel, Inria, COSYS-SII, I4S, Campus de Beaulieu, 35042 Rennes, France

ABSTRACT

Damage detection and damage localization constitute two pillars of Structural Health Monitoring that are highly relevant for applications to large-scale structures. Damage detection is usually achieved through statistical tests of data-driven residuals that monitor changes of a structure from its baseline behaviour. Damage localization investigates changes in damage residuals with respect to parameterized structural models through sensitivity vectors. Among the classic damage-sensitive features used for residual generation are subspace angles and principal components obtained from data spaces, whose evaluation for a decision about damage often boils down to novelty analysis, or statistical likelihood ratio tests. Modal parameter estimates are also employed for this purpose; however, most of the existing approaches appear to neglect the uncertainties related to their estimation. This paper fills this gap and presents a residual for damage detection and damage localization that is based on the difference of modal parameters obtained from data collected in some baseline and some test state of the structural system. The proposed scheme is evaluated in numerical simulations validating its robustness for damage detection and damage localization.

Keywords: damage detection, damage localization, modal parameter estimation, Structural Health Monitoring, Operational Modal Analysis

1. INTRODUCTION

Damage detection and damage localization are two pillars of vibration-based Structural Health Monitoring (SHM) that are well-explored in the literature, e.g., see [1]. Among the many strategies for damage detection and damage localization which are model-based [2, 3], data-driven [4–8], or a combination thereof [9], methods that appreciate the uncertainty in the estimated parameters are particularly appealing from the practical standpoint, as they account for statistical estimation errors related to noise and short data length in the damage diagnosis problem. Such methods include statistical tests on Kalman filter innovations [10], non-parametric change detection tests based on novelty detection [11], or parametric subspace tests [4–6].

Among the classic damage-sensitive features that are often used for the statistical tests about damage are subspace angles and principal components obtained from data spaces. Modal parameter estimates are also employed for this purpose; however, most of the existing approaches appear to neglect the uncertainties related to their estimation. This paper fills this gap and presents a residual for damage detection and damage localization that is based on the difference of modal parameters obtained from data collected in some baseline and some test state of the structure. The statistical properties of the residual are analyzed and are used for a statistical hypothesis test in a metric that boils down to Mahalanobis distance. The proposed scheme is evaluated in numerical simulations validating its robustness for damage detection and damage localization.

2. SYSTEM MODEL AND MODAL PARAMETER PROPERTIES

In this section the parametrized dynamic model for vibration data is introduced, and the statistical properties of modal parameter estimates are recalled.

2.1. System model

Let $\theta \in \mathbb{R}^p$ be a parameter vector that contains p damage-sensitive parameters of the structural elements of interest. This parametrization is defined after the specific monitoring problem at hand, such that θ contains parameters of the dynamic system whose sensitivity to damage is non-zero and which fully parametrize the considered damage, e.g., Young's modulus and density of elements, crack parameters (width, length), among others. The vibration behavior of the monitored linear time-invariant structural system with m degrees of freedom is described by the differential equation

$$\mathcal{M}^\theta \ddot{q}(t) + \mathcal{C}^\theta \dot{q}(t) + \mathcal{K}^\theta q(t) = \mathbf{f}(t) \tag{1}$$

where t denotes continuous time, and $\mathcal{M}^\theta, \mathcal{C}^\theta, \mathcal{K}^\theta \in \mathbb{R}^{m\times m}$ denote mass, damping and stiffness matrices that respectively depend on parameter θ. Vectors $q(t) \in \mathbb{R}^m$ and $\mathbf{f}(t) \in \mathbb{R}^m$ contain the continuous-time displacements at the degrees of freedom (DOF) and the unmeasured external forces, respectively. Let system (1) be observed by sensors measuring accelerations at r DOF of the structure, collected in an output vector $y(t) \in \mathbb{R}^r$

$$y(t) = \mathcal{D}\ddot{q}(t) + \tilde{v}(t), \tag{2}$$

where $\tilde{v}(t) \in \mathbb{R}^r$ denotes the sensor noise and the matrix $\mathcal{D} \in \mathbb{R}^{r\times m}$ selects the acceleration output at the measurement DOF. Sampled at a rate τ, the dynamic behavior of system (1)-(2) can be represented by a discrete-time stochastic state-space model

$$\begin{cases} x_{k+1} = A^\theta x_k + w_k \\ y_k = C^\theta x_k + v_k \end{cases} \tag{3}$$

where $x_k \in \mathbb{R}^n$ are the states, and $A^\theta \in \mathbb{R}^{n\times n}$, $C^\theta \in \mathbb{R}^{r\times n} \in \mathbb{R}^{r\times u}$, are the parametrized state transition and observation matrices estimated at a model order n. Vectors w_k with v_k denote the process and output noises. The eigenfrequencies f_i^θ, damping ratios ζ_i^θ and mode shapes φ_i^θ of the underlying mechanical system are identified for $i = 1 \ldots n$ from the i-th eigenvalue λ_i^θ and eigenvector Φ_i^θ of A^θ such that

$$f_i^\theta = \frac{|\lambda_{ci}^\theta|}{2\pi},\ \zeta_i^\theta = \frac{-\Re(\lambda_{ci}^\theta)}{|\lambda_{ci}^\theta|},\ \varphi_i^\theta = C^\theta \Phi_i^\theta \tag{4}$$

where every eigenvalue of the continuous system λ_{ci}^{θ} is computed with $e^{\lambda_{ci}^{\theta}\tau} = \lambda_i^{\theta}$. The $|(\cdot)|$ denotes the modulus operator and $\Re(\cdot)$ and $\Im(\cdot)$ express the real and imaginary parts of a complex variable.

2.2. Statistical properties of modal parameter estimates

Hereafter assume that $1 \ldots m$ available estimates of modal parameters are consistent, i.e., the estimates converges to their true values when the data length N goes to infinity. Moreover, assume that the estimates of the natural frequencies and the real and the imaginary parts of the estimated mode shapes

$$\hat{z} = \left[\hat{f}_1^{\theta} \ \ldots \hat{f}_m^{\theta} \ \ \Re(\hat{\varphi}_1^{\theta})^T \ \ldots \ \Re(\hat{\varphi}_m^{\theta})^T \ \ \Re(\hat{\varphi}_1^{\theta})^T \ \ldots \ \Im(\hat{\varphi}_m^{\theta})^T\right]^T \tag{5}$$

are jointly asymptotically Gaussian, satisfying

$$\hat{z} \approx \mathcal{N}\left(z, \tfrac{1}{N}\Sigma_z\right),$$

where

$$z = \left[f_1^{\theta} \ \ldots \ f_m^{\theta} \ \ \Re(\varphi_1^{\theta})^T \ \ldots \ \Re(\varphi_m^{\theta})^T \ \ \Im(\varphi_1^{\theta})^T \ \ldots \ \Im(\varphi_m^{\theta})^T\right], \tag{6}$$

and $\Re(\cdot)$ and $\Im(\cdot)$ express the real and the imaginary parts of a complex variable, $\mathcal{N}(\mu, \Sigma)$ denotes a Gaussian distributed variable with mean μ and covariance Σ, and $\Sigma_z \in \mathbb{R}^{m(2r+1)\times m(2r+1)}$ is the joint asymptotic covariance of the natural frequency and the mode shape estimates. Multiple system identification methods satisfy the aforementioned criteria, e.g., stochastic subspace identification (SSI) methods. The computation of a consistent estimate $\widehat{\Sigma}_z$ can be obtained with the statistical delta method [12] and can be found e.g. in [13–15].

3. MODAL PARAMETER-BASED DAMAGE DETECTION AND LOCALIZATION

Based on features extracted from measurement data in the baseline (reference) and in the current test state, the goal of damage detection is to evaluate whether there is a significant change between the states or not. On the other hand, the overall goal of damage localization is to determine the location of the detected damage based on an FE model of the considered structure and its vibration response collected after the damage occurs. While the detection and the localization of damage relate to different engineering problems, both can be scoped to monitoring changes in the system parameter θ. To analyse such changes, the local approach framework is used [16], where the close hypotheses are formulated

$$\begin{aligned} &\mathrm{H}_0 : \theta = \theta_* \ \text{(healthy state)}, \\ &\mathrm{H}_1 : \theta = \theta_* + \delta/\sqrt{N} \ \text{(damaged state)}, \end{aligned} \tag{7}$$

where δ is an unknown change vector. A data-driven damage residual, whose design is the subject of this work, is formulated in a way such that a small change of the (unknown) θ from its assumed nominal value θ_* induces a change therein. Damage detection refers then to monitoring changes in θ via monitoring changes in the expected value of the residual. The damage localization problem boils down to a statistical decision about which entry of θ is linked to the deviation of the residual from its nominal behaviour.

3.1. Residual definition

Let $\hat{\zeta}$ denote a data-driven damage diagnosis residual. In this work a residual based on the difference of modal parameters is used; in principal, however, any data-driven and damage-sensitive Gaussian metric can be adopted for this purpose, e.g., see [4–7]. To define the residual, let $\hat{z}^{\text{ref}}$ denote stacked estimates of natural frequencies and the vectorized estimates of real and imaginary parts of the mode shapes obtained from data collected in some baseline state of the system, and let $\hat{z}^{\text{test}}$ be its counterpart obtained from data collected in some currently tested system state. The modal parameter-based residual is written as

$$\hat{\zeta} = \sqrt{N}\left(\hat{z}^{\text{ref}} - \hat{z}^{\text{test}}\right). \tag{8}$$

The statistical distribution of the residual (8) can be approximated as Gaussian for a sufficiently large data length N thanks to the asymptotic local approach to change detection [16]

$$\text{under } \mathrm{H}_0 : \hat{\zeta} \xrightarrow{\mathcal{L}} \mathcal{N}(0, \Sigma_\zeta), \tag{9}$$

$$\text{under } \mathrm{H}_1 : \hat{\zeta} \xrightarrow{\mathcal{L}} \mathcal{N}(\mathcal{J}^z_{\theta_*}\delta, \Sigma_\zeta), \tag{10}$$

where $\mathcal{J}^z_{\theta_*} = \frac{\partial z}{\partial \theta}\big|_{\theta=\theta_*}$ is the sensitivity of the modal parameters w.r.t. the system parameter evaluated at θ_*, and $\Sigma_\zeta = \Sigma_{z^{\text{ref}}} + \Sigma_{z^{\text{test}}}$ is the residual covariance that accounts for the uncertainty of both reference and test modal parameters. The derivative $\mathcal{J}^z_{\theta_*}$ is obtained based on the FE model of the mechanical system and is of shape

$$\mathcal{J}^z_{\theta_*} = \begin{bmatrix} \mathcal{J}^f_\theta \\ \Re\left(\mathcal{J}^\varphi_\theta\right) \\ \Im\left(\mathcal{J}^\varphi_\theta\right) \end{bmatrix}, \tag{11}$$

where

$$\mathcal{J}^f_\theta = \begin{bmatrix} \frac{\partial f_1}{\partial \theta^1} & \cdots & \frac{\partial f_1}{\partial \theta^p} \\ \vdots & & \vdots \\ \frac{\partial f_m}{\partial \theta^1} & \cdots & \frac{\partial f_m}{\partial \theta^p} \end{bmatrix}\Bigg|_{\theta=\theta_*}, \quad \mathcal{J}^\varphi_\theta = \begin{bmatrix} \frac{\partial \varphi_1}{\partial \theta^1} & \cdots & \frac{\partial \varphi_1}{\partial \theta^p} \\ \vdots & & \vdots \\ \frac{\partial \varphi_m}{\partial \theta^1} & \cdots & \frac{\partial \varphi_m}{\partial \theta^p} \end{bmatrix}\Bigg|_{\theta=\theta_*}. \tag{12}$$

Its computation can be performed analytically [17], or by using, e.g., a finite difference approach.

3.2. Damage detection and localization strategy

The Generalized Likelihood Ratio (GLR) test is used to decide between two distribution functions (9)-(10), which boils down to a weighted Mahalanobis distance

$$t = \check{\zeta}^T \mathcal{A}^{-1}\check{\zeta}, \tag{13}$$

where $\check{\zeta} = \hat{\mathcal{J}}^T\Sigma_\zeta^{-1}\hat{\zeta}$, $\mathcal{A} = \hat{\mathcal{J}}^T\Sigma_\zeta^{-1}\hat{\mathcal{J}}$ and $\hat{\mathcal{J}}$ is a consistent estimate of $\mathcal{J}^z_{\theta_*}$. For a decision about the damage, the test value (13) is compared to a threshold corresponding to a quantile of the theoretical distribution of the reference test statistics. Notice that a parameter-free version of (13) can be formulated by assuming that $\mathcal{J}^z_{\theta_*}$ is the identity matrix of appropriate size.

To locate damage, it has to be decided which entries of θ_* possibly have changed, which boils down to testing each j-th entry of the change parameter δ, i.e., $\delta^j = 0$ (no damage) against $\delta^j \neq 0$ (indicating damage), which yields the test statistic [9]

$$t_j = \check{\zeta}_j^T (\mathcal{A}^j)^{-1}\check{\zeta}_j, \tag{14}$$

where $\check{\zeta} = \hat{\mathcal{J}}_j^T\Sigma_\zeta^{-1}\hat{\zeta}$, $\mathcal{A}^j = \hat{\mathcal{J}}_j^T\Sigma_\zeta^{-1}\hat{\mathcal{J}}_j$ and $\hat{\mathcal{J}}_j = \hat{\mathcal{J}}^z_{\theta^j_*}$ is a column of $\hat{\mathcal{J}}^z_{\theta_*}$ corresponding to the sensitivity of the residual w.r.t. to change of the j-th parameter. The test statistics t_j is asymptotically χ^2 distributed with $d = 1$ degrees of freedom and non-centrality parameter λ_j

$$\lambda_j = \mathcal{A}^j(\delta^j)^2 \tag{15}$$

if $\delta^j \neq 0$ and the other entries of δ are null. When the latter assumption is not satisfied, e.g., when damaged pertains to more than one element, or when testing an undamaged element while others are damaged, the non-centrality parameter does not follow (15) and a minmax test to locate damage should be used [9]. The sketch of the deployed damage detection and localization tandem is presented in Figure 1.

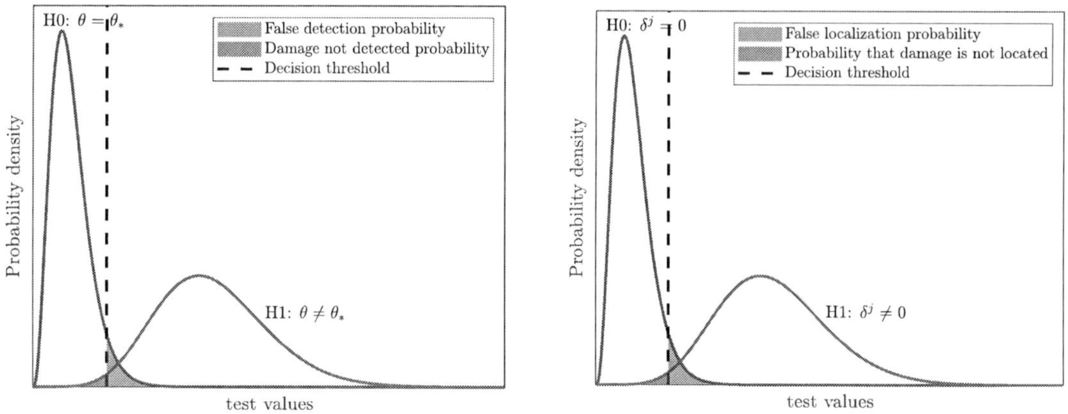

Figure 1: Damage detection scheme (left). Damage localization scheme (right).

Remark 1. *The mode shape contained in* $\hat{z}$ (5) *is called the unnormalized mode shape since its scaling is arbitrary. To make it comparable between different data sets a normalization scheme is needed. On the related note, the covariance of the normalized mode shapes is rank deficient [18], which must be considered in* (13)-(14) *by removing the adequate rows. Two normalization methods were analyzed in detail in [18], from which the normalization with the maximum mode shape component is used herein.*

4. APPLICATION

This section is devoted to the application of the proposed damage detection and localization scheme on data simulated based on Reissner-Mindlin plate model. The model consists of 64 first-order elements, 81 nodes and, consequently, 243 degrees of freedom (DOF). For the sake of simulation, proportional damping is assumed, where the damping matrix is defined such that each mode has a damping ratio of 1%. The translational DOF are constrained to zero at the edge elements of the model. The excitation is modeled as a white noise signal applied on all DOFs. The transverse acceleration data are sampled with a frequency of 6000 Hz and collected with 11 sensors. One damage scenario emulating a 15% increase in mass of element 47 is considered. The plate model is depicted in Figure 2.

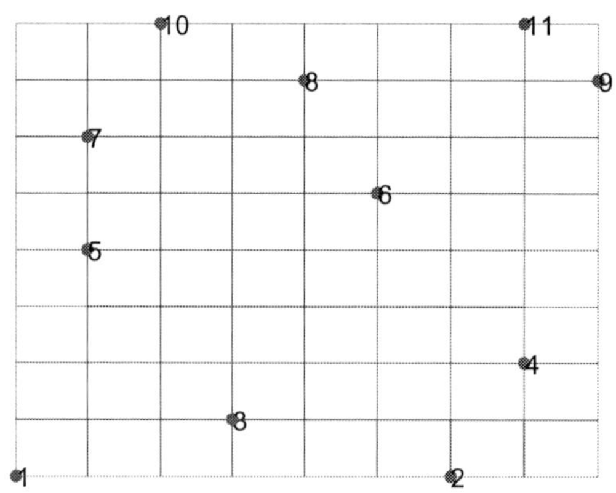

Figure 2: Plate model with sensors.

In total, 200 data sets of length N = 1,000,000 in both healthy and damage states are simulated. For each data set, modal parameters corresponding to the first 8 bending modes of the plate and their corresponding covariance are estimated with stochastic subspace identification and the first-order delta method [14]. The estimates of natural frequencies tracked across the simulated data are shown in the left part of Figure 3.

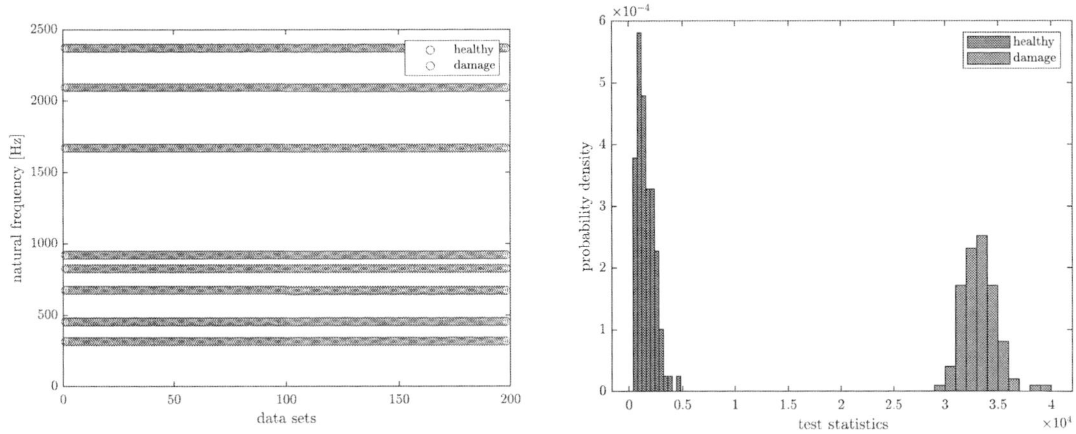

Figure 3: Natural frequency estimates obtained from both healthy and damage data (left). Histograms of damage detection test (right).

It can be viewed that for every data set the complete set of 8 modes is estimated and that the change in the natural frequency estimates due to damage can hardly be distinguished from the visual inspection. To detect damage, the non-parametric modal parameter-based test, i.e., when assuming that $\mathcal{J}^{z}_{\theta_*}$ is an identity matrix, is employed. The distribution of the test statistics is illustrated in Figure 3 (right). The inflicted damages are clearly detected and a clear separation between safe and damaged states is observed.

Subsequently, the localization of the mass change in element 47 is considered. Due to a limited number of sensors compared to the large FE model-based parametrization θ, the sensitivity of the residual with respect to some components of θ may be equal, or be very close. Thus, such parameter components are indistinguishable, and clustering of parameters in $\mathcal{J}^{z}_{\theta_*}$ is performed. For this purpose the hierarchical complete-linkage clustering of the normalized residual sensitivity after [9, 19] is used, and 26 parameter clusters are distinguished. A dendogram diagram showing the clustered parameters is illustrated in Figure 4 and the left part of Figure 5. Subsequently, the minmax damage localization test is performed with using the centers of the clustered sensitivity matrix. The test results are shown in the right part of Figure 5.

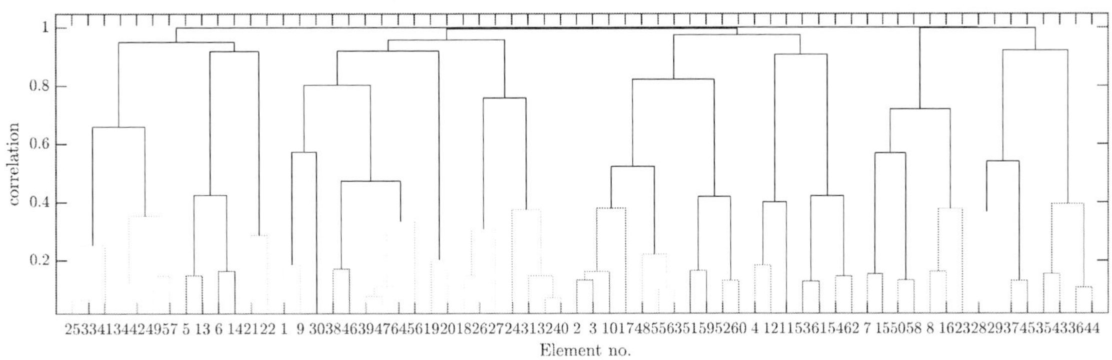

Figure 4: Dendogram showing hierarchical complete-linkage clustering of modal parameter sensitivities.

It can be viewed that the damage localization test yields the highest score for the cluster containing the damaged element, and it can be clearly distinguished from the values of the test corresponding to the remaining clusters.

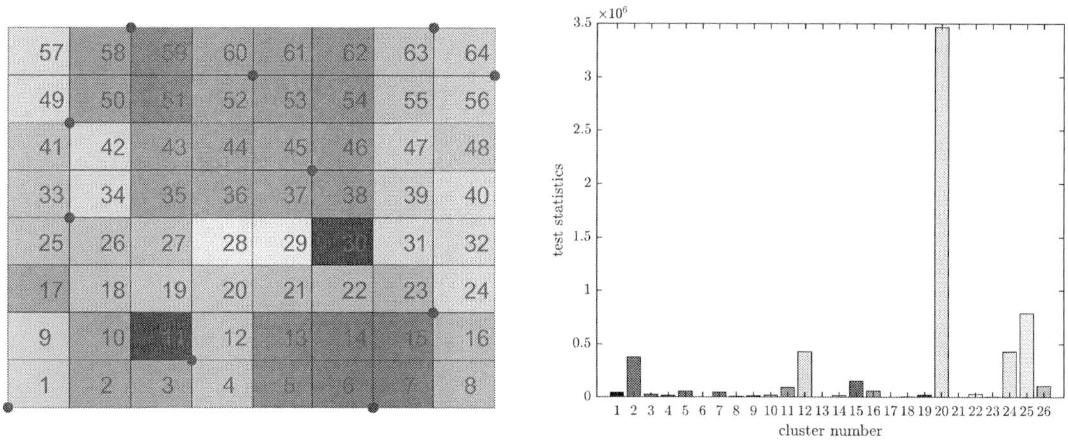

Figure 5: Plate element clusters (left). Damage localization results - damage in element 47, corresponding to the 20th cluster (right).

5. CONCLUSIONS

In this paper, a Gaussian residual for damage detection and damage localization has been derived based on the Mahalanobis distance between modal parameters in different states of the structure. The capabilities of the method were showcased on a numerical simulations of a plate, where a small change in the density of one element were clearly detected, and localized in a clustered parameter space. The proposed approach is applied in the context of detecting damage in large-scale bridges in our companion paper [20].

REFERENCES

[1] O. Avci, O. Abdeljaber, S. Kiranyaz, M. Hussein, M. Gabbouj, D. J. Inman, A review of vibration-based damage detection in civil structures: From traditional methods to machine learning and deep learning applications, Mechanical Systems and Signal Processing 147 (2021) 107077.

[2] D. Bernal, Damage Localization from the Null Space of Changes in the Transfer Matrix, AIAA Journal 45 (2007) 374–381.

[3] M. D. Ulriksen, D. Bernal, L. Damkilde, Shaped input distributions for structural damage localization, Mechanical Systems and Signal Processing 110 (2018) 499–508.

[4] M. Döhler, L. Mevel, F. Hille, Subspace-based damage detection under changes in the ambient excitation statistics, Mechanical Systems and Signal Processing 45 (1) (2014) 207 – 224.

[5] E. Viefhues, M. Döhler, F. Hille, L. Mevel, Statistical subspace-based damage detection with estimated reference, Mechanical Systems and Signal Processing 164 (2022) 108241.

[6] S. Greś, M. Döhler, P. Andersen, L. Mevel, Subspace-based mahalanobis damage detection robust to changes in excitation covariance, Structural Control and Health Monitoring 28 (8) (2021) e2760.

[7] Y. Ou, E. N. Chatzi, V. K. Dertimanis, M. D. Spiridonakos, Vibration-based experimental damage detection of a small-scale wind turbine blade, Structural Health Monitoring 16 (1) (2017) 79–96.

[8] S. Laflamme, L. Cao, E. Chatzi, F. Ubertini, Damage detection and localization from dense network of strain sensors, Shock and Vibration 2016 (2016).

[9] S. Allahdadian, M. Döhler, C. Ventura, L. Mevel, Towards robust statistical damage localization via model-based sensitivity clustering, Mechanical Systems and Signal Processing 134 (2019) 106341.

[10] D. Bernal, Kalman filter damage detection in the presence of changing process and measurement noise, Mechanical Systems and Signal Processing 39 (1-2) (2013) 361–371.

[11] K. Worden, G. Manson, N. Fieller, Damage detection using outlier analysis, Journal of Sound and Vibration 229 (3) (2000) 647 – 667.

[12] G. Casella, R. L. Berger, Statistical Inference, 2nd Edition, Cengage Learning, 2001.

[13] E. Reynders, R. Pintelon, G. De Roeck, Uncertainty bounds on modal parameters obtained from stochastic subspace identification, Mechanical Systems and Signal Processing 22 (4) (2008) 948 – 969.

[14] M. Döhler, L. Mevel, Efficient multi-order uncertainty computation for stochastic subspace identification, Mechanical Systems and Signal Processing 38 (2) (2013) 346–366.

[15] P. Mellinger, M. Döhler, L. Mevel, Variance estimation of modal parameters from output-only and input/output subspace-based system identification, Journal of Sound and Vibration 379 (C) (2016) 1 – 27.

[16] A. Benveniste, M. Basseville, G. Moustakides, The asymptotic local approach to change detection and model validation, IEEE Transactions on Automatic Control 32 (7) (1987) 583–592.

[17] W. Heylen, S. Lammens, P. Sas, et al., Modal analysis theory and testing, Vol. 200, Katholieke Universiteit Leuven Leuven, Belgium, 1997.

[18] S. Greś, M. Döhler, P. Andersen, L. Mevel, Uncertainty quantification for the Modal Phase Collinearity of complex mode shapes, Mechanical Systems and Signal Processing 152 (2021) 107436.

[19] A. Mendler, M. Döhler, C. Ventura, L. Mevel, Clustering of redundant parameters for fault isolation with Gaussian residuals, in: 21st IFAC World Congress, 2020.

[20] N.-J. Jacobsen, P. Andersen, A. Mendler, S. Greś, A general framework for damage detection with statistical distance measures: Application to civil engineering structures, in: IOMAC - 9th International Operational Modal Analysis Conference, Vancouver, Canada, 2022.

9th International Operational Modal Analysis Conference iomac July 3 - 6, 2022 Vancouver, Canada

STRUCTURAL HEALTH MONITORING OF A WOODEN MAST STRUCTURE BASED ON OMA TECHNIQUES

Emmanouil Lydakis[1], *Sandro D. R. Amador*[2] *and Rune Brincker*[3]

[1] PhD Candidate, Technical University of Denmark (DTU), Department of Civil Engineering, elysi@byg.dtu.dk.

[2] Assistant Professor, Technical University of Denmark (DTU), Department of Civil Engineering, sdio@byg.dtu.dk.

[3] Professor, Technical University of Denmark (DTU), Department of Civil Engineering, runeb@byg.dtu.dk.

ABSTRACT

Structural Health Monitoring (SHM) using OMA techniques utilizes the dynamic characteristics, as indicators of the health state of the monitored structure. In fact, changes in these dynamic properties can reflect either a potential degradation of the structural integrity or a change in the environmental conditions (e.g., temperature, humidity, etc.). Therefore, to apply a successful SHM approach to the monitored structures, the damage detection technique must identify and clearly separate the different sources of changes in the monitored dynamic properties. In this context, the present study aims to detect structural changes in a structure exposed to ambient vibrations and varying environmental conditions. The investigated structure consists of a wooden mast and a steel frame topside that is clamped to a concrete block at the bottom. In the monitoring campaign of the wooden mast, the vibration responses are collected by means of a measurement system whose sensors are placed at strategic locations on the topside, whereas the environmental conditions are recorded by a nearby weather station. The collected data is utilized to (i) estimate the environmental conditions; (ii) remove their influence from the estimated modal parameters, and finally (iii) detect structural changes induced by damages added with different severities to the mast.

Keywords: Structural Health Monitoring, Operational Modal Analysis, Damage Detection, Environmental Influence, Environmental Model

1. INTRODUCTION

Critical structural systems, such as bridges, energy plants and offshore wind turbines are significantly related to the economic and sustainable welfare of the modern world. Therefore, it is an essential priority to ensure their structural integrity and safe operation, while reducing the risk of unexpected failures. In an attempt to achieve that, the field of SHM has been rapidly expanding over the last decades and numerous techniques have been developed to evaluate the structural health on a continuous and reliable basis [1].

A widely spread application of SHM is based on Operation Modal Analysis (OMA) algorithms, where vibration measurements are transformed into modal parameters, such as natural frequencies, damping ratios, and mode shapes. Based on that, an assessment of the structural integrity can be achieved by investigating potential changes in these dynamic characteristics [1, 2]. Various identification techniques have been proposed over the years, thus an optimal selection is of high importance to ensure reliable results. Additionally, another crucial parameter for the successful application of SHM is related to the elimination of the environmental influence (e.g. temperature, humidity, wind speed, etc.) on the modal properties [1, 3, 4]. It has been observed that the dynamic characteristics of structures exposed to ambient vibrations and different environmental conditions can be affected to a significant extend by the environmental variability. Therefore, to ensure a reliable vibration-based damage assessment, this environmental impact must be eliminated. Numerous statistical methods have been used to remove the environmental influence on the modal parameters, such as the Principal Component Analysis (PCA), multivariate linear regression and auto regressive models [5, 6].

Along these lines, the present study aims at advancing the previous study conducted by [1], performed in the same outdoor lab at DTU Civil Engineering. The main purpose remains the application of SHM on a medium-sized wooden mast structure using automated OMA techniques. The innovative aspects of this paper with regard to the previous study, however, are related to (i) a longer time duration of the monitoring campaign; (ii) the fact that the mast is moved to new location where it is more susceptible to wind-induced excitations forces; and (iii) to the fact that more accurate specimen's vibration responses are collected owing to the improved calibration of the low-frequency range vibration sensors [7]. Since the experimental model is exposed to varying environmental conditions, it is essential to develop an environmental model to remove the influence on the modal properties. To achieve that a PCA model is utilized, leading to more robust results, mainly due to the increased duration of the monitoring campaign. Moreover, several damage cases are induced to the wooden mast to investigate whether they can be identified based on their influence on the modal parameters. Overall, the proper calibration of the measurement system in combination with an accurate environmental model led to an increased robustness of both OMA-based identification and damage detection.

2. THEORETICAL BACKGROUND

In this section, the theoretical background of the utilized methods is shortly introduced. The OMA-based identification of the modal properties is achieved by the Eigensystem Realization Algorithm (ERA), while the environmental model is obtained using Principal Component Analysis (PCA).

2.1. Eigensystem Realization Algorithm (ERA)

The eigensystem realization algorithm is a time domain identification technique proposed by Juang and Pappa in 1985. The correlation functions of the vibration response can be interpreted as a set of free decays $[\mathbf{y}_1(k), \mathbf{y}_2(k), \ldots]$ in discrete time $t_k = k\Delta t$, thus they can form a free decay matrix expressed as [8]

$$\mathbf{Y}(k) = \mathbf{P}\mathbf{D}^k\mathbf{U}_0 \tag{1}$$

where $\mathbf{P}$ is the observation matrix, $\mathbf{D}$ is the discrete time system matrix and $\mathbf{U}_0$ is the initial condition matrix $\mathbf{U}_0 = [\mathbf{u}_{01}, \mathbf{u}_{02}, \ldots]$. Two block Hankel matrices are subsequently formed with s denoting the number of block rows.

$$\mathbf{H}(0) = \begin{bmatrix} \mathbf{Y}(0) & \mathbf{Y}(1) & \ldots \\ \mathbf{Y}(1) & \mathbf{Y}(2) & \ldots \\ \vdots & \vdots & \\ \mathbf{Y}(s-1) & \mathbf{Y}(s) & \ldots \end{bmatrix} \quad , \quad \mathbf{H}(1) = \begin{bmatrix} \mathbf{Y}(1) & \mathbf{Y}(2) & \ldots \\ \mathbf{Y}(2) & \mathbf{Y}(3) & \ldots \\ \vdots & \vdots & \\ \mathbf{Y}(s) & \mathbf{Y}(s+1) & \ldots \end{bmatrix} \tag{2}$$

As observed in Eq. (2), the only difference between the two Hankel matrices is a time shift of one sample step. Therefore, by utilizing Eq. (1), the two matrices can be expressed as

$$\mathbf{H}(0) = \mathbf{\Gamma}\mathbf{\Lambda} \quad , \quad \mathbf{H}(1) = \mathbf{\Gamma}\mathbf{D}\mathbf{\Lambda} \tag{3}$$

where the observability matrix $\mathbf{\Gamma}$ and the cotrollability matrix $\mathbf{\Lambda}$ are given by

$$\mathbf{\Gamma} = \begin{bmatrix} \mathbf{P} \\ \mathbf{PD} \\ \mathbf{PD}^2 \\ \vdots \\ \mathbf{PD}^{s-1} \end{bmatrix} \quad , \quad \mathbf{\Lambda} = \begin{bmatrix} \mathbf{U}_0 & \mathbf{DU}_0 & \mathbf{D}^2\mathbf{U}_0 & \ldots \end{bmatrix} \tag{4}$$

The singular value decomposition (SVD) of the first Hankel matrix $\mathbf{H}(0)$ is then taken as

$$\mathbf{H}(0) = \mathbf{USV}^T \tag{5}$$

and, by making use of Eq. (2), the observability and cotrollability matrices are estimated as

$$\hat{\mathbf{\Gamma}} = \mathbf{U}\sqrt{\mathbf{S}} \quad , \quad \hat{\mathbf{\Lambda}} = \sqrt{\mathbf{S}}\mathbf{V}^T \tag{6}$$

The discrete time system matrix is finally estimated using the right part of Eq. (2) as

$$\hat{\mathbf{D}} = \hat{\mathbf{\Gamma}}^+\mathbf{H}(1)\hat{\mathbf{\Lambda}}^+ \tag{7}$$

where $\hat{\mathbf{\Gamma}}^+$ and $\hat{\mathbf{\Lambda}}^+$ are the pseudo inverse of the estimated observability and controllability matrices, respectively. The eigenvalues and the eigenvectors of the estimated discrete time system matrix are obtained as

$$\hat{\mathbf{D}} = [\phi'_n]\ [\mu_n]\ [\phi'_n]^{-1} \tag{8}$$

where the eigenvalues μ_n and the eigenvectors ϕ_n are associated with the natural frequencies and the mode shapes, respectively. For a more detailed description of the ERA identification technique, the reader is referred to [8].

2.2. Principal Component Analysis (PCA)

The principal component analysis is a statistical procedure to estimate a lower-dimensional representation of a data set, while retaining most of the variation of the data. According to previous applications of PCA in SHM [3, 4, 5, 6], the implementation starts with the initial data matrix $\mathbf{Y}$ containing N observations of n observed attributes. A singular value decomposition of $\mathbf{Y}\mathbf{Y}^T$ is implemented for the observed features as

$$\mathbf{Y}\mathbf{Y}^T = \mathbf{U}\mathbf{S}^2\mathbf{U}^T \tag{9}$$

where $\mathbf{U}$ is an $n\,x\,n$ matrix containing the singular vectors and $\mathbf{S}$ is a diagonal matrix including the n singular values. The diagonal terms of $\mathbf{S}$ are organized in an ascending order and are associated with the so-called principal components, which represent the directions of the data that explain the maximum amount of variance. Therefore, the first principal components are associated with the desired physical information, while the last ones include residual contributions mainly related to noise effects. The key step to establish a successful PCA model is the optimal selection of $m(< n)$ singular values that represent sufficient amount of physical information. Once this is achieved, the loading matrix $\mathbf{T}$ is formed by taking into account only the first m number of features (i.e. columns) from matrix $\mathbf{U}$. Based on that, an estimate of the observed features can be expressed as [3]

$$\hat{\mathbf{Y}} = \mathbf{Y}\mathbf{T}\mathbf{T}^T \tag{10}$$

To evaluate the loss of information between the initial data matrix $\mathbf{Y}$ and the new estimate $\hat{\mathbf{Y}}$, the residual error matrix $\hat{\mathbf{E}}$ is calculated as

$$\hat{\mathbf{E}} = \mathbf{Y} - \hat{\mathbf{Y}} \tag{11}$$

Finally, the corrected values $\mathbf{Y}_c$ are simply computed by summing the residual error matrix $\hat{\mathbf{E}}$ with the mean value of each feature $\bar{\mathbf{Y}}$.

$$\mathbf{Y}_c = \hat{\mathbf{E}} + \bar{\mathbf{Y}} \tag{12}$$

3. EXPERIMENT SETUP

3.1. Description

The experimental model utilized in this study is a medium-sized monopile structure, which consists of a 3.6-meter high wooden mast with a square cross section 0.1m x 0.1m. A steel topside is placed at the top of the mast, while at the bottom it is rigidly connected to a concrete block. Both connections at the top and the bottom of the mast are bolted steel connections. The measurement system consists of a base station and four geophones, which are vibration sensors with high sensitivity and low noise floor. The sensors are placed on four different corners of the topside, two at the upper wooden plate and two at the bottom one, as illustrated in the middle pane of Fig. 1.

The monitoring campaign lasted approximately three months, starting from November 30, 2021 and finished on March 4, 2022. The monitoring period is split into 20-minute measurements, where the actual measurement duration is 19 minutes, while an 1-minute break follows each measurement. Therefore, 72 measurements are performed per day that finally lead in a total number of 6441 measurement data files.

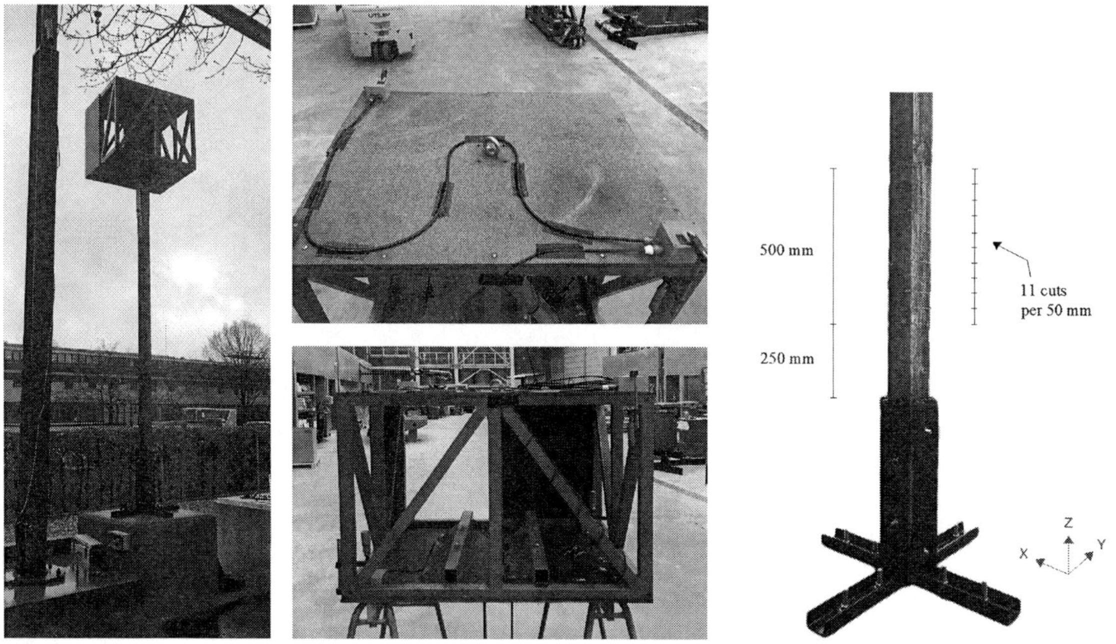

Figure 1: Left: Experimental model; Top middle: Two sensors are clamped on the upper plate of the topside; Bottom middle: Steel topside with the four sensors clamped on the different corners; Right: Damage cases on the wooden mast.

3.2. Damage scenarios

The damage cases are introduced to the experimental model on February 15, 2022. The induced damages are practically 11 cuts on the wooden mast, as illustrated in the right pane of Fig. 1. In the X direction, the depth of each cut is initiated at 2 mm and is gradually increasing by 2 mm, until it reaches the maximum depth of 10 mm on February 23, 2022. On the other hand, the Y direction of the mast is only damaged once, where a cut of 10mm is performed on February 25, 2022. Detailed information regarding the different damage cases are presented in the following table.

Damage case	Date	Time	Severity	Direction
1	02/15/2022	10:10	2mm	X
2	02/15/2022	14:00	4mm	X
3	02/17/2022	09:10	6mm	X
4	02/21/2022	09:00	8mm	X
5	02/23/2022	08:45	10mm	X
6	02/25/2022	08:56	10mm	Y

Table 1: Details about the damage scenarios.

4. RESULTS

The present section includes the obtained results from this experimental investigation. Firstly, the ERA identification results are presented over the whole monitoring period, while a closer examination is subsequently taken in a shorter damage detection period. At last, a PCA application is implemented to eliminate the environmental influence on the modal properties.

4.1. Identified modal parameters

Following the principles of ERA described above, the extracted data from the measurements are transformed into the desired dynamic characteristics. In Table 2, the modal parameters (natural frequencies & damping ratios) obtained during the undamaged state of the structure are presented for the first five vibration modes.

Parameter	Mode 1	Mode 2	Mode 3	Mode 4	Mode 5
Frequency [Hz]	1.1981	1.2078	1.9267	9.8102	12.3966
Damping ratio [%]	0.7126	0.8788	0.8800	0.5824	0.7404

Table 2: Dynamic properties of the first five modes.

To evaluate the performance of the ERA identification, the measurement data are transferred into the frequency domain by estimating the spectral density functions. Transforming a vibration response signal into the frequency domain has the significant advantage of providing a clearer picture of the physical information [8]. In Fig. 2, the singular values of the spectral density matrix are illustrated, where the first five natural frequencies can be identified as the frequency values corresponding to the highlighted peaks. Comparing the natural frequencies from Fig. 2 with the results estimated by ERA, it is evident that the values are identical.

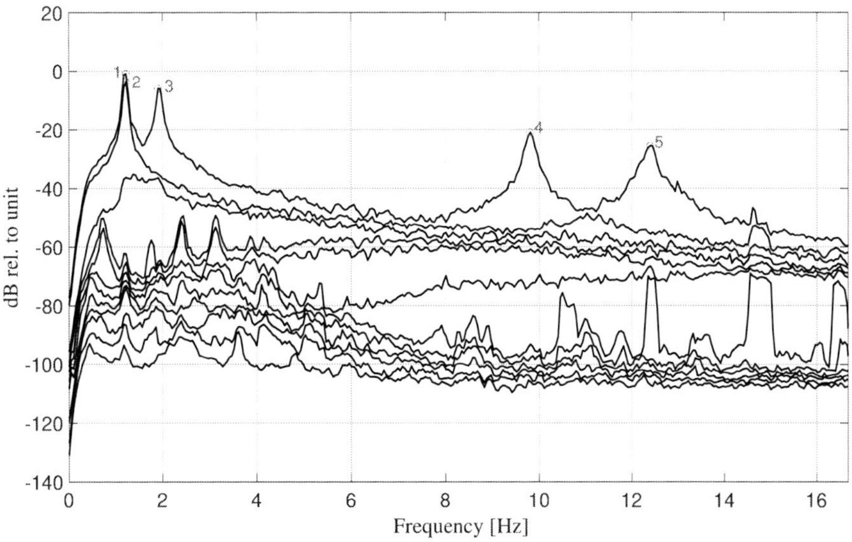

Figure 2: Singular values of the PSD matrix.

Furthermore, to assess the influence from both the environmental conditions and the induced damages, the natural frequency evolution is examined over the monitoring period. The frequency variation is illustrated in Fig. 3, where the damage period is denoted with two vertical lines, indicating the first and the last damage case induced on the structure, respectively.

During the pre-damage period, it can be clearly observed that the natural frequencies of the first two modes remain roughly steady around 1.2 Hz. However, it is evident that after the damage induction, a gradual decrease is caused in the natural frequencies of the first mode, while in the second mode, the natural frequencies seem to be affected only from the last damage scenario in Y direction. Moreover, as soon as the damage period finishes, it can be seen that the natural frequencies reclaim their steady pattern once again in both modes. In addition, it is worth mentioning that the discontinuities observed in Fig. 3 are mainly occurred due interruptions in the power supply of the outdoor lab, causing the measurement system to shut down for short periods.

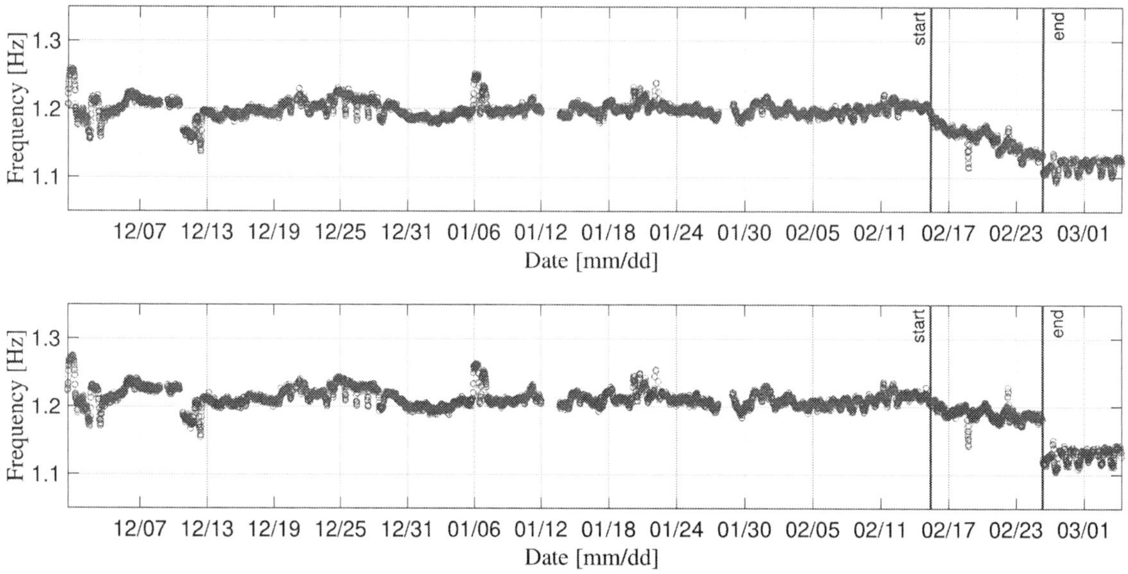

Figure 3: Natural frequency evolution over the whole monitoring period.

4.2. Damage detection

To achieve a better understanding of the damage influence on the modal properties, a shorter period of 24 days is evaluated. This period practically starts one week before the occurrence of the first damage and finishes one week after the induction of the last damage case. The evolution of the natural frequencies over this shorter period is illustrated in Fig. 5, where the different damage scenarios from Table 1 are indicated with vertical lines.

The selection of a smaller window of data provides a clearer picture of the damage impact on the modal parameters. As shown in Fig. 5, the natural frequency of the first mode starts to decrease as the first damage case of 2 mm is induced on the structure. After this point, this decreasing trend continues until the end of the damage period where the frequency fluctuation becomes steady once again.

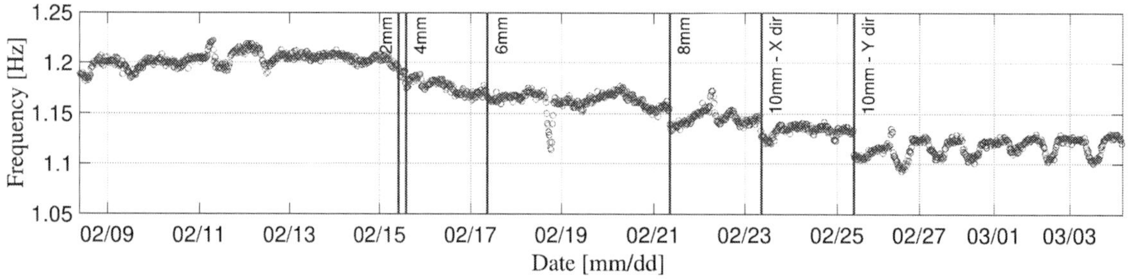

Figure 4: Natural frequency evolution over the damage period for the first mode.

In contrast to the first mode, the natural frequency of the second mode does not appear to be affected by the damages in X direction. In Fig. 5, it is clear that only the 10mm cut in Y direction has a notable impact on the natural frequencies of the second mode. This impact is extremely significant though, as the natural frequency suddenly decreases from 1.20 Hz to 1.13 Hz.

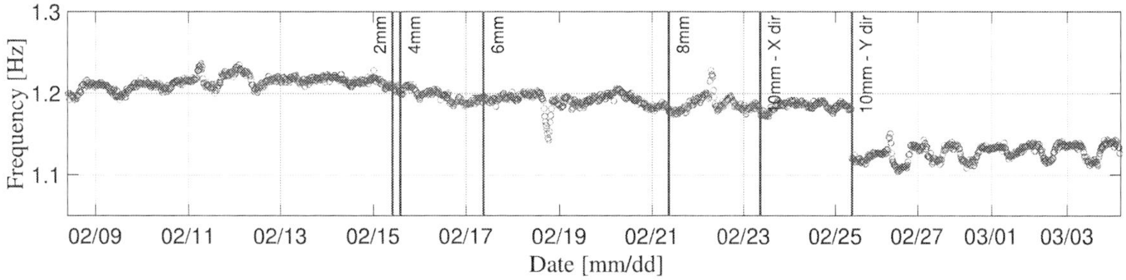

Figure 5: Natural frequency evolution over the damage period for the second mode.

4.3. Environmental model

As previously discussed, the development of an environmental model is essential to eliminate the influence of the varying ambient conditions on the modal parameters. To achieve that, a PCA model is utilized where two principal components are taken into consideration. The results in terms of natural frequencies after the application of PCA are illustrated in Fig. 6.

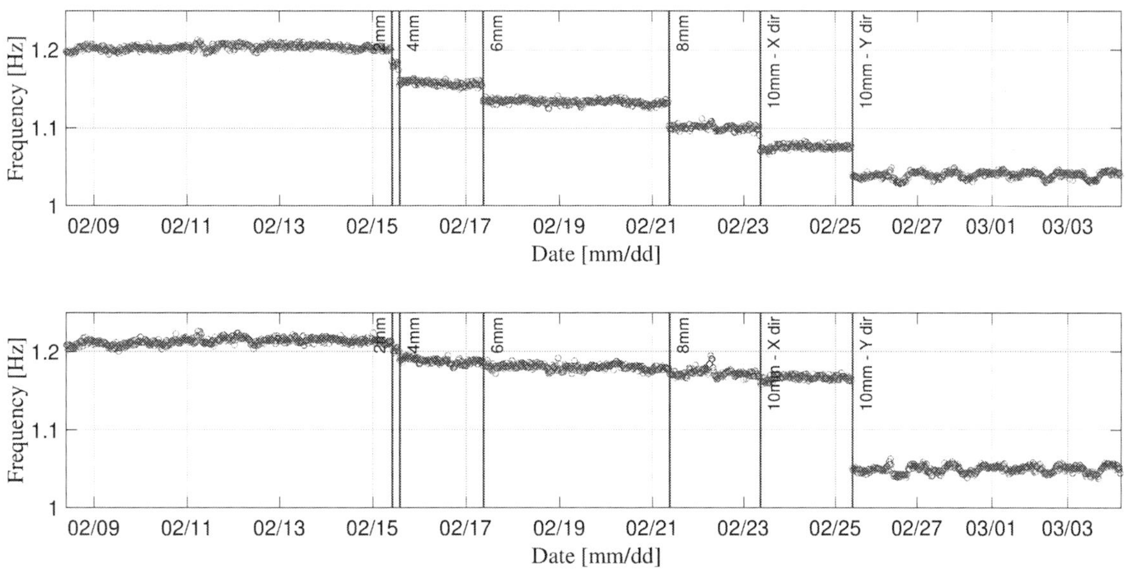

Figure 6: Natural frequency evolution after the elimination of the environmental influence.

After the removal of the environmental effects, it is evident that a clearer picture of the damage effects remains. In both modes, the fluctuation due to the varying environmental conditions is eliminated, leading to a more steady evolution of the natural frequencies. Additionally, the damage presence obviously became more evident in this case, compared to the initial damage detection of the previous section. In Fig. 6, six discontinuities are observed in the evolution of the first natural frequency after the occurrence of each damage case, while only one significant offset is observed in the frequency evolution of the second mode.

5. CONCLUSIONS

The present study focused on the OMA-based SHM on a medium-sized experimental model, while an assessment of gradually induced damages is performed by utilizing changes in the natural frequencies. Furthermore, a PCA model is developed to eliminate the influence of the environmental conditions on the modal parameters. Overall, the obtained results showed that:

- the damage presence in the experimental model led to a reduction of the natural frequencies of the first two modes.
- the gradually induced damage cases in the X direction of the mast resulted a corresponding drop of the natural frequencies only in the first mode, while in the second mode, the natural frequency showed a significant decrease only due to the damage in Y direction.
- after removing the environmental effects, the robustness of the damage detection significantly increased, since each damage case was clearly indicated by discontinuities in the time evolution of the natural frequencies.

REFERENCES

[1] Andersen, P.L., Nielsen, S.T., Amador, S.D.R., Katsanos, E. and Brincker, R. (2019) OMA-based Structural Health Monitoring of a wooden mast structure exposed to ambient vibrations. In: *Proc. 8th International Operational Modal Analysis Conference* (pp. 195-204). Copenhagen, Denmark.

[2] Andersen, P.L. and Nielsen, S.T. (2019) OMA Based Monitoring of a Wind Loaded Structure. *Master thesis*. Department of Civil Engineering, Technical University of Denmark.

[3] Diord, S., Magalhães, F., Cunha, Á., Caetano, E., and Martins, N. (2017) Automated modal tracking in a football stadium suspension roof for detection of structural changes. In: *Structural Control and Health Monitoring* (pp. e2006). Wiley Online Library.

[4] Magalhães, F., Cunha, Á. and Caetano, E. (2012) Vibration based structural health monitoring of an arch bridge: From automated OMA to damage detection. In: *Mechanical systems and Signal Processing*, 28, (pp. 212-228). Elsevier.

[5] Rainieri, C., Gargaro, D. and Fabbrocino, G. (2015) Statistical tools for the characterization of environmental and operational factors in vibration-based SHM. In: *Structural Health Monitoring and Damage Detection*, 7, (pp. 175-184). Springer.

[6] Andersen, P.L., Amador, S.D.R., Nielsen, S.T., Katsanos, E. and Brincker, R. (2021) Vibration-based damage detection using input-output and output-only environmental models: A comparison. In: *Dynamics of Civil Structures, Volume 2* (pp. 29-38). Springer International Publishing.

[7] Irina Gest (2017) Assessment of Vibration Measurement Systems and Sensors, and Experimental Modal Identification on Civil Structures. *Technical report*. Department of Civil Engineering, Technical University of Denmark.

[8] Brincker, R. and Ventura, C. (2015) *Introduction to Operational Modal Analysis*. John Wiley & Sons

9th International Operational Modal Analysis Conference
iomac
July 3 - 6, 2022
Vancouver, Canada

THE USEFULNESS OF OMA FOR EVALUATING THE HEALTH STATUS OF STRUCTURES

Vanni Nicoletti[1], Davide Arezzo[2], Sandro Carbonari[3] and Fabrizio Gara[4]

[1] Post-doctoral researcher, DICEA, Università Politecnica delle Marche, v.nicoletti@pm.univpm.it.
[2] Post-doctoral researcher, DICEA, Università Politecnica delle Marche, d.arezzo@pm.univpm.it.
[3] Associate professor, DICEA, Università Politecnica delle Marche, s.carbonari@univpm.it.
[4] Full professor, DICEA, Università Politecnica delle Marche, f.gara@univpm.it.

ABSTRACT

The health monitoring and the safety assessment of buildings and infrastructures during their life cycle are of paramount importance for assuring the building use with acceptable risks for users, especially after the occurrence of earthquakes or other exceptional events, such as hurricanes, blasts or vehicle impacts. For strategic structures with public functions (e.g., bridges, hospitals, police and fire stations, schools, etc.) the structural health monitoring can provide useful information about the building status, in terms of damage on structural and non-structural elements; if the monitoring system reports alert situations through suitably installed specific sensors, visual inspections and destructive or non-destructive experimental tests can be also executed with the aim of supporting the decision-making process about the building use.

The paper discusses about the effectiveness and usefulness of OMA in the assessment of the health conditions of buildings, and in its suitability within a structural health monitoring framework. An experimental campaign was performed on a laboratory steel-concrete composite frame with infill masonry walls: a progressive damage was produced to the non-structural components through cyclic load tests with increasing amplitude displacements, and vibration-based tests were performed with the aim of tracing the evolution of the frame dynamics and modal properties. Results demonstrate that OMAs are suitable for detecting the damage occurring to the non-structural components, while they are less useful in capturing the dissipative capabilities of the resisting nonlinear mechanisms that develop due to damage.

Keywords: structural health monitoring, operational modal analysis, damage detection, infill masonry walls, laboratory experimental campaign

1. INTRODUCTION

The assessment of the health status of structures during their life cycle is nowadays a topic of great interest, especially for structures with public functions (e.g., bridges, hospitals, police and fire stations, schools, etc.), for which a Structural Health Monitoring (SHM) is often recommended, in case of high hazards (e.g., seismic or hydrogeologic) exposure of vulnerability. Indeed, a monitoring system can provide useful information about the building status, in terms of damage on structural and non-structural elements, occurred during the building life and after exceptional events, such as earthquakes, hurricanes, blasts, vehicle impacts, etc. The SHM of a building permits to get (often continuously) information about some features of the structure (e.g., modal parameters, crack opening, sub-component tilting) that can be correlated with its health condition. If the SHM system reports alert situations through suitably installed specific sensors, visual inspections can be also performed to identify damage on structural and non-structural elements, and destructive or non-destructive experimental tests can be executed to evaluate the residual material mechanical properties.

Among the others, the structural dynamic monitoring is nowadays widely adopted worldwide since it is rather easy to be conceived and very often it does not require the interruption of the building activities for the installation. The dynamic monitoring is based on the use of vibration-based methods [1] that adopt accelerations (or velocities) measured over the structure to characterize its dynamics, in terms of modal parameters (i.e., resonant frequencies, mode shapes and modal damping ratios). The basic idea behind this methodology is that modal parameters vary with the health status of the building (i.e., with the presence and/or the evolution of damage) since they are functions of the structure physical properties (mass, damping, and stiffness). Therefore, damage or changes of material mechanical properties and boundary conditions will cause changes in the modal properties, which can be detected performing dynamic tests on the structure over time.

In the literature, many authors adopted vibration-based tests on real buildings to investigate the damage on structural and non-structural members, both adopting a gradual artificially induced damage [2] and using real excitations, such as earthquake strong motions [3,4]. Other authors adopted vibration-based tests to identify the structural and non-structural damage produced by displacements and forces applied to laboratory specimens [5,6]. One of the most common non-structural components built in framed structures are the infill walls, very often realized with masonry panels [7]. In the technical and scientific literature many works can be found addressing the topic of infill masonry wall damage detection, but only few addressing the use of vibration-based methods for this purpose [8,9]. Unfortunately, differentiating between damage occurred to structural and non-structural members is a hard task, especially when tests are performed on the whole building with infills. At the same time, it is crucial to establish if a structure can be further used or not after an exceptional event.

In this paper, the effectiveness of low-amplitude vibration-based tests for evaluating the health status of structures is discussed. The research is developed based on results of an extensive experimental campaign performed on a steel-concrete composite laboratory frame with light infill masonry walls. The laboratory mock-up was dynamically tested in crucial phases of the experimentation adopting ambient vibration and impact load tests. In detail, dynamic tests were performed on the bare frame, when the infills were built and then during the infill damage, the latter produced by stepped increasing cyclic displacements applied to the whole structure. The experimental campaign is herein described, and the use of dynamic test results is addressed with the main aim to investigate its usefulness in a SHM framework.

2. DESCRIPTION OF THE EXPERIMENTAL CAMPAIGN

The laboratory experimental campaign was performed on a steel-concrete composite mock-up with 2-bay moment resisting frames in the longitudinal direction and 1-bay braced frame in the transverse one (Figure 1). The mock-up is 8.4 m long, 2.8 m wide and 3.0 m high. The floor concrete slab is 12 cm thick, casted on collaborating corrugated steel sheets and connected to the beams of the steel frame by means of Nelson's studs. On the floor, concrete blocks were added to simulate the presence of non-structural and live loads. Two light infill masonry walls were built filling only one of both longitudinal spans. Infills were built with 6 cm thick hollow clay bricks (with horizontally arranged holes) with about 1 – 1.5 cm thick head and bed mortar joints; infills are then plastered on both sides with a 0.7 cm thick gypsum plaster layer, leading to a total thickness of about 7.4 cm for each wall. More information about the mock-up can be found in [10].

An extensive experimental campaign was undertaken on the mock-up and this paper addresses some of the performed tests; in detail, only the low-amplitude vibration-based tests are presented and discussed. Initially, Ambient Vibration Tests (AVTs) and Impact Load Tests (ILTs) were performed: the former consist in measuring the structure accelerations produced by the ambient excitation (in this case mainly microtremors due to the surrounding environment), while the latter foresee the excitation of the structure through instrumented hammer blows and the recording of both impacts and the produced accelerations. Then, the same tests were repeated after the construction of the infills. At this point Cyclic Load Tests (CLTs) were performed applying a stepped increasing longitudinal displacement to the structure, both in push and in pull directions. A total of 25 tests were performed, starting from 1 mm up to 13 mm of longitudinal displacement. These tests mainly aim to produce a progressive In-Plane (IP) damage to both infills, maintaining the steel frame within its elastic range. After each CLT, ILTs were repeated to dynamically characterize the infilled composite structure with different infill damage levels. AVTs are not performed after each load step since they required a long time to be performed and their outcomes are very similar to those obtained from ILTs, which are much faster to be performed. Indeed, it was found that the results obtained from AVTs are very similar to those achieved through ILTs, as it will be shown in the sequel. At the end of CLTs, both AVTs and ILTs were repeated. The experimental campaign is briefly resumed in Table 1.

To perform dynamic tests, six low-noise uniaxial piezoelectric accelerometers (model PCB 393B31) with sensitivity of 10 V/g, frequency range of 0.07 – 300 Hz and resolution of 1 μg were adopted. Sensors were connected by means of coaxial cables to 4-channels dynamic signal acquisition modules (NI-9234) mounted on a USB chassis (NI cDAQ9178) and connected to a notebook equipped with a dedicated software for the data analysis and storage. Moreover, for the impact tests, an instrumented hammer (model PCB 086D20) characterized by sensitivity of 0.23 mV/N, measurement range of ± 22.000 N (peak) and total mass about 1 kg, was also adopted to excite the mock-up. In Figure 1 the layout of accelerometers positioned on the slab, and of the hammer impacts are shown.

Table 1. Summary of the laboratory experimental campaign.

Mock-up description	Performed tests
Bare frame	AVTs and ILTs
Infilled frame (no damage)	AVTs and ILTs
Progressive damage to infills	CLT and then ILT (25 times – from 1 to 13 mm)
Infilled frame with completely damaged infills	AVTs and ILTs

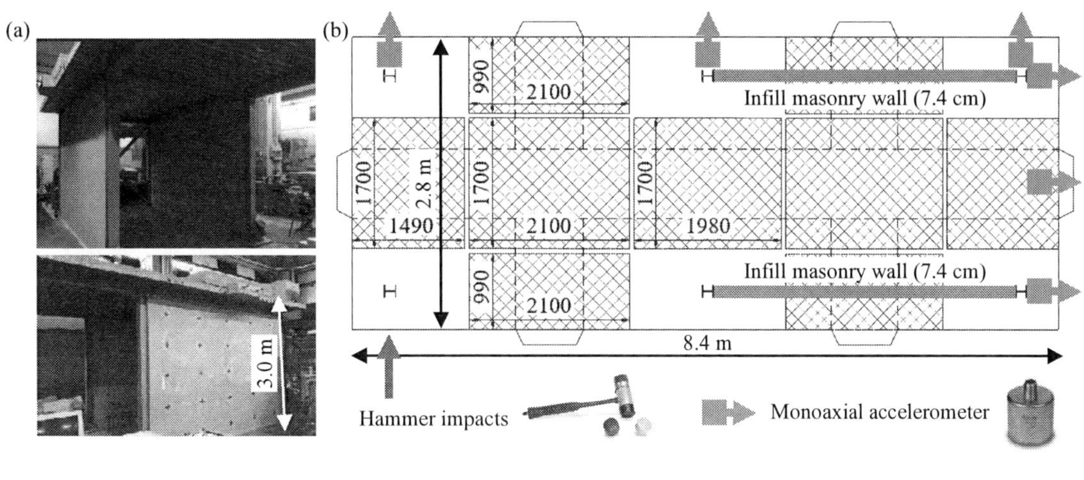

Figure 1. Tested laboratory mock-up: (a) some pictures, (b) dynamic test layout and instrumentation.

3. EXPERIMENTAL TEST RESULTS

During CLTs infills progressively damage due to the increasing IP displacements to which they were subjected. For the sake of completeness, the mock-up hysteretic cycles obtained during the CLTs are reported in Figure 2, even if procedures and the instrumentation adopted to obtain the results are not previously described, as they go beyond the interest of this work. Hysteretic loops are reported only to understand the mock-up behaviour under longitudinal displacements, the latter involving the IP stiffness and strength of the infills. As can be seen from the backbone curves (red lines), infills experienced a first important damage when the mock-up longitudinal displacement reached about 6 - 8 mm (interstory drifts ranging between 1 and 2‰), as demonstrated by a drastic reduction of both infill strength and stiffness. This reduction is attributable only to infills damage since the steel frame always remained in the elastic field. Then, the IP strength of infills increases again after the drop, while the secant stiffness continues to reduce up to the end (the residual stiffness is about the 20% of the initial value). This behaviour is probably due to the development of different resistant mechanisms within the infills during CLTs.

For what concerns the dynamic tests, Operational Modal Analyses (OMAs) are performed based on AVT measurements with the target of identifying the modal parameter of the mock-up, namely natural frequencies, damping ratios and mode shapes; in detail, the Covariance-driven Stochastic Subspace Identification (SSI-COV) [11] output-only technique is adopted, and the relevant modal parameters identified with this methodology are reported in Table 2, Table 3 and Figure 3. As can be seen, three mock-up vibration modes are always identified (for the bare frame, infilled frame and the frame with damaged infills), corresponding to the longitudinal, transversal and rotational vibration modes. For what concerns ILTs, the mock-up modal parameters are identified adopting the so-called Experimental Modal Analysis (EMA) and using the Numerical algorithm for Subspace State Space System IDentification (N4SID) [12], which is an input-output identification methodology working in time domain. The identified modal parameters are listed in Table 2 and Table 3 together with those obtained from OMAs; as can be noted, frequency values and damping ratios obtained through AVTs and ILTs identification procedures are always very close to each other, proving that ILTs can be used instead of AVTs to characterize the dynamic behaviour of the mock-up under low-amplitude excitations. Moreover, all frequencies and damping ratios identified from ILT measurements recorded during the whole experimental campaign (i.e., after each CLT) are reported in the graphs of Figure 4. Finally, the mode shapes obtained through ILTs measurements are not reported for the sake of brevity, but they are compared in terms of Modal Assurance Criterion (MAC) indexes in Figure 5. Here, the mode shape of each vibration mode obtained from ILT measurements is compared with the same mode shape found in the previous cycle load step. MAC indexes provide an indication of how the mode shapes are similar to each other: the closer the index to one, the more the mode shapes are similar.

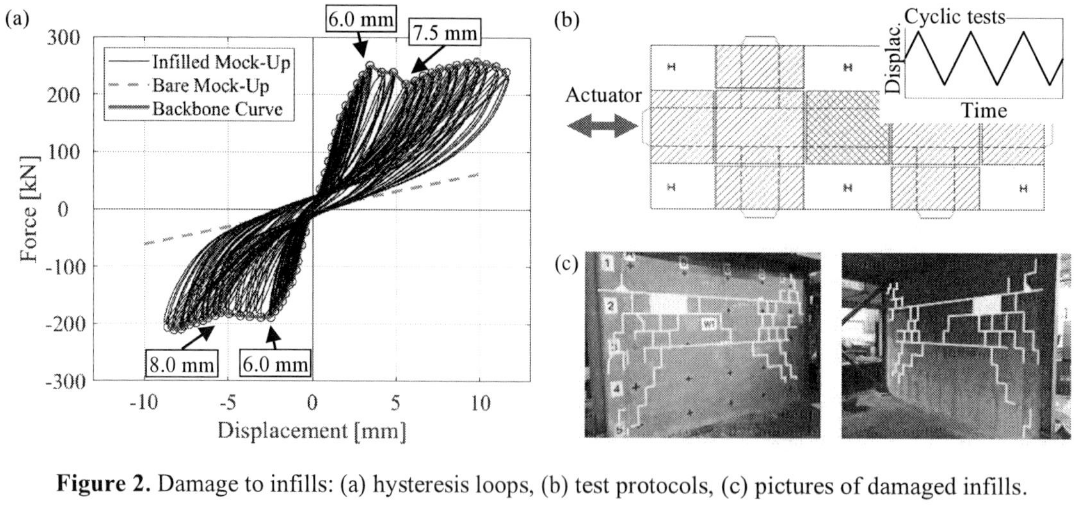

Figure 2. Damage to infills: (a) hysteresis loops, (b) test protocols, (c) pictures of damaged infills.

Table 2. Frequencies [Hz] obtained from AVTs and ILTs for the bare frame and then before and after the infill damage.

Mode type	AVT			ILT		
	Bare frame	**Before damage**	**After damage**	**Bare frame**	**Before damage**	**After damage**
Transverse	8.42	8.37	8.26	8.42	8.35	8.26
Rotational	11.62	13.39	12.35	11.60	13.34	12.28
Longitudinal	2.95	17.69	10.86	2.95	17.26	10.74

Table 3. Damping ratios [%] obtained from AVTs and ILTs for the bare frame and then before and after the infill damage.

Mode type	AVT			ILT		
	Bare frame	**Before damage**	**After damage**	**Bare frame**	**Before damage**	**After damage**
Transverse	0.55	0.67	0.58	0.40	0.77	0.61
Rotational	0.24	0.47	0.35	0.62	1.47	1.43
Longitudinal	0.32	0.98	0.52	0.35	1.32	1.16

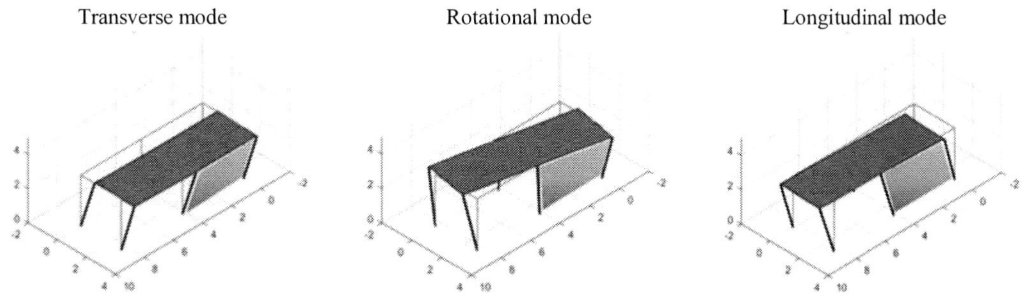

Figure 3. Mock-up mode shapes.

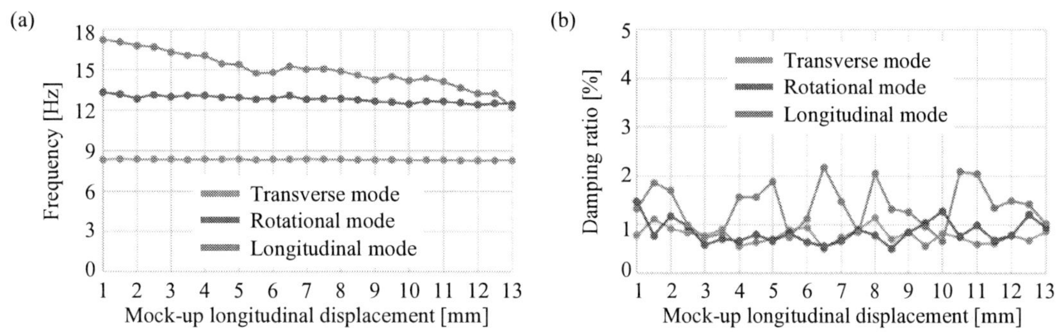

Figure 4. ILT results during the progressive damage of infills: (a) frequencies, (b) damping ratios.

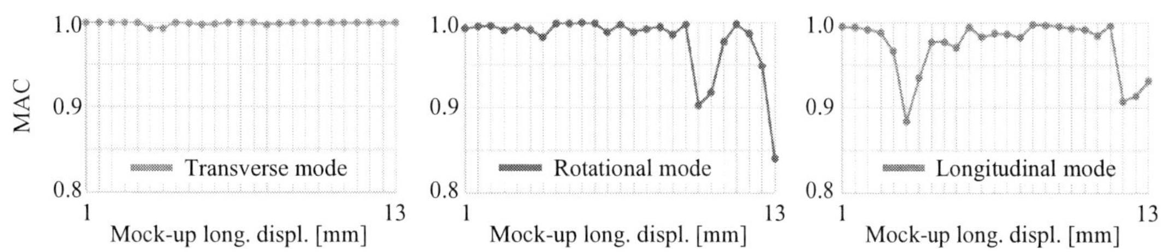

Figure 5. MAC indexes between mode shapes identified through ILT results during the progressive infill damage.

4. USE OF VIBRATION-BASED TEST RESULTS FOR SHM

The results of AVTs and ILTs are analyzed in this section in order to investigate changes in the mock-up dynamics due to the progressive damage of infills and, hence, to evaluate their applicability in a SHM framework. Analyzing the frequencies obtained from OMAs before and after the infill construction (Table 2), it is evident how these non-structural elements affect the dynamic behavior of the mock-up; in particular, the frequency of the longitudinal mode sensibly increases, passing from 2.95 to 17.69 Hz, and also that relevant to the rotational mode varies, even if in a less pronounced way, passing from 11.62 to 13.39 Hz. On the contrary, the frequency relevant to the transverse mode is slightly influenced by the infill presence, and it reduces after the infill construction, probability because the infills mostly contribute to the structural dynamic behavior in term of mass rather than in term of stiffness increase. The infill damage leads to a general decay of frequency values, especially for the longitudinal modes, whose frequency drastically reduces of about 40%. Anyway, it is interesting to observe that, although severely damaged, infills still contribute to increase the longitudinal and rotational (in a less pronounced way) stiffness of the mock-up, being the frequency values obtained at the end of CLTs higher than those obtained for the bare frame. Hence, it can be asserted that the monitoring of frequencies in infilled structures can lead to obtain useful information about their health status and about the condition of their non-structural components. On the contrary, the damping ratios identified in the three key phases discussed before (Table 3) are in all cases under 1% and do not show evident trends, so they cannot help the user to understand if the structure suffered or not a damage. This suggests that, for the structural system at hand, AVTs are not adequate to capture the dissipative capabilities of the damaged system because the latter are essentially due to friction phenomena occurring within the damaged infills that cannot be activated by the low-amplitude vibrations. Same considerations about the usefulness of frequencies and damping ratios in a SHM framework stem from the analysis of ILTs results, which are very similar to those obtained from OMAs. Moreover, analysing the frequency evolutions of Figure 4, different trends can be recognised: frequencies relevant to the transverse mode remain almost constant, those relevant to the rotational mode slightly decrease, while those relevant to the longitudinal one sensibly decrease, showing an almost linear decay trend. In detail, a more pronounced decay is observed in correspondence of longitudinal displacements ranging between 5.5 and 6.0 mm and at the end. The first one is consistent with the infill damage phenomena previously discussed in commenting the hysteretic loops of the system; as already stated, this decay is probably due to an important infill damage that trigger the formation of a new resisting mechanism. Nevertheless, the frequency reduction observed between 5.5 and 6.0 mm is not so evident as to suggest a structural (or, in this case, non-structural) damage activation, especially in a SHM blind procedure (i.e., without performing visual inspections). The evolution of mode shapes (represented through MAC indexes) is not of particular interest in tracing the damage activation and its evolution. Indeed, as can be seen from Figure 5, the mode shapes remain almost the same, without significant modifications and without showing significant trends; moreover, MAC indexes always exhibit high values (higher than 0.84).

The tracing of resonance frequencies during the life of a structure is often not enough to establish its health condition. A SHM strategy for infilled structures that support this type of monitoring can be found in [13]; in the paper, the authors propose to perform AVTs during the main construction phases of the bare structural frame and then during the construction of the non-structural components, as, for instance, infills. This procedure has some advantages: it allows to control the construction correctness, to identify the infill contribution on the building dynamics and permits to support the interpretation of SHM system outcomes during the building life. Indeed, performing AVTs and OMAs during the construction of an infilled frame structure allows to obtain its time-frequency curve, which can be used to interpret SHM data. As an example, Figure 6 shows a typical time-frequency curve obtained monitoring the fundamental frequency of a multi-story infilled frame structure during its construction. Point A represents the frequency value at the beginning of the bare frame construction, point B the fundamental frequency at the end of the bare frame construction, and point C represents the end of construction, when also the non-structural components are built. Two different frequency trends are clearly visible: from A to B the fundamental frequency decreases because the mass addition is predominant with respect to the stiffness increase in the dynamics of the bare structure; contrarily, from B to C the fundamental frequency increases because of the stiffening contribution of infills. Point D represents the fundamental frequency value of the structure when the infills are completely damaged and they contribute to the building dynamics only in terms of added mass. Obviously, this frequency value can be only estimated adopting a numerical model of the structure. Once the time-frequency curve is available it can be adopted to interpret SHM data during the building life: if the measured frequency remains almost constant and equal to point C, then the health condition is verified; if it ranges between point C and D, then a possible damage to the non-structural components occurred; if it drops below point D, then a possible structural damage (together with the non-structural one) may have occurred. It is worth noting that particular attention must be paid to the influence of environmental conditions on the fundamental frequency value. This procedure is applied for the case study at hand; in this case, the time-frequency curve for the mock-up longitudinal vibration mode (the one mostly affected by the infill presence) is built and, as can be seen from Figure 6, this is very simple because the mock-up has only one floor (point A matches B). The frequency corresponding to point D is evaluated based on a modal analysis performed on a Finite Element Model (FEM) of the mock-up already available and that was built for other research purposes [14]. In this FEM, infills are not modelled and they are accounted for only as added masses applied to the bare frame, hence neglecting their stiffness contribution. Then, point X, which corresponds to the frequency measured at the end of the experimental campaign (i.e., when infills were completely damaged) is placed on the graph and it can be seen that it is positioned between points C and B, confirming that (very probably) the frame did not suffer structural damage, as supported by visual inspection performed during the experimental campaign. This simple application confirms that the use of the time-frequency curve could become crucial in case of blind monitoring, where performing visual inspections may be complicated, or even impossible.

5. CONCLUSIONS

In this paper, the applicability of low-amplitude vibration-based tests to investigate the health condition of an infilled structure has been investigated. The study was conducted on the basis of results obtained from an extensive experimental campaign performed on a steel-concrete composite laboratory frame with light infill masonry walls. The laboratory mock-up was dynamically tested in key phases of the experimental campaign, namely without infills (bare frame), when the infills were built and then after the infill damage, the latter produced by a stepped increasing longitudinal cyclic displacement provided to the structure. Low-amplitude dynamic tests (ambient vibration and impact load tests) were performed at each step to identify the system modal parameters.

From the analysis of test results some considerations can be drawn. Firstly, it has proven (as expected) that the infill construction produced a very high increasing of structural stiffness, especially for vibration modes that involve the in-plane stiffness of infills. Secondly, the infill damage produced a frequency reduction that can be detected through both ambient vibration and impact load tests. On the contrary, the evolution of damping ratios is not representative of the increasing damage occurred to non-structural elements since no evident trends were captured during the whole experimentation, being the dissipative mechanisms not activated by low-amplitude excitations.

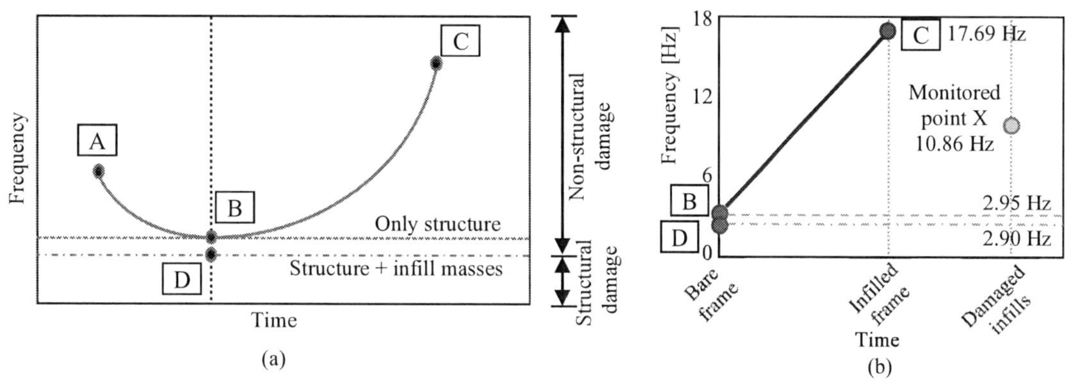

Figure 6. Time-frequency curve: (a) theoretical curve, (b) application to the mock-up.

Finally, a procedure for the structural health monitoring based on the tracing of the time-frequency curve of the structure during its construction process, is presented and then applied to the case study at hand, discussing its advantages.

In conclusion, it can be asserted that tracing frequency values from dynamic tests could be a useful tool to monitor the health status of a structure and to find possible occurred damage of structural and non-structural members.

REFERENCES

[1] Nicoletti, V., Arezzo, D., Carbonari, S., & Gara, F. (2022). Vibration-based tests and results for the evaluation of infill masonry walls influence on the dynamic behaviour of buildings: A review. *Archives of Computational Methods in Engineering*.

[2] Yousefianmoghadam, S., Song, M., Mohammadi, M.E., Packard, B., Stavridis, A., Moaveni, B., & Wood, R.L. (2020). Nonlinear dynamic tests of a reinforced concrete frame building at different damage levels. *Earthq. Eng. Struct. Dyn.*, 49(9), 924-945.

[3] Uebayashi, H., Nagano, M., Hida, T., Tanuma, T., Yasui, M., & Sakai, S. (2016). Evaluation of the structural damage of high-rise reinforced concrete buildings using ambient vibrations recorded before and after damage. *Earthq. Eng. Struct. Dyn.*, 45, 213-228.

[4] Gara, F., Arezzo, D., Nicoletti, V., & Carbonari, S. (2021). Monitoring the modal properties of an RC school building during the 2016 Central Italy seismic swarm. *J. Struct. Eng. (ASCE)*, 147(7), 05021002.

[5] Chellini, G., De Roeck, G., Nardini, L., & Salvatore, W. (2008). Damage detection of a steel-concrete composite frame by a multilevel approach: Experimental measurements and modal identification. *Earthq. Eng. Struct. Dyn.*, 37(15), 1763-1783.

[6] Astroza, R., Ebrahimian, H., Conte, J.P., Restrepo, J.I., & Hutchinson, T.C. (2016) Influence of the construction process and nonstructural components on the modal properties of a five-story building. *Earthq. Eng. Struct. Dyn.*, 45(7), 1063-1084.

[7] Gabbianelli, G., Perrone, D., Brunesi, E., & Monteiro, R. (2020). Seismic acceleration and displacement demand profiles of non-structural elements in hospital buildings. *Buildings*, 10(12), 243, 1-19.

[8] Furtado, A., Vila-Pouca, N., Varum, H., & Arede, A. (2019). Study of the seismic response on the infill masonry walls of a 15-storey reinforced concrete structure in Nepal. *Buildings*, 9(2), 39.

[9] De Angelis, A., & Pecce, M.R. (2019). The structural identification of the infill walls contribution in the dynamic response of framed buildings. *Struct. Control. Health Monit.*, 26(9), e2405.

[10] Nicoletti, V., Arezzo, D., Carbonari, S., & Gara, F. (2020). Expeditious methodology for the estimation of infill masonry wall stiffness through in-situ dynamic tests. *Constr. Build. Mat.*, 262, 120807.

[11] Peeters, B., De Roeck, G. (2001). Stochastic system identification for operational modal analysis: A review. *J. Dyn. Syst. Meas. Contr.*, 123(4), 659-667.

[12] Van Overschee, P., & De Moor, B. (2012) *Subspace identification for linear systems: Theory-Implementation-Applications.* Norwell (MA), Kluwer Academic Publishers.

[13] Nicoletti, V., Arezzo, D., Carbonari, S., & Gara, F. (2022). Dynamic monitoring of buildings as a diagnostic tool during construction phases. *J. Build. Eng.*, 46, 103764.

[14] Nicoletti, V., Regni, M., Speranza, E., Arezzo, D., Carbonari, S., & Gara, F. (2019) Identification of infill masonry walls stiffening contribution on the dynamic behaviour of steel frames. In: *Proc. 8th International Operational Modal Analysis Conference (IOMAC)* (pp. 315-320). Copenhagen, Denmark.

UNCERTAINTIES QUANTIFICATION

9th International Operational Modal Analysis Conference
iomac
July 3 - 6, 2022
Vancouver, Canada

QUANTIFICATION OF STATISTICAL UNCERTAINTIES IN SUBSPACE-BASED OPERATIONAL MODAL ANALYSIS AND THEIR APPLICATIONS

Michael Döhler

Univ. Gustave Eiffel, Inria, COSYS/SII, I4S, Rennes, France, michael.doehler@inria.fr

ABSTRACT

Modal parameters are estimated from vibration data, thus they are inherently afflicted with statistical uncertainties due to the unknown ambient excitation and measurement noise. While the point estimates of the modal parameters can be obtained with several system identification methods, only few of them also provide the associated uncertainties. The quantification of these uncertainties is important for many applications, since they are a means to assess the precision of the estimates, and to evaluate if changes between different datasets are statistically significant or not. As such, they are an added value in modern modal analysis practice and used in applications to e.g., damage detection and localization, reliability analysis, modal tracking and model calibration. For subspace-based system identification, efficient methods for uncertainty quantification have been developed for the last 15 years, yielding reliable estimates of the uncertainties at reasonable computational cost. They cover a wide range of subspace methods and their application areas. In this paper, an overview of the developments is given and the importance of the knowledge of the uncertainties is illustrated.

Keywords: Uncertainty quantification, subspace methods, (operational) modal analysis, monitoring

1. INTRODUCTION

The identification of dynamic system characteristics from vibration measurements is a fundamental task in engineering. Amongst others, subspace-based system identification methods are well-suited for this purpose. They identify the system matrices of a linear time-invariant state-space model that describes the dynamic system behavior [1], from which the modal parameters are retrieved. The estimates based on data are inherently afflicted with statistical uncertainties due to the unknown ambient excitation, measurement noise and limited data length. The quantification of these uncertainties is tied to the deployed identification method. However, the subspace identification methods only produce point estimates but not their related confidence bounds.

The objective for uncertainty quantification is to obtain the modal parameter estimates *and* their confidence bounds from the same dataset. While the statistical properties of estimates from subspace methods have been analyzed in great detail in the automatic control literature in the past, e.g. in [2–4], the expressions therein cannot be directly used for an actual covariance estimation in practical applications, since they require in addition e.g. the estimation of the unknown states and their covariances, which are not computed in the modal parameter estimation. A different approach was proposed in [5], where the covariance of estimated parameters is computed easily from the sample covariances of the underlying output data covariances and their related sensitivities.

The sensitivity-based covariance propagation is a simple and powerful tool for uncertainty quantification, and is theoretically justified by the statistical delta method [6]. It states that a function of an asymptotically Gaussian variable is also asymptotically Gaussian if its sensitivity is non-zero, and gives the respective covariance expression. Since the output covariances that are the basis of any subspace method are asymptotically Gaussian, this strategy can be used for characterizing the statistical distributions and in particular the covariance of the modal parameters and functions thereof.

This paper summarizes some of the developments for uncertainty quantification in the context of subspace methods from the last 15 years. In the first part, theoretical and algorithmic developments are presented regarding the uncertainty quantification of modal parameters for diverse subspace methods, their efficient implementation and the uncertainty quantification of the related modal indicators. In the second part, modal-parameter based methods are presented where the uncertainty information of the underlying modal parameter estimates is integrated, enhancing the originally deterministic methods.

2. BACKGROUND OF SUBSPACE-BASED SYSTEM IDENTIFICATION AND UNCERTAINTY QUANTIFICATION

In this section, the subspace-based system identification method for modal analysis and the associated uncertainty quantification framework are outlined. The schematics of the framework are presented in Fig. 1.

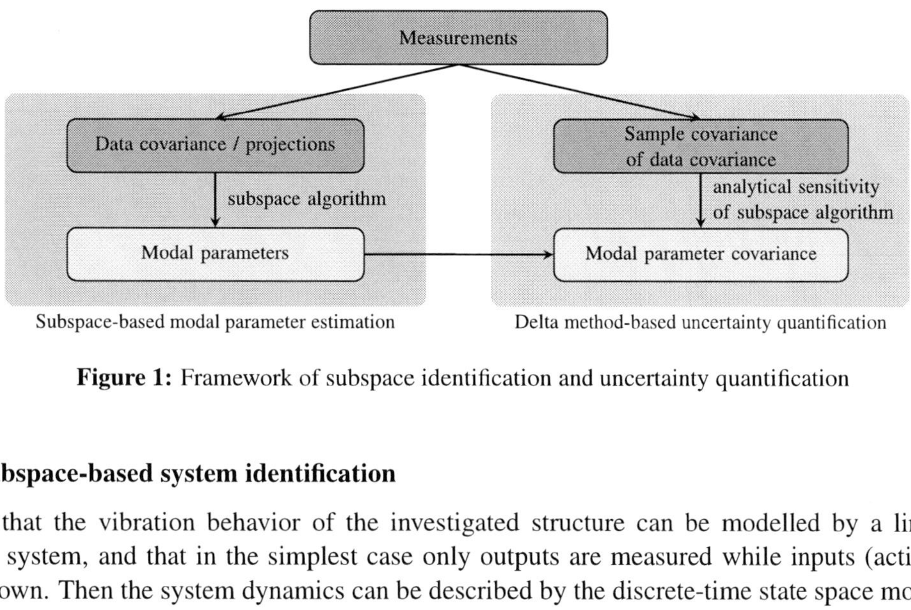

Figure 1: Framework of subspace identification and uncertainty quantification

2.1. Subspace-based system identification

Assume that the vibration behavior of the investigated structure can be modelled by a linear time-invariant system, and that in the simplest case only outputs are measured while inputs (acting forces) are unknown. Then the system dynamics can be described by the discrete-time state space model

$$\begin{cases} x_{k+1} &= Ax_k + w_k \\ y_k &= Cx_k + v_k \end{cases}, \tag{1}$$

where A is the state transition matrix, C is the output matrix, and k is the integer time step corresponding to the system at time $t = k\Delta t$, where Δt is the sampling rate. Vector $y_k \in \mathbb{R}^r$ contains the measured outputs (such as accelerations, velocities, displacements, strains), and $x_k \in \mathbb{R}^n$ is the state vector. The state noise $w_k \in \mathbb{R}^n$ is related to the unknown ambient excitation, and vector $v_k \in \mathbb{R}^r$ is the output noise. The modal parameters are related to the eigenvalues and eigenvectors (λ_i, ϕ_i), $i = 1, \ldots, n$, of A and to C by

$$\mu_i = \frac{\log(\lambda_i)}{\Delta t}, \quad f_i = \frac{|\mu_i|}{2\pi}, \quad \zeta_i = \frac{-\text{Re}(\mu_i)}{|\mu_i|}, \quad \varphi_i = C\phi_i, \tag{2}$$

where μ_i is an eigenvalue of the corresponding continuous-time system, f_i is the natural frequency, ζ_i is the damping ratio and φ_i is the mode shape at the output coordinates.

To estimate the matrices A and C from the output data y_k of length N, $k = 1, \ldots, N$, and consequently the modal parameters in (2), subspace methods are used. They are based on projecting (or simply multiplying) data Hankel matrices with a future and a past time sample horizon obtaining some matrix $\hat{\mathcal{H}}$, such that a consistent estimate of the system's observability matrix can be obtained from the column space of $\hat{\mathcal{H}}$. The respective data Hankel matrices can be defined as

$$\mathcal{Y}^- = \frac{1}{\sqrt{N}} \begin{bmatrix} y_1 & y_2 & \cdots & y_N \\ y_2 & y_3 & \cdots & y_{N+1} \\ \vdots & \vdots & \ddots & \vdots \\ y_p & y_{p+1} & \cdots & y_{N+p-1} \end{bmatrix}, \quad \mathcal{Y}^+ = \begin{bmatrix} y_{p+1} & y_{p+2} & \cdots & y_{N+p} \\ y_{p+2} & y_{p+3} & \cdots & y_{N+p+1} \\ \vdots & \vdots & \ddots & \vdots \\ y_{2p} & y_{2p+1} & \cdots & y_{N+2p-1} \end{bmatrix},$$

where $\mathcal{Y}^-$ can be built also from a subset of reference sensors or projection channels but not necessarily from all sensors.

There are many subspace methods in the literature [1, 7] with different ways to compute $\hat{\mathcal{H}}$, but from which the modal parameters are retrieved in the same way. For example, the covariance-driven subspace algorithm [8] computes $\hat{\mathcal{H}} = \mathcal{Y}^+ \mathcal{Y}^{-T}$, which corresponds to a matrix containing the output covariances of the data for different time lags. Their theoretical values satisfy the decomposition

$$\mathcal{H} = \mathcal{O}\mathcal{C}, \quad \text{where} \quad \mathcal{O} = \begin{bmatrix} C \\ CA \\ \vdots \\ CA^{p-1} \end{bmatrix} \tag{3}$$

with the observability and stochastic controllability matrices $\mathcal{O}$ and $\mathcal{C}$. With the singular value decomposition (SVD) truncated at the desired model order

$$\hat{\mathcal{H}} = \begin{bmatrix} U_1 & U_0 \end{bmatrix} \begin{bmatrix} S_1 & 0 \\ 0 & S_0 \end{bmatrix} \begin{bmatrix} V_1^T \\ V_0^T \end{bmatrix}, \tag{4}$$

an estimate $\hat{\mathcal{O}} = U_1 S_1^{1/2}$ of the observability matrix is obtained. Then, the output matrix C is estimated from the first block row of the observability matrix, and the state transition matrix is estimated from the shift-invariance property in a least-squares sense as $\hat{A} = (\hat{\mathcal{O}}^{\uparrow})^{\dagger} \hat{\mathcal{O}}^{\downarrow}$, where $\hat{\mathcal{O}}^{\uparrow}$ and $\hat{\mathcal{O}}^{\downarrow}$ are the observability matrix estimate without the last and first block row, respectively. Ultimately, the modal parameters are obtained from the eigenvalues and eigenvectors of $\hat{A}$ and from $\hat{C}$ as in (2).

In engineering practice the modal parameters are obtained at different model orders by successively truncating the SVD in (4) and interpreted in so-called stabilization diagrams with the goal to separate (stable) physical modes from spurious ones. An efficient procedure for the multi-order modal parameter estimation can be achieved by exploiting the structure of the least-squares problem at multiple model orders for estimating $\hat{A}$, as detailed in [9].

2.2. Uncertainty quantification

The delta method is a statistical tool that helps to estimate the covariance of a function of an asymptotically Gaussian variable [6]. It is used to propagate the sample covariance of the data-related covariances that are computed in the first step of the subspace algorithms through all steps of the algorithm down to the modal parameters or functions thereof. Finally, confidence intervals of the computed parameters can be derived.

The first step of the subspace algorithms involves data projections that involve the computation of output covariances. If inputs (e.g. due to artificial excitation) are available in addition to the measured outputs, then this step also involves input/output covariances of the data. These data-related covariances are asymptotically Gaussian, i.e.,

$$\sqrt{N}(\hat{\mathcal{R}} - \mathcal{R}) \to \mathcal{N}(0, \Sigma_{\mathcal{R}})$$

where $\hat{\mathcal{R}}$ is a vector containing all covariance estimates involved in the chosen subspace method. An estimate $\hat{\Sigma}_{\mathcal{R}}$ of the covariance can be easily evaluated by the sample covariance based on partitions of the available data. The propagation of this covariance to the modal parameter estimates is then based on the delta method, stating that a function $\hat{Y} = f(\hat{\mathcal{R}})$ is also asymptotically Gaussian with

$$\sqrt{N}(\hat{Y} - Y) \to \mathcal{N}(0, \mathcal{J}_{Y,\mathcal{R}} \Sigma_{\mathcal{R}} \mathcal{J}_{Y,\mathcal{R}}^T).$$

The derivative $\mathcal{J}_{Y,\mathcal{R}}$ of the function with respect to $\mathcal{R}$ is obtained from perturbation theory. For a first-order perturbation it holds $\Delta Y \approx \mathcal{J}_{Y,\mathcal{R}} \Delta\mathcal{R}$. Hence, perturbing the functional relationship between $\mathcal{R}$ and Y analytically and neglecting higher-order terms yields the desired derivative, in particular for cases where the functional relationship is not explicit like for the SVD or eigenvalue decomposition. Subsequently, covariance expressions for the estimates satisfy

$$\hat{\Sigma}_Y \approx \hat{\mathcal{J}}_{Y,\mathcal{R}} \hat{\Sigma}_{\mathcal{R}} \hat{\mathcal{J}}_{Y,\mathcal{R}}^T. \tag{5}$$

With this principle, the uncertainties of the output covariances from the first step of the subspace method can be propagated step by step through the algorithm down to the modal parameters and related quantities. Finally, confidence intervals of the estimates can be established based on the computed covariance and the fact that the distribution of the estimates can be approximated as Gaussian. For example, if $\hat{Y}$ is the vector containing the modal parameter estimates, then the covariance of each component $\hat{Y}_i$ is related to the respective component $\hat{\sigma}^2_{Y_i}$ on the diagonal of the asymptotic covariance estimate $\hat{\Sigma}_Y$, and the 95% confidence interval is given by

$$(\hat{Y}_i - 2 \cdot \tfrac{1}{\sqrt{N}} \hat{\sigma}_{Y_i},\ \hat{Y}_i + 2 \cdot \tfrac{1}{\sqrt{N}} \hat{\sigma}_{Y_i}),$$

i.e. this interval contains the true value Y_i of the estimate $\hat{Y}_i$ with a probability of 95%.

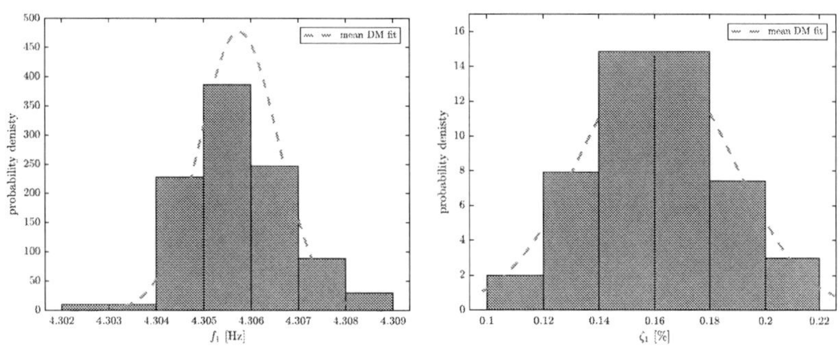

Figure 2: Histograms of modal parameter estimates with the delta method-based Gaussian approximation from [10].

To illustrate the Gaussian character of the modal parameter estimates in a practical setting, histograms of the first frequency and damping ratio are shown in Fig. 2 that are obtained from 100 datasets containing experimental data of a wind turbine blade [10], together with their mean Gaussian approximation provided by the delta method. It can be seen that the Gaussian approximation is appropriate, and that the modal parameter covariance estimated from one dataset (on which the mean fit is based in the figures) describes well the empirical distribution from the histogram.

3. THEORY AND ALGORITHMIC DEVELOPMENTS

3.1. Efficient implementation and uncertainty quantification in stabilization diagrams

The algorithm for uncertainty quantification of modal parameters from covariance-driven subspace identification has been proposed in [5], where the involved analytical sensitivities for the covariance propagation as well as the initial sample covariance are derived. However, in its direct implementation the size of the involved covariance matrices is considerable, which makes it computationally taxing and causing memory problems even for moderately sized problems. To alleviate this problem, a memory efficient and fast computation scheme for this method has been developed in [11] based on a mathematical reformulation of the algorithm, where in particular the structure of the the initial sample covariance estimate is exploited. Moreover, the covariance computation is optimized for multiple model orders in the stabilization diagram in [11], where the fact is exploited that the first columns of the observability matrix estimate at a higher model order are identical to the observability matrix estimate at a lower model order due to the SVD in (4). In this way, redundant operations in the computation of the stabilization diagram uncertainties can be avoided, and the algorithmic speed increased by two orders of magnitude of the maximal model order compared to a direct implementation, resulting in computation times of less than a minute for typical problem sizes.

In Fig. 3, the stabilization diagram from a dataset of the Z24 Bridge is shown, where the estimated standard deviations of the frequencies are shown as horizontal bars. Putting a threshold on the coefficient of variation of the frequencies (standard deviation divided by the frequency) cleans the diagram considerably, as seen in Fig. 3 (right).

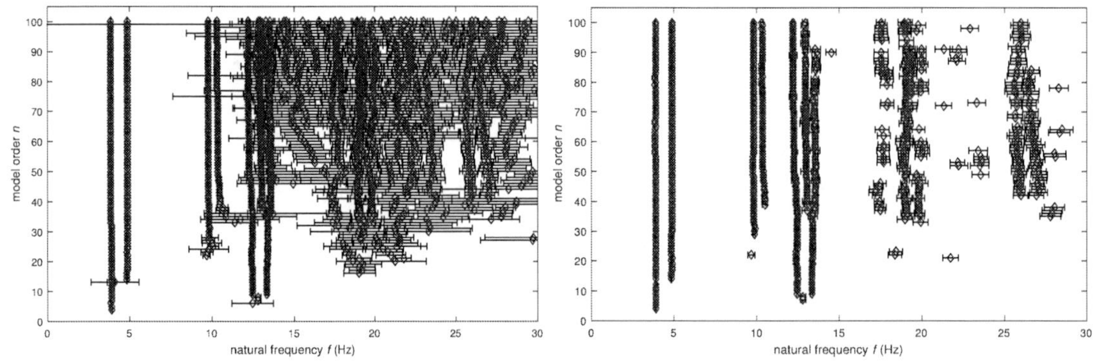

Figure 3: Stabilization diagram of Z24 Bridge without (left) and with threshold on standard deviation of frequencies (right).

The uncertainty information of the modal alignments in the diagram can then be used to obtain global mode estimates [12], and to actually obtain the modal alignments by automated statistical clustering approaches [13].

3.2. Uncertainty quantification for diverse subspace methods

The family of subspace methods is big, including covariance-driven and data-driven methods, methods for output-only (stochastic) system identification, and methods for input/ouput (combined deterministic-stochastic) for the case where some of the inputs are known. The uncertainty quantification strategy for the above-mentioned covariance-driven subspace method has been extended to a wide range of different subspace methods in [14] for the purpose of modal parameter uncertainty quantification.

The main difficulty in the extension to other subspace methods lies in the link between the matrix $\hat{\mathcal{H}}$ and the data-related covariance matrices, in order to perform the first step of uncertainty propagation. The covariance-driven subspace method is the simplest of the subspace methods for uncertainty quantification, since it only depends on one data-related covariance matrix $\mathcal{Y}^+\mathcal{Y}^{-T}$. The sample covariance of this matrix is then propagated throughout the method. In other subspace methods, the construction of the initial 'projection matrix' $\hat{\mathcal{H}}$, from which the observability matrix is obtained, is more complex. For 'data-driven' methods like UPC [1, 8], the projection is not immediately linked to output covariances, but is a matrix that grows with the number of data samples. However, it can be shown that the observability matrix can be equivalently related to $\hat{\mathcal{H}}\hat{\mathcal{H}}^T$ for the purpose of uncertainty propagation, which is again 'covariance-driven'. For the case of UPC where $\hat{\mathcal{H}} = \mathcal{Y}^+\mathcal{Y}^{-T}(\mathcal{Y}^-\mathcal{Y}^{-T})^{-1}\mathcal{Y}^-$, the algorithm depends on two data-related covariance matrices, namely $\mathcal{Y}^+\mathcal{Y}^{-T}$ and $\mathcal{Y}^-\mathcal{Y}^{-T}$. In the presence of known inputs, matrix $\hat{\mathcal{H}}$ depends furthermore on covariance matrices between outputs and inputs, and between inputs. In [14], the related uncertainty quantification schemes are developed for different classes of subspace methods, namely

- Output-only orthogonal projection data-driven algorithm (UPC),
- Input/output covariance-driven algorithm,
- Input/output orthogonal projection data-driven (similar to MOESP),
- Input/output oblique projection data-driven (N4SID).

The developed strategies allow an easy extension also to other subspace methods. While the system matrices A and C and the related modal parameters are obtained from the observability matrix in these methods, there is an alternative way to obtain them based on the state sequences in data-driven subspace methods like UPC, for which the uncertainty quantification scheme has been developed recently in [15].

With the availability of input data, the system matrices B and D of the related input/output state space model can be identified in addition to matrices A and C. With the knowledge of these matrices, the parametric transfer function can be obtained. The associated uncertainties for B and D, and the phase and magnitude of the transfer function have been obtained in [16], showcased in Fig. 4. It can be seen that the computed confidence intervals coincide well with the empirical ones in a Monte Carlo simulation.

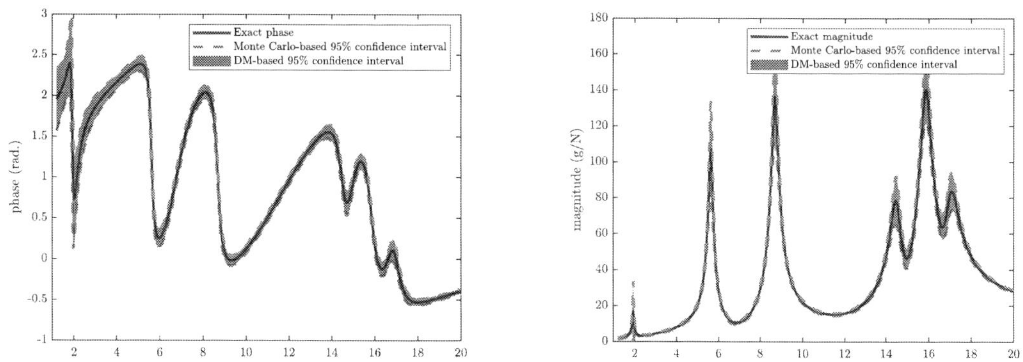

Figure 4: First component of phase and magnitude of $H(z)$ with Monte Carlo and delta method-based confidence intervals from [16].

3.3. Uncertainty quantification of modal indicators

Modal indicators like the Modal Assurance Criterion (MAC) and the Modal Phase Collinearity (MPC) are computed from mode shapes and thus inherit their statistical uncertainties when computed from measurement data. Hence, they will never be exactly one (indicating a perfect mode shape match, or a perfectly real-valued mode shape), but only close to one. Hence, the quantification of the statistical uncertainties is required in order to evaluate if the modal indicators are significantly close to one or not.

The particular difficulty in uncertainty quantification of the modal indicators is their boundedness in the interval $[0, 1]$. When the theoretical value is one, e.g., when the MAC is evaluated for identical mode shapes or when the MPC is evaluated for a real-valued mode shape, then the distribution of the corresponding estimates accumulates near one and is not Gaussian anymore. Hence the previous first-order framework for uncertainty quantification cannot be used anymore. In [17, 18] the distribution properties of the MPC and MAC estimates have been derived, as well as the respective confidence intervals. It turns out that the distributions for theoretical values at the border of the interval (i.e., for MAC or MPC equal to one) can be described by means of the second-order delta method, where the distributions can be approximated by a scaled and shifted χ^2 distribution, whereas in the inside of the interval $[0, 1]$ the distributions are asymptotically Gaussian, as illustrated in Fig. 5.

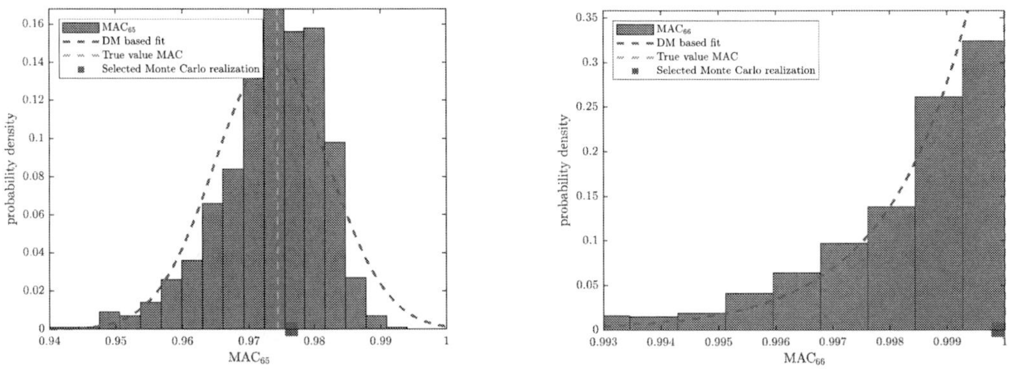

Figure 5: Distribution fits of MAC estimates from delta method, together with histograms from Monte Carlo simulation. Left: MAC of estimates of different mode shapes with Gaussian approximation, right: MAC of estimates of equal mode shape with scaled and shifted χ^2 approximation, from [18].

3.4. Validation

The presented methods for uncertainty quantification of the modal parameters and the modal indicators have not only been extensively validated in simulation studies, but also on experimental data. A first validation of the uncertainties obtained from the covariance-driven subspace methods was reported in [19] using data of a bridge and of a building from different sensor setups. More recently, an extensive validation study on a laboratory test of a large-scale wind turbine blade was carried out in [10] based on 100 experimental data sets, covering all of the presented subspace methods and modal indicators. The results confirm that the delta method is, on average, adequate to characterize the distribution of the considered estimates from all the different methods solely based on the quantities obtained from one data set, validating the use of this statistical framework for uncertainty quantification in practice.

3.5. Some case studies

Modal parameter uncertainties are particularly useful in the monitoring of structures over time. Some large scale case studies have been reported where the modal parameter uncertainty has been evaluated. One example is the S101 Bridge [18, 20], where damages were introduced to the bridge while measurement data was collected continuously during four days. The role of the modal parameter uncertainties was evaluated in [21] for the monitoring the Baixo Sabor arch dam during several years, where it was concluded that the uncertainties are particularly useful for removing outliers in the modal parameter tracking. In [22], the accuracy of the uncertainty estimates during ice-structure interaction was evaluated, and applied to monitoring data of a lighthouse.

4. UNCERTAINTIES IN MODAL PARAMETER-BASED METHODS

Modal parameters and modal indicators are used in many engineering applications. Instead of using their point estimates only, the uncertainties of the estimates are an additional valuable information that can enhance methods. In this section two examples are given where the quantified modal parameter uncertainties are integrated into originally deterministic methods, namely for damage localization and for finite element model updating. Furthermore, some application cases are briefly presented.

4.1. Flexibility evaluation and DLV-based damage localization

The damage locating vector vector approach [23] computes originally a vector in the null space of the change of flexibility matrix that is computed from input/output measurement data from the reference and from the damaged states, and then applies it as a load (at the sensor coordinates) to a finite element model of the structure to compute the stress field. Damage is located where the resulting stress is zero. The approach has been generalized the output-only case [24], where the required load vector is computed from the null space of the transfer matrix difference, which can be evaluated from the modal parameters solely.

Instead of evaluating the resulting stress deterministically to decide if it is zero or not over a structural component, a statistical evaluation is made in [25–27] where the modal parameter uncertainty is propagated to the computed stress field and used for a decision with hypothesis tests. The method has been extended the case of changing temperature in [28], where the temperature influence is removed from the modal parameters. In these works it has been shown that the performance of the damage localization is largely increased when considering the modal parameter uncertainties, as illustrated in Fig. 6. It can be seen that the rate of successful damage localization is always higher when the considering the uncertainties in the statistical tests compared to the deterministic evaluation of the stress estimates.

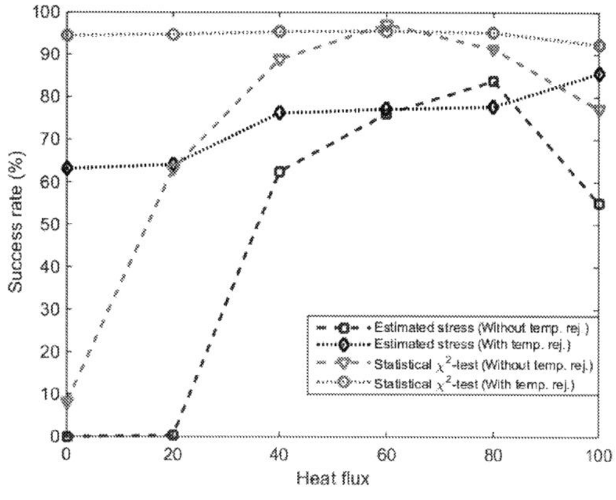

Figure 6: Success rates for DLV-based damage localization with and without considering modal parameter uncertainties for different temperature scenarios, from [28]. Success rates are higher when considering the uncertainties in the evaluation (red vs. black curve, pink vs. blue curve).

In a related work [29], the uncertainty of the modal parameters as well as assumed uncertainties of finite element model parameters have been propagated to the flexibility matrix estimate and associated computed deflections under static loads with the purpose of reliability analysis.

4.2. Finite element model updating

Modal parameters are essential for finite element model updating, and their uncertainties can be valuable for the updating problem. Since the updated model parameters are a function of the modal parameter estimates, the uncertainty of the model parameters due to the uncertainty of the modal parameters can be evaluated by uncertainty propagation. This was carried out in [30], where the propagation is performed through each iteration step of the updating minimization problem in a subspace fitting approach. Furthermore, the uncertainties of the modal parameters can be directly considered in the formulation of the objective function as well as in the stopping criterion for the optimization, as developed in [31]. In this work, model frequencies and mode shapes (via the MAC) are penalized in the objective function when they are outside the confidence bounds of their estimated counterparts, which leads to a steeper objective function. The optimization search can be terminated once the model-based modal parameters are within the confidence bounds of their data-based counterparts, leading to an efficient algorithm for the updating problem.

In Fig. 7, a modal parameter-based objective function is illustrated without and with the consideration of the uncertainties. First of all, it can be seen that the objective function is indeed steeper when considering the uncertainties, which should facilitate the optimization search. Second, it can be seen that the minimum of the objective function (red line) that is computed on the modal parameter estimates is not taken on at the true parameter values (green line) due to the modal parameter uncertainties, but just close to it. This also confirms that convergence of the optimization search to the minimum of the objective function is actually not required, and it is sufficient to stop the search once arrived in the yellow region indicating the values of the objective function where the model-based modal parameters are within the confidence bounds of their estimates.

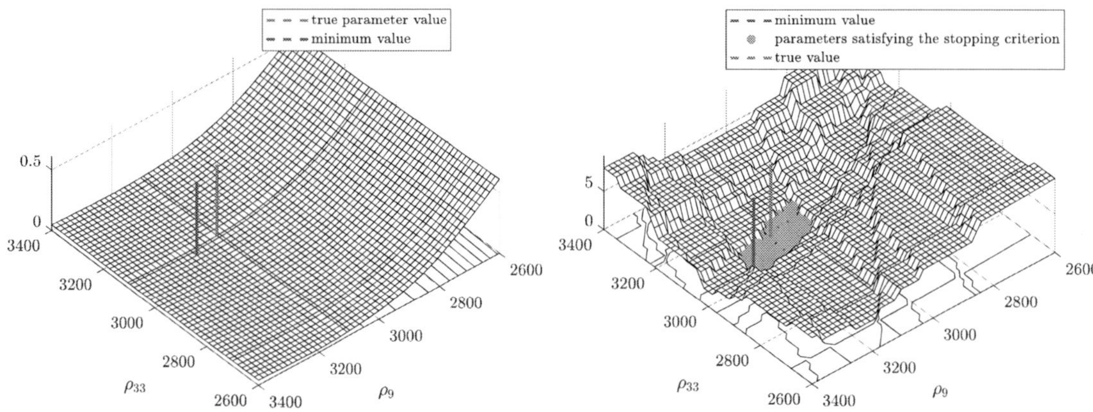

Figure 7: Modal parameter-based objective function to be minimized in the model updating, for two model parameters in the vicinity of their true values. Without (left) and with consideration of modal parameter uncertainties (right), from [31].

5. CONCLUSIONS

The methods for uncertainty quantification in subspace-based operational modal analysis have evolved over the last years, offering computationally efficient tools for a wide range of methods and engineering applications. They also have become part of commercial software [32]. The methods have shown their adequacy in extensive validation studies as well as in diverse case studies on real structures. Future work on the topic should include, e.g., further integration of the quantified uncertainties in methods for damage diagnosis, including in the data normalization step to remove environmental effects, as well as in data-based reliability analysis.

REFERENCES

[1] van Overschee, P., & de Moor, B. (1996). *Subspace Identification for Linear Systems* (1st). Springer.

[2] Bauer, D., Deistler, M., & Scherrer, W. (1999). Consistency and asymptotic normality of some subspace algorithms for systems without observed inputs. *Automatica, 35*(7), 1243–1254.

[3] Chiuso, A., & Picci, G. (2004). The asymptotic variance of subspace estimates. *Journal of Econometrics, 118*(1), 257–291.

[4] Bauer, D. (2005). Asymptotic properties of subspace estimators. *Automatica, 41*(3), 359–376.

[5] Reynders, E., Pintelon, R., & De Roeck, G. (2008). Uncertainty bounds on modal parameters obtained from stochastic subspace identification. *Mechanical Systems and Signal Processing, 22*(4), 948–969.

[6] Casella, G., & L. Berger, R. (2001). *Statistical Inference* (2nd). Cengage Learning.

[7] Benveniste, A., & Mevel, L. (2007). Nonstationary consistency of subspace methods. *IEEE Transactions on Automatic Control, 52*(6), 974–984.

[8] Peeters, B., & De Roeck, G. (1999). Reference-based stochastic subspace identification for output-only modal analysis. *Mechanical Systems and Signal Processing, 13*(6), 855–878.

[9] Döhler, M., & Mevel, L. (2012). Fast multi-order computation of system matrices in subspace-based system identification. *Control Engineering Practice, 20*(9), 882–894.

[10] Greś, S., Riva, R., Süleyman, C. Y., Andersen, P., & Łuczak, M. (2022). Uncertainty quantification of modal parameter estimates obtained from subspace identification: An experimental validation on a laboratory test of a large-scale wind turbine blade. *Engineering Structures, 256*, 114001.

[11] Döhler, M., & Mevel, L. (2013). Efficient multi-order uncertainty computation for stochastic subspace identification. *Mechanical Systems and Signal Processing, 38*(2), 346–366.

[12] Döhler, M., Andersen, P., & Mevel, L. (2017). Variance computation of modal parameter estimates from UPC subspace identification. *7th International Operational Modal Analysis Conference.*

[13] Priou, J., Greś, S., Perrault, M., Guerineau, L., & Döhler, M. (2022). Automated uncertainty-based extraction of modal parameters from stabilization diagrams. *9th International Operational Modal Analysis Conference.*

[14] Mellinger, P., Döhler, M., & Mevel, L. (2016). Variance estimation of modal parameters from output-only and input/output subspace-based system identification. *Journal of Sound and Vibration, 379*, 1–27.

[15] Reynders, E. P. (2021). Uncertainty quantification in data-driven stochastic subspace identification. *Mechanical Systems and Signal Processing, 151*, 107338.

[16] Greś, S., Döhler, M., Jacobsen, N.-J., & Mevel, L. (2022). Uncertainty quantification of input matrices and transfer function in input/output subspace system identification. *Mechanical Systems and Signal Processing, 167*, 108581.

[17] Greś, S., Döhler, M., Andersen, P., & Mevel, L. (2021). Uncertainty quantification for the Modal Phase Collinearity of complex mode shapes. *Mechanical Systems and Signal Processing, 152*, 107436.

[18] Greś, S., Döhler, M., & Mevel, L. (2021a). Uncertainty quantification of the Modal Assurance Criterion in operational modal analysis. *Mechanical Systems and Signal Processing, 152*, 107457.

[19] Reynders, E., Maes, K., Lombaert, G., & De Roeck, G. (2016). Uncertainty quantification in operational modal analysis with stochastic subspace identification: Validation and applications. *Mechanical Systems and Signal Processing, 66*, 13–30.

[20] Döhler, M., Hille, F., Mevel, L., & Rücker, W. (2014). Structural health monitoring with statistical methods during progressive damage test of S101 Bridge. *Engineering Structures, 69*, 183–193.

[21] Pereira, S., Reynders, E., Magalhães, F., Cunha, Á., & Gomes, J. P. (2020). The role of modal parameters uncertainty estimation in automated modal identification, modal tracking and data normalization. *Engineering Structures, 224*, 111208.

[22] Nord, T. S., Petersen, Ø. W., & Hendrikse, H. (2019). Stochastic subspace identification of modal parameters during ice–structure interaction. *Philosophical Transactions of the Royal Society A, 377*(2155), 20190030.

[23] Bernal, D. (2002). Load vectors for damage localization. *Journal of Engineering Mechanics*, *128*(1), 7–14.

[24] Bernal, D. (2010). Load vectors for damage location in systems identified from operational loads. *Journal of Engineering Mechanics*, *136*(1), 31–39.

[25] Döhler, M., Marin, L., Bernal, D., & Mevel, L. (2013). Statistical decision making for damage localization with stochastic load vectors. *Mechanical Systems and Signal Processing*, *39*(1-2), 426–440.

[26] Marin, L., Döhler, M., Bernal, D., & Mevel, L. (2015). Robust statistical damage localization with stochastic load vectors. *Structural Control and Health Monitoring*, *22*(3), 557–573.

[27] Bhuyan, M., Döhler, M., Lecieux, Y., Mevel, L., & Schoefs, F. (2017). Statistical damage localization with stochastic load vectors using multiple mode sets. *Structural Health Monitoring*, *16*(5), 518–535.

[28] Bhuyan, M., Gautier, G., Le Touz, N., Döhler, M., Hille, F., Dumoulin, J., & Mevel, L. (2019). Vibration-based damage localization with load vectors under temperature changes. *Structural Control and Health Monitoring*, *26*(11), e2439.

[29] Li, P., & Zhang, J. (2022). Identification and uncertainty quantification of structural flexibility for reliability analysis. *Mechanical Systems and Signal Processing*, *163*, 108104.

[30] Gautier, G., Mevel, L., Mencik, J.-M., Serra, R., & Döhler, M. (2017). Variance analysis for model updating with a finite element based subspace fitting approach. *Mechanical Systems and Signal Processing*, *91*, 142–156.

[31] Greś, S., Döhler, M., & Mevel, L. (2021b). Statistical model-based optimization for damage extent quantification. *Mechanical Systems and Signal Processing*, *160*, 107894.

[32] Structural Vibration Solutions A/S. (n.d.). ARTeMIS Modal [http://www.svibs.com].

9th International Operational Modal Analysis Conference
iomac
July 3 - 6, 2022
Vancouver, Canada

HANKEL MATRIX-BASED DENOISING FOR STATISTICAL DAMAGE DIAGNOSIS

Szymon Greś, Konstantinos Tatsis, Vasilis K. Dertimanis, Eleni Chatzi

Institute of Structural Engineering (IBK), SMM team, ETH Zürich, 8093 Zürich, Switzerland

ABSTRACT

In data-driven system identification it is assumed that the dynamics of the system can be obtained from a low-rank structure of certain large-size matrices, e.g., an output covariance Hankel matrix. A classical approach to retrieving relevant dynamics is to truncate the singular value decomposition of the considered matrix by retaining only the most significant singular values corresponding to the true order of the noise-free matrix. The elusive true order of the system model is generally unknown; its selection, however, is a fundamental task in application of subspace identification methods for estimation of modal parameters and their uncertainties, often for the purpose of damage diagnosis. In this paper, a statistical methodology to approximate the model order of the output covariance Hankel matrices is derived and applied in the structural damage detection context. It is shown that the model order can be retrieved by analyzing the statistical distribution of the sensitivity of the output covariance Hankel matrix against a random perturbation of its eigenvalues. It is shown that this distribution follows a dual framework, which depends on the covariance of the inputs (loads) acting on the mechanical system. The proposed methodology is applied to the low-rank approximation of output covariance Hankel matrices , extracted as part of the subspace damage detection of a large-scale bridge. It is demonstrated that the robustness of damage diagnosis is enhanced by reducing the number of false alarms.

Keywords: Hankel matrix denoising, statistical damage diagnosis, subspace methods, eigenvalue condition number, Structural Health Monitoring

1. INTRODUCTION

In matrix denoising the aim is to recover a low-rank structure of a large-size matrix minus the noise. A possible way to attain this is to truncate the singular value, or the eigenvalue decomposition of the considered matrix, by keeping only the most significant singular/eigen values corresponding to the *true* order of the noise-free matrix. The true order of a noise-polluted matrix is rarely known; its selection, however, forms a fundamental task in shrinkage [1], estimation of modal parameters and their uncertainties in Operational Modal Analysis (OMA) [2, 3, 4], statistical damage diagnosis in Structural Health

Monitoring (SHM) [5, 6, 7, 8, 9], amongst myriads of other applications.

The choice of the model order has been extensively studied in the engineering community in the context of subspace identification methods [10], where two main lines of work are pursued; a first relying on signal processing, without identification of the system dynamics, and a second involving procedures for assessing the fit of the identified model to data. In the first category, the simplest approach is to search for a sudden decrease, i.e., a substantial gap, between singular values plotted in a decreasing order, i.e., a scree plot, [10]. Despite its widespread use in the modal analysis community, distinguishing a clear separation between the singular values of the signal and the noise can be difficult when data is noisy. Related to the second category are the so-called information criteria, e.g., the Akaike and Schwarz criteria [11], modal contribution [12], or modal dispersion [13]. While each criterion offers a trade-off between the size of the identified model and its predictive capabilities, they require an expensive identification of a system at multiple model orders.

The purpose of this work is to derive a statistical approach to robustly determine the model order in the output-only covariance-driven system identification prior to identifying the system dynamics. In the proposed approach, this is achieved through a statistical analysis of the sensitivity of the eigenvalues of output covariance Hankel matrix towards perturbations. It is shown that the variance of this sensitivity significantly increases when the investigated eigenvalue is spurious, and remains small otherwise. A practical approach to choose the model order and filter the varying eigenvalues is given. The proposed methodology is then applied to denoise the output covariance Hankel matrices in subspace-based damage detection, where the model order is assessed adaptively for different data sets. It is shown that using the denoised damage-sensitive features reduces the number of false alarms in the damage detection of a large-scale S101 bridge.

2. BACKGROUND

The proposed approach for Hankel matrix denoising and the related tools are introduced below.

2.1. Hankel matrix denoising

Let $Y = \{y_1 \dots y_N\} \in \mathbb{R}^{r \times N}$ be a collection of N measurements of an output response of a linear time-invariant (LTI) mechanical system observed by r sensors. The system response is assumed to be generated by an independent and identically distributed zero-mean input process of finite fourth moments, which is persistently exciting the system dynamics of size n [14]. The system is assumed to be stable, observable and with distinct eigenvalues. The dynamic behaviour of the system can be retrieved from a low-rank structure of certain large-size matrices obtained from data, e.g., an output covariance Hankel matrix. Let the theoretical output covariance of the measurements $\mathcal{R}_i = \mathrm{E}(y_k y_{k-i}^T) \in \mathbb{R}^{r \times r}$ be collected in a block Hankel matrix

$$\mathcal{H} = \begin{bmatrix} \mathcal{R}_1 & \mathcal{R}_2 & \dots & \mathcal{R}_q \\ \mathcal{R}_2 & \mathcal{R}_3 & \dots & \mathcal{R}_{q+1} \\ \vdots & \vdots & \ddots & \vdots \\ \mathcal{R}_{p+1} & \mathcal{R}_{p+2} & \dots & \mathcal{R}_{p+q} \end{bmatrix} \in \mathbb{R}^{(p+1)r \times qr}, \tag{1}$$

where p and q are chosen such that $\min(pr, qr) \geqslant n$ with often $p + 1 = q$. In practice $\mathcal{H}$ is not available and a consistent estimate $\widehat{\mathcal{H}}$ is obtained from the output measurements Y. When the true order of the system dynamics n is known, the low-rank structure of $\widehat{\mathcal{H}}$ can be revealed through the eigenvalue decomposition

$$\widehat{\mathcal{H}} = \begin{bmatrix} \hat{U}_{\text{sig}} & \hat{U}_{\text{null}} \end{bmatrix} \begin{bmatrix} \hat{\Lambda}_{\text{sig}} & 0 \\ 0 & \hat{\Lambda}_{\text{null}} \end{bmatrix} \begin{bmatrix} \hat{V}_{\text{sig}}^H \\ \hat{V}_{\text{null}}^H \end{bmatrix}, \tag{2}$$

where $\hat{U}_{\text{sig}} = \begin{bmatrix} \hat{u}_1 & \dots & \hat{u}_n \end{bmatrix}$ and $\hat{V}_{\text{sig}} = \begin{bmatrix} \hat{v}_1 & \dots & \hat{v}_n \end{bmatrix}$ are respectively the n right and the n left eigenvectors corresponding to the n eigenvalues $\hat{\Lambda}_{\text{sig}} = \operatorname{diag}(\hat{\lambda}_1 \dots \hat{\lambda}_n)$ ordered in a decreasing amplitude, and the matrices $\hat{U}_{\text{null}} = \begin{bmatrix}\hat{u}_{n+1} & \dots & \hat{u}_{n+s_1}\end{bmatrix}$, $\hat{V}_{\text{null}} = \begin{bmatrix}\hat{v}_{n+1} & \dots & \hat{v}_{n+s_1}\end{bmatrix}$ are respectively the right and the left nullspace of $\widehat{\mathcal{H}}$, related to the eigenvectors corresponding to $s_1 = (p+1)r - n$ eigenvalues $\hat{\Lambda}_{\text{ker}} = \text{diag}(\hat{\lambda}_{n+1} \dots \hat{\lambda}_{n+s_1}) \to 0$. Assuming knowledge of the model order n, the dynamic characteristics of the underlying mechanical system, e.g., modes, can be retrieved from the observability matrix estimate $\hat{\mathcal{O}} = \hat{U}_{\text{sig}}\hat{\Lambda}_{\text{sig}}^{1/2}$, whose computation is the fundamental step in many subspace system identification and damage diagnosis algorithms.

In practice, however, the model order is unknown. The goal of this work is to assess it in a statistically robust manner and to subsequently retrieve a low-rank approximation of $\widehat{\mathcal{H}}$

$$\widehat{\mathcal{H}} \approx \breve{\mathcal{H}} = \hat{U}_{\text{sig}}\hat{\Lambda}_{\text{sig}}\hat{V}_{\text{sig}}^{H}, \tag{3}$$

which is then used for subspace-based damage diagnosis. For the purpose of finding n, a statistical framework which does not require a prior system identification is derived, where an additional layer of information is added to the eigenvalue scree plot by assessing the sensitivity of the eigenvalue condition numbers to perturbations.

2.2. Eigenvalue condition number

Let $\hat{\lambda}$ be a simple eigenvalue of $\widehat{\mathcal{H}}$ with the associated right and left eigenvector $\hat{u}$ and $\hat{v}$, respectively. The squared condition number of $\hat{\lambda}$

$$\hat{\kappa}^2 = \left(\frac{|\hat{u}||\hat{v}|}{|\hat{u}^H\hat{v}|}\right)^2 = \frac{\hat{u}^H\hat{u}\hat{v}^H\hat{v}}{\hat{u}^H\hat{v}\hat{v}^H\hat{u}} \tag{4}$$

describes an inverted squared cosine of an angle between right and left eigenvectors associated with $\hat{\lambda}$ [15, 16]. The condition number signifies that an $O(\epsilon)$ perturbation in the underlying matrix causes an $O(\kappa\epsilon)$ perturbation in the investigated eigenvalue. Thus, when $\hat{\kappa}$ is close to 1 the perturbation of the matrix entries will have less effect. Conversely, a large value of $\hat{\kappa}$ indicates the enhanced sensitivity of the associated eigenvalue against perturbations [15]. In consequence, the sensitivity of the eigenvalues is controlled by the angle between the corresponding left and right eigenvectors, i.e.,

- when the eigenvectors $\hat{u}$ and $\hat{v}$ are collinear (the underlying matrix is symmetric), $\hat{\kappa} = 1$ for all the considered eigenvalues, indicating that the related eigenvalues are not sensitive to perturbations,
- when the eigenvectors $\hat{u}$ and $\hat{v}$ are not collinear (the underlying matrix is asymmetric), $\hat{\kappa} > 1$ for all the considered eigenvalues, indicating that the related eigenvalues are prone to perturbations.

In both cases, the non-zero eigenvalues of the signal are less prone to perturbations than the non-physical eigenvalues related to noise. In this work, a statistical analysis of the eigenvalue condition numbers is used to distinguish the highly varying eigenvalues of the noise, from the eigenvalues of the signal.

3. DISTRIBUTION OF THE EIGENVALUE CONDITION NUMBER

The statistical properties of the eigenvalue condition numbers inherit the statistical properties of the associated right and left eigenvectors of $\widehat{\mathcal{H}}$. As a consequence of Central Limit Theorem and upon adoption of the statistical delta method [17], the real and the imaginary parts of the right and the left eigenvectors contained in $\hat{X}_{u,v} = \begin{bmatrix}\Re(\hat{u})^T & \Im(\hat{u})^T & \Re(\hat{v})^T & \Im(\hat{v})^T\end{bmatrix}^T$ are asymptotically jointly Gaussian distributed, satisfying

$$\hat{X}_{u,v} = \mathcal{N}\left(X_{u,v}, \tfrac{1}{N}\Sigma_{u,v}\right),$$

where $X_{u,v}$ is the true value of $\hat{X}_{u,v}$ and $\Sigma_{u,v}$ is the joint asymptotic covariance of the right and the left eigenvectors. The expression for $\Sigma_{u,v}$ can be derived using the first-order perturbation of the eigenvalue problem of $\widehat{\mathcal{H}}$, analogously to the expression for the eigenvectors of the state matrix in [2], thus it is omitted here for brevity. Subsequently, a dual framework for approximating the distribution of $\hat{\kappa}$ is devised. Two cases are considered:

- when $\widehat{\mathcal{H}}$ tends to an asymmetric matrix, $\hat{\kappa}$ is shown to be asymptotically Gaussian distributed,
- when $\widehat{\mathcal{H}}$ tends to a symmetric matrix, $\hat{\kappa}$ is approximated by a scaled and shifted χ^2 distribution.

The proof outlining the conditions when $\mathcal{H}$ is symmetric is omitted here due to the space constraints.

3.1. Asymmetric $\mathcal{H}$

When $\widehat{\mathcal{H}}$ tends to an asymmetric matrix, the statistical properties of $\hat{\kappa}$ are inferred by applying the first-order delta method. The delta method is a well-established statistical tool that allows to characterize the probability distribution of a function of a Gaussian variable as also Gaussian, based on the first-order Taylor expansion of the considered function [17]; for $\hat{\kappa}$ it writes

$$\hat{\kappa} \approx \kappa + \mathcal{J}^{\kappa}_{u,v}\hat{X} \ , \tag{5}$$

where $\mathcal{J}^{\kappa}_{u,v}$ is the derivative of the condition number with respect to the real and imaginary parts of the right and the left eigenvector of $\mathcal{H}$, i.e., $\mathcal{J}^{\kappa}_{u,v} = \begin{bmatrix} \frac{\partial\kappa}{\partial\Re(u)} & \frac{\partial\kappa}{\partial\Im(u)} & \frac{\partial\kappa}{\partial\Re(v)} & \frac{\partial\kappa}{\partial\Im(v)} \end{bmatrix}$.

The first-order Taylor expansion of $\hat{\kappa}$ only makes sense if the derivative $\mathcal{J}^{\kappa}_{u,v}$ is non-zero. A necessary and sufficient condition for $\mathcal{J}^{\kappa}_{u,v} \neq 0$ is $\kappa \notin 1 \iff \mathcal{J}^{\kappa}_{u,v} \neq 0$, which can be proved analogously to [18]. In consequence, when $\widehat{\mathcal{H}}$ tends to an asymmetric matrix, the aforementioned first-order Taylor expansion can be applied and thanks to delta method the distribution of $\hat{\kappa}$ is approximated as

$$\hat{\kappa} \approx \mathcal{N}\left(\kappa, \frac{1}{N}\hat{\sigma}^2_{\kappa}\right), \tag{6}$$

where $\hat{\sigma}^2_{\kappa} = \hat{\mathcal{J}}^{\kappa}_{u,v}\widehat{\Sigma}_{u,v}(\hat{\mathcal{J}}^{\kappa}_{u,v})^T$ is the estimate of the asymptotic variance of the eigenvalue condition number and $\widehat{\Sigma}_{u,v}$ with $\hat{\mathcal{J}}^{\kappa}_{u,v}$ are the consistent estimates of $\Sigma_{u,v}$ and $\mathcal{J}^{\kappa}_{u,v}$ respectively.

3.2. Symmetric $\mathcal{H}$

When $\widehat{\mathcal{H}}$ tends to a symmetric matrix, $\hat{\kappa}$ tends to 1 for all the considered eigenvalues. In consequence, the derivative $\mathcal{J}^{\kappa}_{u,v}$ in (5) is null, as indicated by the conditions outlined in the previous section. In this case the first-order Taylor expansion from (5) is insufficient to characterize $\hat{\kappa}$ and the second-order Taylor expansion is used

$$\hat{\kappa} \approx \underbrace{\kappa}_{=1} + \underbrace{\mathcal{J}^{\kappa}_{u,v}}_{=0}\hat{X} + \tfrac{1}{2}\hat{X}^T \mathrm{H}^{\kappa}_{u,v}\hat{X}, \tag{7}$$

where $\mathrm{H}^{\kappa}_{u,v} \in \mathbb{R}^{4(p+1)r\times 4(p+1)r}$ is the Hessian, i.e., the second derivative of κ in u and v. Subsequently, the asymptotic properties of $\hat{\kappa}$ are characterized as a quadratic function of a Gaussian variable $\hat{X}_N = \sqrt{N}\hat{X}_{u,v}$. The corresponding quadratic form $Q(\hat{X}_N)$ is defined as

$$Q(\hat{X}_N) = \tfrac{1}{2}\hat{X}_N^T \mathrm{H}^{\kappa}_{u,v}\hat{X}_N \approx N(\hat{\kappa} - 1) \ , \tag{8}$$

whose distribution can be approximated by a scaled and shifted χ^2 distribution after the methodology developed in [19]. Detailed derivation of this distribution for $\hat{\kappa}$ is hereby omitted; an interested reader can refer to [19, 18] for the outline of the procedure. Consequently, the pdf of the distribution of $\hat{\kappa}$ follows from the relation (8) as

$$f_{\hat{\kappa}}(x) = \frac{N}{\alpha} f_{\chi^2_l}\left(\frac{N(x-1)-\beta}{\alpha}\right), \quad x \in (1 + \tfrac{\beta}{N}, \infty], \tag{9}$$

where the scaling α, the shift β and the number of degrees of freedom l are the parameters characterizing the distribution defined by the probability density function $f_{\chi^2_l}$. The uncertainty in the estimates of κ can be expressed through the quantile of the distribution for a desired confidence level γ, such as

$$t_\kappa = 1 + \tfrac{\beta}{N} + \tfrac{\alpha}{N} t_{\chi^2}, \tag{10}$$

where t_{χ^2} denotes the quantile of the χ^2 distribution with l degrees of freedom.

4. DENOISING ALGORITHM

Since the frameworks proposed in Section 3. are exclusive in theory, a decision between the two must be made. For this purpose only the estimates of κ and the related uncertainties are used. When an appropriate framework to approximate the distribution of $\hat{\kappa}$ is chosen, the noisy eigenvalues must be filtered to obtain an accurate low-rank approximation of $\widehat{\mathcal{H}}$. A sketch of the corresponding denoising algorithm is proposed as follows:

1. To choose between the two approximation frameworks, t_κ (10) is computed. When $\hat{\kappa} > t_\kappa$, the considered $\hat{\kappa}$ is not plausible for the proposed χ^2 approximation, and a decision to assess its statistical properties with a Gaussian distribution is made. Otherwise, $\hat{\kappa}$ is chosen to follow the scaled and shifted χ^2 distribution (9).
2. To distinguish the highly varying eigenvalues when $\hat{\kappa}$ is asymptotically Gaussian, an heuristic threshold on the Coefficient of Variation (CV) of $\hat{\kappa}$, i.e., $\text{CV}_{\hat{\kappa}} = \hat{\sigma}_\kappa/\hat{\kappa} > 5\%$, is enforced. Consequently, if $\text{CV}_{\hat{\kappa}}$ exceeds the threshold, the related eigenvalue estimate is flagged to correspond to noise.
3. To distinguish the highly varying eigenvalues when $\hat{\kappa}$ is approximated by the shifted and scaled χ^2 distribution, an heuristic threshold on the normalized relative shift $\bar{\beta} = \beta/N$ is enforced. If $\bar{\beta}$ exceeds the threshold, the related eigenvalue estimate is flagged to correspond to noise.
4. To compute $\breve{\mathcal{H}}$ only the non-flagged eigenvalues are retained in (3).

5. APPLICATION TO SUBSPACE-BASED DAMAGE DIAGNOSIS OF S101 BRIDGE

This section presents an application of the proposed denoising methodology to the subspace-based damage detection of the well known S101 benchmark bridge study [20].

5.1. Subspace-based damage detection with denoised features

Based on features extracted from measurement data in the reference and in the current test state, the goal of damage detection is to evaluate whether there is a significant change between the examined and reference configuration (state). Let $\breve{\mathcal{H}}_{\text{ref}}$ and $\breve{\mathcal{H}}_{\text{test}}$ be the denoised estimates of the Hankel matrices obtained from data collected in some baseline (reference) and tested states respectively. The subspace-based damage detection residual [5] is defined as

$$\zeta = \sqrt{N}\text{vec}(S_{\text{ref}}^T \breve{\mathcal{H}}_{\text{test}}), \tag{11}$$

where S_{ref} contains columns of the left nullspace of $\breve{\mathcal{H}}_{\text{ref}}$ obtained with, e.g., singular value decomposition. A decision if the system is healthy or damaged is achieved by applying a non-parametric version of the damage detection test

$$t_{\text{np}} = \zeta^T \, \hat{\Sigma}_\zeta^{-1} \, \zeta, \tag{12}$$

where $\hat{\Sigma}_\zeta$ is an estimate of the asymptotic covariance of the residual (11). This test follows a central χ^2 distribution when the system is healthy and a non-central χ^2 distribution in the damaged state. For a decision about damage, the test value is compared to a threshold that can obtained empirically from the values of the test in the reference state.

5.2. Application

The application is carried out on measurement data from the monitoring campaign of the S101 Bridge in Austria, shown in Figure 1.

Figure 1: S101 Bridge before demolition.

The response of the bridge to ambient loads was recorded using 15 acceleration sensors mounted on its deck. Measurements were sampled with a frequency of 500 Hz for a period of 3 days. During this time the bridge was subjected to artificial damage, whose type and extent were controlled. From these measurements, 215 data sets of length $N = 165{,}000$ are selected. The first 130 sets correspond to the healthy state of the bridge, while the remaining data sets correspond to different damage scenarios. From the healthy measurements, 15 data sets are selected to obtain a baseline Hankel matrix estimate $\widehat{\mathcal{H}}_{\text{ref}}$. Note that in existing studies of damage detection on the S101 bridge data [20], the reference features are obtained from a long series of 100 data sets. The current choice of a short baseline aims to emulate the conditions when the reference data availability is scarce. Prior to the damage diagnosis, the Hankel matrix denoising is showcased by following the steps of the pseudo-algorithm described in Section 4.. To illustrate that the simple scree plot is insufficient to chose the model order, the eigenvalues of $\widehat{\mathcal{H}}_{\text{ref}}$ and the corresponding condition numbers are showed on the left part of Figure 2. While no clear drop between successive eigenvalues can be observed, the condition numbers corresponding to 1-4 and 10-12 eigenvalues are relatively small, indicating that these eigenvalues are less prone to perturbation. To determine the eigenvalues that corresponds to noise, first the choice between the two approximation frameworks from Section 3. needs to be made based on the estimation of t_κ (10), as illustrated on the right part of Figure 2.

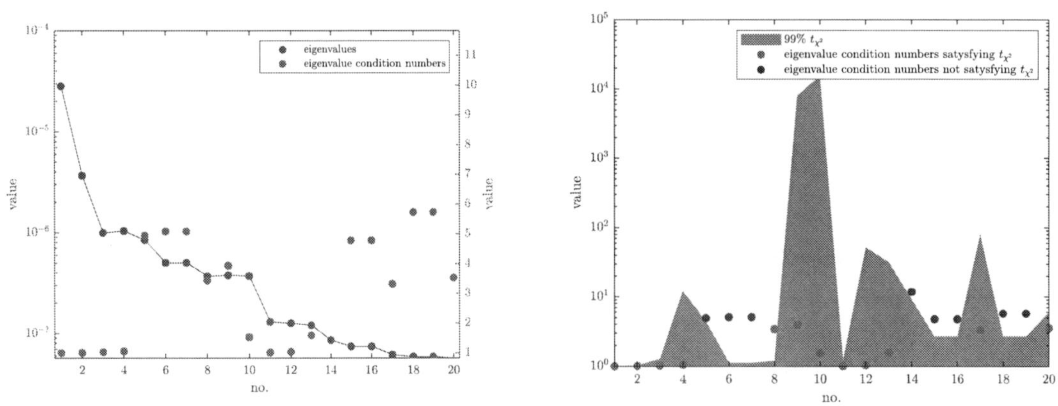

Figure 2: The first 20 eigenvalues of $\widehat{\mathcal{H}}_{\text{ref}}$ and their corresponding condition numbers obtained from the reference data set (left). Quantiles t_κ corresponding to the first 20 eigenvalue condition numbers (right).

The condition numbers not satisfying t_κ are considered Gaussian distributed. The condition numbers satisfying t_κ are considered χ^2 distributed. A 5% threshold on $\text{CV}_{\hat{\kappa}}$ and on $\bar{\beta}$ is used to map the highly varying eigenvalues in the Gaussian case and the χ^2 case respectively. The related procedure is illustrated on Figure 3. In both cases, the eigenvalues corresponding to the condition numbers below the threshold

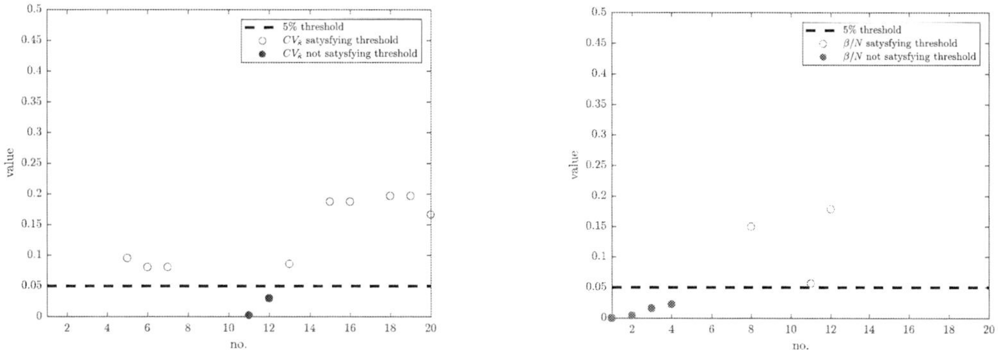

Figure 3: Coefficient of Variation for $\hat{\kappa}$ considered Gaussian (left). Normalized relative shift $\bar{\beta}$ for $\hat{\kappa}$ considered χ^2 (right).

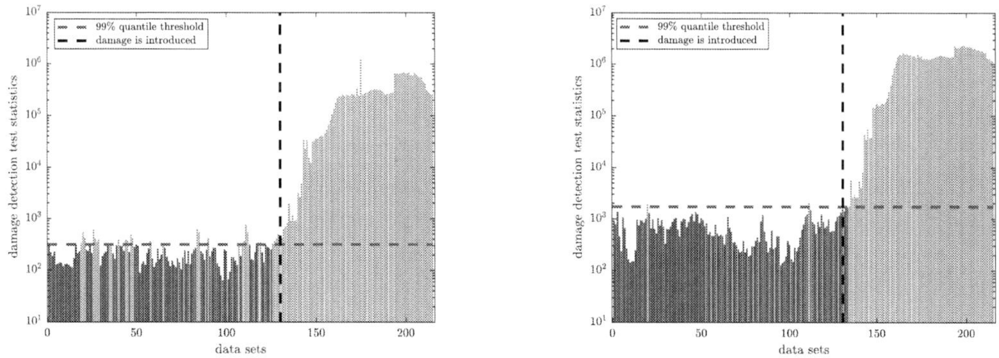

Figure 4: Damage detection test statistics t_{np} without denoising (left) and with the denoised features (right) .

are used to obtain a denoised approximation of $\widehat{\mathcal{H}}_{\mathrm{ref}}$ (3).

The subspace-based damage detection test statistics t_{np} (12) without denoising and with the denoised features are illustrated in Figure 4. In both cases, the same analysis parameters are used, i.e., $p = 20$, the number of blocks to obtain Hankel matrix covariance estimate equal to 100, and the number of columns to obtain its nullspace equal to 255. It can be observed that by using the proposed denoising approach the robustness of damage diagnosis is enhanced, while reducing the number of false alarms.

6. CONCLUSIONS

In this paper, a statistical methodology to approximate the model order of a dynamic system and to consequently denoise the underlying Hankel matrix estimate was derived. The proposed method relies on assessment of the sensitivity of the eigenvalue condition numbers to perturbations. The proposed scheme is applied to damage detection of the S101 benchmark bridge case study, where it is shown to reduce the number of false alarms. The incorporation of this approach within an Operational Modal Analysis setting, bears potential for automated monitoring-based diagnostics.

REFERENCES

[1] M. Yin, R. S. Smith, On low-rank hankel matrix denoising, IFAC-PapersOnLine 54 (7) (2021) 198–203, 19th IFAC Symposium on System Identification SYSID 2021.

[2] E. Reynders, R. Pintelon, G. De Roeck, Uncertainty bounds on modal parameters obtained from stochastic subspace identification, Mechanical Systems and Signal Processing 22 (4) (2008) 948 – 969.

[3] M. Döhler, L. Mevel, Fast multi-order computation of system matrices in subspace-based system identification, Control Engineering Practice 20 (9) (2012) 882 – 894.

[4] S. Greś, R. Riva, C. Y. Süleyman, P. Andersen, M. M. Łuczak, Uncertainty quantification of modal parameter estimates obtained from subspace identification: An experimental validation on a laboratory test of a large-scale wind turbine blade, Engineering Structures 256 (2022) 114001.

[5] M. Döhler, L. Mevel, F. Hille, Subspace-based damage detection under changes in the ambient excitation statistics, Mechanical Systems and Signal Processing 45 (1) (2014) 207 – 224.

[6] K. Tatsis, V. K. Ntertimanis, E. Chatzi, On damage localization in wind turbine blades: a critical comparison and assessment of modal-based criteria, 2018, 7th World Conference on Structural Control and Monitoring (7WCSCM).

[7] S. Greś, M. Döhler, P. Andersen, L. Mevel, Subspace-based mahalanobis damage detection robust to changes in excitation covariance, Structural Control and Health Monitoring 28 (8) (2021) e2760.

[8] G. Oliveira, F. Magalhães, Á. Cunha, E. Caetano, Vibration-based damage detection in a wind turbine using 1 year of data, Structural Control and Health Monitoring 25 (11) (2018) e2238.

[9] O. Avci, O. Abdeljaber, S. Kiranyaz, M. Hussein, M. Gabbouj, D. J. Inman, A review of vibration-based damage detection in civil structures: From traditional methods to machine learning and deep learning applications, Mechanical Systems and Signal Processing 147 (2021) 107077.

[10] D. Bauer, Order estimation for subspace methods, Automatica 37 (10) (2001) 1561–1573.

[11] G. Schwarz, Estimating the dimension of a model, The Annals of Statistics 6 (2) (1978) 461–464.

[12] F. J. Cara, J. Juan, E. Alarcón, E. Reynders, G. De Roeck, Modal contribution and state space order selection in operational modal analysis, Mechanical Systems and Signal Processing 38 (2) (2013) 276–298.

[13] V. K. Dertimanis, On the use of dispersion analysis for model assessment in structural identification, Journal of Vibration and Control 19 (15) (2013) 2270–2284.

[14] R. Bitmead, Persistence of excitation conditions and the convergence of adaptive schemes, IEEE Transactions on Information Theory 30 (2) (1984) 183–191.

[15] G. H. Golub, C. F. Van Loan, Matrix Computations (3rd Ed.), Johns Hopkins University Press, Baltimore, MD, USA, 1996.

[16] Y. Saad, Numerical methods for large eigenvalue problems: revised edition, SIAM, 2011.

[17] G. Casella, R. L. Berger, Statistical Inference, 2nd Edition, Cengage Learning, 2001.

[18] S. Greś, M. Döhler, L. Mevel, Uncertainty quantification of the Modal Assurance Criterion in operational modal analysis, Mechanical Systems and Signal Processing 152 (2021) 107457.

[19] H. Liu, Y. Tang, H. H. Zhang, A new chi-square approximation to the distribution of non-negative definite quadratic forms in non-central normal variables, Computational Statistics and Data Analysis 53 (4) (2009) 853 – 856.

[20] M. Döhler, F. Hille, L. Mevel, W. Rücker, Structural health monitoring with statistical methods during progressive damage test of s101 bridge, Engineering Structures 69 (2014) 183 – 193.

9th International Operational Modal Analysis Conference
iomac
July 3 - 6, 2022
Vancouver, Canada

SELECTION OF DAMAGE-SENSITIVE FEATURES BASED ON PROBABILITY OF DETECTION CURVES

Alexander Mendler[1], *Michael Döhler*[2], *Christian U. Grosse*[3]

[1] Postdoctoral Fellow, Technical University of Munich, TUM School of Engineering and Design, Munich, Germany, alexander.mendler@tum.de
[2] Research Scientist, Univ. Gustave Eiffel, Inria, COSYS/SII, I4S, Rennes, France, michael.doehler@inria.fr
[3] Professor, Technical University of Munich, TUM School of Engineering and Design, Munich, Germany, grosse@tum.de

ABSTRACT
The first phase of each structural monitoring project is the operational evaluation. Its purpose is to define relevant damage mechanisms and environmental conditions, to consider the data acquisition limitations on site, and to justify the investment. Subsequently, relevant measurement quantities and damage-sensitive features are selected, but very few systematic approaches exist in the literature on how to select the most appropriate features. The presented paper fills this gap and develops an approach to select damage-sensitive features based on probability of detection (POD) curves. The POD curves are generated based on a novel method for statistical damage detection tests that requires a finite element model and vibration data from the undamaged structure. However, no data is required from the damaged state, making it particularly suited for unique or large and complex engineering structures. The approach explicitly considers the uncertainties in the features due to unknown loads, measurement noise, and short measurement durations. Although global damage-sensitive features are considered, such as modal parameters and subspace-based residuals, the detectability is evaluated for local structural components. The paper includes a proof of concept study on a laboratory structure. The results demonstrate that the developed method successfully finds the feature with the highest damage detectability for a chosen damage scenario, and that the detectability varies depending on the monitored local component.

Keywords: Structural health monitoring, ambient vibrations, Fisher information, probability of detection

1. INTRODUCTION

National building standards require visual inspections and non-destructive testing for critical engineering structures in periodic intervals. Increasingly, structural health monitoring (SHM) system are installed, meaning sensors are permanently installed on the structure and online damage diagnosis algorithms are trained to automatically diagnose damages in-between the scheduled inspections. The four main stages of each SHM project are the operational evaluation, the data acquisition, the extraction of damage-sensitive features (such as natural frequencies or mode shapes), and their statistical evaluation [1]. Each phase exhibits distinct challenges, for example, the correct parametrization of damage, the selection of appropriate measurement quantities and sensor locations, and the selection of appropriate damage-sensitive features, and algorithms.

Feature selection is a critical topic. Some machine learning experts prefer a 'blind' feature selection, for example, based on neuronal networks whose training process can involve the automated selection of features. Others prefer a 'manual' selection based on engineering judgement, experiences with similar structures, or analytical and structure-specific approaches. Such analytical approaches include sensitivity analyses using finite element models [1], where the effect of individual parameter changes on the data-driven features is studied, or approaches based on confidence intervals, where the changes in the features is put into relation to the statistical uncertainties that are inherent to the features' estimation process. However, few method-specific approaches exist to select the feature with the highest damage detectability. A novel idea is to select features based on probability of detection (POD) curves for critical damage scenarios, as they quantify the reliability of a SHM system. POD curves are standard approaches to verify the effectiveness of non-destructive testing [2], but they are rarely used in SHM. The reason for this is that most methods (e.g., the 29-29 method, the $\hat{a}$ vs. a method, the hit/miss method, the delta method, Bayesian approaches) require empirical data from the damaged state, and this data is typically not available for large and unique structures, such as bridges, highrises, and dams. The main idea of this article is to propose a new method for the creation of POD curves that does not require empirical data from damaged structures. The second objective is to apply this approach to various features and to select the feature that exhibits the highest damage detectability.

The paper is organized as follows: Section 2. recaps state-of-the-art vibration models. Section 3. explains how damage-sensitive features can be formed based on the dynamic system properties, how they can be evaluated statistically, and how POD curves can be predicted based on measurement data from undamaged structures. Section 4. showcases a proof of concept study based on a laboratory beam with extra masses, and Section 5. summarizes the main findings.

2. BACKGROUND

The presented approach is applied to vibration-based features and requires in-depth knowledge on operational modal analysis. This section recaps how modal parameters can be obtained from measurement data using subspace-based system identification. All following considerations are based on linear and time-invariant dynamic systems with m degrees of freedom (DOF)

$$\mathbf{M}\ddot{\mathbf{u}} + \mathbf{D}\dot{\mathbf{u}} + \mathbf{K}\mathbf{u} = \mathbf{f}, \tag{1}$$

where $\mathbf{M}, \mathbf{D}$ and $\mathbf{K}$ are the mass, damping, and stiffness matrices $\mathbb{R}^{m \times m}$, $\mathbf{u} \in \mathbb{R}^m$ is the displacement vector, and $\mathbf{f} \in \mathbb{R}^m$ is the force vector. Sampling the displacement vector at Δt and substituting the state vector $\mathbf{x}_k = \left[\mathbf{u}(k\Delta t)^T \quad \dot{\mathbf{u}}(k\Delta t)^T\right]^T \in \mathbb{R}^n$, the model is transformed to a discrete-time state space model, with $n = 2m$,

$$\begin{cases} \mathbf{x}_{k+1} &= \mathbf{A}\mathbf{x}_k + \mathbf{w}_k \\ \mathbf{y}_k &= \mathbf{C}\mathbf{x}_k + \mathbf{v}_k \end{cases} \tag{2}$$

where $\mathbf{A} \in \mathbb{R}^{n \times n}$ is the state transition matrix, $\mathbf{C} \in \mathbb{R}^{N_{ch} \times n}$ is the output matrix and N_{ch} is the number of measurement channels. The term $\mathbf{y}_k$ is the output vector, and $\mathbf{w}_k$ and $\mathbf{v}_k$ state noise and measurement noise. [3]

2.1. Subspace Decomposition

The first step is to acquire output data $\mathbf{Y} = [\mathbf{y}_1 \ \mathbf{y}_2 \ \dots \ \mathbf{y}_N]^T \in \mathbb{R}^{N \times N_{ch}}$ (displacements, velocities, or accelerations), where N is the number of data points and N_{ch} is the number of measurement channels. Next, output covariance functions are evaluated $\mathbf{R}_i = \frac{1}{N-i} \sum_{k=1}^{N-i} \mathbf{y}_{k+i}\mathbf{y}_k^T$ and arranged in a block Hankel matrix, i.e., a matrix with identical blocks on the anti-diagonals

$$\mathcal{H}_{p+1,q} = \begin{bmatrix} \mathbf{R}_1 & \mathbf{R}_2 & \dots & \mathbf{R}_q \\ \mathbf{R}_2 & \mathbf{R}_3 & \dots & \mathbf{R}_{q+1} \\ \vdots & \vdots & \ddots & \vdots \\ \mathbf{R}_{p+1} & \mathbf{R}_{p+2} & \dots & \mathbf{R}_{p+q} \end{bmatrix} = \begin{bmatrix} \mathbf{U}_1 & \mathbf{U}_0 \end{bmatrix} \begin{bmatrix} \mathbf{S}_1 & \mathbf{0} \\ \mathbf{0} & \mathbf{S}_0 \end{bmatrix} \begin{bmatrix} \mathbf{V}_1^T \\ \mathbf{V}_0^T \end{bmatrix}, \tag{3}$$

where p and q are time lag parameters. Thirdly, singular value decomposition (SVD) is applied to the block Hankel matrix, and the resulting quantities are truncated at the presumed model order, determined through the m physical modes of vibration, yielding the first $n = 2m$ singular values in $\mathbf{S}_1$ and the corresponding singular vectors $\mathbf{U}_1$ (the column space). The remaining singular values $\mathbf{S}_0$ contain noise with the corresponding left null space vectors in $\mathbf{U}_0$.

2.2. Modal Identification

This section revisits how modal parameters can be derived from the block Hankel matrix [3]. First, the observability matrix $\mathcal{O}_{p+1}$ is constructed based on the first n singular values and the column space

$$\mathcal{O}_{p+1} = \mathbf{U}_1\mathbf{S}_1^{1/2}. \tag{4}$$

The output matrix $\mathbf{C}$ can be extracted from the observability in Eq. (4) as the first block row, and the state transition matrix can be approximated through regression, using the shift-invariance property [4]

$$\mathbf{A} = (\mathcal{O}_{p+1}^{\uparrow})^{\dagger}\mathcal{O}_{p+1}^{\downarrow}, \tag{5}$$

where $\mathcal{O}_{p+1}^{\uparrow}$ and $\mathcal{O}_{p+1}^{\downarrow}$ denote the observability matrix without the last and without the first block row, respectively. Modal parameters can be estimated by solving the eigenvalue problem $\mathbf{A\Phi} = \mathbf{\Phi\Lambda}$. Eigenvalues occur in complex conjugate pairs $\mathbf{\Lambda} = \mathbf{\Phi}^{-1}\mathbf{A\Phi} = \operatorname{diag}(\lambda_1, \bar{\lambda}_1 \dots, \lambda_n, \bar{\lambda}_n)$ and so do the eigenvectors. Ultimately, natural frequencies and mode shapes are calculated as follows

$$\mu_j = \frac{\log \lambda_j}{\Delta t}, \quad f_j = \frac{|\mu_j|}{2\pi}, \qquad \mathbf{\Psi} = \mathbf{C\Phi} = \begin{bmatrix} \mathbf{\Psi}_1 & \cdots & \mathbf{\Psi}_n \end{bmatrix}. \tag{6}$$

2.3. Mode Shape Normalization

Mode shapes are unique dynamic properties up to a scaling factor. To enable a comparison of mode shapes, they have to be normalized, e.g., to unit displacement of one of its components l,

$$\bar{\mathbf{\Psi}}_i = \frac{1}{\max\{|\Psi_{i,l}|\}} \cdot \mathbf{\Psi}_i. \tag{7}$$

This forces the maximum amplitude of each normalized mode shape to be equal to one (even when damage has occurred). Consequently, the maximum mode shape component carries no damage-related information after scaling and the mode shape dimension might as well be reduced to $\bar{\mathbf{\Psi}}^{red} \in \mathbb{R}^{N_{ch}-1 \times m}$, which is done in this paper.

3. METHODOLOGY

3.1. Data-driven Residuals

This section shows a selection of damage-sensitive residuals that can be formed based on dynamic system properties from the previous section. In the subsequent sections, the POD curves will be constructed for all features presented in this section. For example, the natural frequencies could be extracted and compared to the baseline values from the training phase

$$\mathbf{r}_1 = \mathbf{f} - \mathbf{f}^0, \tag{8}$$

where the number of entries in the residual vector depends on the number of observed modes of vibration. Another example is the mode shape residual. To reduce the mode shape matrix into a single vector, the vectorization operator $\text{vec}(\cdot)$ is used and all matrix columns are stacked

$$\mathbf{r}_2 = \text{vec}(\bar{\mathbf{\Phi}}^{red}) - \text{vec}(\bar{\mathbf{\Phi}}^{red,0}), \tag{9}$$

where the number of residual entries now depends on the number of modes of vibration and the number of sensors. Since modal frequencies and mode shapes are the results from the same estimation procedure, they can (and should) also be analyzed simultaneously, using a modal vector $\boldsymbol{\eta}$ with the corresponding residual

$$\mathbf{r}_3 = \boldsymbol{\eta} - \boldsymbol{\eta}^0, \quad \text{where} \quad \boldsymbol{\eta} = \begin{bmatrix} \mathbf{f} \\ \text{vec}(\bar{\mathbf{\Phi}}^{red}) \end{bmatrix}. \tag{10}$$

The last considered residual is the subspace-based residual. It takes advantage of the orthogonality between the left null space singular vectors and the block Hankel matrix in the reference state [5]

$$\mathbf{r}_4 = \text{vec}(\mathbf{U}_0^T \boldsymbol{\mathcal{H}}_{p+1,q}) \tag{11}$$

and its size depends on the time lag parameters p and q.

3.2. Damage Detection

This section summarizes the specific damage diagnosis method for which the POD curves are constructed. In this paper, structural changes are analyzed based on a parametrized statistical test, i.e., a statistical test on data-driven residuals that is linked to structural models through sensitivity vectors. The test statistic is defined as [5]

$$t = N \cdot \mathbf{r}^T \mathbf{\Sigma}^{-1} \boldsymbol{\mathcal{J}} \left(\boldsymbol{\mathcal{J}}^T \mathbf{\Sigma}^{-1} \boldsymbol{\mathcal{J}}\right)^{-1} \boldsymbol{\mathcal{J}}^T \mathbf{\Sigma}^{-1} \mathbf{r}, \tag{12}$$

where N is the sample size during testing, $\mathbf{r}$ is one of the damage-sensitive residual vectors from Section 3.1., $\boldsymbol{\mathcal{J}}$ is the first-order derivative of the residual with respect to structural design parameters $\boldsymbol{\theta}$

$$\boldsymbol{\mathcal{J}} = \left. \frac{\partial E_{\boldsymbol{\theta}}[\mathbf{r}]}{\partial \boldsymbol{\theta}} \right|_{\boldsymbol{\theta}=\boldsymbol{\theta}^0}, \tag{13}$$

and $\mathbf{\Sigma}$ is the sample covariance of the damage-sensitive residual which, when evaluated on n_b datasets of length N, is defined as

$$\mathbf{\Sigma} = \frac{N}{n_b - 1} \sum_{k=1}^{n_b} \mathbf{r}_k \, \mathbf{r}_k^T. \tag{14}$$

Structural parameters $\boldsymbol{\theta} \in \mathbb{R}^H$ typically include material properties, cross-sectional values, prestressing forces, or geometric properties of the structure that manifest damage. Defining the relevant damage parameters is part of the first phase of each monitoring phase, the operational evaluation.

The Jacobian matrix $\boldsymbol{\mathcal{J}}$ links structural parameter changes and changes in data-driven features through $\mathbf{r} \approx \boldsymbol{\mathcal{J}}\boldsymbol{\theta}$. It can either be approximated using the finite difference method, or it can be calculated analytically. For the subspace-based residual, the analytical calculation is described in [6] and for the modal residuals, typical approaches include the modal approach [7] or Nelson's method [8].

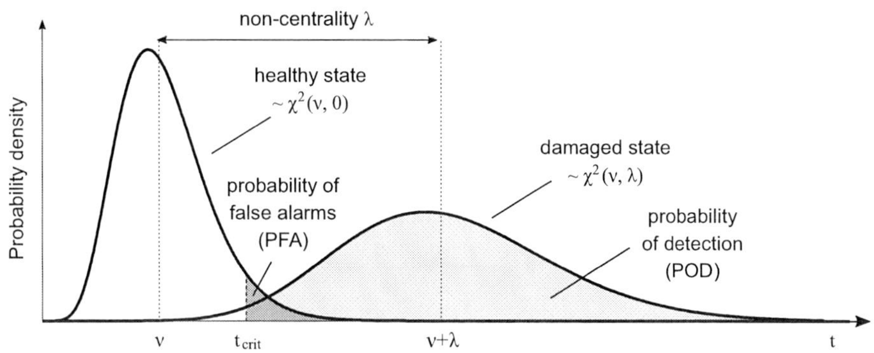

Figure 1: Distribution of the test statistic in the undamaged and damaged state

The covariance matrix is calculated based on data, where the main diagonal holds the variance of each residual entry. It can either be computed empirically based on multiple sets of features from the training phase, or in a combined analytical/empirical approach based on a single measurement record for both the modal residuals [9, 10] and the subspace-based residuals [5, 11].

Uncertainties due to unknown loads and measurement noise cause the test statistic in Eq. (12) to be scattered. Since the damage-sensitive residuals can be approximated by a Gaussian distribution, the tests can be approximated as a chi-squared distribution $\chi^2(\nu, \lambda)$ with $\nu = \text{rank}(\boldsymbol{\mathcal{J}}^T \boldsymbol{\Sigma}^{-1} \boldsymbol{\mathcal{J}})$ degrees of freedom, and non-centrality λ in the damaged state. To make a decision on whether or not the structure is damaged, a safety threshold t_{crit} is introduced, for example, based on the distribution in the undamaged state, and an alarm is issued if the test exceeds the safety threshold, see Fig. 1.

3.3. Probability of Detection Curves

A powerful aspect of the parametric hypothesis tests in Eq. (12) is that the mean test response to a well-defined parameter change can be predicted based on quantities that are available in the undamaged state of the structure. If damage is assumed to be restricted to a single parameter change $\theta_h - \theta_h^0$, the mean test response (the non-centrality) λ is [12]

$$\lambda = N(\boldsymbol{\theta}_h - \boldsymbol{\theta}_h^0)^2 F_{hh}, \qquad F_{hh} = \boldsymbol{\mathcal{J}}_h^T \boldsymbol{\Sigma}^{-1} \boldsymbol{\mathcal{J}}_h, \tag{15}$$

where F_{hh} is the Fisher information and $\boldsymbol{\mathcal{J}}_h$ is the column in the Jacobian matrix that corresponds to the examined parameter θ_h. The larger the mean test response from Eq. (15), the more frequently the test statistic yields values beyond the safety threshold, and the higher the POD. The POD can be quantified as the area under the probability density function of the test statistics beyond the safety threshold, Fig.1,

$$\text{POD} = \int_{t_{crit}}^{\infty} f_{\chi^2}(\nu, \lambda)(t) dt, \tag{16}$$

where the safety threshold could, for example, be defined based on the quantile value of the healthy state distribution of the test statistic. Assuming that the test response λ is known, the formula from Eq. (15) can also be solved for the minimum detectable parameter change

$$\Delta_h = \frac{1}{\theta_h} \sqrt{\frac{\lambda}{N F_{hh}}}. \tag{17}$$

Utlimately, the POD curves can be constructed as follows: First, the non-centrality is fixed to zero $\lambda = 0$. Next, the non-centrality is gradually increased $\lambda = \lambda + \varepsilon$ in steps of ε, while evaluating the POD based on the corresponding probability density function in Eq. (16) and Fig. 1 and the minimum detectable damage Δ_h using Eq. (17). Drawing the POD over Δ_h yields the probability of detection curve for parameter θ_h.

4. APPLICATION

The goal of this section is to analytically construct POD curves based on data from an undamaged structure. Subsequently, actual damage is applied, and it is demonstrated that the empirical POD is close to the analytical one, which was predicted based on undamaged data.

4.1. Laboratory Experiment

The specimen under consideration is a hollow structural steel beam (HSS 152x51x4.78 mm) with a modulus of elasticity of E = 210,000 MPa and a total mass of m = 56.8 kg, Fig. 3. The length of the beam is 4.1 m and pin supports are installed on both ends. The instrumentation consists of eight vertical accelerometers with a weight of 1.28 kg, placed at equal distances, and one shaker with a mass of 3.6 kg and a moving mass of 360 g that injects white noise signals in-between sensors 2 and 3. All other signal processing parameters are given in Table 1.

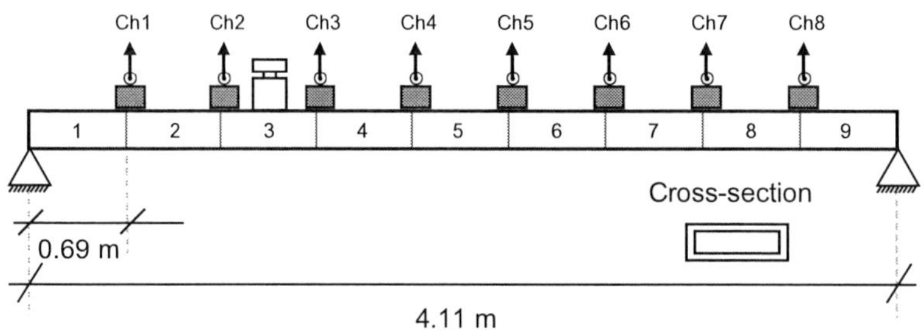

Figure 2: Schematic depiction of the laboratory beam indicating the eight beam segments

Damage is parametrized as a change in mass so the experiments can be conducted non-destructively. A finite element model is built and split into nine beam segments, Fig. 2. Each segment is assigned a different mass value and only mass 8 and 9 are monitored, yielding the parameter vector

$$\boldsymbol{\theta} = \begin{bmatrix} m_8 \\ m_9 \end{bmatrix}. \tag{18}$$

Figure 3: Laboratory HSS beam with eight sensors and one shaker (left) and applied extra masses (right)

4.2. Analytical Results

All studies in this section are based on measurement data from the undamaged structure, where only data from the first four measurement channels is used, Fig. 2. In this state, one long measurement with

Data Acquisition		Data Segmenting	
Measured quantity	acceleration	No. of training segments	100
Sampling frequency	200 Hz	No. of testing segments	100
Reference data length	110 min	Samples/segment	2,000
Testing data length	110 min	Duration/segment	10 s
Modal Parameters		**Subspace-based Residual**	
System order n	14	System order n	14
Time lags p	20	Time lags p	11

Table 1: Data acquisition and signal processing parameters

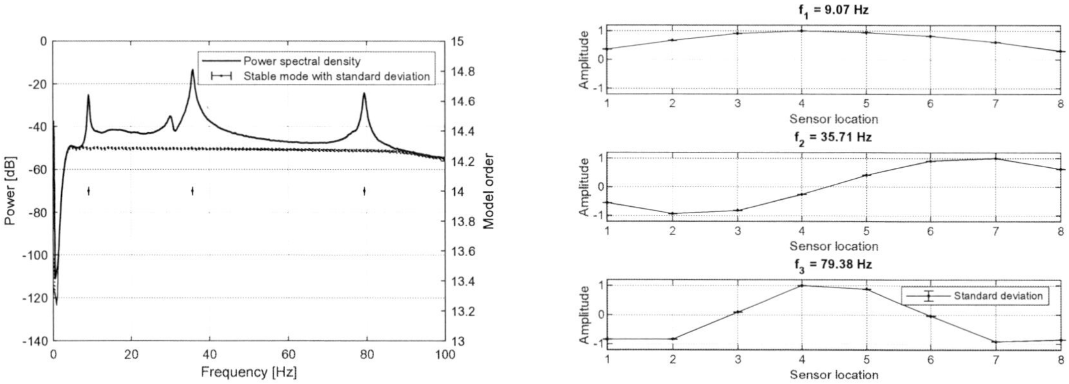

Figure 4: Uncertainty quantification for natural frequencies and mode shapes

a duration of T = 110 min is recorded to be able to estimate the Fisher information, the reference values for the residuals in Section 3.1. (the natural frequencies, the mode shapes, and the nullspace), and the safety thresholds.

The Fisher information **F** can be calculated based on the Jacobian matrix $\mathcal{J}$ and the covariance matrix $\mathbf{\Sigma}$, see Eq. (15). The covariance matrix is calculated based on [5, 10] and for visualization, the standard deviations of the measured modal parameters (i.e., the square root of the covariance's main diagonal values) are shown in Fig. 4 through error bars. For modal parameters, the Jacobian matrix computation can be done based on the numerical model but for the subspace-based residual, data-driven components have to be considered [6]. Once the Jacobian and the covariance matrix are estimated, the Fisher information can be calculated and the main diagonal values F_{hh} can be extracted.

The last required quantity is the safety threshold value t_{crit}. It is different for each damage-sensitive residual, because the χ^2–distribution exhibits a different number of degrees of freedom. In this study, the thresholds are set based on the 0.1% quantile value of the healthy state distribution, meaning one out of 1,000 test statistics is beyond the safety threshold in the undamaged state. The corresponding safety thresholds are 22 for the subspace-based residual, 16 for the frequency-based residual, 16 for the mode shape-based residual, and 22 for the combined frequency and mode shape-based residual.

With the Fisher information and the safety threshold at hand, the POD curves can be predicted for all damage-sensitive residuals from Eq. (8)-(11) with the results being displayed in Fig. 5. The POD curves are drawn for each monitoring parameter, i.e., for parameter 8 and 9 from Eq. (18). The first observation is that changes in parameter 8 lead to a much higher POD than in parameter 9, meaning the damage detectability close to the support is small. According to the POD curves for parameter 8, the frequency-based residual is the most sensitive to changes in the eighth mass parameter, as a parameter change of $\Delta\theta_8 = 5\%$ already leads to a POD close to 87%. The mode shape-based residual, on the other hand, is the least sensitive and a parameter change of 5% leads to a POD of close to 0%, and the subspace-based residual leads to a POD of about 20%. It should be noted that the POD curves are created for particular damage scenarios, captured through the parameter vector in Eq. (18). It appears that the mode shapes do not change for mass changes in beam segment eight and nine, but for other scenarios, they may significantly contribute to the damage detectability and should therefore be considered.

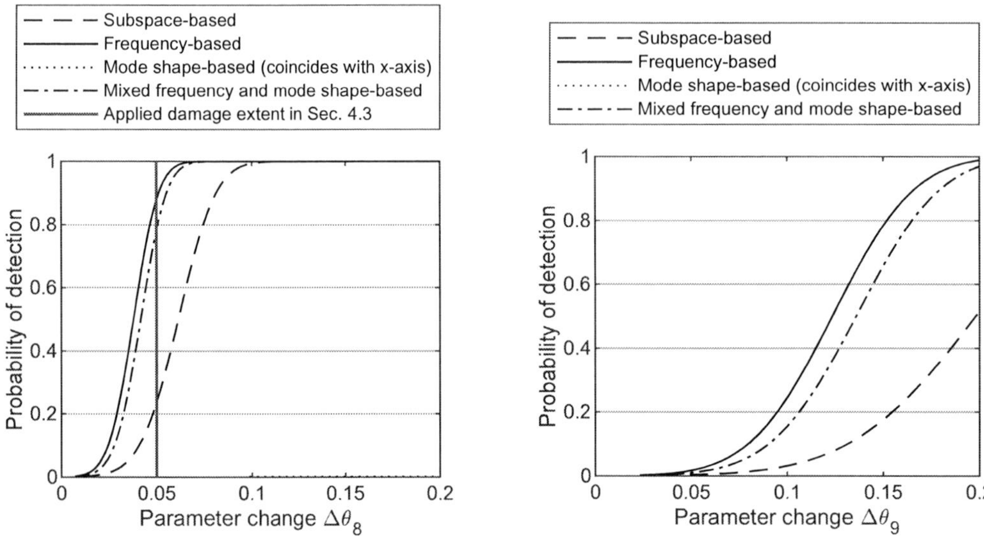

Figure 5: Predicted POD curves based on data from the undamaged state for extra masses on beam segment 8 (left) and beam segment 9 (right) for different residual formulations from Section 3.1

4.3. Empirical Validation

In this section, data from the damaged structure is analyzed for the first time to validate the predictions that were made based on data from the undamaged state. The main idea is to apply a 5% mass increase to the eighth beam segment, simply by placing two washers on top of the beam between sensors seven and eight (see Fig. 3, right side), and to verify whether the empirically evaluated POD is close to the predicted ones from Fig. 5. To evaluate the POD empirically, the test statistic is applied to 100 data sets from the damaged structure, with a measurement duration of 10 s for each segment, and the relative number of tests beyond the safety threshold is counted.

For the frequency-based residual, the empirically evaluated POD is 81.1%, Fig. 6, which is very close to the analytical value of 87%. Likewise, the mode shape-based residual leads to a POD of 0% and the subspace-based residual exhibits a POD of 19.4%, as predicted in Fig. 5. This concludes the validation study, as the analytical POD curves predict the empirical POD for all residuals with sufficient accuracy.

4.4. Discussion

Safety threshold. A peculiar observation appears to be that, in some cases, the mixed frequency and mode shape-based residual leads to a lower POD than the frequency-based residual although more information is available from the structure, see Fig. 5. The reason for this is that the frequency-based residual exhibits a narrower distribution in the undamaged state and a lower safety threshold value of 16 instead of 22. Therefore, an equivalent mean test response leads to a higher POD.

Sensor layout. The study in the previous section concluded that the frequency-based residual is more sensitive to damage than the subspace-based residual. It is important to understand that this result is only valid for the considered sensor layout, because both the sensitivity and the covariance of extracted features depend on the sensor location. To emphasize this, Fig. 7 shows how the POD curves change if the number of channels is increased from 4 to 8. Consequently, the number of mode shape coordinates

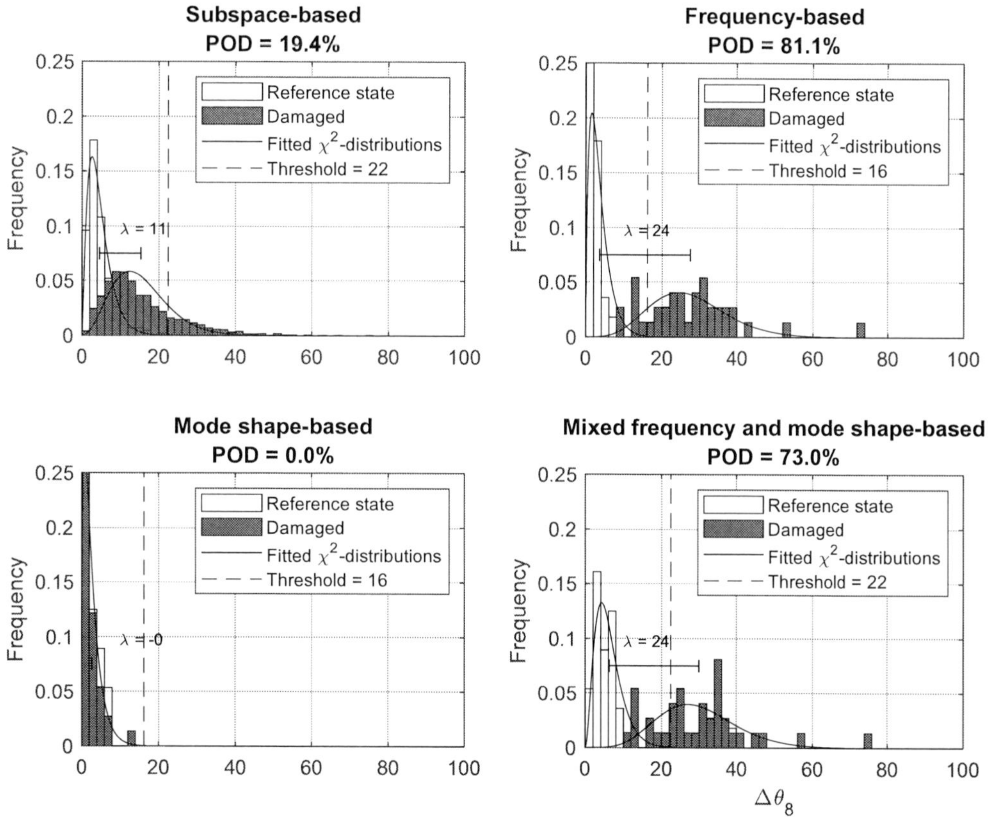

Figure 6: Damaged state: Comparing the empirical POD for different residual formulations from Section 3.1

increases and the POD for the mode shaped-based residual increases for large parameter changes. At the same time, the POD of the subspace-based residual increases from 20% (Fig. 5 left) to almost 100% (Fig. 7 left), making it more sensitive to damage than the frequency-based residual. In other words, the POD curves are powerful means for sensor placement optimization. A systematic approach to optimize the sensor layout can be found in [13].

Measurement noise. One of the advantages of the developed approach is that the uncertainties in the feature due to measurement noise is explicitly considered in the covariance matrix, without having to measure the signal-to-noise ratio. To demonstrate this, vibration data is numerically generated and different noise levels are added to the vibrations. Fig. 7 shows the POD curves for two cases, the mode shape-based residual with a measurement noise level that corresponds to 5% and 10% of the output signal's variance. For the damage scenario $\Delta\theta_8 = 5\%$, the POD increases from about 0% to 12% due to decreased noise level. For other residual formulations considered in this paper, the POD changed as well but the mode shape-based residual appears to be particularly sensitive to measurement noise.

Spatial information. Since POD curves can be evaluated for different structural parameters, they carry spatial information. However, they should not be considered probability of localization (POL) curves, because the statistical test from Eq. (12) is not capable of localizing damage. More advanced statistical tests can identify the parameter that has changed and an approach to determine POL curves can be found in the referenced literature [14].

5. CONCLUSIONS

The main contribution of this paper is an approach to construct probability of detection curves, based on statistical tests and a finite element model. Advantages over other approaches are that no data from the damage state is required and the probability of detection can be analyzed based on data from undamaged

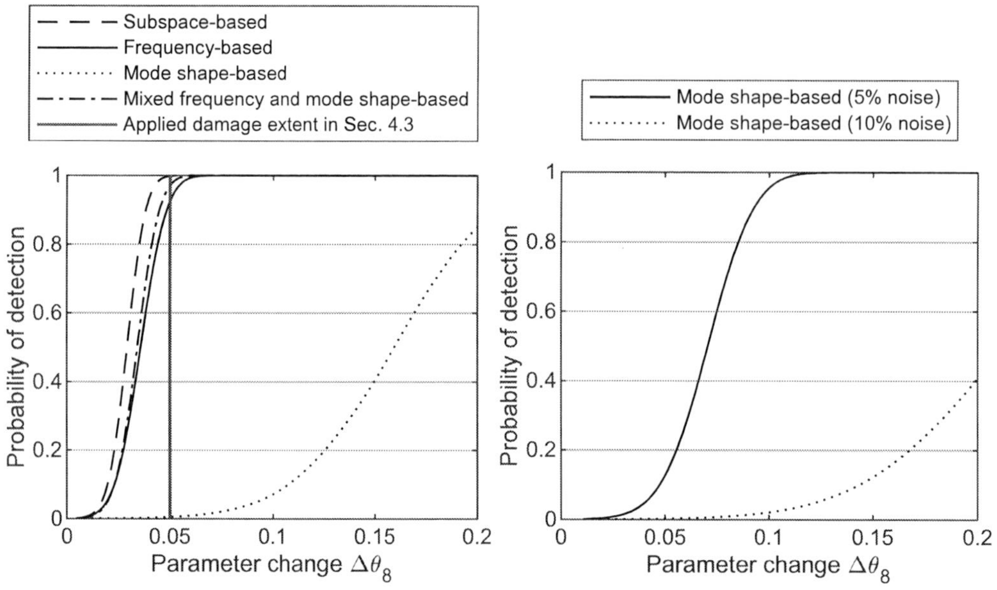

Figure 7: POD curve based on measurement data for an increased number of measurement channels (left), and based on simulated data with varying levels of measurement noise (right).

structures. Moreover, the POD curves can be drawn for different structural parameters, so they include spatial information.

Secondly, it was shown that the developed method for POD curves is a powerful means for feature selection, as features with the highest damage detectability can be chosen before damage occurs. In this paper, the approach is applied to natural frequencies, mode shapes, combined frequency and mode shapes formulations, and the subspace-based residual, but many more features could be incorporated in the framework.

A laboratory case study demonstrates that the POD curves are accurate, even for real data and noisy measurement environments. The main findings are that the POD depends on the structural parameter that is monitored, the sensor layout, and the measurement noise levels. The effect of measurement noise appears to be particularly pronounced for mode shape testing, highlighting the importance of uncertainty quantification in structural health monitoring in general.

An interesting future research topic is the extension to additional features as well as a thorough investigation of measurement noise properties. If measurement noise is modelled accurately, POD curves could be constructed based on numerically generated data and findings can be transferred to real structures.

ACKNOWLEDGMENTS

This research study is funded by dtec.bw – Digitalization and Technology Research Center of the Bundeswehr.

REFERENCES

[1] Farrar, C., & Worden, K. (2012). *Structural health monitoring: A machine learning perspective.* Wiley, Oxford, U.K.

[2] Berens, A. P. (1989). *NDE Reliability Data Analysis–Metals Handbook.* ASM International, United States.

[3] van Overschee, P., & de Moor, B. (1995). *Subspace identification for linear systems: Theory, Implementation, Application.* Kluwer Academic Publishers, Boston/London/Dordrecht.

[4] Magalhães, F., & Cunha, Á. (2011). Explaining operational modal analysis with data from an arch bridge. *Mechanical Systems and Signal Processing*, *25*(5), 1431–1450.

[5] Basseville, M., Abdelghani, M., & Benveniste, A. (2000). Subspace-based fault detection algorithms for vibration monitoring. *Automatica*, *36*(1), 101–109.

[6] Allahdadian, S., Döhler, M., Ventura, C., & Mevel, L. (2019). Towards robust statistical damage localization via model-based sensitivity clustering. *Mechanical Systems and Signal Processing*, *134*, 106341.

[7] Fox, R., & Kapoor, M. (1968). Rates of change of eigenvalues and eigenvectors. *AIAA journal*, *6*(12), 2426–2429.

[8] Nelson, R. B. (1976). Simplified calculation of eigenvector derivatives. *AIAA journal*, *14*(9), 1201–1205.

[9] Reynders, E., Pintelon, R., & De Roeck, G. (2008). Uncertainty bounds on modal parameters obtained from stochastic subspace identification. *Mechanical systems and signal processing*, *22*(4), 948–969.

[10] Döhler, M., & Mevel, L. (2013). Efficient multi-order uncertainty computation for stochastic subspace identification. *Mechanical Systems and Signal Processing*, *38*(2), 346–366.

[11] Viefhues, E., Döhler, M., Hille, F., & Mevel, L. (2022). Statistical subspace-based damage detection with estimated reference. *Mechanical Systems and Signal Processing*, *164*, 108241.

[12] Mendler, A., Döhler, M., & Ventura, C. E. (2021). A reliability-based approach to determine the minimum detectable damage for statistical damage detection. *Mechanical Systems and Signal Processing*, *154*, 107561.

[13] Mendler, A., Döhler, M., & Ventura, C. E. (2022). Sensor placement with optimal damage detectability for statistical damage detection. *Mechanical Systems and Signal Processing*, *170*, 108767.

[14] Mendler, A., Greś, S., Döhler, M., & Kessler, S. On the probability of localizing damages based on mode shape changes. In: *Proceedings of the EWSHM - European Workshop for Structural Health Monitoring*. Palermo, Italy, July, 2022.

9th International Operational Modal Analysis Conference
iomac
July 3 - 6, 2022
Vancouver, Canada

AUTOMATED UNCERTAINTY-BASED EXTRACTION OF MODAL PARAMETERS FROM STABILIZATION DIAGRAMS

Johann Priou[1], *Szymon Greś*[2], *Matthieu Perrault*[3], *Laurent Guerineau*[3], *Michael Döhler*[1]

[1] Univ. Gustave Eiffel, Inria, COSYS/SII, I4S, Rennes, France, {johann.priou,michael.doehler}@inria.fr

[2] Institute of Structural Engineering (IBK), SMM team, ETH Zürich, Zürich, Switzerland

[3] Sercel, Carquefou, France

ABSTRACT

The interpretation of stabilization diagrams is a classical task in operational modal analysis, and has the goal to obtain the set of physical modal parameters from estimates at the different model orders of the diagram. The diagrams are contaminated by spurious modes that appear due to the unknown (non-white) ambient excitation and sensor noise, as well as possible over-modelling. Under the premise that spurious modes will vary and physical modes will remain quite constant at different model orders, the focus is to retrieve the physical modes that constitute the identified model, while rejecting the non-physical, spurious modes. Over the last decade, extensive research has been devoted for developing automated strategies facilitating their interpretation. To this end, the interpretation is in principle disconnected from the identification method and boils down to three stages i.e., clearing the diagram from the spurious mode estimates, aggregating the modal parameter estimates in modal alignments and the final parameter choice. Besides the point estimates of the modal parameters, also their confidence bounds are available with some identification methods, such as subspace identification. These uncertainties provide useful information for an automated interpretation of the stabilization diagrams. First, modes with high uncertainty are most likely non-physical modes. Second, the confidence bounds provide a natural threshold for the automated extraction of modal alignments, avoiding the requirement of a deterministic threshold regarding the allowable variation within an alignment. In this paper, a strategy is presented for the automated mode extraction considering their uncertainties, based on clustering a statistical distance measures between the modes. The relevance of the uncertainty consideration in the automated extraction will be demonstrated on vibration data from two bridges.

Keywords: Operational Modal Analysis, uncertainty quantification, stabilization diagram, automated interpretation, hierarchical clustering, subspace methods

1. INTRODUCTION

Operational modal analysis is a fundamental task in engineering practice. Assuming vibrating structures with a linear time-invariant behaviour, linear system identification techniques such as subspace-based system identification [1, 2] can be used, where the system matrices of a state-space model are estimated before retrieving the modal parameters from their eigenstructure. The model order of the system (corresponding to the number of modes in the data) is in general unknown, and moreover non-physical modes due to colored noise are usually present besides the physical structural modes of interest. Under the premise that spurious modes will vary and physical modes will remain quite constant at different model orders, the identification is repeated at different model orders using efficient algorithms [2] to obtain the stabilization diagram. Then the focus is to retrieve the physical modes that constitute the identified model, while rejecting the non-physical, spurious modes. With subspace-based methods, not only the modal parameter estimates but also their uncertainty bounds can be obtained [3–6], which are valuable information for clearing the diagrams of modes with high uncertainty and their further processing.

Over the last decade, extensive research has been devoted for developing automated strategies facilitating the interpretation of the stabilization diagrams, e.g. [7–9], where an overview is given in [10]. Such strategies usually comprise three stages i.e., clearing the diagram from the spurious mode estimates, aggregating the modal parameter estimates in modal alignments and the final parameter choice. A popular tool for both the clearing and the aggregating stages is clustering based on a distance measure between the modes of the stabilization diagram. A drawback of clustering in this context is that either the number of clusters i.e., the number of modes, is usually assumed to be known a priori, or that thresholds on the allowable distance of the elements within a cluster need to be defined.

The focus of this work is to alleviate these issues to achieve less dependence on user-defined thresholds. First, a distance measure for clustering is proposed that is based on the modal parameters *and* their uncertainties. In this way, the natural variation of the modes between different model orders due to the intrinsic uncertainties is considered. Thresholds for the distances can then be defined based on a chosen confidence level on statistical grounds, instead of defining them in absolute terms on allowable changes in the modal parameters that could be quite different for different noise levels of the data. Second, to further reduce dependence on the user-defined thresholds, an automatic post-processing of the clusters with a merging and a separation step is introduced based on the cluster distances, where too tight or too loose thresholds are alleviated for the final clusters.

This paper is organized as follows. In Section 2., the basics of the subspace-based system identification and uncertainty quantification are recalled. In Section 3., the clustering strategy is developed for the automated interpretation of the stabilization diagrams and applied to vibration data of two bridges in Section 4., before concluding the paper in Section 5..

2. SUBSPACE-BASED SYSTEM IDENTIFICATION AND UNCERTAINTY QUANTIFICATION

2.1. System identification

Assume that the vibration behavior of the investigated structure can be modelled by a linear time-invariant system, then its dynamics can be described by the discrete-time state space model

$$\begin{cases} \mathbf{x}_{k+1} &= \mathbf{A}\mathbf{x}_k + \mathbf{w}_k \\ \mathbf{y}_k &= \mathbf{C}\mathbf{x}_k + \mathbf{v}_k \end{cases}, \qquad (1)$$

where $\mathbf{A}$ is the state transition matrix, $\mathbf{C}$ is the output matrix, and k is the integer time step corresponding to the system at time $t = k\Delta t$, where Δt is the sampling rate. Vector $\mathbf{y}_k \in \mathbb{R}^r$ contains the measured outputs (such as accelerations, velocities, displacements, strains), and $\mathbf{x}_k \in \mathbb{R}^n$ is the state vector. The state noise $\mathbf{w}_k \in \mathbb{R}^n$ is related to the unknown ambient excitation, and vector $\mathbf{v}_k \in \mathbb{R}^r$ is the output noise. The modal parameters are related to the eigenvalues and eigenvectors (λ_i, ϕ_i), $i = 1, \ldots, n$, of $\mathbf{A}$ and to

C by

$$\mu_i = \frac{\log(\lambda_i)}{\Delta t}, \quad f_i = \frac{|\mu_i|}{2\pi}, \quad \zeta_i = \frac{-\text{Re}(\mu_i)}{|\mu_i|}, \quad \varphi_i = \mathbf{C}\phi_i, \tag{2}$$

where μ_i is an eigenvalue of the corresponding continuous-time system, f_i is the natural frequency, ζ_i is the damping ratio and φ_i is the mode shape at the output coordinates.

To estimate the system matrices **A** and **C** from the output data $\mathbf{y}_k$ of length N, $k = 1, \ldots, N$, and consequently the modal parameters in (2), the reference-based covariance-driven subspace algorithm [1, 2] is used. The output covariance estimates with respect to a subset of reference sensors or projection channels are computed as $\hat{\boldsymbol{R}}_i = \frac{1}{N}\sum_{k=1}^{N} \mathbf{y}_{k+i}\mathbf{y}_k^{(\text{ref})T}$. Arranged in block Hankel format, their theoretical values satisfy the decomposition

$$\mathcal{H}_{p+1,q} = \begin{bmatrix} \boldsymbol{R}_1 & \boldsymbol{R}_2 & \ldots & \boldsymbol{R}_q \\ \boldsymbol{R}_2 & \boldsymbol{R}_3 & \ldots & \boldsymbol{R}_{q+1} \\ \vdots & \vdots & \ddots & \vdots \\ \boldsymbol{R}_{p+1} & \boldsymbol{R}_{p+2} & \ldots & \boldsymbol{R}_{p+q} \end{bmatrix} = \mathcal{O}_{p+1}\mathcal{C}_q, \quad \text{where} \quad \mathcal{O}_{p+1} = \begin{bmatrix} \mathbf{C} \\ \mathbf{CA} \\ \vdots \\ \mathbf{CA}^p \end{bmatrix} \tag{3}$$

with the observability and stochastic controllability matrices $\mathcal{O}_{p+1}$ and $\mathcal{C}_q$, and where p, and q are time lag parameters. With the singular value decomposition (SVD)

$$\hat{\mathcal{H}}_{p+1,q} = \begin{bmatrix} \mathbf{U}_1 & \mathbf{U}_0 \end{bmatrix} \begin{bmatrix} \mathbf{S}_1 & \mathbf{0} \\ \mathbf{0} & \mathbf{S}_0 \end{bmatrix} \begin{bmatrix} \mathbf{V}_1^T \\ \mathbf{V}_0^T \end{bmatrix},$$

an estimate $\hat{\mathcal{O}}_{p+1} = \mathbf{U}_1\mathbf{S}_1^{1/2}$ of the observability matrix is obtained for the model order corresponding to the truncation of the SVD. Then, the output matrix **C** is estimated from the first block row of the observability matrix, and the state transition matrix is estimated from the shift-invariance property $\hat{\mathbf{A}} = (\hat{\mathcal{O}}_{p+1}^{\uparrow})^{\dagger}\hat{\mathcal{O}}_{p+1}^{\downarrow}$ where $\hat{\mathcal{O}}_{p+1}^{\uparrow}$ and $\hat{\mathcal{O}}_{p+1}^{\downarrow}$ are the observability matrix estimate without the last and first block row, respectively. Ultimately, the modal parameters are obtained from the eigenvalues and eigenvectors of $\hat{\mathbf{A}}$ and from $\hat{\mathbf{C}}$ as in (2).

2.2. Uncertainty quantification

The computation of the modal parameter covariance results from the propagation of the sample covariance on the Hankel matrix estimate $\hat{\mathcal{H}}_{p+1,q}$ through all steps of the modal identification algorithm. This sample covariance reflect in particular the unknown inputs due to non-measurable excitation sources and the sensor noise, and they contribute in a non-trivial way to the covariance of the modal parameter estimates. The estimation of the sample covariance of the Hankel matrix is straightforward and is done by separating the dataset for $k = 1, \ldots, N$ into blocks. The propagation to the modal parameter estimates is then based on the delta method [11], where the analytical sensitivity matrices are obtained from perturbation theory [3, 5].

Let ΔX be a first-order perturbation of a matrix-valued variable X, like $X = \mathcal{H}_{p+1,q}$. Then, for a function $Y = f(X)$ it holds $\text{vec}(\Delta Y) \approx \mathcal{J}_{Y,X}\,\text{vec}(\Delta X)$, where $\mathcal{J}_{Y,X}$ is the derivative that can be obtained by analytically perturbing the functional relationship between X and Y, and where $\text{vec}(\cdot)$ denotes the column stacking vectorization operator. Subsequently, covariance expressions for the estimates satisfy

$$\text{cov}(\text{vec}(\hat{Y})) \approx \mathcal{J}_{Y,X}\text{cov}(\text{vec}(\hat{X}))\mathcal{J}_{Y,X}^T. \tag{4}$$

In this context, the modal frequencies and damping ratios satisfy

$$\Delta f_i \approx \mathcal{J}_{f_i,\mathcal{H}}\text{vec}(\Delta\mathcal{H}), \quad \Delta\zeta_i \approx \mathcal{J}_{\zeta_i,\mathcal{H}}\text{vec}(\Delta\mathcal{H}), \tag{5}$$

where the analytical sensitivities are derived in detail in [3, 4], and the modal parameter covariance follows from (4) based on the Hankel matrix sample covariance and estimates of the respective sensitivities.

3. AUTOMATED INTERPRETATION OF STABILIZATION DIAGRAMS

Clustering techniques are well-suited for the automated interpretation of stabilization diagrams [8, 12], where data (the modes in the stabilization diagram) are regrouped according to similar properties into clusters (the modal alignments) with respect to a chosen distance measure. If the distance between two modes is "small", they are grouped together in one cluster. The clusters should contain modes with stable properties over several model orders. This section will first define appropriate distance measures, and in a second part will describe the clustering process to obtain alignments.

3.1. Definition of distance

Amongst several distances for clustering [8], a basic distance is based on the frequency difference and the MAC between two modes i and j in the stabilization diagram, defined as [7]

$$D_{ij}^{c} = \frac{|f_i - f_j|}{\max(f_i, f_j)} + (1 - MAC_{ij}). \tag{6}$$

Here the absence of the damping ratio can be noticed, which is often not used for clustering due to its high variability. The distance is normed in the sense that both the (normed) frequency and the MAC are in the interval $[0,\ 1]$, leading to $D_{ij} \in [0,\ 2]$ where D_{ij} indicates a perfect match between the modes.

Despite its high variability, the damping ratio is an important information to be considered in the distance measure, which can be achieved by appropriate weighting in

$$D_{ij}^{n} = \alpha_1 \frac{|f_i - f_j|}{\max(f_i, f_j)} + \alpha_2 \frac{|\zeta_i - \zeta_j|}{\max(\zeta_i, \zeta_j)} + \alpha_3 (1 - MAC_{ij}), \tag{7}$$

with the weighting factors $\alpha_l \in [0,\ 1]$ with $\sum \alpha_l = 1$ the distance can be interpreted as a change in percent between two modes. In the classical distance (6) a 50% weighting is chosen by default. Here a weighting is chosen as $\alpha = [50\%,\ 5\%,\ 45\%]$ between the modal parameters, reflecting the high uncertainty of the damping ratio. The threshold of the distance for elements in the same cluster is chosen ad-hoc as $D_{\text{lim}} = 0.9$, corresponding to 10% allowable variation in each of the weighted modal parameter components.

The normed distance (7) is based on the (deterministic) relative difference between the modal parameters. Since the modal parameter uncertainties are available from their estimation as outlined in Section 2.2., this uncertainty can be used as a natural weighting in the computation of the distance. Considering the uncertainties of the frequencies and damping ratios, the first part of the distance can be evaluated statistically by

$$S_{ij} = \begin{bmatrix} f_i - f_j \\ d_i - d_j \end{bmatrix}^T \Sigma_{ij}^{-1} \begin{bmatrix} f_i - f_j \\ d_i - d_j \end{bmatrix} \tag{8}$$

where

$$\Sigma_{ij} = \mathbf{E}\left(\begin{bmatrix} \Delta(f_i - f_j) \\ \Delta(d_i - d_j) \end{bmatrix} \begin{bmatrix} \Delta(f_i - f_j) \\ \Delta(d_i - d_j) \end{bmatrix}^T \right),$$

which can be evaluated based on Equations (4) and (5). Since the modal parameter estimates are asymptotically Gaussian distributed [5], the variable S_{ij} is asymptotically χ^2 distributed with two degrees of freedom. Its non-centrality parameter is different from zero if the theoretical values of the frequencies and damping ratios are different. Hence, a known value for a target percentile of the distribution is available for verifying the assumption that the theoretical values of the frequency and damping ratios are equal, thus belonging to the same cluster. When targeting a 99% percentile, the corresponding threshold obtained from the χ^2 distribution is around 9.2, so modes with $S_{ij} < 9.2$ can be considered to be a member of the same cluster. A criterion for the MAC can also be added on statistical grounds based on [13]; however, for ease of presentation its deterministic format is kept in the following, defining the combined distance, also called statistical distance,

$$D_{ij}^{s} = S_{ij} + \tilde{\alpha}(1 - MAC_{ij}). \tag{9}$$

with an appropriate weighting $\tilde{\alpha}$. This weighting factor can be chosen as follows. Considering a weighting of 45% of the MAC to the distance measure (9) as in (7), and the remaining 55% to S_{ij} having a threshold of 9.2, a total threshold for D_{ij}^{s} in (9) is set to $D_{\mathrm{lim}}^{s} = 16$. Then, assuming a criterion for the allowable change of the MAC in the order of $MAC_{ij} > 0.9$, this corresponds to $\tilde{\alpha} = 70$.

3.2. Clustering

There are many methods for clustering in the literature; amongst the most known are k-means and hierarchical clustering [14] which are both in use for automated modal analysis. The k-means clustering requires the number of clusters as an input, which is hard to know beforehand in modal analysis. However, it is mostly used to distinguish spurious modes from physical ones [8, 15]. Hierarchical linkage clustering is based on a tree format where elements are clustered according to their distance, starting with the smallest one and stopping when a maximal distance D_{lim} is reached. In the first step, each element defines a cluster. In an iterative process, the two clusters with the shortest distance are combined into a larger cluster, where the distance between two clusters is defined in different ways. Setting a limit on the distances between the modes instead of defining the number of modes seems to be more natural for clustering the stabilization diagram; hence the hierarchical linkage clustering is chosen in the following.

3.2.1. Linkage

The linkage is the choice of how the elements (i.e., the modes) form a cluster. Two popular ways of linkage are complete and single. Single linkage regroups elements together by the minimum distance, i.e., the distance between two clusters is defined by the minimum of the distances between their respective elements when combining them. It can also be called nearest neighbor. On the other side, the complete linkage regroups the clusters by the maximum distance of their elements, also known as farthest neighbor. The direct consequence is that the complete linkage is more strict as the maximum distance of elements should be under a specified value, while the single linkage allows more flexibility. For the first clustering step, complete linkage is chosen to ensure that the distances between all cluster elements are below the respective threshold D_{lim} as defined previously. Resulting clusters with too few elements are deleted. In a second step, a post-processing of the retained clusters is carried out. To avoid modal alignments that are split over the model orders due to too low thresholds, the clusters are checked with the single linkage distance for merging. Furthermore, to avoid the contrary effect of over-agglomerated clusters with several modes at single model orders due to too high thresholds, a separation step is introduced.

3.2.2. Post-processing

As presented before, the clustering depends on the threshold D_{lim} which is an *a priori* choice to a greater or lesser extent – greater when considering deterministic distance measures and lesser when considering statistical distance measures. If the threshold is too low physical modes will be missing; if it is too high different modes will be agglomerated in the same cluster. For less impact of the choice of this parameter several correction steps have been developed.

Merge

The first correction step is merging. The complete linkage for the initial clustering is strict and may tends to divide single mode alignments into different clusters. To correct this, a near neighbor merging was implemented comparing close neighbors between them based on the single linkage approach. The *minimum* distance between two close clusters is computed, then if this distance is below the limit D_{lim} the two cluster are merged.

Separation

The second step is a separation. A global mode cannot have different estimates at the same model order, yet this can happen when the threshold is too big, or when noise modes with similar properties are nearby. The purpose is then to clean some outlier points that could have been mixed with a real mode, and to possibly separate two modes that are close. To clean these clusters, a reference "mono-order" subset is defined by the elements of the cluster with unique model orders, i.e. at the corresponding model orders there is only one mode estimate in the cluster. For the remaining model orders with multiple estimates the closest element to the reference sub-set is kept, and the others deleted if too close.

The final step is a size verification of the found cluster. Every cluster whose number of elements is under a stability criterion nb_{stab} is deleted. The criterion nb_{stab} is chosen as 20% of the maximum order computed. The modal parameters are then determined from the means of the cluster elements when using the classical normed distance, or from the weighted mean of the elements, where the weights are related to the modal parameter uncertainties at the different model orders [16].

Algorithm 1 Clustering

Require: Frequencies f, damping ratios ζ, mode shapes φ, model orders n, maximum distance D_{lim}, minimum number of modes per alignment nb_{stab}
Ensure: Clusters
Compute distance D_{ij} between every pair of elements (Equation (7) or (9))
Compute the clusters with complete linkage with respect to D_{lim}
Sort the clusters by frequency and delete every cluster whose size is below nb_{stab}
Merge
Compare the neighboring clusters and merge the closest if their single linkage distance is below D_{lim}
Separation
for Every cluster **do**
  while There are model orders with several modes **do**
    Compare the different modes at each order to the mode set at orders with single modes
    Keep the closest and delete the other
  end while
end for

---

4. APPLICATIONS

Vibration data of two bridges, namely S101 Bridge [17] and Z24 Bridge [18, 19] are used to apply the developed cluster algorithm 1 using either of the two distances defined in (7) and in (9), denoted by *normed distance* D^n and *statistical distance* D^s, respectively.

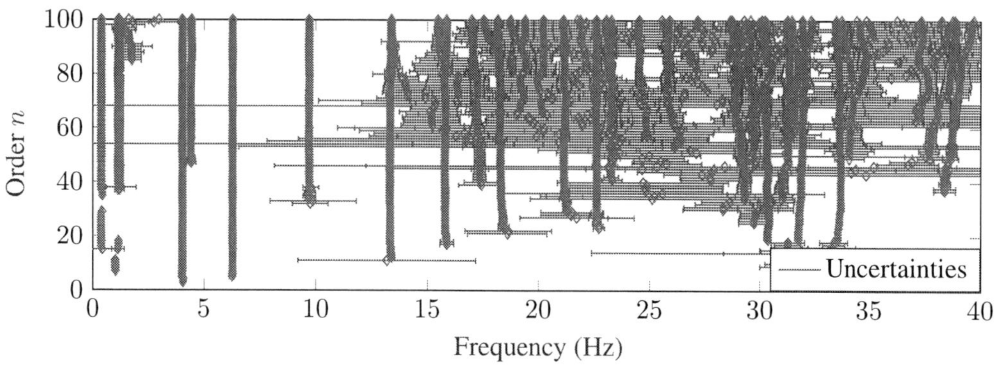

Figure 1: Full stabilization diagram of the S101 Bridge

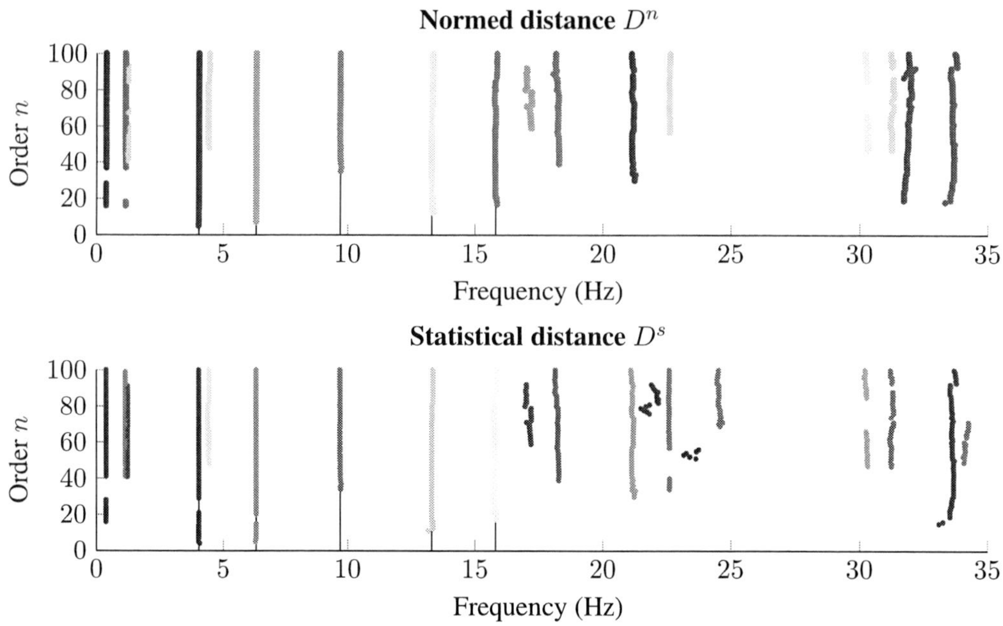

Figure 2: Hierarchical clustering from full stabilization diagram of the S101 Bridge (Figure 1) based on normed distance D^n (top) and statistical distance D^s (bottom)

4.1. S101 Bridge

One dataset of the reference state of S101 Bridge before damage [17] has been chosen for analysis, containing measurements from 45 sensors during 5.5 min. The respective stabilization diagram with the uncertainty bounds on the frequencies is shown in Figure 1, where the modal alignments are already quite clear.

In Figure 2, the clustering results with the developed algorithm are shown based on the classical normed distance (top) and the statistical distance (bottom). The five modes that were previously identified in [17] are shown as vertical lines in Figure 2. They are clearly present with both distances. This validates the use of statistical distance.

The uncertainty bounds of the modal parameters can also be used as hard criterion to delete very uncertain modes.With a threshold on the coefficient of variation of the frequencies (standard deviation of the frequency divided by the frequency), the stabilization diagram becomes clearer as shown in Figure 3 and seemingly easier to analyze. The clustering results based on the cleaned stabilization diagram are shown

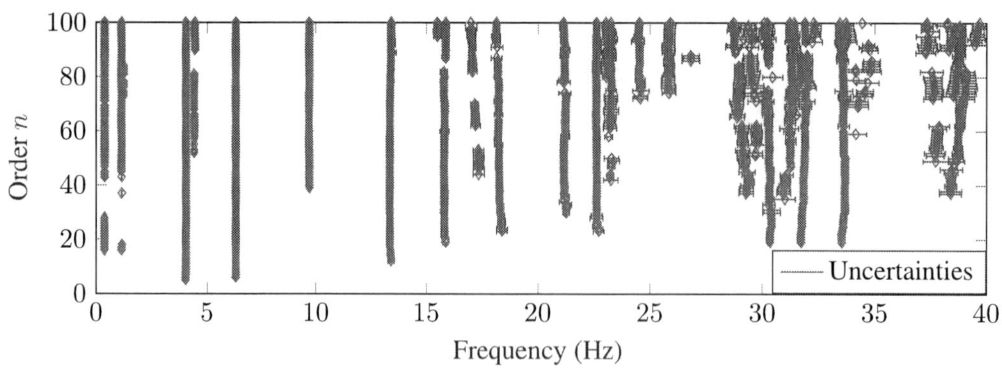

Figure 3: Cleaned stabilization diagram of the S101 Bridge with threshold on the coefficient of variation of frequencies of 1.5%

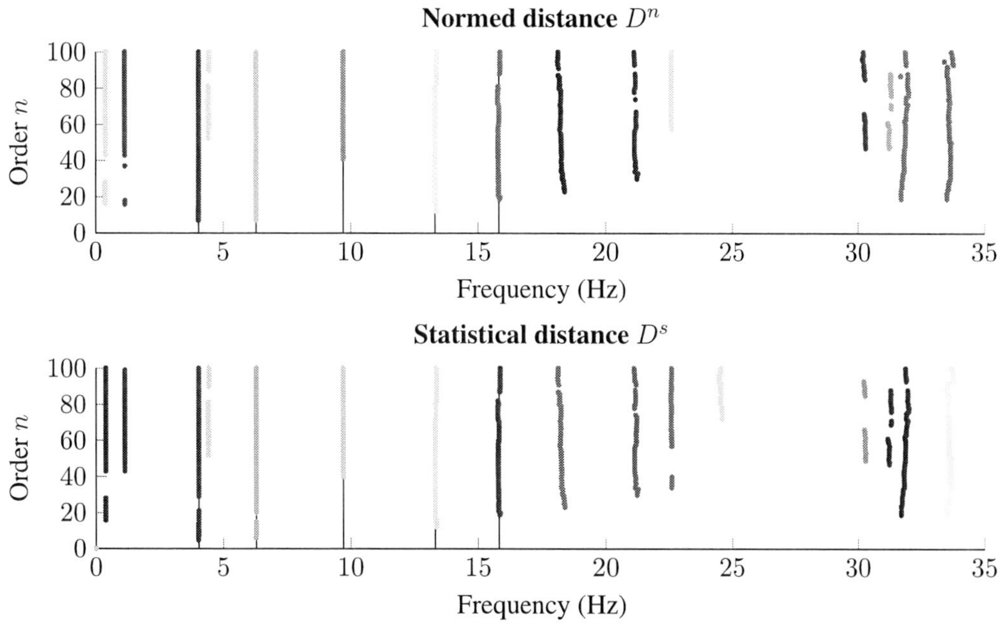

Figure 4: Hierarchical clustering from cleaned stabilization diagram of S101 Bridge (Figure 3) based on normed distance (top) and statistical distance (bottom)

in Figure 4, where they do not seem to be impacted by the application of the uncertainty threshold, while allowing as faster computation of the clustering.

The clustering algorithm is efficient to automatically retrieve stable alignments; however some alignments of spurious modes are also stable but tend to vary between different datasets. In order to retrieve the modes that are stable over different datasets, the same clustering technique can be applied on the set of modes that is obtained from each of the datasets in the spirit of "cross-validation" of the modes. Assuming only little change of the physical modes between the analyzed datasets, the same threshold for their distances as in the analysis of a single stabilization diagram can be used.

The results of this second clustering on the modal parameters obtained from 21 successive datasets in the reference state of S101 Bridge is shown in Figure 5 (left), where the five reference modes are

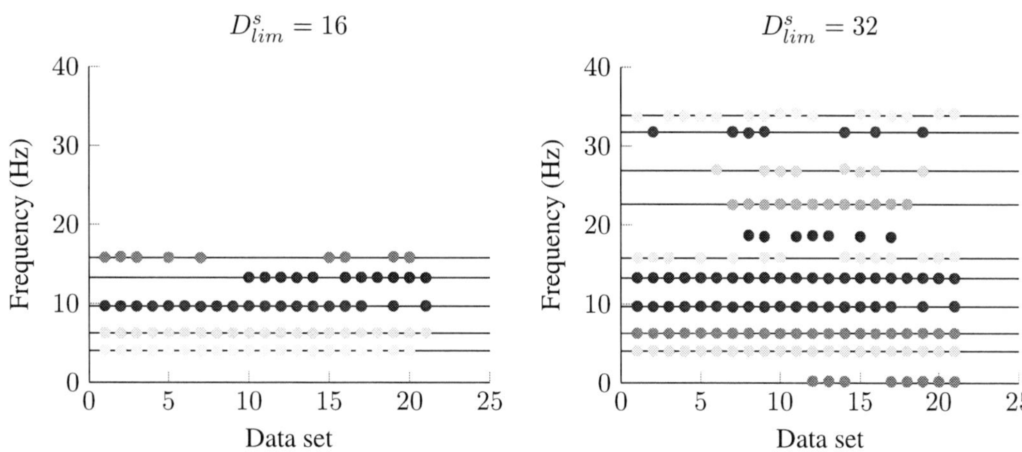

Figure 5: Hierarchical clustering of modes obtained from clustering of 21 stabilization diagrams using the statistical distance with the same threshold $D^s_{\mathrm{lim}} = 16$ as in the clustering of the diagrams (left), and the doubled threshold (right)

well recognized and other modes with higher variability are dismissed. To account for higher mode variability between different datasets (as e.g. in tracking applications [12]), the threshold is usually increased. Results with the doubled threshold are shown in Figure 5 (right), where more stable modes are found. An in-depth analysis of these additional modes showed that the modes at 1 Hz and 18 Hz are most probably non-physical, while the other modes are indeed physical modes with lower excitation.

4.2. Z24 Bridge

The second example is the Z24 Bridge [18, 19], where one dataset of the multi-setup measurements has been used as in [4]. Measurements are more noisy, resulting in higher uncertainties of the modal parameters and more spurious modes, as shown in Figure 6, making the automated analysis more difficult. Nevertheless, the same thresholds as in the previous example are used for the clustering, and the impact of the developed steps for post-processing (merge and separate, see Algorithm 1) as well as the impact of the statistical distance measure are analyzed.

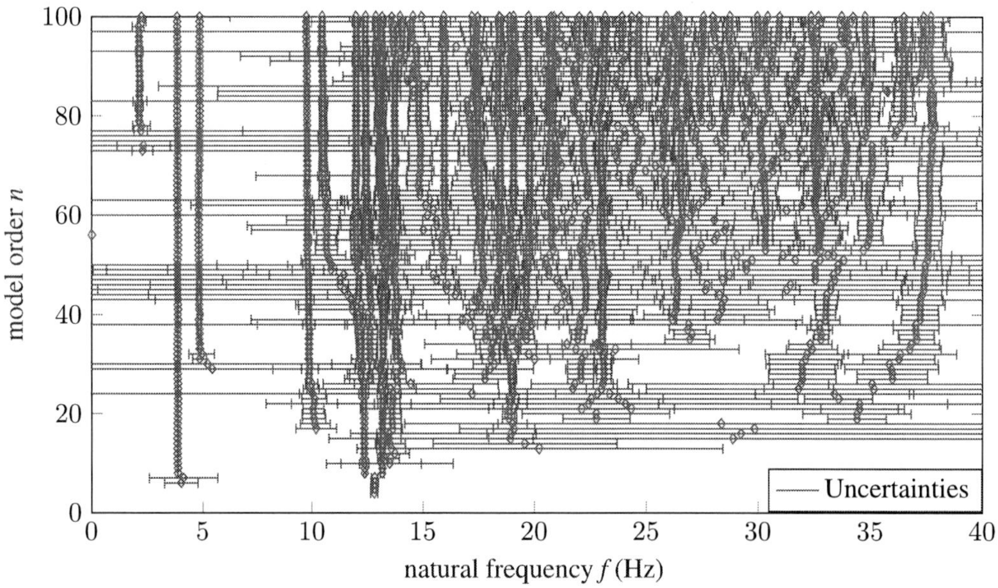

Figure 6: Full stabilization diagram of Z24 Bridge

In Figure 7 the result of the clustering is shown without any of the post-processing steps described in Section 3.2.2.. The black vertical lines represent the reference modes identified in [19]. Indeed, some of the alignments are split due to the more noisy data that would possibly require more relaxed thresholds. After the post-processing steps, the final clusters correspond well to the structural modes in Figure 8. However, there is one exception, namely the mode at 17 Hz that is very lowly excited and shows high variability. It is missing when using the classical normed distance; however the statistical distance considers its higher uncertainty intrinsically where it is well recognized. This shows that the statistical distance is more robust in a noisy situation.

It should be noted that it the effect of cleaning the diagram was tested by putting a threshold on the coefficient of variation of the frequencies, similarly as in Figures 2 and 3. First, since data is noisier, the threshold of 1.5% needed to be increased in order to keep modes with higher estimation uncertainty. Second, the results did not show improvement of the clustering, as already seen in Figure 3; moreover the mode at 17 Hz (which has a higher variation) tends to get lost if the threshold is not set very carefully. This shows that clustering strategy does not require a previous cleaning of the diagram, whereas such a cleaning may be helpful for a manual visual inspection of the diagram.

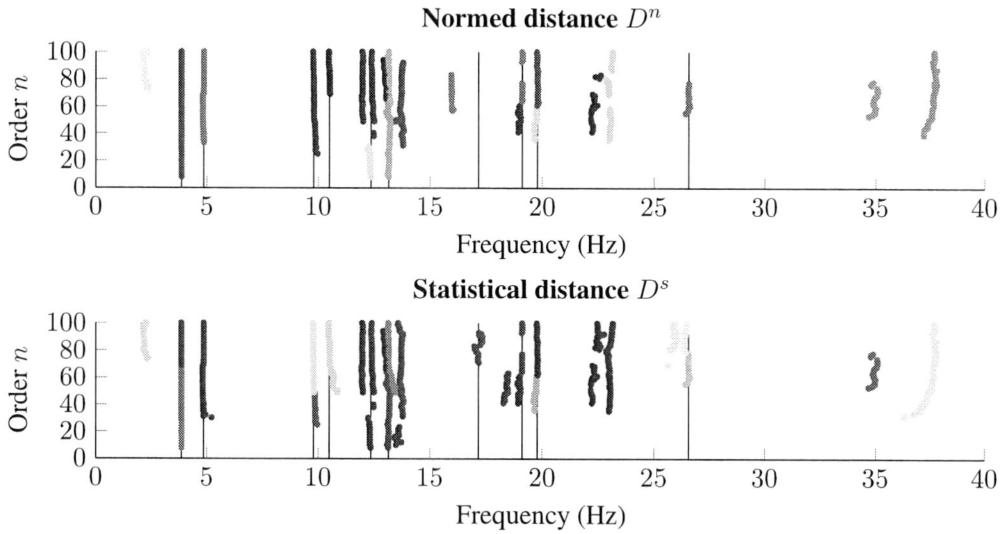

Figure 7: Hierarchical clustering without post-processing of the full stabilization diagram of Z24 Bridge based on normed distance (top) and statistical distance (bottom)

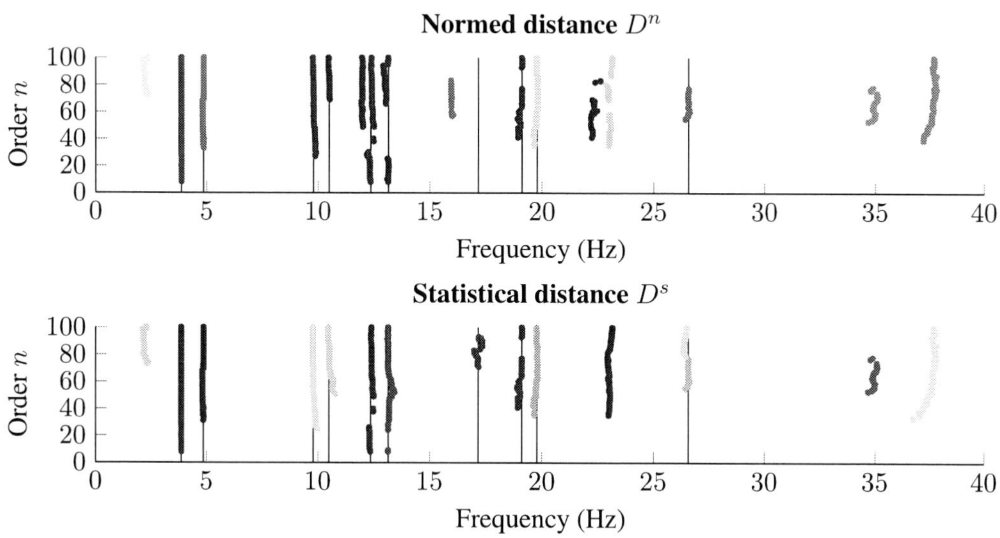

Figure 8: Hierarchical clustering after post-processing of the full stabilization diagram of Z24 Bridge based on normed distance (top) and statistical distance (bottom)

5. CONCLUSIONS

The proposed statistical distance for clustering of stabilization diagrams has been validated on the S101 Bridge data. Then an application on the Z24 Bridge showed that in difficult noise condition the statistical approach allows to find modal alignments even of very noisy modes due to its intrinsic consideration of the uncertainties, leading to a more robust algorithm. The examples also showed that clearing the diagrams with a hard criterion on modal uncertainty bounds may not be necessary, since the clustering algorithm takes them into account directly, and may even be counterproductive. Furthermore, it has been shown on the S101 Bridge data that the clustering approach is a means for cross-validation of modes from several datasets.

ACKNOWLEDGMENTS

The support from the ANR "France Relance" program is gratefully acknowledged.

REFERENCES

[1] Peeters, B., & De Roeck, G. (1999). Reference-based stochastic subspace identification for output-only modal analysis. *Mechanical Systems and Signal Processing*, *13*(6), 855–878.

[2] Döhler, M., & Mevel, L. (2012). Fast multi-order computation of system matrices in subspace-based system identification. *Control Engineering Practice*, *20*(9), 882–894.

[3] Reynders, E., Pintelon, R., & De Roeck, G. (2008). Uncertainty bounds on modal parameters obtained from stochastic subspace identification. *Mechanical Systems and Signal Processing*, *22*(4), 948–969.

[4] Döhler, M., & Mevel, L. (2013). Efficient multi-order uncertainty computation for stochastic subspace identification. *Mechanical Systems and Signal Processing*, *38*(2), 346–366.

[5] Mellinger, P., Döhler, M., & Mevel, L. (2016). Variance estimation of modal parameters from output-only and input/output subspace-based system identification. *Journal of Sound and Vibration*, *379*(100), 1–27.

[6] Greś, S., Riva, R., Süleyman, C. Y., Andersen, P., & Łuczak, M. (2022). Uncertainty quantification of modal parameter estimates obtained from subspace identification: An experimental validation on a laboratory test of a large-scale wind turbine blade. *Engineering Structures*, *256*, 114001.

[7] Magalhães, F., Cunha, Á., & Caetano, E. (2009). Online automatic identification of the modal parameters of a long span arch bridge. *Mechanical Systems and Signal Processing*, *23*(2), 316–329.

[8] Reynders, E., Houbrechts, J., & De Roeck, G. (2012). Fully automated (operational) modal analysis. *Mechanical Systems and Signal Processing*, *29*, 228–250.

[9] Yaghoubi, V., Vakilzadeh, M. K., & Abrahamsson, T. J. (2018). Automated modal parameter estimation using correlation analysis and bootstrap sampling. *Mechanical Systems and Signal Processing*, *100*, 289–310.

[10] Zini, G., Betti, M., & Bartoli, G. (2022). A quality-based automated procedure for operational modal analysis. *Mechanical Systems and Signal Processing*, *164*, 108173.

[11] Casella, G., & Berger, R. (2002). *Statistical inference*. Duxbury Press.

[12] Pereira, S., Magalhães, F., Gomes, J., & Cunha, A. (2022). Modal tracking under large environmental influence. *Journal of Civil Structural Health Monitoring*, *12*.

[13] Greś, S., Döhler, M., & Mevel, L. (2021). Uncertainty quantification of the Modal Assurance Criterion in Operational Modal Analysis. *Mechanical Systems and Signal Processing*, *152*, 107457.

[14] Duda, R. O., Hart, P. E., & Stork, D. G. (2001). *Pattern Classification* (2nd). John Wiley & Sons.

[15] Neu, E., Janser, F., Khatibi, A. A., & Orifici, A. C. (2017). Fully Automated Operational Modal Analysis using multi-stage clustering. *Mechanical Systems and Signal Processing*, *84*, 308–323.

[16] Döhler, M., Andersen, P., & Mevel, L. (2017). Variance computation of modal parameter estimates from UPC subspace identification. *7th International Operational Modal Analysis Conference*.

[17] Döhler, M., Hille, F., Mevel, L., & Rücker, W. (2014). Structural health monitoring with statistical methods during progressive damage test of S101 Bridge. *Engineering Structures*, *69*, 183–193.

[18] Reynders, E., & De Roeck, G. (2009). Continuous vibration monitoring and progressive damage testing on the Z24 bridge. *Encyclopedia of Structural Health Monitoring*.

[19] Döhler, M., Lam, X.-B., & Mevel, L. (2013). Uncertainty quantification for modal parameters from stochastic subspace identification on multi-setup measurements. *Mechanical Systems and Signal Processing*, *36*(2), 562–581.

WIND TURBINES

9th International Operational Modal Analysis Conference iomac
July 3 - 6, 2022 Vancouver, Canada

HARMONIC REMOVAL FOR WIND TURBINES

Miroslav Zivanovic[1], *Aitor Plaza*[2], *Xabier Iriarte*[3], *and Alfonso Carlosena*[4]

[1] Dr. Zivanovic, Public University of Navarre, miro@unavarra.es.
[2] Dr. Plaza, Public University of Navarre, aitor.plaza@unavarra.es.
[3] Dr. Iriarte, Public University of Navarre, xabier.iriarte@unavarra.es.
[4] Dr. Carlosena, Public University of Navarre, alfonso.carlosena@unavarra.es

ABSTRACT

We present a novel approach to harmonic disturbance removal in single-channel wind turbine acceleration data by means of time-variant signal modeling. Harmonics are conceived as a set of quasi-stationary sinusoids whose instantaneous amplitude and phase vary slowly and continuously in a short-time analysis frame. These non-stationarities in the harmonics are modeled by low-degree time polynomials whose coefficients capture the instantaneous dynamics of the corresponding waveforms. The model is linear-in-parameters and is straightforwardly estimated by the linear least-squares algorithm. Estimates from contiguous analysis frames are further combined in the overlap-add fashion in order to yield overall harmonic disturbance waveform and its removal from the data. We describe a case study that illustrates the advantages of the algorithm in gaining insight in the structural vibration features of a particular data record. The algorithm performance is validated through the stabilization diagrams, which are a standard tool for determining modal parameters in many time-domain modal identification algorithms. The results show that the proposed approach is suitable as a pre-processing stage in operational modal analysis.

Keywords: *Wind turbine, harmonic disturbances, non-stationary signal modeling.*

1. INTRODUCTION

Operational modal analysis (OMA) is a generic name for output-only system identification strategies, which provide characterization of large structures – wind turbines, bridges, etc. – from vibration signals under operating conditions. An extensive overview of the principal techniques in the context of structural health monitoring is given in [1]. Often measured output signals contain a mixture of the structure response (stochastic) and harmonic perturbation (deterministic) which typically arise in presence of rotating components e.g. periodic aerodynamic effects created between the tower and blades in a wind turbine – the tower shadow effect. If not properly taken into account, those disturbances may seriously hamper the OMA procedure by introducing bias in the estimation of the structural modes or identifying the harmonics as structural modes [2].

A large body of methods has been developed in order to assess the aforementioned identification problem. Most techniques introduce pre-processing extensions to OMA by means of harmonic detection and removal from the response. They either assume no a priori knowledge about the harmonic content – the random decrement vibration signature[3][4], cepstrum editing[5][6], spectral kurtosis [2] [7][8], entropy [9] – or need an initial estimate of the harmonic fundamental frequency – time-synchronous averaging [10] and constant-amplitude nonlinear-phase sinusoidal modeling [11]. Other methods modify existing OMA algorithms by incorporating the knowledge on the harmonic disturbances into the identifying scheme: the least-square complex exponential identification [12], the eigensystem realization algorithm [13], the stochastic subspace identification [14], and the linear time-periodic system identification [15]. Let us also mention an approach which emphasize structural modes by combining transmissibility functions from different excitation points [16].

A major constraint of the majority of the state-of-the-art methods is related to the assumption that the harmonic content is quasi-stationary, which means that their instantaneous parameters generate a negligible bandwidth around the nominal frequencies. This assumption is, however, not valid for wind turbines because persistent wind field fluctuations in the rotor plane induce constant time changes in aerodynamic loads [17], [18]. These loads acting on the rotor affect the azimuth that, in turn, give rise to non-stationary instantaneous amplitude (IA) and phase (IP) in the harmonics [19]. The result is a harmonic spectral peak broadening – harmonic bandwidth increase – which can jeopardize the estimation of structural modes [20]. This is especially important for low-order harmonics (e.g. 1P – rotor rotational frequency and 3P – blade passing frequency), which possess a considerable energy and are clustered together with the first bending Fore-Aft moment (FA).

Aware of the drawbacks mentioned above, we have designed a novel approach to harmonic estimation and removal in wind turbines inspired by the techniques which appear in speech and audio signal synthesis and coding [21]–[24]. It turns out that audio signals are similar in nature to vibration signals, in the sense that tonal music sounds are made out of time-variant deterministic plus stochastic contribution. In the present work, the harmonic disturbances in vibration signals are conceived as a collection of time-varying harmonically related sinusoids whose instantaneous amplitude and phase change over the time record. Those variations are simultaneously captured by low-degree polynomials, whose coefficients describe the relationship between harmonic instantaneous amplitude and phase in the analysis frame. Assuming that the harmonic dynamics evolve in time around some mean fundamental frequency, we show that a proposed model is unique and computationally reduces to resolving an overdetermined linear system of equations. The minimum-norm solution yields an estimate of the harmonic polynomial coefficients, which can readily be plugged in the signal model to obtain the corresponding waveform. The full record harmonic disturbance is synthesized by combining neighboring analysis frames via the weighted overlap-add method (WOLA), which ensures smooth waveform transitions over the frames [25]. The final step in the proposed method consists in subtracting the estimated harmonic waveform from the input data, which is now harmonic-free and can further be analyzed by well-known OMA techniques. An additional benefit of the present algorithm is that it provides an estimate of the harmonic instantaneous frequency, which can be useful in tracking applications. A schematic overview of the herein proposed method is outlined in Fig.1.

2. METHOD

Fig.1 outlines the chief signal processing steps in the proposed algorithm. The input single-channel vibration data $x(t_m),\ m = 1,2,\dots,M$ is split into a series of overlapped analysis frames, whose processing yields the corresponding short-term harmonic components $\hat{h}_l(t_n), n = 1,2,\dots,N$. Next, those components are windowed and merged by means of the WOLA method to obtain the long-term harmonic component $\tilde{h}(t_m)$. In the last step, the estimated harmonic perturbation is subtracted from the input and the residue $r(t_m)$ is harmonic-free.

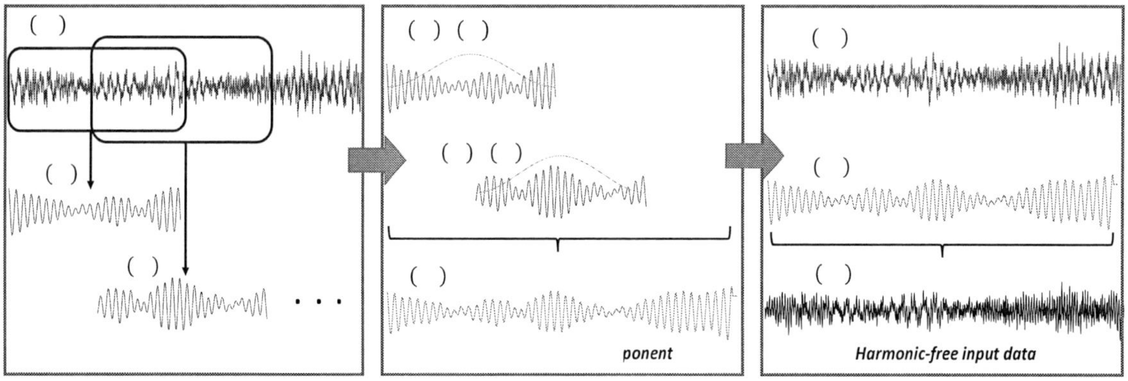

Figure.1. Schematic pipeline of the proposed harmonic removal algorithm.

2.1. Short-term harmonic signal modeling

Structural analysis of wind turbines is based on acceleration registers taken at different tower heights, when available, or at the nacelle, under natural excitation conditions. One such register can be modeled in a length-N analysis frame [23], [24]:

$$y(t_n) = h(t_n) + r(t_n) = \sum_{k=1}^{K} A_k(t_n)cos\big(2\pi k f_0 t_n + \varphi_k(t_n)\big) + r(t_n), \quad n = 1,2,\dots,N. \tag{1}$$

The harmonic component $h(t_n)$ has its origin in the rotating behavior of the structure, remarkably the tower shadow effect (3P). It is therefore represented by a set of harmonically related sinusoids with instantaneous amplitudes $A_k(t_n)$ and phases $2\pi k f_0 t_n + \varphi_k(t_n)$, being f_0 the average fundamental frequency which is usually known (e.g. a rotary encoder) and $\varphi_k(t_n)$ the non-linear instantaneous phase deviation which can also accommodate errors in the initial estimation of f_0. The residue $r(t_n)$ is stochastic in nature and contains the contribution from the structural modes and noise. The model (1) cannot be uniquely identified because analytically, it represents a non-linear underdetermined system of equations. In order to relax the non-linearity constraint, we rewrite (1) as a combination of the in-phase and quadrature terms:

$$y(t_n) = \sum_{k=1}^{K}\big(p_k(t_n)sin(2\pi k f_0 t_n) + q_k(t_n)cos(2\pi k f_0 t_n)\big) + r(t_n), \tag{2}$$

$$p_k(t_n) = -A_k(t_n)sin\big(\varphi_k(t_n)\big), \qquad q_k(t_n) = A_k(t_n)cos\big(\varphi_k(t_n)\big). \tag{3}$$

The system (2) is now linear-in-parameters but it still has more unknowns than equations. Let us assume that both $p_k(t_n)$ and $q_k(t_n)$ are in origin continuous functions of time. Accordingly, the products (3) are also continuous and can therefore be approximated in the analysis window by low-degree polynomials:

$$p_k(t_n) \approx p_{k,0} + p_{k,1}t_n + \dots + p_{k,D}t_n^D, \qquad q_k(t_n) \approx q_{k,0} + q_{k,1}t_n + \dots + q_{k,D}t_n^D. \tag{4}$$

Combining (3) – (4) with (2) we obtain the signal model for the input data:

$$y(t_n) = \sum_{k=1}^{K}\Big(\sum_{i=0}^{D} p_{k,i}t_n^i \, sin(2\pi k f_0 t_n) + \sum_{i=0}^{D} q_{k,i}t_n^i \, cos(2\pi k f_0 t_n)\Big) + r(t_n). \tag{5}$$

The last expression is next rewritten in the computationally more convenient matrix form:

$$\boldsymbol{y} = \boldsymbol{B\theta} + \boldsymbol{r}. \tag{6}$$

Vectors $\boldsymbol{y} \in \mathbb{R}^N$ and $\boldsymbol{r} \in \mathbb{R}^N$ contain the observations and noise samples respectively whilst the model parameters are stored in a vector $\boldsymbol{\theta} = (p_{1,0}\ p_{1,1} \dots p_{1,D}\ q_{1,0}\ q_{1,1} \dots q_{1,D} \cdots q_{K,1} \dots q_{K,D})^T \in \mathbb{R}^{K(2D+2)}$, with $(\cdot)^T$ being the transpose operator. The regression matrix $\boldsymbol{B}$ is a block matrix whose structure is given as:

$$\boldsymbol{B} = (\boldsymbol{B}_1\ \boldsymbol{B}_2\ \dots\ \boldsymbol{B}_K) \in \mathbb{R}^{N \times K(2D+2)}\ , \tag{7}$$

$$\boldsymbol{B}_k = (\boldsymbol{\alpha}_k\ \ \boldsymbol{\beta}_k) \times \begin{pmatrix} \boldsymbol{Z} & 0 \\ 0 & \boldsymbol{Z} \end{pmatrix} \in \mathbb{R}^{N \times (2D+2)}\ , \tag{8}$$

$$\boldsymbol{\alpha}_k = diag([sin(2\pi k f_o t_1)\ sin(2\pi k f_o t_2)\ \dots\ sin(2\pi k f_o t_N)]) \in \mathbb{R}^{N \times N}\ , \tag{9}$$

$$\boldsymbol{\beta}_k = diag([cos(2\pi k f_o t_1)\ cos(2\pi k f_o t_2)\ \dots\ cos(2\pi k f_o t_N)]) \in \mathbb{R}^{N \times N}\ , \tag{10}$$

with $\boldsymbol{Z}_{n,i} = t_n^{i-1}, i = 0,1,\dots,D$ being the time Vandermonde matrix. The estimation of the parameters $\boldsymbol{\theta}$ reduces to minimizing the following cost function:

$$\widehat{\boldsymbol{\theta}} = \underset{\boldsymbol{\theta}}{argmin}\|\boldsymbol{y} - \boldsymbol{B}\boldsymbol{\theta}\|_2^2 = (\boldsymbol{B}^T\boldsymbol{B})^{-1}\boldsymbol{B}^T\boldsymbol{y} = \boldsymbol{B}^+\boldsymbol{y}\ , \tag{11}$$

where $(\cdot)^+$ designates the pseudoinverse of a matrix. A straightforward combination of the solution in (11) with (6) – (10) yields the estimate of the harmonic component in the analysis frame

$$\hat{h}(t_n) = \sum_{k=1}^{K}\left(\sum_{i=0}^{D}\hat{p}_{k,i}t_n^i\, sin(2\pi k f_0 t_n) + \sum_{i=0}^{D}\hat{q}_{k,i}t_n^i\, cos(2\pi k f_0 t_n)\right),\quad n = 1,2,\dots,N. \tag{12}$$

In addition, we estimate the instantaneous amplitude and phase deviation for each harmonic in the analysis window:

$$\hat{A}_k(t_n) = \sqrt{\left(\sum_{i=0}^{D}\hat{p}_{k,i}t_n^i\right)^2 + \left(\sum_{i=0}^{D}\hat{q}_{k,i}t_n^i\right)^2}\ , \tag{13}$$

$$\hat{\varphi}_k(t_n) = -atan\left(\frac{\sum_{i=0}^{D}\hat{p}_{k,i}t_n^i}{\sum_{i=0}^{D}\hat{q}_{k,i}t_n^i}\right),\quad k = 1,2,\dots,K. \tag{14}$$

Expressions (13) and (14) will be useful for calculating the harmonic bandwidth as part of the stochastic synthesis.

2.2. Long-term harmonic signal modeling

Let us suppose that we have acquired from the response analogue signal a total of M samples at the time instants $t_1, t_2, \dots, t_M = Mf_s,\ M \gg N$, with f_s being the sampling rate. A vector $\in \mathbb{R}^M$, which contain the aforementioned samples, is segmented in L overlapped analysis frames $x_l(t_n) = x(t_n + lt_d),\ l = 1,2,\dots,L$ where t_d is the time delay between contiguous frames whilst L is the number of frames covering the total duration of the input data. A successive application of the above algorithm to the overlapped analysis frames $x_i(t_n)$ (Fig.1, left panel) generate a set of short-term harmonic segments $\widehat{h_l}(t_m - lt_d),\ l = 1,2,\dots,L$. The synthesis of the long-term harmonic waveform is carried out by means of the weighted overlap-add technique [25], which consists in the following steps (Fig.1, central panel):

1) Each segment $\widehat{h_l}(t_m - lt_d)$ is scaled by an analysis window $w(t_n)$, whose role is to mitigate potential discontinuities at the boundaries of adjacent analysis frames. The typical choice is a raised-cosine window e.g. Hann, which possesses a convenient scaling property:

$$\sum_{l\in\mathbb{Z}} w\left(t_m - l\frac{N}{2f_s}\right) = 1\ .$$

2) The windowed segments are linearly combined with an appropriate weighting, which compensates the windowing effect. The resulting waveform is the estimate of the harmonic disturbances in the data whose length covers M samples:

$$\tilde{h}(t_m) = \frac{\sum_{l=1}^{L} w(t_n)\hat{h}_l(t_m - lt_s)}{\sum_{l=1}^{L} w(t_m - lt_s)}, \qquad m = 1,2, \dots M. \tag{15}$$

By combining (13) – (15), we also obtain the harmonic instantaneous amplitude and phase deviation for the duration of the input data:

$$\tilde{A}_k(t_m) = \frac{\sum_{l=1}^{L} w(t_n)\hat{A}_l(t_m - lt_s)}{\sum_{l=1}^{L} w(t_m - lt_s)}, \tag{16}$$

$$\tilde{\varphi}_k(t_m) = \frac{\sum_{l=1}^{L} w(t_n)\hat{\varphi}_l(t_m - lt_s)}{\sum_{l=1}^{L} w(t_m - lt_s)}. \tag{17}$$

Finally, by subtracting the estimated harmonic contribution from the input data we obtain the residue, which contains only the structural information:

$$r(t_m) = x(t_m) - \tilde{h}(t_m), \qquad m = 1,2, \dots, M. \tag{18}$$

2.3. Model tuning

For the sake of implementation of the proposed harmonic signal model, we need to adjust the following analysis parameters: the number of harmonics K, the polynomial degree D and the analysis frame duration Nt_s. The number of harmonics will utterly depend on the application. For instance, in the context of the present application, often harmonics at integer multiples of the 3P frequency concentrate most of the energy and thus can potentially shadow the structural modes. Accordingly, in the harmonic signal model (5) only the corresponding terms in the sum (k = 3, 6, 9, etc.) should be considered. In other circumstances, we may need to monitor the dynamics of the tower's first bending mode in strong wind conditions, so that it does not get coupled to the 1P component and possibly provoke structural damages. In that case, the harmonic signal model would contemplate a single term corresponding to the fundamental rotational component (k = 1).

The polynomial degree and analysis frame time duration determine the goodness-of-fit of the model to the data in the given bandwidth around the harmonic frequencies. They act in a mutually correlated fashion in order to constrain the model to the specific bandwidth and avoid possible undesirable effects of under and overfitting. Given the polynomial degree, shorter analysis frame yield small modeling bias but can inflate variances of the estimated parameters - overfitting. Conversely, enlarging the analysis frame duration, the uncertainty of the estimates reduces and modeling bias gets larger - underfitting. Moreover, we want to keep the polynomial degree as low as possible (the parsimony principle) in order to avoid numerical instabilities when evaluating the Moore-Penrose pseudoinverse matrix in (11).

The minimum frame duration is clearly conditioned on the mean period of the fundamental harmonic (1P or 3P as the case may be). As the signal model (5) represents sinusoids whose energy is clustered around the harmonic frequencies, the analysis frame must cover at least one period of 1P. In the context of the present application, we adjust the number of observations N in the way that the analysis frame covers approximately two 1P periods: $N = 2\,f_0/f_s$.

As for the polynomial degree, we will assume that the instantaneous amplitude and phase deviation evolve linearly in the analysis frame. Accordingly, the expressions (3) become:

$$p_k(t_n) = -(A_{k,0} + A_{k,1}t_n)sin(\varphi_{k,0} + \varphi_{k,1}t_n), \tag{19.a}$$

$$q_k(t_n) = (A_{k,0} + A_{k,1}t_n)cos(\varphi_{k,0} + \varphi_{k,1}t_n). \tag{19.b}$$

Applying the sum-of-angles trigonometric identities to the last expressions and making use of the small argument Taylor series approximation ($sin(\varphi_{k,1}t_n) \approx \varphi_{k,1}t_n,\ cos(\varphi_{k,1}t_n) \approx 1$), we have:

$$p_k(t_n) \cong -A_{k,0}sin(\varphi_{k,0}) - (A_{k,0}\varphi_{k,1}cos\varphi_{k,0} + A_{k,1}sin\varphi_{k,0})t_n - (A_{k,1}\varphi_{k,1}cos\varphi_{k,0})t_n^2 =$$

$$= p_{k,0} + p_{k,1}t_n + p_{k,2}t_n^2 \,. \tag{20.a}$$

$$q_k(t_n) \cong A_{k,0}cos(\varphi_{k,0}) - (A_{k,0}\varphi_{k,1}sin\varphi_{k,0} - A_{k,1}cos\varphi_{k,0})t_n - (A_{k,1}\varphi_{k,1}sin\varphi_{k,0})t_n^2 =$$

$$= q_{k,0} + q_{k,1}t_n + q_{k,2}t_n^2 \,. \tag{20.b}$$

Subsequently, we choose the second-degree polynomials for the estimation of the harmonic model (5). Observe in (20.a) and (20.b) that the parameters $p_i, q_i, i = 0,1,2$ possess certain internal structure, which depend on $(A_{k,0}, A_{k,1}, \varphi_{k,0}, \varphi_{k,1})$. Albeit this information might enclose certain relationships between the instantaneous amplitude and phase deviation, it will not be dealt with in the present work. In the next section, we show that this choice for the polynomial degree and analysis frame duration is well suited to real wind turbine signals.

3. RESULTS

We will include here a representative case, out of the many analysed, of a wind turbine operating in the below-rated region (between cut-in and rated wind speed). The blade pitch is constant whereas the generator torque is varying, so that both the blade tip speed and rotor speed increase proportionally to the wind speed, [26]. The wind speed, shown in figure 2.a, is increasing at about constant rate of 0.13 m/s per minute; as expected, the 3P frequency, figure 2.b, is increasing proportionally as well. A typical 10 minute record is shown in figure 2.c, and its power spectrum in figure 2.d shows superimposed the frequency locations of the principal vibration modes and harmonic components. A substantial energy dispersion around average harmonic frequencies, due to the presence of non-stationarities, is clearly visible; moreover, observe in 2.e that visual identification of 1ºFA is hampered by the fact that 3P harmonic dominates low-frequency spectrum. As the 3P frequency is gradually changing, it is clear that the harmonic bandwidth will be determined by the combined dynamics of both the instantaneous amplitude and phase. This is further illustrated by the spectrogram of the input data, figure 2.f, where 3P noticeably pop out regarding 1ºFA, especially in the first three minutes of the recording. Furthermore, it is evident from the energy time evolution that 3P harmonic exhibits a gradual increase in frequency, whilst the 1ºFA vibration mode's frequency is fairly stable over time. The estimated harmonic waveform and individual harmonics are shown in figures 2.g and 2.h. 3P harmonic is evidently the most prominent, followed by 9P harmonic.

The stabilization diagram of the raw acceleration data, figure 2.i completely fails in identifying stable vibration modes. This case study illustrates the fact that the SSI-COV is seriously jeopardized by the presence of non-stationarities in data, as well as colliding components. The suppression of the estimated harmonics from the data delivers the residue, whose stabilization diagram shows two stability lines located at the frequencies of the principal vibration modes: 0.39 Hz (1ºFA) and 1.85 Hz (2ºFA).

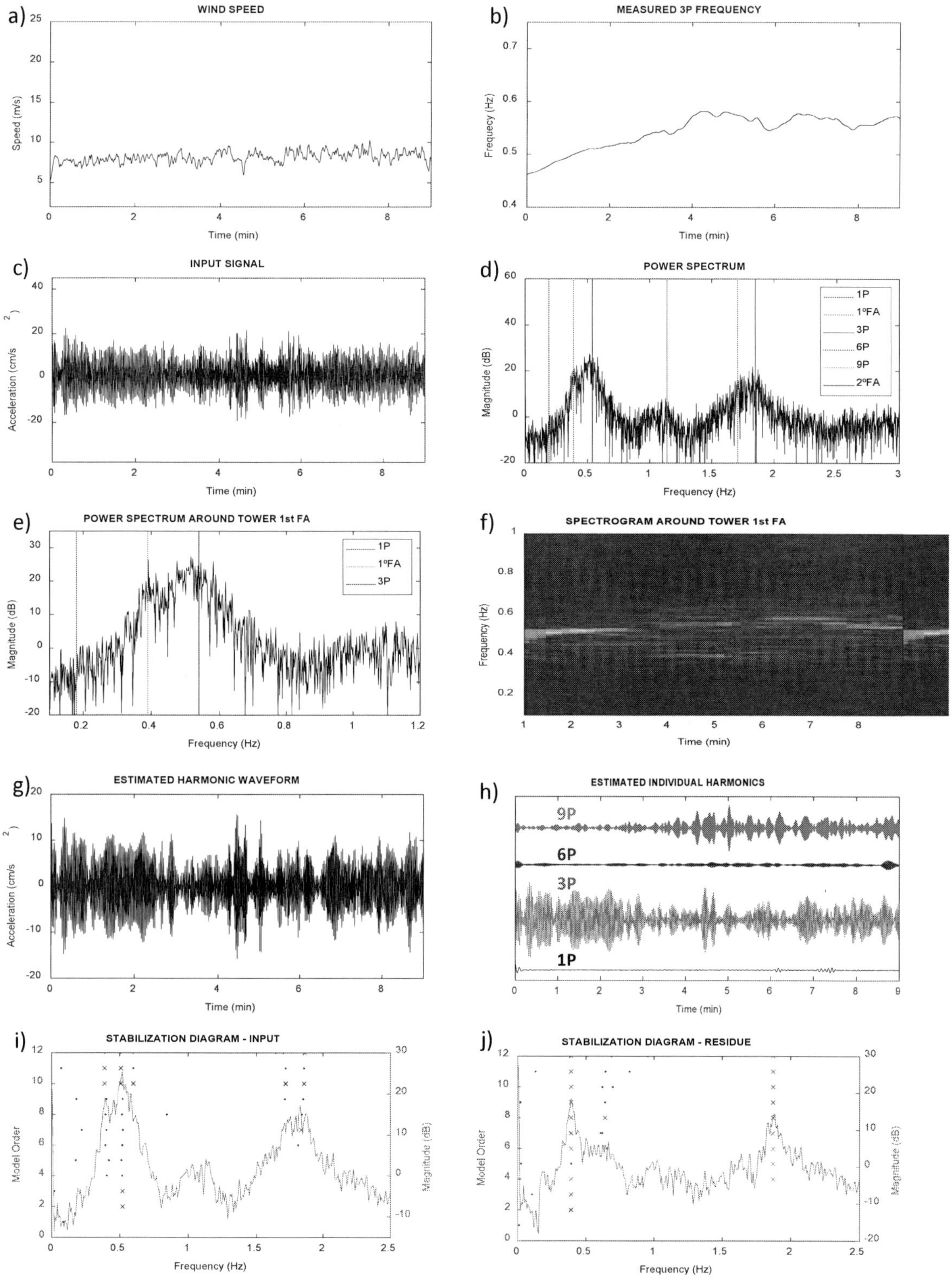

Figure 2. Raising low speed wind with approximately constant positive slope.

4. CONCLUSIONS

As the main conclusion of our work we can say that the method proposed in this paper is highly effective in removing the influence of the harmonics in acceleration data acquired from the tower of a wind turbine, while keeping intact the information required to properly calculate the structural vibration modes. This affirmation is validated with a number of experimental tests, from where we have selected a single illustrative case presented here. It is important to stress that the signals taken from sensors at the nacelle were not intended to perform structural health monitoring (SHM); therefore, the presence of the harmonics in the data has rendered the analysis scenario far more complex.

The main benefit of our approach, in contrast with other previously proposed techniques, is that it deals with non-stationarities in the harmonics in both amplitude and phase. We have used the information of the rotation speed provided by the SCADA, sampled at 100 milliseconds, but we also estimate instantaneous frequency/phase variations. This means that the algorithm could also work with an initial guess of the rotations speed, and then update its value from the estimated phase. In addition, an estimate of the instantaneous harmonic amplitude is also obtained in by the algorithm.

The fact that we have introduced a precise non-stationary model for all relevant harmonics allows not only removing them from the original signal, but also obtain information about the harmonics themselves, and eventually, we believe, information of the structure. For instance, it seems noteworthy to us that there seems not to exist any correlation between wind speed and the 3P harmonic. Much in the same way, the harmonic envelopes, and therefore the instantaneous power of the different harmonics exhibit seemingly unrelated time patterns. These observations suggest a deeper analysis to find out what kind of factors, external or internal, influence the characteristics of the harmonics, and if they contain information on the structure which may be useful to determine possible failures in the turbine mechanical structure. This is an open area for future research.

ACKNOWLEDGEMENTS

This work has been supported by the Spanish Research Agency under grant AEI/FEDER, PID2019-107258RB-C32, and also by the Government of Navarre (Dpt. Of Economic and Business Development) under grant 0011-1365-2021-000199.

REFERENCES

[1] E. Reynders, "System Identification Methods for (Operational) Modal Analysis: Review and Comparison," *Arch. Comput. Methods Eng.*, vol. 19, no. 1, pp. 51–124, 2012.

[2] R. Jacobsen, N.J. Andersen, P. Brincker, "Eliminating the Influence of Harmonic Components in Operational Modal Analysis," 2007.

[3] C. S. Huang and C. H. Yeh, "Some properties of Randomdec signatures," *Mech. Syst. Signal Process.*, vol. 13, no. 3, pp. 491–507, 1999.

[4] S. V. Modak, C. Rawal, and T. K. Kundra, "Harmonics elimination algorithm for operational modal analysis using random decrement technique," *Mech. Syst. Signal Process.*, vol. 24, no. 4, pp. 922–944, 2010.

[5] R. B. Randall, M. D. Coats, and W. A. Smith, "Repressing the effects of variable speed harmonic orders in operational modal analysis," *Mech. Syst. Signal Process.*, vol. 79, pp. 3–15, 2016.

[6] S. Manzato, C. Devriendt, W. Weijtjens, E. Di Lorenzo, B. Peeters, and P. Guillaume, "Removing the influence of rotor harmonics for improved monitoring of offshore wind turbines," *Conf. Proc. Soc. Exp. Mech. Ser.*, vol. 4, pp. 299–312, 2014.

[7] N. M. R. Brincker, P. Andersen, "An Indicator for Separation of Structural and Harmonic Modes in Output-Only Modal Testing." Proceedings of the International Modal Analysis Conference - IMAC (2000) 2 1649-1654, 2000.

[8] J. L. Dion, I. Tawfiq, and G. Chevallier, "Harmonic component detection: Optimized Spectral

Kurtosis for operational modal analysis," *Mech. Syst. Signal Process.*, vol. 26, no. 1, pp. 24–33, 2012.

[9] A. Agneni, G. Coppotelli, and C. Grappasonni, "A method for the harmonic removal in operational modal analysis of rotating blades," *Mech. Syst. Signal Process.*, vol. 27, no. 1, pp. 604–618, 2012.

[10] B. Peeters, B. Cornelis, K. Janssens, and H. Van der Auweraer, "Removing disturbing harmonics in operational modal analysis," *Proc. 2nd Int. Oper. Modal Anal. Conf. IOMAC 2007*, no. May, pp. 1–2, 2007.

[11] R. Pintelon, B. Peeters, and P. Guillaume, "Continuous-time operational modal analysis in the presence of harmonic disturbances," *Mech. Syst. Signal Process.*, vol. 22, no. 5, pp. 1017–1035, 2008.

[12] P. Mohanty and D. J. Rixen, "Operational modal analysis in the presence of harmonic excitation," *J. Sound Vib.*, vol. 270, no. 1–2, pp. 93–109, 2004.

[13] P. Mohanty and D. J. Rixen, "Modified ERA method for operational modal analysis in the presence of harmonic excitations," *Mech. Syst. Signal Process.*, vol. 20, no. 1, pp. 114–130, 2006.

[14] S. Gres, P. Andersen, C. Hoen, and L. Damkilde, "Orthogonal projection-based harmonic signal removal for operational modal analysis," *Conf. Proc. Soc. Exp. Mech. Ser.*, vol. 6, pp. 9–21, 2019.

[15] M. S. Allen, M. W. Sracic, S. Chauhan, and M. H. Hansen, "Output-only modal analysis of linear time-periodic systems with application to wind turbine simulation data," *Mech. Syst. Signal Process.*, vol. 25, no. 4, pp. 1174–1191, 2011.

[16] C. Devriendt and P. Guillaume, "The use of transmissibility measurements in output-only modal analysis," *Mech. Syst. Signal Process.*, vol. 21, no. 7, pp. 2689–2696, 2007.

[17] E. Smilden, A. Sørensen, and L. Eliassen, "Wind model for simulation of thrust variations on a wind turbine," *Energy Procedia*, vol. 94, pp. 306–318, 2016.

[18] D. Tcherniak, S. Chauhan, and M. H. Hansen, "Applicability limits of operational modal analysis to operational wind turbines," in *Structural Dynamics and Renewable Energy, Volume 1*, Springer, 2011, pp. 317–327.

[19] A. Lazkano *et al.*, "Case study: Flicker emission and 3P power oscillations on fixed-speed wind turbines," *Proc. Int. Conf. Harmon. Qual. Power, ICHQP*, no. January 2016, pp. 268–273, 2012.

[20] P. G. K. Motte, W. Weijtjens, C. Devriendt, "Operational Modal Analysis in the Presence of Harmonic Excitations: a Review," *Conf. Proc. Soc. Exp. Mech. Ser.*, vol. 77, p. V, 2015.

[21] X. Serra, "Musical sound modeling with sinusoids plus noise," *Music. signal Process.*, pp. 91–122, 1997.

[22] Y. Stylianou, "Applying the harmonic plus noise model in concatenative speech synthesis," *IEEE Trans. speech audio Process.*, vol. 9, no. 1, pp. 21–29, 2001.

[23] M. Zivanovic and J. Schoukens, "Single and piecewise polynomials for modeling of pitched sounds," *IEEE Trans. Audio, Speech Lang. Process.*, vol. 20, no. 4, 2012.

[24] M. Zivanovic and J. Schoukens, "On the polynomial approximation for time-variant harmonic signal modeling," *IEEE Trans. Audio, Speech Lang. Process.*, vol. 19, no. 3, 2011.

[25] W. Verhelst, "Overlap-add methods for time-scaling of speech," *Speech Commun.*, vol. 30, no. 4, pp. 207–221, 2000.

[26] J. Aho *et al.*, "A tutorial of wind turbine control for supporting grid frequency through active power control," in *2012 American Control Conference (ACC)*, 2012, pp. 3120–3131.

This page intentionally left blank.

9th International Operational Modal Analysis Conference
iomac
July 3 - 6, 2022
Vancouver, Canada

DATA ACQUISITON FRAMEWORK AND SYSTEM IDENTIFICATION OF AN IN-SERVICE WIND TURBINE

Onur Ozturkoglu[1], *Veysel Yurtseven*[2], *Yasar Taner*[3], *Ozgur Ozcelik*[4], *Serkan Gunel*[5]

[1] Research Assistant, Dokuz Eylul University, onur.ozturkoglu@deu.edu.tr.
[2] *Graduate Student*, Dokuz Eylul University, veysel.yurtseven@ogr.deu.edu.tr.
[3] Research Assistant, Dokuz Eylul University, yasar.taner@deu.edu.tr.
[4] Prof. Dr., Dokuz Eylul University, ozgur.ozcelik@deu.edu.tr.
[5] Assoc. Prof. Dr., Dokuz Eylul University, serkan.gunel@deu.edu.tr.

ABSTRACT

During recent years, wind energy has become an important renewable energy source, and a more attractive alternative to conventional ways of energy generation due to higher capacity utilization factors and shorter return of investments. Demand for larger wind turbines, which can produce more energy in the short term, is increasing rapidly in the market. To ensure that the turbine continuously generates energy, and stays perfectly operational during its lifespan, there is an increasing need to have a comprehensive understanding of their dynamics from a structural point of view. In this study, a novel distributed data acquisition system is designed and deployed throughout the tower height on a 2.5MW in-service fully operational wind turbine in Izmir/Turkey. Using the collected response data, the dynamic properties of the turbine tower are estimated by using operational modal analysis methods and compared with the modal analysis of the detailed finite element model.

Keywords: Wind Turbine, Data Acquisition, Operational modal analysis

1. INTRODUCTION

Wind energy has become an important renewable energy source, and more attractive alternative to conventional ways of energy generation due to higher capacity utilization factors and shorter return of investments. Consequently, in energy investment enterprises there is an increasing demand for building taller/bigger and more advanced wind turbines. To ensure that the turbine continuously generates energy, and stays perfectly operational during its lifespan, there is an increasing need to monitor the structural integrity of these large structures.

In many parts of the world, large number of wind turbines have been installed in areas where earthquake hazard is high and this trend is still on-going, e.g., Turkey. When looked at in conjunction, Disaster and Emergency Management Authority's publication (AFAD) "Seismic Hazard Map of Turkey" [1] with Republic of Turkey Ministry of Energy and Natural Resources's "Wind Energy Potential Map of Turkey" [2], it can be seen that the regions with high potential of wind energy have high earthquake hazard levels. Therefore, majority of wind farms built in Turkey are in high earthquake hazard regions. Due to the obstacles set by wind turbine manufacturers and technical difficulties due to turbines operational conditions, the studies on the seismic behavior of wind turbines have so far been limited in literature [3].

Field-testing of full-scale structures plays an important role in determining the dynamic properties of structures under realistic operational and environmental conditions. Operational Modal Analysis (OMA), also known as only-output modal analysis, is based on measuring only the response (output) of a structure and using its ambient vibrations. under natural operational conditions, as unmeasured input for modal identification. As opposed to input-output methods for modal identification, OMA techniques are used under actual operating conditions and in situations where it is difficult or impractical to externally excite the structure. These techniques are used on structures under actual operating conditions so as to estimate operational natural frequencies and operational aerodynamic damping that are naturally different from the ones obtained under non-operational conditions [4-5].

Originally developed for system identification of civil engineering structures, e.g., buildings, towers, bridges, and offshore structures, OMA techniques today are also used on highly complicated mechanical structures such as aircrafts, ground vehicles, ships, and any type of rotating and moving machinery. While civil engineering structures are mainly excited by ambient stochastic forces like wind, waves, traffic and/or seismic micro-tremors, mechanical structures are typically excited by a combination of harmonic forces originating from rotating and reciprocating parts, and broadband excitations originating from either self-generated vibrations [6].

In this study, a distributed data acquisitions system, composed of accelerometers, thermocouples and humidity sensors, is deployed on an operating full scale-wind turbine. In addition to these data, operational (e.g., rotor speed, pitch angles, nacelle direction, generated power) and environmental (e.g., wind speed, wind direction, temperature, humidity) data from the SCADA system is collected synchronously with the vibrational data. Accelerometer data is processed using OMA techniques and modal parameters of wind turbine are estimated.

2. WIND TURBINE

The subject of the research is a wind turbine with 2.5 MW capacity operating by a local energy company in Urla/Izmir/Turkey (Figure 1). The hub height of this horizontal axis turbine with 3 blades is 90 meters. The turbine tower is a thin-walled steel cylinder fixed to the reinforced concrete foundation with bolts. The nacelle, hub and blades are located on the turbine tower. Various features of the aforementioned wind turbine are presented in Table 1.

Table 1. Properties of wind turbine

Properties	Value
Rated power	2,5 MW
Rated wind speed	13 m/s
Cut-in wind speed	3 m/s
Cut-out wind speed	25 m/s
Rotor speed	9,6 – 16 rpm
Rotor diameter	90 m
Tower height	80 m
Hub height	90 m
Nacelle mass	91 tons
Rotor mass	55 tons

(a) (b)

Figure 1. a) The monitored wind turbine **b)** a general view of the wind farm.

The wind turbine tower consists of four parts connected by flanges. The tower diameter and wall thickness change along the height (Figure 2). The material (S355) properties of the tower are as shown in Table 2.

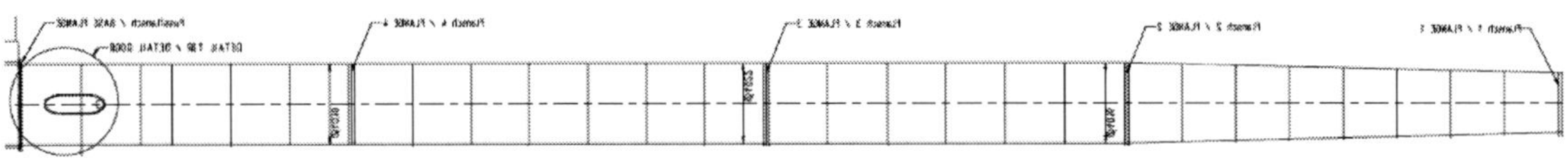

Figure 2. Tower geometry (flipped - right is top).

Table 2. Material properties (S355).

Properties	Value
Yield strength	355 MPa
Tensile strength	510-630 MPa
Modulus of elasticity	210 GPa
Shear modulus	81 GPa
Density	7850 kg/m^3
Poisson ratio	0,30

The wind turbine sits on a relatively rigid ground. Some of the ground features found in the ground survey report conducted in December 2008 are presented in Table 3.

Table 3. Soil properties.

Properties	Value
Bearing capacity	3 kg/cm^2
Coefficient of soil reaction	15000 t/m^3
Primary wave speed	399-910 m/s
Secondary wave speed	173-267 m/s

A horizontal axis wind turbine generally consists of four parts: foundation, tower, rotor and nacelle. It is decided that the foundation and the tower to be modelled with a detailed finite elements model (Figure 3), and the rotor and nacelle with a simplified approach (Figure 4) as detailed in literature [7].

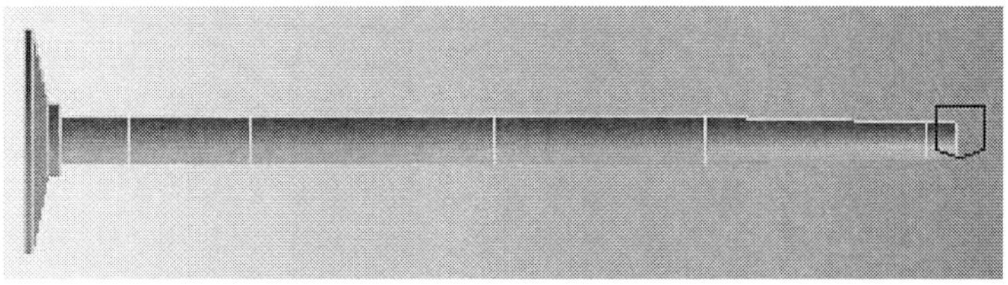

Figure 3. ANSYS model of the turbine tower and foundation.

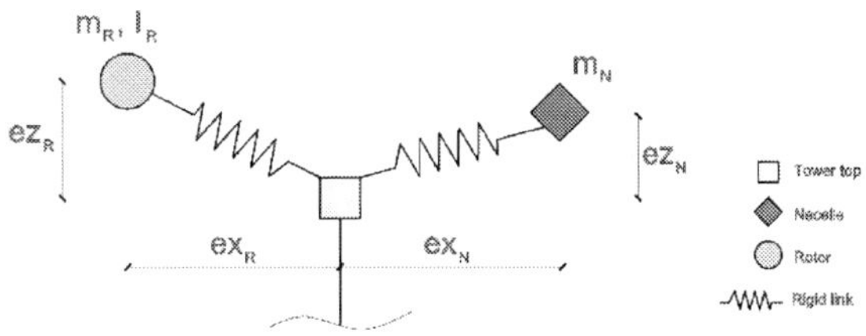

Figure 4. Model illustration of rotor and nacelle.

Where m_R is rotor mass, I_R is moment of inertia of rotor, m_N is nacelle mass, ez_R, ex_R, ez_N and ex_N are eccentricity of nacelle and rotor. After the wind turbine model was created in the ANSYS environment, modal analysis is performed and the first 3 structural modes are presented in Table 4.

Table 4. Mode frequencies.

Frequency (Hz)	Description
0.36	1st structural
3.03	2nd structural
8.32	3rd structural

3. DATA ACQUISITION SYSTEM

Turbine tower height is 80 meters and there are horizontal platforms that can be walked on at every 20 meters. These levels are named as follows according to their ground clearance; Level 1: 0 meter (foundation), Level 2: 20-meters, Level 3: 40-meters, Level 4: 60-meters, Level 5: 80-meter (top of the tower). Information regarding the components of the system installed along the height of the tower and the introduction of the system's general features are given in Table 5.

The sensors and the data acquisition system components used to collect data from the aforementioned levels are listed as follows (Figure 5):

- **Level 1 (0-meter):** One triaxial accelerometer, three uniaxial accelerometers, and one temperature/humidity sensor are on this floor. To collect data from the sensors, two NI 9239 and one NI 9203 module modules is connected to a cDAQ-9185 chassis. In addition to these, industrial box PC, PoE switch, power supply, UPS and P2P antenna are on the foundation level.
- **Level 2 (20-meter):** Two uniaxial accelerometers are on this floor. To collect data from the sensors, a NI 9239 module is connected to a cDAQ-9185 chassis.
- **Level 3 (40 meter):** Two uniaxial accelerometers and one temperature/humidity sensor are on this floor. To collect data from the sensors, a NI 9239 module is connected to a cDAQ-9185 chassis.
- **Level 4 (60-meter):** Two uniaxial accelerometers are on this floor. To collect data from the sensors a NI 9239 module is connected to a cDAQ-9185 chassis.
- **Level 5 (80-meter):** Two uniaxial accelerometers and one temperature/humidity sensor are on this floor. To collect data from the sensors, a NI 9239 is connected to a cDAQ-9185 chassis.

Table 5. Components of the Data Acquisition System

Device	Description
Uniaxial Accelerometer	Measures acceleration
Triaxial Accelerometer	Measures acceleration
Temperature and Relative Humidity Sensor	Measures temperature and relative humidity
NI 9239 Analog Input Module	Converts continuous-time and continuous-amplitude analog signals to discrete-time and discrete-amplitude digital signals
NI cDAQ-9185 Chassis	Controls timing, synchronization, and data transfer (at most four modules can be attached)
NI PS-16 Industrial Power Supply	Provides power for all system in the tower
P2P Wireless Antenna	Transfers data from the switchyard to the turbine tower
Industrial Box PC	Runs Labview codes to operate the system and controls data streaming
Workstation	Runs various codes for analyses
NAS	Backs up all collected data
UPS	Prevents system shutdown in case of power failure
Industrial Ethernet Switch	Allows devices to communicate with each other
Splitter	Separates data signals from power signals

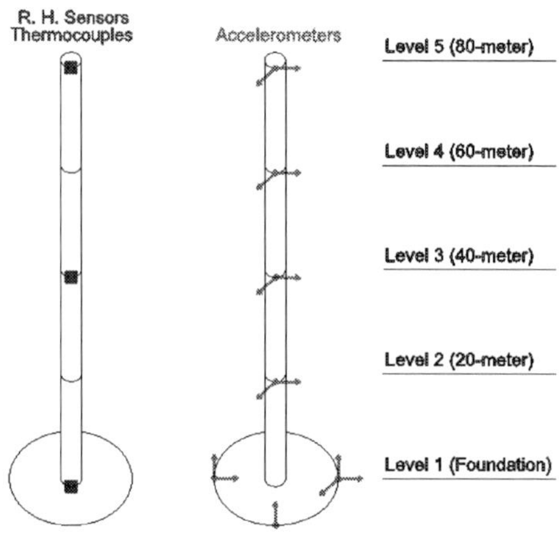

Figure 5. Deployment of sensors along the tower

Before the data acquisition system is deployed on the turbine, it is assembled and tested in the laboratory. System elements assembled together in the laboratory are shown in Figure 6 along with their short descriptions.

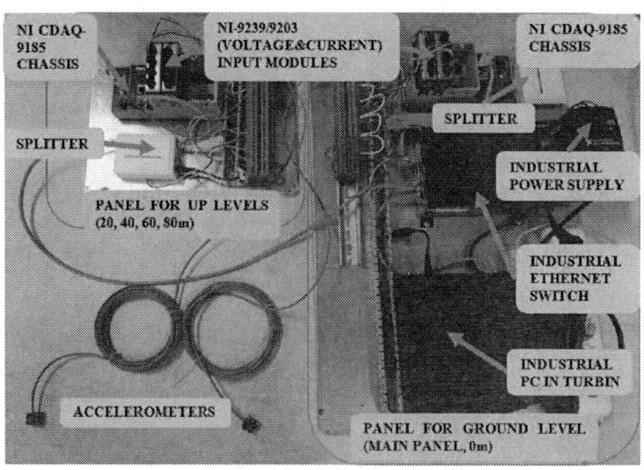

Figure 6. Assembly of the system components in the laboratory.

In the system, NI 9185 cDAQ chassis are used to collect data synchronously on each level. Compatible inputs to the modules are provided by these chassis. The 8-port industrial switch, specifically manufactured for this project, enable all devices in the turbine tower to communicate with each other. At the same time, both data flow and energy flow is provided through the switch with PoE cables.

One triaxial and three uniaxial accelerometers at foundation level and at each level (e.g., 20, 40, 60 and 80 m) along the tower, two uniaxial accelerometers are placed perpendicular to each other. Technical characteristics of the accelerometers are shown in Table 6.

Table 6. Specifications of accelerometers.

		Uniaxial/Triaxial Accelerometer
Acc. Range	(g)	±5
Sensitivity	(mV/g)	540
Frequency Range	(Hz)	700
Noise	(μg/√Hz)	0.1
Bias Temperature	(mg/°C)	17
Shock Survivability	(g)	2500
Operating Voltage	(V)	5-20

Since proper placement of the accelerometers along the horizontal and vertical directions is a critical issue in order to obtain the acceleration data correctly, they were placed with a spirit level as shown in Figure 7 and the position of the accelerometers relative to each other is measured with a laser meter and set as 20 m. It may be seen in Figure 7 that the accelerometers are attached by using strong magnets attached to the tower turbine wall. Temperature and humidity meters have been installed at three different levels (0, 40, 80 m) on the inner part of the tower.

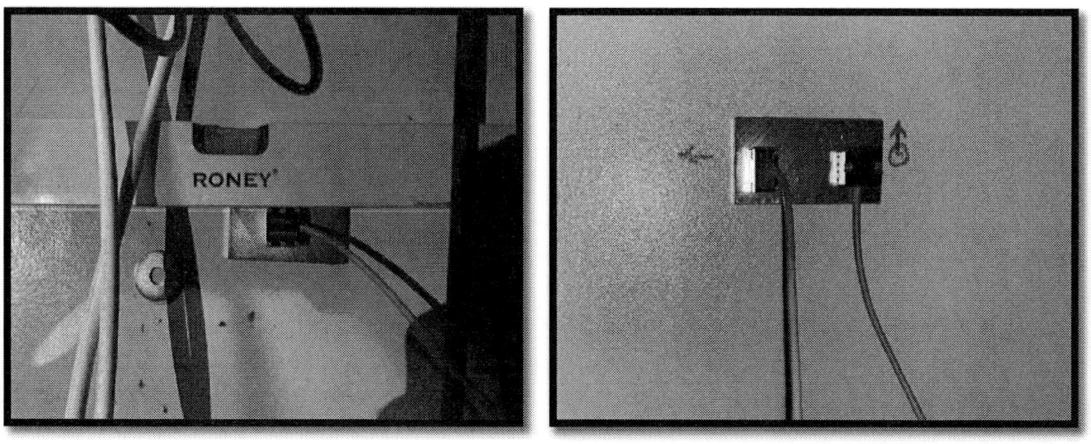

Figure 7. Attachment of the accelerometers.

In addition, rotor speed, nacelle direction, pitch angle, actual power, outside temperature values are instantly transferred to the workstation on the campus from the SCADA system. The data collected from the switchyard where the SCADA system is located and from the turbine where the data acquisition system is installed are transferred to the workstation located in the campus. Communication and lossless data transfers between these three points are provided by a custom code developed using LabVIEW for this project.

4. ANALYSIS AND CONCLUSION

To estimate the modal properties of the wind turbine, 600 seconds acceleration data sampled with 2048 Hz is recorded under the environmental and operational conditions given in Table 7. The turbine is at rest while the data was being collected. This is done to minimize the effect of the operational conditions.

Table 7. Enviromental and operational conditions.

	Parameter	Value
Environmental	Average Wind Speed	2 m/s
	Average Wind Direction*	272°
	Average Temperature	21° C
	Average Humidity	43%
Operational	Rotor Speed	0 rpm
	Pitch Angle	87°
	Nacelle Direction*	265°
	Generated Power	0 kW

*from north-clockwise direction

Before processing the data for parameter estimation, the following post-processing scheme is applied: first raw acceleration data filtered with a low-pass filter having 128 Hz corner frequency, and then the filtered data is decimated to obtain more manageable file size with a sample rate of 256 Hz. As presented in Table 4, fist three structural modes of the turbine are within the frequency range of 0-10 Hz. To prevent aliasing effect on the lower frequencies another low-pass filter with a corner frequency of 30 Hz is used. Finally, acceleration data is detrended.

The acceleration data processed accordingly is imported to the Artemis software [8], and each channel is assigned to a DOF point at the created turbine model. Operational modal analysis is performed using EFDD method and the structural modes are estimated. The power spectral density of the system and the mode shapes are shown in Figure 8 and Figure 9, respectively. The modes estimated from the analytical model and using the real-world data are presented together in Table 8.

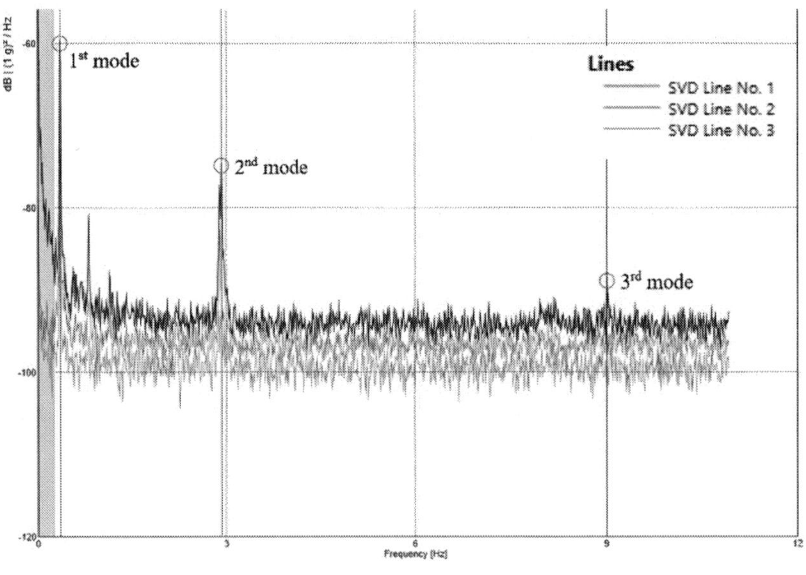

Figure 8. Estimated power spectral densities.

Table 8. Comparison of the experimental vs. analytical natural frequencies.

Frequency (Hz)			Damping (%)	Description
Experimental	Analytical	Difference (%)	Experimental	
0.36	0.36	-	1.25	1st structural
3.08	3.03	1.6	0.19	2nd structural
8.26	8.32	0.7	0.07	3rd structural

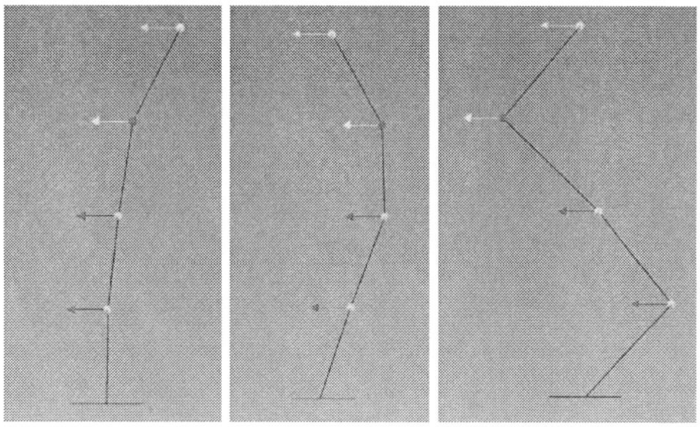

Figure 9. First three structural mode shapes estimated using the real-world experimental data.

Experimentally identified structural modes with their numerical counterparts are presented in Table 6. As can be seen from the numbers presented in the table, there is a good agreement between the experimental and numerical natural frequencies. Slight differences on mode frequencies originate from modelling assumptions. In the upcoming studies, the numerical model will be calibrated using the experimentally identified modal parameters. Acceleration data will be recorded under different environmental and operational conditions, and an extensive correlation work will be conducted to identify their effects on the estimated modal parameters.

ACKNOWLEDGEMENTS

Authors greatly acknowledge the financial support provided by The Scientific and Technological Council of Turkey (TUBITAK) under the grant number 120M218. Any opinions, findings, conclusions or recommendations expressed in this publication are those of the writers, and do not necessarily reflect the views of the sponsoring agency.

REFERENCES

[1] Disaster and Emergency Management Authority (AFAD). "Seismic Hazard Map of Turkey". https://deprem.afad.gov.tr/deprem-tehlike-haritasi Last access date: 27 April 2022.

[2] Republic of Turkey Ministry of Energy and Natural Resources. "Wind Energy Potential Map of Turkey". https://repa.enerji.gov.tr/REPA/bolgeler/TURKIYE-GENELI.pdf Last Access date: 27 April 2022.

[3] Katsanos, E. I., Thöns, S., & Georgakis, C. T. (2016). Wind turbines and seismic hazard: a state-of-the-art review. *Wind Energy,* 19(11), 2113-2133.

[4] Tcherniak, D., Chauhan, S., & Hansen, M. H. (2011). Applicability limits of operational modal analysis to operational wind turbines. In *Structural Dynamics and Renewable Energy, Volume 1* (pp. 317-327). Springer, New York, NY.

[5] Tcherniak, D., & Allen, M. S. (2013). Experimental characterization of an operating Vestas V27 wind turbine rotor using harmonic power spectra and OMA SSI. In 6th *International Operational Modal Analysis Conference*. Spain.

[6] Gade, S., Schlombs, R., Hundeck C. and Fenselau, C. (2009). Operational Modal Analysis on a Wind Turbine Gearbox, In *Proceedings of the IMAC-XXVII* Orlando, Florida USA.

[7] Ali, A., De Risi, R., & Sextos, A. (2021). Seismic assessment of wind turbines: How crucial is rotor-nacelle-assembly numerical modeling?. *Soil Dynamics and Earthquake Engineering*, *141*, 106483.

[8] Weir A. (2017). Artemis. Del Rey.

INDEX OF AUTHORS